A SOCIAL
AND RELIGIOUS
HISTORY OF
THE JEWS

By SALO WITTMAYER BARON

Second Edition, Revised and Enlarged

Late Middle Ages and Era of European Expansion,
1200–1650

VOLUME X

ON THE EMPIRE'S PERIPHERY

Columbia University Press
New York and London 1965

The Jewish Publication Society of America
Philadelphia 5726

CONTENTS

A SOCIAL AND RELIGIOUS HISTORY
OF THE JEWS

PUBLISHED VOLUMES

ON THE EMPIRE'S PERIPHERY

XLII

GERMANY'S NEIGHBORS

AMONG the Central-European principalities, bishoprics, and free cities harboring Jews were a number whose connection with the Holy Roman Empire became ever looser as the Middle Ages drew to their close. While the emperors still claimed some sovereignty in those territories, their power was even more circumscribed there than in the areas which permanently remained parts of the Empire. Before long both Switzerland and the Low Countries emancipated themselves completely from the imperial tutelage. To all intents and purposes Switzerland, which had started with the union of the three Forest districts, was growing into an ever larger and more independent country by the end of the fifteenth century. In 1499 it was in fact, if not *de jure,* an independent nation. Theory followed suit, and the Peace Treaty of Westphalia of 1648 formally recognized its independence.[1]

Somewhat different was the development in the Low Countries. In the early modern period Habsburg preponderance took the shape of Spanish domination, rather than that of the emperor. It was also in a revolt against Spain that Holland achieved her complete liberation in the sixteenth century. Here, too, the Treaty of Westphalia formally recognized an incontrovertible reality of several decades.

On the other hand, Hungary essentially belonged to east-central Europe and had more in common with Poland and the Balkan areas than with the West. However, toward the end of the Middle Ages, she became, through her Luxembourg and Habsburg kings, deeply involved in the imperial policies. Even in the sixteenth and seventeenth centuries, when she was, for the most part, incorporated into the Ottoman Empire, large parts of her territory, varying in size according to the fortunes of war, became permanent Habsburg possessions sharing the destinies of the adjoining Austrian and Bohemian lands to the end of the First World War. While she did not thereby become a formal member of the Holy

Roman Empire, Hungary's military and civilian manpower and economic resources were to play a significant role in the rise and decline of the dynasty's imperial authority.

Nor can Poland's medieval history be at all understood without constant reference to developments in the neighboring Empire. She achieved her very unity and independence only as a result of her centuries-long struggle against German dukes and barons, and particularly against the Teutonic Order, the military-religious arm of German expansion to the adjacent parts of the Slavonic East. Internally, too, the colonization of many Polish cities by newcomers from Germany, both Christian and Jewish, significantly contributed to the remarkable evolution of the Polish economy and culture. In many respects, therefore, the historic evolution of the rising Jewish communities in Poland may be treated in conjunction with that of the larger and more fully developed communities located within the Empire. Only in the sixteenth century did Poland, together with Lithuania, become a major center of Jewish life, which it remained until its devastation by the Nazi extermination squads during the Second World War. This new role of Polish-Lithuanian Jewry, as well as the fate of the communities which came under Ottoman sway in the early modern period, will be more fully analyzed in later chapters.

SWITZERLAND

Jewish history in Switzerland is even more diffuse and diverse than in other German-speaking territories. Frequently cities and regions joining the original alliance of the Forest districts associated themselves with one group of allies but not with others. Members of these unions still enjoyed much leeway in their military and foreign relations; they had complete freedom of action in their domestic legislation. At first limited to the German-speaking areas, they began expanding southward and finally, in a constant struggle with the Milanese, reached Italian Ticino. Toward the west and southwest they embraced the areas around Lake Geneva which, French-speaking, had previously been under the control of French rulers, particularly the dukes of Savoy. The Jewries of these localities often shared the fate of their coreligionists on the periphery of royal France, rather than that of the imperial communities.

Despite that enormous diversity, one may perhaps draw some generalizations from medieval developments in the principal Jewish communities of Basel, Zurich, Constance, as well as in the somewhat less important centers of Biel (Bienne), Berne, Soleure (Solothurn), Lucerne, Schaffhausen, Diessenhofen, St. Gallen (St. Gall), and, in the southwest, Fribourg and Geneva. Contemporaries doubtless saw little unity in these areas, but rather looked across the borders to neighboring German and French communities. Basel had immemorial ties with Strasbourg and the rest of Alsace, while Constance often participated in the regional Swabian combines. Moreover, all through the Middle Ages Habsburg rulers, whether or not occupying the imperial throne, exercised special authority in various parts of that region in a way greatly affecting the position of the Jews.[2]

No reliable information for any Swiss Jewish community antedates the twelfth or thirteenth century. If in his ninth-century *capitulare* Bishop Hatto of Basel enjoined the Christians to observe their Sundays from morning to evening, "lest they be captivated by Judaism," he merely echoed an old theological tradition without reference to contemporary Jews. The first reliable reference to a Basel Jew dates from 1213, when Bishop Lüthold set aside six marks "for the redemption of pawns, namely of an episcopal seal-ring and a silk garment from the Jew Meier [*Villicus*]." Ten years later Bishop Henry mentioned that the church treasury was paying interest "to Jews" (*apud Judaeos*). Yet by 1241 the Basel community appeared among the contributors to the imperial tax with the fairly substantial amount of 40 marks. Half a century later it occupied some twenty buildings. Constance, too, must have embraced a sufficiently large community in 1254 for Pope Innocent IV to complain to its bishop that "the Jews of your province and diocese do not observe this decree [of the Lateran Council concerning the Jewish badge] and hence may dare to commit the sin of damnable intercourse [with Christian women] under the excuse of an error." It has been suggested that about that time Meir b. Baruch of Rothenburg served as rabbi of Constance. If true, it must have been a community of substantial size to compare with the other residences of that distinguished scholar. On the other hand, one Rasor, recorded in a Basel document of 1293, may really have been called R. Asher, but it is unlikely that he was Asher b. Yeḥiel, Meir's famous disciple who, in 1303, was to emigrate to Spain. From that period we also possess evidence for Jewish settlements in Geneva, Biel, Berne and other communities. In 1291 the abbot and monks of Murbach (Guebwiller) sold some of their possessions to Emperor Rudolph I for his sons because they needed the purchase price of 2,000 marks to pay off heavy debts to Jewish moneylenders in Berne and Ensisheim. Incidentally, none of these monks knew how to write; their names had to be signed for them and confirmed by the bishop of Constance.[3]

Compared to their coreligionists in other areas, Swiss Jews lived a rather undisturbed life during the thirteenth and early fourteenth centuries. The cities which admitted Jews usually tried to treat them on the basis of near equality, as may be deduced from some still extant "letters of protection" in favor of individuals. After reviewing the recorded names of early settlers, Augusta Steinberg has shown that their majority had immigrated not only from neighboring Alsace, Baden, Bavaria, and the Franche-Comté, but also from more distant Lower Rhenish communities, the Champagne, even Flanders and the Provence. Not surprisingly, Alsatian influence was preponderant. This is seen, for example, in the various Hebrew tombstone inscriptions in Basel, which have been closely investigated ever since Johann Tonjola published his *Basilea sepulta* in 1661, although only a few of the 570 tombstones allegedly available to him and his immediate predecessors are still extant. Characteristically, they reveal the stress laid by contemporaries upon charity. For example, the 1320 epitaph of a R. Samuel son of R. Joseph, designated one of the "heads of the province" (probably because he participated in the communal management of a larger district around Basel), emphasizes far less his learning or piety than the fact that "he had always joyously given his bread to the poor . . . never withheld his hand from extending charity to all who asked him for it . . . and hence was lovingly accepted by great and small." This is not surprising, as social welfare and mutual aid were the very mainstay of any young community. Since the possession of cemeteries was often attained only after protracted negotiations and heavy payments to cities, churches, or private owners, a central burial place often had to serve a number of adjacent localities, although the transportation of corpses was not only arduous and insecure but also frequently subject to special tolls. When a modern excavation (for the building of a medical institute) in Basel led to the discovery of the medieval Jewish cemetery, the remains of twenty-five corpses, and particularly the fourteen preserved crania, were subjected to close anthropological investigation. Even this tiny sample showed a variety of racial characteristics among the medieval Swiss Jews.[4]

No such early epigraphic evidence is available from other Swiss cities. In the case of Berne we have some equivocal reports concerning a major affair of 1288 or more likely 1294. We are told by several chroniclers that because a Jew named Joli murdered a little Christian boy, allegedly for ritual purposes, he and several other Jews were executed, while the rest of the community was banished from the city forever. On the other hand, Emperor Rudolph I, angered by this arbitrary act against his "serfs of the Chamber" and having other scores to settle with the city, sent down an army variously given as consisting of 5,000 or 30,000 men which placed it under siege. First repulsed by the staunch resistance of the burghers, the army returned later and stormed the city walls. More recent critical historians removed some of the drama of that narrative and shifted the date to 1294. According to the revised story, it was King Adolph of Nassau who intervened and appointed an investigating committee headed by Bishop Peter of Basel. Neither the city nor the Committee was particularly interested in ascertaining the truth. Even six years later the official documents speak only of an "alleged" (*ut dicitur*) crime. Nevertheless, the Jews were ordered to deliver to the city of Berne all their pawns and writs of indebtedness and pay it 1,000 marks in addition to the 500 marks due to the magistrate (*Schultheiss*). The city was to inherit, moreover, all the property of the Jewish fugitives. While speaking of "the excesses perpetrated against the burned Jews by the Berne burghers," King Adolph confirmed this judgment, which was reconfirmed by King Albert in 1300. Only after they had met these exorbitant demands were the Jews allowed to return to the city and to continue plying their accustomed trades. As elsewhere, most of our information about the presence of Jews in Swiss localities is derived from incidental references in contemporary documents primarily related to Jewish moneylending. When a noble, Haymo of Montenach, sold in 1259 some property to a church in Interlaken, we are told that he needed (*evidenti necessitate compulsus*) the 21 pounds he had thus obtained in order to pay off Jewish loans. It has long been assumed that the Jewish creditors figuring in this and in similar transactions recorded in Interlaken in 1263 and 1268 were then living in Berne. In Fribourg, perhaps as an adumbration of the great role Jewish physicians were to play in that city, the early records, beginning with 1356, relate to at least seven Jewish doctors. At the same time non-Jewish healers seem to have consisted only of surgeons-barbers.[5]

Legally, Swiss Jewry was treated as part of the imperial "serfdom of the Chamber." Louis the Bavarian in particular stressed that over-all supremacy of the German kings and introduced here, too, the "golden penny." At the same time the Austrian dukes maintained their claims on specifically Jewish, as well as general, controls over large parts of that region. Whenever a Habsburg happened to combine the royal-imperial office with his hereditary rights, he was prone to legislate with even greater freedom concerning Jews.

In a remarkable decree of 1317, Frederick the Handsome, Louis' long-time rival to the royal throne, jointly with the Dukes Leopold and Henry of Austria and Styria, recognized the services rendered them by Constance Jewry, which doubtless included substantial monetary advances, and provided:

For this reason We declare them free and liberated from all taxes and services. They will not be obliged to render such to Us nor Our bailiffs from today until next Christmas and from then during the full following four years. Should it happen that We might forget it and act against this provision or some one else should do so in Our behalf, We request you [the authorities of Constance] with utmost seriousness and order you to remind Us of it so that We may desist. Should We nevertheless persevere, We give you with this letter the power to protect and aid the Jews residing among you with Our good will, with no anger or hatred, and with no quarrel against you on Our part on this score.

In 1324, while this conflict was still raging, Duke Leopold II of Austria concluded an alliance with Charles IV of France, promising to support the latter's candidacy for the royal throne of Germany. In return, the French king promised, if elected, to pay Leopold 30,000 marks. So long as this amount remained unpaid, he was to mortgage to the Duke the cities and castles of Basel, St. Gallen, Constance, Schaffhausen, and several others, with the various rights thereto held by Roman emperors, the treaty specifically including the authority over the Jewish residents of these localities. After Frederick's defeat Louis himself recognized the rights of the Austrian Habsburgs when, in 1330, he mortgaged to Dukes Albert and Otto the cities of Zurich, Schaffhausen, St. Gallen, and Rheinfelden, together with their Jewish revenues, until the dukes would receive the 20,000 marks promised them for their services. This act did not prevent the emperor from signing, five years later, a receipt for 50 florins paid by Zurich Jews for two years' taxes—not a small sum considering the tiny size of most Swiss communities. Until the battle of Sempach of 1386, which ended in the decisive defeat of Austrian troops, Habsburg protection of Jews far outweighed that of the bishops. Not even those of Basel and Constance exerted any great influence, although, for instance, the early developments in Biel largely depended on the good graces of the Basel bishops. Here, too, the progress of municipal autonomy proved decisive, the ultimate course of Jewish history being largely determined by the composition of the city councils. As elsewhere, the artisan classes were far more hostile to Jews than were the patricians or even the clergy. Not only did the city mobs often stage anti-Jewish riots, but whenever the artisan guilds attained power they used their legislative weapons to restrict the rights of Jews or even completely to withdraw their toleration.[6]

Nor did the Swiss communities escape those perennial suspicions which all over Europe generated the accusations of Jewish desecration of hosts and ritual murder. We recall the tragedy of Berne Jewry late in the thirteenth century. Not long thereafter (in 1312) a number of Jews of Constance lost their lives because they had allegedly desecrated a host. Again in 1333, it sufficed for the Jews of that city to be accused vaguely of contempt for the

Christian religion and some mischief against the "sacrament of the altar" (probably an allusion to another alleged defacement of the host) in order to have twenty-seven of them slain (twelve by burning and six by drowning). Much more severe and widespread were the persecutions in the Black Death era, when most Swiss communities, too, suffered total eclipse. In fact that mass hysteria had its starting point in Chillon, in the Swiss part of Savoy. From there it spread to other communities, especially Berne and Zofingen, which in turn stimulated Basel, where an extended correspondence with Strasbourg preceded the final tragedy. Zurich, Schaffhausen, Constance, and others followed suit. According to a chronicler, 330 Jews were burned in Constance alone, "a part of them dancing, another singing psalms, and a third weeping." The few survivors were executed half a year later. The Habsburg Duke Albert II, to be sure, who had successfully protected the Jews in his Austrian territories, long resisted the demands of Swiss communities to execute the Jews who had escaped to the castle of Kyburg. But when representatives of the cities of Diessenhofen and Winterthur insisted that if he failed to annihilate the alleged criminals they themselves would burn them "according to justice" (*per justiciam*), the duke, not wishing to see his controls flouted, decided to burn the Jews on his own. At first Charles IV claimed damages to the Empire through the losses in manpower and property sustained by his Jewish "serfs." But he was quickly enough placated and forgave the burghers for their excesses; he only demanded a share of the spoils. Apart from a few lucky escapees, the survivors seem to have consisted only of those who adopted Christianity, including numerous forcibly converted children. On the other hand, according to contemporary writers, some earlier converts were so inspired by the ready submission to the divine will by the Jewish martyrs that in the crisis they retracted and joined their former coreligionists in their "sanctification of the name of the Lord." [7]

Very soon thereafter, however, Jews were allowed to return to many communities, the few who had gone underground reappearing publicly soon after the restoration of order. In Lucerne they were formally readmitted in the very year of the Black Death, 1349. A generic "letter of freedom" was issued by the city of

Zurich to its Jewry in 1354. In the same year we also hear of Jews in Soleure and, in 1355, we find a Jew Manassès employed as a tax farmer in Geneva. In the following decades Jewish communities were reestablished also in most other places, in some for avowedly utilitarian reasons. The scribe of Diessenhofen unabashedly wrote in its old *Stadtbuch:* "In 1426, we have accepted a Jew as a burgher, for we had unfortunately contracted large debts and it became necessary for us to take in Jews and other persons so that we might the better carry the large taxes which we must pay annually." Similarly, the destruction of 652 homes in Berne by two conflagrations in 1405 caused the burghers to welcome the Jews back to their city. Some banking families now opened branch offices in several cities, thus entering the evolving Swiss capitalistic economy on a fairly high level. One Jäcklin of Ulm, who had resided for a while in Constance, persuaded that city to admit his brother-in-law as a burgher in 1378. In the same year his son Fidel opened a branch in Zurich. Other members of that family resided in Nuremberg and Strasbourg. Thus they ran a far-flung net of business establishments in Switzerland and southern Germany.[8]

Such business advances were not seriously hampered by the legal uncertainties associated with the growth of municipal controls. Typical of the legal instability was the situation in Basel, where in 1365 Charles IV formally conferred upon the council the duty of protecting the Jews. The city had but shortly before begun readmitting Jews, since, in addition to the severe population losses sustained by the Black Death, it had also suffered from an earthquake. Jews were to help to repopulate the city and to furnish the additional revenue needed for its reconstruction. While negotiating an alliance in 1362 with several other cities in Colmar, Alsace, the city elders even invited the Jew Eberlin, a recent arrival in Colmar, to settle in Basel. Eberlin was followed by many others, 31 families appearing among those admitted between 1365 and 1371 alone. In 1374, to be sure, by another decree of Charles IV, protection over the Jews reverted to the house of Austria, but it was taken back by the city on Duke Leopold III's defeat and death at Sempach in 1386. The city rights were expressly confirmed by King Wenceslaus in 1390. The Basel council now assumed control also over the Jews of Little Basel. Doubtless in this connection the burghers of that town secured from a Jewish couple a general release. In this interesting Hebrew document of 1387, one Ḥayyim son of Jacob and his wife "took an oath on the entire Torah and what is written in it not to do anything against the burghers of Little Basel, that is not to detain them, nor to cause them damage in any locality where they may find them, neither by themselves nor through their representatives to the end of days." [9]

More remarkably, among the Swiss cities only Constance seems to have benefited from Wenceslaus' cancellation of debts in 1385 and again in 1390. Although Basel had likewise belonged to the Swabian Confederation with which the king had made the original agreement, it still was formally under Habsburg control in 1385; five years later it was involved in a controversy with Wenceslaus about its general authority over Jews, which the king ultimately recognized. It appears that, on both occasions, the city council refused to deliver its share of the payments demanded by the king. Thus this blow seems to have affected the Swiss Jewish money-lenders less than it did their coreligionists in other parts of the Empire. Moreover, Wenceslaus' subsequent reversal of these policies came to the fore also in Switzerland. On December 23, 1397 he actually ordered the cities of Basel, Zurich, Berne, and Lucerne to assist two Jews (Solomon and Abraham) in the collection of debts from the counts of Gruyère. Lucerne's prohibition of Jewish moneylending on interest in 1383, on the other hand, was much more serious, although moneylending was not Swiss Jewry's exclusive occupation. Apart from those engaging in commerce and certain trades, there were a number of more or less distinguished physicians, not only in Fribourg. In Berne, which extended to individual Jews "letters of protection" for a limited period of two or three years, Jewish doctors are mentioned in 1375 and 1384. Among Basel's new arrivals in 1370 was a physician Jocet who, during the preceding fourteen years, had practiced medicine in Fribourg. Two years later Jocet was appointed the city's medical officer (*Stadtarzt*) with an annual salary of 25 livres. In 1398 the council invited another Jewish doctor, Gutleben, a local resident for some twenty years, to serve it in a similar semiofficial capacity for ten years at an annual salary of 50 florins. Nor were all inter-group social relations altogether hostile. In 1378 a Constance Jewish banker, Gutmann, was fined 100 pounds because his son had entertained illicit relations with a Christian girl. While elsewhere such a trial might have ended with the couple's execution, the Constance authorities were satisfied with conducting the pregnant girl, clad in a Jewish hat, through the streets of the city and banishing both her and her paramour to a distance of at least one German mile from the city.[10]

The growing fifteenth-century tensions proved as catastrophic for Swiss Jews as for their coreligionists in other German-speaking areas. At the onset of another pestilence in 1397 many Basel Jews, with memories of the Black Death still fresh in their minds, hastened to leave the city, putting an end to its second organized Jewish community. It took several years before a new functioning association could be established. This panic was followed by a serious Blood Accusation in Diessenhofen in 1401, which dragged on for ten years, and had widespread repercussions. The neighboring city of Schaffhausen took such interest in this affair that it pursued some of its own Jewish residents who tried to escape, although the latter's involvement in that "crime" seemed extremely farfetched. Forced by prolonged torture to confess, these men were executed. Not satisfied with this local blood bath, the Schaffhausen authorities urged several other cities, including Fribourg and Zurich, to follow their example. Fribourg seems to have ignored this suggestion, whereas Zurich, in order to appease its own aroused populace, instituted an independent investigation. After hearing the testimony of several witnesses from the original locales, it became convinced of the spuriousness of the entire accusation. Nevertheless a similar libel in Ravensburg in 1429 again led to complications far beyond that city's borders. In 1443, because of another blood libel in neighboring Ahausen, many Constance Jews were imprisoned. On the intervention of Frederick III the defendants were liberated, but only after they had spent five years in prison and had signed a receipt that their previously confiscated property had been restored to them minus certain discounts and expenses. Other accusations, unchecked by royal intercessions, led to riots, the burning of a number of Jews even if not involved in the alleged crimes, and large-scale plunder of Jewish property either through direct seizure or in the form of negotiated settlements with the Jewish communities.[11]

Apart from such recurrent tragedies, the struggling Swiss communities suffered from the unceasing pressures of the ever money-hungry imperial and municipal administrations. No sooner did Sigismund convoke the Ecumenical Church Council to Constance than he imposed a tax upon all German Jewry to help defray its costs. The Jewish community of Constance was called upon to extend public welcomes to the king and the newly elected pope, Martin V. It also was the recipient of Martin V's first favorable decree, copies of which were distributed to various Jewish communities throughout the Empire. But it was deeply shocked when Sigismund exacted from it the enormous contribution of 20,000 florins. Although among the largest in the Swiss region, it had never embraced more than thirty-two taxpaying households; it was able to pay this large amount only with the assistance of both the municipality, which assumed part of the obligation, and other German-speaking communities. Hardly had it recovered from that financial emergency when the Ravensburg affair of 1429 embroiled it in new difficulties, from which it freed itself only through another payment of 20,000 florins. It is small wonder, then, that some of its wealthiest members left the city.

Among the major Swiss Jewish financiers of the early fifteenth century were Solomon of Rheinfelden, his son Löw, and another Löw "of Constance." In 1424 they were all admitted to burghers' rights in Zurich, although its city council knew well enough that the latter Löw had left Constance without that city's permission and that he had not fully met his obligations toward the king. This unusual eagerness of the Zurich council to admit him to a relatively lengthy twelve-year residence stemmed from his promise to lend money to the local burghers at the low interest rate of 22 percent, and extend to the city itself an annual loan of 2,000 florins at 5 percent. Eleven years later it was Schaffhausen's turn to compete for Löw, now of Zurich, to whom, together with several associates, the council extended a comprehensive privilege in which it wrote:

We pledge ourselves and promise to protect, shield and uphold all the liberties and rights which these Jews and their households enjoy in respect to their bodies and property as granted to Jewry as a whole or to them specifically by our Holy Father, the Pope and our Lord, the Emperor, or as is provided in the following. We shall extend that protection inside and outside the city against any adversary, no one excepted, on a par with that given our native-born burghers. [It is to last] until St. Martin's day following the date of the present document and subsequently as long as we or our descendants shall fail to revoke it and to announce that we no longer wish to keep any Jews among us. After such an announcement it is to continue without qualification for a whole year.

This document contained the usual regulations concerning the badge and interest rates, but it also provided that the newcomers should be allowed to hold congregational services twice a year, for which purpose they might import foreign scholars and students and keep them at their homes for the required periods. In return, they were to donate on each such occasion two glass windows for the city hall.[12]

Relative prosperity of a few wealthy bankers could not conceal, however, the basic insecurity of the Jewish position in Switzerland. The rise of the artisan classes, combined with the new permissiveness, however qualified, to charge interest, extended by the Council of Basel to Christian moneylenders, undermined the foundations of Jewish life in the Swiss districts as it did in Germany. After the Council of Basel, moreover, religious intolerance, exemplified by the missions of Nicolaus Cusanus and John Capistrano, was steadily gaining ground. In his pastoral letter of 1448, Bishop Henry IV of Constance not only restated the old canonical postulates concerning segregation, the nonemployment of Christian servants, and the badge, but he also demanded that Christians abstain from doing business with Jews altogether. Going beyond the canonical requirements, he enjoined the clergy of his diocese to prevent Jews from building new synagogues and even from restoring old ones. Although the Jewish communities in the diocese continued to decline in the following half century, Bishop Hugo von Landenberg restated some of these restrictions in his epistle of 1497, and published it for wider distribution.[13]

Nor was the example set by neighbors from England to Vienna lost on the Swiss burghers. The resulting local expulsions showed many variations in detail; the cities themselves often reversed their actions after a short period. But the ultimate outcome was the gradual elimination of Jewish communities from the Swiss soil.

The best dates for the definitive expulsions of the Jews may be given as follows: Lucerne in 1384, Berne in 1408 and 1427, Fribourg in 1428 (notwithstanding a ten-year contract it had concluded in 1420 with the Jewish physician Ackimus de Vixou), Zurich in 1436, Schaffhausen in 1472–75, Geneva (where a formal ghetto, the so-called *cancellum judaicum,* had been established in 1428) in 1490, St. Gallen, Soleure, and Basel (where but few Jews resided after 1397) in the early sixteenth century. Where some individuals were subsequently allowed to sojourn on a temporary basis, their life was governed by discriminatory laws much more adverse than those under which their ancestors had lived in the Middle Ages. Not until the latter part of the nineteenth century did Swiss Jewry achieve a standing comparable to that of the other Jewish communities of modern Europe.[14]

LOW COUNTRIES

Even more diffuse and numerically less significant were the Jewish settlements in the Low Countries. The territories now included in Holland, Belgium, and Luxembourg constituted a political entity only during the very brief period after the treaty of Verdun of 843, when, together with other areas, they were assigned to Lothair I. In the fifteenth century some of these districts were reunited under the dukes of Burgundy, especially Philip the Good. But as a rule Brabant, Flanders, Gelderland (Guelders), and Holland had little in common with one another. Luxembourg, whose dynasty furnished four emperors to Germany, was a somewhat more integral part of the Empire until the death of Sigismund and its incorporation into Burgundy. The linguistic division between French and Flemish or Dutch likewise contributed to that great diffusion of power. "French villages," rightly observes Thomas Harrison Reed, "have confronted Flemish villages, the Flemish side of the street the French side, time out of mind, without one tongue gaining on the other, and without any tendency toward the formation of a common speech." [15]

Little is known about Jews in the Low Countries before the thirteenth century, although Jewish culture may well have radiated there from the large region of "Lotharingia." We recall that some thirty Jews, headed by one Jacob, were reputedly invited by Count Baldwin IV of Flanders to settle in his county (*ca.* 1024). More reliably, we hear of a Jewish street in Tirlemont (Tienen) in 1232. This seems, indeed, to have been one of the largest Jewish communities of the region; it probably owned the cemetery from which came a tombstone recording the passing of one Rebecca a quarter century later (1255–56). Jews also settled in Louvain where the conversion of a six-year-old Jewish girl and the clergy's subsequent refusal to return her to her parents caused quite a stir in the city and was even recorded by outsiders like Caesarius of Heisterbach and Thomas of Cantimpré. Some Jews are also referred to in Brussels (*ca.* 1260), and in Malines (Mechlin) where a Jew Hagin helped Henry Bate in 1273–74 to translate a number of astrological treatises by Abraham ibn Ezra. Jews from these communities, as well as from Gelderland, appear also from time to time in the records of the city of Cologne, which entertained close economic relations with the Low Countries. As pointed out by Jean Stengers, all eight Brabant cities where Jews are mentioned in the thirteenth and early fourteenth centuries were located on or near the important trade route from Cologne to Bruges. Jews must have been sufficiently important there, both numerically and economically, for Duke Henry III, in his aforementioned testament of 1261, to recommend their expulsion along with that of the Cahorsins unless both groups were prepared to give up money-lending and turn to other branches of commerce. The failure to implement this recommendation and the ensuing correspondence with Thomas Aquinas concerning the princes' right to derive benefits from Jewish taxation likewise attest the significance of the Jewish question in the duchy.[16]

Nevertheless the position of the Jews still was extremely tenuous. For the most part they lived not on the basis of broad privileges extended to entire communities, but rather on temporary permits granted to a few individuals by local rulers. Several extant safe-conducts by the counts of Hainaut, where the Jews seem to have settled first after their expulsion from royal France in 1306, are dated in 1307, 1308, 1310, and 1337; they emphasize the recipients' right to settle in the entire county except in such localities as Binche (1310), or those in which there were Lombards (1307–1308). Evidently the latter had thus sought to safeguard their banking monopoly. The safe-conduct of 1310 further specifies:

If the aforementioned Jews, or any of them, should seek haven because of the fear of wars, should such occur in the country, or because of some adventure of Crusaders, as it happened before, they should be given shelter in Our fortress at Binche and at all other fortresses in Our land. We shall protect them there on a par with Our burghers.

In return for these privileges Jews were to pay either specific annual amounts or stated lump sums. The temporary character of their settlement did not seriously interfere, however, with their business enterprises, which at times were conducted on a fairly large scale. We even hear of a regular company of Jewish moneylenders, headed by one Godschalk of Recklinghausen, and consisting of his daughter, Hannah, Leon of Münster, another Godschalk of Werden, and Moses of Cologne. This interterritorial association of Jews stemming from northwestern Germany centered in Overijssel in the years 1332–49.[17]

Fear of the Crusaders, alluded to in the Hainaut safe-conduct of 1310, was not a mere historic reminiscence. On Pope Clement V's call in 1308, another Crusade had started to form in central and western Europe, but lacking proper leadership the unorganized mob, assembled in Avignon, was dismissed by the pope. On their way, however, these would-be Crusaders often attacked Jews, whereupon Duke John II allowed the Jews of Brabant to foregather in the castle of Genappe, and when the Crusaders laid siege to it he attacked and dispersed them. Probably few Jews lost their lives in 1309, but in view of the tiny size of their communities even such small-scale losses had enduring consequences. In 1326 a Jewish convert, Guillaume, allegedly attacked a picture of the Virgin in Cambron and pierced it with his lance. Around this so-called "sacrilege of Cambron" began cluttering legends which further envenomed the relations between Jews and their neighbors. Yet apart from the burning of Guillaume, there were no immediate reprisals against the Hainaut Jews, whose privileges were, in fact, renewed in 1337. On this occasion we learn about the presence of eighteen Jewish families, scattered in some ten communities throughout the county.[18]

Jewish life was not to endure there, however, any more than it did in most other parts of central Europe. In 1349–50 the massacres by the Flagellants and the panicking mobs, supplemented by more formal trials and condemnations, terminated for a while the development of most Jewish communities in the Low Countries as well. Where they began recovering slowly from that ordeal, as in Brussels, Louvain, or Luxembourg, they faced an ever more hostile public opinion. According to Treasury reports of 1368–70, there were at that time altogether two Jewish families in Louvain, while the seven families living in Brussels in 1368–69 were reduced to four in the following year. The three who had departed were fortunate, for in 1370 the remaining families were prosecuted for an alleged desecration of the host and burned at the stake. This "sacrilege" has ever after been commemorated in Brussels by an annual celebration of the so-called "holy sacrament of the miracle," centered on two chapels, one erected on the site of the former synagogue. The semicentennial celebrations in particular of 1670, 1720, 1770, and 1820, were observed with a fanfare merited by a better cause. Certainly, at the end of the Middle Ages no one could have foretold that within two centuries Holland would become one of the major centers of Jewish life and that Amsterdam, which seems to have harbored no Jews at all during the Middle Ages, would legitimately be nicknamed the "New Jerusalem." [19]

Luxembourg, which even in modern times had only a small population, attracted relatively few Jews in the Middle Ages. Mentioned in passing in a document of 1276, their presence was sufficiently significant for Charles IV to order on July 24, 1349 the officials of the capital city, then called Lützelburg, to protect Jewish lives and property. That this order was not carried out is evidenced from the inclusion of that city, as well as of neighboring Echternach, in the long list of martyred communities later commemorated by various German congregations. In 1391 the Jews of Luxembourg, or rather the few who had settled there again after 1350 (a Jewish gate is mentioned in the capital in 1376), were expelled from the whole duchy. If in the course of the fifteenth century some hardy souls reappeared on the scene, they were victimized by a riot in 1478, after which we encounter only a few scattered individuals in that entire district.[20]

HUNGARY

At the southeast of the Empire, the kingdom of Hungary succeeded from the outset in maintaining its independence. Efforts by Henry III and Henry IV to impose German overlordship were defeated by both the Hungarian resistance and the Empire's protracted struggle with the Papacy. The subsequent threats to Hungarian independence emanating from the expansive Byzantine Empire were permanently averted by the latter's collapse during the Fourth Crusade. To balance the two empires against one another Hungary often allied itself with the Papacy. Beginning with King Geza I, its monarchy intermittently acknowledged being but a papal fief, which in practice involved but slight limitations in international relations and meant even less in domestic affairs. Internally, its situation was in so far unusual as a large part of the population professed Islam, Greek Orthodoxy, or even outright paganism. Religious toleration was, therefore, not a mere ideological postulate here but an irresistible historic imperative.[21]

Under these conditions, Jews, who had lived in the country long before the Magyar conquest, constituted an integral part of the population and played a particularly important role in its growing trade. King Coloman (1095–1116), bent on facilitating commercial transactions (his famous road known as *magna via Colomanni regis* served for many centuries as a most important artery of communication), effectively protected the Jews against the passing Crusaders. We recall the Hebrew chronicler's exaggerated gloating over the latter's destruction. At the same time the king tried to keep his Jewish subjects under stricter supervision by limiting their residential rights to episcopal cities. Under ecclesiastical pressure (especially the Gran Council of 1112), he forbade them to hold Christian slaves. Yet he and his successors made good use of Jews not only as mintmasters, whose craftsmanship was not easily duplicated, but also as Treasury officials, purveyors of salines, and in other semiofficial capacities. Some of them rose here to the ranks of nobility, particularly the aforementioned Count Teka, the distinguished financier and diplomat of both Hungary and Austria.[22]

Not surprisingly, both the Church and the lower nobility looked askance at such "excessive" toleration. Utilizing their great influence upon the Hungarian monarchs, the popes, seconded by the local clergy, vigorously protested against the opportunities thus given to Jews to exercise dominion over Christians. Not long after ascending the throne, Innocent III addressed to Hungary, as well as to France, England, and Sicily, a circular letter demanding the enforcement of a moratorium on the capital, and cancellation of all interest, on debts owed by Crusaders. Several subsequent papal communications emphasized particularly the withholding of public offices from Jews, as pledged by King Andrew II (1205–35) in his famous Golden Bull of 1222. This charter, confirmed by Louis the Great in 1351 and made a permanent part of Hungary's constitutional law, has sometimes been compared with the contemporary English Magna Carta. In fact, however, it merely favored the gentry at the expense of the high aristocracy, the king thus seeking a counterbalance to the frequently rebellious grandees. In this bull the king provided that "only the nobles of the realm shall be eligible [to become] counts of Our Mint and purveyors of salines and customs, but not Ishmaelites [Muslims] and Jews." He repeated that pledge in 1231 and 1233. It was easy, therefore, for Honorius III to demand in 1225 the observance in Hungary of the old canon legislation barring "blasphemers of Christ" from public office and to complain of the infidels' possession of Christian slaves. The pope claimed that the Saracens' prosperity encouraged many Christians to convert to their faith. While the pope referred specifically to Saracens, he clearly also had Jews in mind. A few years later (in 1231) Gregory IX repeated the same complaints to the Archbishop of Gran (Esztergom) with even greater vehemence, adding that the Cumans (a pagan tribe rather recently converted to Christianity) were particularly prone to abandon the faith. A year later this energetic pope also tried to enforce in Hungary, too, the seventeen-year-old Lateran canon concerning the badge.[23]

Despite the general submissiveness of the Hungarian kings to ecclesiastical demands, particularly if they were also supported by the gentry—the monarchy's closest allies—the sociopolitical realities proved stronger. The king soon realized that he simply could not get along without Jewish fiscal advisers, tax collectors, and saline managers. Doubtless informed that, because of similar needs, the pope had yielded on this score to the wishes of the Portuguese king, Béla IV (1235–70) obtained a partial retraction from Gregory in 1239. Only to "save face," the pope insisted that if the king "should perchance sell his revenues to Jews or pagans, he should deputize a Christian not suspect of causing hardships to clerics or churches through whom the Jews or Saracens might collect the royal dues without injury to Christians." This concession was doubly important at that time, since the country was speedily approaching the catastrophic denouement of the Tartar invasion. In 1241 the Mongolian hordes overran Hungary, practically with no resistance, leaving behind utter ruination of cities and villages. As in other periods of great crisis, the populace was prone to blame Jews for sympathizing with the enemy. A contemporary German chronicler wrote:

They [the Tartars] invaded parts of Hungary, Bohemia, Poland and the adjoining regions, devastating everything, sparing no men, old or young, rich or poor, and killing women with their little children. . . . Many Jews, however, began to rejoice, for they believed that their Messiah was coming and their liberation would begin in that year, for this was the year 1241 since the Lord's incarnation.

We recall that similar rumors were spread in Germany, Jewish hopes doubtless surging higher and higher at the coincidence of this tremendous upheaval with the beginning of the sixth millennium of their era of Creation. Another German chronicler even reported a popular assumption that the Mongols were but descendants of Jews once transplanted by Alexander to the Caspian mountains; he was only wondering how the few original exiles could have proliferated into the vast multitude of thirteenth-century Tartars.[24]

We have no evidence of any Hungarian attacks on Jews during the Tartar invasion similar to those in more distant Frankfort, although they obviously suffered together with their neighbors from the general devastation. Before long, however, some Jews bore the brunt of the newly introduced accusation of the desecration of a host. An otherwise unknown Pressburg scholar, Rabbi Jonah b. Saul, tried to save himself through flight, but he was apprehended and, apparently together with a number of associates, publicly stoned. Regrettably, the elegy written on this occasion by an anonymous poet, beginning '*Agumah nafshi* (My Soul is Disturbed) gives neither further biographical data nor the date of the execution. This event, unconfirmed by any other source, seems to have been quite exceptional, however. Even relations with foreign Jews were quickly resumed. Isaac b. Moses Or Zaru'a of Vienna encountered no difficulty on his journey to Buda and Gran (about 1250), from where he reported the presence of warm springs similar to those of Tiberias.[25]

The tremendous task of reconstruction facing the returning king and his advisers made them doubly appreciate the cooperation of Jewish counselors and administrators. Jews apparently had no difficulty in persuading the king that, in order to attract their coreligionists to the depopulated country, he should issue a broad privilege in their favor. They found a ready model in the extensive charter promulgated in 1244 by Frederick II of Austria. In 1251 Béla IV copied that charter almost verbatim and promulgated it as the basic law for Hungarian Jewry.[26]

So slavishly did the Hungarian king follow the Austrian text that he apparently paid little attention to the differences in the social structure and the peculiar position of Jews in the two countries. Even the penalties for attacking Jews were repeated, and included the same monetary fines with no differentiation as to the value or purchasing power of the respective currencies. Only the death penalty, which together with the confiscation of property was imposed by Frederick upon any Christian murderer of a Jew, was modified here, as well as in the similar charter issued by Přemysl Ottakar II three years later; it was replaced by the vague statement that such a murderer should be punished by an "appropriate judgment" (*digno iudicio*) as well as confiscation. Obviously, the medieval tradition that murder was under the sanction of a *wergeld* rather than death was still too strong in both Hungary and Bohemia. On the other hand, Béla sharpened the Frederician decree by adding the conclusion that "if the judge of a city in which Jews live should not wish to judge them according to the tenor of this Our privilege, but should desire to oppress them in contravention of their hitherto observed statutory customs and liberties, he shall be removed as soon as We are informed by them [of his action] and another man appointed in his stead according to Our will." Béla also spoke of the "perpetual validity" of this privilege, a validity which he tried to reinforce by confirming it in 1256 and extending it to territories interveningly occupied. In consonance with this charter, Andrew III, a year after being crowned king in 1290, made it clear to the city of Pressburg (Pozsony or Bratislava) that, while renewing its municipal privilege, he also intended that "the Jews residing in the city should enjoy the same liberties as the very burghers." Clearly, Béla's decree was taken seriously in practice. Despite the papal perorations, and despite the sharply phrased canons adopted by the large provincial Church Council of Buda in 1279 which stressed above all the exclusion of Jews from public offices as well as the badge, we find Jewish counts in the latter part of the thirteenth century. One of them, Count Henok (Ḥanokh), ancestor of a distinguished Hungarian Jewish family, was awarded by the king control over the fortress of Komorn (Komárom or Komarno).[27]

With Andrew's death in 1301 the long line of the Arpad dynasty, the real founders of the Hungarian kingdom, came to an end. After a seven-year period of anarchy and civil strife, the royal crown was conferred upon the capable prince Charles Robert of Anjou. As Charles I (1308–42) he was mindful of the traditions of the Capetian, Habsburg, and Comnenian, as well as the Arpad, dynasties, all of whose blood coursed in his veins. Combining great diplomatic skill with perseverance and military ability, Charles ultimately overcame the centripetal regional rulers, reunified the kingdom, and expanded its boundaries. The reign of his son, Louis the Great (1342–82), was generally regarded by a grateful posterity as the Golden Age of medieval Hungary. Louis not only enlarged his kingdom (for the last twelve years of his life he simultaneously served as king of Poland), but he also promoted domestic peace, prosperity, and culture. His regime was marred only by the outbreak of the Black Death in 1349, which intermittently devastated Hungary until 1360, and which was followed by another pestilence in 1388–89. Their cumulative effect is said to have caused the decline of Hungary's population by fully one-quarter.

Jews who had previously shared in the growing prosperity were, more than their neighbors, victimized by the Black Death. Although spared the massacres and public burnings which destroyed so many communities in the neighboring Empire, they became here, too, objects of suspicion and hostility, and in 1360 Louis decreed their general expulsion. According to the chronicler, Joannes de Turóczi,

as a zealous searcher for salvation Louis desired to convert the Jews to the Christian faith and to make them tributary [*lucrari*] to Christ. But when he was unable to carry out his intention because of the obstinate stiff-neckedness of the said Jews, he ordered their expulsion from the entire kingdom of Hungary. But he did not wish to acquire or possess any of their goods and objects which had been accumulated through voracious usury and which he despised like dirt. In this way all of them left Hungary for Austria and Bohemia where they continued living scattered [in various communities].

Evidently the king did not mind appropriating the real estate left by the exiles, which they could not dispose of in the limited time allowed to them. In 1361, for instance, he gave the synagogue of Pressburg, "which had fallen to the royal Treasury," to a physician, Magister Francis, for perpetual possession. This total suppression of Judaism was evidently adopted by the king without due consideration, and he soon regretted it. After four years he revoked the decree and invited the Jews to come back. It seems that many exiles, who had interveningly found new homes in Wallachia and elsewhere, failed to return, but their places were speedily taken by immigrants from the more inhospitable western lands.[28]

So convinced had Louis now become of the usefulness of his Jewish subjects that, upon their return, he appointed in 1365 a dignitary by the name of Simon as "justice of the Jews," a sort of minister for Jewish affairs whose duty it was both to protect the Jews and to exploit them financially for the benefit of the Crown. This office lasted for almost a century, the last justice being the highest court dignitary, Palatine Lawrence Héderváry, appointed in 1440. At the same time Louis tried to restore the preexpulsion system of

Jewish taxes, insisting that, for instance, the Pressburg Jews must pay the accustomed imposts from their vineyards to the city (1371). The fiscal contributions became particularly burdensome under the long reign of the Luxembourg Sigismund (1387–1437). As in later years, when he also wore the Bohemian and the Imperial Crowns, Sigismund alternated protective measures for Jews with their extreme fiscal exploitation. His usual inconsistency was well illustrated by the two enactments he issued in quick succession in 1393. On the one hand, informed by a Jew, Salomon, that the Cathedral of Stuhlweissenburg (Szekesfehervár) possessed a document (doubtless a copy of Béla IV's privilege) which "might prove highly necessary for the ratification of their [the Jews'] liberties and the pursuit of their rights," he ordered the chapter of that church diligently to search for this document and to deliver authorized transcripts to Salomon and other interested Jews of the realm. On the other hand, to reward two dignitaries, Nicholas and Johannes de Gera, for their services, he allowed them to attract Jews from Germany, Bohemia, and other lands and to settle them in their private possessions. These nobles were not only permitted to tax such settlers at their discretion, but all royal officials, including the treasurer and the *judex Judaeorum*, were specifically forbidden to interfere in their affairs. The king thus lightheartedly diffused the royal controls over Jews and undermined the very flow of revenue to the royal coffers, on which he was so greatly to depend in later years. In Hungary he could still justify his excessive demands by the patriotic need to defend the country against the advancing Turks. However, Hungarian Jewry was also taxed to fill the royal chest for the king's struggle against the Bohemian Hussites and his other numerous domestic and foreign enemies in the Empire. The king felt free to dispose of the property of his Jewish "serfs," introducing on occasion the Austrian system of *Tötbriefe* (letters of cancellation) of debts owed by individuals. In 1426 he canceled the entire debt owed by the city of Pressburg to Jewish lenders. More frequently he merely "forgave" the debtors' accrued interest, justifying it by the high rates legitimately charged by Jews before and also after his reign. A document of 1357 mentions the prevailing rate of interest of 3 pfennigs a week per pound, or the yearly rate of 65 percent. In

1452 a lengthy discussion refers, as a matter of fact, to a Jewish loan of 32 florins which in the course of nine years snowballed into a debt of 310 florins. Another debt of 45 florins turned within a brief period in 1487 to one of 150 florins, while still another 25-florin debt, having increased tenfold by 1493, was reduced by the king to 50 florins. Willy-nilly the Jewish lenders took these cancellations or reductions in their stride.[29]

Such speedy accumulation of profits naturally enabled some Jews to acquire large fortunes. A Pressburg Jew named Isaac, banker of the Moravian Palatine Jodocus, came, through a forfeited mortgage, into the possession of a house belonging to the son of a city judge. This house was distinguished by a tower. The city, perhaps resentful of its Jewish ownership, acquired it in 1387 from Isaac for the large amount of 447 florins and converted it into its city hall. This incident also illustrates the protection extended to individual Jews by some Hungarian magnates. Isaac's negotiations with the Pressburg council were doubtless smoothed by his patron Jodocus' letter of November 20, 1386, asking the city fathers to be helpful to Isaac in all possible ways. A year and a half later (March 12, 1388), Jodocus assumed a more threatening tone. He informed the council that he would hold it responsible for any mishap to the Jewish residents of Pressburg during the forthcoming Easter holiday, indicating that, if need be, he would use his armed forces against the city.[30]

Frequent emphases on loans in the extant documents should not mislead us, however, into believing that Hungarian Jewry consisted exclusively, or even primarily, of moneylenders. By their very nature credit transactions often led to litigations, and appear in court and other records with much greater frequency than, for example, the sales of objects by petty merchants or deliveries of goods by artisans. Since monopolistic guilds developed in Hungary much more slowly than among its western neighbors, we hear relatively little about Christian competitors trying to curtail Jewish industrial opportunities, as did the Ödenburg (Sopron) tailors, for instance, when they demanded in 1507 "that Jews should in no way be allowed to acquire entire bolts of cloth and to work them up into clothing whereby the [Christian] tailors must necessarily suffer great damage and want." [31]

However, moneylending was not only the most lucrative occupation but, by bringing the lenders into contact with borrowers from among the highest aristocracy and state officialdom, it also gave them an opportunity to intervene in behalf of their coreligionists in times of stress. This situation was formalized under Matthias I of the house of Hunyadi (1458–90), equally distinguished as a statesman, general, and patron of letters, when he appointed a Jewish banker, Jacob Mendl of Buda, as "prefect of the Jews," formally in charge of the defense of Jewish rights. This office was held by the Mendl family for four generations until the downfall of the kingdom at the battle of Mohács in 1526. Its vast authority may be gauged from Wladislaus II's (1490–1516) later confirmation of its privileges. Addressed in 1516 to all Jews of Buda and the rest of Hungary, this decree insisted that the "prefects" alone appoint all presbyters from among "the Pharisaic Jews" (*judeis phariseis*) and threatened all opponents with royal displeasure. In return, Jacob Mendl and his successors led the Jewish communities in their manifestations of patriotic allegiance to the king. Not only did the Jews of Buda solemnly greet Matthias upon his accession to the Throne in 1458, but Mendl also headed a large Jewish delegation which in 1476 rode together with other dignitaries to welcome the king upon his second marriage with the ambitious Neapolitan princess Beatrice. According to a lengthy contemporary description, they seem to have displayed on this occasion their own flag with the star of David. Reciprocally, Matthias confirmed the privileges of Pressburg Jewry, together with those of the city, in 1464. Nor did he appear to be seriously affected by his anti-Jewish friends among the foreign and domestic "humanists" whom he helped to support, including the sharply Jew-baiting polemist, Peter Schwarz (Nigri). In general, in emphasizing royal supremacy also in the ecclesiastical domain, Matthias simultaneously stole the thunder of pro-Hussite trends toward a national church and pursued a course independent of Rome. On the other hand, during his short-lived occupation of Lower Austria in 1482–90, he did not feel it incumbent upon himself to readmit the Jews to that province. More remarkably, for local reasons he consented to the expulsion of Jews from the city of Tatatóváros (Tata, Dotis, or Totis), an exclusion which remained in force until 1518.[32]

Otherwise the fifteenth century proved an unfavorable period for the Hungarian Jews, though not to the extent it did among that country's western neighbors. In 1490, even the Blood Accusation made its appearance in Hungary. Utilizing the insecurity created by Matthias' sudden death on April 4, 1490, the burghers of the Slovakian city of Tyrnau (Nagyszombat or Trnava) seized a number of Jews and held them captive under trumped-up evidence. This act immediately called forth the intervention of the widowed Queen Beatrice, who on April 21 informed the city council that "the Jews whom you so greatly oppress [*turbatis*] belong to no one else but the royal Chamber. At the present time, when the kingdom is without a monarch, you ought to defend, rather than to oppress them." Nevertheless, the ensuing trial in the presence of the palatine, combined with the confessions of the accused obtained by torture, led to the execution of twelve men and two women in 1494, and to anti-Jewish riots in various communities. Even more extensive attacks occurred at the beginning of the sixteenth century in Pressburg, Buda, and elsewhere, attacks which the greatly weakened regime of Wladislaus II was unable to stem. Yielding to various pressures Wladislaus decreed in 1503 a general cancellation of all debts owing to Jews, whereupon the latter, led by Jacob Mendl (sometimes called in contemporary Latin documents "Nigri" or "Niger," the equivalent of "Schwartz" or "Schwarz"), turned to Emperor Maximilian I for protection. The Habsburgs, who ever since Albert II (Sigismund's son-in-law) had claims on the Hungarian Throne, might gladly have assumed that responsibility. But they did not really attain a foothold in the Hungarian regime until after the catastrophic battle at Mohács and the death of Louis II (1516-26). During the final years of Hungary's independence, a Jew Isaac became in 1524 manager of the royal mint in Kaschau (Kassa or Košice), while a convert Imre Szerencsés (Fortunatus) served as treasurer of the whole country. Rumor had it that this former Polish Jew, named Solomon Glück, continued secretly to adhere to Judaism (possibly a reflection of the widespread suspicion of the Spanish *conversos*) and that he ultimately died as a repentant Jew. But unfortunately for him, as well as for the Jews, he had to conduct his office during a highly inflationary period, when fiscal pressures were compounded by the Treasury's urgent need of funds for the preparation of a defense against the Turks. The hatreds generated by his doubling the existing taxes were partly responsible for the anti-Jewish riots in Buda in 1525.[33]

Deterioration of Jewish status came to the fore in many forms. As late as the fifteenth century the oath *more judaico* was extremely simple and inoffensive. One recorded formula read:

The Jewish oath. "You the Jew shall swear in the following form, namely in the name of the Omnipotent God Father Sabaot who appeared to Moses in the bush or in that of the true Father Adonai that you will answer correctly and tell the truth about whatever you may be asked." He shall answer: "I swear." "And if you should prove culpable and should perjure yourself, you shall be dispersed among the nations and dwell in the land of your enemies and the earth shall swallow you up as it did Dathan and Abyron [Abiram]." He shall respond: "Amen."

The sixteenth-century codifier Stephen Werböczy changed this formula to one of much greater length and derogatory implications, which bore a much closer resemblance to those interveningly developed in other Christian lands.[34]

Jewish autonomy, too, was less fully respected now than it had been in previous generations. Largely in connection with the disturbances following 1526, but in part adumbrated earlier, even Jewish cemeteries were frequently violated. As a result, only a dozen tombstones from Buda and Tyrnau have come down to us, but hardly any from the other four Jewish "houses of eternity" (in Gran, Pressburg, Ödenburg, and Eisenberg [Vasvár]) recorded in documents. Ödenburg's Jewish cemetery, which had claimed existence since the ninth century, was wilfully destroyed after the expulsion of Jews from the city in 1526, and only one inscription has turned up. It was discovered in a suburban cave in 1944. Nor have medieval Jewish writings survived the stormy transition of the sixteenth century. If a number of manuscript fragments, used for bindings in later libraries, have been pieced together in recent years by Alexander Scheiber, they all are of non-Hungarian authorship and range from the Talmud to Maimonides. In fact, only the work of one outstanding medieval Jewish Hungarian halakhist is known to us. But Isaac of Tyrnau's "Book of Custumals," written about 1420, has probably been preserved only because the author moved to Vienna and thus joined the then flourishing

German-Jewish school of recorders of local customs. There doubtless were many other rabbis and scholars who carried the torch of
Jewish learning in the Hungarian communites. But, working outside of the main centers of Jewish learning, they remained as inarticulate in a literary way as did most of their confreres in other
peripheral lands of Jewish settlement such as medieval Poland or
Lithuania.[35]

POLAND'S SLOW BEGINNINGS

Jews were recorded in Poland from the tenth century on. Dis-
counting both the equivocal archaeological findings and the old
legends concerning the first Jewish king of Poland, Abraham Pro-
chownik, to which reference was made in an earlier volume, there
is little question that Jewish minters and other individuals served
princes of that region in various capacities before any regular communities were established. In view of the paucity of sources, we
can as a rule postulate the presence of Jews only from a few incidental references; for instance, the decree reputedly issued by
Mieszko III (1173–1202) which, according to the chronicler
Wincenty Kadłubek, imposed the severe fine of "seventy" (probably seventy skins, or the equivalent of 14 to 17 silver marks) for
the bloody assault on a Jew. A similar fine was usually provided
only for lèse-majesté or sacrilege. Even such a negative qualification as that of the 1262 privilege, which allowed the Cistercian
order in Koprzywnica to admit to settlement in its area all sorts of
persons "except Jews," clearly indicates that elsewhere their presence had made itself felt. These Jewish settlements still were very
small, however, as is attested by a responsum of Rabbi Eliezer b.
Isaac of Bohemia (ca. 1200). Replying to Rabbi Yehudah b. Samuel the Pious, who had complained about the "misuse" of the
Purim collections destined for charity for the payment of salaries
of synagogue readers, Rabbi Eliezer pointed out that

in most localities of Poland, Russia and Hungary there are no students
of Torah; because of their poverty, the communities hire any competent man they can to serve as their reader, judge and schoolteacher
[promising him all these revenues]. If you should prohibit these payments, the ordinary salaries would not suffice to maintain them. As a

result the Jews of those countries would remain without Torah, without prayer and without persons to dispense justice to them.

By "Russia" the rabbi doubtless understood the areas of Red Russia (roughly corresponding to modern eastern Galicia) and parts of the Ukraine including the venerable city of Kiev.[36]

Early settlements of Jews in the Polish area are reliably reported only in its western parts, particularly in Silesia. Most Jewish settlements have to be postulated by scholars merely on the basis of names of localities derived either from Jews or from Khazars. Otherwise Polish sources are quite inarticulate. In the case of Cracow, for example, we hear nothing about Jews there until 1304, when suddenly a "Jewish street" appears in the records. Soon thereafter we learn about a synagogue, a Jewish cemetery, a Jewish gate, and the like. The effect of this reticence of non-Jewish writers is compounded by the almost total absence of literary works produced by the medieval Jews themselves in Russia or Poland. The little information we have about their intellectual interests stems from their occasional appearance in western lands, whether in person or through correspondence. Just as Moses of Kiev, a twelfth-century scholar, became known to us only through his association with the school of R. Jacob Tam of Rameru, France, so do we learn about a Cracow Jewish scholar in the late thirteenth century through a brief reference to him in a responsum by R. Meir b. Baruch of Rothenburg. Only toward the end of the fifteenth century did one Samuel of "Russia" leave behind a voluminous talmudic work, preserved in the Vatican Library.[37]

From the thirteenth century on, Jewish settlements gradually expanded without necessarily being recorded in the sources. In the important city of Kalisz in Great Poland, which under the name of Kalisia had been mentioned by Claudius Ptolemy as early as the second century, Jews appear in the records for the first time in 1283. Yet it stands to reason that the famous privilege issued by its Duke Boleslas (Bolesław) the Pious in 1264 had been secured by local Jews. They probably were there already in the days of Mieszko I. Similarly, in the other Great-Polish community of Poznań (Posen), where some Jews may have lived in the eleventh century, they are not formally recorded until 1367. The important

Little-Polish community of Sandomierz is also first mentioned in that year. The Jews of Lwów in Red Russia appear first in 1356, although neighboring Przemyśl may have had, as early as the eleventh century, Jews who furnished the Arab geographer Idrisi with information about the trade route from Breslau to that city. A young Przemyśl Jew may also have been mentioned in an eleventh-century responsum by Yehudah b. Meir ha-Kohen. We would know even less about the Jewish communities of Lithuania, were is not for Grand Duke Vitovt's (Witold's) special privileges for several Jewish communities in 1388–89. This happened shortly after Lithuania's conversion to Christianity and her entry into the orbit of West-European civilization. Another text mentions Vitovt's gift of two Lithuanian villages to a Jewish leader named Shakhna.[38]

Not that progress was steady and unhampered. The entire country, including its Jewish population, suffered severely from the devastating Tartar invasion of 1241, repeated on a lesser scale in 1259. Since most of the nascent cities lying in the path of the ruthless invaders were laid waste by fire and sword, many Jews, too, were either slain or forced to flee for their lives. This wholesale destruction was hardly compensated for by the earlier arrival of refugees escaping the wrath of the Tartar conquerors from other southeastern territories which had maintained some vestiges of the old Khazar settlements. On the other hand, Jews apparently were not accused in Poland, as they were in parts of Germany and possibly in Hungary, of having conspired with the Tartar invaders.[39]

Even after having overcome that crisis, Polish and Lithuanian Jewry permanently had to contend with the opposition of both the Church and the rivaling German burghers. Without being vehemently opposed to the Jewish settlement as such (the anti-Jewish intent, if any, of the aforementioned privilege of the Koprzywnica Cistercians of 1262 appears to have been a singular exception) the Church's leading organs began, through various synods, to agitate for the restriction of both the number of Jews and their rights. In quick succession the synods of Kalisz (1264), Breslau (1267), and Łęczyca (1285) adopted a number of important anti-Jewish resolutions. So did the aforementioned provincial Council of Buda of 1279, which, presided over by the papal legate,

Philip, had a strong representation of the Catholic clergy from Poland. The acceptance in Poland, too, of the underlying ecclesiastical ideology is well illustrated by an anonymous memorandum dated by its editor at about 1267, although it may have been written much later. Here the author insisted that:

The Jewish people committed a great sin and, for that reason, it became homeless like the fratricide Cain. . . . They [the Jews] are rightly to be treated as serfs condemned to the yoke of servitude. . . . Some Jews living in parts of Poland acquire through money public offices from their Christian holders and administer them, being favored by many noble and non-noble participants, even some prelates of the Church. They hire Christian women to nurse their children whom they force to cohabit with them to the injury of Christ and the Christian name. They have built several synagogues in a city against [the law], covered them with lead roofs painted in various colors [plumbo tectas . . . inter diversis coloribus depinguntur], and erected them at such height that the distinction [decorum] of the house of the Lord [the church] appears to be lost in Poland.

The anti-Jewish conciliar resolutions were later included in the decisions of the synod of Kalisz of 1420, adopted under the leadership of Mikołaj Trąba, archbishop of Gniezno and primate of Poland. Having just returned from the Ecumenical Council of Constance where he had led the Polish delegation, Trąba and his associates imbued the decisions of the Kalisz synod, often considered the first codification of Polish canon law, with that Council's antiheretical and anti-Jewish spirit. Twenty years later the archbishopric of Lwów adopted the same resolutions and thus extended them to the rest of Poland.[40]

Equally persistent was the opposition of the German colonists. Their number and contribution to the rise of the Polish economy have long been under heated debate among German and Polish nationalists. But there is no question that their jealously guarded privileges, often referring to the Magdeburg or other German city law, had almost totally exempted them from the jurisdiction of the local authorities. Even appeals from local German courts were long referred to the respective tribunals in the German mother cities. Only one Jewish community that of Troki (Trakai) in Lithuania, was put under the Madgeburg law, by decree of King Wladislaw III in 1441. Utilizing this privileged position, the German burghers, together with their Polish followers, tried with all means at their disposal to stave off the Jewish competition.[41]

On their part, Jews also enjoyed an extensive autonomy, though of a different type. Because it was buttressed by their religious law and solidarity, it was in some respects even more effective. Thus most cities of Poland in the late Middle Ages had side by side two communities, a German-Polish and a Jewish, which sharply competed not only in business but also for residential space and rights. Moreover, most Germans had brought with them from their home country much anti-Jewish feeling, and together with local mobs they often staged riots against Jews. Here, too, the Black Death and the subsequent pestilence of 1360 caused much suffering. The Chronicle of Oliva includes the following brief entry under 1349 which could have been written by any German chronicler: "Jews poisoned springs and wells. . . . Hence they were cut down in all of Germany and almost all of Poland, some dying at the point of the sword, others being burned, and still others drowned in water." Though lacking confirmation from any other chroniclers, this report is partially borne out by brief references to Cracow in western *memor* books, and in a Hebrew poem surveying the sufferings of the Jews in central Europe. This disturbance, even though it led to the killing of but relatively few Jews, nonetheless augured badly for the future.[42]

Anti-Jewish agitation received increasing nourishment from the introduction into Poland, too, of the folkloristic accusations of ritual murder and the desecration of hosts. As early as 1347, the first Polish Blood Accusation caused the Jews to appeal to the pope for protection. However, the papal bull of 1349 was no more effective in Poland than were earlier bulls and imperial decrees in the Holy Roman Empire and elsewhere. In 1598 an ardent Jew-baiter, Father Przecław Mojecki, claimed that these papal bulls had been outright forgeries, and that at best they testified to the purity of the Jewish faith but not to the innocuous nature of contemporary Jews and of their magic practices. He enumerated no less than thirty-four ritual murders and fourteen host desecrations allegedly committed by Polish Jewry up to his time. The Jewish defense usually proved ineffective; for instance, the Cracow Jew who, according to the unsympathetic German merchant, Justus Ludwig

Dietz (Decius), had "strongly and courageously defended himself" against the allegation of having desecrated a host, was nevertheless burned (1508). Apart from the individual victims of trials, entire communities suffered from attacks such as occurred in Poznań in 1367 and in 1399, the latter in connection with the first host accusation recorded in Poland. Cracow was stricken as a result of rumors spread against Jews during the pestilence of 1360, and again in 1407. The latter outbreak started with inflammatory sermons by one Magister Budek, who described in graphic detail the Jews' alleged slaying of a Christian child and throwing of stones at a priest carrying a crucifix on his way to visit a dying patient. Although some Cracow Jews found shelter in St. Anne's church, the rioters set the church afire and thus forced the inmates to surrender. Only a few saved their lives by adopting Christianity. That greed was at least partially responsible is clearly reflected in Jan Długosz's narrative: "They looted many valuables and precious articles found in Jewish homes. Numerous Christians suddenly became wealthy and lived in luxury. After the suppression of the tumult the authorities found many treasures in their houses, some of them hidden in the sand and in outhouses." The reappearance of such accusations in various parts of the country caused much concern to the royal administration, which, as we shall see, tried to stem them by various ordinances, until by the end of the sixteenth century even its struggle against these superstitious libels had gradually weakened.[43]

Nevertheless the Jewish settlements increased by leaps and bounds. By 1350 at least sixteen organized Jewish communities existed in the seventy-five Polish cities. At the end of the fifteenth century Great Poland alone embraced twelve Jewish communities, Little Poland ten, Red Russia eighteen, Mazovia and Kuyavia jointly twelve, Lithuania four. Most of these communities still were quite small. Yet the total number of Jews in the realm, variously estimated, appears to have reached 30,000. As usual, the very establishment of organized Jewish communities added new stimuli to Jewish immigration.[44]

Such growth was not seriously impeded by the occasional privileges *de non tolerandis Judaeis* secured by a number of Polish cities. Among the more important localities which then or later refused to admit Jews altogether were Bydgoszcz (Bromberg), Sambor, Drohobycz (Drogobych), Łomża, Piotrków, and Radom. The uncertainties of Jewish settlement even after admission are well illustrated by the story of Warsaw. Belonging to the duchy of Mazovia, Warsaw may have had Jews quite early, since Płock in the same duchy had Jewish residents as early as 1237. Yet their first mention in Warsaw dates only from 1414, and frequent references to their business transactions do not begin to flow until 1421. By 1427 no fewer than 173 such transactions were entered in the local court records. It seems, however, that in connection with the animosities aroused by John Capistrano's arrival in Cracow in 1454, Warsaw, too, became the scene of anti-Jewish riots. The Mazovian Duchess Anna, who on her visit to Cracow was sufficiently impressed by Capistrano to establish a Bernardine monastery in Warsaw upon her return home, may have been coresponsible for the toleration of these attacks. Yet it is unlikely that the later historian of the Franciscan order had Warsaw in mind when he wrote that "he [Capistrano] caused the expulsion of these people [the Jews] from many cities as irreconcilable enemies of the name of Christ." Nevertheless, the preacher's seeds bore fruit thirty years later, and Jews were told to leave Warsaw in 1483. But they were allowed to return after three years, to be definitely banished after the permanent union of Mazovia with the Polish Crown in 1527. The prohibition against Jewish settlement was renewed "with the consensus of the councilors of Our realm" by Sigismund Augustus in 1570, Stephen Bathory in 1580, and Wladislaw IV in 1633.[45]

Such exclusiveness was more practical than ideological; it was mainly intended to reserve the entire local trade for Christian burghers. Nor was enforcement always effective. When, because of its more central location, the capital of the realm was transferred to Warsaw, Jews were allowed to visit it as litigants before courts, as royal suppliers, and as other interested parties, particularly during the protracted sessions of the Polish Diet. From such occasional visitors, reinforced by "lobbyists" representing communities or individuals, there gradually arose a small permanent settlement. Elsewhere, too, Jews often managed to establish residences in immediately adjacent localities, or even in small enclaves within the cities themselves belonging to certain nobles or the Church and therefore exempted from the jurisdiction of the municipal organs.

More frequently Jews and burghers reached some general agreements concerning the location of the Jewish quarter and the commercial activities of its inhabitants. In Lublin, for instance, where Jews are first mentioned in the second half of the fifteenth century, they were largely concentrated in a district called *Podzamcze* (under the castle), which by 1568 had assumed the character of an almost independent Jewish municipality. This was indeed the case in Cracow, where the Jews, after a struggle lasting several decades, in part led by the influential churchman and royal councilor, Zbigniew Oleśnicki, were first compelled to sign in 1485 a very restrictive covenant with the city. It clearly was only under duress that they agreed to limit their trade to forfeited pledges, of which they were to dispose only on Tuesdays, Fridays, or at fairs. Contravention was put under the severe sanction of three marks, payable to the governor. Even the sale of artisans' products was restricted to caps and collars manufactured by the "poor" Jews themselves. It sounds like pure irony when the Jewish representatives confirmed with their signatures and seal that this compact had been adopted by "the unanimous vote of our entire community and we have accepted it of our own free will and with no compulsion." Yet it did not satisfy the Cracow burghers, and in 1495 they forced the Jews to leave their old habitats in the center of town and to move to a suburban township named Kazimierz (Kuzmark) in honor of its founder, King Casimir the Great, where Jewish settlers had but sporadically been mentioned before. Despite the burghers' stubborn resistance, however, this new Jewish community constantly expanded its area and jealously guarded its minimal trading privileges in the old Polish capital itself. From the outset many Cracow burghers must also have realized that by transplanting the Jews to Kazimierz they would enhance the latter's competitive position. Characteristically, Jews there and in many other places (in Lublin in 1568, in Poznań in 1633, and in the Lithuanian cities in 1645) secured quasi-privileges *de non tolerandis christianis,* by virtue of which they were able to preserve the uniformly Jewish character of their quasi-municipalities.

Even where no such legal enactments were in operation, the Jewish community, which, as we shall see, had developed in Poland into an even more powerful autonomous institution than in the western countries, succeeded in keeping non-Jewish settlers out of their quarters for cultural as well as for economic and political reasons.[46]

More threatening was the sudden decree of expulsion from Lithuania issued by Grand Duke Alexander in the same year of 1495. The background of this significant, if temporary, episode has not yet been fully clarified. Although undoubtedly imbued by his tutor, Jan Długosz, with the spirit of religious intolerance, Alexander (1492–1506) had at first renewed the privileges of the Karaite community of Troki, employed Jewish tax farmers, and generally maintained the regime's traditional pro-Jewish attitude. Perhaps his wife, Helena, daughter of the Muscovite Tsar Ivan III, instilled in him a fear of Jewish proselytism, which, in her own country, had been held responsible for the flowering of the great sect of *Judaizanti*. These "Judaizers" had penetrated the highest circles of court, aristocracy, and the very Church. The expulsion of Jews from Spain three years before, which had created a great sensation all over Europe, the more readily invited emulation as the king and his advisers saw in it an easy expedient to enrich the Treasury and to relieve it of its burdensome debts. In actual execution, however, this operation proved to be far less profitable than expected, for Alexander was much too profligate in bestowing the confiscated Jewish property on monasteries, Jewish converts, whose number had greatly increased among the settlers reluctant to leave their old homes, and other favorites. On their part, the Jewish exiles seem to have realized the impulsive nature of this grand-ducal ordinance. Many moved to the neighboring Polish town of Ratno, from which they could maintain some commercial relations with Lithuania and where they hoped to weather the temporary storm. Their expectation proved justified when, upon the death in 1501 of his brother John Albert, Alexander also assumed the Polish Crown. He not only renewed the traditional privileges of Polish Jewry, but in 1503 he also readmitted the Jewish exiles to his Lithuanian possessions and even ordered the restoration of their confiscated property. The king's change of heart was further demonstrated by the numerous privileges he issued in favor of individual Jews from 1503 on. For instance, he sweepingly proclaimed that the physician Ezekiel was "freed by Our royal Majesty from all imposts and taxes which the Jews have hitherto been wont to pay at royal discretion." The king also conferred upon Ezekiel a free mansion in Lublin.[47]

In this exceptional treatment of a Jewish doctor, Alexander likewise followed in his brother's footsteps. In 1501 John Albert had granted his physician Isaac, a Spanish exile, a stipend of twelve marks to be collected from the revenues of Sandomierz Jewry. He also freed him from any jurisdiction other than the king's own and from the payment of taxes. These privileges were renewed by John's successors, Alexander and Sigismund I. Alexander had an additional reason for being grateful to Isaac Hispanus, who, at his request, undertook in 1504 the long and arduous journey to the khan of the Volga Tartars, then in need of expert medical treatment. True, such royal favors were never completely dependable, as Isaac himself was to learn when, in 1507, Sigismund granted Jan of Buczacz, the district governor of Rawa, a lifelong annual rent from the revenue of the Lwów Jews, as an indemnity for Jan's large war losses. Yet the king did not hesitate, in the very same year, to order that official to disburse to Isaac one hundred zlotys annually from that rent. More, after Isaac's death in 1510 Sigismund ordered that the latter's widow, Barsabea, should continue enjoying her husband's prerogatives. These favors evidently caused much jealousy even within the Jewish community, and some of Isaac's enemies spread rumors that he was of illegitimate birth. But this gossip was squelched by the king. At royal request two Polish nobles visiting Jerusalem investigated the family background of the doctor, whose sister was living in the Holy City, and reported back that according to the testimony of Jerusalem Jews both siblings were the legitimate offspring of one Abraham, member of a fine Jewish family.[48]

Less spectacular were the interventions of Polish kings in behalf of their Jewish merchants abroad, including their reiterated efforts to secure the admission of Jewish traders to the intolerant Muscovite Empire. As early as 1453, Casimir IV wrote to Grand Master Ludwig von Erlichhausen of the Teutonic Order in behalf of "iudeus noster," Sloma of Grodno (Gardinas). Having previously obtained for Sloma trading rights and an immunity for goods in the Grand Master's territory, the king now protested that his protégé had been illegally detained and deprived of his merchandise. This letter was successfully presented to the Grand Master by four Mazovian Jews, who, curiously, refused to take back the Grand Master's reply to the king. Conversely, in 1464 the Venetian doge complained to King Casimir about a Venetian citizen, Nembrot, who after his arrival in Poland had been "furtively deprived of his merchandise by some Jews." Intertwined with this international concern for Jewish commerce was also some special treatment of immigrants. When Abraham of Bohemia arrived in Poland with warm recommendations from Emperor Maximilian I and the Hungarian King Wladislaus, Sigismund accepted him with open arms. The king not only tried to safeguard the new arrival, in 1518, against his enemies' accusations and provided that only the royal court or the Cracow governor could adjudicate litigations against him, but in addition he quickly elevated him to a leading position in Polish Jewry. Sigismund also took under his special protection certain prospective immigrants from such Bohemian cities as Leitmeritz (Litoměřice) and Komotau. More astonishingly, he was so sure of the forthcoming arrival of many Bohemian Jews that in 1517 he informed the Bohemian Chancellor Vladislav Sternbergk that all possessions of the prospective émigrés were under the protection of the Polish Crown. Hence the chancellor sought to shield those Jews against any injury, to enable them freely to transfer their property to successors, and generally to let them enjoy the rights of other Bohemian subjects. There is no evidence that the Bohemian authorities in any way repudiated this outside interference in their domestic affairs.[49]

EXPANSIVE ROYAL PRIVILEGES

In contrast to that in most western lands, the legal status of Jews in Poland and Lithuania was constantly improving in the later Middle Ages. The foundations were laid by the princes of divided Poland in the twelfth and thirteenth centuries. But there was little continuity in these local regulations and observances (few records of which are extant), except perhaps in each region's customary laws, which more or less permanently accompanied the written enactments emanating from the Crown. So long as the Jewish population was small and for the most part transitory, no extensive legislation was needed. But as the number of Jews increased, together with that of the non-Jewish western arrivals, and as the unification of Poland into a powerful monarchy and its later union with Lithuania injected into the social fabric more distinctive class divisions as well as many ethnic and cultural strains, including Armenians and Muslims, formal privileges or statutes assumed new importance. They now governed at least some major facets of the Jews' relations with their neighbors.[50]

Such general charters did not necessarily enjoy automatic validity throughout the realm, however. The kings themselves repeatedly issued special privileges for Jews of the respective provinces and cities, or even granted special rights or exemptions to individuals. Alexander, for instance, saw himself forced by the pressure of "Our spiritual and secular councilors" to cancel in 1506 a three-year contract he had concluded a year before with the Jew Josko for the farming of the royal customs duties in the districts of Lwów and Bełz. He nevertheless insisted upon maintaining Josko's exemption from all local taxes and his immunity from all jurisdictions except the king's own. On the other hand, when four years earlier Duke Conrad of Mazovia had complained to Alexander about undue exactions by the Jewish toll master in Głowno, the king ordered all his Głowno toll collectors "not to introduce any innovations," but he otherwise upheld all their established rights.[51]

For a long time the Jewish status thus lacked both uniformity and clarity, and there were considerable variations between regions and cities. This is the less surprising as the more numerous German settlers, who were in a much better bargaining position, likewise received privileges which followed different German municipal systems and often greatly diverged from one another. Next to those using the Magdeburg law, there were enactments based upon the Kulm, Neumarkt, and other German municipal regulations. Ultimately, the nexus between these German "colonies" and their "mother cities" was greatly loosened when Casimir the Great forbade his subjects to appeal in their litigations to the Magdeburg tribunals—an important step, indeed, in the gradual Polonization of the burghers. Nonetheless, since Jagiello the country remained not only binational in the sense of permanently embracing both Poles and Lithuanians, but multinational with a large predominantly Ukrainian area, in addition to mixed settlements of Germans, Jews, Karaites (Karaims), Tartars, Armenians, and others. This ethnically heterogeneous character prevented Poland from ever going the way of the West-European lands, which in their drive toward national homogeneity, found in the Jewish communities an unassimilable ingredient of which they usually tried to rid themselves either by unruly popular massacres or by formal decrees of expulsion. Except for the temporary outburst of intolerance in Lithuania under Alexander, no expulsion of Jews ever occurred from a major Polish-Lithuanian region, and even large-scale massacres for the most part skirted the ethnographic settlements of the Polish majority.[52]

German influence manifested itself clearly in the first privilege issued for the Jews of a major Polish duchy in 1264. Boleslas the Pious of Kalisz followed in the footsteps of Frederick II of Austria and his Czech and Hungarian imitators in formulating this significant decree, which unbeknown to him was to become the foundation stone for Polish Jewry's constitutional law. We recall how deeply indebted Frederick II had been to his imperial predecessors, from Henry IV to his contemporary and namesake, Emperor Frederick II. Boleslas was in turn to find imitators, particularly among the later thirteenth-century dukes of Silesia who copied his text almost verbatim. While his decree had merely regional validity, and, like other contemporary privileges, was subject to modification by his successors, the Polish Jews were to benefit from the growing trend toward Poland's unification achieved by Casimir the Great (1333–70).[53]

We possess the texts of three decrees issued by Casimir in 1334, 1364, and 1367, and of another without a date. The first two are essentially but renewals of Boleslas' statute; the third appears as Casimir's independent formulation without direct reference to that of his predecessor, although it largely agrees with it in its tenor. The fourth is a restatement of Boleslas' privilege in a much expanded form (it contains 46 as against 36 articles of the latter charter), and has legitimately been called the Boleslas-Casimir statute. Here the powerful ruler of united Poland laid down the basic principles which were to govern Polish legislation regarding Jews until the partitions of Poland in the eighteenth century. The aim of this privilege was not only to protect the Jews in life, limb, and property, but also to open to them vast economic opportunities so that they might assist in the exploitation of the country's natural resources for their own and the Crown's benefit.

Casimir's sympathetic attitude to his Jewish subjects was the more remarkable as he constantly was under the pressure of his anti-Jewish councilors, which came clearly to the fore in his statute in favor of Little Poland (*ca.* 1347), Art. xxvi of which reads: "Since the aspirations of the perverse Jews are aimed at depriving Christians not so much of their faith as of their riches and property, it was decided that henceforth no Jew shall advance money to any Christian in the realm nor lend him on mortgage deeds but only on sufficient pledges according to the long-observed custom." One easily senses behind this phrasing the influence of Jarosław Boria Skotnicki, leading jurist and primate of Poland, who, though generally quite moderate, had brought back with him from his law studies in Bologna some of the anti-Jewish prejudices of the contemporary Italian churchmen. The fifteenth-century historian, Jan Długosz, felt prompted, therefore, to explain the king's pro-Jewish legislation by his love affair with a Jewess, Esterka, who, like her biblical predecessor, had allegedly intervened with him in behalf of her coreligionists. Modern historians have rightly cast doubts on the historicity of that affair, notwithstanding the persistent popular traditions clustering around the alleged house of Esterka's birth, as well as a mountain named after, and a tombstone attributed, to her. Most dubious are the legends concerning Esterka's two daughters from that morganatic union, who were supposedly raised in the Jewish faith while her two sons grew up as Christians, and about her violent death after the demise of her lover. Whatever one may think of these personal impulses, Casimir, great statesman and administrator that he was, had perfectly valid political and economic reasons to try to attract to his country numerous Jews who, even if not styled *servi camerae* as in the Holy Roman Empire, were likely to serve as the Crown's most loyal subjects. Personally a pious Catholic, Casimir could foresee the growing trend toward the formation of two powerful and independent estates of Church and nobility, which were ultimately to undermine the power of the Polish monarchy. He must have regarded, therefore, as highly desirable the presence in the country of another class of royal subjects, even more dependable than that of the German burghers, to counterbalance these centrifugal forces.[54]

Casimir's successors, the Hungarian King Louis of Anjou (1370–82), the latter's daughter, Jadwiga, and her Lithuanian husband, Wladislaw Jagiello (1387–1434), were far less friendly to Jews. Although Jagiello had only been baptized into the Christian faith after assuming the Polish throne, he speedily came under the influence of the Polish clergy. If we are to believe Zbigniew Oleśnicki, Jews often tried to persuade him to renew their charters, which they submitted to him in forged copies, but the king resisted their blandishments and their pecuniary offers. Jagiello once even declared, "Jews are obnoxious to many people, and almost all Christians hate having relations with them. I, too, heartily dislike their infidelity." Nevertheless, throughout his reign he maintained good relations with individual Jewish bankers, especially Lewko, son of Jordan, who had extended credit to both his wife and his father-in-law, as well as with Wołczko of Lwów. At times Jagiello even entertained Jewish guests at meals. An entry in the king's account book refers to the expenditure of three groszy for meats served on such an occasion. One merely wonders how, in such cases, the hosts got around the limitations of Jewish ritual law in serving meat to Jewish guests. Even in his relations with Wołczko, however, Jagiello, with the zeal of a neophyte, pursued conversionist aims. After allowing Wołczko to found, in 1427, the village of Karcz and even to lease the position of the magistrate there, he stated expressly that he hoped that "through the gifts of Our munificence he [Wołczko] would be rendered more inclined . . . to give up the error of his blindness and be led to the recognition of the holy Christian faith." But it is possible that here and in a privilege granted for three years to two Ravensburg Jews who had settled in Krosno, the king merely mouthed pious phrases to cover up his purely mundane objectives.[55]

Be this as it may, we have good evidence that at least, in her general privilege of 1387 for the city of Lwów, Jadwiga had included the Jews as well as the Ruthenians, Armenians, and Saracens, in her guarantees of all existing privileges. Her husband did the same with respect to the Jews of Grodno in that year, and apparently again in 1424. In 1432 Jagiello issued a decree for the inhabitants of Volhynia, in which he provided that "the Jews and Armenians should have the same [law] as that enjoyed by the Jews and Armenians in Our cities of Cracow and Lwów." On the other hand, he did not resist the demands, supported by both clergy and nobility, that Jews not be allowed to lend money on landed estates. These demands were espoused particularly by Bishop Mikołaj Trąba, who had also initiated the segregationist resolutions of the church synod of Wieluń-Kalisz in 1420. Three years later the Estates, assembled at Warta, adopted a statute against Jewish loans on mortgages which was confirmed by the king. In the meantime, however, Jagiello's brother Vitovt, left behind as grand duke of Lithuania, largely copied the old Boleslas document and in three independent decrees granted full privileges to the Jews of Brest, Troki, and Grodno in 1388–89. Through these privileges the distinguished duke laid the foundations for the future rights of Lithuanian Jewry along lines similar to those established in the Polish "Crown." [56]

It was not too difficult, therefore, for their successor, Casimir IV, who had assumed the government of Lithuania in 1440 and that of Poland in 1447 and continued to reign over both parts of the realm until his death in 1492, to unify these privileges in comprehensive documents of his own. First approached by the Jews of Poznań, who claimed that their original charter had been burned during the city's great fire of 1447, the king confirmed, in 1453, the document submitted to him by the Poznań elders in an authenticated transcript. He simultaneously confirmed a similar privilege for the Jews of Little Poland, and despite an enforced temporary retreat in 1454 he adhered to this policy for the entire Polish-Lithuanian realm for the rest of his life.[57]

Casimir's hesitation in the early years of his reign arose from the ecclesiastical pressure exerted upon him not only by Zbigniew Oleśnicki but also by the influential preacher, John Capistrano, who, after causing many misfortunes to German Jewry, arrived in Cracow in 1454. After earlier interventions Oleśnicki wrote to the king:

A short time ago your Majesty has granted the Jews certain liberties and privileges, supposedly enacted for them by King Casimir, to the detriment and insult of our religion. However, your father [Jagiello] in my presence, I being an eyewitness, and reading these perverted privileges, had refused to confirm them despite the offer of many gifts by Jews. But your Majesty has confirmed them without consulting me who was in Cracow at that time, nor any of the numerous barons. You have permitted the inclusion of certain articles which are contrary to the Christian religion. In the meantime you have learned from the lips of the venerable Father John Capistrano how offensive these privileges are to God, how much they dim your fame and place you under opprobrium, and how greatly the people find them objectionable and hateful. May your Majesty not underestimate the importance of that measure and believe that you may act as you please in matters of faith and the Christian religion. Hence I beg and adjure your Majesty to revoke these confirmations and liberties. Let your Majesty show that you are a Catholic king by removing causes from which can only arise infamy to your name and lead to even worse results.

On his part Capistrano urged the king to revoke the Jewish privileges, "lest the Lord become angry . . . and transfer the reign" to someone else. He also sent Pope Nicholas V copies of the confirmed privileges which the king had theretofore refused to revoke. The populace of the Polish capital, in part still consisting of German Jew-baiters, readily listened to the harangues of that bewitching preacher. But except for local disorders of a minor nature and the indirect role Capistrano played in the exclusion of Jews from Warsaw, nothing untoward happened to the Polish Jews. At first Casimir IV yielded to the popular clamor and ecclesiastical demands—which reached the point of Oleśnicki's threats to secure from the pope an interdict on all of Poland—and revoked, in 1454, the Jewish privileges. But as in other policy matters he thus gave way in form rather than in substance, and in reality the Jewish status remained unaltered until Casimir's death in 1492.[58]

Casimir's sons and successors John Albert and Alexander were, as we recall, far less sympathetic. It was at the beginning of John Albert's reign that, after negotiations continuing for almost a year, Jews were ousted from Cracow in 1495. This happened despite the objections raised by the young king's mentor, Philip Callimach Buonaccorsi. The Italian humanist's intervention aroused the ire of John Albert's Polish advisers, including his brother, Cardinal Frederick, who complained that "the persistence and importunities in favor of Jews by one foreigner counts more with your Majesty than the authority and fidelity" of all royal councilors. Similarly, even after the revocation of his decree of expulsion from Lithuania in 1503, Alexander evinced few sympathies for Jews and the Jewish community as a whole, even if he made special allowances for such favorites as the physician Ezekiel.[59]

Among Alexander's restrictive measures was his order to the jurist, Jan Łaski, to include Boleslas' privilege in his compilation of Polish laws completed in 1506. While it is cited here from Casimir the Great's confirmation of that statute in 1334, it is much less comprehensive and pointed than that confirmed by Casimir IV. The king made it clear that its inclusion in Łaski's code was to be "a defensive safeguard *against* the Jews." Not surprisingly, therefore, this oldest extant text of the Kalisz privilege contains obvious alterations in disfavor of Jews, whether newly introduced by king or jurist or taken over by them from earlier anti-Jewish redactors. For instance, the old provision that if a Jew were murdered the ruler would place a duelist at the accuser's disposal was replaced by the vague formula that the latter would be given "the protection of justice." This alteration may have antedated, however, Łaski's codification, since public ordeals in criminal trials had been falling into disuse for several generations. This new formula is, indeed, included also in the Hungarian and Bohemian charters. More directly inspired by contemporary biases was the elimination of the right of Jewish lenders to take over lands of insolvent debtors. This right, to which the Polish nobility had been raising strenuous objections, as in the statute of Warta of 1423, was here completely abrogated, making that paragraph totally meaningless. Another textual change may have been owing to a simple copyist's error, possibly also antedating Łaski's compilation. The threat that a Christian violating a Jewish woman (*alicui judee*) would be punished according to the law of the land was transformed into an attack upon a Jew (*alicui judeo*), which had already been placed under more severe sanctions in preceding articles.[60]

Neither king nor jurist, however, was able to turn back the wheel of history. Alexander's successor, Sigismund I, restored the line of continuity by confirming the old privilege in the Boleslas–Casimir the Great combination, as confirmed by Casimir IV in 1453. It is substantially this final text, as issued by Sigismund I in 1539, that remained the cornerstone of all subsequent legislation. It was reconfirmed by Sigismund Augustus, Stephen Bathory, Sigismund III, Wladislaw IV, and their successors down to the last king of Poland, Stanislaus Augustus Poniatowski, soon after their accession to the throne. Poniatowski's confirmation of June 14, 1765 remained valid until the disintegration of Poland and the replacement of the Polish legislation by those of the three occupying powers, Russia, Prussia, and Austria. However, even the latter took some cognizance of the provisions of this traditional statute. It doubtless was to influence the attitude of their new masters that the Poznań elders submitted in 1793 seven of these privileges in a certified German translation to the Prussian authorities. A comprehensive "summary," officially confirmed by the last Polish king in 1765, was also kept in the Cracow Jewish archives for use under the Austrian occupation.[61]

These brief remarks must suffice here. The content of the extensive privileges and their bearing upon the position of Polish Jewry will be more fully clarified in our later chapters devoted to an analysis of the medieval Jewish legal status and economic life in general. They will also be the subject of fuller exposition in connection with the far richer and more amply documented history of the Jews in early modern Poland and Lithuania.

RISE OF EAST-CENTRAL EUROPE

On the periphery of the Holy Roman Empire we thus witness basic differences among the west, south, and east. The Low Countries gradually loosened their ties with Germany and, economically as well as culturally, were drawn into the orbit of western Europe, particularly France and England. Like those more powerful neighbors, they grew less and less tolerant of Jews and by the end of the Middle Ages eliminated them completely. In the south, Switzerland, though likewise partially drawn into non-German (French and Italian) spheres of cultural influence, remained predominantly a German-speaking country. But like their confreres in the Empire itself, the Swiss burghers, and particularly the artisans, increasingly resented Jewish competition and moneylending and they gradually succeeded in ousting these "aliens" from the confines of their cities.

In contrast, Hungary and Poland forged ahead as major areas of Jewish settlement. This evolution was, understandably, slow and gradual. It was made possible only by the Christianization of both peoples, which established their close contact with western Christendom. True, in their earlier pagan periods, too, they (ever since Roman Pannonia) had admitted Jewish residents and transients. The relatively few Jews engaged in slave trade with the Muslim East had found the Slavonic countries an inexhaustible reservoir of unfree manpower. In this respect the adoption of Christianity by the Poles and Magyars actually interfered with the Jews' export and import business. But they could continue to handle the other articles of trade between the Baltic and the Middle-Eastern heartlands of Islam, as described by Ibn Khurdadhbah in 846, were it not for the intervening dissolution of the Caliphate. Yet, in the long run, their losses were more than made up by the new opportunities opened to them through the growing exchanges with western lands, the improved farming techniques, and the rise of cities.[62]

Growth of new urban centers, to be sure, was not an unmitigated blessing for Jews. Many of them were founded, or at least developed, by German colonists who often brought with them their deep-rooted anti-Jewish feelings and who, sooner or later, sought to eliminate the unwelcome Jewish competition altogether. However, in contrast to their counterparts in the imperial and Swiss cities, these burghers were themselves as alien an element in Hungary and Poland as were the Jews. Even in cities placed under the Magdeburg or some other German municipal system, the German ethnic group as a rule constituted but a minority lording it over a majority of Poles and other racial and religious groups.

Moreover, both countries witnessed the rise to power of a nobility which, divided between a high landowning aristocracy and a lesser gentry, often pursued economic policies at total variance from those of the German-dominated bourgeoisie. By balancing these divergent class interests against one another, the kings were able for a time to establish their supremacy over the country, and incidentally also to protect the Jews against their German antagonists. While those divided powers eventually became the source of great instability, and ultimately led to Poland's ruination, they enabled the Jews to find shelter among the various local authorities whenever intolerant winds blew in either the major urban centers or at the royal court. The Church itself often had to tone down its anti-Jewish program or to propagate it with less fervor and conviction. Compromises like those agreed upon by such an extreme advocate of papal supremacy as Gregory IX with Béla IV of Hungary in 1239 were frequently repeated in practice, if not in theory, in the following generations. The very anti-Jewish resolutions adopted by the synods in Buda, Breslau, or Wieluń-Kalisz could rarely be implemented because of lack of cooperation by either the royal power or the gentry, or both.

It is small wonder, then, that the last three centuries of the Middle Ages prepared the ground for the later remarkable evolution of the two great civilizations of Hungary and Poland-Lithuania. Even more revolutionary was the transformation of the Jewish community in the latter area from a relatively minor segment of the Jewish people, dependent for its very cultural and religious sustenance on the older western centers, into a great focus of Jewish learning, which, within a brief span of one century, achieved cultural hegemony over the Ashkenazic—in fact the entire Jewish—world. If Hungarian Jewry did not quite share in this grandiose evolution, this was owing to the country's division into an Ottoman segment which included the capital of Buda, that of semi-independent Transylvania, and the western provinces which came under the sway of the Habsburgs and were subordinated to that dynasty's far-flung imperial ambitions and responsibilities. Despite these difficulties, Hungarian Jewry, too, was to make considerable progress during the sixteenth and seventeenth centuries and was ultimately to become a leading center of modern Judaism.

FRANCE AND ENGLAND

POLITICALLY wholly independent, most West-European countries were nevertheless tied to the Holy Roman Empire
through the common bonds of Christian civilization and the
basic similarity of their religious and sociopolitical organization
dating back to the Carolingian period. On the Jewish question, in
particular, the principles laid down by Charlemagne and Louis the
Pious, as well as the arguments advanced against them by Archbishops Agobard and Amulo, remained a common heritage of all
countries north of the Alps and Pyrenees.

During the great struggle for supremacy between the Papacy
and the Empire, however, the contradictory claims of those universalist institutions necessarily provoked a reaction also among
the rulers and jurists in France and England. The latter realized
the implications for the status of their own Jewries of the Church's
clamor for control over all Jews because they had been condemned
to "perpetual servitude" since their repudiation of Christ, and of
the Empire's insistence on the submission to it of all Jewish "serfs
of the Chamber" by virtue of its inheritance of the rights of the
ancient Roman conquerors of Judea. We need not take too seriously the aforementioned report of the Austrian chronicler that
because of this imperial claim Philip IV expelled the Jews from
France in 1306 since he did not wish to tolerate in his land subjects owing allegiance to a foreign monarch. And yet we may believe that Frenchmen or, to a lesser extent, Englishmen found
these imperial pretensions quite irksome. They advanced therefore the contrary theory that the Jews outside Germany and the
Papal States owed their exclusive allegiance to their respective territorial masters. By the thirteenth century this was an indisputable
historical reality. But it still required some theoretical justification.

ROYAL SUPREMACY

Such a new evaluation of the true position of the West-European Jewries was but part of a general revolt against the pervasive universalist ecclesiastical and imperial postulates. The growing nationalist undercurrents in France, England, and the Iberian Peninsula nurtured the rise of both a lay culture and a growing spirit of political independence from under the temporal "sword" of either the Papacy or the Empire. Ultimately, the conflict between the Roman Church and the ever more centralized French monarchy not only terminated the Papacy's drive for world domination but it also led to the ignominious "Babylonian exile" of the fourteenth-century popes in Avignon. These new trends generated rationalizations of the independent "divine right" of kings and their prerogative as well as duty freely to pursue what they considered the best interest of their countries. From different angles these new principles were effectively argued by influential political thinkers from the Norman "Anonymus" writing in English Normandy around 1100 to Marsiglio of Padua in the fourteenth century.

Protagonists of these principles, from which was later to evolve the doctrine of national sovereignty, claimed that every king was an emperor in his kingdom and that he served directly as the vicar of God and His minister on earth. As the thirteenth-century English jurist, Henry de Bracton, explained it, "the king shall have no peer, not to mention a superior, especially when exercising justice." Before long King Philip the Fair of France vigorously protested against Boniface VIII's attempt to impose upon him a truce with both the Empire and England. Probably at the advice of the staunchly royalist Peter Flotte, Philip informed the French churchmen that the government of the temporality of his realm belonged to him alone, as king, and to no one else, and that "in temporal matters he recognized no superior, just as his ancestors had none, as is generally known throughout the world." In practice, after Innocent III such royal independence was fully established. In his communications with the other monarchs Frederick II himself frequently toned down some of those grandiloquent im-

perial aspirations with which he was regaling his German and
Italian subjects. The popes, too, usually ran into a stone wall of
passive resistance when they tried to dictate the domestic behavior
of individual kings. Even in the case of Jews, we recollect, pope
after pope urgently, but ineffectively, appealed to the Western
kings for the collection from Jews of ecclesiastical tithes, or against
the appointment of Jewish officials. Papal appeals proved, as a
rule, persuasive only in such preeminently religious matters as the
Jewish badge or missionary sermons, which were of minor concern to the kings. But few monarchs were ready to relinquish their
jurisdictional authority over their Jewish subjects or their self-
interest in Jewish property. It took prolonged external and internal pressures before the kings were ready to compromise in
allowing recent converts to retain all or part of their property.[1]

In arrogating to themselves full control over Jews, the kings
could invoke the existing practices and the power of tradition.
Otherwise they merely fell back on Church doctrine, the fountainhead of almost all ideologies in medieval Christendom. They
accepted the concept of the Jews' condemnation to "perpetual serfdom" because of their "guilt" for having repudiated Christ. But
they insisted that the Jews were serfs of Christian rulers, whoever
these may be, rather than specifically of the Church or the Empire.
This royal interpretation appeared so simple that it did not require
elaborations of the type found in papal or imperial letters.

In England, particularly, the total dependence of the Jews on
the royal power had become manifest almost from their settlement
under William the Conqueror. A twelfth-century compilation
attributed to Edward the Confessor of the pre-Norman period the
sweeping assertion that "the Jews and all theirs belong to the
king." Reviewing the conditions in the thirteenth century, Henry
de Bracton, with involuntary humor, observed, "The Jew can
have nothing that is his own, for whatever he acquires, he acquires
not for himself but for the king; for the Jews live not for themselves but for others, and so they acquire not for themselves but
for others." This oft-quoted assertion by the eminent English
jurist has often led to extreme interpretations of the alleged Jewish "rightlessness" in medieval England. Even such distinguished
students of medieval British law as Frederick Pollock and F. W.

Maitland, though admitting that the term *servus* is not to be found in any medieval text, nevertheless insisted that the status of English Jewry in the latter part of the twelfth and during the thirteenth century was that of villeins belonging to the king. We shall see that this interpretation requires considerable modification, since similar phrases were often used to justify special *privileges* conferred upon Jews. In his charter of 1201, John Lackland provided among other matters:

And wherever Jews be, be it lawful for them to go wheresoever they will with all their chattels, as our proper goods [*sicut res nostre proprie*], and be it unlawful for any to delay or forbid them. And We ordain, that throughout the whole of England and Normandy they be quit of all customs and tolls and prisage of wine, as our proper chattel [*sicut nostrum proprium catallum*]. And We command you and ordain, that you have them in ward and guard and countenance.

In later years, to be sure, John, and still more Henry III, began interpreting this royal supremacy in the sense of the kings' right of unlimited fiscal exploitation. Yet even they realized that their controls were circumscribed by custom. During the reign of Edward I, jurists trying to impress upon the Jews obedience to the kings' statute knew of no greater sanction than that, in case of violation, a Jew or a Jewess would "be at the mercy of our Lord, the king touching life and limb, and all his or her goods and chattells"—a condition which, in legal theory, had existed even before the offense. Nonetheless there is no question about the total dependence of Jews on the royal power and the underlying conviction of kings like John and Henry that, whatever they may have understood by that term, the Jews were really *their* serfs.[2]

In the Spanish kingdoms and Portugal the actual conditions of the Jews were far better. Certainly the exploitation of the Jewish financial resources was more limited. Nevertheless here, too, we find clear expressions of the peculiar nexus between the Jews and the royal Treasury. As early as 1176 the important *Fuero* of Teruel evidently expected no contradiction to its statement, "Be it known that a Jew has no part in the fine paid for an assault or homicide on him, but that it all belongs to the Lord King. For the Jews are serfs of the king and always belong to the royal Treasury [*nam iudei servi regis sunt et semper fisco regio deputati*]."

Equally succinct was the assertion included in the collection of Castilian custumals (*Libro de los Fueros de Castilla*), "The Jews are the king's. No matter whether they live under the authority of all the great lords or the nobles or others or under that of monasteries, all of them belong to the king, live under his tutelage and for his service." Unabashedly some Castilian and Aragonese rulers admitted their self-interest in maintaining the Jews' taxpaying ability. In trying to stem, for instance, Ferrant Martinez' incendiary sermons, John II stated sharply in 1382, "You should know that it is Our will and grace that the said Jews be protected, defended and maintained as Our and Our chamber's property." As late as 1481, Ferdinand the Catholic, in consultation with Isabella, severely censured the prior of the Saragossan Cathedral for his unauthorized public appeal to confine Jews to their quarter. "It appertains to none," the king declared, "but Ourselves and Our own person to provide and ordain in matters relating to Jews, who are Our chests and Our patrimony." In this document Ferdinand did not call the Jews his "serfs," but rather "Our vassals and chests." Going beyond the Spanish boundaries, James I sweepingly lectured the municipal authorities of Montpellier in 1252 not to tax the local Jews, as such action would run counter to the royal jurisdiction and honor, "for the Jews in almost all lands are subject to the serfdom of Christian princes [*fere in terris omnibus Christianorum principum subiacent servituti*]." Such utterances can easily be multiplied. Here, too, the practical application of such phrases depended on changing local conditions. But at least in theory the postulate of Jewish serfdom under royal tutelage seemed to enjoy universal acceptance in both Aragon and Castile.[3]

In France, on the other hand, no such universal supremacy of the king could be established so long as the country was generally broken up into multiple feudal regimes. Perhaps for that very reason each principality tried to arrogate to itself complete control over its Jews. Sometimes an individual city, like Narbonne or Marseilles, could have Jewish communities paying allegiance to different rulers. In Narbonne there apparently existed a tripartite division into sections under the jurisdiction of the viscount, the bishop, and the Jewish "king." In Arles it was Frederick Barbarossa who gave the archbishop power over the local Jews "who belong to Our chamber." Not surprisingly, therefore, the early part of the thirteenth century witnessed a series of extradition treaties between the king and some powerful vassals, in which the contracting parties pledged themselves to return one another's Jewish subjects. It was particularly Philip II Augustus who, after his readmission of the Jews to the royal domain in 1198, attempted to undergird his control over Jews by a series of such treaties with various dukes and barons. In 1223 Louis VIII concluded a more general compact in which the parties promised not to seize each other's Jews. Louis IX renewed such a convention in Melun in 1230, adding the provision that it extended over all the barons of the realm. "No one in the entire kingdom," Louis ordained, "shall be able to retain a Jew of another lord. Wherever a master shall find his Jew, he may freely seize him like his own serf, no matter how long the Jew might have dwelt under the dominion of another lord or in another kingdom." Later he reinforced this agreement by a series of treaties with individual barons and even by having it incorporated in the resolutions of the provincial council of Béziers of 1255 (canon 27). In time, however, with the growth of royal authority, the Jewish "serfs" were increasingly attached to the Crown. That the latter pursued a rather inconsistent policy and time and again tried to get rid of all these faithful "serfs," by no means diminished the submission to it of more and more French Jews so long as they lived in the royal domain.[4]

FRENCH VAGARIES

In contrast to the German, the French evolution tended toward an ever more centralized royal power. But centralization here did not accrue to the benefit of Jews. The French monarchy spearheaded the movement toward sharper fiscal exploitation, stricter limitations of Jewish economic endeavors, and, finally, complete elimination of the Jews from the country. As the boundaries of royal control extended, particularly by the inclusion of England's continental possessions, the Champagne, and other provinces, the once flourishing French Jewish centers of commerce and culture declined rapidly. After 1394 only a few remnants of Jewish com-

munities residing on the fringes of royal France precariously clung
to their ancient privileges until they, too, were gradually ousted.
The only surviving groups in the early modern period lived in
Avignon and the Comtat Venaissin, which remained under papal
suzerainty until the French Revolution. The intervening grave
inconsistencies, partly owing to the ever changing boundaries of
royal supremacy, but largely resulting from the alternating fits of
tolerance and intolerance of the various monarchs and their leading counselors, often defy systematization. They will best be illustrated by the following chronological survey.

At the beginning of the thirteenth century the French kings
were bent upon safeguarding their Jewish source of revenue. Having been disillusioned by the effects of his drastic expulsion and
despoliation of Jews in 1182, Philip II Augustus (1180–1223) recalled them to Paris and his other possessions in 1198. In the subsequent two decades he strove to keep, even to increase, his Jewish
population. He made the returning exiles swear that they would
not leave his realm, and even kept a number of Jewish hostages
from various communities (some were still held in 1204) to make
sure of the Jews' keeping this pledge. He also concluded, as we
have seen, several treaties with his more powerful vassals providing for the mutual return of their respective Jewish "serfs." He
thus tried to prevent his Jews, doubtless made apprehensive by his
highhanded policy at the beginning of his regime, from emigrating to the Champagne and other more hospitable regions. Occasionally, he specifically reserved his jurisdiction over Jews in
localities which he gave away to such friendly vassals as an abbot or
a countess. This policy of holding on to the royal serfs was pursued
after his death by Louis VIII (1223–26), and in the early years of
Louis IX (1226–70) by the latter's mother, Blanche of Castile.
Three months after his coronation Louis VIII, together with
twenty-four lords, issued a *stabilimentum* which tried both to curtail Jewish usury and to safeguard the respective controls over
Jews. The provision against receiving or keeping Jews of another
master was expected to be binding on all lords, even if they happened not to be among the signers. This policy culminated in the
aforementioned treaty of Melun of 1230 in which the king and
most French lords pledged themselves not to raid one another's

Jewries. Connected with these measures were regulations concerning the collection of debts owed to Jews who, according to the original treaty between Philip II and Thibaut III of the Champagne in 1198, were not supposed to lend money to subjects of the other lord. Since France followed the English example and demanded the registration of Jewish loan deeds, Count Thibaut IV of Champagne himself had to secure in 1224 from Louis VIII a seven-year extension for the repayment of a large loan of 10,500 livres which he owed to two royal Jews. All these provisions derived, of course, from the doctrine that, as masters of their Jewish serfs, the kings and barons had a stake in their property, the Treaty of Melun stressing the fact that Jews were the *proprii servi* of their lords. At the same time these treaties enabled the Capetian kings to extend their power over all of France. As Gavin I. Langmuir observes, "the Capetians had enacted their first measure of effective general legislation—over the bodies of the Jews." [5]

These conventions were frequently enforced by the courts. In 1260 the Paris Parlement assigned a Jew who for a long time had resided in Chauvery to the lord Philip de Chauvery, provided only that the latter would promise "that he would not mistreat [*turpiter*] the said Jew." Similarly, the archbishop of Reims successfully reasserted in 1270 his authority over the local Jews by proving that two Jewish families had lived from time immemorial in a separate quarter of his city (a *vicus Judaeorum* is indeed recorded in a Reims document of 1103), and that they "used to enjoy there much freedom because of an Isaiah scroll [*rotulum Ysaie*] which they were said to be guarding." In many cases, on the other hand, the court upheld the royal claims; in one instance even against the duke of Burgundy (1270) Surveying these court records, Count A. A. Beugnot was led to observe that "at no time has there been more trafficking in, nor more pleading about, Jews as objects of commerce than in the thirteenth century." [6]

When Louis IX, gratefully remembered by the Catholic Church as Saint Louis, assumed a greater personal share in the administration, he injected into the royal policies his strong religious orientation. As a devout Catholic he viewed the French throne as a bastion of Christianity and its doctrines. While at times resisting papal encroachments in French domestic affairs, he nevertheless twice embarked on a Crusade, and generally tried to live up to the highest Christian ideals. He spent many hours daily on devotional exercises which would have been considered exacting in many a monastery. Nudged on by occasional papal epistles, he also endeavored to regulate Jewish affairs in accordance with the canonical doctrines espoused in his day particularly by the vigorous Popes Gregory IX and Innocent IV. He was the only European monarch to lend a willing ear to Gregory IX's denunciation of the Talmud, France becoming the scene of the first burning of that classic in 1242. His personal bias was also reflected in his aforementioned exclamation that a Christian layman ought not to argue with Jews the merits of his religious convictions, but rather plunge his sword into any Jewish debater's vitals "as far as it will go."

Unlike most of his predecessors or successors, therefore, Louis IX, levelheaded statesman though he often was, allowed his policies to be determined less by fiscal considerations than by an attempt to convert the Jews through persuasion and other measures short of outright force. L. Lazard contends that, under Louis' reign, "the sums devoted to the conversion of Jews to Christianity doubtless exceeded those drawn from them by the Treasury." The following data concerning converted children living at royal expense in various cities are undoubtedly incomplete, yet they show that the king's missionary program was moderately successful. According to extant records, there were between 1253 and 1256 no less than 25 such children in Bourges, 14 in Laon, 25 in Orléans, 17 in Amiens, and 56 in Tours. The number of adult converts must also have been large enough for them to form a sufficiently recognizable group to be set apart in official documents. In a manuscript, found of all places in a Leningrad library, a rented house in Paris is designated as belonging to "Dyonisius called conversus son of the deceased Baldwin conversus." The neighboring structure had belonged to the "deceased Thomas conversus." Evidently by 1266, when this document is dated, the converts had left the Jewish quarter and acquired property on St. Martin Street.[7]

Not surprisingly, the king took an uncompromising stand on usury, the major source of income for his Jewish subjects and, indirectly, also of the royal revenue from them. Going beyond anything enacted by his predecessors between 1176 and 1223 and even beyond the letter of canon law, as expressed in contemporary papal decrees and epistles which primarily tried to restrict usury among Christians, he decided to outlaw moneylending on interest among Jews as well. Particularly after returning from his first Crusade in 1254, he issued a decree which reads in part (Art. xxxii): "Let the Jews abstain from usury, blasphemies, sorceries, and magic arts [caracteribus]. Let their Talmuds and their other books containing blasphemies be burned; Jews not wishing to respect this order shall be expelled and transgressors shall be adequately punished. Let them all live from the fruits of their hands or from commerce without usury." Louis meant what he said and in 1257–58 he appointed a commission to investigate Jewish usury and to return such unlawful gains to the debtors. If need be, it was to sell Jewish real estate, other than synagogues or cemeteries, for the satisfaction of such claims. That is probably why an agreement concluded by the canons of Notre Dame with Jews in Paris for the establishment of a new Jewish cemetery contained the clause that, "if under whatever circumstances the Jews should cease owning" the plot, it should revert to the church. In 1260 Louis actually restored to the city of Tours 600 livres which he had collected indirectly from Jewish usury.[8]

Such idealistic postulates could more easily be enacted than carried out, however. In the upsurging French economy of the time credit transactions became a vital necessity. If Jews abstained from that trade, their place was quickly taken by Christian usurers who, because they engaged in that occupation illicitly and with even greater risks, understandably charged still higher rates of interest. In the subsequent decades the administration had to make all sorts of compromises, such as trying to divert Jewish moneylending from the lower classes to the nobility and upper bourgeoisie. These measures resulted in but another distortion of the economic trends, making it doubly difficult for small artisans and shopkeepers to secure the necessary capital for initiating and expanding their businesses. Even under Louis IX, moreover, much Jewish moneylending continued under various disguises, particularly in the provinces administered by his brother, Count Alphonse de Poitiers, who in many ways was more typical of the

Capetian kings. Primarily concerned with empire building, these rulers had found themselves constantly in financial straits, which were to reach a climax in the Hundred Years' War. The Crusades led by Louis IX, with Alphonse's participation, likewise involved large expenditures. The kings did not hesitate to lay their hands on Jewish property; they were mainly concerned with the methods of seizing it most expeditiously. The example set by Philip II proved extremely tempting. Time and again Jews of certain localities or entire regions were suddenly arrested and not released until they paid a substantial ransom. At times such imprisonment, combined with torture, was used to make Jews reveal their holdings and deliver them to the authorities. Not surprisingly, the officials entrusted with the execution of these expropriatory decrees sometimes concealed Jewish holdings and collected outstanding loans for their private benefit.

Typical of these difficulties is the procedure employed by Alphonse de Poitiers. In 1243, three years after assuming the government of his appanage, Alphonse approved an agreement with the Jews that they should pay him 2,500 livres in the course of the following three years and 500 livres during each of the subsequent four years. But before the expiration of this seven-year compact he decided to increase his cash flow for the forthcoming Crusade by decreeing, in July 1248, the expulsion of all Jews from the cities of La Rochelle, Saint-Jean-d'Angély, Saintes, Poitiers, Niort, and Saint-Maixent. He revoked this decree only after the burghers had failed to indemnify him for his prospective tax losses and when the Jews offered to pay him 1,000 livres, that is, more than he could reasonably expect to collect after their departure. Even before that time (March 8, 1248), however, he sent the following characteristic instructions to two commissioners:

Through the complaints addressed to Us by Our Jews of Poitou We have learned that, since the confiscation of their property by Our bailiffs, Our provosts, and other persons, many things have been taken, disposed of, or retained illicitly—to Our detriment as well as to that of the Jews. Hence We order you, after hearing the Jews' testimony, summoning those who are to be assembled, gathering proofs from here and there, and carefully weighing the presumptions and circumstances which are to be examined in such cases, you will devote yourselves diligently to this matter and to no other facts concerning Jews. This you will do exactly according to the methods prescribed to you in other letters. You will faithfully communicate all your findings to Me under your seal.

In preparation for another Crusade in 1268, Alphonse again ordered the arrest of all Jews and the seizure of their movable property. His fiscal objectives became doubly apparent in his letter to the seneschal of Poitou dated October 8, 1268 (amplified in other epistles eight days later and on March 9, 1269), in which he ordered the immediate release of all impecunious Jews and particularly the infirm, women, and children under fourteen, whose movable goods he had confiscated. "As to the rich Jews and their wives, about whom it may be assumed that they will employ subterfuges in order to conceal their fortunes and the pawns they possess, you shall hold them captive until they will render the said goods and pawns. Once you will have determined that, you shall release them, too." Alphonse also had to make allowances for certain independent claims advanced by local lords. Once again he settled with the Jews for a lump sum ransom of 4,000 livres.[9]

Whatever compunctions Louis IX may have had concerning the Church injunctions on maintaining Jews to the end of days, he paid them little heed in his legislation. They were wholly disregarded by his immediate successors, Philip III the Bold (1270–85) and Philip IV the Fair (1285–1314). Of a rather unstable character, Philip III often pursued contradictory policies. His personal animus had come to the fore soon after his accession to the throne in a sharply anti-Jewish decree which not only reintroduced the badge, but also prohibited the Jews from exercising the medical profession and from possessing more than one synagogue or cemetery in a diocese (1271). These regulations went beyond the accepted canon law, and encouraged anti-Jewish churchmen like Bishop Gautier of Bruges to initiate further restrictive legislation in such diocesan synods as that held in Poitiers in 1280 (canon 6). Philip the Bold also continued his father's conversionist policies. According to a Hebrew chronicle (unconfirmed from other sources), he encouraged a Spanish controversialist, Paul, who had come to France "to eliminate the remnant of the holy people from all the lands of the King of France," to stage in 1272–73 public disputations at the royal court or a monastery. Apparently these debates attracted large crowds of Jews. The chronicler claims that, despite frequent assaults by mobs, a thousand Jews appeared at such assemblies, but not one of them was swayed by the missionaries to give up his faith. In 1283 Philip reminded his officials of his confirmation of his father's *établissements* with respect to the Jewish badge. He also paid lip service to Louis' antiusury decrees. At the same time out of sheer self-interest he sought, particularly in an ordinance confirmed in Carcassonne in 1282, to facilitate Jewish pawnbroking, and he even enabled the lenders to collect debts on the basis of notes of indebtedness alone. As if to underscore the usual medieval legislative inconsistencies and royal favoritism, he freed in 1282, at the request of the Duke of Brabant, the Jew Avram de Faloie (Falaise) of his share in the large Jewish tax of 60,000 livres. Notwithstanding such occasional acts of "generosity," at the expense of other Jewish taxpayers, Philip III did not wish to relinquish one iota of the royal control over Jews achieved by his predecessors. True, at times he had to recognize the barons' specific claims, but he tried to curtail their authority as much as possible through the instrumentality of the Paris Parlement.[10]

Under the impact of these uncertainties, further intensified by royal whims and bureaucratic inefficiency, the Jewish communities in the royal portion of France constantly diminished in number and affluence. According to the extant tax records for the capital, there were in 1292 only 124 Jews (in 86 households) among some 15,200 taxpayers, and they contributed but 126 livres, 10 sous to the total intake of 12,218 livres, 14 sous. In contrast, the number of persons enumerated as "Lombards" at the beginning of the list included 205 individuals contributing the substantial sum of 1,513 livres, 14 sous. In 1296–97, the number of Jews declined further to 82 households contributing in the aggregate only 101 livres, 8 sous. Elsewhere, however, the Jewish taxes kept on increasing. In the province of Tours, for example, the total receipts from Jewish taxpayers had risen from 120 livres in 1234 to 2,077 livres in 1299. At the same time the Jewish population in that province had not substantially increased, since the church council of Bourges of 1277 had, with the king's approval, forbidden their settlement in small localities.[11]

These tax lists date, of course, from the reign of Philip IV. But they show the cumulative effects of the regimes of his grandfather and father. If anything, Philip the Fair was even more ruthless than either of his predecessors, and pursued his political and nationalistic aims with even less regard for fairness and religious restraints. By his time, moreover, arbitrary incarceration, and even partial or total expulsion of Jews, had become a traditionally accepted means for French rulers to secure funds. It makes little difference whether Philip was personally responsible for these decisions or whether he too readily followed the advice of his influential counselors. But he himself rightly admitted his responsibility. On his deathbed he is reputed to have said that whatever bad advice he had received he had been "himself the cause of that bad advice." While more fundamental factors operated on the scene which, as we shall see in another context, were ultimately responsible for the total elimination of Jewry from the French realm, partial expulsions or threats thereof had become simple Treasury expedients.[12]

Philip IV employed these and other methods quite ruthlessly. On the one hand, he refused admission to the Jewish exiles from England in 1290, probably because he considered them too poor to become an immediate source of revenue. The Parlement of La Chandeleur of 1291 ordained in his presence that all Jews arriving from England or Gascony be speedily expelled (*infra mediam quadragesimam expellantur*). On the other hand, exceptions were made for wealthy Jews such as one Bonus Amicus son of Jose who was allowed to settle together with his family in any locality which had Jews, for an annual fee of 100 livres. Domestically, too, Philip tried to increase the number of his Jewish subjects; once he even acquired a single Jew for 300 livres. In 1297 he quarreled with his brother Count Charles de Valois about the control over forty-three Jews residing in the latter's possessions. The dispute was settled by two Jews, acting as the main arbiters. The king was represented by Calot (or Kalot) de Rouen, *procurator communitatis Judeorum regni nostri*, while the count delegated Joucet de Pontoise. Ten of the contested Jews were assigned to the count, the rest to the king. Two years later Philip purchased all Jews living under his brother's control, for 20,000 livres—a fair investment expected to yield immediately some 4,000 livres annually which presumably could be raised in the following years. No sooner did the king acquire direct sovereignty over the Champagne when he collected, in 1285, 25,000 livres from the Jews of that county. Three years later he utilized the Blood Accusation of Troyes to confiscate the property of the Jewish martyrs. On one occasion (in 1298) he imposed a general levy of one-fourteenth of all Jewish property, which, although less than the one-third sometimes demanded by the English and German monarchs, amounted to a sizable sum. At the same time, he instructed the seneschal of Carcassonne twice (in 1288 and 1291) to maintain the Jews of his district in the undisturbed possession of their synagogues, schools, and cemeteries. While mouthing, especially in an ordinance of 1299, the old professions of wishing to spread virtue and prohibit usury, he nevertheless insisted, in his order to officials of the realm three years later, upon the collection of all older Jewish debts. Generally involved in an arduous struggle with the Papacy and frequently evincing anticlerical tendencies, Philip IV also sought, by decree of 1302, to restrain the jurisdiction of inquisitors over Jews as a matter both of principle, in order to secure the royal supremacy, and of expediency, the better to safeguard Jewish property. On the other hand, he did not hesitate to use the threat of expulsion from Poitou in 1291. In return for the Jewish revenue thus lost, he was going to impose a tax of 6 sous on each Christian hearth. But he was readily assuaged by the Jews' offering larger payments, which by 1296 yielded no less than 3,300 livres, despite the reluctance of many communities, abetted by their local lords, to fulfill their quotas.[18]

With all these Draconian measures, Philip found the flow of Jewish revenue too slow to satisfy his urgent need of cash for his costly campaigns against England and the Flemish republics and his no less expensive acquisitions of vassal lands in the East. In 1305 he expostulated with the newly elected pope, Clement V, for appropriating some possessions of the Church as well as of Jews and Lombards by emphasizing the large costs of his defense against both the English and domestic enemies. Such confiscations, the king argued, had become doubly necessary because of the imperative need he had felt to stabilize the French currency. Before long he was to lay hands upon the accumulated wealth of the Knights Templars, who, having been forced to abandon their original activities in the Holy Land, had waxed rich from successful business enterprises which were in many ways similar to those of Jews. Aided by jurists well trained in Roman law, the king dealt harshly with the Templars, many of whom he kept imprisoned for years until they revealed to him the hidden resources of the order, which he confiscated without restraint (1307–13). It is small wonder, then, that the sudden appropriation of the whole wealth of his Jewish "serfs" appeared to him as an even more legitimate, indeed time-honored, expedient. In 1306, a year before despoiling the Templars, he issued a universal decree of banishment of Jews not only from the royal possessions, which had interveningly grown to cover most of France, but also from those of his vassals. He merely promised subsequently to allot a share in the plunder to the individual lords. Although disobeyed in some regions, this order might have put an end to the French Jewish settlement, which reached back to Roman times, were it not for Philip's cupidity. Being unable to locate all holdings left behind by the exiles and fully to identify their claims against the Christian residents, he began recalling, in 1311, certain rich Jews to testify concerning their rights for the Treasury's benefit. This method proved ineffective, for the Jews had little interest in enriching their foe. Finally, Philip's successor, Louis X (1314–16) decided in 1315 to reopen France to Jewish settlement.[14]

SPASMODIC TOLERATION

Louis X's charter of 1315 resembled a bilateral treaty between the Crown and the returning Jews. Its affinity to the *condottas,* wherewith Italian cities of the fourteenth and fifteenth centuries were to invite Jewish moneylenders to settle in their midst, was further underscored by the king's justification of his reversal of the previous policy. He insisted that he had done it because of the "clamor of the people" in need of credit, a need which was doubtless aggravated by the general economic crisis brought about by the expulsion. A near-contemporary chronicler claimed that "on the day following" the Jewish exodus the French currency had

depreciated by two-thirds to four-fifths. Yet the decree sanc-
timoniously asserted that "since the Jews are obliged to work and
labor with their own hands, or to engage in commerce, as said before, it is not Our will that they should be able to lend money on
usury, which We herewith expressly forbid. But if it should perchance [*par aventure*] happen that they would lend it, they
should not be permitted to charge more than two deniers per livre
a week," or the customary rate of 43⅓ percent. Clearly, the
alleged "clamor of the people" and the Crown's fiscal interests
were based upon the expectation that this "chance" occurrence
would turn into a regular feature. The Jews were invited to return to the communities they had previously inhabited, but to no
others, and to resume their allegiance to the previous lords. However, the king could keep any baronial Jew he wished to have in
his own domain. This reversal of the earlier extradition treaties
was but another sign of the intervening growth of royal power.
Otherwise the legal *status quo* of the preexpulsion period was to
be restored intact, including the Jew's repossession of their former
synagogues and cemeteries, but they were to indemnify the intervening Christian owners for their investments. Where such establishments were no longer available, they were allowed to acquire
new ones without any hindrance. Similarly, their books, as yet un-
sold, were to be returned, except for the outlawed talmudic literature. They were also to collect all debts owed them before their
departure, provided they delivered two-thirds of the proceeds to
the Treasury. Doubtless at the insistence of the Jewish contracting
parties, the king added a clause guaranteeing the validity of this
charter for twelve years. If, after that time, the Crown should decide to terminate it, the Jews were to be granted a year's delay to
wind up their affairs in an orderly fashion.[15]

Returning exiles who thus entertained hopes of enjoying at
least a dozen relatively peaceful years were quickly dissillusioned.
In fact, the following decade was filled with some of the most har-
rowing episodes in the entire history of French Jewry. To be sure,
both Louis and his successor, Philip V the Tall (1316–22), at first
tried effectively to protect them. At the Blood Accusation of
Chinon in 1317, Philip ordered the apprehension of the real cul-

prits, a chaplain and a Jewish convert. In the same year he issued a lengthy decree again prohibiting the confiscation of Hebrew books, thus assuring Jews of the undisturbed pursuit of their most cherished studies. He also instructed the bailiffs to protect Jewish lives in the future. Under his direction the French tribunals intervened quite frequently in favor of Jewish individuals. At the same time, Philip sharply reacted to rumors about excessive Jewish contacts with Christians. In his decree to the bailiff of Troyes of February 26, 1319 [1320] he ordered the curbing of such excesses by Jews who

inject themselves and mix openly and publicly in the meetings of Catholics in the latter's houses and, what is more serious, in churches. They do not wear the marks imposed upon them so that they be differentiated and distinguished. From this circumstance frequently arises the inconvenience and absurdity that religious persons and, even more seriously, the very priests greet them with reverence.

Philip also lent full credence to complaints that loud prayers in synagogues often interfered with the worship in churches. Evidently these rumors and accusations reached the king's ear from local Franciscans and Dominicans whose churches he specifically mentioned as being disturbed by the Jews' prayers. How exaggerated these aspersions were can easily be gauged from the informants' assertion that many prominent Jews, clad as dignitaries, were frequenting churches and receiving undue homage from both priests and worshipers—a most unlikely occurrence among pious adherents of Jewish law.[16]

Nor did the royal administration overexert itself in forestalling the sudden attacks of the Pastoureaux in 1320. It is estimated that no less than 120 Jewish communities were destroyed, though Paris and other communities under strong royal control remained unscathed. No sooner was this emergency over than the Jews were accused of having acted in concert with lepers in poisoning wells. According to one of many obviously fabricated stories, Archbishop John I, lord of Parthenay, intercepted in Poitiers a circular letter stemming from the Muslim ruler of Granada which urged the conspirators to exterminate all Christians. Reputedly this rumor so frightened the king that he hurriedly left Poitiers for Paris. Treating the matter as high treason rather than as a religious offense, the Paris Parlement condemned the French Jews to the enormous fine of 150,000 livres, estimated by some scholars as the equivalent of 30,000,000 gold francs today. In any case, this was a convenient way not only for the government to secure substantial funds but also for the populace to get rid of unwelcome lepers. While physically the latter were the main sufferers, some Jews were burned along with them. The lepers' immediate financial losses also exceeded those of Jews. At least, the royal account books for the province of Toulouse in 1322 list the income from estates of Jews slain by the Pastoureaux as totaling only some 66 livres, while the yield from the lepers' estates exceeded 258 livres. However, according to another account for the same province in 1324, the revenue from Jews amounted to 4,881 livres as against a mere 105 livres collected from the lepers. Obviously this increase was the result of Philip the Tall's intervening expulsion of Jews from France in 1322 under the excuse that the Jews' part in the conspiracy entitled him to break the twelve-year pledge to maintain them in France given by his predecessor in 1315. The unpaid balance of the fine of 150,000 livres was still being collected from the Jewish property in liquidation when, according to some unverified assertions by chroniclers, the Jews were recalled in 1328 by Philip VI (1328–50)—not necessarily for their benefit. If true, few Jews availed themselves of that invitation. When, in 1340, the king forbade all French debtors to pay their Jewish or Lombard creditors, he emphasized that he had mainly creditors living outside the country in mind. Such export of funds was placed under the sanction of another full payment to the Treasury, in addition to a severe fine. If in 1346, as is sometimes asserted, Philip proclaimed another expulsion of Jews unless they were willing to accept conversion, his decree could have affected only a few hardy individuals.[17]

Compared with these vagaries of royal policies in the first half of the fourteenth century, the last period of the Jews' settlement in royal France, from their recall in 1359 to their final expulsion in 1394, was relatively stable. The immediate impetus to their return was given by the great financial stringency under John II the

Good (or rather the profligate "no-good"; 1350–64). The king, taken prisoner in 1356 by the English, and his son, Dauphin Charles, were unable to raise the enormous ransom of 3,000,000 gold crowns, particularly since they were also involved in a constant struggle with rebellious vassals and restive Estates General. These fiscal needs were aggravated by the accelerating inflation, as exemplified in the rising value of silver marks. At the same time the Estates, which might have put up some serious resistance, were fairly inactive in 1359–60 and their newly admitted members representing the Paris burghers exerted little influence on their noble and clerical colleagues. Charles, who had already initiated a pro-Jewish orientation in his own Dauphiny, now recalled the Jews to France in 1359 and granted them a new privilege in 1361. This charter, confirmed by the imprisoned king, as given "for certain and legitimate reasons relating to the benefit of the Kingdom," was the result of negotiations with Jewish representatives, headed by Menecier of Vesoul. In its twenty articles, the Crown extended to Jews the right of settlement anywhere in France for the following twenty years under direct royal protection, with no reference to any prior baronial rights to them or the king's duty to extradite them to their former masters. They were given considerable socio-religious autonomy, allowed to acquire all houses and lands needed for their synagogues and cemeteries, and promised to be freed from missionary sermons and the seizure of books. In addition to enjoying extensive judicial self-government, they were to be protected by local officials against false rumors and accusations. In order to enable them to pay larger imposts (these began with the substantial admission fee of 14 gold florins for each Jew and his wife and one florin more for each child), they were to be free to engage in all commercial and industrial activities and to lend money at interest rates up to 86⅔ percent.[18]

Disregarding the immediate opposition from many quarters, particularly the clergy, Charles V upheld this policy throughout his own reign (1364–80). He found effective collaborators in Menecier, whom he charged with the general collection of Jewish taxes, and in his own relative, Louis d'Evreux Count d'Étampes. The latter's duties as *gardien général des Juifs et conservateur de leur privilèges* may be reconstructed from a letter issued in 1359 for D'Evreux's southern counterpart, Robert d'Outreleau, which stated:

We give you and those deputized by you full and free power to guard them [the Jews], to pass judgment on any of their litigations and the latter's implications. You shall act in their behalf and defend them against . . . those who would molest and oppress them. You may punish and reprove them as will seem appropriate to you according to the tenor of their privileges.

How seriously Count d'Étampes took his duties may be gauged from an incident in 1380, which must have caused a general sensation. When the mayor of Versigny refused to pay his debts to a Jew of Laon, the provost of that city, on the count's orders, personally appeared in Versigny accompanied by four sergeants and arrested the stubborn debtor. On various occasions, and particularly during the great economic crisis of 1370, to be sure, some councilors advised the king to relieve the court's financial stringency by again expelling the Jews and confiscating their property. Although wavering for a while, however, and recalling that three years before he had himself contemplated such a move, the king staunchly adhered to his twenty-year pledge and actually reconfirmed the Jewish privilege for the moderate payment of 1,500 francs.[19]

It is truly surprising how secure the Jews felt in France within a few years after their return. They could indulge in internal squabbles and even bring them before royal courts without fearing their effect upon their general status in the country. In one remarkable trial before the Paris Parlement in 1355 two leading Jews of Paris, Vivant and Menessier de Viergon, were accused by one Jacob de Sainte Maxence, supported by the royal procurator, of a variety of crimes. They were supposed to have placed Jacob under excommunication (*nidnich,* a misspelling for *niddui*), refused to circumcise his son until forced to do so by royal command, removed the synagogue to Menessier's house in order the more effectively to exclude Jacob from services, and even supposedly hired killers to do away with him. More directly in violation of government orders, they allegedly failed to wear badges, preached to Jews and Gentiles, and also improperly accounted for Jewish taxes. Menessier denied all these allegations or invoked the autonomous rights of the Jewish community in dealing with recalcitrant members. Despite this sound and fury the matter seems to have been settled amicably within a short time. Another more significant controversy raged over the succession of Mattathiah Trèves as chief rabbi of the French communities. We shall see in another connection how this matter assumed international dimensions; it was not settled until it involved leading rabbis in Spain and Austria, who finally decided the controversy in favor of Mattathiah's son.[20]

After Charles V's death, however, the dissensions at court and the uprisings of the burghers and peasants contributed again to the feelings of Jewish insecurity, although young Charles VI (1380–1422) at first tried to maintain his father's tolerant policy. A contemporary chronicler describes in graphic detail the excesses and the pillage committed by the populace against the Jews of Paris during the early years of the new regime. On the other hand, the king not only frankly admitted his fiscal interest in the Jews, but in July 1387 he promised them a twenty-year immunity from prosecution for charging compound interest. In February 1388 he ordered the suspension of all prosecutions of Jews for alleged transgressions against the usury laws and other crimes, since the previous fines imposed upon them for this reason had undermined the economic strength of the Jewish communities "and they will thenceforth be unable to offer as substantial an aid toward the prosecution of Our war as they have been accustomed to do." But no sooner did the king reach real maturity than he began listening to his anti-Jewish councilors, as well as to the popular clamor. Suffering, moreover, from mental derangement and being under the pressure of divided counsels from his uncles, he impulsively reacted to the rumor of an alleged Jewish attack upon a rich convert by issuing a decree of expulsion on July 15, 1394. The Jews were "in perpetuity" to be excluded from France under the sanction of capital punishment for illicit entry. This time the Crown proved rather disinterested; the Jews were allowed to carry away their movable property. Although everything left behind was confiscated, Charles canceled all outstanding Jewish loans without benefit to the Treasury.[21]

Jewish life in fourteenth-century France thus offers a picture of such unmitigated gloom that one wonders why so many Jews appeared ready to return there after each mass imprisonment and expulsion. Even during the relatively peaceful thirty-five years which preceded the tragic finale of 1394 they were affected by constant territorial readjustments. After the recapture of certain districts of Poitou from the English in 1372, Charles V did not hesitate, in the following year, to allow Jews to settle there for ten years and to lend money at the maximum rate of 86⅔ percent. But twenty years later the new community of Poitou suffered a sudden eclipse along with the rest of royal Jewry.

One must also bear in mind that our extant records give a somewhat one-sided picture. They are concerned principally with Jewish moneylending and its excrescences on the one hand, and, on the other, with the fiscal exploitation by the monarchy, the ensuing wholesale arrests, expulsions and revocations. Interspersed are tales of popular uprisings, Blood Accusations and other dramatic events. Little do we hear, at least from French legislative and narrative sources, about daily Jewish life during the not infrequent, fairly quiet, intermissions. We have to go back to Hebrew letters, particularly the responsa concerning individual cases, as well as somewhat similar decisions by French courts, to secure some glimpse of the ordinary life of the Jewish communities. French Jewry was, moreover, widely distributed throughout the country, living not only in the cities but also in small hamlets and villages. Only under Philip III do we hear of a concerted drive by the French clergy to eliminate Jews from the countryside, lest "they deceive the simple country people and induce them to share their errors." Such a resolution was adopted by the provincial council of Saumur-Brouges in 1276 (canon 14). In 1284 the king provided that Jews must not live in the smaller communities "among simple Christians" but only in the more famous cities "where they had lived of old." This decree was followed by his successor's sweeping order to the royal officials to expel Jews from all places without public markets, even if the latter had lived there from time immemorial (1291), and by another instructing the royal officials to cooperate with the inquisitors in apprehending Jews guilty of abetting Christian heresies (1299). Unlike Germany, to be sure, northern France was controlled primarily by kings or feudal lords, whereas the burghers and city councils exercised but relatively little control over the Jewish inhabitants. Nevertheless local developments left a permanent mark on Jewish day-to-day living.[22]

UNDER POWERFUL VASSALS

Until the death of Louis IX in 1270, only a minority of French Jewry was affected by the occasional outbreaks of royal intolerance. The very boundaries of the royal possessions were unclear, the term "frontier" apparently appearing for the first time in a document of 1315. As Robert Fawtier pointed out, at the beginning of the fourteenth century the king of France himself had but a blurred picture of his domain in mind and was prone to cherish his crown, as a symbol of royal authority, much more than one or another parcel of his scattered territories. Yet the growth of royal power in both breadth and depth was incontestable. In contrast to the decree of banishment of 1182, which had affected only the Jews of the Île de France and a few neighboring districts, those of 1306 and 1394 were promulgated for the whole country including the areas still controlled by dukes, barons, or bishops. Only a few of those regional or local rulers were still able to disregard the royal wishes. Among them at first also was John, duke of Berry, uncle of Charles VI. There is no record that he opposed the expulsion of 1394, although we know that the much-needed counsels of the uncles of the unstable king were often sharply divided. Sharing with his brother, Charles V, "the Sage," a love for learning, the duke lacked Charles' prudence and spent vast sums on monumental buildings and other undertakings which he could not afford. He had to borrow heavily from both Jews and Lombards and, on his death in 1416, he left behind an enormous indebtedness to members of both those outlawed groups.[23]

Jewish life under the lesser powers was not necessarily more stable and prosperous. Lorraine (an area of very fluid boundaries) had been one of the oldest centers of French Jewish culture, the tenth-century "sages of Lotharingia" often being quoted with reverence in rabbinic letters. Yet by the time Duke Simon decreed, in 1176, an expulsion of Jews, it affected directly but a few communities. On the other hand, just as Jewish life in Paris was

quickly revived after 1198, the Jews also reappeared speedily in
Metz, Nancy, and Saint-Dié. One of the Lorraine dukes, Ferri III
(1251–1304), actually tried to attract Jews from neighboring Germany to stimulate the growth of cities as a counterbalance to the
baronial power. Occasional acts of intolerance, to be sure, marred
this record. From a Hebrew elegy we learn that in 1276 a Jewish
scholar, R. Samson, was burned after a ten-year imprisonment. We
are not told about the reason for that execution, it being a mere
surmise by the modern editor that R. Samson may have been
guilty of encouraging the relapse of a converted Jew. These more
or less tolerable conditions continued until the Black Death. All
along, the number of Jewish residents must have been quite small.
Even a purported profanation of a host seems to have led to the
execution of but one Jew (*ca.* 1385). The community of Metz
really entered upon its great historic career only under Bishop
Conrad Bayer de Boppard, who granted it in 1422 a fairly favorable privilege.[24]

Neighboring Burgundy was long divided into a duchy, which
on the whole followed the French kings, and the so-called Free
County (Franche-Comté) where German influence long predom-
inated. Duke Odo III (1193–1218), to be sure, transferred his
Jewish rights in Dijon to the city in 1196. But he and his successors nevertheless retained their overlordship. Fourteen years later
he signed a treaty of mutual nonretention of Jews with Blanche of
Champagne. This appreciation of Jews was reflected also in the
dukes' protection of their Jewish subjects. One of the latter,
Jocesinus, felt strong enough to defy the bishop of Mâcon, who
threatened to forbid Christians to have any contact with him because he had allegedly violated the immunity of several churches
and had turned a priory into a "hide-out of burglars and rapists."
Even the final boycott of Jocesinus, proclaimed by the bishop with
the approval of the papal legate in 1230, apparently remained
without effect. The bishop's accusation fails to go into specific details, but it appears that Jocesinus had offended the Church in
connection with his financial dealings. More serious was Hugh
IV's decree of 1256, ordering the explusion of Jews and the confiscation of their property. While pretending to follow the example
of Louis IX, he merely imitated Alphonse de Poitiers. Like that

rapacious count, he revoked his decree under the promise of receiving from the prospective victims a huge "ransom," which was still being collected in 1304 shortly before the new exile. Obviously, by that time the Burgundian Jews, many of whom had originally derived their living from viticulture, had turned to moneylending, encountering, as elsewhere, the sharp competition of Lombards with whom they also shared the debtors' hatred. In response to the growing antiusury agitaton, Duke Robert II (1272–1309) inserted into his testament of 1302 the pious wish that Jews (he did not mention Lombards) should live from the labor of their hands. Nonetheless he and his successors continued to make ample use of both taxes and loans received from Jewish moneylenders. But at crucial moments they followed the French kings in expelling their Jews, too, in 1306, 1322, and 1394. The 1306 banishment proved very remunerative; as it turned out, Hugh V collected over 33,000 livres from the estates left behind by the Dijon Jews alone. The readmission of Jews after 1359, and the new constitutions enacted in 1374, 1380, and 1384, likewise closely followed the contemporary French patterns.[25]

On the other hand, the counts of Franche-Comté, though stemming from a branch of the Capetian dynasty, pursued more independent policies. The county itself was hardly a stable unit, many areas changing hands from time to time. Here a group of Jews, apparently negotiating for certain rights in several localities, took an unprecedented initiative in recognizing Jean de Chalon, lord of Rochefort, as their master and swearing on a scroll of law that they would submit to no other ruler. In this remarkable document of 1269, the Jewish representatives declared:

We wish and concede to our aforementioned lord that he may freely, either by himself or through his officials, seize our persons and those of our wives and children wherever they may be found, without a judge and without any judicial proceedings. He may also retrieve us for his dominion as his own property.

Such a declaration was so manifestly rendered under duress that the abbot and priors who certified it felt prompted to attest that "all the aforementioned statements were made to us spontaneously by the said Jews and have been expressed here at their bidding and request." Despite this harking back to the earlier French extradition treaties, the County followed the French policies so little that Philip the Fair's decree of expulsion of Jews of 1306 remained a dead letter even in a district which was under the king's direct administration. In 1312 Duke Hugh de Bourgogne, in a fit of remorse over the excessive taxation he had imposed upon traders (he probably had but Christians in mind), provided in his testament for the refund of these overcharges. If this will was ever executed and if it also applied to Jews, it offered a telling study in contrasts to Philip the Fair's ruthless exploitation of all, and especially the Jewish, taxpayers. It is difficult to take such pious utterances at their face value, however. Had not Philip IV himself often sharply spoken up against usury? In 1304, but two years before he was to fall heir to the vast accumulation of profits accrued from Jewish usury over the years, he forbade the royal officials in Burgundy to extend any assistance to Jewish creditors with respect to loans "contracted in a usurious fashion or under usurious fraud [evasion]." In those very years, as we shall see, the Jewish banker, Héliot of Vesoul, reached the apogee of his international banking career and in 1315 actually negotiated for the Jews' return to royal France.[26]

In 1322, however, the expulsion hit the Burgundian Jews very hard, although even then not all of them departed. The survivors soon were joined by some newcomers so that by 1330 several Jewish communities were functioning again. But not for very long. Here the catastrophe of 1348–49, though less sanguinary than in the adjacent regions, ended with their banishment from the county and the confiscation of their property. Some Jews were conducted under guard to the frontier. Yet despite a pledge exacted in 1349 by the nobles from the countess-regent, Jeanne de Boulogne, that she would get rid of all remaining Jews and Lombards within six months, it is doubtful whether all of them actually left. Within a quarter century (September 24, 1374) the clergy of the important city of Salins petitioned the new Countess Marguerite of France for another expulsion "of the very vile and perfidious Jews, whose contact soils the Christians and gives rise to innumerable sins," from both their city and the hamlet Bracon. In recompense for the loss of her taxpayers the countess was promised free masses during her lifetime as well as in perpetual commemoration of her death. Similarly, the Estates assembled in 1382 to vote subsidies for the war in Flanders, did so under the condition that Duke Philip (Charles V's brother) would expel all Jews and Lombards. The duke promised, but failed to issue the required ordinance and most of his Jewish subjects tenaciously clung to their posts until the final expulsion of 1394. Only in Besançon the Jewish community, perhaps the largest in the entire region because it enjoyed the protection of the "imperial" city, persevered and even temporarily increased in size through the influx of exiles from the rest of France. However, its days, too, were numbered; its end was graphically demonstrated when its cemetery was sold in 1465 for the city's benefit.[27]

More remarkably, the Dauphiny, even when governed by heirs to the French throne, did not automatically follow the French example. Jewish communities of the archbishopric of Vienne had made general Jewish history because of the Blood Accusation in Valréas in 1247, which prompted Innocent IV to issue the first major papal bull against the blood libel. On the other hand, six years later the same pope first authorized the archbishop to expel from his archdiocese the rabbis and later also the other Jews because of the danger they allegedly created for the orthodoxy of the Christian people. This authorization, which was to be executed "by yourself or by others," was not carried into effect and Jews continued living in the archdiocese and the rest of the Dauphiny long after the expulsions of 1306, 1322, and even 1394. In fact, in 1306, and again in 1322, Jewish refugees were admitted to the Dauphiny from both royal France and Avignon (where a total expulsion appeared imminent in 1322, but, as we shall see, was successfully averted). That liberality was in part due to the influence of such wealthy Jews as Vivaud, whom the Dauphin entrusted in 1319–21 with the recovery of revenues in Auvergne. This Jewish factotum not only lent the prince funds but he also supplied him with horses and oversaw repairs of the castle of Beauvoir. By 1345 Vivaud's monetary advances were still outstanding, as were his additional loans to the new Dauphin Humbert II (1333–49), for which he was but slightly repaid by a lifetime annual rent of thirty florins. Yet Humbert soon turned on all Jews and in 1345 not only expelled them from the Dauphiny proper but also sent out officials

to banish them from his outlying possessions. Perhaps unfortunately for the Jews these orders were not fully carried out, and
enough of them remained to be victimized in the Black Death
massacres of 1348–49. Ninety-three suffered death in the small
town of Veynes alone. Once again the dauphin sent messengers
through his provinces to confiscate the property left by the
martyrs.[28]

Within a few years the situation changed. The new dauphin,
Charles (who was soon to become King Charles V of France),
after annexing to his territory parts of Savoy, extended in 1355 a
comprehensive privilege to the Jewish community of Saint-
Symphorien, which in some respects served as a model for the all-
French charter issued with his father's approval in 1361. The Jews
enjoyed, indeed, considerable liberties in the Dauphiny even after
Charles's son had turned his back on the Jews of France in 1394.
Although few in number (in 1401–1402 their fiscal contributions
amount to only about one-third of one percent of the total),
they felt indispensable enough to threaten in 1409 that they would
leave the duchy unless their tax burdens were alleviated. In 1439
the authorities had to remind the municipality of Montélimar
that the Jews ought to wear badges. Two years later the bishop of
Valence, Jean de Poitiers, had to emphasize that these "guests
ought not to be regarded as citizens [*ne pro civibus hospites
haberentur*]." Nor did the clergy relax their conversionist efforts.
They forced the Jews to attend missionary sermons and in 1453
persuaded the consuls of Montélimar to appoint a special preacher
for the conversion of both bad Christians and Jews. At the same
time the Parlement of Grenoble intervened in 1468 in favor of
Jews maltreated by the inhabitants of that city. Some Jews were
even reckless enough to take part in the political struggles between Dauphin Louis, later King Louis XI (1461–83), and his
father Charles VII. Although in the early years of his reign as
dauphin (1440–61) Louis had shown himself quite favorable to
his Jewish subjects, upon his return from his five-year exile and his
ascension to the royal throne he wreaked vengeance on all his
opponents. In the case of Jews this retribution took the form of a
large fine of 1,500 gold écus imposed by the Parlement of
Grenoble upon the whole community, rather than upon the indi-

vidual culprits. Before long, however, the general anti-Jewish trends in France made life less and less bearable for Jews in the Dauphiny, too, particularly after its incorporation into the royal domain in 1456. By 1463 only four communities, protected by special earlier treaties, were still in operation. Twenty-three years later two of these (Vienne and Valence) were eliminated, and eight years later a royal decree of expulsion suppressed also the final Jewish remnant.[29]

In part, the tolerant attitude evinced in the Dauphiny by King Charles VI himself after 1394 was owing to the treaty he concluded in 1404 with the count of Savoy. In taking over two Savoy districts he promised that "the king and his successors, the dauphins of the Vienne area, will behave, after the death of the said count, in such a fashion as to satisfy the Jews and Jewesses inhabiting these districts with his and his said successors' upholding the liberties and franchises granted them in earlier times." Such toleration was even more consistently practiced in Savoy itself—of course, for a price. The remarkable document of 1254, describing how in a small village about twenty miles west of Chambéry eight Jews had appeared before a notary and "spontaneously" renounced forever all their possessions in favor of Count Peter II of Savoy, furnishes a telling illustration of the pressures to which Jews were subjected from time to time. Nor was the public always friendly. In 1329, rumors about a blood ritual committed by two Jews, supposedly "with the knowledge and consent of all Jews in the county of Savoy," found ready acceptance. Only after a close investigation did Count Edward scotch them, with special reference to the bulls of Innocent IV and Gregory X which had sharply condemned the Blood Accusation. The counts were less successful in preserving Jewish life and property during the Black Death. Actually the attribution to Jews of poisoning the wells had started in Savoy and thence spread its baleful wings over the rest of Europe. Nevertheless some Jews remained in the county and continued to prosper under its tolerant regime. In 1355 Magister Palmerius appears among the wealthy citizens lending money to the city of Chambéry. Five years later Amadeus VI (1343-83), whose physician-in-ordinary Palmerius was, bestowed upon him some revenue as a feudal benefice in return for a personal loan of

900 gold florins. The high standing and free behavior of some Savoy Jews is well illustrated by a court decision of 1404. One San-sinus de Luent, a Jew of Burg, was fined 120 florins because of the following allegations: he had said that if Jesus were to return he would again be crucified; he accused a priest of being the real usurer for charging a florin for a mass which cost him nothing; and he cohabited with many Christian women because of "the abun-dance of his finances." We need not take such judgments at their face value, and yet admit that some Jewish financiers may have abused their financial power under Savoy's fairly tolerant re-gime.[30]

A major reversal came only under the reign of Amadeus VIII (1391–1440) who was so deeply imbued with the doctrines of the Church that, although not an ordained priest, he was elected pope by the Council of Basel in 1439. An expulsion from Châtillon-les-Dombes in 1429 may have been caused by local pressures and need not be laid at his door, since he generally adhered to the papal principles of tolerating Jews. But his decree of 1430, which re-placed the older Jewish privileges, was largely a restatement of the ecclesiastical postulates relating to the Jews' segregated quarters, abstention from public appearance during the Holy Week, the badge, and the nonemployment of Christian servants. In line with these postulates many Hebrew books were suppressed in 1466. Ultimately, disturbed by the large influx of Spanish refugees in 1492, the regents for Charles II (1490–96) tried to banish all Jews from their country. Nonetheless a few persisted and continued their historic progression also after Savoy was joined by Piedmont and became principally an Italian, rather than a French princi-pality.[31]

SOUTHERN HOSPITALITY

Most differentiated was the Jewish position in southern France. Wherever the royal power reached directly for longer or shorter periods, the southern Jews largely shared the fate of their northern coreligionists. However, the frequent changes of real overlordship and the relative independence of some of the ancient municipali-ties long prevented the application of royal laws with any degree of consistency. On the whole, southern French Jewry succeeded in overcoming the evil effects of the Albigensian Crusade, which at first, as in conquered Béziers, threatened to engulf it.

The royal administration itself often departed here from its own principles. A specific article in the Treaty of Paris of 1229, which handed over Languedoc to the royal power, barred the appointment of Jews to public office. Yet soon thereafter a Jew Astruguet served as "royal official . . . who collects for the lord king the judicial fees and fines" of the province of Carcassonne. Other Jews were employed in similar capacities throughout that region. The resolutions of the Councils of Béziers (1246) and Albi (1254), which forbade Christians to consult Jewish physicians under the threat of excommunication, but slightly impeded the widespread medical practice by Jewish doctors. Ultimately, King John the Good himself merely tried to restrict it in 1362 to candidates passing a preliminary examination before Christian experts. True, Alphonse de Poitiers attempted to apply here, too, his northern policy and in 1268 arrested the Jews of Toulouse and the neighboring communities. But this policy was totally reversed by his brother Charles I, who actually sought to attract new Jewish settlers. Similarly, when Philip III took over the Comtat Venaissin he endeavored, in 1269, to expel the Jews. Within five years, however, he recognized the Papacy's sovereignty over Avignon and the Comtat, and their Jewish communities thenceforth shared the ambiguous, but fundamentally consistent, status of the Jews in the Papal States.[32]

Languedoc Jewry fared better, on the whole, under the rule, however arbitrary, of feudal lords, both lay and ecclesiastical, than under the undisguisedly rapacious administrations of the French kings. The bishops and barons, although likewise primarily interested in Jewish revenue, acted under restraints imposed upon them by ancient privileges and customs. Some remonstrated against the royal excesses and often secured even from Alphonse de Poitiers or Philip the Fair a grudging recognition of their long-established rights, although at times the kings merely let barons share in the fruits of their despoliations. The kings also had to settle many controversies among the local lords. Even a Blood Accusation could become an object of jurisdictional disputes, as happened in the city of Uzès in 1297. Before long the ritual libel appeared secondary while the conflicting claims of the bishop who usually controlled one quarter of the city and the lay lords who exercised authority over the rest of Uzès became the paramount issue, which ultimately had to be decided by Philip IV. The long-established local customs likewise often diverged greatly from one another, as well as from the royal law. The custumal of the important commercial city of Alais (issued with the approval of its local lord) mainly echoed the postulates of the Church. It demanded that Jews wear badges, not work on Sundays and Christian holidays, and refrain from appearing publicly on holy Wednesdays, Fridays, and Saturdays. Without regard to royal law it also borrowed from the Montpellier custumal the provision that interest accruals must never exceed 100 percent of the principal. Likewise in agreement with canon law, the custumal of Carcassonne of 1204 forbade the calling of Christians of Jewish or Saracen descent, Jews or Saracens. Montpellier, on its part, insisted in 1205 upon the continued use of the accepted moderately phrased formula of the Jewish oath.[33]

Such local divergences, the result of several centuries of a checkered political and economic evolution, deeply affected Jewish life throughout southern France. The important Jewish community of Béziers had long lived under the joint jurisdiction of a viscount and a bishop. When, after the disastrous siege of 1209, the king took over the rights of the viscount, the bishop tried to assume control over all Jews, but he was rebuffed by the monarch in 1230 and 1278. The king, nonetheless, recognized the continued supremacy of the bishop in the old episcopal quarter. In 1284 Philip III had to order the seneschal of Carcassonne closely to investigate the background of twenty-seven Béziers Jews so as to prove that they belonged to the king and not to the bishop. Even more confusing was the situation in the old community of Narbonne because of the competitive controls exercised in various districts by the bishop, viscount, and Jewish *nasi*. Apart from other feudal possessions the Jewish chief also owned, within the Jewish section, several buildings popularly called the *cortada regis Judaeorum* (the court of the Jewish king). Although still parading its "king," however, and claiming independent jurisdiction over its own quarter, the Narbonne community suffered greatly from the city's general decline. Its legal situation became so thoroughly confusing that when, in 1321, the Paris Parlement had to decide between the conflicting claims to certain Jewish property by the Narbonne archbishop and the royal procurator of Carcassonne, it could not reach an immediate decision and had to postpone the trial. Nevertheless the Jewish community carried on as best it could, celebrating a special annual "Purim Narbonne" to commemorate the preservation of its autonomy after a disturbance in 1236. Certainly, compared with the northern communities, the life of Narbonne Jewry must have appeared calm and contented, until it, too, was overcome by the expulsions of 1306 and 1322.[34]

Among the other Languedoc communities, that of Lunel lost much of its great intellectual distinction, but it continued to prosper economically during the thirteenth century. As late as 1293 its lord, Rosselin, mortgaged with a Jew Thauros of Montpellier the revenue from his barony "for the value of a rent of 40,000–50,000 livres." This arrangement was ratified by Philip the Fair, under the condition that Thauros would either declare himself "the king's Jew," or else pay him the equivalent of six years' income from the barony.[35]

Montpellier Jewry likewise continued its historic evolution, notwithstanding the transfer of sovereignty over it from Aragon to France. A curious compact was made in 1208 by the city consuls and the Jewish community regarding the Jewish share in the city's defense. To forestall more excessive demands the Jews agreed to furnish, at the approach of a besieging army, 20,000 arrows "on the first hour of the third day." After three months, or at the approach of another enemy force, they had to repeat that contribution. In return they were to be freed from all other taxes. In the following centuries, however, the status of the Jewish community deteriorated even more than that of the city as a whole, although the royal regimes of both Aragon and France occasionally intervened on the former's behalf. In 1252 King James I wrote, "We firmly forbid the consuls of this city, present and future, to place any exaction or demand on the Jews there living, or who will be living there in the future, to the prejudice of Our jurisdiction or honor." In 1365 it was the turn of the French conservator of Jewish rights to safeguard the community from being evicted from its well-placed quarter, allegedly because it opened the city to incursions of soldiers. More decisively, the entire city suffered greatly from the Black Death and its aftermath. It has been estimated that Montpellier's population had amounted to some 40,000 persons before 1348, but that it declined to 18,080 by 1367 and to but 15,000 in 1404. The Jewish community could no more maintain its old luster than did, for instance, Montpellier's famous old university, which in 1378 had only twelve students enrolled in its Faculty of Arts.[36]

In fact, the expulsion of 1306 must have come as a greater shock to the old and long-prosperous communities of Languedoc than to the northern Jews living under the shadow of recurrent persecutions since the days of the First Crusade. Many individuals doubtless found a way of remaining behind while many others returned in 1315. Only thus can one explain their large share in the expected Languedoc contribution to the fine of 150,000 livres imposed upon all French Jewry in 1321. The districts of Carcassonne and Beaucaire alone were taxed to the extent of 22,500 and 20,500 livres, respectively. Languedoc Jewry also seems to have suffered less, or more speedily recovered, from the expulsion of 1322. At any rate, when in 1359, under John the Good's regime, Jews were readmitted to France and provided with a highly placed *gardien général* by Regent Charles, the latter's younger brother, Count John de Poitiers, governor of Languedoc, appointed a similar official for the communities under his administration. The post was first held by Robert d'Outreleau and ten years later by Deys or Doys Quinon.[37]

Occasional royal favors of this kind did not stem the progressive decline of most Languedoc Jewries. In 1391 the once flourishing community of Toulouse—where in 1180 a Jew Heliazar could be elected city consul—may have embraced no more than fifteen families. Even Narbonne seems to have numbered in 1305 only 1,000 Jews in a population of 15,000. Their formerly flourishing commerce, too, declined greatly on account of the warlike disturbances and the growth of Mediterranean piracy, as well as of the establishment of direct communications between the great mercantile centers of Flanders and Italy which displaced many southern

French intermediaries. If, owing to changes in commercial techniques, the once vital function of the great Champagne fairs was now taken over by such regional markets as Pézenas and Montagnac, the Jewish traders fell behind their Christian competitors. Probably more than before they now turned to moneylending, giving rise to the usual complaints about their excessive usuries. Even the friendly King John the Good had to order in 1360 an investigation of Jewish practices in the province of Beaucaire, where, it was asserted, the Jews were exacting "in one year usuries exceeding the principal contrary to the royal ordinances promulgated on this subject which may be found in our Beaucaire archive." This constant erosion of the Jews' numerical and economic strength prepared the ground for their total elimination in 1394 also from most southern areas. Only where the Jewish economic differentiation persisted and the French kings did not exercise sole authority were the Jewish communities given a lease on life of varying duration.[38]

Such was the case in Provence, which, under the reign of Charles of Anjou and his descendants, managed to maintain a large measure of independence until its incorporation into royal France in 1481–86. Its ancient cities, particularly Marseilles, successfully invoked their old privileges and enjoyed a higher measure of self-government than the northern municipalities. Their local ordinances took greater cognizance of Jewish religious scruples. A regulation enacted in 1363 that all houseowners must clean the streets in front of their houses every Saturday specifically permitted Jews to perform that chore on Fridays. Twenty-four years later all Marseilles residents were ordered to carry lights while walking at night, but Jews were exempted from doing so on their Sabbaths and holidays. The latter were also able to pursue their diversified callings with greater freedom and a higher recognition of their ancient rights. In some Provençal cities, including Arles and Marseilles, they actually were treated as *cives* enjoying a fair degree of equality with their Christian compatriots. Most proclamations of the Marseilles authorities were addressed to both the Christian and the Jewish "burghers" of the city. In 1472 the muncipal council informed Count de Valmont that, as citizens of Marseilles, the Jews were not subject to taxes in Orgon. This legal status was greatly enhanced by the Jews' significant role in Marseilles' flourishing North-African trade (which declined, however, in the fifteenth century) and among its medical practitioners, of whom at one time they seemed to have constituted the majority. Only with respect to East-Mediterranean trade did Marseilles' Christian burghers pursue monopolistic policies. The municipal statutes allowed the accommodation of but four Jewish passengers on each Marseilles ship; this permission did not apply to "a voyage to Alexandria to which they may not and must not go." Most local Jews were workers, particularly skilled in the production of corals and other beads, which they almost monopolized at both the labor and commercial ends. They also played a preponderant role among the numerous commercial agents in the city, benefiting from the municipality's agreement with the bishop in 1290 which virtually converted Marseilles into a free city. These peaceful conditions prevailed to the last third of the fifteenth century, when anti-Jewish forces began to make themselves strongly felt.[39]

In other Provençal cities, too, the greater economic differentiation and populousness of the Jewish communities, some of which had had a long career even before the onset of the Capetian rule, helped to maintain their legal rights in a state of relative equilibrium. In 1306, to be sure, Robert of Calabria, acting in behalf of his father Charles II, then in Italy, tried to carry out the royal decree of banishment and we possess some records of arrests and confiscations. But Robert's order was speedily abrogated by Charles on his arrival in Marseilles—not without a substantial subsidy from the Jews—when he also expressly reconfirmed the Jewish privileges. The position of Jews in the ancient city of Arles was fairly typical. Although according to a recent author Jews were neither citizens nor aliens there, they were basically treated on a par with the burghers. The very archbishops did not hesitate to employ Jews in the service of their churches. However, the old luster of the community as one of the great centers of Jewish learning and enlightenment did not last beyond the thirteenth century.[40]

In the lesser municipalities, the power of the counts, later kings of the Provence, was more decisive. In the fifteenth century the Provence resembled a flourishing Jewish oasis within the deserted regions of the rest of France. Imitating the example set by Charles V after 1359, the Provençal rulers placed their Jews under the protection of high-ranking conservators of their rights, who also served as their judges in criminal affairs. Ten such influential officials have been identified in the period from 1403 to 1499; among them Ferry de Lorraine, Count of Vaudemont, the king's son-in-law and grand-seneschal of the Provence who served as protector of Jews from 1462 to 1470. To the complaints of the Provençal Estates in 1417 and 1419 that this institution infringed upon their jurisdiction, the king bluntly replied, "They [the Jews] belong to Me and the request presented is contrary and prejudicial to the rights of My dominion." True, Jews too sometimes suffered from the heavy hand of their "protectors" and particularly from the latter's deputies, an office usually secured by the highest bidders. But only at the beginning in 1403 did eight Jews from Marseilles and Aix, summoned by the conservator to appear in Tarascon, succeed in reversing his decision by appealing to the king with the aid of their cities, which effectively invoked their old privileges *de non extrahendo*.[41]

Conservators were but a link in a variety of legislative and administrative measures designed to make the life of Provençal Jewry more secure. Even with respect to criminal prosecution, Queen Yolande provided in 1423 that Jews should not be incarcerated on the basis of anonymous accusations and that their accusers must deposit a bond to be forfeited in case of the defendants' acquittal —a veritable habeas corpus act, as it is called by Raoul Busquet. During the long reign of the enlightened King René (1434–80) Jews enjoyed even broader freedoms. In 1447 (and again in 1474) the king went so far as to accept the suggestion of a Jewish delegation from Aix, Arles, Marseilles, Tarascon, Saint-Maximin, and Salon and to pronounce a general pardon for all crimes (including blasphemy) committed by Jews, with the exception of *lèse-majesté*, the falsification of currency, forging documents, homicide, and arson. In 1454 René reduced the size of the Jewish badge, abolished the compulsory attendance at missionary sermons, specifically permitted Jews to practice medicine, and allowed them to serve as collectors of taxes and customs. He also rejected the very idea of their segregation, stating bluntly:

We ordain that the said Jews may with impunity converse with Christians, as they have hitherto been accustomed to do, to walk back and forth, deal, do business and negotiate with them anywhere; to keep

Christian employees and servants, as they wish, without regard to contrary edicts.

At the same time he encouraged conversions to the extent of occasionally serving as godfather at baptismal ceremonies. But he sharply repudiated the use of force to achieve that aim. In all these respects Provençal Jewry resembled its coreligionists of Spain or Italy more than those who had resided in royal France. Similarly, in the neighboring counties of Roussillon and Cerdagne (Cerdaña), which for the most part were under Majorcan or Aragonese domination, the Jews of the fourteenth and fifteenth centuries largely shared the fate of their Spanish rather than their French brethren.[42]

Although thus sheltered by law and their own economic and cultural strength, the southern Jews could not completely escape the ravages of the Pastoureaux, the lepers' conspiracy, and the Black Death. In fact, some northern communities fared better than their southern counterparts in 1320, until the combined action of Pope John XXII and the seneschal of Beaucaire led to the destruction of the roving bands. That some local officials themselves had been involved in the assaults was proved by subsequent investigations. Even Bishop Béraud of Albi was accused of "having allowed the Pastoureaux to enter the city of Albi with their flags deployed, to make an inquiry into the Jews' possessions, and to commit various acts of violence." He was absolved, however, in 1324. Blood Accusations also cropped up quite frequently, and in 1348 Toulon, and even such a small town as Vergnes-en-Gapençais, became the scenes of violent anti-Jewish outbreaks. In the following century there were occasional riots in other cities and the formerly friendly burghers now began agitating for the expulsion of Jews. Sometimes these outbreaks were inspired by religious fanaticism. In one attack of 1475, a Capucin monk marched at the head of the mob which carried two large crosses. Hearing of this incident, indignant King René exclaimed: "Is it not abominable to make use of the cross for the shedding of blood? To act in this way means transforming an outstanding symbol of peace and love into a standard of hate and revolt." But there also were serious economic jealousies, particularly after the great destruction wrought by the attack of the Aragonese navy in 1423 from which the city recovered very slowly. Among the leaders of the anti-Jewish faction in Marseilles were members of the family Forbin (of Genoese origin), which had many a quarrel with Jewish competitors and employees. Ultimately, in 1481, Jacques Forbin delivered a sharp anti-Jewish tirade at a session of the municipal council. Claiming that the Jews were planning the city's ultimate ruin, he tried to persuade his colleagues to send a delegation to the king demanding their expulsion. His motion was rejected, but it was a clear indication of the approaching storm.[43]

All these changes clearly reflected the fundamental trends in French public life. Sooner or later the growing unification of France, without completely eliminating the legal and economic differences between the two sections, enabled the French kings to extend their anti-Jewish regime into the southern regions. True, in 1482, when the Provence was being reincorporated into France, Louis XI hastened, at the request of several Jewish communities, to reaffirm their ancient privileges. But soon the tensions mounted, and for reasons which will be explained in another context the trend toward excluding Jews proved irresistible. Antagonisms were sharpened after the expulsion of Jews from Spain and the arrival of many Spanish refugees in 1492. Louis XII's decree of May 23, 1500, ordering the Jews' departure within three months from their remaining French settlements (in Provence by November), sealed the fate of these old communities. The last to go were the Jews of Arles and Marseilles in the years 1500–1501. At the beginning of the sixteenth century the only Jewish communities lawfully established in French territories were those living under papal rule in Avignon and the Comtat Venaissin. Only a few Jewish individuals made sporadic appearances in one or another city. In Poitiers, for example, a Jewish physician, Raphael, is mentioned in 1528. A few years later (ca. 1532) there was born in Fontenay-le-Comte Amatus Lusitanus, who later settled in Italy and became one of the medical luminaries of the century. At the same time, however, new life sprouted from the debris with the arrival of Iberian New Christians. These settlers included numerous clandestine Jews. Because they outwardly lived as Christians, they suffered from few legal disabilities and were able to open a totally new chapter in the history of Jews on French soil.[44]

ENGLAND

In war and in peace the English treatment of Jews was intertwined with that accorded them in France. Apart from maintaining some traditional Norman attitudes and institutions, the Plantagenet kings, who were themselves often more Angevin than either English or Norman, retained large French possessions after the loss of Normandy to Philip II in 1203–1206. Exchanges between the Jewish communities under the two regimes were in many ways even more intimate. Most English Jews had come from France; they continued to speak French to the very end of their stay in England, and looked to the Franco-Jewish leaders for intellectual guidance. The renowned Jewish synods in twelfth-century France included representatives from England. If the English Jews did not share the exile of their French coreligionists under Philip II in 1182 and its revocation in 1198, most French communities outside the Île-de-France had likewise remained intact. Time and again, the English kings intervened in favor of their Continental Jewish subjects; for instance, through the instruction issued in 1221 to the city of Niort by Henry III (1216–72), or rather by the regents during his minority: "We order you to maintain and protect Our Jews of Niort, not to tax them, nor to let them be taxed in any fashion without Our order, not to cause them nor to allow others to cause them any damage." [45]

Not that the lot of English Jewry was altogether enviable. The same adverse combination of factors, economic, political, social, and religious, ultimately led here, too, to the complete elimination of Jews in 1290; in fact, long before they gave up their last footholds in France. At the beginning of the thirteenth century, however, the outlook for the English Jews still appeared relatively rosy. Many were led to disregard the warnings implicit in the popular outbreaks of 1189–90, and were lulled into a sense of security by the apparently effective royal protection.

The century began with the unequivocal confirmation of their old privileges by John Lackland (1199–1216). The first article of his Charter stated succinctly:

Know that We have granted to all the Jews of England and Normandy to have freely and honourably residence in Our land, and to hold all that from Us which they held from King Henry, Our father's grand-father, and all that now they reasonably hold in land and fees and mortgages and goods, and that they have all their liberties and customs just as they had them in the time of the aforesaid King Henry, Our father's grandfather, better and more quietly and more honourably.

Other provisions renewed the Jews' right to be judged by their own peers and to be convicted only by the mixed testimony of Jewish and Christian witnesses. Their corpses were to be protected against detention by creditors, the heirs alone being responsible for their debts. They were to be free to trade in any objects except church implements and bloodstained cloth. As moneylenders they were to be protected in disputes with their Christian debtors and allowed to sell their pledges after a year and a day. "And wherever the Jews may be, let it be lawful for them to go when they will with all their chattels just as Our own property, and let none stop or prevent them in this." In such journeys throughout England and Normandy they were not to pay any customs and tolls. "And We order you to guard, to defend, and to maintain them." The Jews' expectations based on this charter were heightened by its claim of being essentially but a renewal of such older privileges as that granted by Richard Lion-Heart to an individual, Ysaac son of Rabbi Jose, in 1190, and its ancient precedents going back to the revered Henry I—a matter of great moment in the subsequent con-stitutional struggles with the barons. Here and in his other enact-ments John laid great stress upon the Crown's exclusive mastery over Jews. Unlike the earlier Continental enactments which had promoted frequent transfers of royal controls to lesser authorities, the English decrees, including one attributed to the pre-Norman king, Edward the Confessor, insisted that no Jew "ought to place himself under any mighty man without the king's license." Not even during Stephen's weak and divided reign (1135–54) had there been actual transfers of Jews to baronial jurisdiction, al-though many Jews seem to have stayed away from the areas most affected by the civil war and some may have acquired special pro-tection from powerful lords. But even they continued to live under royal authority and merely secured some additional protec-tion by voluntary payments to one or another lord.[46]

Soon, however, the real nature of King John, his insatiable greed and utter unreliability, came to the fore. The charter of

1201 was secured only after the Jews' substantial contribution of 4,000 marks, which—in view of their rather impoverished state after the upsets of the preceding decade and a half—they were allowed to pay in four instalments. In the following years John and his advisers employed ever new means of shearing their Jewish sheep. To help finance his French wars the king often canceled the debts owed Jews by volunteers enlisting for service across the Channel. Without such motivation he arbitrarily freed some favorites from the payment of interest or even the entire debt owed to Jews. While the financial resources of the Jewish community thus greatly diminished, its direct contributions to the Treasury grew by leaps and bounds. In addition, innumerable fines were collected from wealthy individuals under flimsy excuses. For one example, after the so-called Bristol tallage of 1210 (to be mentioned presently), Isaac of Norwich was imprisoned in the Tower of London and fined the enormous sum of 10,000 marks. In order not to become instantaneously ruinous, this fine was to be paid at the rate of one mark daily over a period of almost three decades, such instalments still being mentioned in the sources of 1220. Royal revenue from the Jews' judicial fees, usually amounting to 10 percent of the sums under litigation, also was quite considerable. For better control, as well as for more effective protection of Jewish property, John appointed, in 1200, Thomas de Neville and other "justices of the Jews" to adjudicate litigations between Jews and Christians. Thenceforth these courts handled most disputes, although they could not prevent occasional direct royal interventions, or prosecutions by justices of the Eyre. Further to insure effective tax collection, John ordered all sheriffs, under their personal responsibility, to assist the collectors.[47]

It was particularly after the loss of Normandy in 1206 and his campaign in Ireland that John found himself in great financial straits and sought relief in violent extortions. Among them was his ruthless attack on the Jews, from whom he tried to collect the enormous levy of 66,000 marks. Clearly imitating Philip II Augustus' highhanded method of 1182, he ordered, after his return from France in 1210, the imprisonment of "all" Jews and a careful scrutiny of their resources. Specially appointed local sheriffs were to exact the minimum of 40 shillings even from the poorest men under the sanction of expulsion from the realm. True, this staggering "Bristol tallage" of 66,000 marks (it probably approximated the purchasing power of some $18,000,000 today), was a third less than the Jewish share of £60,000 in the Saladin tithe of 1188. Obviously, that tithe and the following massacres of 1189–90 had so reduced the Jews' ability to pay that even John had to be satisfied with the smaller assessment which was still being ruthlessly collected after his death in 1216 (in one recorded Oxford case, as late as 1228). According to a widely repeated tale, a Bristol Jew (Abraham?) who had pleaded poverty, was made to yield by the successive extraction of seven teeth. On another occasion six rich Jews were tortured by John's henchmen and lost their right eyes, while two were hanged "and not a small multitude of others who did not have enough to give more were ejected from England." [48]

John's cruelties affecting almost all classes of the population ultimately aroused concerted opposition. They led to a protracted civil war and the enactment in 1215 of the Magna Carta. They also caused many discouraged Jews to emigrate from England—or rather flee, as they were not allowed to depart without a royal license. Even some leading scholars, after a meeting in London in 1211, decided to join the group of French rabbis who settled in Palestine. This migration of three hundred rabbis understandably made a great impression not only in France and England but also in the Near East, where it was commented on by Yehudah al-Harizi and an anonymous author. More permanently, the tallage of 1210 set an ominous precedent which, with many variations in detail, was frequently employed also by John's successor.[49]

Henry III's long reign of fifty-six years started rather auspiciously for the Jews. During his adolescence (1216–24) the regents, William Marshal, Earl of Pembroke (d. 1219) and Chief Justiciar Hubert de Burgh (to 1227), kept a close check on budgetary expenditures; they also tried to safeguard the resources of the Crown's Jewish subjects. Curiously, one of the provisions of the treaty of Lambeth of 1217, in which Prince Louis (later King Louis IX) of France renounced his claims to the English throne, was the restoration to the regency of some archives, including Jewish bonds which had been seized by the rebels during the civil war.

To reassure prospective Jewish immigrants as well as returnees from the flight of 1210, William ordered the local constables in 1217 to appoint in each major city twenty-four burghers to guard Jewish lives and property against attack, particularly by roving would-be Crusaders. In 1219 he issued a royal mandate to the wardens of English harbors to facilitate the entry of Continental Jews with their possessions under the condition that they would speedily register with the Jewish Exchequer. If, in 1218, the badge was introduced into England, which thus became one of the earliest countries to implement the Lateran canon of 1215, the regent and his advisers seem to have viewed it more as a security measure for Jews than a discriminatory regulation against them. The public, too, responded cheerfully to this friendly policy. The interfaith relations became so amicable that the churchmen, assembled in Oxford in 1222 under the chairmanship of Archbishop Stephen Langton of Canterbury, felt prompted to adopt sharply segregationist resolutions. But when the archbishop tried to interfere with the usual Judeo-Christian economic contacts, his order was sharply countermanded by Hubert de Burgh.[50]

As soon as Henry took the reins of government into his own hands, however, his reckless profligacy, his love for monumental buildings—such as Westminster Abbey on which alone he was to lavish more than £500,000—his extremely costly pageants and festivities, as well as his frequent wars with France, preparations for the Crusades, and imperial ambitions for his brother and son in Germany and Sicily, involved him inextricably in heavy debts. In desperation he seized funds from whomever he could, arousing the sharp opposition of the higher and lower nobility, which finally rose up in arms against him under the leadership of Count Simon de Montfort, Earl of Leicester, son of the leader of the Albigensian Crusade.

Jews could not react with an armed rebellion. In 1233 Henry not only imposed a new tallage on them but also tried to collect all their arrears. In an ordinance, recorded in a clerk's chance transcript three years later, he also ordered the speedy deportation of all Jews unable to be of service to the king. At the same time, rather inconsistently, he limited the rate of interest on Jewish loans to 43⅓ percent. This rate was quite customary on the Continent, but it appeared rather low in England, particularly in view of the Crown's excessive demands. It was, indeed, to be doubled in the subsequent legislation. All Jewish appeals for royal moderation remained unheeded. On one occasion, in 1255, when they pleaded for mercy, Henry pathetically answered, "It is no wonder that I covet money for it is dreadful to think of the debts in which I am involved. . . . I am a mutilated and diminished king. . . . I am, therefore, under the necessity of living on money obtained in all quarters, from whomsoever and in what manner soever I can acquire it." A partial list of his Jewish tallages, compiled some two centuries ago by D'Blossiers Tovey, shows the following imposts during Henry's reign: 1230–31, 15,000 marks; 1233 and 1236, 18,000 marks each; 1241 and 1244, 20,000 marks each; 1245, 60,-000 marks; 1246, 10,000 marks; 1247, 5,525 marks; 1249, 10,000 marks; 1251, 5,000 marks; 1252, 3,500 marks; 1253, 5,000 marks; 1259, 5,000 marks; 1271, 6,000 marks. This list is definitely incomplete. Other accounts have shown that in the years up to 1259 more than 250,000 marks were levied from English Jewry in tallages alone. The significance of these contributions can readily be gauged by a comparison with the Crown's total tax intake, which in 1245, according to the English envoys at the Council of Lyons, allegedly amounted to only £40,000 (60,000 marks), or exactly the sum supposedly paid by Jews alone during that year.[51]

Apart from these general tallages there were severe fines in connection with Blood Accusations and other purported Jewish crimes; death duties as a rule amounting to one-third of the estate; large penalties imposed upon individual wealthy Jews under manifold, often flimsy, excuses; an *auxilium* (a feudal term usually relating to noble vassals) for the marriage of the king's sister Joan to King Alexander of Scotland in 1221; similar other donations for weddings and other royal festivals; presents to the queen or queen mother; special levies for the preparation of Crusades, and the like. The *auxilium* of 1221 included also a fine which English Jewry had to pay for one of its coreligionists, Moses son of Brun, convicted for forgery of a writ of indebtedness allegedly given his father by Thomas, a former prior of Dunstaple. The sum of £654 3s. 5½d. collected on this occasion from seventeen Jewish communities amounted to nearly 20 percent of Princess Joan's total dowry of 5,000 marks. When, in 1236, Henry married off his sister, Princess Isabel (who in the preceding year had secured for a friend the cancellation of a debt of 40 marks to Jews), to Emperor Frederick II of Germany, he offered the emperor a dowry of 30,000 marks. Here the Jewish contribution was raised to 10,000 marks, or fully one-third. Aaron of York and nine other Jews were appointed as sureties for raising that subsidy. Nor was the "aid" of 1221 altogether voluntary, even in the limited sense that *auxilia* by barons or cities were obtained through formal consent. In more devious ways Jews were made to contribute funds, for instance, through their repurchase of "blasphemous" books seized by royal officials in 1245. If some royal princes, moreover, used Jews as agents in a variety of business dealings, the latter were completely at the mercy of their highly placed patrons.[52]

In some cases fiscal exploitation went hand in hand with an outspoken anti-Jewish bias. Henry III's extravagant consort, Eleanor of Provence (from 1236 on), contributed much to the fiscal pressures on the Jews, whom she nevertheless disliked intensely. After Henry's death she secured from her son, Edward I, a grant "that no Jew shall dwell or stay in any towns which she holds in dower." This animosity did not prevent her in earlier years from allowing Jews to cover the enormous costs of entertainment of her Continental relatives. In 1240 Henry was persuaded to tax the English Jews 20,000 marks so that she could extend lavish hospitality to her uncles; three years later Aaron of York and other Jews bore a large part of the cost of the wedding of the queen's sister Cynthia to the king's brother Richard, Earl of Cornwall, at which allegedly 30,000 dishes were served. The end effect of half a century of Henry's misrule was the almost complete ruin of that English Jewry, which only a century earlier had belonged to the most prosperous Jewish communities in Europe.[53]

In all those exploits the thirteenth-century English kings relied heavily on the cooperation of Jewish leaders, each of whom bore the honorific title of *presbyter omnium Judaeorum Angliae*. This office of presbyter or archpresbyter, which, despite its designation, had few ecclesiastical functions, was established in 1199 and was expected to be exercised by its occupants "freely, quietly, honorably, and with integrity—so that no one may presume to molest or trouble them in any way." Supposed to grant a lifetime occupancy, each appointment could be terminated at the king's discretion; in Henry III's case usually after the particular archpresbyter had been squeezed dry. Six men are recorded to have held that office: Jacob of London (1199–1207), Jose of London (1207–36), Aaron of York (1236–43), Elias l'Eveske of London (1243–57), Hagin son of Magister Moses of Lincoln (1257–73?), and Hagin son of Deulecresse of London (1281–90)—all of them selected because of their wealth and influence rather than on the basis of learning or piety. But theirs was a thankless task, and had tragic consequences, particularly for Aaron of York and Elias l'Eveske. Long before his death in 1268 Aaron, in his prime one of the richest businessmen in England, had been totally ruined. In addition six of the wealthiest Jews of England were selected to serve as tax assessors during the regency of William Marshal in 1219. In the pertinent royal decree the new appointees were told that they

should not hide anybody possessing chattels of the value of 40 shillings and upwards, and should be careful to assess the taxation upon all who ought to be taxed, whether a kinsman such as a father or mother, brother or sister, son or daughter, nephew or niece, grandfather or grandmother, father-in-law or son-in-law, or the husband of a niece, or any person who stands in any sort of relationship.

Nor did Henry hesitate to imprison the wealthiest Jews and to collect the entire Jewish tax from them under the assumption that they would subsequently be reimbursed by their coreligionists. On one occasion, he convoked a Jewish "parliament" to Worcester in 1241 with an enforced attendance of six delegates from each of the larger Jewish communities and of two delegates each from lesser townships, to secure from them a vote for a new tallage.[54]

In order to protect this source of revenue, Henry was perfectly willing to let the Jews enjoy considerable rights. They could own land and houses, and engage in various trades. Their disabilities largely stemmed from the canonical postulates of segregation, badges, nonemployment of Christian servants, and the like. Henry III, though personally pious, did not follow Louis IX's example in outlawing or even restricting Jewish usury. On the contrary, he encouraged Jewish moneylending and, by controlling all Jewish credit transactions through the long-established Jewish Ex-

chequer, chirograph offices, and the royally appointed justices of
the Jews, he was able to reduce evasions of taxpayers to a minimum. On their part, Jews often required royal aid in collecting
debts owed to them by Christian debtors, especially if the latter
felt excessively burdened by accumulated interest. It should consequently have been to the Jewish creditors' own interest to obey
the law and have each writ of indebtedness registered at the
Exchequer. Royal searches of the *archae* are indeed recorded on
several critical occasions. Yet, as the king's arbitrary exactions
multiplied, it was often to the advantage of both lenders and borrowers to make clandestine deals and refrain from registering their
bonds. This practice, readily attributed by the royal officials to
"the Jews' obnoxious malice and falsity," continued unabated,
often with the connivance of the keepers of the *archae* themselves.
It was but partially stemmed by the ever stricter regulations of
1210, 1233, and 1239, and such punitive actions as the wholesale
dismissal of the chests' personnel in the latter year.[55]

Of course, there also were Jewish tax evaders. The king himself
frequently compromised with a taxpayer, or his rapacious councilors and corrupt justices helped the culprit to escape the royal
wrath. On the other hand, the "hosts of hungry Poitevins and
Bretons" (John Richard Green), whom Henry had imported
from his wife's French possessions, often enriched themselves at
Jewish expense far beyond the law. Ultimately, the Jews formally
joined the accusers of Peter de Rivaux, Robert Passelewe, and
their associates. But the king himself was almost congenitally unable to keep his word. After arranging with such a rich individual
as Aaron of York for some special payments by promising him
immunity from the general Jewish tallages, he went right back
and collected from Aaron his share in the tallage, sometimes under
the guise of a "gift" to the queen. Another noteworthy royal trick
consisted in the imposition of anticipatory estate taxes. Since, in
legal theory, all estates of deceased Jews were supposed to be
escheat to the king, the heirs were usually expected to pay the
Treasury the equivalent of one-third of each estate, just as the
king "demanded a relief from the heir of a landowner before his
homage was accepted" (H. G. Richardson). In the case of Aaron
of York, Henry went a step further and made the latter's prospec-

tive heirs pay him 200 marks annually for nineteen years before Aaron's death, at which time, as it turned out, the estate had practically no assets. The financial situation of English Jewry became so untenable that on two occasions (in 1254–55), according to Matthew Paris, Elias l'Evesque argued with Henry that the monarch

has papal merchants, or rather his own (I will not call them usurers), who amass endless heaps of money; let the king depend upon them and gape after his emoluments by them: they it is who have destroyed and impoverished us. The king conceals his knowledge of this, and demands of us what we have not the power to give, though he should pluck out our eyes or skin us and afterwards cut our throats.

Elias asked, therefore, that his coreligionists be given safe-conducts to leave the country. They would "seek a place of abode elsewhere, under some prince who has bowels of compassion, and will properly observe truth and good faith." This was, of course, a counsel of despair which the king did not accept. In fact, as early as 1238 two Bristol Jews trying to leave the country without a license, and others who thus tried to evade the severe taxes, were apprehended by the local authorities or the custodians of the Cinque Ports.[56]

CLASS ANTAGONISMS

Utilitarian objectives thus dominated the relationships between the English Crown and her Jewish subjects. To such ends the kings encouraged Jewish moneylending and closed their eyes to the excessive rates of interest. At the same time, they used the Jews' economic power as a leverage in their quest to wield effective controls over the various other groups in the population. Obviously neither objective appealed to the numerous disaffected groups, whose resentment of the royal "pretensions" readily extended to the Crown's Jewish wards, who were made doubly "obnoxious" by their monetary demands.

Even the clergy, who had many other financial dealings with Jews, as when synagogues or cemeteries were erected on lands belonging to churches, often borrowed heavily from them. The famous Minster at Lincoln was built partly with funds lent by Jews. Yet repayment was not always easy and, as with other classes, caused much dissatisfaction. When Peter de Blois, then serving at the Cathedral of Canterbury, found himself in financial difficulties, he addressed a pathetic letter to his friend, the Bishop of Ely:

Drawn by extreme urgency, I am going [from Bath] to Canterbury to be crucified by the perfidious Jews, who torture me by their debts and afflict me with their usury. I expect to bear the same cross through the London Jews, unless you free me out of pity, and I feel confident that you will show me compassion, and will fully redeem me. Therefore, my father and dearest friend, I pray that you will remove this cross from me, and take upon yourself the payment of the £6 that I owe Samson the Jew, and, by this act of liberation, turn my debts into a cause of profound gratitude to you.

It is small wonder, then, that Peter became one of the leading anti-Jewish controversialists. William de Blois, bishop of Worcester, to one of whose predecessors Peter had addressed his polemical tract, issued on his own a prohibition against Jews' lending on interest funds received from non-Jews, since thereby they caused Christians to benefit from usury. He also forbade them to deposit any valuables for safekeeping in churches (1219, repeated by him in 1229, and by his successor in 1240). Similarly, Archbishop Stephen Langton of Canterbury, although "he virtually shared the regency" with the pro-Jewish justiciar, Hubert de Burgh, consistently favored discriminatory policies. In contrast to his predecessor, Hugh, whose passing the Canterbury Jews had, for good reasons, deeply mourned, Langton was probably responsible for the inclusion in the Magna Carta of the provision protecting estates belonging to minors against foreclosure by Jewish money-lenders (Art. x). To be sure, the same restriction applied also to non-Jewish creditors (Art. xi), but this was before the full development of the Cahorsin trade in London. More, after promoting the aforementioned anti-Jewish canons by the synod of Oxford in 1222, Langton, together with the bishops of Lincoln and Norwich, forbade Christians to have any social contacts with Jews or even to sell them food. Such a boycott would, of course, have made Jewish life in England unbearable. It was immediately countermanded by Hubert de Burgh, who wrote to his officials, "And if you find any who denies them [the Jews] victuals or other necessaries in the city of Canterbury and elsewhere, you will seize him and keep his body safely until we send you a further command." The regent's intervention was the more remarkable as, during those stormy years, he often needed Langton's support. Other Church assemblies likewise offered the clergy a forum for the venting of its anti-Jewish grievances and personal spleen. After Oxford came the synods of Worcester in 1240, Chichester in 1246, Salisbury in 1256, Merton in 1258, Lambeth in 1261, and others, most of which adopted increasingly sharp anti-Jewish canons.[57]

Little did the Church realize that such hostile measures merely stiffened the Jews' resistance to its conversionist efforts, which were greatly intensified as the thirteenth century wore on. The more effectively to persuade Jews to accept baptism, William de Arundel, archdeacon of Huntingdon, wished to translate into Hebrew a missionary pamphlet he had completed in 1240. At his request the king ordered the viscount of Huntingdon to allow a Jew considered competent to assist the author in this task to settle in that city. Remarkably, despite the sufferings of its adherents, the Jewish faith still appealed to some Christian Englishmen. Most dramatic were the conversions to Judaism of an Oxford deacon in 1222, and a Dominican friar, Robert of Reading, half a century later. The Church, particularly concerned about the frequent relapses of baptized Jews, made strenuous efforts to safeguard the property rights of new converts against royal confiscation and to foster the new *Domus Conversorum*. Finally, even Pope Honorius IV was to complain, in his bull *Turbato corde* of 1286, about the successful Jewish mission among the Christians in England. Obviously exaggerated, his assertions nevertheless impressed not only the clergy but also pious laymen, including Henry III and particularly his son Edward I, who in many ways sought to follow in the footsteps of Louis IX across the Channel.[58]

More radically anti-Jewish was the nobility, both higher and lower. Apart from nursing the usual resentments of borrowers toward creditors, the baronage saw in the Jews, not without justification, an instrument of royal supremacy, especially if, through their loans, some baronial estates were channeled to the Treasury. Jewish moneylending created further distortions when the creditors transferred their rights to one or another magnate who then seized the land of the impoverished debtor. Typical of such adverse effects on an old heritage was the sale, by Aaron of York to William of Valencia, "the king's brother," of a debt of 400 marks owed by one Roger Bertram. A document of February 26, 1257, informs us that

the king confirms the said sale, granting that if the said Roger or his heirs do not keep the terms of payment it shall be competent for the said William and his heirs or assigns to sue and restrain the said Roger and his heirs according to the assize of Jewry, up to the full payment of the whole debt; and further grants that neither the king nor his ministers will take this debt into their hands for any debt which Aaron or his heirs may owe to the king, nor for any tallage, nor for any other reason.

This specific form of concentration of landed property in fewer and fewer hands became a social ill which the kings ineffectively combated. On its part, the higher nobility, the main beneficiary of that concentration, bitterly resented its own indebtedness to Jews, and particularly the occasional foreclosures of some of its large feudal estates to Jewish creditors or to churches and monasteries which had advanced them the money. For example, the Earl of Vavasour borrowed £330 from Aaron of York and pledged his estates at Hazelwood, which had originally been allotted to his ancestor by William the Conqueror. The debt of another great lord, Peter de Wadworth, was paid for him to Aaron by the Roche Abbey, which thus took over part of Wadworth's land. Many other illustrations can readily be culled from the numerous extant *starrs*. Much of that indebtedness arose from the growing profligacy of the baronial class while prices were steadily rising until the 1260s and continued on a high level for more than a century thereafter. Once deeply indebted, the landowners could hardly meet the high rates of interest out of the far lesser rates of return from agriculture. Many nobles also were traditionally charitable toward churches and monasteries, which at times involved them even in the transfer of serfs to the clergy. "To combine a donation," writes Reginald Lennard, "of tithe with the assignment to the recipient monastery of a peasant's service was clearly a very common practice in Norman England." [59]

At first the barons succeeded in inserting into the Magna Carta of 1215 only two, rather moderate, provisions aimed at some more obvious shortcomings of the credit system. One article required, as we recall, that Jewish lenders abstain from collecting interest from minor heirs. Another provided that heirs of mortgaged property received by the king from Jews would be responsible only for the original capital, not the accrued interest. Moreover, the livelihood of widows and orphans constituted a prior claim on the estate; only surplus revenue was to be used to pay off debts. These two articles of the famous charter (x–xi) were not repeated in its subsequent renewals, for when the new regime consented to transform it from a revolutionary document, "won at the point of the sword, into a manifesto of peace and sound government" (William Stubbs), it left the management of Jewish affairs to the king's discretion. But similar provisions were included in later royal ordinances, such as the Statute of Merton of 1236.[60]

Before long, however, the barons, locked in bitter conflict with the Crown, began striking more severe blows at the king's defenseless "serfs." Even before leading the antiroyal rebellion, Simon de Montfort, Earl of Leicester, decreed the expulsion of Jews from his own city of Leicester in 1231, and carried it out in 1253. In the barons' grievance of 1258 the petitioners complained about the loss of their lands through the collusion between the Jews and "powerful personages [potentioribus regni]," which was a clear hint that the king himself, as well as some magnates, were involved. In subsequent attacks of the "disinherited knights" before and during the Barons' Rebellion of 1264–66, the first to suffer severely were the Jews of Worcester in 1263, while London Jewry was attacked for the second time in 1264. During the latter year Northampton and Canterbury felt the brunt, whereas Lincoln and the Isle of Ely were affected only toward the end of the revolt in 1266. True, these attacks were not always premeditated. The baronial leaders, upon arriving in the neighborhood of Cambridge, were at first satisfied with the burghers' paying them an indemnity of £10; "and the Jews paid a fine of ten pounds for themselves." But before long the rebellious army demanded 300 marks from the burghers and proceeded to stage a regular massacre and pillage in the Jewish quarter. A subsequent inquest showed that the assailants had carried away all the captured Jewish goods, so that, upon the restoration of peace, none could be recovered in Cambridge. This at least was the information given by the city, which tried to exonerate its inhabitants from any part in the attack on the local Jewry. While this uprising was ultimately quelled by Prince Edward's victory at Evesham in 1265, the baronial party was never completely repressed. In its constant struggle for the enlargement of its liberties it nurtured a growing resentment against Jews as tools of their royal masters.[61]

No less hostile were the burghers, and particularly those especially dependent on petty loans. The populace was prone to listen to any rumor about Jewish wrongdoings and the alleged Jewish hatred of Christianity and the Christians. As early as 1204, John had to address a warning letter to the mayor and barons of London:

We say this for Our Jews and for Our peace, for if We have granted Our peace to anyone it should be observed inviolably. Henceforth, however, We commit the Jews residing in the city of London to your custody, so that if any attempt to do them harm you may defend them, coming to their assistance with an armed force. For We shall require their blood at your hand if by your fault any ill happen to them, which may God forbid. For We well know that things of this sort happen by reason of the unwise of the towns and not of the discreet, and the discreet ought to check the folly of the unwise.

Similar precautions had to be taken before the proposed Crusades of 1215, 1237, and 1271, lest the tragic experiences of the Third Crusade be repeated. Such royal "interference," however, probably added fuel to anti-Jewish feeling in the English towns. In the 1230s several important communities were eliminated entirely. Such local expulsions took place from Newcastle, Wycombe, the entire county of Warwick and parts of East Anglia in 1234, from Southampton in 1236, from Northamptonshire but not the town of Northampton itself in 1237, from Berkhamsted in 1242, from Newbury and Speenhamland in 1243. Royal legislation had to take cognizance of these facts, and in 1253 it specifically provided "that no Jew be received in any town but by special license of the King, save only in those towns in which Jews have been wont to dwell." Thus the old freedom of movement was severely curtailed —except, of course, for Jews obtaining a special royal license for a fee.[62]

Such restrictive policies are doubly noteworthy as thirteenth-century England was rapidly expanding then, both demographically and economically. "It saw towns," observes G. H. Martin in a recent study, "at the height of their prosperity before the calamities of depression and plague, and the last burst of town-making." Yet the burghers' hostility made them receptive even to the belief in Jewish ritual murders, a libel which assumed ever increasing dimensions. The affair of the Christian child, Hugh of Lincoln, in 1255, in particular, implicated all of English Jewry, since the king's justiciars had allegedly "discovered and decided that the Jews of England had by common consent [*communi consilio*] crucified" the boy. This accusation not only had immediate serious repercussions but, through ballads and other dramatizations, continued to envenom Judeo-Christian relations for generations thereafter, and far beyond the confines of England. Tensions mounted further through certain misdeeds of individual Jews protected by mighty personages. In 1250 Abraham of Berkhamsted allegedly committed many crimes, which included coin clipping and the murder of his wife for her failure to participate in his defacement of a painting of the Virgin. Protected by the king's brother Richard Earl of Cornwall, he defied the Jewish community, which tried to punish him, and ultimately denounced all Jews to the authorities. Even an offer by the Jewish elders of 1,000 marks for his imprisonment and execution was of no avail; with the earl's aid Abraham succeeded in having his sentence of perpetual imprisonment converted into a fine of 700 marks for the king, upon the payment of which he was released.[63]

Sensing the rising wave of hostility around them, the Jews blamed it on such occasional misdeeds by members, which, through the process of facile generalization affecting minorities, cast a bad light on the whole community. Some local Jewries tried, therefore, to exclude newcomers of tarnished reputation from settlement in their midst. A pertinent communal ordinance, known as the "Canterbury Treaty" of 1266, read in part:

The Jews of Canterbury had come to the resolution, and thereto bound themselves by oath, that no Jew of any other town than Canterbury shall dwell in the said town, that is to say, any liar, improper person, or slanderer, and that should anybody come to dwell there by the writ of their Lord the King, the whole community shall pay to the king such sum as . . . [he] shall lay upon the community in order that that person may be disqualified by the king from residing there; and, if any of the community should oppose the disqualification of such a Jew who has shown himself a liar, an improper person, and a slanderer, or has obtained such a writ from the king, let both be disqualified.

This was but a phase of the more general controls exercised by the Jewish community over the admission of new members, which was often styled the *herem* or *hezqat ha-yishub* (ban or presumption of settlement). Supported by internal religious sanctions, this treaty probably was but infrequently broken through individual licenses granted by the Crown. Yet it could hardly stem the tide of anti-Jewish feelings. Although during its last forty-five years in the country English Jewry was essentially restricted to some twenty-one communities, these were located in the most important cities of the realm, and the Jews' exposure to the bourgeoisie's resentments remained unabated. Together with the accumulated hatreds among the clergy and the nobility, this hostility of fellow urbanites was to play a decisive role under Edward I's regime.[64]

UNDER THE "ENGLISH JUSTINIAN"

Edward's influence on English Jewry did not begin with his coronation. As victor of Evesham he was the recognized leader of the royalist party, and generally took an active hand in counseling his aging father on all affairs of state. With respect to Jews, he as well as his uncle, Richard Earl of Cornwall, enjoyed for a time even a more formal authority, which the king had conferred upon them in return for their loans. Prince Edward's mortgage over the entire Anglo-Jewish community "to hold with all issues and profits, debts and customs [*consuetis*] which could fall to the king if he kept it in his hands," was to last for three years (1262–65). After that time the prince was to restore "the said Jewry in as good state as he received it or better." In fact, after one year he transferred his mortgage to the Cahorsins. In contrast, Richard's authority, granted in 1255, had continued for fully five years. The king had promised that "he will not permit any extent to be made of the debts of Jews in the meantime and that he will not give or pardon the debts of them to anyone, that he will not tallage the said Jews or exact anything from them in the meantime except customary pleas and reliefs of Jews according to custom of the

Jewry." Unlike his brother, Richard was an excellent administrator and husbander of funds, and offered the Jews considerable relief from Henry's arbitrary and cruel exactions. True, he did not behave in England as he did in Germany, where, after his election as Roman king, he sought to secure the support of Jews as well as Christians. But he generally neglected his hopelessly entangled duties in the Empire (during the fifteen years of his purported reign he appeared there for only a few brief visits) while he carefully administered his large estates in England. He also personally supervised the affairs of his Jewish wards, whose deteriorating economic situation was well illustrated later by their tallage of 1271 to help defray the cost of Prince Edward's Crusade. Not only was the assessment of 6,000 marks far below their previous imposts, but they were unable to raise even that amount, Richard advancing them the balance of 2,000 marks in return for the right to collect the regular Jewish revenue for a year. By no means moderate in his exactions, Richard was at least more prudent and predictable than Henry. Prince Edward, too, tried to take care of his Jewish "pledges" somewhat more effectively than did his father.[65]

Unlike his father and grandfather, Edward I addressed himself primarily to the economic problems arising from Jewish moneylending. At no time did he abrogate the original laws enacted by Henry II, Richard I, and John. But while Henry III, in his two major legislative acts of 1233 and 1253, had laid the main accent on either the Jew's utilitarian value to him ("No Jew shall remain in Our realm unless he can serve the King and is able to furnish good pledges for his loyalty") or on the Church-sponsored legisla tion concerning low-voiced prayers, the payment of ecclesiastical tithes, nonemployment of Christian servants, outlawry of religious disputations, and the like, Edward I made a real effort to deal with the Jewish question from the standpoint of the general needs of state and society. At the same time he was deeply imbued with Christian religious doctrines and often set before himself Saint Louis' example. During Edward's active collaboration with Henry III, two important edicts were issued concerning Jews. In 1269 Chancellor Walter de Merton suspended Jewish moneylending on rent-free lands and provided for the cancellation of all feudal fees then in the hands of Jews if "not assigned or sold to Christians."

For the future, Jews were not to extend such loans altogether "on pain of forfeiture of life and chattels," while each Christian purchaser of illegal bonds was to be punished with the "forfeiture of his chattels and his inheritance." This sharp decree, a concession to the reform party, paid little attention to the economic realities, and apparently was widely disobeyed. No less a dignitary than Archbishop Walter Gifford of York made such acquisitions in 1270. In one case he personally defended his claim before the Exchequer of the Jews against the rabbi-banker Benedict (Berakhiah) of Lincoln. Perhaps slightly more effective was the royal decree of 1271, providing that in the future

no Jew do have a freehold in manors, lands, tenements, fees, rents or tenures of any kind whatsoever by charter, grant, feoffment, confirmation, or any other kind of obligation, or in any other manner: so nevertheless that they may continue to dwell in the houses in which they dwell in cities, boroughs or other towns, and have them as they have been wont in time past; and also that if they have other houses to let, they may lawfully let them to Jews alone, and not to Christians.

Other provisions were intended to appease the prelates, who together with the nobles were largely responsible for this enactment. The main objective of the laws of 1269 and 1271 clearly was to eliminate Jews from regular landholdings, however temporary, especially of feudal benefices which, though nowhere expressly conceded, had theretofore been open to them. Understandably, the baronial class, and in particular the segment which constituted the driving force behind the reforms, sought to remove the threat to its feudal holdings, and to some extent to the feudal order as a whole, which loomed from the possible large-scale foreclosures of feudal estates by Jews. In whatever form the latter might administer such estates (their religion certainly offered a serious handicap to their acting as regular feudal lords), they might unduly shift the balance of power to the Crown.[66]

From the outset Edward's reign must have filled English Jewry with grave apprehensions. While still in Gascony this Crusader appeared as their outright persecutor. Certainly, his order to all sheriffs who had served during the preceding seven years to appear "before Our Justices assigned to the custody of the Jews . . . with all summonses received by them from the Exchequer of the Jews

for the levying of debts in Jewry due to Our said father to render
account thereof," seemed to set in motion a new wave of fiscal extortions. Within a year after Edward's return to England (1275),
his mother, Queen Eleanor, doubtless with his approval, expelled
the Jews from her four dower towns. Jewish fears were but partially allayed by his order, according to a contemporary source, to
resettle the Gloucester Jews in "Our town of Bristol with their
chirograph chests and all their goods, and they were henceforth to
dwell and abide among Our other Jews in that place." Jews of the
other three localities were similarly assigned residences in three
other cities. This procedure merely illustrated Edward's general
penchant for the maintenance of public order. No sooner did he
ascend the throne than his regent, Earl of Gloucester, appeared in
the London Guild Hall and proclaimed peace for all, Christians
and Jews alike. The London municipal administration fell in line
and the ordinances issued by Mayor Gregory de Rokesle, probably
in 1276–78, began with the provision demanding peace *inter
christianos et judaeos*. Public order was indeed rather effectively
maintained even during Blood Accusations, as well as in 1278–79
when the government prosecuted the entire community for coin
clipping and imprisoned a large number of wealthy Jews. That
Jews, whose major business consisted in handling coins, should be
found among the coin clippers is not astonishing. Yet in two of the
three London cases brought before the Exchequer of the Jews in
the Trinity Term of 1277, a year before the bloody prosecution,
the defendants were acquitted. Only one trial, that of a woman,
Floria of Kingston, resulted in a fine of 40 shillings. Certainly,
their alleged mass participation in that outlawed activity in 1278
and the tragedy of their wholesale executions (the figure of 293
culprits hanged, a very large segment of the entire adult membership of the Jewish community, is doubtless exaggerated) was ex-
plainable only in the light of both governmental rapacity and the
intervening legislation which had gravely impeded the earning of
a legitimate livelihood by the majority of Jews.[67]

Such was the effect of the ordinance issued by Edward I in 1275.
His *Statutum de judeismo* was intended radically to transform the
whole life of Jewry and to pave the way for its socioeconomic
integration into English society. Edward's main intent, like that of

Louis IX, was to outlaw Jewish usury. In order to open to Jews alternative avenues for making a living, he encouraged them to engage in commerce and crafts and even to cultivate the soil, for which purpose he gave them permission to rent lands for a period of ten years, with the option to extend the lease for five more years. Yet he did not force the merchant and artisan guilds to admit them to membership. Nor did he abruptly cancel the current debts owed to Jews, but rather sought to have them liquidated in a slow and orderly fashion. He used for this purpose the existing machinery of the Jewish Exchequer, the justices of the Jews, and the newly appointed archpresbyter, Hagin son of Deulecresse, who was to serve for life (*pro vita sua*). However, like many other reformers, Edward was disappointed by the slow effects of his legislation. Nor could he completely forego the traditional methods of exacting money from Jews, although he must have realized that, if effectively applied, his laws would make it difficult for them to earn a bare livelihood. Quite in line with his father's procedures, he ordered the sudden imprisonment of all English Jews in 1287 and freed them only after they paid him 20,000 marks silver.[68]

All these proved to be half measures only, which satisfied neither the king nor the Jews, nor any other important social group. In the 1280s the clergy's fulminations against Jewish religious transgressions, and particularly attempts to reconvert baptized Jews, grew in a powerful crescendo. They led to Honorius IV's sharply worded bull, *Turbato corde,* of 1286 and Archbishop Peckham's drastic closing of a London synagogue. In 1279, one Abraham, son of Deulecresse, was burned for "blasphemy," the only such case known in Anglo-Jewish history. Many barons and cities, too, now clamored for the exclusion of Jews. In 1280 the number of petitions aimed at Jews, as well as on other subjects, had so greatly increased that in order to relieve the king it was decided to channel them respectively to the Chancellor, the Exchequer, or the Justices, and "those which pertained to the Jewry shall come to the Justices of the Jewry." The rise to power of the artisan class in London, beginning in 1285, likewise brought to the forefront a traditionally anti-Jewish group of aldermen. Most decisively, the Crown began losing interest in its impoverished

Jewish serfs. The place of the wealthy Jewish taxpayers and lenders was now taken by the Cahorsin and Italian merchants, whether resident in England or doing business from their Florentine or other foreign headquarters. If in 1239–43 the Jewish tallages had apparently amounted to one-sixth of the entire royal revenue and had risen further to one-fifth in 1243–49, they dropped off sharply thereafter. In contrast, Italian loans and taxes increased in the years 1269–90 to 11,500 marks, a sum which English Jewry was no longer in a position to match. Outside England, Edward owed in 1289 no less than £107,000 to the Riccardi firm in Florence alone. In short, Jews, at least superficially, now seemed expendable.[69]

Reacting to the growing pressures, Edward decided to cut the Gordian knot and about July 18, 1290 ordered the expulsion of all English Jews. The latter were forewarned by his preceding banishment of their coreligionists from Gascony (Wasconia) in 1288 or early in 1289. Although as late as 1281 he himself had issued two pro-Jewish decrees, after expressing concern over the progressive decline of Gascony's Jewish population so that "where fifty taxable Jews used to live but few have now remained," he changed his mind during another year's stay in that domestically and externally turbulent country (August 1288 to August 1289) and expelled the Jews.[70]

Even more than his French counterparts of 1182, 1306, and 1322, Edward tried in 1290 to camouflage his fiscal objectives behind the cloak of pious professions. The text of his decree is not extant and hence its motivations can only be conjectured. But a later statute offers the following reason for its nullification of all penalties claimed by owners of bonds left behind by the Jewish exiles:

We, prompted by solicitude for the honor of God and the welfare of the people of Our Kingdom, have ordained and decreed that no Jew of this realm should thenceforth lend to any Christian at usury on the security of lands, rents, or anything else, but that they should all live from commerce and crafts. However, these Jews have thereafter, through a malicious conspiracy, contrived a new form of usury, more pernicious than the old, which they have called *curialitas,* and have under its guise oppressed Our said people in many ways, thereby making their latest error twice as reprehensible as the first. For this reason We, in retribution for their crimes and for the honor of the Crucified, have banished them from Our realm as infidels.

True, in England Jews were given three months to wind up their affairs and to take along their movables. But their landed hold-ings, especially houses, became escheat to the king. Parliament recognized the Crown's financial "sacrifice" involved in this sub-mission to the popular clamor, and offered to compensate it with the impost of a fifteenth of all movable property owned by nobles and burghers, and a tithe from the *temporalia* of the clergy.[71]

Thus ended the medieval chapter in Anglo-Jewish history. Sup-ported as the expulsion was by public opinion, it was more effec-tively carried out than even in Edward's French possessions. In Gascony the king had to repeat at least twice (in 1292 and 1305) that "We do not want that the Jews should dwell anywhere within Our land and under Our reign, and We order you totally to expel all Jews from Our aforementioned duchy." This order was re-stated again by his son, Edward II (1307–27) in 1313 and 1317— not with complete success, since Jews reappear from time to time in the records of Bordeaux and other localities in the following generations. No such repetition was necessary in the British Isles, although later some Englishmen may have had second thoughts about the wisdom of the total exclusion of the Jewish minority. When the Lincoln merchants asked for relief from their economic crisis under Richard III, they dolefully recalled that at one time Jews had brought much trade to the city. A general decree of ex-pulsion did not necessarily prevent a few individuals from insinu-ating themselves into both Gascony and England during the long era between Expulsion and Resettlement in the mid-seventeenth century. On at least three occasions Jewish physicians were invited from the Continent by Edward II, the London Mayor Richard Whittington, and Henry IV for medical consultations (1309, 1409, and 1410). The first of these, Magister Elias, allegedly tried to persuade the king to readmit the Jews to England—with no effect. The records of the *Domus Conversorum* likewise reveal the presence in London of prospective Jewish converts all through the fourteenth century. However, the number of Jewish settlers began to become significant only after the expulsion of Jews from Spain in connection with migratory movements set in motion among the Iberian Marranos by the inquisitorial trials.[72]

We must bear in mind once again, however, that the constant governmental harassment of wealthy leaders, the occasional riots in the cities, the blood libels and other accusations, and even the tragic finale do not tell the whole story of Anglo-Jewish life during the thirteenth century. Notwithstanding all difficulties, the Jewish population seems to have increased almost to the middle of the century. The extant records, including the dramatic narratives of Matthew Paris, pay attention principally to the great financial exploitation of Jews through tallages and the kings' completely ruthless behavior toward individual wealthy taxpayers. They also bring to the fore certain extraordinary incidents which caught their authors' fancy. On the other hand, we do find evidence that Jews could freely sue before English courts and frequently obtained redress in accordance with the law. While occasionally officers of the Jewish Exchequer, the justices of the Jews, and the archpresbyters proved corrupt, their professional ethics were not inferior to those of the contemporary judiciary, and were far above those of the average administrative personnel in the realm. Regrettably, medieval English Jewry left behind few rabbinic responsa and ethical writings such as those in which much of the day-to-day living of Continental Jewry was reflected. Hence we do not quite possess the necessary correctives. Nevertheless, it appears that during the first two centuries of their life in Norman England (1066–1233), and to some extent even in the following two or three decades, despite Henry III's grandiloquent introduction to his decree of 1253, the average English Jews, particularly the scholars and poorer wage earners, pursued their historic career in relative independence from the outside hostile forces.[73]

NADIR OF ASHKENAZIC JEWRY

The last three medieval centuries, which at first witnessed the greatest flowering of Jewish communities north of the Alps and Pyrenees, also saw their rapid decline and even large-scale extinction. During the thirteenth century, Jews, though facing enormous difficulties and growing hostility on the part of many segments of the population, increased in number and affluence throughout France, England, and the Holy Roman Empire. Having overcome the crisis of the partial expulsion of 1182, French Jewry now exerted great influence on the affairs of the country as a whole.

Not for very long, however. Its powers of survival were undermined by the occupational restrictions enacted by the ever more centralized royal administration under Louis IX and his early successors. Royal greed and popular hostility finally brought about the expulsion of 1306, which was superimposed upon the earlier banishment from the large English possessions of Wasconia (Gascony and neighboring lands). The span between their readmission in 1315 and renewed exile in 1322 was too brief to allow for a substantial recovery of the Franco-Jewish communities. Although French Jewry continued to flourish in many provinces outside royal France, and upon its readmission by the king in 1359 it developed a strong and cohesive communal structure, it could not prevent the tragic repercussions of the Black Death in many areas and the somber finale of the third royal banishment of 1394. The posts which it still precariously occupied on the fringes of the royal domain, in Lorraine, Burgundy, the Dauphiny, Savoy, and the Provence, likewise had to be vacated in the course of the fifteenth century. By 1502 France had become almost wholly *judenrein,* a fate which had befallen the Anglo-Jewish settlements in 1290.

While still living in these western lands, moreover, Jews had increasingly fallen prey to arbitrary administrations and ruthless fiscal exploitation. Allied as they thus became with the respective monarchies, they also had to absorb much of the animosity generated by the powerful revolutionary movements which were then transforming the western countries from medieval conglomerations of feudal baronies into precapitalistic, centrally, though not yet absolutely, governed societies.

If German Jewry escaped the fate of total elimination, this was owing much more to the diffusion of power within the Holy Roman Empire than to any pro-Jewish tendencies in society or government. Here, too, powerful forces operated in the direction of their elimination from their ancient habitats in western Germany and of their increasing concentration in the emperors' hereditary possessions in Austria, Bohemia, and Moravia, as well as, for a while, in the newly colonized, formerly Slavonic, "open spaces" of eastern Germany. It was indeed fortunate for the Jews that that eastward movement continued into the adjacent lands of Poland and Lithuania, which, at the end of that period, began inheriting the mantle of leadership from what was left of Ashkenazic Jewry.

Concomitant with that general decline in political status and economic prosperity was the growing insecurity of West-European Jewry in the face of widespread massacres and unpredictable fits of governmental intolerance, all contributing also to the progressive decline in its cultural creativity. The generations after the Black Death lived largely on the intellectual heritage left behind by their more fortunate ancestors of the eleventh, twelfth, and thirteenth centuries. No giants of the type of Rashi, Jacob Tam, Eleazar Roqeah of Worms, Yehudah the Pious, or Meir b. Baruch were now to be found in the decimated western communities. Jews continued to cultivate their traditional talmudic and hasidic learning along the lines laid down by those more creative ancestors. Their chief contribution to Jewish culture resulted from their concentration on salvaging for posterity the records of their daily living and religious rituals. In the vast literature of custumals, written in the fourteenth and fifteenth centuries, they succeeded in erecting a living memorial to the great variety of mores and observances which had, in the course of the preceding centuries, evolved in the various parts of the Ashkenazic world. Together with their assiduous labors in preserving and commenting on the works of their predecessors, they were thus able to transmit a rich intellectual patrimony to the nascent Polish communities which soon carried the torch of traditional Jewish learning with a new brilliance and effervescence.

XLIV

RISE OF IBERIAN JEWRY

IN THE Mediterranean communities of Spain, Portugal, the Provence, and southern Italy, no geniuses of the caliber of an Ibn Gabirol or Halevi, Alfasi or Maimonides, arose after 1200. But the generally high educational level of their members was effectively maintained, or speedily restored, after the shocks of the *Reconquista*. In other chapters we shall see how much the Iberian, Provençal, and Italian Jewries contributed to the sustained intellectual efforts of the Jewish people the world over. Legally and economically, too, Iberian Jewry speedily recovered from its severe losses under Almoravid and Almohade intolerance. Despite all manifestations of Jew-baiting, religious controversies, and unrestrained taxation, Spanish Jewry, in particular, was still able to write some of the most glorious chapters in the annals of medieval Jewish history.

SPANISH *RECONQUISTA*

Iberian Jewish history during the last three medieval centuries fundamentally differed from that in other western lands. In numbers, wealth, political connections, and cultural diversity it far exceeded the aggregate of all other Jewish communities under Christian domination. Spain's geographic position, too, on the border between Western Christendom and Islam, continued to affect deeply the entire socioeconomic and cultural structure of the realms which gradually emerged, and finally united, under the impact of their perennial struggle with the Muslim "infidels." The very presence of numerous Saracens left behind in the territories reconquered by Christians created here a situation wholly unparalleled in France, England, and Germany. In Castile the Jews constituted but the second largest and politically more dependable religious minority. Even Aragon, whose age-old ties with France, reinforced by Aragonese sovereignty over Montpellier and the counties of Roussillon and Cerdagne, made it more open to French political and religious influences, steered a course with respect to Jews that was radically different from that of the Capetian and Valois dynasties.

Anti-Jewish trends which had come to the fore during the twelfth century were greatly moderated during the rapid stages of the *Reconquista* before 1250. The friendly Alphonso VIII (1158–1214), whose victory over the Almohades in the battle of the Navas de Tolosa in 1212 had set the scene for the speedy rise of Castile, died two years later, but his successors Ferdinand III (1217–52) and Alphonso X (1252–84) continued to treat the Jews fairly. Deeply engaged in the reconquest and the subsequent consolidation of his domain, Ferdinand, whose Christian piety was to earn him the designation of Saint, nevertheless impartially called himself "king of the three religions," that is, of Christians, Muslims, and Jews. Alphonso X, on the other hand, styled *el Sabio* (the Wise or Learned), was too deeply involved in interdenominational scientific studies, which yielded the famous Alphonsine Tables, to introduce sharply discriminatory measures against Jews. Their celebrated Aragonese contemporaries James I the Conqueror (1213–76), and Pedro III the Great (1276–85), despite their personal Catholic piety and temporary submission to the Papacy, likewise extended effective protection to their Jewish subjects.[1]

On the whole, the first decades of the thirteenth century resembled the early period of the Christian reconquest in the ninth and tenth centuries. Now, as then, the newly occupied areas were decidedly underpopulated; this time because of the ravages of the preceding Almohade regime, intensified by the mass flight of Muslim inhabitants before the approaching Christian conquerors. Once again, Jewish manpower was appreciated by the rulers, as well as by society at large. The reconquest of Andalusia with its famous cities of Cordova (1236) and Seville (1248) called for a new policy of resettlement and economic rehabilitation. Such repopulation was needed also in the Balearic Islands and Valencia, occupied by James in 1229 and 1238. Time and again Jews were invited to establish their residences in quarters abandoned by, or forcibly taken away from, the Muslims. As during the first era of

resettlement, they were frequently assigned castles or other fortified positions within the cities. Typical of Alphonso VIII's promotion of Jewish "castles" is a decree of uncertain date issued for the
Jewry of Haro (Faro). He wrote:

Be it known and manifest to those present and to future generations
that I, Aldeffonssus, by the grace of God king of Castile and Toledo,
together with my wife Queen Alienor, with a glad mind and sponta-
neous will give and concede the Castle of Faro to you, the entire community of Jews of Faro, to inhabit it. This castle, together with all its
approaches and exits and with all its possessions . . . is to be owned
and possessed by you and all your descendants in hereditary succession.

The decree goes into great detail in protecting Jewish lives and
limiting the community's responsibility for crimes committed outside this area. It states, for example, that "he who will attack the
castle with a stone, arrow, lance, or any other weapon shall pay a
fine of 1,000 gold pieces to the king." Other provisions safeguard
Jewish economic rights such as fishing, and running mills, as well
as trading and moneylending. This decree was subsequently confirmed by Ferdinand III in 1221 and by later kings. Responding to
these friendly gestures, Jews in large numbers left their old, but
now inhospitable, settlements in the Almohade provinces, and established themselves in the more backward but rapidly expanding
northern territories. Nearly everywhere they soon formed a sizable
segment of the population and greatly contributed to the gradual
rise of commerce and crafts.[2]

Nevertheless, both the Aragonese and the Castilian Jewish legislation during the thirteenth century remained quite ambiguous.
To begin with, the monarchy was still too weak to exercise effective dominion domestically while it was engaged in its ambitious
conquests, for which it needed the wholehearted cooperation of
the powerful magnates and high churchmen. For a long time the
king was considered merely a *primus inter pares,* the most important among a number of substantially equal territorial lords. Only
the progress of the *Reconquista* itself, which handed over to the
kings the control over large territories, substantial new revenues,
and strong armed forces, tipped the balance in favor of the monarchy over the centrifugal baronial powers. Yet the struggle continued for several generations and ended only with the decisive

centralization of administrative authority in the hands of the Catholic monarchs Ferdinand and Isabella late in the fifteenth century.

In the thirteenth century the conquering kings still had to seek the active cooperation of their powerful vassals. They often transferred, therefore, their authority over Jewish communities or individuals to some local lords or churches. In 1187, for instance, Alphonso VIII handed over a Jew, Abraham, resident of Medinaceli, to the bishop of Sigüenza to be "subject to your usages, needs and undertakings; he is to be exempted from all royal or anybody else's servitude and freed from any [royal] tribute and exaction." At the same time the king forbade any molestation of that Jew by outsiders and entrusted him to the bishop's effective tutelage. Alphonso and other kings also had to yield to the ecclesiastical demands that Jews pay tithes from possessions they had acquired from Christians. Such provisions, which as we recall had often been enacted in other Christian countries too, are recorded in Valladolid in 1177, in Calahorra, and other localities. Nevertheless, the Church still felt aggrieved by what it regarded as excessive favors conferred upon Jews. Evidently on information which had reached him from the bishop of Burgos, Innocent III addressed a sharp reprimand to King Alphonso on May 5, 1205. Here the pope complained not only about the taxation imposed upon the generally tax-exempt Castilian clergy, but also about Jews being allowed to demand full indemnity at the market value for every slave converted to Christianity whom they were forced to liberate, rather than the far lower maximum price set by canon law. In defense of his earlier apostolic letters, the pope added, "you have not only refused to induce them [the Jews] to pay the [ecclesiastical] tithes, but given them greater opportunity of evading them and of acquiring ever larger possessions. In this fashion the Synagogue grows, while the Church declines in power, and the handmaiden is favored over the free woman." In 1239, but three years after Ferdinand III's conquest of Cordova, Gregory IX considered it his duty to urge the bishop to introduce the Jewish badge there. The pope claimed that many Jews, utilizing the absence of the Spanish Crusaders, often insinuated themselves into their homes under the disguise of being Christians, stole many objects and even seized some Christian boys to sell them to Saracens across the border. This papal demand is the more remarkable as the Jews in the older Castilian provinces had long repudiated the badge with royal approval and even with a partial papal dispensation.[3]

Serious administrative difficulties likewise influenced the royal attitude to Jews. The kings often needed their services in reorganizing the administration in the newly conquered territories previously handled by Muslim officials who had either fled before the approaching Crusaders or were distrusted by their new masters. Certainly, some local Jews, familiar with the Arabic dialect and legal procedures, were in a much better position to maintain the necessary continuity than were Christian officials imported from the older provinces. The fiscal administration, in particular, which required intimate knowledge of the differences among the various classes and religious groups, as well as of the financial resources of communities and leading individuals, could only be handled adequately by experienced financiers. For this reason all through the thirteenth century, and to a lesser extent in the following decades, Spanish kings leaned heavily upon their Jewish advisers.

Much of recorded political history of Spanish Jewry during that period consists indeed of the vicissitudes of numerous Jewish grandees. Apart from being in charge of the fiscal reorganization of the new provinces, they were often entrusted with tax collections in the older provinces as well. Occasionally, the kings simply farmed out the entire tax revenue to prominent Jewish businessmen against the payment of stipulated annual amounts. On their part, these tax farmers had to engage in protracted negotiations with the various groups of taxpayers, whose resistance often grew in direct proportion to their power and influence in the realm. The representatives of the Estates assembled at the Cortes from time to time agitated for the removal of all Jewish tax agents and, more generally, demanded that Jews not be entrusted with any public offices. These postulates, long sanctioned by canon law, found ready support among the Spanish churchmen, who took a clue from Innocent III's aforementioned censure of Alphonso VIII of Castile in 1205. The kings resisted these concerted attacks and, because of the exigencies of their treasuries, they made but half-hearted promises not to employ Jewish tax farmers while refusing point blank to dismiss all Jewish officials. There was much less opposition, needless to say, to Jewish participation in Spain's armed forces. In contrast to the battle of Zalaqa of 1086, however, Jews were found only on the one, the Christian, side of the battle. Under the Almohade outlawry of Judaism, no overtly professing Jews could serve in the Muslim forces. The Christians, however, despite such hostile legends as that about the alleged surrender of a Jewish wing in the battle of Uclés of 1109, welcomed the reinforcement of their armies by Jewish combatants. The observation by the German rabbi, Eliezer b. Joel ha-Levi, in the twelfth century was still largely true a century later. He wrote: "It still is a general practice in Spain for the Jews to go out to war together with the king." This statement was repeated by Isaac Or Zaru'a in the thirteenth century, very likely as a reflection of contemporary conditions rather than as a purely literary reminiscence.[4]

Not that the clergy, the nobility, or the cities refrained from utilizing the Jews' financial resources and commercial ingenuity for their own benefit. Intergroup business transactions of various kinds are frequently recorded in the sources. Even with respect to the controversial ecclesiastical tithe, Archbishop Roderic of Toledo arranged in 1219 with the Jewish communities of his diocese that they substitute for it an annual capitation tax of one-sixth of a gold piece for each male member aged twenty or over. This agreement was confirmed by King Ferdinand III. The Knights Templars were particularly prone to employ talented Jewish neighbors in their far-flung business activities. On the other hand, these Jewish agents not only ran the usual business risks and faced the resistance of powerful taxpayers, even of entire cities, but sometimes became involved in the endless palace intrigues and factional struggles, courting retribution on their entire community. For instance, the eminent royal revenue official, Don Çag (Isaac) de la Maleha, Alphonso X's long-time favorite, in a moment of weakness yielded to the entreaties of the rebellious Crown Prince Sancho and handed him in 1280 (or 1279) some accumulated Treasury funds. As a result, the Treasury was unable to pay the wages of soldiers then besieging Algeciras (in the Muslim kingdom of Granada) and the siege had to be lifted. Angered by this "treasonable" act of his trusted Jewish adviser, the king without much ado had Çag executed and his property confiscated. Not satisfied with punishing the revenue agent and his associates, Alphonso blamed the whole Jewish community for Don Çag's misdeeds. At the same time, hard pressed for cash, he took a leaf out of the French book and ordered the sudden seizure of all Jewish communal leaders on a Sabbath (January 19, 1281). They were released only after they pledged themselves to raise speedily the large sum of 4,380,000 maravedis, or approximately double their usual annual assessment. There also were cases of individual assassinations or attempted assassinations of Jewish grandees by political opponents, enraged debtors, or religious fanatics.[5]

Apart from suffering from the effects of such individual miscalculations, the Jewish community was exposed to collective dangers. In Spain, too, riots were intermittently staged by their enemies, even though the kings were no longer in as forgiving a mood for assaults on their Jewish protégés as they had been in the earlier period of monarchical weakness. In fact, Alphonso VII's pardon of 1127 absolving the inhabitants of Soldaña, Céa, Carrión and other localities from responsibility for damages they had inflicted upon Jews, extended also to the destruction wrought by them on the king's own palaces and other possessions. A less dramatic, but in the long run equally disturbing, source of insecurity was the frequent change in administrative practices. The same Alphonso VIII who, together with the queen, had in 1177 transferred the Saracens and Jews of Palencia to its bishop Raymond and the latter's successors, did not hesitate eight years later to order the Palencia community to pay its taxes exclusively to the royal Treasury. Yet once such a transfer had been recorded, it invited repetition under favorable circumstances. In 1256, Alphonso X confirmed the original decree of 1177 and restored to the Palencia bishop exclusive authority over the local Jewish community. Such shifts were quite frequent. Even in Spain Jews thus had to learn to "live dangerously" and to adjust themselves to the ever changing legal and political conditions.[6]

Royal insistence upon employing Jewish officials is doubly remarkable, as canon law generally played a very great role in shaping the legal status of the Jews in both Castile and Aragon. The

Castilian regime, though somewhat more independent of the Papacy and deeply engaged in assimilating the diverse population strains within its borders, wholly accepted the ecclesiastical outlook on Jews and Judaism. This submission to the priestly ideology came clearly to the fore in Alphonso X's *Las Siete Partidas* (the Seven Divisions). This code, which according to a modern historian "still finds a place in the library of every Spanish lawyer from Barcelona to Valparaiso," did not achieve full force until 1348. Yet it clearly reflected the thinking of both Alphonso and his predecessor, Ferdinand III. Apart from various specific regulations pertaining to Jewish behavior toward Christian sacraments, the Jewish oath, and particularly mixed marriages, scattered throughout the code, a whole chapter in the last section (vii.24) is devoted to Jews. It begins by giving a threefold explanation:

Jews are a kind of people who, although they do not believe in the faith of our Lord Jesus Christ, were nevertheless suffered by the grand masters of Christianity to live among them. . . . A Jew is called one who believes in and observes the law of Moses according to the letter and performs circumcision and other duties ordered by that law. The name is derived from the tribe of Judah which was the noblest and most powerful among all the tribes; and from it issued the king of the Jews. . . . And the reason why the Church, emperors, kings, and other princes have allowed Jews to live among Christians is that, by forever living in captivity, they are to serve as a reminder to the people that they come from the lineage of those who had crucified our Lord Jesus Christ.'

Among the restrictions spelled out in the following ten articles was one forbidding Jews to attack Christianity in any form or to try to convert Christians to Judaism. On the other hand, Jewish converts to Christianity were to be protected in their rights (Arts. 2, 6, 7). Jews were to live a segregated life, no Christian being allowed to live among them. Nor were they to employ Christian servants, while their Muslim slaves turning Christian were to be instantly freed. Sex relations with Christians were put under the sanction of capital punishment. Jews were also to be forced to wear distinguishing marks (Arts. 8–11). At the same time, Jewish religious requirements were to be respected, judges being forbidden to summon Jews on Sabbaths and the communities being allowed to keep their older synagogues under repair. Most significantly, Jews were not to hold any public office which might give them control over Christians. "In ancient times the Jews were most honored and had great privileges over all the other nations, for they alone were called the people of God." Since their crucifixion of Christ, however, they had no priests and the ancient emperors found it appropriate to deprive them of all their honors and privileges (Art. 3). This entire legislation clearly betrays the great influence exerted on Alphonso and his advisers by the outstanding Aragonese canon jurist, Raymond de Peñaforte, who was applying the principles of the papal Decretals he had codified in Rome to the secular legislation of his home country. Peñaforte not only impressed the ruling circles of Aragon with the need of converting its large Jewish population, but he also boasted of having secured the cooperation of Alphonso X, as well as of James I, in the establishment of his new college for Arabic and Hebrew studies to serve the Christian mission. We have the testimony of Alphonso's nephew Juan Manuel that, notwithstanding the king's deep scientific interest, he was dedicated to the Church's missionary ideals and that for this purpose he had inspired a Spanish translation of the Qur'an and the Talmud.[8]

Many of these and other royal provisions were not only disregarded in practice, but also ran counter to many of the king's own enactments. For instance, on the intervention of Ferdinand III, Pope Honorius III had issued, on March 20, 1219, a general dispensation for all Castilian Jewry from wearing the badge postulated by the Fourth Lateran Council. He had been informed, the Pope wrote to Archbishop Roderic of Toledo, that many Jews of Castile were so wrought up over that canon "that some of them choose rather to flee to the Moors than to be burdened with such signs. Others make conspiracies and hold secret assemblies on such occasions. As a result, the king, whose income in large measure derives from these very Jews, may suffer grave damage and misfortune may befall the kingdom." In time, of course, the badge was introduced into both Castile and Aragon and much energy was spent by royal officials on enforcing it. More difficult was adherence to the prohibition against investing Jews with public offices which, in a greater or lesser degree, was violated all through the years.[9]

Fully to comprehend the meaning of the secular legislation relating to Jews, one must turn, therefore, to specific royal enactments and particularly to the numerous local *fueros* (custumals) promulgated, or at least approved, by the kings. Being of local origin, many of these compilations reflect usages and observances haphazardly accumulated over generations, and are often devoid of any guiding principles and inner consistency. They are in part survivals of the anti-Jewish legislation of the Visigothic age, which because of the intervening changes in the sociopolitical situation had often been greatly moderated. Some cities, perhaps the majority, were now ready to treat the Jews, as we recall, almost on the basis of equality. Because of the great disparity in such local developments, many of which went unrecorded and are even now shrouded in total darkness, these *fueros* greatly vary from one another. All of these inconsistencies did not prevent the kings from confirming them or even, by taking some of them over into the *Fuero real,* from lending them more general validity. Not surprisingly, some provisions, as well as many specific acts of government, ran counter to other enactments by the same kings, and to privileges granted by them to cities on the spur of a moment. These inner contradictions led to endless complaints by injured parties, both Jewish and Christian, the kings frequently settling the ensuing controversies by other *ad hoc* regulations which merely compounded the existing confusion.[10]

Some regulations pertained to the inner life of the Jewish communities. Internal administration was otherwise left to the discretion of communal elders whether or not their election had been confirmed by royal authorities. In this respect, the thirteenth-century official *Fuero real* greatly differed from the private collection known as the *Libro de los Fueros de Castilla.* The former was primarily concerned with intergroup relations. It provided that Jews should not serve as attorneys or testamentary executors for Christians, nor inherit Christian estates, and that Christian fathers begetting illegitimate children from Jewish or Moorish mothers should raise them in the Christian faith. Jews were forbidden to proselytize, blaspheme against Christian doctrines, or keep books attacking either the Christian or the Jewish faith. The maximum rate of interest was set at $33\frac{1}{3}$ percent, with the proviso that the accumulated interest must never exceed the principal of the debt. On the other hand, Jews were not to be summoned to court, nor were they subject to judicial execution, on their Sabbath, but neither could they appear as plaintiffs against Christians on that day. Equally egalitarian was the demand that neither Jews nor Christians should employ nurses of the other faith and that none, except Catholic priests, should be allowed to acquire church objects. The *Libro de los Fueros,* on the other hand, while likewise regulating intergroup credit transactions and procedural methods, nevertheless included a number of commercial provisions and set fines for assault and battery, profanation of a Sabbath, and illicit sex relations, even if all parties concerned were Jewish. The communal elders were also told to cooperate in the search for criminals hiding in the Jewish quarter and to force reluctant witnesses to testify under the sanction of a Jewish ban. In justification the compiler of the *Fueros* merely needed to invoke the general principle "that the Jews are the king's; much as they may be under the power of some great lords, nobles, and other persons, or under that of monasteries, all of them belong to the king and live under his protection and for his service." [11]

No substantial changes seem to have occurred during the brief regime of Sancho IV (1284–95). Involved in rather constant warfare with either rebellious nobles or Morocco, the king could not afford to dispense with the services of his Jewish advisers. At the same time he did not wish to antagonize the Cortes, which demanded from him in 1286 the dismissal of the judges specially assigned to mixed litigations between Jews and Christians. Sancho did not reject this demand outright, but he simply failed to implement it. In 1293 he promised the Cortes not to employ Jews as tax farmers. But evidently unable to renounce that reliable source of revenue, he failed to fulfill his promise. The king did not even enforce his own prohibition of 1288 against some Jews of Valladolid acquiring land in the city environs, because they had usually paid taxes only on movable property. In short, the policies laid down by Sancho's predecessors carried over with little change into the fourteenth century.[12]

ARAGON'S PIONEERS

Inner contradictions were even more pronounced in the policies of James I and Pedro III of Aragon. In the newly conquered territories of Valencia and Majorca, James the Conqueror generously allotted land and castles to Jews from the older provinces. He even tried to attract newcomers from North Africa. In 1247 he issued a blanket safe-conduct and letters of naturalization for two Jewish families from Sigilmassa, Morocco, if they were to come by land or sea and settle in the provinces of Majorca, Valencia, or Catalonia. This policy was pursued also by some of his later successors, Pedro IV granting in 1343 a general permission to Jews and Saracens coming from Muslim countries to settle and trade in the city *(civitatem)* of Majorca "like the other Jews of that city." No less than 104 Jews benefited from the distribution of Valencia land left behind by fleeing Muslim landlords and farmers. Privately, too, three Catalan nobles in 1240 mortgaged to Solomon Alfachim (Alconstantin?) for a loan of 150 maravedis a fortress and a village near Tarragona with all their revenues. Solomon was given the right to administer the estate through his own men and, after the stipulated period, to charge 20 percent on the balance unpaid.[13]

Such royal encouragement of Jewish immigration often contrasted sharply with the efforts to get rid of many Saracens, ever suspect of possibly turning into a "fifth column" in later campaigns against the Muslim kingdom of the South. In fact, James granted a license and safe-conduct to the Jew, Abraham Albanna of Tortosa, to transport Saracens from Castile and the territory of Aladrach by sea to the port of Dénia and thence to North Africa. He only demanded from him a per capita payment of two gold besants in addition to the usual harbor fees in Dénia. Very likely, these Moorish émigrés included many free inhabitants who had given up hope for the return of a Muslim regime. At the same time the favorable reception accorded Jewish arrivals by the authorities paid off so well that, within a few decades, the newly conquered territories had populous and prosperous Jewish communities. This is evident from such extant data on the fiscal contributions of the various communities as were compiled for the year 1274. Apart from Barcelona, where no figures are given, the old Jewish communities of Saragossa and Calatayud paid the largest amounts, totaling 15,000 (or 17,000) and 10,000 solidi jac., respectively. At the same time the newly acquired community of Valencia contributed 5,000 solidi jac., favorably comparing with the older wealthy community of Perpignan which in that year paid the same amount, though in a different currency (solidi melg.). Of course, Valencia Jewry consisted not only of newcomers but also of older settlers from Moorish times who had remained in their places of residence upon the approach of the Christian Crusaders. Majorcan Jewry's contribution is not recorded in this connection, but among assessments made a few years before (*ca.* 1271) it appears with an impost of 5,000 solidi regal. This amount compared with but 3,000 then expected from Valencia, as against 8,000 from Calatayud, 9,000 from Saragossa, 15,000 from Perpignan, and fully 40,000 from Barcelona.[14]

Legally, too, the kings drew a fairly sharp distinction between the newly acquired lands, where they had to give the Jews wider privileges, and the old provinces of Catalonia and Aragon where the conditions of the Jews had long been determined by the interplay of various local factors and vested interests. In the new regions, too, the royal officials often conferred privileges on cities or monasteries which ran counter to those granted the Jews. For example, in his desire to acquire a certain castle owned by the Cistercian order, James I conferred upon it, in 1219, a monopoly on the *alcacería* (shopping center) of Calatayud, which included exchange counters and even some artisan shops. Jews and others often protested in vain against the ensuing high rents. In his renewal of that privilege in 1249, James emphasized "that no Jew shall dare or presume to have any other shops or stores or to sell in any other location of that city, except in the aforementioned *alcacería*." He repeated this injunction in another renewal of 1262. These inconsistencies were but a facet of the instability of medieval Jewish and non-Jewish life in the face of the strains and stresses imposed upon the royal policies by the clash of classes, parties, ideologies, and even by personal whims of kings and their counselors.[15]

One outstanding difference between some older and newer communities in the provinces of Catalonia and Aragon consisted in the presence or absence of provisions recognizing Jewish capital jurisdiction. This right was considered so integral a part of municipal liberties that many a newly established Spanish town started by erecting gallows on its market place as an outward sign of its municipal independence. In his charter of 1229, James I conceded it to the Jewish community of Calatayud. According to this charter, which undoubtedly restated many older rights, the Jews were allowed to elect four elders entrusted with the authority to expel members from the community, imprison them, and even condemn them to death. Only in the latter case was the community to indemnify the royal Treasury by the payment of 1,000 solidi for the loss of a taxpayer. With respect to two specifically named individuals of ill repute, however, exiled by the king, the elders were given the right, upon the culprits' illicit return to the district of Calatayud, to execute them without the payment of any indemnity. These elders were also entitled to issue ordinances in consultation with the membership at large. In conclusion, the king instructed both the royal officials and the municipal councilors of Calatayud that they "should maintain you [Jews] and all your things wherever you may go, stay or return, should protect and defend you like [tamquam] Our own property, should assist you and uphold your customs and regulations in every matter . . . and not permit anyone to disturb you." This charter was renewed by James II in 1306. Slightly more circumscribed was the privilege granted by James I to the community of Barbastro in 1273. Here the ten elected Jewish elders were empowered only to recommend to the royal bailiff the execution of Jewish informers and other men of ill repute, against an indemnity of 500 solidi to the Treasury. They merely had to swear on the Law of Moses that the accused had been lawfully convicted.[16]

No such latitude was given to the Jews of the old county of Barcelona or the entire province of Catalonia, although in a famous incident of 1279 James' successor, Pedro III, actually forced the distinguished rabbis, Jonah b. Joseph (a cousin of the more famous Jonah b. Abraham) of Gerona and Solomon ibn Adret of Barcelona to sentence a Jewish informer to death. Even the privilege of 1239 for the Jewish community in newly conquered Valencia, though quite broad and considerate of the demands of Jewish autonomy, reserved to the king the exclusive right to pass judgment over Jews accused of homicide. But this privilege stated bluntly that in litigations between Jews and Christians no Jews should be convicted except on the mixed testimony of a Christian and a Jew, and that all such litigations must take place before the defendant's judge. Each party had the right to appeal from his judgment to a higher tribunal. In taking an oath, Jews were to swear only on the Law of Moses. A noteworthy concession was made in favor of Jewish prisoners, who were to be temporarily released from jail on each Friday afternoon, while no Jew was to be summoned before the authorities on a Sabbath or Jewish holiday. The king declared:

Finally, We receive you all, collectively and individually, as well as your property under Our protection, custody, and command, and under Our special safe-conduct [*guidatico*] wherever you go, stay or return through all the localities of Our kingdoms and Our dominions on land and on the sea. Nor shall anyone dare to aggrieve you, invade, seize or detain you or your property, except in the case of your own debt or transgression.[17]

Such communal charters were often supplemented, as well as violated, by innumerable privileges granted to individual members. To cite but a few examples from a single source collection relating to the district of Barcelona under the reign of James I: On January 15, 1258, one Astrug, son of Isaac of Gerona, was given the specific right, in case of a lawsuit being filed against him by any Jew or Christian, to appear only before a Jewish judge. He was also told that "all cases instituted against you shall be discussed and determined in accordance with Jewish law and mores." Such a special privilege was apparently needed in Catalonia, whereas in the newer provinces this rule applied to all Jews. On the same day another Astrug named Buenseñor was given permission to break through parts of the city wall of Barcelona facing his houses and to open windows and entrances in them wherever he pleased. A year later James gave a blanket permission to one Juceff de Grassa to marry another wife, whether or not he divorced his spouse or had other wives, although Jewish representatives had appeared before the king and told him that he "ought not to do it in defiance of the Jewish law and ritual." Yet, apart from safeguarding the contractual rights of Juceff's first wife, Gima, the king forbade all Jews under the severe penalty of 500 morabetinos to interfere with that bigamous marriage through any kind of prohibition or excommunication. Nor did he hesitate in other cases affecting his Jewish favorites to run counter to established canon law. In 1263

James absolved one Isaac, son of Bonjuda Fusel, of the accusation of having cohabited with a Christian woman in remote parts of Sicily. Claiming that this transgression "had hitherto not been proved against you nor have you been accused of it by anyone before Us," the king made it clear that he did not wish to see Isaac prosecuted, "whether it be true or not that you have committed that crime." Similarly disregarding the canonical fulminations against the erection of new synagogues, James permitted one Bonanasco Salamón "to erect a chapel or synagogue in the midst of your houses or in any location you may wish in the Jewish street of Barcelona in which you may place the book of the Law of Moses which is called *Rotle,* as well as any other Hebrew books. All Jews wishing to pray there may legitimately congregate and come to services held in this chapel or synagogue without any obstacle on Our part or that of Our [subjects]." He also issued orders to the bailiffs and provosts of Barcelona, "present and future," to protect that synagogue during Bonanasco's entire lifetime. These examples can readily be multiplied.[18]

In other respects, however, Aragon was indeed under much stronger ecclesiastical influence than Castile. Apart from the direct impact of the Papacy, the example of the revered French king Louis IX helped nurture governmental as well as popular antagonisms toward Jews. Moneylending on interest, in particular, became here a major issue, strong economic as well as ideological factors tending to limit the interest rates. Not that the country could get along without credit, which was, in fact, badly needed for the upbuilding of the deserted regions. Hence even Christians were finally allowed to charge 12 percent per annum. But the rate of 20 percent, set for Jews in 1228, was far below the prevailing charges even in Castile. At the Cortes of Tarragona in 1234–35 this maximum was restated under the severe sanction of confiscation of property and public flagellation for offending lenders. Six years later, at the Cortes of Gerona, the king added the limitation that the total debt owed to a Jewish lender at the end of a year must not exceed the principal by more than one-sixth. Usury also served as the springboard for general accusations against Jews at both Cortes and ecclesiastical synods, such as that likewise held in Tarragona in 1235. James was, moreover, under the constant pressure of his advisers to cancel debts owed to Jews or else to follow the French example and to confiscate them for the benefit of the Treasury. Jewish fears were sufficiently aroused for the king to issue several decrees (in favor of the Jewish communities of Barcelona, Villafranca, Tarragona, and others in 1257, of Barbastro in 1260–61, and so forth) in which he pledged himself not to cancel such debts for a specified number of years.[19]

In purely religious matters James even more willingly followed the lead of Raymond de Peñaforte and other ecclesiastical advisers. True, he did not imitate Louis IX's example in the outlawry and burning of the Talmud, although he, too, had received Gregory IX's circular letter of 1239. He was satisfied, as we recall, with the expurgation of incriminated passages, which established a precedent for similar compromises in many lands. But he consented to stage the famous disputation at Barcelona between Naḥmanides and Pablo Christiani. Subsequently, his wavering policies made life sufficiently miserable for the aged Gerona rabbi to cause him to leave his country and to spend the last years of his life in Palestine. Shortly after the disputation James yielded to papal pressure, renewed by Urban IV's bull of October 1263, and more strictly enforced the Jewish badge. Soon thereafter a Tarragona Jew was severely fined for failing to appear in public wearing the prescribed red sign. The king also forced Jewish audiences to listen to frequent missionary sermons. Despite its subsequent modifications, James' pertinent decree of 1263 outdid those of the pope and was not emulated in Rome until several generations later. On the other hand, while upholding the prohibition enacted in 1228 against the conversion of Muslims to Judaism and vice versa, "the Conqueror" tried to safeguard Jewish slaveholding in Majorca, where at that time it still was a major economic necessity. In 1252 he restricted the baptism of the Jews' Muslim slaves to Easter, Pentecost, and Christmas. On any other days the new converts had to pay the prohibitive fine of 12 maravedis. In 1273 he added the proviso that all newly baptized Saracen slaves would become royal property, thus removing a major incentive from their conversion. These inconsistencies are well reflected in the comprehensive Fuero de Aragón enacted by James in 1247. While in the main summarizing older legislation, this compilation betrayed the newer biases by restating the interest limitations of 1241 and the recently introduced humiliating formulas of the Jewish oath.[20]

Many vicissitudes of the Jewish communities can be understood only against the background of the existence throughout the thirteenth century of numerous influential Jewish courtiers, diplomats, fiscal agents, and physicians in both Spanish kingdoms. As a rule they were superior to the Christian nobles and the relatively few burghers by business training, linguistic skills, and familiarity with conditions in the newly acquired territories as well as in the neighboring Moorish possessions. They also proved to be the more reliable servants of the Crown, as their entire status depended on the good will of their royal masters. Their financial resources, too, could be more readily tapped by the Crown than those of the more recalcitrant nobles and Christian merchants. Even an infante like Pedro could readily borrow from Jews; for instance, 1,000 solidi from Vives in Valencia in September 1267, and 5,360 solidi from the Gerona Jew, Astrug Ravaya, at the Castle of Peratallada two months later. By January 1274, Pedro's indebtedness to Vives rose to the large sum of 64,000 solidi.[21]

Jewish aid appeared particularly important during the critical thirteenth century, when the Aragonese monarchy tried to establish its undisputed supremacy over the various classes of the population. In this endeavor the kings encountered the sharp opposition of powerful nobles, particularly of the thirty-nine families which constituted the first "arm" (*brazo*) of the Cortes. At one time the king was told by a member of this group that "every one of us is as important as you; all of us together are more important than you." Seeking allies among the clergy and burghers, as well as the lower nobility, the kings had to grant each of these groups extensive concessions, which, rather than strengthening the monarchy, undermined its power. From time to time they even had to transfer the control over some Jews to knightly orders or individual magnates. In an interesting decree of March 31, 1211, Pedro II donated the city of Cabañas to the Order of Hospitallers in exchange for some Jews. He added:

Except Rabbi Aser Abentalca, his son and nephews, since the king knows that Rabbi Aser would prefer to belong to the Order of Hospitallers and does not wish to be associated with the other Jews. Taking into account the good services rendered [by Aser] to the previous kings, his [Pedro's] ancestors, he ceded him to the Order together with all his property and rights.

The Order's chapter assembled in Saragossa accepted Aser and his son and nephews, and promised to defend them against any mishaps. In 1258 James I enacted an extensive privilege in favor of the Knights Templars; it included the obligation "to defend the said militia at his own expense against whatever litigation the relatives of the Jew Aaron who had died in Morocco" may institute against it. On the whole, however, the kings rather jealously guarded their Jewish patrimony and, over the resistance of both nobles and churchmen, made excellent use of their Jewish officials to reorganize and administer their far-flung possessions.[22]

Opponents of the monarchy or of the Jews, however, often cast aspersion on the loyalty of Jewish officials. Pope Honorius III lent a willing ear to these suspicions and, in 1220, lodged protests with the kings of Aragon, Castile, Leon, and Narvarre, as well as with several Spanish bishops and abbots. In his letter to James I of Aragon he wrote:

Know ye that it has come to Our notice that much harm comes to Christians from the circumstance that, whenever the occasion arises for you to send envoys to the noble Miramoline [Emir Yusuf abu Ya'qub] or to his subjects, you rarely, if ever, send anyone but Jews. These men betray to them the plans and the positions of the Christians and reveal to them the latter's secrets. . . . You ought rather to send Christians, for you cannot expect faithfulness from infidels.

While the papal apprehensions may have been heightened by the critical situation on the Peninsula following the victory at the Navas de Tolosa in 1212, this sharpening of the traditional canonical prohibition of the appointment of Jews to positions of trust doubtless was but an echo of similar aspersions spread in Spain by the enemies of the Jewish diplomats. The kings paid no attention to these unsubstantiated rumors. They considered them wholly unjustified in their diplomatic relations with Almohade princes, whose continued religious intolerance must have greatly antagonized any Jewish envoy. They found some Jews particularly useful because of their familiarity with foreign languages, especially Arabic, and their acquaintance, through travel or personal origin, with conditions in many neighboring lands. This need for Jewish experts in the Arabic epistolary and contractual style even in many domestic chancery services continued well into the fourteenth century. We learn, for instance, that James II appointed one Abrahim Abenamies as his secretary and official interpreter in the Arabic language. Conversely, the Muslim rulers of Granada, who had in the meantime moderated the Almohade exclusiveness, used their own Jews for diplomatic missions to Christian courts. On the very day of Abrahim's appointment (September 1, 1291), James II also ordered his officials to guard over the security of two envoys of the king of Granada, who, after accomplishing their mission, were about to return home. Curiously, one of these two envoys bears the identical name of Abrahim Abennamies [sic]. It may well be that Abrahim had changed his mind and, rather than return to Granada, decided to enter the services of the Aragonese king. Such transfers of allegiance to another sovereign were far from unusual among diplomats then and long after.[23]

Occasional depositions and despoliations of these Jewish dignitaries after years of devoted service no more discouraged their would-be successors than did the similar instability in royal favors affecting Christian statesmen and officials. Don Çag de la Maleha's execution because of his mistaken generosity toward the Castilian infante is a case in point. This unfortunate victim of royal moods had been forewarned ever since the demise of his own father, Don Çulema (Solomo ibn Sadoq), whose entire estate accumulated in years of public service had been confiscated by the Treasury. True, the leading royal advisers from the houses of Alconstantin and Ibn Shoshan, or Abraham al-Barchilon, in Castile; and their Aragonese confreres like Jahuda (Yehudah) ibn Labi de la Cavalleria, Benvenist de Porta, Astrug Jacob Xixon, Bonastrug de Porta (a namesake of Nahmanides), Muça de Portella, and particularly Astrug Ravaya or Ravailla and his sons, Jucef or Yusuf and Musa (Joseph and Moses), escaped the effects of such sudden reversals of royal amity. In some cases, perhaps after bargaining, the Jewish officials were appointed bailiffs for life. Such appointments are recorded in the cases of Astrug Jacob Xixon in Tortosa in 1265 and of Moses Abinbinag in Lérida in 1268. At times Jews were asked to take over more than one bailiwick, at least during an emergency. The leading Jewish magnate of Aragon, Jahuda de Cavalleria, who had been bailiff of Saragossa since 1257, was asked by James to put down a Muslim insurrection in Valencia in 1275, a task in which the Jewish financier acquitted himself to the king's satisfaction. Appointed by James' successor, Pedro, governor of the entire kingdom of Valencia, Jahuda reestablished peace so effectively that he ventured to return to his old post in Saragossa, where he died in 1276. Even more dramatic was the career of the two brothers Ravaya who, during Pedro's successful expedition to Sicily, were left behind in effective, if not nominal, control of the entire realm. On the other hand, although we have no clear-cut documentary evidence, these officials must have frequently resorted to the then customary strong, even ruthless methods. They thereby antagonized some of their own coreligionists. In 1272, two Jewish arrivals from Germany joined some local Saragossans in charging Jahuda with extorting usury. A similar accusation was hurled by four Jews and a Moor against another Jewish bailiff, Vives Abenvives, in 1270 and again in 1274. The latter denunciation included allegations that Vives fraudulently acquired from Moors many objects below their real value and that he was guilty of sodomy. But in all these cases the charges proved unfounded and the Jewish officials were quickly restored to power.[24]

Some of these royal councilors, long active under James I, were still employed by Pedro the Great in his diplomatic negotiations with the Muslim kings of Granada and Morocco, and entrusted with important missions in the newly annexed kingdom of Sicily. Domestically, too, they were in charge of the reorganization of many disjointed fiscal and administrative functions in the loosely united territories. In time of war they served not only as contractors supplying the royal armies, but, as in the case of Yusuf Ravaya, were allowed to issue in their own names orders even to such important vassals as the king of Majorca. If such a Jew's "overbearing" behavior irked some of these powerful lords, it was doubly resented by the whole noble class bent upon wresting from the kings many royal prerogatives. In the civil war of 1286, in particular, the noble opponents of the monarchy were deeply aggrieved by the Crown's effective Jewish allies.[25]

FOURTEENTH-CENTURY AMBIGUITIES

On principle, the legislation in both Spanish kingdoms remained substantially unaltered during the fourteenth century under the reigns of Ferdinand IV the Summoned (1295–1312), Alphonso XI the Judge (1312–50), Pedro I the Cruel (1350–69), Henry II de Trastamara (1366–79), and John I (1379–90), of Castile, as well as under James II (1291–1327), Alphonso IV (1327–36), and Pedro IV the Ceremonious (1336–87), of Aragon. However, many factors combined to cause a constant deterioration of the Jews' legal and, even more, of their socioeconomic status. The *Reconquista* was largely completed, only Granada remaining in Muslim hands till 1492. The Christian rulers now expended most of their energies in fighting one another or in trying to pacify the ever rebellious nobles in their own lands. Notwithstanding these internecine struggles the Christian population, augmented by Moorish converts and immigrants from other lands, increased sufficiently in numbers and stability so that Jews were no longer needed to supply manpower for the colonization of deserted areas. On the contrary, their presence was often resented now by the competing and ever more self-assertive bourgeoisie.

In their domestic policies the kings needed the cities' assistance in subduing the nobles; they rewarded the burghers by extensive municipal charters, which often involved curtailment of Jewish rights. In their anti-Jewish demands the cities' representatives at the Cortes received much support from both the nobles and the clergy, although their petitions frequently included requests that neither nobles, clerics, nor Jews be appointed tax collectors. Such a resolution, adopted by the Cortes of Burgos in 1315, was accepted by the regents for the adolescent Alphonso XI. Seven years later it was repeated by the Cortes of Valladolid, which added the provision that the king no longer appoint clerics or Jews to any post in the royal chancery. Moreover, the burghers' spokesmen from Castile, Leon, and the Estremadura insisted that loan contracts between Jews and Christians should not be concluded before a vicar or an archpriest, whereby "the royal jurisdiction is replaced by that of ecclesiastical courts." In view of this persistently hostile attitude of the muncipalities, it is not at all surprising to find Jewish lenders occasionally preferring ecclesiastical over secular jurisdiction. That both clerical and Jewish tax collectors were lumped together as exploiters of the population may be attributed to the general penchant of taxpayers for complaining of fiscal burdens and the real abuses of power by many such governmentally authorized businessmen-officials. Nor did the Jewish tax collectors necessarily spare their own coreligionists. According to the complaint submitted by the master of the renowned Order of Calatrava to Alphonso XI in 1316, the Jewish community of Maqueda had once before been depopulated by the emigration of many overtaxed members, whereupon Alphonso's father, Ferdinand, had reduced its tax burden from 8,000 to 5,000 maravedis. In 1316, however, during the allocation by the Jewish representatives of the respective communal shares in the overall Jewish contribution, the Maqueda community was assessed 8,281 maravedis, which had already caused the departure of "all" Jews. The king recognized the legitimacy of this complaint and once again reduced the total assessment to 5,000 maravedis.[26]

In the fourteenth century Jews constituted a significant segment of the population of every major and of many minor Spanish cities, their ratio often being as high as one-third. Side by side with them lived many substantial communities of Moors (so-called *mudejares* or *moriscos*), while the Christian majority itself often embraced some French or Italian merchants more or less permanently residing in the Spanish emporia, as well as nobles, clerics, and newly settled landless peasants. In essence many Spanish cities consisted of three semi-independent municipalities of members of the three faiths. Without any compulsion Jews and Moors lived in their own *juderías* or *morerías,* many surrounded by walls, within which they enjoyed extensive municipal liberties. Not only did Jewish elders exercise the right of admitting or expelling members but, in 1294, James II of Aragon ordered his officials in Valencia to prevent the local burghers from sheltering Jews expelled from their *aljama.* In the same year the king also condemned the *jurados* (municipal elders) of Saragossa for employing illegal methods in their controversy with Jews over a missing Christian child. Even in that early period of the spread of the blood libel in Spain, such a disappearance raised the specter of serious involvement of the whole Jewish community. The city council of Saragossa decided, therefore, to employ a magician to locate the corpse of that Christian child in order the more readily to convict the Jews, who were so intimidated that "they did not dare to show themselves anywhere among the Christians." Fortunately, the Jewish elders instituted a search throughout Aragon and Navarre and finally found the child living with his purported father in Calatayud. Many other controversies between municipalities and Jewish communities arose from diverse interpretations of the conflicting privileges and regulations enacted by kings to meet *ad hoc* situations, or of the different customs observed by the two groups. Such a clash over the divergent treatment of Muslim slaves converted to Christianity induced Pedro I of Castile, on complaint of the city of Toledo, to summon in 1353 representatives of both the municipality and the *aljama* to appear before his court for judicial decision. On the other hand, we shall see that, notwithstanding these official suspicions and animosities, the day-to-day relations between the Christian and Jewish city folk in Spain became so close as to call forth frequent counteraction by both the state and the Church.[27]

Under these circumstances the kings had no option but to disregard the Cortes' reiterated petitions to dismiss their Jewish tax agents or tax farmers. More successful, as we shall see in a later chapter, were the Cortes' fairly unanimous demands concerning the reduction of interest rates, one- to three-year moratoria, and even partial cancellation of debts owed to Jews. The kings realized, of course, that by yielding to the petitioners they would substantially reduce an important source of their revenue. But they were forced to meet them halfway with sufficient frequency for the Jewish communities to continue seeking advance reassurances against such sudden losses, at least for certain specified periods. Needless to say, the personal attitudes of monarchs likewise varied, depending on the exigencies of the time as well as on their individual characters or temporary moods.

On its part the Church likewise went over to an offensive against both Jews and Muslims. The newly introduced preaching friars and inquisitorial courts embarked upon ambitious schemes to convert the large religious minorities in the country. These efforts, which had led to the dramatic disputation in Barcelona in 1263, were crowned at times with considerable successes. Even a moderate preacher like Raymond Lull persuaded, in 1299, James II "firmly" to order all Jewish communities in his realm to listen to Lull in their synagogues on Sabbaths and Sundays, adding, "If they wish they may take the opportunity of answering his preachment and exposition without, however, being forced to do so." Somewhat later, as we recall, Lull induced the Ecumenical Council of Vienne in 1311 to establish chairs in Hebrew, Chaldaic, and Arabic at the Universities of Salamanca, Paris, Oxford, and Bologna, in order to train a corps of more effective missionaries. Personally, to be sure, James was not unprejudiced. In perusing his private correspondence one finds that, when he congratulated the Infanta Doña Constanza on her giving birth to a son, he added: "But, my daughter, you ought not to do as you are wont to do, and raise him according to the advice of Jews." Three years later he assigned to Infanta Maria "all the income of Our Court which has come, or is yet to come, from the condemnation by the inquisitor of heretical depravity of certain Jews of the community of Calatayud." In public, however, the king exerted a moderating influence and tried to protect the rights of his Jewish subjects also against the inquisitorial tribunals. On one occasion, in 1305, he reduced the penalties imposed by the inquisitors upon two Jewish proselytes from Germany, while in 1312 and 1318 he completely acquitted two rich Jews accused of blasphemies.[28]

Not that churches and monasteries ceased deriving direct benefits from Jews. Even in the fourteenth century we still hear of new transfers of Jews or their taxes to ecclesiastical groups. In 1313, Alphonso XI of Castile allotted some Jewish taxes in Ocaña to the master of the Order of Santiago. On the other hand, an abbot of Eslonza, Castile, seems to have had no compunction against transferring to a Jewish couple some real estate, together with the vassals living there, in payment of a debt of 3,000 maravedis contracted by the abbot's predecessor several years before (1300). In 1359, a Seville burgher served as arbiter in a litigation between the local monastery and a Jew. Most remarkably, in 1386 Archbishop Pedro

Tenorio of Toledo, defying the increasingly anti-Jewish agitation in the county, followed a plea of the Christian citizens of Brihuega and changed its weekly market from Saturday to Wednesday because the Jews were "one of the great elements [*gran meneo*] of that market." Don Pedro, and the master of the Order of Calatrava who had fifteen years earlier instituted a similar change in Pastrana, evidently did not realize that a corresponding alteration in the Carolingian Empire had been furiously denounced by Archbishop Agobard of Lyons as a mark of "Jewish insolence." [29]

Even before the resolution of the Council of Vienne some Dominicans sought to acquire a knowledge of Hebrew from their Jewish neighbors. In 1297, Pedro III actually freed the monks' Hebrew teacher from taxation, on a par with rabbis serving Jewish communities. The popes, too, on occasion proved quite lenient. In 1342 Alphonso XI requested Pope Clement VI to allow the use of a synagogue newly built in Seville by his close adviser, Joseph de Ecija. To justify this violation of the ancient canonical prohibition against new synagogues, the king pointed to the large increase of the Jewish population in that southern community where "the Jews are most needed, for they contribute to the city's necessities and also frequently go out together with the Christians against the Saracens, not fearing to expose themselves to death." On the other hand, in 1379 the pope permitted the Dominicans of Saragossa to accept a synagogue given them by King Charles of Navarre and to convert it into a convent. In the same year Queen Joan of Castile confiscated a synagogue in the diocese of Oviedo and gave it to the bishop because the Jews had dared to enlarge and embellish it in defiance of the canonical prohibition. Yielding to ecclesiastical pressure, Castilian kings outlawed the daily recitation in the synagogues of the antiheretical prayer which, notwithstanding persistent Jewish denials, the Church considered anti-Christian. In 1280, John I even forbade that prayer to be included in any book owned by Jews and demanded its total expurgation from all existing copies. Long before Ferrant Martinez, moreover, many churchmen contributed through their sermons to sowing hatred of Jews. During the stormy year of 1348, in particular, Pedro IV felt obliged to warn the episcopal vicars and chapter in Barcelona to see to it that "the words uttered by preachers and others in the

churches of the said city from which scandals and perils could arise
for the said Jews should be totally silenced." Most frequently, the
Church clashed with the state with respect to the inquisitorial
prosecutions of Jews beyond the mutually agreed purely religious
concerns for alleged blasphemy, the conversion of Christians, or
the aid to relapsed converts.[30]

Churchmen often joined hands with the cities in the growing
agitation against Jewish moneylending. To the economic interests
of burghers, who often tried to get rid of debts and particularly
their increment through interest, the Church added its strong
ideological opposition to usury of any kind. Although Jews were
not directly subject to canonical legislation, the clergy, particularly in Aragon where French influences were most pronounced,
tried to stimulate legislation of the kind enacted by Louis IX in
France and Edward I in England. The Castilian Council of
Zamora attempted in 1313 to subject the Jews to the general antiusury canons adopted by the Council of Vienne in 1311 and
promulgated as binding laws for Christians by Pope Clement V.
This action was taken despite the promise of the Toledan Cathedral Chapter but six years before, in the face of severe royal sanctions, not to interfere with Jewish moneylending on interest. This
pledge had been exacted by Ferdinand IV's sharp ordinances
issued in quick succession on February 3, 22, and 24, 1307. Here
the chapter was particularly enjoined from applying papal commands and forcing Jews to restore the interest received to their
Christian debtors. Ferdinand's commissioner, Ferrant Yuanas
Pantoja, recited these ordinances to the assembled clergy; they included passages like the following:

I, the king, have been astonished how they [the archdeacons and canons
of the church] have dared to use such writs [cartas] without My order
and to impose a sentence for this reason upon My Jews. You understand well that this should never have been done without My consent,
for no such thing ever happened in the time of the kings My ancestors;
it is a matter which impinges upon My authority. . . . You well know
that all Jews and whatever they own are Mine. Should such an action
against them be allowed to pass they would be ruined and be unable to
pay My taxes. For this reason I firmly order that none of you should
dare to use such writs nor make use of a sentence of excommunication

nor of any other [pressure] against any Jew for this reason. Should something like that have already been done, you should instantly undo it.

The royal official actually intimated that, by further pursuing such a course, the clergy would be guilty of treason.[31]

Nevertheless, in time the kings yielded to these persistent attacks, and at the very least limited interest rates—for the most part to 20 percent in Aragon, and to 33⅓ percent in Castile, both below the rates prevailing in other European countries. Although lower rates were to some extent justified, as we shall see, by the greater availability of cash and credit on the Iberian Peninsula, these legal restrictions were largely the effect of the public propaganda by the clergy and the vociferous demands of the cities' representatives at the Cortes. Attempts were also made to follow the Anglo-French example and to force Jews of the entire Aragonese monarchy to register their bonds with the authorities. Jews, both domestic and foreign, were threatened, in case of failure to register within the prescribed term, with the forfeiture of their claims. True, in his detailed ordinance of November 14, 1333, Alphonso IV defined its objective as purely fiscal and being "for your common good and utility and those of the other Jews of Our land, as well as to avoid the frauds, expenses and damages frequently arising among you while filing your tax declarations." But, incidentally, such registration, if fully carried out, would doubtless have made evasions of the antiusury laws much more difficult. Yet Alphonso himself realized how unprepared the Aragonese bureaucracy was to carry out this gigantic undertaking, and he revoked his decree after but fifteen months. Its renewal by Pedro IV in 1346 proved no more successful. That these legal restrictions, whether effective or abortive, and even the frequent moratoria and partial cancellations of debts, did not totally undermine the economic strength of Spanish Jewry, nor envenom Judeo-Christian relations to quite the same extent as they did north of the Pyrenees, was largely owing to the greater economic differentation within the Iberian communities, in which moneylending was but one of several important occupations and was not always vital even for the wealthy Jewish tax collectors, officials, and physicians.[32]

Missionary efforts were aided and abetted not only by the personally pious, but also by the ruthless, if frequently indecisive, kings. Especially during the long reigns of James II and Pedro IV in Aragon and those of Ferdinand IV, Alphonso XI, and their successors in Castile, the Jewish communities suffered from sudden changes of royal policy. Disturbances of public order, too, often led not only to destruction of Jewish lives and property but also, as a means of escaping the wrath of assailants, to numerous conversions. Such was the case in the northern areas affected by the attacks of the Pastoureaux and the accusation of the lepers' conspiracy brought over from France in 1320–21. In the small Aragonese community of Montclus, which in 1307 had been greatly strengthened by the admission on royal command of expellees from France, the Pastoureaux were given free rein. Although in July and August, 1320, James II issued several orders to his officials to protect Jews, the Montclus alcalde himself was subsequently condemned for involvement in the massacre of Jews. There were but few such punitive actions, most guilty persons being finally amnestied by the king in 1333. Certainly, royal weakness in the face of these riots served to encourage imitators. No preventive action at all was taken against the unleashing of the popular fury accompanying the Black Death in 1348–49, although the king had an inkling of the contagious nature of the pestilence and did not believe in any responsibility of Jews for its spread. The latter were, of course, also victimized by that pestilence, which did not completely die down until 1356, and by another contagion which struck Spain severely in 1369–70. The combination of the Black Death mortality with anti-Jewish riots reduced the Jewish population of Saragossa to one-fifth of its former size. In Lérida the membership of the Jewish community council declined from thirty to ten. The Jews of Inca, Majorca, had to give up their plans for erecting a quarter of their own. In many communities the death rate had reached such proportions that new Jewish cemeteries had to be quickly improvised. The economic disaster, too, occasioned by the panic of the terror-stricken population, was aggravated by the long-term effects of that catastrophic mortality. In the sphere of moneylending alone the death or hurried departure of many debtors and lenders not only rendered the subsequent collections of loans or interest extremely arduous, but it made a shambles of all long-established business relations.[33]

To these destructive forces were added the frequent foreign and civil wars, particularly those between the Spanish kingdoms themselves. The internal disturbances were climaxed in Castile in the fratricidal struggle between Pedro I and his half brother, Henry II, during which the contending parties called to their aid English and French detachments from the armies then locked in combat across the Pyrenees. These foreign mercenaries were not only permeated with the anti-Jewish feelings of their home countries but were bent on wholesale pillage. Wherever they passed they left behind them a trail of blood and smoldering ruins of destroyed Jewish quarters. No sooner did the Jews, together with the rest of Castile, recover from these shocks after the firm seizure of power by Henry II and under the fairly strong rule of John I, than they were rudely awakened by the so-called "Holy War" against them initiated in 1391 by Ferrant Martinez.[34]

Long before this catastrophic dénouement, the Jews' growing insecurity affected also their daily life. From the outset they had often been assigned a castle (*castrum Judaeorum*), especially in communities where they were newly settled or resettled. With the growth of both the cities and the Jewish communities, however, these original Jewish quarters often became overcrowded. Jews were frequently granted additional quarters, or else allowed to move into the Christian districts. This situation created a vicious circle of increased insecurity for the Jewish residents, the breakdown of their segregation from the Christians, and the ensuing agitation for locking the Jews up in formal ghettos.

Nor did the Jewish community as a whole greatly profit from the continued influence in court circles of some leading Jewish fiscal advisers and physicians. While the Castilian and, to a lesser extent, the Aragonese kings still found Jewish administrators of their revenue indispensable, it was difficult for the latter to resist the frequent court intrigues. Alphonso XI may have left the financing of his war with the Muslim rulers of Granada and Morocco entirely in the hands of his trusted Jewish adviser, Don Joseph de Ecija, "than whom there was none more powerful in the kingdom of Castile." Yet among the latter's protégés was a Christian noble, Gonzalo Martinez de Oviedo, who quickly rose in the

ranks to become the official "dispenser of the royal court." Before
long Gonzalo turned against his former benefactor and demanded
from the king Don Joseph's dismissal. According to Solomon ibn
Verga's picturesque description,

he went to the king and said to him: Sire, if you will listen to me I shall
provide you with large funds for the pursuit of your war. The king inquired: How is that going to happen? Gonzalo said: Sell me ten Jews
of your realm and I shall weigh eight talents of gold to be brought into
the royal treasury. Said the king: Who are they? Gonzalo replied: The
first is your official, Joseph, who has depleted your Treasury and diminished the wealth of the nation. Also Samuel ibn Waqar, the physician,
whom you have appointed councilor, together with eight others among
the wealthy men of your realm. Sell them to me as well as their children.
The king said: Let it be as you say. Said Gonzalo: Let it be written and
sealed with the royal ring and I shall weigh the currency.

This speech is imaginary; it is used as part of the accepted techniques of contemporary historiography to express the motivations
of acting personalities. But the intrigue resulted in such a royal
sale, a procedure not uncommon at that time, although Alphonso
ultimately regretted and saved Don Joseph from prison. Also,
going back on his word, he canceled Gonzalo's claims on this Jewish favorite, but he apparently failed to spare Samuel, who died in
prison. Similar ups and downs are recorded in the case of many
other Jewish, as well as non-Jewish, grandees of the realm. Pedro
the Cruel, in particular, indulged (at least according to his sworn
enemy, the chronicler Pedro López de Ayala) in wholesale butch-
eries. Among his victims was his distinguished Jewish adviser,
Samuel ha-Levi, whose beautiful synagogue in Toledo, later converted into the church of El Tránsito, has become one of Spain's
national shrines.[35]

Apart from the fiscal administration and some contracting for
the armed forces, diplomatic service and medical assistance still
offered the broadest opportunities for Jews in public service. The
ever changing relationships with the neighboring Muslim kingdoms of Granada and Morocco—sometimes welcomed as allies but
for the most part considered hereditary enemies of the Spanish
kingdoms—continued to demand frequent negotiations and the exchange of missions. Jewish experts in the respective languages and
diplomatic usages, who also often were intimately acquainted with

the general commercial and political affairs as well as with the foibles of leading personalities on either side of the frontier, were in a strategic position to render excellent mediating services to all parties concerned.[36]

NAVARRE

Developments in these Spanish realms affected also the Jewish communities of northwestern Spain and southern France. We recall that Montpellier and Perpignan had been under Aragonese rule before they became parts of the French kingdom. Conversely, Navarre was for a time under French domination. The poet-king, Thibaut I (IV) of Champagne (1234–53), despite his attachment to King Louis IX of France, long pursued the previous tolerant policy toward Jews. But he followed the French kings' example in 1238 in securing funds for his second military expedition by the wholesale confiscation of Jewish, together with some non-Jewish, property. To justify his move, this imaginative king, whose popular songs were admired even by such a competent judge as Dante, claimed that he had been unable to locate the original owners of these funds gained by usury, or their heirs. He appealed, therefore, to Gregory IX to allow him to spend this revenue on the Crusade. The pope could not quite suppress his suspicion of the purity of the king's motives. Yet he advised Abbot Garnerius of the Cistercian order that:

Since the king had devoted himself and his property to the service of Jesus Christ and We intend to show him all favors possible, God willing, We leave it to your discretion by these Apostolic letters, after carefully investigating the above assertions, to make the necessary provisions in this matter for his sake, just as you have been providing for the salvation of his soul.

We have no information about the outcome of the investigation, if any, but it is very unlikely that any funds were returned to Jews. Even earlier many debtors of various classes tried to use the transition to the French regime as an excuse to get rid of their obligations, claiming that the barons of France had taken an oath not to repay money to Jews. Unable to secure redress at home, the Jews appealed to Pope Innocent IV, who in a strong letter to the king of July 6, 1247 urged him to treat the Jews "humanely and as you used to do" and to force the debtors to pay, notwithstanding any such alleged oaths. In general, the pope added, "you ought to preserve them [the Jews] in the good customs observed at the time of your predecessors." [37]

Crusading fervor showed its ill effects on Jews in Navarre as it did elsewhere. Thibaut II (1253–70), who at the beginning of his reign tried to treat the Jews rather fairly, soon came under the spell of his father-in-law, Louis IX of France, whom he joined on the crusading expedition to Africa. Following French precedents, Thibaut ordered in 1268 a general imprisonment of Jews in his realm and the confiscation of much of their property. He also assigned the synagogue of Sangüesa to the local Dominicans, who speedily converted it into a church. Nor was his donation of a vineyard in Estella to other monks in 1265 particularly welcome to Jews, since that vineyard is described as extending "from the little castle [casticillo] to the portal of the Jewish quarter." The friars thus became the Jews' immediate neighbors, which doubtless added incentive to their conversionist efforts. Jews fared even worse under Philip the Fair of France who, through his marriage with Queen Joan, became the ruler of Navarre in 1284. Philip began his reign by squeezing out of Navarrese Jewry a huge contribution of 20,000 livres, only 5,000 less than he exacted from their coreligionists in the Champagne. This blow struck the Jews at a time when they were still recovering from the severe losses they had sustained during the warlike disturbances of 1277–78, particularly in the capital of Pamplona. Although in the treatment of certain individuals Philip could demonstrate his sense of justice, in regard to the community at large he implacably pursued expropriatory policies in his Spanish, as well as in his French, possessions. Only the transfer of sovereignty over Navarre to his son Louis le Hutin (the Quarreler, later Louis X of France) in 1305, spared the Navarre communities of Pamplona, Estella, Tudela and others the catastrophic effects of the decree of expulsion of 1306, but slightly tempered by its revocation in 1315. However, the attacks of the Pastoureaux made themselves felt immediately, although the Jews of Pamplona, apparently trained in defense and aided by a knight, were able to repel the invaders.[38]

Nevertheless the basic principles laid down by Sancho VII the Wise in the latter part of the twelfth century still determined the Jews' general status in the country. In fact, Sancho's privilege for the Jews of Tudela of July 1170, itself modeled after the provisions of Najéra and an earlier charter issued by Alphonso I in 1115, was confirmed by Charles II in May 1355, at the request of Jewish representatives. From the outset the possession of the Tudela castle was entrusted to Jews, the king reserving only the larger tower for his own use. Jews were also granted complete immunity from prosecution if, in defense of their quarter, they killed some assailants. Such defensive functions of Jewish quarters, aimed at foreign as well as domestic enemies, continued through the thirteenth century. According to a responsum by Solomon ibn Adret, the community of Estella had adopted a communal ordinance which forbade the weakening in any form of its ghetto walls and the consequent undermining of the Jewish defenses. As observed by Isidore Epstein, this ordinance may well have been adopted before the French first occupied the city in 1234, but it was upheld for several decades thereafter, to be cited by the distinguished Barcelona rabbi as a current regulation. In his even more extensive privilege of April 1171 for the Jews of Funes, Sancho VII not only repeated the protective safeguards of the Tudelan decree but added further guarantees. He prescribed that "if a Christian slays a Jew be it by day or by night the Christian inhabitants of the particular locality shall pay the fine to the king." Such collective responsibility was particularly helpful in the case of the murderer's disappearance or the authorities' inability to collect enough evidence to convict him. It also made all Christian inhabitants aware of their duty to surrender the culprit and, more importantly, to prevent the crime from being committed. More generally, in their ordinary relationship with their Christian and Muslim neighbors Jews were treated on a basis of equality before the law. Were it not for the growing fiscal pressures, the Jews of Navarre might have pursued their peaceful careers undisturbedly even under the more intolerant regime of French princes.[39]

Curiously, just as the arrival of the French spelled trouble, so did the subsequent uprisings against the French rulers, and the reestablishment of a native regime in 1328 lead to renewed massacres of Jews, particularly in Estella. Once again the Jews fought back. In Estella they manned the walls of their quarter and held off the attackers until these were reinforced by gangs of neighboring peasants thirsty for blood and loot, who by sheer numbers overwhelmed the defenders. On their part Navarrese Jews, too, included numerous hotheaded individuals who did not refrain from resorting to violence. Although practically no cases of homicide by Jews are recorded in contemporary documents, the local courts had frequent occasion to deal with Jewish defendants accused of assault and battery against fellow Jews or Christians. One such extended litigation in Tarazona, Aragon, involved also the famous apologist, Shem Ṭob ibn Shapruṭ (appearing in Spanish documents as Sento Isach Xaprut), who, in 1375, had publicly debated in Pamplona the merits of Judaism versus Christianity with Cardinal Pedro de Luna (the later Antipope Benedict XIII). A former resident of Tudela, Shem Ṭob moved to Tarazona, where, preoccupied as he was with both medical practice and banking, he found time to compose in 1380–85 his polemical tract, *Eben boḥan* (Touchstone). He and his family, most of whom had remained in Tudela, were accused in 1384 of having wounded one Reyna Francès in a family dispute. Aroused by thus being dragged before Gentile courts, Shem Ṭob and his faction denounced their main accuser as an informer (*malsin*), an offense recognized also by Spanish laws as a serious menace to the Jewish communities. While this affair did not seriously hurt the pugnacious scholar, it caused him and his family to leave Aragon and return to their native Tudela.[40]

Apart from entailing immediate loss of lives (exaggeratingly estimated by some contemporaries and later historians at 6,000 to 10,000 persons) and of property, the outbreaks of 1328 had many untoward consequences for the Navarre communities. The fact that the king imposed collective fines upon many municipalities for having failed to defend the Jews served further to embitter the relations between the Jews and the burghers. Even if Estella's penalty, set at the high amount of 10,000 livres payable over eleven years, was forgiven after two years, its memory rankled and strengthened the local anti-Jewish forces. The Church, too, now became more deeply involved, since the Franciscan Pedro Olligoyen was generally considered one of the main ringleaders of the pogromists. Although jailed for a time, Olligoyen, together with other fanatical preachers, carried on with their Jew-baiting campaign. Understandably, Jewish usury was their major target. They succeeded in forcing the government in 1330 to limit the interest rate to 20 percent; any higher charge automatically made the loan subject to confiscation. The same penalty was imposed on loans running for more than five years. Doubly to assure enforcement of this Draconian law, the king demanded that each year the rabbis recite these restrictions from their pulpits, and threatened them in case of disobedience with deposition from their posts and a fine of 50 livres. However, these regulations affected only the minority of Jewish financiers, while they had little effect on the Jewish masses making a living from other occupations including dyeing, medicine, and the arts. For one example, a "royal juggler" Bonafos and his son Santo are frequently mentioned in documents from 1365 to 1389; in the latter year Bonafos received some houses as a gift from the king.[41]

The Church's segregationist agitation now likewise celebrated many victories. Even before the concerted Peninsular move to shut the Jews up in their *juderias*, which was to follow the catastrophic year 1391, Charles I of Navarre ordered the Jews of Pamplona in 1324 to stay within the narrower limits of their own quarter in the old district of the Navarrería. Although that district suffered severely from the ravages of the uprising four years later, the governor invoked Charles' order and, in 1336, empowered two Pamplona burghers to supervise the resettlement in it of all Jews. Perhaps with tongue in cheek the governor contended that this order would accrue to the benefit of the Jews themselves, for in this fashion "no one would cause them annoyance, evil or damage in their bodies or property and they would be able to behave and live safely and securely in the said *juderia*." At the same time he also asserted that the previous system of Jews leasing houses and living among Gentiles had "resulted in much loss to the government and in great shame and dishonor to the Christians." If in the following years less was heard about forcible measures to confine Jews within their quarters, this was doubtless owing more to biological reasons than to any moderation of the anti-Jewish faction. The outbreak of the Black Death in 1348 so decimated the Jewish as well as the non-Jewish population that most Jewish quarters, still largely limited to the originally assigned environs of the "Jewish castles," were now underpopulated, and could accommodate practically all Jews without difficulty.[42]

Not that these strained relations necessarily weakened the Jews' fealty to the kings or undermined their traditional alliance with the Crown. The royal concept of Jewish serfdom, as viewed by a princess of the house of Capet, found a curious expression in the letter addressed in 1349 by Queen Joan to Alphonso XI of Castile. Having fallen ill on a visit to her native country, the queen invited a Jewish doctor of Tudela, Magister Solomon, to come to her bedside in France. Since at that time Jews were not allowed to reside in the royal possessions of France, she asked the governor of Navarre to dispatch Solomon "honorably and with a good escort." For some reason the doctor refused, and rather than fulfill his queen's wishes left the country. Joan now tried to enlist the aid of both the Castilian and Aragonese kings in tracking down the fugitive and in sending him to her, for "We should be quickly restored to health, as soon as he is with Us." We hear no more about this incident, for the queen passed away in that very year. The Navarrese kings continued to appoint Jewish fiscal agents and use Jewish physicians. On his death in 1342, the prominent Jewish merchant, Don Ezmiel (Ishmael or Samuel) de Ablitas, left an estate, the liquidity of which was greatly impaired because Ezmiel's loans to Pedro IV of Aragon alone, amounting to 70,000 solidi, were not readily collectible. Nevertheless Charles II the Bad (1349–87) did not hesitate to employ Ezmiel's grandson and namesake, as well as numerous other Jews, as his fiscal agents. He made particularly good use of the services of one Juda (or Judas) Levi of Estella. Having entrusted several Jews, he wrote in 1365, with the collection of sales taxes in their respective localities, he now appointed Juda as the chief commissioner in charge of these collections throughout the realm. In his noteworthy letter of appointment the king emphasized:

Convinced of your loyalty and discretion, We confer upon you the power and give you the authority to journey through all the districts and to see and get acquainted with every one of the said commissioners and to learn how diligent they are and how they conduct themselves.

We give you the power to censure them and, if need be, to discharge them from their posts and appoint others in their stead who may more diligently attend to their duties. You may also receive the funds gathered, deliver them to Our Treasury, as well as issue regulations instructing each commissioner what he might and should do so that the said impost be most expeditiously collected.

In 1366 Charles also entrusted Levi with the supervision of imported goods and the care for the security of foreign merchants. Juda Levi's work proved so eminently satisfactory to the king that his and his associates' names recur in the tax records of the realm quite frequently during the following eighteen years.[43]

Despite such opportunities in public service and other economic adjustments, the Jewish population seems to have constantly diminished from the high point reached in the thirteenth century. This decline was but partially alleviated by the occasionally recorded immigration of Jews from France and even Portugal, which may have exceeded their emigration from Navarre. With the decline of the Jewish population also went a progressive alienation of Jewish property, despite the age old prohibition for Christians and Muslims to acquire any land owned, or to share in estates left, by Jews, since ultimately such transfers accrued to the disadvantage of the Treasury. In 1380 the authorities instituted a searching inquiry in Estella and the neighboring communities, listing the names of all local Jews who had in the past sold their holdings, and of all Christians and Moors who had purchased them. The largest Jewish community of Tudela, for one instance, was reduced from some 500 families before 1300, to 270 in 1366, and to 90 in 1391. It was very fortunate, indeed, for Navarrese Jewry that in this weakened condition it did not have to face the full impact of the catastrophe of 1391 which so thoroughly ruined the larger and more prosperous communities in the other Spanish kingdoms.[44]

PORTUGAL

On the whole, Portuguese Jewry shared the destinies of its Spanish coreligionists. Even after its separation from Leon at the turn of the twelfth century, Portugal long remained a part of the

Iberian system, which despite internecine wars among the Christian states grew at the expense of Islam. In the decisive battle of the Navas de Tolosa in 1212 Portuguese detachments fought alongside other Iberian armies and laid the foundation for the southward expansion of the Portuguese regime. In these crusading efforts which, as early as 1147, had led to the capture of Lisbon with the aid of English Crusaders, the country understandably revealed many earmarks of religious intolerance and submission to the Church, canon law influencing its legislation even more than that of its neighbors.

Nevertheless, in the long run the relative stability of the regime, Portugal's entry into the growing maritime commerce of the Mediterranean world, and finally the Portuguese voyages of exploration on the Atlantic Ocean, opened also untold possibilities for Jewish merchants and bankers, who increasingly combined profitable enterprises of their own with eminent services to Crown and country. The fact that the same dynasty maintained itself until 1383 to be followed by another long-lived royal family, and that certain kings like Alphonso III (Affonso III, 1248–79), Dinis (1279–1325), Alphonso IV (1325–57), John I (1385–1433), and Alphonso V (1443–81) ruled for more than thirty years each, helped to keep the internal tensions under control. For this reason the Jews of Portugal, too, suffered less than their neighbors from such large-scale outbreaks as accompanied the Crusade of the Pastoureaux, the spread of the Black Death, and the "Holy War" of 1391. Even the internal upheaval which brought John I to power in 1383 and inspired many fears among Jews affected only a few Jewish individuals.

Needless to say, there was a good deal of anti-Jewish feeling in Portugal, too. Economic rivalries, envy of the prosperity of some upper-class Jews and their conspicuous display of luxuries, as well as the usual resentments of borrowers toward lenders—all combined with religious bigotry to induce the Portuguese Cortes to voice manifold complaints about the Jews' behavior and to demand remedial action. At times popular feeling also ran very high. On its part, the Church preached full compliance with canon law and pursued its general discriminatory and segregationist program. But it was not until 1496 that the policy of total exclusion was adopted under the direct pressure of Spain's Catholic monarchs.

Regrettably, research in Portuguese Jewish history has not kept pace with the noteworthy progress made in the course of the last several decades in the investigation of Jewish history in neighboring Spain. True, the country's size, the number of its Jews, and their contributions to Jewish and general culture lagged far behind those across its eastern border. However, Portugal, too, was developing into a world power, with far-flung discoveries leading to the establishment of a vast empire. Culturally, it became one of the most advanced European countries in the fourteenth and fifteenth centuries. Its social structure was influenced by its large Moorish and Jewish populations, on a par with that of Castile or Aragon. And yet relatively few modern Jewish scholars have evinced an equally deep interest in the past of their people in medieval Portugal. Nor has general scholarship, domestic or foreign, concentrated on that segment of Iberian life in a degree comparable to the accomplishments of non-Jewish scholars in the field of Spanish-Jewish history, even before the establishment of the Instituto Arias Montano at the Universities of Madrid and Barcelona. With respect to general Portuguese history, a prominent German student observed some forty years ago that "the centuries of the age of exploration, which have for a long time elicited great interest among both Portuguese and foreign scholars, are relatively best known. But the medieval period lies almost totally fallow." Our general historical knowledge has greatly advanced in the last decades, but the exploration of the Jewish past still leaves much to be desired.[45]

For a long time the Portuguese Jews had to contend with both ecclesiastical demands and certain anti-Jewish customs which had grown in the preceding centuries. Portugal's dependence on the Papacy, acknowledged by its founders, Count Henry of Burgundy and Alphonso I in the twelfth century, opened the gates to papal interventions in its internal administration. When, in 1231, the bishop of Lisbon complained to Gregory IX about the alleged "preferment" of Jews in appointments to public office in his diocese, the pope responded with his usual zeal. In a bull addressed to the bishops of Astorga and Lugo on October 20, 1231, he referred to the care the Church had taken of King Sancho II during his minority; nevertheless the king was behaving contrary to the statutes of the general (Fourth Lateran) council "to the opprobrium of the Christian faith and the serious scandal to many." Gregory conceded that existing circumstances might force the king to farm out some revenues to Jews or pagans (Muslims), but he urged the appointment of Christian supervisors who would see to it that these collections would cause no injury to the Christian population. This concession was evidently exacted from the obdurate pope by strong royal assertions that the country could not get along without "infidel" fiscal advisers and agents. It was also obtained, as we recall, by the Hungarian regime with special reference to that papal modification for Portugal. There is no evidence that either country seriously sought the cooperation of a Christian supervisory personnel. In 1239 the pope included Portugal in the countries to which he transmitted Nicholas Donin's accusations against the Talmud. But, preoccupied with their grave tasks of reconstruction of the deserted areas wrested from Islam, the Portuguese rulers almost totally ignored the papal message.[46]

More important from the practical angle were the custumals compiled at the end of the twelfth and in the early thirteenth centuries in various Portuguese localities. The *foros* of Castelo Bom, Alfaiates, Castelo Rodrigo, and Castelo Melhor even found imitators across the Castilian border, some of their provisions being included, for instance, in the *Fuero* of Usagre enacted by Don Pelay Correa, Master of the Order of Santiago (1242–75). Apart from many widespread discriminatory provisions, we find here a few less usual prohibitions. For example, Jews were forbidden to acquire fish on Friday lest they compete with observant Catholics. They were not to represent other parties before courts. While testimony in mixed litigations was to consist, as elsewhere, of both Christian and Jewish witnesses, the latter were not allowed to abstain from testifying. Jews were not to engage in pawnbroking except in the presence of witnesses. For the conviction of a defendant accused of forbidden sex relations with a member of the other faith, one required merely the testimony of two Christians and one Jew, or two Jews and one Christian. Unusual fines were also set for intergroup assault and battery. Other *foros,* including those of Santarém and Beja, tried to reduce controversies between Jewish moneylenders and Christian debtors by insisting that the repayment of loans be made in the presence of both Christian and Jewish witnesses, or else that the amount be deposited with a trustworthy third person. Insults to Jews or Moors by Christians were not to be subject to prosecution.[47]

Ecclesiastical and popular prejudices were clearly reflected also in the royal legislation. Following the example of the monk Theotonio, who even under the Muslim domination had refused to exchange greetings with Jews, many churchmen now made strenuous efforts to erect thick walls of separation between their flocks and the "infidels." Among the grievances presented in 1258 by the Portuguese bishops to Alphonso III, one article referred particularly to the king's disregard of the canonical provisions relating to Jews in public office, their distinguishing marks and their payment of ecclesiastical tithes. Another complaint of the bishops submitted to Pope Clement IV (1256–68) culminated in the assertion that the king

restricts the free position of Jews and holds them as well as the Moors in serfdom; that he confiscates for the Treasury the property of Jews converted to Christianity; that he allows Moorish slaves converted to Christianity to be retained by their Jewish masters as before; and that by a general law he exempts from tithes and dues of the first fruit all lands acquired by Jews or Moors from Christians.

These grievances were but halfheartedly acted upon by Alphonso and his successors. In fact, at times the royal interests demanded that Jews be encouraged to acquire land and cultivate it for the benefit of the Crown. This was the case not only in the southern, newly reconquered areas whose repopulation by Jews, as well as Christians, appeared as an urgent task. In a remarkable contract of 1279 with the new King Dinis (surnamed *O Lavrador* or the Farmer because of his deep interest in the country's agricultural production), nineteen Jews of northern Braganza had to promise to pay him annually 600 Leonese maravedis in taxes, as well as to acquire from the state 2,000 maravedis' worth of vineyards, 1,000 maravedis' worth of fields, and 500 maravedis' worth of houses. They had to pledge themselves not to dispose of these properties but to keep the fields and vineyards under permanent cultivation.

Of course, future Jewish settlers in Braganza were expected to contribute additional taxes. At the same time the authorities were enjoined to extend to both old and new Jewish residents effective protection.[48]

Least satisfactory from the standpoint of both the clerical and lay Jew-baiters was the Crown's attitude to the employment of Jewish officials. To the very end the kings felt that replacing all their trusted Jewish fiscal advisers as well as court physicians would cause them great harm. As in Castile, one or another royal confidant was also asked to serve as "chief rabbi" of all Jews in the country even if his learning did not entitle him to a rabbinical post. Beginning in 1278, such an *arrabi moor* appears in the records with increasing frequency. In both countries the chief rabbinate was indeed more a political than a religious office, the Jewish communities often submitting to it only because they derived direct benefits from the presence at court of an influential Jewish spokesman. True, at times these political leaders became embroiled in the factional strifes rampant in court circles, failed to supply the kings with expected sums of money, or gave them wrong advice in the conduct of foreign affairs. In such cases the royal wrath was often vented on the entire community. But this was merely a facet of the general insecurity of Jewish minority existence in all medieval lands.[49]

Dinis' unyielding attitude toward ecclesiastical pressures was owing in part to his numerous other differences with the clergy resulting from his consistent endeavors to establish national independence from the Papacy. In their complaint addressed to Pope Clement V of 1309, the Portuguese hierarchs not only repeated their traditional grievances against the appointment of Jewish officials and the frequent neglect of distinguishing marks, but they also claimed that the king used Jews to imprison bishops in their monasteries or churches and that "the Jews are haughty and boastful; they adorn their horses with toupees and indulge in luxuries which leave a very bad impression on the population." The pope was too busy at that time with international politics and the transfer of the papal residence to Avignon to evince any direct interest in the Portuguese clergy's complaints against Jews. More persuasive was the action of the Cortes, particularly under Dinis' successor, Alphonso IV. Immediately after the latter's accession to the throne in 1325, the Cortes of Évora renewed the ordinance concerning the Jewish badge, which was now defined as a yellow six-cornered star to be worn on either the hat or the outer garment. Other complaints led the king to set in 1353 a maximum interest rate of 33⅓ percent and to outlaw evasive "usurious contracts." Even he, however, recognized the indispensability of Jewish wealth for the country, particularly after the severe losses in population and the dislocations in both city and countryside occasioned by the Black Death, which hit Portugal with great severity from September to December, 1348. In 1352, he issued a sharp ordinance against the unauthorized emigration of well-to-do Jews. He provided that owners of property in excess of 500 livres trying to depart without a permit would lose all their possessions and, together with their families, become the king's private property.[50]

Alphonso's successor, Pedro I (1357–67), nicknamed "the Severe," administered justice impartially to all, including Jews. On the one hand, he rigidly suppressed acts of violence against them. The execution of two noble youths personally close to the king, because they had robbed a Jew, created a widespread sensation. Pedro also tried to facilitate the collection of funds due to Jewish lenders. At the same time he approved in 1361 the resolution of the Cortes of Elvas aimed at Jewish usury and residence among Gentiles (Arts. x and xl). The king strictly forbade Jews or Moors to appear outside their quarters after sundown; conversely, Christian women were forbidden to enter these areas at any time during the day or night without a male escort. It was during Pedro's regime that Samuel ha-Levi of Toledo arrived in Lisbon in 1358 on a diplomatic mission from the king of Castile and successfully negotiated a pact of friendship between the two countries. This amity did not last very long, however. Under Pedro's successor, Ferdinand (1367–83), their differences led to outright hostilities. Jews became involved in these high policies in so far as one leading adviser, Dom Judah, had helped the king in the manipulation of currency which entailed many losses for the Treasury, while another Jewish leader, Gedaliah b. Solomon ibn Yahya, joined the court faction which counseled the king not to embark upon a winter campaign against the Castilian usurper-king, Henry de Trastamara. Disregarding that advice, Ferdinand continued his attack, which ended disastrously with the Castilian occupation of Lisbon in 1373, on which occasion a part of the city including the Jewish quarter was consumed by fire. Apparently resentful of these prudent councilors, whose motives he may have suspected, Ferdinand removed Gedaliah from office, whereupon the latter entered the services of King Henry.[51]

After Ferdinand's death ten years later, his widow Leonore first tried to seize the reins of government for herself. To captivate the benevolence of the ruling classes, she eagerly listened to their grievances and made promises to remedy the deteriorating economic situation. Among the main complaints presented to her by the "good men of the city" of Lisbon were, according to the chronicler Fernão Lopes, the following:

Know that canon and civil laws as well as the laws of the kingdom strictly forbid Jews or Moors to hold offices over Christians. This is not unjustified, since they, especially the Jews, have been brought up in hatred and unbelief in Jesus Christ, whose law and faith we maintain. The ancient kings of these realms behaved accordingly, but for our sins it pleased the King [Ferdinand], whose soul may God keep, to appoint them [Jews and Moors] to public offices which required the greatest fidelity and devotion to service, trusting them more than the Christians. Wherefore we beg you to do us the favor of observing the laws which prohibit this and to discharge them [the infidels] from such posts. [In the future you ought not] to allow them to be tax gatherers in our realms, nor collectors of any dues, nor serve as officers in your household.

The queen pledged herself to follow this rule, piously adding that she would rather lose money than act against law and ethics. She realized soon, nevertheless, that she could not stem the tide of discontent sweeping over the country and entered negotiations with her son-in-law, the Castilian king John I. She wished to see John crowned king of Portugal as well, but broke with him, curiously, over the appointment of the Jewish chief rabbi of Castile. John disregarded her recommendation and instead of her favorite, Dom Judah, he appointed Don David Negro. The ensuing breach between John and Leonore turned out to be a blessing in disguise for Portuguese Jewry, since the aroused patriots, not wishing to surrender Portugal's independence to the Crown of Castile, rejected both these claimants and chose one of their own grandees,

John, Ferdinand's illegitimate half brother, as their new king (1385). His illegitimate birth was no more held against him than that of his opponent's father, Henry, in Castile, or of Henry's descendant, Ferdinand I in Aragon, or of John II in Navarre. Although previously a master of the Order of Avis and personally quite pious, John I pursued a very moderate course with respect to Jews.[52]

As an able soldier and good administrator John was bent upon the preservation of public order. His determination was of great importance to Jews, since even their close social relations with many non-Jews did not prevent segments of the population from nurturing deeply hostile feelings toward them. During major disturbances particularly, rabble-rousers easily excited the passions of a populace further stimulated by greed and the expectation of abundant loot in the reputedly wealthy Jewish quarter. Nevertheless, Portugal's record in this respect is much cleaner than that of its neighbors. As on previous occasions, particularly in 1348–49 and 1383, the authorities took the necessary precautions against such violent outbreaks as occurred all over Castile and Aragon in 1391. When Vicente Ferrer wished to continue his missionary campaign on Portuguese soil he was refused admission by John I, who allegedly informed the spellbinding preacher that he could come only "with a crown of glowing iron [*corõa de ferro ardendo*] on his head." The Jewish communities, too, helped to forestall the anti-Jewish propaganda when in 1391 their chief rabbi, Dom Moses Navarro, handed the king a Portuguese translation of Pope Boniface IX's bull of July 2, 1389. This bull, largely a restatement of that issued by Clement VI on July 5, 1347, renewed the traditional papal safeguards for Jewish life and religious institutions. The king ordered that it be circulated throughout the country, and in July, 1392 added a similar protective edict of his own. By thus averting the great catastrophe from Portuguese Jewry, John enabled it to write some of the most glorious chapters of its entire history.[53]

IBERIAN JEWRY'S LEADERSHIP

Within the few decades of the *Reconquista* Iberian Jewry regained much of its former glory. The communities, downtrodden and muted under Almohade oppression, now sprang to life and expanded much beyond the borders of their original concentration. If Cordova, as both a city and a Jewish community, never staged a complete comeback and thenceforth remained a mere provincial center rather than the grandiose capital of 'Abd ar-Raḥman III, its place was now taken by Seville. Without serving as a major seat of government, this Mediterranean port, situated at the crossroads between Africa and Europe and between the Mediterranean and Atlantic, became a great emporium of international trade and a city of beauty and gracious living. Lucena was no longer the locale of the greatest Spanish Jewish academy. But it was replaced by such new foci of Jewish learning as Naḥmanides' Gerona, Ibn Adret's Barcelona, or Asher b. Yeḥiel's Toledo.

In fact, during the thirteenth century Jewish settlements began, for the first time, to dot the entire Peninsula. They now spread out into the remote corners of Portugal and Navarre, places unknown in the annals of Jewish history before the Christian reconquest. Numerically, too, Iberian Jewry recovered with astonishing rapidity. By the end of the thirteenth century, it appears, more Jews lived on the Peninsula than at any time during their Golden Age in the Spanish Caliphate. Their impact on world Jewry was enormous. In most fields of Jewish and general learning they achieved undisputed supremacy, and only in the discipline of Jewish law did they share their leadership with the disciples of the Franco-German schools of Tosafists. In Asher b. Yeḥiel and his sons, Spanish Jewry was able organically to blend the best fruits of its own and of the northern halakhic heritage. At a crucial point in their communal evolution, during the struggle for succession in the chief rabbinate of royal France, the northern leaders turned to two Spanish and one Austrian rabbi for final decision. Except for their Provençal coreligionists, whose cultural evolution was in many ways but an elongation of their own, the Iberian Jews had practically no rivals in the development of Jewish mysticism, Hebrew poetry, or general science and medicine. In no other country of the mid-fourteenth century could a Jewish leader erect for himself a monument of the magnificence of the Toledo synagogue (later known as *El Tránsito*), left behind by Samuel ha-Levi. Nor would any Jew outside the Peninsula venture to prepare such a self-assertive and grandiloquent inscription proclaiming to the world that "since Ariel's [the Jewish people's] exile none like him had arisen in Israel." [54]

When these words were inscribed, however, Spanish Jewry had passed the apogee of its power and influence. During the fourteenth century it lost much of its expansive *élan* and it merely tried to consolidate its position, which was being gradually undermined by the growing intolerance of the Spanish and Portuguese peoples. No longer were the Jews so badly needed to repopulate the deserted areas and to marshal the major resources of the respective realms for the benefit of their Crowns in peace or war. The role of their leaders as royal councilors and fiscal administrators steadily declined, but it still was sufficiently conspicuous to arouse the bitter enmity of influential rivals. One of the mainsprings of these leaders' power, the speedy accumulation of profits from moneylending, encountered increasing resistance on the part of the indebted population, egged on by the fulminating anti-usury preachments of churchmen. Even their royal patrons were torn between the desire to preserve the Jewish financial resources for future exploitation, and the pressures of the various groups in the population clamoring for relief from Jewish "usury" in the form of moratoria, partial or full cancellations of debts, or, at the least, the setting of maximum rates of interest, prohibition against the piling up of interest arrears over years, and procedural advantages for debtors over lenders.

Popular resentments manifested themselves also in occasional attacks on individual Jews or Jewish quarters. Farsighted Jewish leaders sensed the dangers facing their communities in periods of inner upheaval. Poets often gave vent to their coreligionists' feelings of despondency over endless chicaneries by predominantly hostile neighbors and fiscal extortioners. But the majority seems to have lulled itself into a feeling of security because it saw how effective royal intervention was in stemming the attacks of the Pastoureaux or of the frenzied mobs during the Black Death panic. They also saw that the great crisis of dynastic transition in Portugal in 1383 passed without causing permanent damage to their community. On the other hand, a similar transition in Navarre in 1328 victimized many Jewish lives, and the Castilian

Civil War of 1366–69 caused untold sufferings to Jewish communities of the whole realm. Taking little heed of such warnings, however, the Spanish Jewish leadership seemed totally unprepared for the severe blow which struck its people in 1391.

DECLINE OF IBERIAN JEWRY

IN THE latter part of the fourteenth century most of the Iberian Peninsula was in a state of ever deepening crisis. The population losses sustained during the Black Death were not made up for several generations. Economically, the various realms suffered from growing inflation, governmental manipulations of currency and costly military ventures. On the international scene, the Peninsula lived under the shadow of the Hundred Years' War with the individual kingdoms aligning themselves from time to time with either France or England. Aragon's expansion into Italy and the eastern Mediterranean may have enhanced the glory of its dynasty and added to its numerous Spanish and Italian titles those of "Dukes of Athens and Neopatria." But the modest advantages which the country derived from its increased maritime commerce were outweighed by the extension of its limited resources over too vast an area.

Nor was the domestic situation altogether reassuring. The revolutionary trends, aimed at weakening the monarchy, received new nourishment from the tainted claims to office advanced by the occupants of the various thrones. It was a strange spectacle, indeed, to see all four Iberian Crowns in the hands of bastards or their issue who had in quick succession replaced the legitimate descendants of the old dynasties, doubtless raising in the minds of many subjects serious misgivings about the charismatic nature of the monarchy.

Socially and ideologically, too, Spain was greatly weakened in that period of transition from medievalism to early modern life. There was considerable loosening of family ties, concubinage having become a widely recognized social institution. Synod after synod fulminated in vain against priests' maintaining concubines even in their own parish houses. Ecclesiastical discipline and religious guidance suffered severely also from the far-reaching religious crisis generated by the great Papal Schism. One of the contenders for the Papacy, Cardinal Pedro de Luna (Antipope Benedict XIII), may have received considerable support from his Spanish countrymen. But he did not possess sufficient authority to control even the Spanish ecclesiastics and still less to direct the religious orientation of the growing lay intelligentsia, deeply confused by the breakdown of the old uniform *Weltanschauung,* which had not yet been replaced by any all-embracing new philosophic outlook.

Gone were the well-rounded and intrinsically consistent approaches to life of the theretofore regnant Thomistic school, while the incipient signs of revival of classical culture were mere harbingers of the dawning era of humanism. They certainly could offer no acceptable rationale for the new attitude to life. Jews, whose internal cultural evolution had greatly suffered from the incursion of these and other non-Jewish ideas and the growing assimilation of Spanish-Averroist ideologies and criteria of value, were doubly unprepared to face the chaotic conditions created by the general, as well as the specifically Jewish, crisis.[1]

AFTERMATH OF "HOLY WAR"

After the massacres of 1391, the background and extent of which will be analyzed more fully in another connection, the Jews of both Castile and Aragon emerged in greatly reduced circumstances. Only small parts of the two realms, such as Leon and the district of Murviedro (Sagunto) in the province of Valencia, escaped the vengeance of the pogromists. All major communities from Seville and Cordova in the south to Barcelona and the Balearic Islands in the north and east lay prostrate. In addition to the many thousands of lives lost at the hands of rioting peasants and urban mobs, and the numerous Jews who escaped to the more hospitable Muslim lands of Granada and North Africa, a host of others accepted baptism. In many localities the number of converts was extremely large. With considerable exaggeration a contemporary poet Samuel described the massacre of the "delightful community of Cordova," by saying that "there remained none among them, great or small, who had not changed his faith." In its complaint of 1392 to the king, the monastery of Santo Domingo el

Real of Madrid stated that it had received none of the 3,000 maravedis which in the preceding seven years it had collected from the local Jews "because of the pillage and destruction which the said Jews of the said city had undergone; they had been robbed, destroyed and all had become Christians." According to a contemporary estimate, "many [Spanish Jews] were sold for bondmen and bondwomen to the Mohammedans and about 140,000 abandoned Judaism and turned Christian." While the ratio of such renegades to the total number of Jews living in the two realms before the catastrophe cannot be accurately ascertained, this newly emergent large and influential class of *conversos* injected serious new complications into all aspects of Jewish life throughout the Peninsula.[2]

Reconstruction of the shattered communities now became the major task of the Jewish leadership. Unfortunately, during these decisive years the thrones in both realms were held by immature or weak kings. Perhaps the catastrophe might have been averted or mitigated in Castile, where it started, had Martinez' preaching been staunchly opposed by a vigorous regime. However, upon John I's death in 1390 the reins of government were weakly held by an ineffective regency and, in subsequent years, by Henry III the Invalid (1390–1406). Royal futility is well demonstrated by the vain attempt of Henry's administration to punish Martinez for having destroyed two synagogues in provincial communities even before the outbreak of the Sevillian riots. On December 22, 1390 the king's advisers appealed for support to the clergy of Scville. They cited the opinion of the deceased Sevillian Archbishop Pedro, who had previously suspended Martinez from officiating at the Cathedral because of his antipapal utterances, including his contention that even the pope had no right to grant licenses to Jews to erect new synagogues. But the archdeacon undisturbedly continued with his agitation. Six months later (June 16, 1391) Henry III with equal lack of vigor tried to stem the outbreaks in Burgos by referring to the intervening attacks on the Jews of Seville and Cordova. In asking the Burgos city council to take the necessary preventive measures, the king wrote:

Some of the small people of the said cities, crude [*rosicos*] and of little understanding, paid no heed to their great error and Our [damage.

Not] fearing God nor My justice, nor considering the time and age in which I find myself, they arose against the Jews living in the *aljamas* of the said cities, killed many of them, robbed others, and used force on still others to become Christian. For this reason the Jews who lived in the said *aljamas* have greatly diminished in number [*espoblados*] which caused Me very great annoyance and accrued to a great disservice to Me.

This letter did not prevent the bloodshed in Burgos, while the city council of Madrid insisted after the tragedy that the main responsibility for punishing the pogromists rested with the royal officials. Many culprits were indeed imprisoned, but others fled the scene of their crime and formed gangs of robbers attacking travelers outside the cities. Here and there some criminals were seized and executed, but the weak regime, doubly insecure because it had been the real target of the uprising, was bent mainly upon restoring some sort of order and largely suspended the prosecutions.[3]

Even the first thirteen years of John II's long reign (1406–54) —he was less than two years old when he became king—were marked by lack of long-range planning and vigor in execution. The original regency, consisting of the bigoted queen mother Catalina and the equally narrow-minded Infante Ferdinand, the future king of Aragon, acted with divided counsel and was generally quite unfriendly to Jews. It was assisted by an equally antagonistic Council, which included the newly converted Rabbi Solomon ha-Levi, then serving as bishop of Cartagena. Solomon, renamed Paul, had functioned for four years (1403–1407) as nuncio of the anti-Jewish Benedict XIII; he had also been designated in Henry III's testament as its main executor and as tutor of the royal heir till the latter reached maturity at the age of fourteen.[4]

In Aragon the situation was somewhat more favorable. John I the Hunter (1387–95) used his royal prestige to stem the excesses which were spreading like wildfire through his realm. While his orders to local officials often were issued "too little and too late" or were disobeyed, in some cases his intervention prevented more widespread bloodshed; in others it set in motion some punitive actions against the assailants. In his own place of residence, Saragossa, the king's presence doubtless served as a deterrent and helped salvage this major Jewish *aljama*, which soon assumed the direction of all attempts at rebuilding the destroyed communities. Even in Saragossa, to be sure, the reconstruction was fraught with many difficulties. According to the testimony of its leading official, Pardo de la Costa, some recent converts were exciting the local population through their incendiary sermons, "to such an extent that for the most part the Jews do not dare to go through the Christian quarter without being maltreated and insulted." As a result of the large Jewish emigration, both the government and the Jewish community were also confronted with great fiscal deficiencies. At times the Treasury had to renounce all income from Jews for five years, as it did in Tortosa. It also had to reduce from 500 to 300 florins the contribution of the Saragossa community to the wedding of Infanta Maria and John II of Castile, "out of consideration for the diminution and poverty of the *aljama*." However, neither John nor his successor Martin, surnamed the Humane (1395–1412), pursued any consistent policies in the face of the strongly anti-Jewish alliance between the revolutionary forces, in both the countryside and the cities, aimed at the royal regime and the Spanish Church led by Cardinal Pedro de Luna.[5]

Conditions became even more critical during the short-lived, but for the Jews very momentous, reign of Ferdinand I the Honest (1412–16). The new king, brought over from Castile, was not only personally intolerant but he also had a peculiar viewpoint concerning the sanctity of royal promises. Encouraging King Sigismund at the Council of Constance to violate his safe-conduct for John Hus, Ferdinand wrote: "It is no breach of faith with one who breaks faith with God." In this he was perhaps unconsciously echoing Innocent III's dictum. Moreover, in many ways he owed his throne to the intercession of the famed preacher, Vicente Ferrer, who, as we recall, now concentrated his efforts upon the mass conversion of the rest of Jewry by all means short of direct force. On his missionary journeys through Aragon and Castile before 1412, Ferrer had transformed a number of synagogues into churches (Toledo's Santa Maria la Blanca, Salamanca's Vera Cruz, and others) and had converted an estimated total of 20,000 to 35,000 Jews to Christianity. Now Ferdinand, together with Benedict XIII, staged the disputation at Tortosa where dramatic pageantry and "defeat" of the Jewish spokesmen generated another Jewish stampede to the baptismal font. The sum total of Jewish conversions since 1391 may indeed have reached 200,000, as suggested (under the date of 1412) by the distinguished astronomer and chronicler, Abraham Zacuto.[6]

Not surprisingly, the quarter century of 1391 to 1415 brought about a sharp decline in the numbers, affluence, and legal status of Spanish Jewry, a decline from which it was never fully to recover. As early as September 22, 1391, that is within a few weeks after the massacres, John I ordered the various bailiffs to collect information about the possessions previously held by the ravaged Jewish communities or by individual Jews who were either killed by rioters or had committed suicide to escape baptism. Obviously, that property, as part of the royal domain, was now to be recaptured for the king's benefit. John also appointed Andreas Denari, the queen's treasurer, as his attorney general to prosecute the murderers. In practice, however, he found it difficult to persuade the public that the massacres had taken place without his approval and that he viewed them as "ignominious dangers to Our authority." On September 16 he dispatched a special messenger, Don Lope de Gurrea, to Huesca to counteract the rumors of his tacit approval and to declare that "We consider this matter an evil and a bad example which is apt to bring disrepute and damage to Our royal prerogatives and to the general public welfare." As early as July the queen had sent an envoy to Avignon with the request that the pope not intercede in behalf of those guilty of the excesses nor do anything in this respect without previously communicating with the king. John also severely censured his brother, Don Martin, for the latter's laxity during the attacks upon the Jews and Moors in Valencia. Being present during the riots, the king told him, Martin should have hanged 300 or 400 ringleaders on the first day, whereupon the rioters would have desisted. Perhaps this was an overoptimistic estimate written in the early stages of the massacres (July 16, 1391); it also might have been encouraged by reports of the successful defense of Jews by the authorities of Murviedro, not far from Valencia, for which John dispatched a letter of thanks to them on the same day. On royal orders a number of ringleaders were indeed executed in various places, and city authorities who had failed to do their duty in preserving public order were subjected to severe fines. In one instance, an heiress of a noblewoman who used to receive 5,000 maravedis from the taxes of the Jewish community of Cuenca filed in 1408 a civil suit against the city council blaming its inactivity seventeen years earlier for the community's dissolution and the ensuing losses she had sustained.[7]

In most cases, however, the municipal authorities shifted the blame to either irresponsible city mobs or neighboring peasants, among whom the then widespread revolutionary spirit had indeed inflamed passions against the Jewish allies of the ruling classes. Confronted with such enormous resistance of almost all classes, the king was forced to moderate his punitive measures. His gradual retreat is well illustrated by the events in Majorca. While on August 9, 1391 the local authorities, standing up to the rebellious peasants, prohibited the destruction of any notarial Jewish records under the penalty of death, the peasant delegates continued demanding their wholesale elimination (September 30). A few days later (October 4) the governor yielded and decreed the cancellation of all debts owed the Jews if contracted during the preceding ten or more years. Nine months later the king granted a general amnesty to all Majorcans who had participated in the outbreaks of 1391. Elsewhere, too, the prisoners who had escaped execution were released; fines imposed upon cities were sharply reduced, and wherever the terms of payment ran over years were simply canceled. In short, the punishment in no way fitted the crime, and to all intents and purposes left the impression of relative impunity for lawless assaults on Jews.[8]

Even the simple restoration of Jewish property to its former owners or their heirs was quite difficult. In many areas the Jewish quarters, including their fortified castles, had been completely destroyed. Elsewhere houses abandoned by Jews were occupied by Christian neighbors, who were reluctant to vacate them, especially if they had invested funds in their acquisition or remodeling. Not infrequently, whole families were wiped out leaving no known heirs. Exercising its right of eminent domain, the government frequently reclaimed such property but only rarely restored it to the Jewish community. Many city councils, even if they escaped punishment for their part in the massacres, viewed with misgiving the

Jews' return to their former quarters. Since many Jewish communities dated back to the very foundation of these cities, the *juderías* had usually occupied choice locations in the centers of the respective towns. Yielding to governmental pressure, the municipalities now began assigning to Jews new quarters in outlying districts. Jews frequently complained that the new locations were not only smaller in size (this could be justified by the decline in the Jewish population) but also unsanitary, difficult of access, and detrimental to their business. Resettlement also gave additional impetus to the trend toward stricter segregation of Jews from Christians. Some cities refused readmission of the Jews altogether and occasionally managed to secure government approval. Having for nearly a decade succeeded in postponing the return of Jews, the city of Barcelona obtained from King Martin, in 1401, a decree altogether prohibiting the reestablishment of a Jewish community. This prohibition was renewed in 1424, in the privilege granted the city by Alphonso V, although small groups of Jews sporadically reappeared in later years. Thus formally ended the once glorious community which had belonged to the most ancient and renowned centers of Jewish life under Western Christendom. The same obstructionist and delaying tactics were also employed by Valencia and other cities.[9]

Other Aragonese cities resisted Jewish reconstruction far less strenuously. In Gerona, where the Jewish community (curiously declared "dead" by the municipal elders in 1389) had defended itself more fiercely and more generally rejected the alternative of baptism, Queen Violante, as early as July 16, 1392, allowed the remnant to elect a new communal council and reestablish its ancient communal organization. Five years later, to be sure, King Martin's wife, Queen Maria, issued in his name a rather restrictive decree for that community. Using harsh language, she demanded that, in order to stem "the infidelity and obstinacy of the Jews and their malignant spirit," they should be clearly distinguished by their attire. She also prescribed how Jews ought to behave at Christian processions and forbade Jewish doctors to attend Christian patients because "the said infidel Jews, as enemies of the Christians, drink the latter's blood, and it is dangerous for Christians to make use of Jewish doctors." Upon his return from Sicily,

however, King Martin revoked this decree, without altering
the existing older laws relating to the Jewish badge or to the
segregation of Jews particularly from recent converts. Such a decree had been specifically issued by John I in 1393 for Tortosa and
temporarily also for Barcelona; it ended with a sharp declaration
that if a Jew be found copulating with a Christian woman "both
of them shall be burned without any mercy." Nevertheless even in
Gerona the Jewish quarter was not functioning to the full satisfaction of the authorities, and half a century later the municipality
had to issue a new series of regulations concerning it (1445–48). In
any case, whether the main aim of the new royal legislation was to
protect the Jews or more effectively to segregate them from the
non-Jewish population, the Gerona community never regained its
former strength in either numbers or intellectual eminence.[10]

More protracted were the negotiations concerning the reconstruction of the community of Lérida. Acting on numerous petitions by communal elders, King Martin approved in 1400 such
important provisions as that the new settlers would not be held
responsible for the debts of the previous *aljama* but rather enjoy a
moratorium even on their private debts, and that they would be
granted immunity from prosecution for earlier transgressions.
Landlords were ordered to put their houses in good shape for undisturbed Jewish occupancy. Other Jewish communities were asked
to collaborate in Lérida's reconstruction by allowing members
freely to move there after settling their communal obligations.
These protective regulations were further expanded in 1404 when
the king approved another set of petitions by the communal secretaries, including the permission for Lérida Jews to appeal to the
"protector or conservator" of Jewish rights against the local
bailiff's arbitrary moves. Despite such warm royal support, however, the restoration of the ruined community progressed very
slowly. In 1408 the problem of the synagogue, interveningly converted into a church, was still unsolved. In their new petitions to
the king, the communal elders requested that either the bishop
pay the required compensation as ordered by the king, or else return the building to them. They also asked that the king arbitrate
between the city and the community concerning the Jews' share in
the payment of indirect taxes, and that they be freed from the

indemnity of 50 pounds theretofore paid to the bailiff for the execution of a Jewish informer. This freedom was sought for a period
of three years, and was justified by the general poverty of a community facing manifold dangers, which must have greatly increased in that period of tense relations between Jews and the
numerous new converts to Christianity. Most of these concessions
were confirmed even by the generally unfriendly Ferdinand I in
1413. That the government took its efforts to rebuild the Jewish
communities quite seriously may be seen from its payment in 1402
of the large sum of 100 gold florins to one Mosse Içach for his
expenses "in augmenting and newly populating the Jewish quarter in the city of Lérida." As a result, the city witnessed the formation of a small but influential Jewish community, which later
included the distinguished ophthalmologist Crescas Abnarrabi,
known for his cure of John II's severe eye malady at a crucial juncture of the latter's reign.[11]

Permanent effects of the great tragedy were felt also in localities
where the Jews had suffered fewer casualties. According to Ḥisdai
Crescas, the outstanding leader of Aragonese Jewry, the majority
of the community in Palma, Majorca was saved from destruction
by escaping to the royal castle. In his succinct report to his
Avignonese coreligionists, he estimated that "some 300 souls had
perished in sanctification of the name of the Lord, whereas
approximately 800 found refuge in the king's castle and the rest
accepted conversion." One of the governor's first acts upon the return to normalcy was to reintroduce the badge, now defined as a
circle, one-half of which was to be vermillion and the other half
yellow (*groga*). "And this," the governor added, "under the
penalty of the loss of the garment of whatever kind the latter
might be. It is to be at the mercy of the lieutenant [governor];
one-half of the garment shall become the property of the royal fisc
and the other half shall belong to the denouncer." Yet these
chicaneries and even the presence of a large number of new converts, who before very long were to be known under the specific
pejorative name of *chuetas* (swine), did not completely interrupt
the continuity of Jewish communal life on the Balearic Islands. In
fact, in 1395 John I issued a safe-conduct for all Jews returning
from Muslim lands to Majorca; they were to enjoy immunity from

prosecution for illicit emigration and be free from all extraordinary taxes. The Islands' geographic location close to the North African shores, which had made them a convenient way station for refugees from the Peninsula to the more hospitable Muslim lands, now exerted that attraction in reverse on the returning exiles. However, as we shall see, this prosperity was not to endure for even half a century.[12]

On the whole, even where they were readmitted, the Jews sensed the hostility of their neighbors and they often failed to return in large numbers. At first, John I actually sought to force them to resettle in Barcelona and Valencia. In 1393 he ordered Ḥisdai (Azday) Crescas, together with two representatives from each of the relatively intact communities of Saragossa and Calatayud, to choose sixty Jewish families and to make them establish their residence in the Catalan and Valencian capitals. (Incidentally, he similarly used force to persuade an individual Jew to follow the Infante to Sicily.) Many smaller communities had even greater difficulties in reconstituting themselves. As late as 1398, thirty-six Jews left their desolate quarter in Fraga and settled in ten neighboring villages. Reminding them of their duty to pay their share in the communal debts, Queen Maria ordered them to return to Fraga within a month and not to leave it until they fulfilled their obligations. To encourage resettlement the government granted full or partial tax exemptions for a number of years to a few communities. For instance, Queen Violante released the Jews of Tarragona from taxation for five years and allowed them to appeal for funds to other communities.[13]

We have much less information about the reconstruction of the Jewish communities in Castile. Young Henry III's ineffectual, but rapacious, regime was much more interested in its immediate gains from taking over the heirless Jewish property (only to squander much of it on some court favorites) than in rebuilding the Jewish *aljamas* as a constant source of royal revenue. The elders of the small towns of Cala and Santolalla in the district of Seville were told by the king in 1395, within five days after the receipt of his order, to render account to the archbishop of Toledo "for what reason and at whose order you have destroyed and made to be destroyed the synagogues which were there so that the said archbishop should know [that reason] and certify its veracity." Such an order was also issued to the city council of Carmona. The implication of these orders, of course, was that the rioters who destroyed synagogues without good reason would be severely punished. It may be noted that even the clergy of Ecija, where the entire disturbance had started, now expostulated that they had had no part in the demolition of the local synagogue. They claimed that in their passive resistance they had actually disobeyed express orders which they had received from the archdeacon of Ecija, Ferrant Martinez. Curiously, the mere rebuilding of synagogues created new legal problems. Since the age-old canonical prohibition against the erection of new synagogues applied also to such structures in newly established quarters, special permits often had to be secured from the ecclesiastical authorities. Even hostile Benedict XIII had to allow the Jews of Toro to construct a new house of worship in lieu of the two which had been converted into churches (1404). Similarly, the Abbot of Oña permitted the restoration of an older synagogue, with the understanding that it not differ in shape from the neighboring residential buildings. Despite these concessions and notwithstanding the reappointment of quite a few Jews as fiscal agents by the two Crowns, the task of reconstruction proved to be extremely slow and burdensome to numerous Jewries.[14]

Internally, too, Jews found it necessary to readjust their individual as well as communal lives to meet the new exigencies. Among the numerous semipublic and semiprivate transactions, we need but mention the remarkable agreement of 1395 between a Burgos Jew, Dumzagus b. Abraham Levi, and the Republic of Venice concerning a two-thirds reduction of tolls for Venetian merchants arriving at certain Castilian ports in the course of the following two years. Evidently, Dumzagus expected to profit from the ensuing increase in trade. The reconstruction of the Jewish communities was handicapped not only by their huge property losses during the massacres and the sharp decline in the number and affluence of their members, but also by the difficulties they often encountered in recruiting qualified personnel. Many leading citizens, whose faith had been undermined by general humanistic and Averroistic studies, had been prone to give up their religious allegiance rather than to suffer martyrdom. Later on, during the disputation at Tortosa, too, some of the wealthier and better educated Jews more readily acknowledged defeat and adopted Christianity. In some instances, therefore, the old communal leaders had to be completely replaced. At times their posts were taken over by craftsmen, paralleling the then widespread clamor of the artisan classes for participation in municipal governments. On the other hand, these new leaders often lacked both the learning and experience needed to handle communal affairs in that critical period.[15]

It is small wonder, then, that Crescas and other scholars resented the new leadership and, with gov*e*rnental aid, championed the adoption of communal statutes allotting more power to the upper classes. In their aforementioned petition of 1408, too, the Lérida elders sought royal approval for the provision that no Jew owning less than 50 florins' worth of property be eligible for any communal office without express consent by the secretaries and councilors. However, the statute enacted in June 1396 for the community of Saragossa proved so unpopular that in February 1399 Queen Violante had to modify it sharply by reestablishing fuller democratic controls. In general, after a period of hesitation the authorities gradually restored the extensive Jewish autonomy, hoping thereby to revive Jewish life also for the benefit of the Treasury. In these endeavors they found full support among the Jews themselves. Even in Navarre, which in 1391 had escaped the brunt of the popular hysteria, the Jews felt that by closing ranks and practicing more fully the orthodox rites of their religion they would stave off future catastrophes. The community of Tudela now renewed its statute of 1303 and strengthened it by new disciplinary provisions, such as entrusting a new committee of twenty to punish all transgressors against the ritual law. It explained these new controls by stating:

Considering that everything depends on the worship of the Creator, that the evil decrees come upon the world because of the sins of the generation, and that the preservation of the communities depends on their good deeds—this has been true in the case of all past generations and is doubly so in that of our generation when, on account of our sins, we have remained but a few in lieu of many—we need to mend our ways and to set up fences and regulations concerning the service of the Creator as well as the service of our lord the king so that we may continue living in his realm. Also when members of other communities located in the other kingdoms will learn of the good order we have established for the maintenance of our faith, they will come to live among us. For these reasons the whole community resolved as follows. . . .[16]

GOVERNMENTAL REACTION

Complicating all efforts to restore the earlier status was the presence in many communities of a large mass of *conversos* and their twilight position between Judaism and Christianity. Formally, they were Christians. None of the Iberian rulers emulated the example of William II of England and Henry IV of Germany, who in 1097 had allowed the New Christians left behind by the onrushing Crusaders to return to their former faith. The monarchs of 1392 generally shared the view of the Church that, although the methods employed by the pogromists had been illegal, the sacrament of baptism was not to be desecrated by the public profession of Judaism of such persons baptized under pressure. The *conversos* could, therefore, publicly revert to their ancestral faith only after escaping to other countries, mainly Muslim. The majority remained in Spain, some continuing to perform Jewish rites secretly. The ecclesiastical organs did not yet pursue the sharp policy of repression which was to characterize the later, more efficient, inquisitorial tribunals. However, there was much room left for suspicion on the part of both the clergy and the public, suspicion aimed not only at the *conversos* but also at their Jewish friends and neighbors who were accused of aiding and abetting their relapses. Needless to say, many *conversos* had no intention whatsoever of returning to their Jewish faith. Some of them had been outright agnostics at heart and they now became just as questionable Christians as they had been unreliable Jews. Others took their conversion more seriously; a few with the zeal of neophytes tried to convert their Jewish brethren. From among them arose such sharp polemists against their former faith as Paul (Pablo) de Santa Maria, bishop of Burgos, and Geronimo de Santa Fé. There was no end to individual tragedies when parents were separated from each other or from their children, an occurrence frequent enough to create difficulties also in the settlement of property rights.[17]

In some cases the government had to intervene to prevent blackmail, as when a *converso*, with the aid of the governor of Valencia, tried to extort money from the childless widow of his Jewish brother by withholding from her the *ḥaliṣah,* the ceremony required by biblical law before she could remarry. Conversely, the wife of another convert, who had refused to join him in adopting Christianity, nevertheless did not wish to release him from his marital bonds unless he paid her the contractual marriage settlement. Such insistence, fully justified from the standpoint of Jewish law, clearly ran counter to the canonical provisions which automatically dissolved marriages of converts with their unconverted mates. At the same time we also hear of numerous amicable property settlements. We even possess certain wills of Jewish parents providing for the distribution of their estates among their children, both Jewish and baptized. No less complicated became the relations between the *conversos* and their old communities. As late as 1414, Ferdinand I of Aragon had to issue a decree freeing the New Christians from their share in communal taxes, since as former members they were considered liable for their share in the debts of their *aljamas*. On the other hand, the community of Saragossa was persuaded to raise funds for the support of a priest who wished to study in Avignon, and for that of a *converso* preacher. Even more remarkably, the archbishop of Toledo tried, in 1395, to foist his personal physician, apparently a convert, upon the Jewish communities as their chief judge, although the Jews strenuously opposed this appointment. Some diplomats continued serving their communities even after conversion. We learn, for instance, that in 1414 Gonzalo de la Cavalleria, formerly Don Vidal Benveniste b. Labi, collected from the Saragossa community 2,000 solidi for his expenses after he had intervened in its behalf with Antipope Benedict XIII. In another case, the Jewish community of Fraga was forced by the king retroactively to pay the expenses of its spokesman at the disputation of Tortosa until the day of his conversion.[18]

All these complications paled into insignificance, however, compared with the stimulus they gave to some leading churchmen, such as St. Vicente Ferrer, to redouble their efforts in converting the remaining Jews as well as in segregating more sharply those who rejected baptism. They also gave impetus to Benedict XIII's convocation of the disputation of Tortosa, the objective of which was clearly stated in his letter of invitation to Aragon's Jewish communities. In that addressed to Rabbi Juce Abinarduc of Huesca he wrote:

Since it is Our duty by virtue of Our office [to take care] not only of the faithful but also of the infidels, We wish to give you and other Jews of the Huesca community instruction and information concerning the Catholic faith for the salvation of your souls. This is done in order that, purged of the Judaic superstition, you should be able to acknowledge the precious truth of the eternal light. We order, therefore, you as well as the other Jews of the *aljamas* of the kingdom of Aragon to come before Our presence on a certain day as is more fully explained in Our pertinent letters.

We know that the antipope to a large extent achieved his aim, although it took his partisans much longer and required much more exertion than he had anticipated.[19]

More significantly, this new hostility toward Jews communicated itself also to the two governments. While in the early years after the massacres both regimes showed real interest in reestablishing the Jewish communities, be it only for fiscal reasons, a decade later they began concentrating on restricting Jewish rights and promoting the conversion of the surviving remnant. In 1405 Henry III approved resolutions of the Cortes of Valladolid which, apart from renewing some older laws, added the provision that, whenever one was in doubt concerning the amount owed by a Christian to a Jew, "only one-half of the outstanding debt should be paid, on the presumption that the other half consists of [accrued] interest, as Jews and Moors generally take bonds for double the amount they lend to Christians." Only if the Jewish creditor could prove by reliable Christian witnesses that the entire amount represented capital was he to collect his debt in full. The king accepted also another significant alteration of the age-old Jewish privileges: "It is My will and pleasure that in all civil and criminal cases Christians may and can serve as witnesses against Jews and Moors, the same as against Christians, without the testimony of a Jew or Moor being required, provided the Christians are reputable persons." The exemption from wearing distinguishing marks, previously granted to Jews appearing at the royal palace, was now abrogated. Only one concession was made to the Jews. The law prohibited the arbitrary removal by any passer-by of a garment worn by a Jew without a badge; such action was restricted to persons specifically authorized by courts. A far-reaching decree issued by the Queen Mother Catalina in the name of the minor King John II on October 25, 1408 represented a self-imposed sweeping renunciation by the Crown of the valuable services of its Jewish fiscal agents. Unable to refer to more recent precedents, the regents cited the pertinent provisions of the *Siete Partidas:*

Know ye that, according to the laws of the *Partidas,* it is akin to a sacrilege to give Jews power over Christians, so that they may judge them and collect from them the tolls. Nor must one appoint Jews collectors and receivers of other dues which Christians pay to the lords of the land, or else allow Jews to farm these imposts. By virtue of these arrangements the Jews assume great authority over Christians and have the opportunity, in many ways, to cause them much harm and grief, which entails great disservice to God and Me and accrues to the great injury of My kingdoms. Therefore, desirous to provide a remedy, I intend that, for the benefit of My service and the welfare of My kingdoms, the said *Partidas* and the other laws enacted in this matter be observed.

The decree actually shifted the blame from the authorities to the appointees themselves; they were to be publicly flogged and fined an amount double the revenue collected by them. Christians parading as a "front" for Jewish agents were likewise to pay a double indemnity. To encourage both denunciations and enforcement by local authorities, the law provided that all such fines be divided between the informers, the sentencing courts, and the Treasury.[20]

Equally hostile and clearly betraying the spirit of Ferrer and his associates, was the more comprehensive law enacted by the Regency in the name of John II on January 2, 1412. This conglomeration of sharply Jew-baiting ordinances also embraced many secular provisions demanded by burghers and other anti-Jewish groups. It begins with the pious declaration that every king or prince is appointed by God to reign over his people and that particularly Catholic kings and princes should exercise their power "so that the Christians who believe in the holy Catholic faith should not fall into errors by participating in conversations with infidels who are neither believers, nor obedient to our Lord Jesus Christ, nor are members of His holy Catholic faith." This aim was to be accomplished by twenty-four provisions which pursued mainly the objectives of: (1) strictly segregating Jews and Moors from Christians; (2) promoting the former's conversion to Christianity; (3) limiting the Jews' economic activities and particularly their services to the Crown; (4) restricting Jewish judicial autonomy; and (5) preventing the emigration of Jews not only to foreign countries but also to the districts under the jurisdiction of more friendly nobles.[21]

In order to achieve strict segregation, the authorities of the various cities were ordered to assign to Jews and Moors separate quarters surrounded by walls, each having but a single gate for entry and exit. All Jews and Moors were to move into such quarters within eight days; otherwise they were to be subject to the confiscation of all their property and corporal punishment at royal discretion (Art. 1). Christian women were forbidden to visit them at any time of day or night. A transgressor, if married, was to be fined 300 maravedis for each entry, an unmarried or kept woman was to lose the clothes she had on, while a prostitute was to receive 100 lashes and be driven out of town (Arts. 6 and 11). Even outside their quarters Jews and Moors were not allowed to sell food to Christians, supply them with drugs, attend them in their illness, employ them as servants, farmworkers, or shepherds, or perform such services for them. They were also prohibited from peddling in Christian houses. In fact, they were told not to eat with Christians except on journeys or at the royal court. Christians and "infidels" were also forbidden to attend one another's weddings or funerals, under the penalty of 2,000 maravedis for each offense (Arts. 2, 4, 5, 10, 19–21). To emphasize their inferiority, Jews and Moors were not to be addressed as Dons; they had to wear their distinctive garb (both men and women had to be dressed in robes or mantles reaching to their feet and adorned with red badges), and were forbidden to trim their beards and hair with scissors (Arts. 12–15 and 18).

If Jews or Moors wished to be baptized, "they were not to be prevented or impeded by force or in any other manner by Moors,

Jews, or Christians, both men and women, even if one be their father, mother, or brother." No Jews or Moors were to be employed as tax farmers, attorneys, collectors, house stewards, or rent receivers by the king or by any other lord under the penalty of 1,000 maravedis to be paid by the person thus employed (Art. 5). The old privileges of the Jewish and Moorish communities to exercise civil and criminal jurisdiction were to be abrogated; all their litigations were to be dealt with by the local judges who would take into consideration their usages and customs. Nor were their communities to continue taxing their members without special government authorization (Arts. 7–9). Jews and Moors were not permitted to change their domiciles under the penalty of losing all their property; any Christian lord sheltering alien infidels was to be penalized 50,000 maravedis for the first offense, and the loss of that dwelling for the second offense. Jews and Moors caught in an attempt to leave the country were to lose all their possessions and become the king's perpetual slaves (Arts. 16, 17, and 23). In conclusion, to assure the execution of these drastic measures, the decree enjoined the local judges from in any way reducing or altering the civil penalties (Art. 24).

This decree of the bigoted queen regent has been summarized more fully here, because it reproduced in essence the whole array of ecclesiastical and lay postulates of the anti-Jewish faction led by Ferrer and his ally Benedict XIII. It soon became clear, however, that the legislators had gone too far. Within half a year (July 17, 1412) the law was modified by another decree issued in Cifuentes by coregent Infante Ferdinand, at least for the southern regions administered by him. Yet its basic objectives and the drastic methods of execution remained unaltered. Soon thereafter, as a result of the so-called "Compromise of Caspe," secured with the aid of Benedict XIII and Ferrer, Ferdinand ascended the throne of Aragon. On March 20, 1413, he enacted there a Catalan version of the modified decree of Cifuentes. Aragonese Jews (including the residents of Majorca) thus immediately felt the brunt of their country's importation of this Castilian prince. Finally, these Castilian-Aragonese provisions served as a basis for Benedict XIII's papal bull *Et si doctoris* of 1415, which attempted to incorporate the severe Spanish regulations and basic approaches into the universal canon law. Benedict's ukase was confirmed by Ferdinand for Aragon in the same year. Not that Ferdinand and the antipope always saw eye to eye. In the case of a Sargossan Jew, Açach Nageri, who had been summoned to the papal court but had left on royal business, the king insisted on Açach's innocence (1414). Even before the great disputation Ferdinand ordered the royal officials in Tortosa, Gerona, and Tauste effectively to protect the Jews against attacks and to prosecute those who stirred up anti-Jewish riots. In Gerona the royal intervention doubtless found support among the local authorities, since the city council itself, concerned about the forthcoming papal enactment, soon ordered its envoy to the royal court to intercede in the Jews' behalf, and to demand that they be maintained in their *status quo.* On the other hand, the city of Teruel, inspired by Ferrer's sermons, enacted a sharply segregationist ordinance and dispatched a special envoy to the king to secure its confirmation. Not surprisingly, Teruel also sought support from Benedict XIII.[22]

A contemporary Hebrew moralist, Solomon ibn Leḥamias Alami (Al'ammi), graphically described the immediate impact of that hostile legislation, particularly in the area under Catalina's direct control. Characteristically, in his "Epistle on Ethics," written in 1415, Solomon did not blame the regime or the Church, but in the traditional vein he expatiated on the sinful behavior of his Spanish coreligionists which had brought down God's wrath upon their heads. In his opinion, the punishment was exactly commensurate with the Jews' overbearing behavior:

Because we had striven to dress like the Gentiles, we have been forced instead to wear some strange clothing so that we should be singled out for shame and contempt before the onlooking public. Because we had despoiled our beards and hairdos [against the traditional law], we have been ordered to grow our hair long and to wear beards like mourners. Because, oblivious of the destruction of our Temple, we have built spacious and beautiful mansions and palaces, we have been expelled and driven into open fields and slum-like corners.

Not that Solomon particularly regretted the disappearance of the earlier luxuries. The entire tenor of his ethical treatise is aimed at both the inner divisions in Jewry and the love of luxuries among its upper classes. He attributed the catastrophe principally to the wealthy leaders of Spanish Jewry who, having acquired a superficial knowledge of Greek science, had ridiculed their ancestral traditions and "cast off everything that reminds them of their Judaism. They seek to dazzle by princely luxury; their wives and daughters array themselves in jewels like princesses; and, swelled with pride, they deem themselves the princes of the land." In contrast thereto, he claimed, the Christian grandees outdid one another in promoting and glorifying their religion.[23]

FRUSTRATING READJUSTMENTS

After 1415 came a period of relative calm, interrupted only by sporadic local outbursts of popular hostility or governmental fits of intolerance. The legislation which had climaxed the turbulent quarter century of 1391–1415 proved untenable in the long run. Although but partially abrogated and even occasionally restated in subsequent decrees, these sharply discriminatory laws were largely honored in their breach. Benedict XIII was deposed by the Council of Constance, and although he never acknowledged defeat he and his rivals were replaced by the new, more humane Pope Martin V. Similarly, Ferdinand I of Aragon died in 1416 and his successor Alphonso V was not undeservedly styled "the Magnanimous" (1416–58). Under him and under John II (1458–79) Aragonese Jewry secured a certain respite from the constant legislative and administrative harassment. In his important decree of March 21, 1419, Alphonso to all intents and purposes nullified Ferdinand's and Benedict's anti-Jewish decrees. He even provided for the return of synagogues and books owned by Jews, the latter subject to expurgation of incriminated passages. For this purpose two Saragossa clerics were appointed to review, in cooperation with an informed convert, all questionable Hebrew manuscripts. In this way the king resolved a thorny problem raised by a petition of Jewish communities asking for the return of the confiscated rabbinic works. We do not know whether this was the result of deliberations of a committee of jurists and theologians to which he had originally intended to submit the Jewish request. But it stands to reason that he had obtained Pope Martin V's approval for this drastic decision which, probably more than any other, induced the city council of Gerona to declare that "the Jews secured all they wished from the lord King." Their Castilian coreligionists likewise breathed a little more freely when their king John II grew into maturity and personally assumed, until his death in 1454, the responsibilities of government even if he often delegated them to such a favorite as Álvaro de Luna. The situation remained substantially unchanged under his successor, Henry IV the Impotent (1454–74).[24]

Spanish Jewry's main difficulties during the six decades following the disputation of Tortosa lay in their countries' anarchical situation, rather than in outright Jew-baiting. Not that the anti-Jewish voices were ever silenced; they actually swelled into a mighty chorus in the Spanish literature, lay as well as ecclesiastical, during its renowned *siglo d'oro*. But the furor of the pogromists and the frenzied proselytism of Ferrer's kind had largely spent themselves. Jews still were obliged to listen to missionary sermons. Even an Italian Franciscan, Matteo d'Agrigento, was allowed to address the Jewish remnants of Barcelona and Valencia in 1427–28, King Alphonso V repeatedly ordering the royal officials to assist the preacher in his conversionist endeavors. On the other hand, when in 1422 the Dominican Pedro Cerdán began delivering incendiary sermons in various localities, Alphonso wrote from Naples that these homilies had gone beyond all permissible limits and must be stopped. In general, a certain *modus vivendi*, with occasional close personal relations, was now established even between the Jews and the clergy. The so-called Alba Bible is, indeed, a remarkable monument of the intellectual collaboration of a rabbi, Moses Arragel of Guadalajara (on the title page spelled Guadalfajara), and Luis de Guzman, the grand master of the Order of Calatrava (*ca.* 1430). The rabbi did most of the translation and provided it with a commentary largely based upon older Jewish exegetical literature. The accompanying illustrations, doubtless prepared by a Christian artist under De Guzman's supervision, showed the rabbi attired in Jewish garb but otherwise in a proud and dignified posture, presenting the Bible to the grand master and other ecclesiastical dignitaries.[25]

In lieu of the expected mutual hostility, in part reflected in the polemical literature of the period, the relations between Jews and *conversos,* too, were often quite friendly. The remarkable absence of venom within certain divided families is well illustrated by the notable testament left behind in 1443 by the widow of Benveniste de la Cavalleria. In bequeathing a substantial amount to the Jewish community of Saragossa, this loyal Jewess expressed the wish that this legacy be administered by the closest of kin bearing the name of Cavalleria or, in the absence of such a person, by the closest Jewish relative having another name. The testator further added that, if the Saragossa community "should for any reason be destroyed, depopulated or change its faith," the legacy should be transferred to the next largest Jewish community of Aragon. Her deep attachment to the Jewish faith, however, did not prevent the lady from providing in her will for four of her converted children along with two daughters specifically designated as Jewesses. In another remarkable will, dated April 3, 1470, one Estelina, widow of a Gerona Jew, requested that "my Christian daughter Margarita and my sons, heirs of Vidal de Piera, the Jew, should properly behave toward each other and should live in peace, unity, and love." [26]

Nor did the kings hesitate to make the best use possible of the services of Jewish fiscal agents. Despite the law of 1412, they themselves almost uninterruptedly entrusted responsible positions to Jewish fiscal advisers, the latter's titles alone being somewhat camouflaged in order to mitigate popular resentment. No camouflage was needed in the case of Jewish court physicians. In all three Spanish kingdoms their medical ministrations were often combined with the leadership of Jewish communities, especially with the chief rabbinate. In Navarre, in fact, where the popular and governmental reaction after 1391 was far less virulent, Joseph Orabuena effectively served in both capacities until 1413. [27]

On several occasions John II of Castile also tried to protect the rights of less prominent Jews. On the petition of Sancho Alpullate (Pullate) of Alcalá, "procurator of the Jewish communities" in the realm, he issued on March 29, 1447 a circular letter to all royal and municipal officials forbidding them without previous royal approval to impose upon Jews payments in kind or to force them to contribute to the billeting of government functionaries, other than the king, the queen, the crown prince, and members of the

royal Council and Chancery. This decree was subsequently confirmed by Henry IV in 1455 and even by Ferdinand and Isabella
in 1483 and 1485. All three confirmations, it may be noted, were
likewise secured by Jewish spokesmen—in 1455 by Pullate himself.
Jews also possessed extensive landholdings in many parts of both
realms. In 1453 the city council of Haro actually protested against
a real estate covenant allegedly concluded by the local Jews and
Moors not to sell any land to Christians. According to the council,
members of these minority groups were acquiring land from
Christians "every day because of the latter's poverty" and there
was real danger that ultimately they would monopolize all landholdings.[28]

Jewish communities recovered also most of their autonomous
functions. In the course of the fifteenth century several prominent
personalities held the ever more influential office of the Castilian
rab de la corte (court rabbi). This official served as the main intermediary between the Crown and the Jewish communities.
True, at the beginning of the century Court Rabbi Meir Alguades
could not stem the onslaught of the anti-Jewish forces, although he
succeeded in preventing some individuals from deserting their
faith. Ultimately, he himself fell victim to the aroused passions
and was executed by Queen Mother Catalina, allegedly because he
had confessed after torture that he had taken part in a conspiracy
to desecrate the host and that he had poisoned his patient, King
Henry III. But in the more quiescent period of John II's adult
reign Abraham Benveniste could undertake to reform Jewish
community life in Castile on a grand scale. With the king's aid, he
convoked in 1432 an important assembly of Jewish community
leaders at Valladolid. This synod adopted a series of resolutions,
which, preserved in both their original mixture of Hebrew and
Castilian and in an old Castilian translation, belong to the most
remarkable Jewish communal records of the Middle Ages. While
many provisions, which will be more fully analyzed in other connections, could not be implemented under Castile's then growingly anarchical conditions, the Valladolid assembly undoubtedly
helped the Jewish communities to regain some of their self-
confidence and pride in their religious heritage. A few decades
later, another Abraham, surnamed Seneor, played an even more

prominent role as both Jewish communal leader and the Crown's fiscal aid. His career, begun under Henry IV, shone ever more brightly under Ferdinand and Isabella until it ended in the anticlimax of his conversion to Christianity under royal pressure. In 1492, he chose this alternative to the hardships of exile, which at his advanced age of over eighty might indeed have been suicidal.[29]

The reforms of 1432 came at an opportune time for the Castilian communities whose controls had been greatly undermined by the catastrophe of 1391 and its aftermath. As late as 1427, Catalina, John II's sister, was still greatly concerned about the consecration into a church of a former synagogue in Ocaña, in the district of Toledo. Without mentioning the massacre she merely claimed that, as a result of the "Jewish preachment of Brother Vicente [Ferrer], many Jews had become Christian." Hence the greatly diminished Jewish community of Ocaña did not require the use of its two synagogues, and one could readily be converted into a Christian house of worship. In Aragon, too, the general weakness of most Jewish communities during the early decades of the fifteenth century is illustrated by many incidents and legal enactments. In Gerona the Jewish population had dwindled to such an extent that when the last treasurer of a Jewish philanthropic foundation accepted baptism in 1431, Alphonso V instructed him to continue in his office and to distribute the funds among Christian as well as Jewish poor. The king claimed that the number of remaining Jews had become so small that one could hardly speak of a Jewish community. Twenty-eight years later, however, John II considered it incumbent upon himself to issue a new comprehensive statute for the Gerona community, which was to serve it for twenty years. The tenuous nature of many communities was also ostensible in such arrangements as made by that of Valladolid in 1413; it leased from a monastery space for a new Jewish quarter under the condition that, should all its members be converted, the lease would automatically expire. Similarly, the large community of Saragossa through most of the fifteenth century drew up its budgets with a view toward the possible apostasy of its members. The communal statute concerning the wine tax, recorded in a notarial act of August 11, 1434, provided for the payment of 15 solidi by each contributor departing for another city or turning Christian.[30]

Jews suffered, moreover, along with other citizens from the general anarchy then ravaging both Aragon and Castile. The drive of the nobles and cities to achieve almost total independence from the Crown, combined with a growing agrarian revolution, sharply divided the classes and converted their internecine conflicts into a more or less permanent civil war. On the whole, Jews sided with the Crown, such communities as Saragossa in 1460 and Cervera in 1474 being rewarded by tax concessions for their help. In the privilege for the latter, John II of Aragon emphasized that the Cervera Jews had been "greatly oppressed and molested because of their having been consistent in Our service." In Castile, too, John II rewarded the community of Tordesillas for its services with a ten-year tax exemption on a par with that granted to the Christian population (1443). In 1465 Henry IV liberated the Jews of Soria from all taxation permanently because of the service they had rendered in defending the castle. In the following year he reduced by 50 percent the taxes of the Alfaro community (until such time when it would embrace a membership of 70 families) because of its outstanding part in the defense against the French. At times royal protection extended beyond the state's boundaries. In 1458 John II of Aragon sent letters to the king of France and Count de Foix protesting against the kidnaping of two Jews of Tudela and their removal to French territory. Pertinent instructions were also given to two Aragonese envoys in Paris.[31]

Such attachment to the Crown was not seriously diminished by the fact that, living in the constant shadow of attack, some Jews as well as *conversos* secretly rejoiced over the expansion of the Ottoman Empire. The fall of Constantinople in 1453, which made a deep impression throughout the West, evoked in the minds of many messianically minded Jews the picture of the gigantic wars of Gog and Magog which were to precede the end of days. *Conversos*, better informed about Christian doctrines, were prone to identify the Turk with Antichrist. But such messianic yearnings were hardly ever translated into disloyal acts against their own kings. On the contrary, time and again Jews became victims of attack precisely because of their royalist partisanship. One such anti-Jewish riot in Segovia is described in the introduction to a Hebrew sermon preached there on June 17, 1452. Far more serious were the assaults on the Jewish communities of Cordova and Jaén in 1473, which, though followed by the punishment of ringleaders, ended with the expulsion of the Jews from Cordova and all of Andalusia.[32]

Nor was the life of Jewish statesmen and Treasury officials altogether secure. In a period when even an Álvaro de Luna, constable of the realm and grand master of Santiago, "the boldest knight, the ablest intriguer, the most fascinating companion at the king's court," ended a career of nearly forty years of almost unlimited power under the ax of an executioner, no one in authority could be certain of a peaceful end. True, the leading Jewish official in the 1430s, Abraham Benveniste, De Luna's close associate and in his own right an influential army contractor, fiscal agent, and court rabbi, was able to transmit his wealth and social position to his son, Joseph, and other members of the Benveniste family. When the Cortes of Burgos of 1430 reminded the Castilian John II that his father and Pope Benedict XIII had outlawed the appointment of Jewish officials, the king replied evasively: "Whatever is for the service of God, his divine law, My service and the welfare of My kingdom, shall be observed." Equally influential in later years was the distinguished scholar and royal adviser, Joseph ibn Shem Tob, who for a time combined in his hands the offices of superintendent of royal accounts and court physician. For the latter service alone he received the substantial salary of 40,000 maravedis in 1453. As a patron of humanistic studies, moreover, John II allowed his Jewish favorite considerable intellectual freedom and listened with much interest to the religious debates carried on at court between this Jewish controversialist and his Catholic opponents. Joseph was nevertheless diplomat enough to be entrusted with delicate missions, as when he was sent to Lisbon to secure the hand of the Portuguese princess, Isabella, for his king—a choice of the great Constable, though John himself would have preferred a French princess royal as his second wife (1450). Ibn Shem Tob survived De Luna and also continued serving under the new king Henry IV. But before long his name disappeared from the records and ultimately he seems to have died the death of a martyr.[33]

Such relative freedom of expression deeply irked the Spanish hierarchy, which never quite gave up its anti-Jewish stance. It heartily disliked Martin V's sharp reversal of Benedict XIII's policies, and pleaded with the new pope that his pro-Jewish enactments aroused much unrest among the Spanish people. Thereupon in 1423 Martin instructed the archbishops of Tarragona, Valencia, and Gerona, together with a number of qualified persons of their choice, to submit these privileges to renewed scrutiny. He even allowed them to suspend some especially explosive provisions. He repeated this order two years later. Perhaps nothing came out of these negotiations because of the intervening changes in the attitude to Jews and Judaism within the ruling Spanish circles themselves. The Spanish Church now had to struggle against the equally moderate Jewish policies pursued by John II after he achieved adulthood. Under its influence Pope Eugenius IV tried to revive the anti-Jewish legislation of Benedict XIII, and in his bull, *Dudum ad nostram,* of August 8, 1442, specifically addressed to Castile and Leon, he renewed most of his predecessor's sharply segregationist provisions of 1415. Doubtless echoing the complaints of Castilian churchmen, the pope insisted with particular vehemence that Jews must not be allowed to serve as:

arrendators, collectors, tenants or leaseholders of produce and property held by Christians, as their bookkeepers, caretakers, managers, agents, mediators, go-betweens in betrothals, marriage brokers, or obstetricians. Nor are they to perform any work in Christian houses or estates, or hold any partnerships, offices, or administrative posts in any joint enterprise, craft, or construction job with Christians. No Christian shall be allowed to bequeath them anything in his testament or last will, nor to leave any legacy to Jews, to their communities, or to Saracens.

This bull was confirmed by Nicholas V in 1451. That these papal ordinances largely resulted from the persistent pressures of the Spanish churchmen is evident. Otherwise neither pope was consistently unfriendly to Jews. In 1435, Eugenius IV had sharply forbidden preachers to arouse the public against them and to urge that Christians not bake bread for Jews nor kindle fires for them on Sabbath. Because of Spanish complaints, however, he revoked this order in 1442, which revocation was confirmed by Nicholas on December 6, 1447. On his part, Nicholas, too, had a few weeks earlier (November 2, 1447) reacted favorably to petitions of Spanish Jewry against the agitation of monks during Christian holidays, which had often resulted in attacks on Jewish houses, the conversion of synagogues into churches, forced conversion of individuals to Christianity, and blood libels. The pope declared, therefore, that he must forbid "by a perpetual and irrevocable constitution" all Christians, including archbishops and other dignitaries, to incite people publicly or clandestinely against Jews, or to hinder them in any way in the celebration of their Sabbaths and holidays, or in the observance of their other rituals.[34]

Such papal inconsistencies must have shocked the royal advisers. But the latter could not reject outright even some extremely anti-Jewish bulls for fear of further aggravating the ever deepening inner tensions. Without completely contradicting Eugenius, therefore, John II issued a lengthy decree on April 6, 1443. Here he not only failed to renew the Castilian provisions of 1412 which had underlain Benedict's legislation, but with a good deal of sophistry, somewhat camouflaged by wordiness and repetition, he toned down the papal demands as if they were in agreement with his own. At the same time he scolded the lesser authorities who had allowed themselves without royal permission to enact severe statutes and ordinances against Jews and Moors. "Were the like permitted, they [Jews and Moors] would, without cause or crime, be deprived of, and interdicted from, participation and communication with Christians"; all that under the guise of complying with the papal bull, "published when I was at Toledo." This was an indirect censure of those who had circulated the papal ordinance without the Crown's special permission—a procedure sharply opposed by John and his successors. The king was particularly aroused about the economic restrictions attributed to the papal bull:

It does not follow therefrom that they [Jews and Moors] should be forbidden to contract, buy, sell, or exchange any goods and wares among and with Christians; nor that they should be kept out of such lowly trades and serviceable handicrafts as the occupations of rag dealers, silversmiths, carpenters, barbers, masons, confectioners, shoemakers, tailors, clothiers, milliners, braziers, bridlemakers, saddlers, ropemakers, potters, curriers, basketmakers, money changers, and all other similar trades, mechanical arts, and lowly and servile ministrations, in which they employ manual labor. Christians should be allowed to be their servants in such trades and handicrafts for just wages and hire, for there is not much dignity in these occupations, nor are they [Jews and Moors] honored thereby, neither do they derive any authority or assume any power from such trades; nor can they thereby injure, molest, or administer justice to Christians; nor would such ministrations lead to too much familiarity, constant company, or association among the parties concerned . . . provided only that the said Jews and Moors do not form partnerships with the said Christians in the said arts and trades, or become too familiar, or keep constant and assiduous association with them.

At the same time John conceded the need of separate quarters for Jews and Saracens. But he insisted that wherever no such existed, streets should "be allotted to them in populous and suitable districts, where they can live and reside comfortably." [35]

John's weaker successor, on the other hand, often yielded ground more readily. Henry IV's gradual retreat in the Jewish question is doubly remarkable, as he started his reign with a sweeping protective decree. Responding to another appeal by Santo Alpullate (Sancho Pullate) in behalf of the Jewish communities of the realm, he forbade in 1455 the forcible expropriation of synagogues and Jewish cemeteries. "Nor must one enact against them [the Jews] statutes or ordinances or introduce any [other] innovations without first securing My special authorization." This decree, occasionally invoked by local Jewish leaders, was never revoked and was, in fact, confirmed by Ferdinand the Catholic in 1479. Yet its effective implementation under the country's unstable conditions would have required more strength and will power than Henry was able to marshal. On the contrary, at the demand of the Cortes of Toledo, he tightened up in 1462 the regulations concerning bills of indebtedness, because the laws of 1377 and 1405 had allegedly been too greatly modified in favor of Jewish lenders. More significantly, he accepted in 1465 the judgment of a court of arbitration in a controversy between himself and the estates of lords and nobles. Headed by a leading monk, Alphonso de Oropesa, this court understandably injected many canonical postulates into its decisions. It reemphasized the elimination of Jews from public office and total segregation to the extent of declaring Jews and Moors illegally living outside their quarters *eo ipso* slaves of either the king or the lord on whose property they lived. Perhaps the most remarkable items related to the newly expanded inquisitorial proceedings. The judgment provided that the bishops should urgently but circumspectly prosecute all persons suspected of heresy or the observance of non-Christian rituals, so that the guilty be punished but the innocent be protected against undue molestation and insults. No one was to interfere with such inquisitorial prosecutions, to which the secular arm was to extend full support.[36]

Remarkably, these changes of papal policy and the royal reactions to them are attested only for Castile, not Aragon or Navarre. There seems to have been a general diminution of the virulence of anti-Jewish agitation on the part of the Aragonese Church of the period, the hostile feelings apparently being nurtured primarily from the economic antagonisms between burghers and Jews. Nor did Alphonso V, who was spending most of his time in his Italian possessions, take any direct interest in the possible attempts of the local Church to impinge upon the royal authority. He was far more concerned about his diplomatic relations with the Papacy, and particularly Eugenius IV, during the crucial period of their estrangement and subsequent reconciliation with respect to his reign over Sicily in 1442–43. Nevertheless, in Aragon, too, the state and Church relations could not fail to affect also the Jewish position.

With the growth of heresy-hunting in Aragon, it was of paramount importance to the kings to stave off ecclesiastical interference with the royal jurisdiction over Jews. In 1457 Alphonso V inserted into his privilege for the Saragossa community (primarily concerned with the Jews' civil rights) special pledges to protect its members against excesses of the ecclesiastical judiciary as well as against imprisonment or seizure of property by powerful lay personalities. This privilege, secured by petitions of the Saragossa community, was reissued in the following year by John II in favor of the communities of Calatayud, Huesca, Jaca, Teruel, Tarazona, Albarracín, and Tauste. In a sharply worded letter in 1475 to the inquisitor of the diocese of Vich, who had started proceedings against one Astruch Adret, the king firmly reiterated that "all Jews residing within Our royal authority are subject to no one but Ourselves in their spiritual or temporal concerns both from the civil and the criminal point of view. Hence none but Ourselves and Our officials are allowed in any way to decide what should and ought to be done about them." On certain occasions the Crown directly intervened in safeguarding the Jews' opportunities for making a living; for instance, through the untrammeled sale of their agricultural produce (Huesca, 1436) or their plying the tailoring trade against the opposition of local Christian rivals (Monzón, 1461). We recall the various tax exemptions John granted to Jews loyal to him during the Catalonian uprising. Time and again he reduced the amounts due to the Treasury because of the hard times upon which one or another community had fallen. Nor did he mind retracing his steps, as when he revoked a specific tax exemption he had granted to one of his Jewish favorites upon learning that it ran counter to the interests and privileges of the beneficiary's community. In 1474 he informed the royal officials in Cervera, that because of their loyalty to the Crown, the Jews had sustained many hardships during the uprising and they were now entitled to the full restoration of their property. Nor were they to be made to share in the punitive contribution imposed upon the city after its surrender, or be forced to stand guard and perform other military services in Cervera's fortress in peacetime. All of these friendly gestures, however, had not prevented the same Aragonese government, acting through Queen Maria, from approving the flagrant miscarriage of justice perpetrated on the Majorcan Jews in 1435. This affair began with a typical accusation that four Palma Jews, including their rabbi, had used a Muslim slave to imitate the passion of Christ. The ensuing prosecution soon became the subject of a major jurisdictional conflict between the royal and ecclesiastical authorities, quickly expanding into a threat of a wholesale massacre of Jews. It ended with the conversion of the entire Jewish community of some two hundred souls. Through Maria's approval and the closing of the local synagogue, the Majorcan community thus terminated its historic career some fifty-seven years before the rest of Spanish Jewry.[37]

Closely related to the Aragonese developments were those in fifteenth-century Navarre. In 1417 Charles III still evinced considerable interest in preserving Jewish self-government. He summoned a group of the most learned Jews of the realm to interpret for him the provisions of their law "according to the Talmud and the true intentions of their doctors." But after his death in 1425 Navarre came under the influence of Aragon first through John II, Charles' son-in-law, and later through Ferdinand the Catholic. In principle the old laws remained intact. But there was increasing emphasis on segregation. Princess Leonore, John's second daughter, ordered in 1469 that all Jews living in Pamplona be made to return to their quarter and to keep their houses there under good repair. A similar action was taken in 1488 by John de Labrit, the last Navarrese king, with respect to the Jews of Corella. These chicaneries were far overshadowed, moreover, by the country's general political instability and economic decline. The numerous losses sustained by the Jews through the severe pestilences, floods and other elementary catastrophes between 1410 and 1435 were never made up, particularly since many refugees had little incentive to return to their homes. Navarre Jewry was thus dying on its vine even before it was struck down by the formal decree of expulsion in 1498.[38]

CRISIS OF HOMOGENEITY AND CENTRALIZATION

Events in Majorca and Navarre adumbrated the great crisis of the age, which in both Castile and Aragon had, in part, arisen from the equivocal status of the *conversos*. The rich and complicated story of this large and influential mass of citizens, who precariously hovered between Judaism and Christianity, will be analyzed in another context. Suffice it to say here that the sudden appearance of perhaps 140,000 new converts in 1391 alone and their sharp numerical increase during the following quarter century injected unprecedented problems into the relations between the state and the Church and deeply colored the attitudes of both the public and the respective government agencies.

In time those *conversos* who secretly professed Judaism, and were derisively called "Marranos" by the populace, developed ever more refined techniques for hiding their true faith and in clandestinely observing at least some Jewish rituals. The Jewish communities, though on the whole rather averse to proselytizing among Gentiles, often aided and abetted such relapses into the ancestral faith. At first they tried to whisk away secret Jews to some Muslim country. Later, emigration became not only suspect and hence dangerous, but also less and less indispensable for carrying on the Marranos' newly adjusted mode of life. At the same time all *conversos*, whether genuine or not, were formally Christians and as such not subject to any disabilities affecting Jews. The highest honors were open to them and they could achieve positions of eminence even within the Church itself. Many joined the learned professions and penetrated the ranks of royal bureaucracy and city councils. As members of a secret society they also developed the usual feelings of solidarity and readiness for mutual aid which could but promote their careers. At the same time this very secrecy nurtured among their neighbors exaggerated suspicions, which found frequent expression in contemporary letters. Since satires were then extensively used for political purposes, quite a few poems of this genre were also aimed at the false New Christians. Of particular interest is a satire written in terms of a diploma allowing a true Christian to call himself a Marrano. In a more factual vein, the so-called "Green Book of Aragon" listed many prominent families of Jewish descent in the kingdom, in order to discredit them.[39]

Before long these accumulated hatreds began to be focused on this large, economically and politically powerful, and socially conspicuous class. As we shall see, demands were made ever more vociferously that these secret Jews be treated on a par with overt Jews, segregated from the Old Christians in separate quarters, distinguished by badges, and shut out of public offices and other economically profitable occupations. Of course, if seized and convicted of heresy the *conversos* were liable to be executed, while professing Jews were rarely molested on that score. Popular agitation rose to such a high pitch that by the middle of the century *anticonverso* feeling exceeded in sharpness that aimed at Jews. In 1449 a regular pogrom against *conversos* was staged in Toledo while the Jews remained unscathed. Begun as a revolt against a new war tax imposed by the hated Álvaro de Luna, this generally antiroyalist movement soon found a gifted leader in the commander of the fortress, Pedro (Pero) Sarmiento. Similar disturbances took place in neighboring Ciudad Real. As a result, the city of Toledo declared all *conversos* to be "of ill repute, unable, incapable, and unworthy" to hold public office or to serve as public notaries and witnesses. When news of these developments reached Rome, Pope Nicholas V immediately (September 24, 1449), protested against such discrimination. Contending that this agitation was likely "to undermine the salutary foundation of the unity and peace of our faith," the pope confirmed the older status, unequivocally declaring that *conversos* had the same rights to public office, ecclesiastical or secular, as Old Christians. Only those among them who proved unreliable in their faith were to be prosecuted by competent tribunals. Despite Sarmiento's flight to Aragon and his death within two years, the agitation continued in so vehement a fashion that in 1451 the pope, at the king's behest, felt obliged to issue another bull, appointing two high Spanish churchmen as inquisitors in charge of prosecuting and ferreting out all cases of dissimulation. But papal bulls and royal enactments proved ineffective either in reducing the popular animosity or in preventing the *converso* group from achieving influence and power wholly disproportionate to its numerical strength.[40]

At this point the couple who came to be known as the "Catholic kings" of Spain entered upon the arena of history. Isabella, Queen of Castile (1474–1504), had married, not without the cooperation of both *conversos* and professing Jews, Ferdinand who was to succeed John II as king of Aragon (1479–1516). Abraham Seneor, in particular, actively helped to arrange the secret meeting between the young couple, and was subsequently instrumental in placating the irate King Henry IV, who had had different plans for his sister. According to the chronicler, Alonso de Palencia, Abraham was rewarded by Isabella with an annual stipend of 100,000 maravedis. Rumors later circulating among the Spanish exiles explained this friendliness of Seneor, as well as of several highly placed Marranos, toward Ferdinand, by the latter's alleged Jewish ancestry. One such story reported by Elijah Capsali, placed in Isabella's mouth a reproach to her husband, "You have cause to love the Jews, for you are bone of their bone and flesh of their flesh. That is why the Jews have married me off to you, so that you may serve as their staunch supporter." We may wholly discount these legends, but there is no question that most Jewish leaders favored this marriage. The royal pair had still another reason to be grateful to Jews. Disregarding, as did their predecessors, the old canonical prohibition against using the services of Jewish physicians, they consulted a Jew, Lorenzo Badoç, in the hope of securing male progeny. We have the testimony of Ferdinand himself, who wrote to the physician: "The august Queen, Our consort, who for a number of years could not conceive, became pregnant through your praiseworthy ministrations by the will of God. She gave birth to Prince John, Our most beloved first-born." [41]

Nor was Jewish advice and financial assistance negligible in the Catholic monarchs' persistent efforts to unite the two large Spanish realms, to be joined not long thereafter by most sections of the kingdom of Navarre. Ferdinand and Isabella thus laid the foundation for a united Spain, which was to play a preeminent role in the history of Europe and the New World in the following two centuries. From the outset these capable rulers went about their task of unifying the country by reducing the unruly nobles and city councils to a position of impotence and by allying themselves with the Church, whose mainstay they and their descendants were to be in the approaching storms of the Reformation and the Catholic Restoration.

Jews were at first attracted to the energetic, purposeful couple. They anticipated that the new rulers would bring peace and stabilization to the deeply torn country and that under their powerful regime business, both domestic and international, would flourish, as indeed it did. Together with the rest of the population, they must have been tired of the anarchical conditions under Henry IV and hoped that the new sense of security would make possible the display of their commercial and fiscal talents to the mutual benefit of the Crown and themselves. It doubtless was more than a formality that on December 18, 1474, Isabella's accession to the throne of Castile was celebrated by the Jews of Ávila and other communities in a public festival with the display of scrolls of law, music, and benedictions. Despite their deep personal piety (Isabella especially always remained a preeminently Catholic monarch) the couple reciprocated by utilizing the energies of both the Jews and the *conversos* to their best advantage.[42]

Ferdinand and Isabella seemed, for a while, to fulfill the Jewish expectations. During the first years of their reign the monarchs had frequent occasion to protect Jewish rights. At the outset they ordered the authorities of Bilbao to revoke the ordinances issued against foreign Jews which made it impossible for some residents of other cities to pursue their accustomed trade of purchasing goods in Bilbao for resale in their own areas (March 12, 1475). Isabella was quite irate when she heard that in Trujillo Jews were forced by certain knights to clean their stables, collect the dung, and do other distasteful chores under the threat of maltreatment by ruffians placed in their houses. Having learned of these abuses from Salamon Romi, a representative of the Jewish community, Isabella issued a sharp order to the corregidor, alcaldes, and other justices of the city of Trujillo to stop these practices. In explanation she added:

Inasmuch as all the Jews of My kingdoms are Mine and are under My protection and shield and it appertains to Me to defend, protect, and maintain them in justice, I find it appropriate to order that this edict be issued to you for the said reason. Therefore I command you all and each one severally that from now on you should not consent and give room [to such abuses]. . . . For through this edict I take and receive the said *aljama* and all the good Jews, each one of them, together with all their property and possessions, under My royal safeguard and defense.

On other occasions Isabella, or Ferdinand, or both, insisted that Jews not be forced to stand guard, for instance, in the city of Ávila except together with the rest of the city, while at the same time Isabella confirmed the privileges of such communities as Huete and Alfara, where Jews did perform military services but were not supposed to share in the general taxes imposed upon their localities. This was indeed a frequent bone of controversy. While the cities tried to make the Jewish inhabitants participate in the heavy imposts levied on them by the governmental authorities, the Jews claimed that they were subject to special taxation allocated to each community by their own country-wide or regional organizations. In some cases special relief was granted to individual groups. The Crown favorably considered, in 1479, the petition of the Cáceres Jews who claimed that the tax load of their 130 families was as great as that of the 2,000 Christian families of the district.[43]

The royal pair was particularly insistent upon upholding the supremacy of the state. On learning in 1481 that the prior of the cathedral of Saragossa had issued anti-Jewish ordinances without previous royal approval, Ferdinand sharply censured the cleric and told the bailiff to suppress the ordinances. In 1485–86 the king and queen ordered a careful investigation of the Jewish community's complaints against the city of Burgos concerning unlawful limitations of Jewish residence rights and obstacles placed in the path of Jewish tailors and other artisans, as well as of Abraham Seneor's accusations that the Jews of his native Segovia felt threatened by incendiary speeches and were prevented from baking unleavened bread. In all such cases the monarchs sensed a threat to their major program aimed at suppressing the excessive jurisdictional rights of nobles and cities and establishing a nearly absolutist regime in the country. In 1476 they forbade one Diego Pizarro to assume the office of alcalde of Moors and Jews until a decision would be made by the Royal Council. In the same year they also forced the authorities of Monzón, Castrojeriz, and Carrión to fulfill their contracts with the Jews. More remarkably, despite their alliance with the Church they ordered the ecclesiastical judges of Osma in 1479 to suspend the bans they had issued against the debtors of Jews. They even tried to restrain their beloved "brotherhoods." When in that year the provincial deputy tried to impose upon the Jewish community of Ávila a double contribution for the hermandad, he was told by the President of the Royal Council, Don Lope de Ribas, that he must desist from this unlawful procedure.[44]

On the other hand, the Catholic monarchs frequently yielded to anti-Jewish demands of both the Cortes and the Church. Quite early in their career (1476) they approved the demands of the Cortes of Madrigal which restated with special sharpness the laws relating to the Jewish badge and the restrictions imposed upon Jewish usury. Cortes and monarchs also renewed the suspension of Jewish criminal jurisdiction first proclaimed in 1380 by earlier Cortes and King John I. For several years thereafter the courts

were kept busy with controversies arising particularly from the
Madrigal regulations relating to loans. At times Jews, too, invoked
these new formulations to good effect. For the most part, however, the Christian debtors were led to believe that the intent of
the legislators was to free them from all payments. Because of the
confusion generated by the new decrees, the Jewish moneylenders
of Ávila decided, so to say, to go on strike and refused to lend
money to anyone. This sudden stoppage of the flow of credit
quickly played havoc with much of the city's business and incon-
venienced many individuals in need of funds. Reports on the ensuing controversy with the municipal authorities reached the
Crown, which was particularly perturbed by the damage which
might arise therefrom for its own war against the king of Portugal,
and the development of its much-cherished *hermandades*. A decree
promulgated on December 15, 1477 merely prolonged the debate
and forced Isabella to issue still another decision on September 18,
1479, in which she restated at some length the opposing arguments
of the two sides. As a result, the opportunities for Jewish moneylenders were now sharply curtailed, and even a charge of 30 percent was considered exorbitant. In 1490 Ferdinand and Isabella
lent a willing ear to the complaints of the Cortes of Toledo, and
ordered that all Jews without exception be removed to separate
quarters within two years. More significantly, yielding to popular
clamor and the pressure of the Inquisition, they seemingly approved in 1483 a decree of expulsion of the Jews from the districts
of Seville and Cordova, and three years later set in motion a
similar expulsion from the archbishopric and city of Saragossa and
the bishopric of Albarracín. However, the latter decree apparently
was not implemented until the general expulsion of 1492.[45]

Disregarding the canonical prohibitions against entrusting Jews
with public office, the Catholic couple appointed many Jewish, as
well as Marrano, fiscal agents and tax farmers, who helped to raise
the royal revenues in an unprecedented degree. A Polish traveler,
Nicholas of Popielowo (in German, Nikolaus von Popplau), who
visited Spain in 1483–84, reported that he had heard the inhabitants of Catalonia and Aragon complain publicly

that the queen is a protector of Jews and the daughter of a Jewess [here
Nicholas doubtless confused the rumor about Ferdinand's Jewish descent with Isabella's ancestry]. Besides, I have observed with my own

eyes that she has more confidence in baptized Jews than in Christians. She entrusts to them all the revenues and imposts; they are her, as well as the king's, councilors and secretaries, which does not prevent them from hating their sovereigns rather than respecting them.

As late as 1491 Ferdinand and Isabella still concluded four-year contracts with Jewish tax farmers, either because they expected them to accept baptism and thus remain in service even after the expulsion, which they seemingly then had under advisement, or else in order to enrich themselves by confiscating the property of the "voluntarily" departing agents under the guise of merely collecting the latter's contractual obligations. Among these royal servants were some newcomers from other countries. Overshadowing them all in learning and financial as well as diplomatic skills was Don Isaac Abravanel, who, together with a nephew, had to leave his native Portugal after having become involved in an unsuccessful factional intrigue against the king. Don Isaac had probably succeeded in salvaging only a small portion of his capital, but in the eight years of his service for the Spanish Crown he amassed another large fortune. His departure in 1492 caused Ferdinand and Isabella to issue an order to the officials "of all cities, villages, and localities of all Our kingdoms and possessions" exempting for the state's benefit the claims left behind by Abravanel from the general suspension of payments of debts owed the Jewish exiles (October 6, 1492). When the Catholic monarchs organized the famous brotherhood, the *hermandad,* which became their fighting arm against all rebellious forces in the realm, they did not hesitate ultimately to appoint Don Abraham Seneor, their court rabbi, as its chief treasurer (1488). In his various fiscal capacities, Seneor and his associates helped provide the sinews of Spain's war against the remaining Muslim strongholds in Granada. Characteristically, the Jewish communities seem not to have strongly opposed the special taxes imposed upon them to finance that war against the remnant of Islam's ancient glory on the Peninsula, although the latter's territory had so long served as a haven of refuge for their coreligionists in despair and, even in 1492, may still have harbored some 20,000 Jews.[46]

Even more signal were the services rendered by some leading *conversos*; among them Gabriel Sanchez and Luis de Santangel, who were to achieve immortality through their role in promoting Columbus' expedition to the New World. However, while enjoying the cooperation of questionable Christians, Ferdinand and Isabella were determined to stamp out all heresies in the country. They were prompted to do so not only by their personal Catholic piety and their acceptance of the dictates of canon law, but also because they sought to submerge all existing regional and religious differences and to forge, in the crucible of domestic suppression and international expansion, the new, united Spanish nation. They evinced particular impatience with the ambiguous position and the ever suspect behavior of many *consersos*. They believed that a stronger surveillance would eradicate the recalcitrant minority of secret Jews and absorb the rest in the large body of Old Christians. For this purpose they persuaded Pope Sixtus IV in 1478 to establish the new centralized Inquisition, which was to pursue this task more efficiently than the inquisitorial courts theretofore attached to each episcopal see. At first the new tribunals were established only in the province of Andalusia, where from time immemorial Jewish, and now also *conserso*, communities had played a distinctive role. From there the Inquisition spread to the other provinces of Castile and soon also to Aragon. Under the leadership of the fanatical Dominican Tómas Torquemada it was to write some of the most sanguinary chapters in the history of human intolerance.[47]

It did not take long for the inquisitors, as well as the monarchs, to realize that the extirpation of the Judaizing heresy was greatly hampered by the presence of Jewish communities in the country. So long as professing Jews publicly performed their rites, congregated in their synagogues, and cultivated their Judaic lore, it was not difficult, though risky, for their Marrano neighbors to secure from them important implements of worship, instruction on questionable points of law and religion, and general guidance as to how to meet the minimum requirements of clandestine Jewish observance. Moreover, as we shall see in a broader context, the very presence of a rather large and culturally influential Jewish group was felt by some Spaniards to be an obstacle to that national unification which now became the overpowering goal of both the monarchs and forward-looking patriots. Little did the Jews realize that, by helping to reestablish order and unity in the faction-riven Peninsular society, they were undermining the very foundations of their continued existence in Spain. Together with other factors, religious, economic, and political, this drive for unity led to the decree of expulsion proclaimed by Ferdinand and Isabella within four weeks (March 31, 1492) after their conquest of Granada on March 4. Ostensibly, the Crown proceeded humanely, from the standpoint of contemporary practices, and allowed the would-be exiles "to sell, exchange, or transfer" all their movable and immovable possessions and freely to dispose of them as they wished. But it did not protest when, within less than a month, the Inquisition sabotaged this permission by threatening with excommunication Christian purchasers of such property.[48]

The expulsion of this large and influential group of the population made a tremendous impression in Spain and abroad, especially in countries which soon began receiving waves of penniless, harassed, and yet often welcome refugees. The Marranos who remained in the country continued to occupy many minds and to arouse much suspicion for generations to come in Spain, and much longer in Portugal. Some dramatic incidents from the preexpulsion era, and particularly the alleged martyrdom of the La Guardia infant, were frequently dramatized. The permanent Jewish heritage in the physiognomy and thinking of Spain have even longer been the subject of heated debates. The differing evaluations of the role played by Jewry in the rise and decline of modern Spain contributed greatly to the new liberal economic theories in eighteenth-century Holland, as well as to the early postemancipatory antisemitic formulations of Christian Friedrich Rühs, a professor of history in post-Napoleonic Berlin. Nor has the problem lost its actuality today. According to one recent anthropological investigation, 15 percent of the population of Valladolid still reveal typically Jewish features—whatever this may mean—as against 65 percent of those physiognomically belonging to the Mediterranean race and some 15 percent betraying their Teuton origin. The situation in Valladolid is probably typical of conditions in most other Spanish regions as well, although the underlying racial assumptions are clearly hypothetical. The permanent impact of the Jewish cultural heritage on the subsequent destinies of the Spanish people has likewise been extensively discussed in recent years, particularly in the wake of theories advanced by Américo Castro. To some extent the pros and cons of similar earlier debates have had some effect even on Spanish policies and legislation in the nineteenth and twentieth centuries.[49]

PORTUGUESE FINALE

Because of the close interrelations between the two countries, Spain's domestic relations and particularly its attitude toward Jews had frequent repercussions in Portugal. Although the battle of Aljubarrota of 1385 had, not without Jewish cooperation, brought John I to the throne and definitely established Portugal's independence, the commercial and intellectual relations with neighboring Castile remained close even when the two regimes pursued opposing international policies. There also was a constant movement of Jewish residents from one country to the other. In periods of stress, in particular, such as followed the massacres of 1391 in Spain, many refugees settled in Portugal. They were followed by a considerable number of *conversos*, who, after accepting baptism in Castile or Aragon, voluntarily or under duress, regretted their apostasy from their ancestral faith and looked for a neighboring country which would tolerate their return to Judaism. Next to Muslim lands, Portugal proved to be their most important haven of refuge.

Among the new arrivals from Castile was Samuel Abravanel of Seville who, though a leading member of the Jewish community, seems to have yielded to the pressures generated by Ferrant Martinez' rousing sermons and submitted to baptism, perhaps before 1388. Under his new name of Juan Sanchez, he served as the royal treasurer of Andalusia and chief paymaster (*contador mayor)* of Castile. He also played a considerable political role. However, sometime after 1397, whether stricken by remorse or for some other reason, he emigrated to Lisbon where he overtly rejoined the Jewish community. Even more prominent was his son, Don Yehudah Abravanel, who entertained particularly close relations with John I's younger son, Ferdinand. In 1437, before departing on his ill-fated expedition to North Africa where he was to die in captivity six years later, Ferdinand ordered in his will the payment of a large sum (52,000 and 45,000 reis blancos) which he owed Don Yehudah. The Infante, later celebrated as both martyr and soldier, was also indebted to many other Portuguese Jews, and while in captivity he used a Jewish surgeon, Magister Joseph, to transmit letters from Fez to Portugal. The House of Abravanel reached the heights of its Portuguese achievements in Yehudah's son, Don Isaac, who, in contrast to his grandfather, staunchly adhered to his faith during the great crisis of the Spanish exile. He had come to Spain in 1481 because, upon Alphonso V's demise, he was accused by the new king John II of having participated in the conspiracy hatched by John's relative, the Duke of Braganza. In his immediate autobiographical record, inserted into the Preface to his Commentary on Joshua, Don Isaac graphically described how he had been prepared to follow the king's summons when he suddenly was warned by a friend that, like the duke, he was in peril of immediate execution. He succeeded in evading the pursuers dispatched after him by the king, and he crossed the Castilian frontier. Here he devoted himself for a while to his exegetical work, including the Joshua commentary. Another arrival from Portugal was the aforementioned Vidal Astori, whom Ferdinand appointed chief rabbi of many Castilian communities only to revoke that order in 1477 because of Seneor's prior claims. Astori, who as early as 1467–69 had served as silversmith (*argenter*) to the then Infante Ferdinand, may in some way have become involved in Portuguese politics, because in 1484 the Catholic monarchs had to extend to him special protection against his personal enemies. On the other hand, Castilian Jews often served as diplomatic intermediaries in negotiations with the Portuguese Court. We remember Samuel ha-Levi's effective negotiations in Lisbon in 1358, which led to the conclusion of a peace and friendship treaty between the two countries. Almost a century later it was the turn of Rabbi Joseph (ibn Shem Ṭob) to be dispatched by Infante Henry to negotiate a marriage agreement with a Portuguese princess. This compact was soon replaced by another, and finally resulted in a wedding in May 1455.[50]

As in fifteenth-century Spain, there was a persistent agitation to segregate Jews in separate quarters and in a lesser degree to force them to wear badges. The latter provision was often observed in its breach, however. The Cortes, as well as some Jewish moralists, frequently complained of the display of luxuries by rich Jews whom they accused of riding on mules, with both rider and animal attired in costly garments, and of displaying expensive jewelry, while the masses of the population suffered from starvation. A most graphic description of this "conspicuous consumption" was offered by the Cortes of 1481–82 at the height of the anti-Jewish propaganda:

We speak thus, Sire, because we see the horrible dissoluteness that is rife among the Jews, Moors, and Christians, in their style of living and in their dress, while in their manners and conversation are seen things repugnant and abominable. We see Jews made knights, mounted on richly caparisoned horses and mules, and clothed in fine gowns and hoods, silken doublets, gilt swords, and masks and turbans, so that it is impossible to know what race they belong to. They enter the churches and scoff at the Holy Sacrament, mixing criminally with the Christians.

The Cortes attributed this effrontery to the Jews holding high positions as tax farmers. They further complained that many visiting Jewish craftsmen entertained illicit relations with wives of peasants while the latter worked in the fields. At times the kings yielded to these demands and, apart from enjoining the Jews to display the prescribed distinguishing marks (some Portuguese peculiarities in this matter will be discussed in another context), ordered them to wear only wool, rather than silk, garments and forbade them to place tufts on the heads of their mules, which was also prohibited to Christians.[51]

Separate Jewish quarters became a major public issue from 1361 on, even before they became the subject of violent anti-Jewish agitation in neighboring Spain. Their legal enforcement was often Draconian. According to an ordinance issued by King Pedro the Severe, any Jew found outside the *judaría* after the first three clangs of the bell was to be flogged on the city's streets; in repeat cases the culprit's entire property was to be confiscated. On the concerted petition of the Jewish communities, John I modified these drastic penalties. In 1412 he provided that thenceforth every Jew aged fifteen or more found outside the *judaría* after the given signal was to be fined 5,000 livres; he was to pay 10,000 livres when apprehended for the second time, and to be flogged on the third occurrence. If these penalties still were exceptionally severe, their edge was considerably blunted by the numerous exceptions stated in the ordinance. There also were exceptions made in favor of certain individuals such as a Rabbi Cad and his wife, of Elvas, who were specifically allowed "to live and dwell outside the Jewish quarter among the Christians" (November 25, 1451). The fervor of this segregationist propaganda was, in part, nurtured from the legislators' genuine concern about mixed sex relations. More consistently than elsewhere, they forbade Christian women to visit Jewish quarters unless accompanied by Christian men. They also prohibited Jewish peddlers and traders from entering peasant houses while the husbands worked in the fields. Exceptions were stated, however, in favor of Jewish physicians, craftsmen, and other indispensable visitors, revealing how integrated the Jews had become into the fabric of Portuguese society not only in the cities but also among farmers. If, on the other hand, on May 24, 1451, Alphonso (Affonso) V permitted the Jews of Lamego to consume "Christian" wine without the penalties theretofore exacted for such a "transgression," he may have had the rabbinic efforts to outlaw "wine of libation" as much in mind as any state regulation.[52]

Actual integration came to the fore also in all phases of cultural and economic life. Jews actively participated in the progress of science and exploration. Among the major events of the 1420s, observes Charles E. Nowell, was "the arrival in Portugal of Jafuda Cresques, a renowned cartographer from the island of Majorca." Jewish sailors are said to have participated in 1415 in the Portuguese conquest of Moroccan Ceuta, a key harbor for the further penetration of the west coast of Africa; one of them reputedly fell in battle. Little did they know that, before long, the king would develop an interest in lions brought from his new possession and that the Lisbon Jews would be called upon to take care of these animals. Only in 1450 was this obligation commuted into a daily tax of 25 reis per head. In some areas, such as the newly invented art of printing, Jews were the leading pioneers. The first Hebrew book printed in Portugal appeared in 1489, to be followed by the first Latin book in 1494 and the first Portuguese work in 1495. Although the "expulsion" of 1496 put an end to Hebrew printing, almost one-half of all known Portuguese incunabula (11 of 24) are Hebrew. Several more may have been published in Portugal, for a number of incunabula of Iberian provenance cannot be attributed to any specific locality.[53]

Portugal's leading role in international commerce, stimulated by the great discoveries and scientific advances made under the sponsorship of its famed Prince Henry the Navigator, produced ever sharper economic rivalries between the rising bourgeoisie and the wealthy Jewish merchants and financiers. Even churchmen now used the economic lingo together with their accustomed religious arguments. In a remarkable memorandum, addressed to Alphonso V by a monk of São Marcos who apparently had the king's ear, great emphasis is laid upon these competitive aspects:

Now, Sire [the friar wrote], in its [the Crown's] desire to obtain a larger income, the Christian population is subjected to the jurisdiction of Jews, while strangers to the country are carrying off most of the commodities of your kingdom, and the native merchants are perishing of want. For this state of affairs I would that your Majesty might find a remedy, as so often you have been requested to do; for it would be more honor and profit to you if your fellow countrymen were rich than for foreigners to be, for they bring loss and not gain to the country.

Although Alphonso V was on the whole favorably inclined toward Jews, he had to yield some ground to the aroused public opinion. In 1449 the authorities suppressed with great difficulty an incipient anti-Jewish riot in the capital during the king's absence in Évora. Hastening back to Lisbon, in order to prevent an even more serious outbreak, Alphonso ordered the imprisonment of ringleaders. The police, facing the usual difficulties of identifying assailants after the event, may have incarcerated some innocent persons, one of them actually pleading that he had aided the Jews, all of which merely increased popular hostility, now directed also against the royal power.[54]

Economic appetites also were behind the clamorous demands of the Cortes, whether they voiced old or new arguments, and called for the enforcement of existing or the introduction of novel restrictions. These parliamentary debates on the Jewish question swelled into a regular chorus in the second half of the fifteenth century. In quick succession the Cortes of Santarém complained in 1451 of Jews wearing silk garments; in 1455 the Cortes meeting in Lisbon accused the Jews of riding on mules on Sundays; in 1461 those of Cintra demanded that Jews should not be allowed to sell merchandise to Christian customers on Sundays and Christian holidays until after the completion of church services; in 1473 those of Coimbra clamored against Jews being allowed to farm ecclesiastical revenues and demanded that the right of asylum extended by churches be granted only to converts, not to professing Jews. More significantly, the latter Cortes also insisted that the rabbis exercise civil jurisdiction only in purely Jewish litigations, whereas Judeo-Christian controversies even if involving a Jewish defendant be submitted exclusively to Christian judges. In 1475 the representatives of the Estates demanded outright that in all civil litigations with Jews Christian plaintiffs or defendants be given a favored status. How strong the anti-Jewish feelings ran among these influential spokesmen may be seen in the decision of the Cortes of Lisbon in 1460. While voting a substantial voluntary contribution of 15,000 gold doubloons to the Treasury, the Cortes insisted that neither Jews nor Moors be allowed to participate in that impost. Their intention doubtless was to prove to the king that, from the standpoint of the country's fiscal needs, these minorities were expendable. Yielding to these popular pressures, Alphonso V renewed many older anti-Jewish provisions and included them in his *Ordenaçoens*.[55]

At variance, however, with both Castile and Aragon, fifteenth-century Portugal was not plagued by the complex *converso* problems. Not having suffered from mass assaults, intensive propaganda, and sharply discriminatory legislation as did their Spanish coreligionists in 1391–1415, the Portuguese Jews had but a more or less normal quota of apostates. Conversions were frequent enough for the Beja custumal to provide that "he who calls a convert from another religion to Christianity a *tornadisso* [turncoat] shall pay the alcalde 60 solidi." This provision was subsequently amplified by John I to include the prohibition against calling a convert "Jew," under the penalty of 30 corvas to be paid to the informer. Such sporadic baptisms, whether undergone for worldly reasons, under moderate duress, or out of genuine conviction, usually led to the speedy amalgamation of the new converts and their offspring with Christian society. Portugal faced, therefore, only such derivative complications as arose after 1391, when some Spanish converts, who had escaped the hands of pogromists, wished to return to the old faith and settled on its more hospitable soil. But this crisis was overcome after a few years, and the newcomers were rather effectively absorbed by the existing community. In the subsequent decades only relatively few relapsing Castilian or Aragonese converts sought shelter behind the anonymity granted them by resettlement in Portugal. So long as this movement was limited to a few individuals, it created few difficulties. After the establishment from 1478 on of the Inquisition in Andalusia and the other Spanish provinces, however, the number of its prospective victims, and hence also that of émigrés to Portugal, increased rapidly. This mass influx of *conversos* and, after 1492, the even greater immigration of professing Jews from the Catholic regime of Ferdinand and Isabella, injected into Portuguese society, too, new complicating factors.[56]

Characteristically, the law provided that insults against converts be adjudicated by a secular, rather than an ecclesiastical judge. Evidently, the clergy could not be fully trusted with the prosecution of defendants motivated by an excess of Catholic zeal. On the other hand, Jewish communal leadership secured from John an important regulation safeguarding Jewish wives of converts against blackmail. The law provided that if a wife refused to follow her husband to the baptismal font, she had to be handed a writ of divorce immediately so that she would be free to remarry. This provision was somewhat weakened by Alphonso V, who delayed the enforcement of such divorces for a year after the husband's conversion, in order to test the wife's determination to remain Jewish. At the same time, following the Church's demands, the law insisted that converts not be deprived of their property or even their inheritance rights. An attempt was even made to secure for them the immediate payment of their share in the prospective estates while the parents were still alive. But this provision was hardly ever fully carried into effect.[57]

Upon ascending the throne, John II (1481–95), "doubtless the ablest king ever to rule Portugal" (Charles E. Nowell), resisted fiercely the pressures of both the Cortes and his own councilors to alter the royal policies in the light of the intervening establishment of the Spanish Inquisition and the subsequent expulsion of the Jews from Spain. This firmness is doubly remarkable, as he was of a rather unfriendly disposition and might have generalized Don Isaac Abravanel's "treasonable" activities by condemning all Jews. Yet he refused point blank the Cortes' demand that he replace Jewish by Christian tax farmers. He pointed out that that occupation had been in Jewish hands for many generations and that whenever Christian tax farmers had been used, they insisted on such enormous profits that little was left for the Crown. The king yielded, however, sufficiently to extend the existing prohibition against employing Jews in public office to include their services as higher officials on the estates of the royal family or the barons.[58]

After 1492, John was under tremendous pressure to close the frontiers to both Jews and *conversos* arriving from Spain. But he reached an agreement with the Portuguese communities whereby the Jewish exiles were to be admitted at five designated frontier posts (Olivenza, Arronches, Castelo-Rodrigo, Braganza, and Melgaço) for the payment of an entry fee, variously reported as one cruzado to eight escudos in gold per capita. Such permits, however, entitled the visitors only to a sojourn of eight months, after which period they were to leave at their own expense on ships provided by the government. Only 600 rich families were admitted to permanent residence after paying the huge amount of 60,000 cruzados. Illegal immigrants, on the other hand, were to be sold into slavery. In fact, many of those who smuggled themselves through the extended frontier were robbed or killed by the peasants. In all these matters the king acted against the advice of most of his councilors, some of whom argued that a Christian regime should not offer the Spanish Jews the alternative of emigrating, rather than of adopting Christianity in their own country. The public at large was even more antagonistic toward that mass influx.[59]

Such resentments made themselves doubly felt after John II's death and the assumption of the throne by his cousin Emanuel (1495–1521). Although the new king's first act was to liberate the Jewish slaves, he yielded to the combined pressures of the local population and of the Catholic monarchs of Spain. The Spanish princess, Doña Isabella, actually consented to marry Emanuel only under the condition that all *converso* fugitives from the Inquisition be expelled within a month. In December 1496, even before the formal marriage contract was signed in August 1497, Emanuel grudgingly consented to issue a decree of expulsion of all Jews. But rather than allow them to leave the country some eight months later, as was promised them in the decree, he forced nearly all of them to submit to baptism.[60]

INEXHAUSTIBLE VITALITY

In this fashion the long and glorious career of Jews on the Iberian Peninsula apparently drew to an end. Having survived an antagonistic Christian Roman Empire, having come to grips with an extremely intolerant Visigothic regime, Spanish Jewry not only survived the tremendous onslaughts which would have destroyed many a less persistent group of people, but soon thereafter it reached unprecedented heights of achievement in its Golden Age under the rule of Islam. When this period ended in another wave of total intolerance under the Almohades, the Jewish communities bent their heads in silence and awaited the great change which was bound to come. It did come in the shape of the *Reconquista* by the Christian Crusaders who, instead of bringing with them the accustomed fire and sword of religious intolerance, opened up new opportunities for Jewish religious and communal self-assertion. Even Granada, Islam's remaining outpost on the Peninsula, gave up its exclusivist policies and became a stronghold of heterogeneity adjacent to the growingly homogeneous Spanish and Portuguese realms. It not only harbored a substantial residue of the old Arabic-speaking Jewry, but it also kept its gates open to many Jewish expatriates escaping the discrimination against their faith in the neighboring Christian lands.

Before 1391, however, one might have questioned the survivalist power of the Spanish and Portuguese Jews. So integrated did the Jewish community become in its Spanish environment, that for centuries thereafter its descendants were using their Castilian dialect even while living for many generations in foreign lands. A rabbi like Santob de Carrión could produce Hebrew books, but in his *Proverbios morales* he could significantly contribute to four-teenth-century Spanish belles-lettres. With the spread of Aver-roism and other radical interpretations of philosophy and religion, there was indeed a danger that, as a result of its peaceful amalgamation with the Spanish majority, the Jewish people would vanish or at least dissolve into warring camps.[61]

This process was rudely interrupted by the massacres of 1391. Now the real menace was that, because of the severe blood-letting by pogromists, the conversion of large segments of survivors and the mass emigration of others, few Jews would remain in Castile and Aragon to carry on their traditional mode of living. Assimila-tory pressures were even more irresistible. Behind them was arrayed the whole power of government and Church, which, through legislative discrimination and disputatory suasion, tried to sway the remnant to give up its struggle for survival. It is, in-deed, a testimony to the tremendous vitality of Spanish Jewry that while suffering from these external and internal forces of disinte-gration it gradually rebuilt its shattered communal ruins and em-barked upon a new historic career of high attainment.

The fifteenth century, which had started with the aftermath of the massacres of 1391, a sharply antagonistic legislation, and the spectacular disputation of Tortosa, nevertheless witnessed the resurgence of many old and the growth of some newer communi-ties whose leaders often played a significant role in the economic and political affairs of their countries. Intellectually, too, though failing to produce the great leaders of Jewish thought of the earlier centuries, the Spanish remnant embraced a considerable number of jurists, mystics, and poets who stand comparison with their compeers of other lands. At the same time their cultural integration into the Spanish environment continued unabated. Precisely those forces which were shaping the destinies of Spain's national unification, its progression to the position of a leading world power, and the cultural richness of its *siglo d'oro*, also operated to undermine the internal Jewish cohesiveness and to re-inforce the trends toward the final elimination of Jews by royal fiat.

However, such vitality withstood even this heaviest of blows. As it turned out, the events of 1492–98 marked for neither Spain nor Portugal and still less for the Iberian Jewish people a final chapter in the long history of Judeo-Christian symbiosis. As we shall see, Spain and even more so Portugal were to wrestle with the problem of the surviving *converso* minority for generations thereafter. On the other hand, the Jewish and Marrano dispersions, while still carrying the torch of their Iberian heritage, were to inject a powerful ferment into many West-European and Mid-Eastern societies. They simultaneously penetrated also the vast expanses of the newly discovered Western Hemisphere. Like some other great migratory movements, this almost world-wide dispersal of descendants of the Spanish-Portuguese refugees became, in the long run, a major vehicle of progress in the history of European and Jewish civilization.

XLVI

ITALIAN POTPOURRI

P RACTICALLY all trends shaping the political and legal evolution of medieval Jewry, which have been described in the
preceding chapters, were reflected in Italy. Medieval Italy
was not really a country but a conglomeration of principalities,
republics, and free cities, each of which pursued a distinct policy,
had a different constitutional structure, and treated Jews from the
standpoint of its own needs and ideas. Discussing the conditions in
the early twentieth century, Giuseppe Prezzolini observed:

It is Europe that one finds in the valley of the Po, and, to all intents
and purposes, Africa in Sicily. For the last seven centuries the history
of Italy has been that of Lombardy, Tuscany, Venice and the South.
It has been that of France, Germany and Austria rather than that of
Italy herself. Italy has a dozen capitals, some of which have had closer
connections with foreign countries than with other Italian centers.[1]

In short, the Apennine Peninsula and its adjacent islands resembled a United Nations rather than a single country. That some of
these states developed into leading economic and cultural powers
whose influence was felt far and wide, underscored this uniqueness
of the Italian people.

Foremost among these Italian sovereignties were the Papal
States, themselves a combination of diverse Italian and French
possessions, the boundaries of which were often fluid and ill-
defined. Papal overlordship made itself felt in different degrees
among the neighboring localities, some of which like Ferrara were
later reincorporated into the States of the Church. Apart from its
territorial claims the Papacy exercised great political and cultural
influence on all of Italy; as a most peculiarly Italian institution it
vitally contributed to the development of Italian culture. At the
same time its international character made its outlook and influence reach out to the extreme ends of Christendom. In the Jewish
question, particularly, which was in essence an international
religiously colored problem, all of Christendom followed the

Papacy's lead in one form or another. As in the earlier Middle Ages, the international Church and interterritorial Jewry were locked in their perennial dialogue without ever resolving the existing differences between them but also without ever completely severing their powerful links. Not by accident, among all major medieval Jewish communities it was only that of Rome which at no time suffered from total exclusion.

Quite different was the situation south of the Papal States, particularly in the so-called Two Sicilies. During the late Middle Ages this largest and most populous Italian state had come under the sway of Hohenstaufen, Angevin, and Aragonese dynasts. Alphonso V the Magnanimous of Aragon actually spent more time in Naples and Palermo than in Barcelona and Saragossa. Yet quite apart from the hegemony of Spanish military and naval power, the southern Italians shared with the Iberians the fruits of a splendid Roman-Byzantine and Saracen heritage. Sicily in particular long embraced, in addition to Moors and Jews, a substantial Greek-speaking population. While wave after wave of immigrants from the Italian mainland gradually lent it a preeminently Italian character, it still retained many peculiarities of its own, among them its different attitude to the Jewish question from that regnant in either Rome or the North-Italian commonwealths. Here, as well as in Naples, Calabria, and Apulia, the Jewish communities were able to maintain their unbroken historic continuity from the earlier Middle Ages.

In contrast, in northern Italy, which soon assumed the political, economic, and cultural hegemony over the entire Peninsula, the Jews' position was often quite precarious. From some areas they were permanently locked out. To many others they were admitted under specific treaties of limited duration, renewable only by mutual consent. Despite their geographic proximity, such extraordinary city-states as Florence and Genoa pursued widely divergent policies with respect to the toleration of Jews. The difference between Piedmont (soon permanently associated with Savoy) and Venice in the treatment of Jews was as great and ramified as was that of their general sociopolitical structures. The Venetian regime, moreover, had to consider the interests of its numerous colonies in the eastern Mediterranean, the population of which,

exceeding in size that of the mother city, embraced substantial segments of Jews, recruited from Aegean and Balkan natives as well
as from Italian, Spanish, and northern immigrants.

It would be futile, therefore, to look for simple generalizations
concerning the historic evolution of late medieval Italian Jewry.
While the south largely followed the example set by the Iberian
Peninsula, the north strongly felt the impact of the Holy Roman
Empire and France. Central Italy, too, was open to constant foreign penetration, both warlike and pacific. Yet, because of the
papal regime it succeeded in preserving much of its ancient
Roman heritage. Even Roman law, however modified by canon
law, still played a preeminent role in shaping the status of its Jewish as well as non-Jewish subjects.

SOUTHERN ITALY

More than any other Italian region, that of Naples and Sicily,
together with their adjoining outposts in Malta, Gozo, and
Pantelleria (often joined also by the island of Sardinia), was more
or less under permanent foreign domination. When, after the
death of Emperor Frederick II (I in southern Italy, 1197–1250),
the regime of the Hohenstaufen gradually gave way in 1263–65 to
the Angevin dynasty under Charles I (1266–85), the influence of
imperial Germany was replaced by that emanating from southern
France. After the "Sicilian Vespers" of 1282, however, the
Angevins lost Sicily to the Aragonese while retaining control over
the mainland kingdom of Naples. The original Angevin line of
Charles II (1288–1309), Robert the Wise (1309–1343), and
Joanna I (1343–82) was succeeded in 1382 by rulers from another
branch, previously established in Hungary: Charles III of Durazzo
(1382–86), Ladislaus of Hungary (1386–1414), and Joanna II
(1414–35). Among the outstanding Aragonese rulers of Sicily
were Frederick III (really II in Sicily, 1295–1337), Frederick IV
(III, 1355–77), and Martin V (I in Aragon, 1392–1409). As in
Aragon proper, the rule shifted in 1412 to Ferdinand I, originally
of Castile, who was followed by Alphonso V the Magnanimous
(1416–58). Under that king's regime, Naples was temporarily reunified in 1442 with Sicily and Sardinia. However, after Al-

phonso's death in 1458 the kingdom was split again between his sons, John II, who ruled over Aragon, Sicily, and Sardinia (1458–79) and Ferrante (Ferdinand I), king of Naples (1458–94). Before long, however, Ferdinand II the Catholic, who had ruled Sicly as coregent since 1468 and wholly succeeded John in 1479, took over Naples as well in 1502. Through his marriage to Isabella and his conquest of Spanish Navarre in 1512, his realm extended over all of Spain and southern Italy during the last years of his life (he died in 1516), and Spanish connections continued to dominate the entire area during the following two centuries.

Southern Italian Jewry, too, was drawn into these imperialist clashes, and its status was affected as much by the institutional forms and attitudes imported by foreign rulers as by the local evolution. Only the deep-rooted respect for local customs prevailing throughout the Middle Ages preserved it from undergoing more radical changes. On the whole, Sicilian, Sardinian, and to a lesser extent Neapolitan, Jewry led a relatively prosperous life during the last three medieval centuries. While suffering from wars and invasions and having carefully to steer clear of entanglements with the various political factions, the Jewish communities maintained their autonomous structure and greatly contributed to that region's industrial and agricultural economy, even more than to commerce and banking. However, here, too, the antagonistic trends manifest all over western Europe during the fifteenth century made themselves increasingly felt.[2]

Subject to the usual vagaries and inconsistencies of medieval administrations, the Norman and Hohenstaufen policies were generally continued under the Angevin and Aragonese regimes, although Emperor Frederick II's program of transforming southern Italy into a model state with an advanced economy and an effective military and bureaucratic organization could not be sustained. The emperor had used the Jews in expanding the agricultural and industrial production and in running some of the newly established government monopolies of dyeing and silk manufacture. As "serfs" of the Chamber (Frederick's own coinage) they were also to supply the Treasury with some financial means for maintaining his growing military establishment and centralized bureaucracy. Their intellectual leaders finally were to help the enlightened emperor, whose own vast learning was greatly admired by contemporaries, to acquire for his country the fruits of the advanced Muslim civilization, principally by translating major Arabic works into Hebrew and thence into Latin. At the same time the presence of strong Saracen and Greek-speaking minorities removed from the Jews the stigma of being the only "infidel" and "alien" group in an otherwise homogeneous population.[3]

In the early years of his regime, to be sure, Frederick followed the dictates of the Church. In 1221 he fulfilled the demand of the Fourth Lateran Council and ordered Jews to wear distinguishing marks under the drastic sanction of confiscating any culprit's property, or in the case of impoverished transgressors of branding them on their foreheads. He also continued to endow churches with royal largesse, often transferring to them the control over Jewish revenue, or at least renewing privileges to this effect enacted by his predecessors (Cosenza, 1212; Salerno, 1221; Rossano, 1223).[4]

As his relations with the Papacy deteriorated and as his fiscal needs steadily grew, Frederick began exploiting the country's resources more intensively, in defiance of the vested interests of barons and churchmen. He subjected the very clerics to the jurisdiction of royal judges, characteristically threatening with the confiscation of property all those "who in the contempt of Our jurisdiction would repair to a court other than those appertaining to Our *curia.*" In his aforementioned Constitution of Melfi of 1231 he not only extended protection to Jews and Saracens, but he entirely omitted the provision relating to badges. By emphasizing that canon law prohibited usury only among Christians—a prohibition violated by himself when he borrowed heavily from Christian creditors at high interest rates—he allowed the Jews to extend loans provided they charged no more than 10 percent per annum. The more effectively to enforce public order, he imposed upon any locality failing to apprehend a murderer a uniform fine of 100 augustals if the victim was Christian, and of 50 augustals if he was a Jew or a Saracen. Frederick also tried very hard to attract foreigners to settle in his realm, with the only difference that Christian arrivals were to be free from taxation for a period of ten years, while Jews had to start paying taxes immediately. This regulation may have been enacted, however, at the instigation of Jewish leaders who, in accordance with rabbinic law, wished to see newcomers participate after a brief sojourn in all communal burdens, including the community's part in government imposts. In Palermo, whose municipal prerogatives over Jews he himself had expressly confirmed, the emperor ordered the city to admit some African Jewish immigrants and to set aside a new quarter for them so that they might develop the cultivation of dates. He merely added, "We do not consider it expedient at present to permit them the construction of a new house of worship, but they should be allowed, if they so desire, to rebuild some old, vacant synagogue." [5]

It is small wonder, then, that under Frederick's protective, though despotic, regime southern Italian Jewry increased in number and affluence. It also successfully weathered the storms following the emperor's death in 1250 and the subsequent struggles for succession. Utilizing the demise of its sworn enemy, the Papacy contested the succession of Frederick's heirs, treated the country as if it were Rome's vassal state, and plunged it into a succession of wars which ended only after thirteen years with a transfer, by the pope, of the sovereignty to Charles I of Anjou. As early as 1254, the apostolic vicar general in Sicily transferred to the church of Girgenti (Agrigento) all revenue from Jews and (doubtless related with it) from the local dyeing plant, in order to augment the income of the church, "of which the former Emperor Frederick had despoiled it." In the following year, on the other hand, Pope Alexander IV granted to five Jewish merchants, styled *cives Romani,* and their associates immunity from Sicilian road taxes. To be sure, according to certain traditions preserved by Samuel Usque, followed by Joseph ha-Kohen and Solomon ibn Verga, there were widespread persecutions and forced conversions of Jews about 1240. According to one version, Frederick II's testamentary injunction to his son to treat Jews well and to repay them all outstanding loans led the son to believe that the best service he could render them was to make them Christians. Another report has it that a priest purposely disfigured a crucifix in order to place the blame on Jews, whereupon the aroused populace forced the latter either to accept baptism or to perish. Both these reports doubtless reflect but a garbled recollection of what actually happened a few decades later, Ibn Verga in fact synchronizing these events with the expulsion of the Jews from England in 1290.[6]

When Charles I of Anjou seized the reins of government in 1263 (he did not begin effectively to rule until three years later), Jews undoubtedly suffered, along with the rest of the population, from the ruthless fiscal exactions and tyrannical behavior of French officials and soldiers, but nothing untoward happened, as far as the records go, to curtail their basic rights. True, dependent as his regime was on the Church's good will, Charles had to make the usual concessions. In 1267 he assigned to the convert, Manoforte of Trani, an annual stipend of six gold ounces not only because "he firmly persists" in his new faith, but also because "he tries by his preachment and exhortation to bring also other Jews back to the way of truth." Three years later, at the denunciation of Manoforte, now designated as "formerly a teacher of the Jewish synagogue," the king ordered the seizure of Hebrew books, including the Talmud, "carrboct" (qerobot, or certain prayers for holidays), and the Hebrew prayerbook, all of which allegedly contained blasphemies against Jesus and Mary. These books were to be delivered to the royal court. Probably the entire proceedings ended with a handsome gift from the Jewish communities, and we hear no more of that affair. On the other hand, Charles' greed and dire need of funds (in 1268 he had to pawn his gold crown with its jewels for a loan of 1,040 gold ounces from a Sienese Christian banker, Niccolò Orlandini) made him often go against the wishes of the Church. Just as in Anjou he had freed his Jewish subjects in 1273 from their obligation to wear badges in return for an annual tax, he sharply censured the archbishops of Trani and Bari in that year for trying to extort from their Jews more than the customary revenue by imprisoning Jewish leaders and by keeping those in Bari on a diet of bread and water. With equal vehemence he outlawed in 1269 forced conversions even of his Saracen subjects, who, because they had aided the Hohenstaufen in their last struggles, appeared as legitimate prey for missionaries. He tried to safeguard the very autonomy of his Muslim subjects, "For they are Our serfs and their possessions are Ours." Charles also disregarded the canonical prohibition against employing Jewish physicians. He once ordered a surgeon, Johaede (Yehudah), to come to him "without delay . . . for his presence is greatly needed by Us," and provided him with the necessary travel expenses. After the Sicilian Vespers of 1282, too, during which the oppressed Sicilian population indiscriminately massacred all Frenchmen it could reach and permanently freed itself from the French domination, the Jews of the remaining parts of the Angevin kingdom carried on as before. In the constitution enacted in 1283 by Prince Charles (later Charles II), based on an agreement with the Neapolitan estates, a special article relating to the privileges and immunities of the churches provided that "in so far as they are subjects of the Church, Jews should not be entrusted with public offices; nor shall one inflict upon them any aggravation or oppression." By implication this provision indicated that other Jews could be appointed to public office—a clear breach of a basic canonical prohibition.[7]

After ascending the Neapolitan throne in 1285, however, Charles II became less tolerant; at least he did nothing to stem the growing anti-Jewish agitation. As elsewhere, inquisitors of the southern French kind, who beginning in 1268 sought to stamp out heresies, often accused Jews of favoring heterodox individuals. More and more frequently, the Jews themselves now had to submit to listening to missionary sermons. According to a curious report of 1293, two Spanish monks, John and Sancho, were moving from city to city preaching to Jews in Hebrew—a medium which was rarely used even by Jewish preachers of that period. An influential Dominican friar, Bartolomeo da Aquila, persuaded Charles II that the Jews of Apulia had crucified a Christian child in ceremonies designed to mock Jesus' passion. From later Hebrew chronicles, as well as from some tombstone inscriptions recovered in Trani, it appears that in the early 1290s the persecution of Jews spread through most of the kingdom, many Jews being allowed to remain only after submitting to baptism. This persecution may have been stimulated by Charles II's general decree of 1288, banishing Jews, as well as Lombards and Cahorsins, from his home provinces of Anjou and Maine. While many professing Jews remained in many parts of the kingdom of Naples, the persecutions resulted in the emergence of a fairly numerous class of *neofiti*. As early as 1294, no less than 1,300 formerly Jewish families had to be granted immunity from the taxes they had previously paid as Jews.

Characteristically, their largest concentration (310 or 376) was in Trani, whose community had boasted of generations of distinguished Jewish scholars and royal advisers. The next largest groups existed in Taranto (172), Salerno (150), and the city of Naples itself (138). Many other communities, including the venerable seat of rabbinic learning at Bari, were likewise deeply affected. A royal decree of May 1, 1294 provided for the assumption by the *neofiti* of Christian family names, as a rule those held by their godfathers (including members of the high nobility), and for their immunity from their share in the indebtedness of their former communities. As in other countries, this mass conversion left behind a trail of insincere converts who, even if not formally classified as *relapsi* subject to execution, for generations thereafter were to envenom Judeo-Christian relations at the foot of the Apennine Peninsula.[8]

Not that this enforced conversion was universal. Although we have no pertinent records, it appears that the Jewish communities calmly endured the persecution. Many individuals left for more hospitable regions, including the city of Mantua, but some returned to their native places as soon as the storm blew over. As early as 1294 a group of such refugees successfully negotiated with the king for their safe return "under his trust." But their feeling of security apparently was not fully restored until Charles II was succeeded by the enlightened Robert the Wise (1309–43), who considered it his supreme task to develop the economic and cultural resources of his realm.

In those endeavors the Jews were very useful. Trying to stem the recurrent fiscal and other abuses, the king exclaimed, "So long as the Jews commit no transgression against the [Christian] faith, and so long as the Church tolerates them, they ought to be treated humanely." Even the Church must have been seriously disappointed with the effects of the preceding mass conversion. In 1311 it had to secure from the new regime a specific decree forbidding the converts' return to Judaism. It still had to seek a confirmation of that decree thirty-two years later. Not surprisingly, the provincial Council of Benevento, meeting in 1374, passed a resolution that Jews should not be forced to accept conversion. The populace, too, became less unfriendly. True, the Jewish quarter of

Gerace was attacked during the Easter week of 1311, and to avoid future riots Jews were ordered to remain in their homes behind closed doors and windows during the entire Holy Week. Thereupon the community of Gerace complained that its houses had greatly lost in value, and demanded tax reductions. It also secured, probably in connection with these events, permission to carry arms and to restore its old synagogues. In 1324, the same permission was granted to the Jews of Rossano and Cotrone (Crotone). Twenty-one Jews of Trani and twenty-three of Salerno were allowed to bear arms at least during their perilous commercial journeys (1315–16). In 1329 King Robert went so far as to invite Jews from the Balearic Islands to settle in his kingdom. He is also reported to have intervened with Pope John XXII to forestall a threatened decree of expulsion of Jews from the Papal States. This tolerant policy was continued by Robert's successor, Queen Joanna I. She employed a Jewish court physician and generally allowed her Jewish subjects to carry on their trade and medical practice among Christians, "and do other things according to the Hebrew mores." The fourteenth century was, indeed, a relatively happy period for Neapolitan Jewry, and Robert was not altogether wrong when, in demanding in 1328 a special levy from the Jews, he claimed that they were better off in his country than in any other Christian land.[9]

During the disturbances following Joanna I's death and the transfer of sovereignty to the Hungarian line of the Angevin dynasty, the position of Jews remained unaltered. Charles of Durazzo and particularly Ladislaus of Hungary proved themselves quite amenable to granting important privileges to individual Jews and, through them, to entire communities. In extending, for instance, such a privilege to Ligucio son of Dattolo, and to Gaio son of Ligucio, and their familes and associates, to settle and trade in various cities of the Abruzzi, Ladislaus went into lengthy details to protect Jewish rights. This decree of July 27, 1400 is summarized by Nicola Ferorelli as follows:

They were permitted to have synagogues and cemeteries of their own; they did not have to observe Christian holidays, work on Jewish festivals, wear distinguishing marks; nor be subject to forced loans and other common burdens and imposts; they were to enjoy the privileges,

prerogatives and concessions granted to the totality of Jews in the kingdom, to be able to acquire immovable property, and to be cited in civil
or criminal suits exclusively before the royal captains of the city; they
were to restore stolen objects pawned with, or sold to, them only after
the repayment of their investments; they were to pay taxes only on immovable property and to be allowed to sell pawns after a year from the
date of the loan; . . . they were to be treated like the Christian
burghers with respect to all excise taxes and the purchase or sale of
merchandise and goods and to be dressed like all other subjects; nor
were they to be detained or arrested in any place and particularly not
in Monreale and its district.

The king also ratified certain pacts concluded by these Jews with
several municipalities. Similar privileges were extended to other
Jewish families. Since the rapidly expanding economy had created
a shortage of capital, some Christian cities themselves took the
initiative of inviting Jewish moneylenders, who appeared as welcome accessions both because of their loans to the local population
and their contributions to the fiscal revenues of city and state. For
this reason Brindisi, which on several previous occasions had registered strongly anti-Jewish complaints, now approached Ladislaus
for permission for its local Jews to lend money on interest without
fear of prosecution. The king's agreement, subject only to the
limitation of the interest rate to 40 percent, was greeted by the
Brindisi population as "a great favor under the iniquitous conditions of these days, for otherwise the poor citizens are forced to sell
their property at a low price." This interest rate was actually
raised by Ladislaus' successor Joanna II to 45 percent.[10]

So certain had the Jews become of their indispensability that
they demanded, and often succeeded in securing, various tax
immunities from Joanna. The Jews of Catanzaro obtained assur-
ances that they would not be molested by inquisitors or royal officials, and were granted a general dispensation from wearing
distinguishing marks. Otherwise, they threatened, they would
leave the country. Curiously, the increase in the high interest rate
was enacted by the moody queen on August 13, 1427; it marked a
complete reversal of her anti-Jewish attitude three months before.
Greatly impressed by John Capistrano upon his arrival in Naples
as inquisitor, she had issued on May 3, 1427 a decree annulling
many previous concessions. More, she allowed the preacher to at-

tack Jews in many cities, to demand their strict segregation in separate quarters, and in many ways to impede their business. Her
subsequent change of mind was doubtless facilitated by Martin V,
who, at the request of a Jewish delegation aided by the influential
Salomone di Ventura of Anania, had called Capistrano to order by
pointing out that the Church had always tolerated Jews. Once
again Joanna embarked on an anti-Jewish course when she heard
in 1429 that the Jerusalem Jews had been responsible for the
seizure of the Franciscan chapel on Mount Zion. Unlike the
Venetian authorities, however, she merely imposed a severe contribution of one-third ducat per capita on her Jewish subjects. But
we know neither how much of this tax was fully collected, nor
whether it really served to indemnify the Franciscans for their loss.
Only in Lanciano payment by no less than 638 individuals is recorded in 1429, a sizable number of Jews in a total population of
some 4,000 according to a census of 1449. In any case, the chapel
was apparently returned to the Jerusalem Franciscans within three
or four years, and this storm, too, blew over, Joanna returning to
her generally tolerant treatment. Although thus dependent on individual whims and abrupt changes of policy, the status of
Neapolitan Jewry was far from unfavorable in 1442, when Naples
joined Sicily, Sardinia, as well as Aragon, under the single rule of
Alphonso V.[11]

UNDER ARAGONESE RULE

In the preceding hundred and sixty years of Aragonese domination, Sicily's historic evolution greatly differed from that of the
dynasty's Spanish possessions. The Aragonese rulers themselves,
and particularly the princes left in charge of the island's administration, were often as much Italian as Spanish. Alphonso V, too,
comported himself more like one of the contemporary Italian
humanist rulers, combining moderate despotism with deep interest in and patronage of arts and letters. Not surprisingly, Sicilian
Jews did not instantaneously suffer from the reversal in the fortunes of their Aragonese brethren. Their economic stratification,
too, with their greatest concentration in crafts, made their presence as a rule quite welcome to their Christian neighbors.

The powerful Greek and Moorish traditions in Sicily likewise continued to create some good will and understanding among the various segments of the population, particularly since there was no Moorish or Greek irredenta to endanger the Christian domination. The small size of the Moorish population surviving after 1209 made any political aspirations entirely illusory. Although by the end of the Middle Ages Sicily, too, had an overwhelming Italian majority, its nationalistic feelings were greatly restrained because of its persistent sociocultural divergences from north-central Italy and its permanent foreign domination. Hence we hear also of relatively few riots against Jews. Selig Cassel observed that of the known sixty Jewish communities of the island only twelve had been the objects of some disturbances, and only three had been victimized by really sanguinary attacks. Even the catastrophic years of 1348–49 and 1391 passed there without major upheavals. True, Palermo became, in 1392, the scene of an anti-Jewish riot, but it was less severe than that of 1339. The smaller town of Monte San Giuliano (Erice) alone staged a bloody attack, placing the Jews before the alternative of baptism or death. The more general effects of Martinez' "Holy War" on this Aragonese dependency were a few restrictive laws issued by the administration in 1392. But these, too, were on the whole short-lived.[12]

From the outset, the Aragonese rulers, like their Norman and Hohenstaufen predecessors, had to struggle against powerful centrifugal forces. Often at loggerheads with the Crown, the barons did not hesitate to rebel and even to conspire with foreign nations. The bishops and cities, too, sought to preserve their traditional autonomous rights, and during periods of the Crown's weakness to enlarge them at the latter's expense. This struggle necessarily affected the Jews, the kings finding it necessary time and again to reemphasize the theory of Jewish "serfdom" proclaimed by Frederick II. They thus sought to safeguard this reliable source of revenue against encroachments by lords, churchmen, and cities.

Soon after his occupation of Sicily, Pedro II (1282–95) strictly forbade the syndics of San Marco to impose upon Jews more than the customary local tax of 10 percent or a total of 7 ounces of gold. He enacted a protective decree in favor of Jews' running the local dyeing establishment. At the same time he forbade his

Aragonese officials to interfere with a business journey to Sicily by two Barcelona Jews who were to be allowed to take with them "their merchandise, except articles prohibited" by law (1285). Pedro's successor, Frederick III (or II) likewise issued a number of protective ordinances for the Jews of Palermo and other cities. In 1310, to be sure, he tried to placate the opposition by renewing Emperor Frederick II's early anti-Jewish decree with its canonistic overtones relating to segregation, Christian servants, public offices, and physicians. He even sought to abrogate whatever local customs excluded Christians from testifying against Jews. But it is not likely that these pious declarations, the very date of which is not altogether certain, were taken too seriously by either the king or the population at large. In 1312 he himself restored the right of Palermitan Jewry to live within the city walls, while retaining their quarter interveningly established outside. Most insistently, he tried to defend the Crown's exclusive supremacy over Jews. In a sweeping decree issued on October 11, 1324 he wrote:

It has come to Our Majesty's notice that some of Our faithful have shown so much audacity and temerity that they have taken under their protection Jews whom We consider serfs of Our kingdom. They parade as their [the Jews'] defenders, not realizing that such action results in the detriment to the allegiance owed by those Jews to Our Chamber. Properly to prevent such occurrences, We order with Our present constitution that none of Our realm's nobles, be he count, baron, or knight, or else a burgher, or anyone else, should accept any Jew commended to him and constitute himself the latter's protector; nor shall he intercede for, or defend those Hebrews whenever Our officials try to exact from them the payments and services due to Our Chamber.

The penalties for infractions were scaled down from 50 gold ounces for counts and barons to 25 for lesser nobles, and to 10 for burghers. The Jews, soliciting and obtaining such outside protection, were to be penalized by fines of 20 (in another version, 5) ounces.[13]

Characteristically, the decree did not prohibit churchmen from assuming such protective functions. In fact, many high ecclesiastics had long claimed special jurisdiction over Jews, and produced pertinent privileges of earlier rulers. Sometimes Frederick was forced to retrace his steps. He restored, for instance, the jurisdiction of the bishop of Mazzara (Mazara del Varro) over the local

Jewish community in 1326. Reluctantly he also yielded to a similar demand of the archbishop of Palermo, supported by texts of privileges dating from 1210, 1215, 1247. He did it only after lengthy hearings in 1333–34 regarding precedents for such episcopal jurisdiction, one witness testifying that he had himself seen Archbishop Bartholomew "sentencing two Jews, the community's elders, to be flogged with perforated paddles through the [streets of] the aforementioned city." [14]

Nor did the cities completely relinquish their control over Jews. The so-called *Consuetudines Palermitanae,* compiled about 1300, offered a recapitulation of local customs which had gradually evolved over several generations and which betrayed many an anti-Jewish bias. In defiance of all laws of equity, this custumal demanded that testimony of Christian witnesses against Jews be accepted, but not vice versa, and that the right of preemption, granted according to ancient tradition to both relatives and neighbors, should not apply to Jews or Saracens. In the latter case, however, the government, churches, monasteries, counts, and barons, were likewise to be excluded, since the burghers were in dread of the ever increasing concentration of ecclesiastical mortmain and other irretrievable real estate ownership. On the other hand, the validity of Hebrew deeds was fully recognized. Even the exclusion of Jews from the professions of law and medicine was secured indirectly by demanding from each practitioner an annual oath couched in Christian terms. In contrast, the Messina and Syracuse custumals were fairly egalitarian and provided that neither Christians nor Jews could testify against one another. Some cities tried to arrogate to themselves exclusive jurisdictional rights over all inhabitants including Jews, thus infringing upon the autonomous rights of the Jewish communities, fully guaranteed by royal decrees. The *Consuetudines* of Catania achieved the same purpose by stating certain specific exceptions from the municipal controls without including Jews in these exceptions. [15]

In line with the decree of 1324, Frederick IV referred to his Syracuse officials on February 20, 1369 (1370), complaints about the city's fiscal oppression presented to him by two Jewish representatives, "burghers of that city," in behalf of their community, "serfs of our Chamber." The king ordered the officials "to protect the aforementioned Jews with the favor of Our arm and not to allow them to be afflicted in any way by undue exactions, on the part of any persons, whether ecclesiastical or secular, to the injury of the law." In 1374 he reduced the Jewish taxes in various Sicilian communities. At the same time he insisted upon the literal application of accepted canon and state laws relating to badges and new synagogues. In 1369 he actually appointed a special *custos rotellae rubeae* (custodian of the red wheel), the better to supervise full compliance with that law.[16]

In this welter of conflicting jurisdictions, the Jews fared best when the Crown was strong and in full control of the situation. If, under the impact of the hostility transplanted from the Spanish mainland, King Martin V renewed the general enforcement of the ghetto, he also confirmed, at the request of Palermitan Jewry, the earlier protective decrees, especially those outlawing forced baptisms. Wherever local riots broke out, as in Monte San Giuliano and Syracuse, the royal officials severely punished the ringleaders. The Jews of Marsala secured in 1399 a royal decree against enforced attendance at Christian missionary sermons, which had usually been followed by stone-throwing upon the Jewish listeners returning from churches. Three years later the Marsala Jews even dared to submit a whole series of grievances, asking that they be freed from personal services other than those owed the king, and be obliged to contribute no more than one tenth to the municipal imposts, in the exact ratio of their population. Determined to get rid of the episcopal jurisdiction, they suggested that all their civil and criminal affairs be adjudicated exclusively by royal tribunals, while inquisitorial decisions in religious matters be subject to appeal to the king. Curiously, these and similar other demands did not seem too farfetched to the king, who approved them in a special decree. Other Jewries were less fortunate. For instance, that of the small community of Vizzini was expelled by the burghers in 1415, Queen Blanca's prohibition to the contrary. It appears that few, if any, Jews were allowed to return.[17]

These conditions remained substantially unaltered under the long and prosperous domination of Alphonso V (1416–58). If the king had to be richly recompensed for every favor, no one, least of all the Jews themselves, took umbrage. The Jews of Catania prevailed upon him in 1420 to restrict the number of Christian holidays during which Jews had to abstain from work in public, a ruling which was essentially upheld by the municipal authorities in subsequent controversies between the Jewish community and the Church. This quarrel ultimately led to another ordinance, issued *ca.* 1450, which enumerated 16 to 17 Christian holidays, in addition to all Sundays, on which Jews were so to abstain from work. It added the provision that during Christian processions "Jews should close their windows and doors. They should also reverently stand by until the passing of the cross, lest they offend the feelings of faithful Christians." On occasion, Jews even secured tax concessions. Following Marsala's example, the Jews of Palermo complained in 1453 that, although numbering less than 10 percent of the population, they supplied fully one-quarter of all municipal revenues, including the city's contribution to the 200,000 florins shortly before voted by Parliament for the royal Treasury. The king agreed to cut the Jewish share to one-seventh, and within half a year repeated this concession, over the city's protests. At the same time, by invoking a law of 1400 which had forbidden the export of precious metals, he condemned some prospective Jewish émigrés to Jerusalem to actual slavery and forfeiture of their property, but he quickly settled for a ransom of 1,000 gold ounces. More for show, Alphonso also renewed several times the old provisions concerning Jewish quarters and badges. On one occasion, when the Dominicans of Taormina complained that Jews had erected a synagogue and cemetery in the vicinity of their cloister, it required direct papal intervention for the king to order the Jews to remove those institutions to another locality. No one, however, seems to have raised the issue of Jews' not being allowed to build new synagogues at all.[18]

This "forgetfulness" is the more remarkable as the king was perfectly familiar with that ancient prohibition. Personally, too, he was a devout member of the Church, deeply cherishing the ideal of a Christian Crusader against infidels. The contemporary chroniclers do not tire of extolling his daily personal devotions, which allegedly began at dawn, his regular church attendence, and even his various extraordinary acts of charity and self-mortification down to washing the feet of beggars. Queen Maria, too, encouraged such missionary preachers as Fra Matteo of Girgenti and Fra Bernardo of Palermo, and in 1432 wrote in behalf of the former to the authorities of Syracuse, assuring them that the friar had said nothing against them and urging them to support him in his "good work." But such personal religiosity interfered even less with the king's pro-Jewish orientation than with his extensive amours and his fathering a number of illegitimate children, including the later King Ferrante of Naples. When in 1453 a Jewish delegation, representing the communities of the whole realm, complained to Alphonso of the disturbances created by the enforced attendance at missionary sermons, he specifically revoked the pertinent permits granted to Fra Matteo. More sweepingly, he renewed in 1451 and 1453 (?) all the ancient Jewish privileges and proclaimed the Jews' full freedom to sell or purchase land, houses, or any other objects, both movable and immovable, to draw up any kind of contract with Christians, and to engage in monetary transactions of every description with them. Jews were also to be allowed to "maintain synagogues and schools, to preserve, rebuild or repair the older structures, and to select some ordinary locations for use as cemeteries in accordance with their religious requirements." Alphonso strictly ordered all officials, high and low, ecclesiastical and lay, to observe these provisions under the sanction of royal displeasure and the enormous fine of 10,000 florins for each transgression.[19]

In all these matters Alphonso followed not only his own humanitarian and enlightened inclinations but also the well-conceived interests of the state—a consideration which in that period of the nascent dominance of the *raison d'état* played an ever increasing role in shaping governmental policies throughout Italy. Reverting to the policy of his predecessors, the king tried to establish full royal control over Jews. In appointing, on May 29, 1456, Francesco Martorel as "general bailiff and ordinary judge" of all Jews, he insisted that his Jewish subjects obey exclusively their new bailiff or his representatives. Any other person intervening in their affairs would be severely punished. In another decree of August 17, 1456 Alphonso spelled out Martorel's competences in detail, emphasizing that, although "the said office of bailiff and judge had not heretofore effectively secured the full-fledged protection and safeguard of the said Jews who are Our serfs," it would now replace the "wide diffusion of commands and authority" (*generalitas verborum et auctoritatum*). Alphonso even tried to tackle the ever worrisome problem of *neofiti*. In accordance with a decree of Eugenius IV he absolved all such suspects of any inquisitorial prosecution if they merely signed an oath of abjuration. The text of such an oath, taken by the *neofiti* of Lucera in 1454, has been published. To demonstrate their penitence tangibly, the Lucera suspects contributed sixty ducats to the prosecution of the war against the Turks and pledged themselves during the following fifty years to marry exclusively Old Christians.[20]

On their part, the Jews proved their usefulness to the Crown not only through manifold direct contributions to the country's industrial, commercial, and cultural endeavors but also, like their Spanish coreligionists, through diplomatic services, particularly in negotiations with Muslim neighbors. As early as 1393 a Jew was dispatched to Tripolis to offer the Muslim king an alliance against Muslim Tunisia in return for his support of King Martin's reconquest of the adjacent island of Djerba. Sixteen years later another Jew, Samuel Sala of Trapani, served as the official envoy in negotiating a truce with the Tunisian king. King Martin's letters to the Jewish minister, couched in unusually familiar terms, involved among other matters the king's demand of 30,000 doubloons as ransom for Saracen prisoners. On his part Sala once redeemed with his own funds the bishop of Syracuse taken prisoner by Saracens. Later on, however, the rise of the Ottoman Empire and the Turkish conquest of Constantinople served to undermine the confidence of Christian rulers in the loyalty of their Jewish advisers, particularly since many Jews preferred to leave the Christian lands for the more hospitable Ottoman regions. The government actually began clamping down on Jewish emigration. It was in connection with these suspicions that Alphonso V took the aforementioned drastic action against the export of precious metals, which often accompanied their owners departing to eastern lands.[21]

Jewish settlements on the island of Sardinia, at least since its gradual occupation by the Aragonese in 1297–1326, were but smaller variants of those in Sicily. Although reaching back to an-

cient times when Emperor Tiberius had condemned 4,000 young
Jews to forced labor in the Sardinian mines "and employed
[them] in suppressing brigandage," the Jewish community left behind but few Hebrew inscriptions, some adorned by a seven-
branch candelabrum or another Jewish symbol, principally in the
southwestern district around Sulcis (Sant' Antioco). Perhaps life
was too calm and undisturbed for Jews to write and preserve historical records. Only two major misfortunes are more or less
reliably mentioned. In 790 nearly the entire Jewish quarter of
Cagliari was consumed by fire. Rather than being guilty of arson,
as suggested by some historians, the Christian population tried to
assist the stricken Jews. Five centuries later (in 1174), the latter's
descendants suffered from a sudden decree of expulsion, for reasons not yet satisfactorily explained. While such a decree may not
have been fully carried out, the existing tiny settlements doubtless
suffered further diminution in numbers, since many members
must have left for other lands and some others were converted to
Christianity. In any case, under the Pisan domination in the thirteenth century there were but few Jews on the island, mainly in
Cagliari, where they were assigned parts of the castle for habita-
tion.[22]

Aragonese rule brought with it an influx of immigrants from
other Italian, as well as Spanish, communities. From the outset the
new regime favored Jewish settlers and kept them under the
Crown's direct tutelage. Their privileges, on the whole resembling
those of their Barcelona coreligionists, were confirmed in 1370 and
again in 1397. When in 1391 the Cagliari bailiff sought to exclude
Jews from the castle, where only persons of Aragonese or Catalan
origin were allowed to live, he was informed by King John that
Jews, of whatever nationality, ought to be admitted, for they are
"serfs of Our chamber and are considered Our treasure." During
his short reign Ferdinand I (1412–16) tried to force Sardinian
Jewry to wear distinguishing marks of the kind worn by the Jews
of Majorca—apparently with little success. Such insistence on royal
controls and the occasionally stubborn resistance to them by the
local population were greatly facilitated by the absence of sharply
drawn lines between state and municipal jurisdictions. Although
the Crown was less in need of the burghers' good will in Sardinia

than in the Aragonese homeland, it was ready to concede that, "in all civil and criminal matters the jurisdiction over [the local] Jews belongs in the first instance" to the municipal vicar of Cagliari. When in 1399 the governor arrested a Jew, Sabbatino, because he allegedly had "through magic arts discovered an underground treasure," King Martin ordered the prisoner's surrender to the vicar. Only with respect to the sale of Jewish meat did the kings insist on the exclusive jurisdiction of their officials. Invoking several earlier decrees (of 1335, 1355, 1380, 1399), Alphonso V in 1428 sharply called the city to order for interfering with this phase of the royal administration.[23]

Quite unusual in many ways was the establishment of the rather prosperous Jewish colony in Alghero in the northwestern part of the island. That city became both a center of the mining industry and a major harbor, with many Jewish traders enjoying there privileges resembling those of a modern free port. While originally there was opposition to Jews' exploiting the silver mines (some orders to that effect are recorded in 1327), early in the fifteenth century two Jews of Alghero obtained a special license for prospecting and working the mines under the condition that they would pay half of the proceeds to the Treasury. When in 1432 the local Jews complained to Alphonso V about violations of the letter and spirit of their privileges, the king sweepingly declared that they ought to enjoy "all [general] and special franchises and liberties which are enjoyed and used by the Christian inhabitants of the city of Alghero." Occupationally, Sardinian Jewry included many craftsmen and petty workers of all kinds. There also was a sprinkling of physicians, among them Bonjudes Bondavin (Yehudah b. David), formerly employed by Queen Maria of the Provence, who settled in Alghero in 1390 and often personally attended King Martin. Another Jewish doctor, Eahim di Hipre (Ḥayyim of Cyprus), apparently an arrival from the East, wrote a book about the medicinal herbs of the island, casually mentioning its unhealthy climate (ca. 1459). The latter statement involved him in a protracted controversy with a Christian physician, which ended, however, in their public reconciliation. As in the Spanish homeland, there also were numerous Jewish fiscal agents, including several members of the Carcassona family, who advanced funds to the Treasury (1459, 1481). Maimon Carcassona played host to the viceroy during the latter's visits to Alghero, while Moses was a leading tax farmer and in charge of customs. Some feudal lords, such as the counts of Oliva, likewise extensively employed Jewish agents. Bishops and cities, too, were often aided by Jewish financiers such as Vidal de Santa Pau. This relatively favorable status of Sardinian Jewry was demonstrated when in 1448 the secretaries of the Jewish community cooperated with the city elders of Cagliari in a joint petition to Alphonso V. Their request for a general amnesty for their respective members was largely granted. In 1451 Alphonso extended to Sardinian Jews an important privilege, exempting them from the badge and enforced attendance at conversionist sermons. He even allowed them to keep slaves turned Christians for the full period of twelve months provided by Jewish law, a much longer period indeed than had been allowed by other Christian rulers.[24]

Remarkably, the presence of a number of influential Jews apparently aroused little jealousy among the Sardinian burghers. We hear neither of violent outbreaks, such as afflicted other communities in 1348 and 1391, nor even of any sustained complaints against Jewish exploitation through commercial and banking operations. This is the more remarkable as the Sardinian public possessed a ready mouthpiece in its well-developed parliamentary institutions. From the hitherto published materials it appears that the Sardinian Parliaments, meeting ever more frequently in the fifteenth century and sometimes resounding with popular grievances against the royal administration, had little to say about the Jewish question. Even toward the end of the century, when developments on the Aragonese mainland were increasingly pointing toward the tragic dénouement of 1492, the Sardinian representatives maintained their silence.[25]

FINAL HALF CENTURY

With the passing of Alphonso V, there set in a gradual decline in the position of the Jews. Relatively most favorable remained their status in the Neapolitan kingdom ruled by Ferrante (1458–94). True, a great uprising of barons and peasants during the first five years after Alphonso's demise affected the Jews severely. The rebels expelled them altogether from Lecce and Bari. But no sooner did royal troops recapture those cities than the government reestablished Jewish rights. To pacify the populace, however, King Ferrante extended to all debtors a two-year moratorium which proved even more detrimental to Jewish merchants than to moneylenders, since much of the trade in cloth was done on credit. In 1469, 1475, and 1494 some Jews obtained general privileges to settle throughout the kingdom, including the baronial possessions, and to enjoy all residential rights on a par with other citizens. The law specifically provided that any contrary provisions included in the privileges of Christian burghers be disregarded. At times the king claimed to have thus acted for the benefit of the burghers themselves. In his privilege of March 1, 1463 he gave the following reason:

The said district of Lanciano now possesses some Jewish families who have lived and are living there and the said city has received and continually receives assistance through their business and support through their moneylending. Therefore the said city wishes that they should be kept and treated like the other citizens and that they should enjoy and be able to enjoy every privilege, grace, franchise and exemption possessed and enjoyed by all the other native citizens and residents of that district of Lanciano.

Ferrante might have added that he was thereby merely renewing a privilege granted the Jews of that area by his predecessor, Ladislaus of Durazzo, sixty-three years earlier. In general, Ferrante belonged to those medieval monarchs who were most favorably disposed toward Jews. On one occasion, in 1476, he is reputed to have exclaimed: "We love and take delight in those Jews and every one among them, and We have always been and shall be a protector and supporter of those Jews and every one among them." [26]

Many churchmen, reacting to the then growing anti-Jewish tendencies throughout the Peninsula, strenuously objected to this governmental "favoritism." Some outstanding preachers, including Giacomo della Marca and Bernardino da Feltre, traversed the country preaching against Jews. Fra Giacomo established in 1466 the first *monte di pietà* in Aquila, but it proved unsuccessful. Operating from the same city in 1488–89, Da Feltre attacked the

southern Italian Jews and extolled, in particular, John Capistrano's earlier visit to Naples. Summoned by Infante Alphonso, Da
Feltre expostulated that he was working in the cause of God and
the poor and had merely sought to eliminate the plague of Jewish
usury. But he did not refrain from censuring those Christian
princes who "unduly" favored their Jewish subjects. Even after his
departure, Fra Bernardino took the occasion of his visit to Duchess
Eleonora of Ferrara, Ferrante's daughter, to urge her to intercede
with her brother Infante Alphonso that he cease supporting the
Jews' exploitation of the poor. Otherwise, he warned, a prophecy
would come true and the prince would be expelled from his
kingdom—a prediction which was to be fulfilled with the French
invasion of 1495–96.[27]

Interveningly, however, the Sicilian and Sardinian Jewries had
ended their historic careers. Being part of the Aragonese—now
Spanish—kingdom, they were immediately affected by Ferdinand
and Isabella's decree of expulsion of 1492. The deterioration of
their status had been foreshadowed under John II (1458–79)
through several local incidents, which had also reflected the ever
deepening social unrest culminating in the 1464 revolt in Messina.
In 1456 the Jewish quarter in Marsala was set on fire while the
Jews attended a missionary sermon. The community of Trapani
suffered in 1473 a sharp reprisal for its purported admission to
membership of the daughter of a Jewish mother and a Christian
father, which was in accordance with Jewish law. In the following
year several communities were attacked because of alleged Jewish
blasphemies. The shout, "Long live the Virgin and death to the
Jews" reverberated through the island, and in the ensuing riots
Jews, variously estimated at 360 to 470, lost their lives. On his full
accession to the throne in 1479, to be sure, Ferdinand the Catholic
tried to prevent the recurrence of such sanguinary attacks, and renewed a number of Jewish privileges. Local authorities, too, collaborated in safeguarding Jewish rights. In 1486 they allowed,
with the viceroy's approval, the enlargement of the synagogues of
Santa Lucia and Castroreale. In 1489, the very Dominicans were
given permission to use Jewish doctors. As late as November 2,
1491, a formal agreement between the city of Palermo and the
Jewish community provided for mutual aid in securing the main-

tenance of their respective privileges. Independently, the viceroy had issued in 1474 an amnesty for all *neofiti* against the payment of a contribution of 50,000 florins toward the war.[28]

The polarity of the governmental attitude may be seen, however, in the dispatch, on the one hand, by the Duke of Montblanc of a Jewish ambassador to Abu'l Aḥmad of Tunis and, on the other hand, in Ferdinand's appointment of Gerardo Agliato as his chaplain, evidently because as a student of Hebrew and Chaldean he was expected to be an effective missionary among Jews (1483). Another Christian preacher, the convert Maestro Paolo, traveled during those years up and down the island preaching against Jews. Even more prominent was another convert, Guglielmo Raimondo Moncada (born in Girgenti to a Spanish émigré, Nissim Abulfaraj), who later made a distinguished career in Rome. All this reflected the change of policy from the days of Alphonso V, who in his decree of 1431 had freed all Sicilian Jews from involuntary attendance at sermons. By 1467 the viceroy specifically authorized the Dominican John da Pistoia to force all Sicilian Jews to listen to his homilies. This increasingly vehement agitation caused the community of Sciacca to appeal to the government in 1486–87 to restrain the preachers. As late as May 28 and June 1, 1492, the viceroy himself renewed the pledges of royal protection for Jews and threatened their assailants with serious penalties.[29]

Sicilian Jewry knew, however, of the decree of banishment issued in Spain on the preceding March 31, although it had not been formally promulgated until several weeks later. Reading the signs on the wall, many islanders made preparations for departure while there still was time to take funds with them. The government, which had for several decades discouraged Jewish emigration and particularly the resultant export of precious metals to the Ottoman Empire, now clamped down, and in a special decree of June 9, 1492 threatened with severe corporeal and financial penalties all Jews attempting to escape, sell their property, or conceal their merchandise. For better control they were ordered to register all movable property and to deposit their deeds with notaries within forty-eight hours. The final blow came a few days later. On June 18, all Jews refusing baptism were told to leave the country within three months. Except for later extensions to December 18 and the following January 12, this decree was rigidly enforced, no professing Jew being subsequently allowed to live in Sicily or Sardinia until the nineteenth century.[30]

The Sicilian tragedy did not immediately affect the mainland possessions of the other Aragonese branch. Undeterredly, Ferrante and his son Alphonso continued to treat the Jews with much fairness, and even opened the gates to the Spanish and Sicilian exiles of 1492. Jews, old and new, not only contributed much to the country's commercial life and to the Treasury (for instance, through their share in the emergency tax of 30,000 ducats to repel in 1480 the Turkish occupation of Otranto and of some 80,000 ducats for staving off the French invasion in 1494), but also helped improve its agricultural economy and injected new cultural ingredients into the rich humanistic movement of the region. Among the new arrivals were Don Isaac Abravanel and his son, later renowned as the philosopher Leone Ebreo. Perhaps stirred up by the new fermentation, southern Italian Jewry pioneered in employing the newly invented art of printing in the publication of Hebrew books. The first Hebrew incunabulum, that of Rashi's *Commentary* on the Pentateuch, appeared in Reggio di Calabria. Another Hebrew printing press was soon established in Naples. "The names of those," observes Joshua Bloch, "who in one way or another were connected with Neapolitan Hebrew printing betray the cosmopolitan character of the city's Jewish population. . . . They were German, French, Italian, Portuguese and Spanish Jews." [31]

However, the French invasions, followed by attacks from Spain, threw the Neapolitan provinces into a state of chaos which adversely affected also the Jewish population. Their final occupation by Ferdinand the Catholic in 1502 presaged the end of the Neapolitan Jewish communities as well. Despite their secrecy there may have been "leaks" about the king's intentions as expressed in his correspondence with his "Gran Capitán," Hernandez Gonzalo de Cordova. As early as October 11, 1501, while the campaign was still in progress, Ferdinand had written that he expected "that the Jews would leave these duchies . . . without any delay." Less than two years later (July 11, 1503), in full possession of the Neapolitan territories, he was more explicit:

You know that many years ago We have ordered all Jews living there to leave Our kingdoms in order to avoid the offenses against Our Lord which arose from their presence there. Since We do not wish that there should be any Jews [left] in any part of Our kingdoms and still less in this kingdom [of Naples], We instruct you to work toward that accomplishment in all matters in which they offend Our Lord, and that, when you see the time ripe, to make all Jews depart from the said kingdom.

According to a report sent home on April 10, 1504 by Antonio Giustinian, the Venetian ambassador to Rome, he had seen a letter written by De Cordova after the latter's victory over the French. The general had spoken about the Catholic monarchs' objective "that for the pacific and quiet living of their subjects, the entire realm ought to be reformed. In this way everyone will be able to recognize the difference between the dominion of their highnesses and that of others." In his capacity as viceroy, De Cordova soon suggested the establishment of an Inquisition along Spanish lines, though the country evidently was not ready for it. Such innovations could not but augur badly for Neapolitan Jewry. The ax fell in 1510. Although Ferdinand's decree of expulsion was not completely carried out, this remnant of the once flourishing southern Italian communities had to carry on its bitter struggle for survival under most adverse conditions, until it, too, was snuffed out by another decree in 1541.[32]

STATES OF THE CHURCH

In contrast to the south's scores of old and populous Jewish settlements, central Italy had only one major Jewish community of truly venerable antecedents. Rome not only was the spiritual capital of Catholic Christianity but it also harbored the oldest and most enduring Western Jewish community. On the other hand, such Jewish settlements as those of Ancona, Fano, Orvieto and Viterbo in the Marches, Umbria and the Patrimony of St. Peter in the narrower sense, or the Tuscan cities of Florence, Pisa, and Siena, were of relatively recent vintage. Only Ravenna in the Romagna and Lucca in Tuscany had communities looking back to a cultural history of several centuries, adorned with legends resembling those of southern Bari. The newly acquired southern French territories, including the Jewish communities of Avignon and Carpentras, assumed real significance only during the popes' "Babylonian Exile" (1305–78) and their subsequent permanent attachment to the Papal States until the French Revolution. The important communities of Bologna, Ferrara, Modena, Rimini, and Urbino, too, reached the heights of their achievement only in the Renaissance age, in part under the enlightened rule of the House of Este. Most of these Jewries were so intimately associated with the destinies of their coreligionists in the Papal States that they may legitimately be treated here as a connected geographic area.

Of course, the Jews' fate under papal rule was to a large extent determined by the Papacy's international status and ambitions. The *Constitutio pro Judaeis* not only became the foundation stone of the structure of Roman Jewry but also served as a guidepost for the Catholic Church in all Christian lands. On the other hand, papal letters and decrees addressed to distant kings and bishops reflected back on the status of Jews at home. Some of these "foreign" interventions, particularly if intended to protect Jewish rights, were secured with the aid of Roman Jewish elders or individual Jewish favorites of popes or cardinals. This constant intermingling of international and domestic affairs involved the Papacy in an endless series of wars and foreign invasions, which at times destroyed the economic well-being of the entire population. It also nurtured domestic factionalism and unceasing clashes between Ghibellines and Guelphs, pro- and anti-French partisans, which undermined the country's security and often forced the very popes to abandon their residence.

Rome's constitutional life, too, with the popes sharing power with the Roman "senators," who sometimes included such powerful foreign monarchs as Charles I and Robert the Wise of Naples, added to the instability of the regime. This imbalance was further aggravated by the frequent popular upheavals culminating in the days of Cola di Rienzo in the dramatic revival of the ancient Roman republic. During this entire period, moreover, the city of Rome as such retained a great measure of municipal self-government. Ordinances of the city council helped to regulate the legal status of the Jewish inhabitants, who were often treated as Roman burghers. These confusing crosscurrents were further confounded by the frequent changes in the occupants of the Papal throne. No less than thirty-nine popes are offically counted as having held the tiara during the last three medieval centuries (1198–1503). There also were several "antipopes" not recognized by the Church at large, as well as lengthy interregna extending over months or years before the cardinals managed to elect a successor to a deceased pope, who had perhaps reigned but a few months or weeks. Almost all popes, moreover, reached their high office at a very advanced age. Although the octogenarian Gregory IX acted with vigor and dispatch, others responded with greater lassitude to the challenging problems of their age.[33]

The Papacy's general attitude toward Jews and Judaism, discussed in an earlier chapter, was not always the decisive factor in Rome's local evolution. Perhaps because of their very proximity, the popes exerted less influence upon their Italian subjects than upon the Catholics of other countries. Was not anti-Catholic Otto von Bismarck once cynically to suggest that the pope, dispossessed by the unification of Italy in 1870, should be allowed to establish a residence in Germany, so that "direct observation of Rome's priestly regime would help cure the Germans" of their "political Catholicism"? At the same time, the splendor of court life and the intellectual patronage of the more prominent Renaissance popes, made possible by the generous contributions from all Catholic countries, set the pace for a cultural evolution of the papal capital paralleled by few other cities.

Curiously, the powerful thirteenth-century popes had relatively little to say about the Roman Jews. Perhaps they were so busy with world politics that they left Roman affairs largely to the determination of local officials. The badge, so solemnly proclaimed by the Fourth Lateran Council in 1215, made its first appearance in the papal capital in 1257, later than in most Western countries. It is even doubtful whether Gregory IX's circular letter to the Western monarchs, demanding the seizure and scrutiny of Hebrew books, was followed by similar orders to his own subordinates in the Papal States, and whether any copies of the Talmud were burned in Rome in the 1240s. The apprehensions of the Roman Jewish community on this score, which found expression in a locally proclaimed fast day in 1239 and dirges by local poets, evidently did not materialize. In any case, Roman Jewry continued to participate in the welcoming ceremonies for every newly elected pope, who reciprocated with the standardized formula of accepting the Torah scroll handed him by the Jewish representatives but rejecting their interpretation. Such ceremonies are attested again in connection with Gregory IX's entry in 1230, and with Boniface VIII's triumphant procession in 1295. On the other hand, the popes were often powerless to protect Jews during the frequent local disturbances, such protection being sometimes extended to them by Roman senators, including Charles I of Anjou (1271). Individual acts of grace by popes are also recorded, as when Alexander IV freed certain Jews from all customs duties (1255). Extensive privileges were granted to Jewish physicians, including Magister Gaio and a southern French Jewish doctor who attended Martin IV (1281–85). The same pope, Nicholas III (1277–80), who in 1278 entrusted the preaching orders with the task of delivering regular missionary sermons to Jewish audiences, did not hesitate to listen favorably in the same year to the Jewish envoy, Bonjudas of Montpellier, seeking papal intervention in behalf of his community. That such interventions were secured only by the mediation of Roman Jewish leaders and after the presentation of valuable gifts surprised no one; this was part of the mores of the age. Most remarkably, the daring appearance of the mystic Abraham Abulafia in 1280, which seemed graphically to bear out the accusation of Jewish proselytism in Clement IV's *Turbato corde* of 1267, passed without untoward consequences for the Jews of Rome.[34]

Even the rise of the Dominican and Franciscan orders affected the Roman community far less than the more distant Jewries of southern France, where the Inquisition soon began celebrating its sanguinary victories. True, as has been shown, Nicholas III's *Vineam sorec* of 1278 was addressed to both orders in all lands. The bitter denunciations of Jewish proselytism in *Turbato corde* were likewise intended for general consumption by the issuing popes, Clement IV (1267), Gregory X (1274), and Nicholas IV (1288), the latter specifically repeating its provisions in his order of 1290 to the Franciscans of the Papal States. Yet there is no record of either major anti-Jewish prosecutions by Roman inquisi-

tors or of special missionary preachers among Roman Jews until
the sixteenth century. Only one communal elder, Elias de' Pomis,
died a martyr's death at the hand of inquisitors in 1298, causing
his immediate family of distinguished lineage to emigrate to
Spoleto. But a year later Boniface VIII, in a special bull, severely
restrained the inquisitional zeal aimed in particular at the
wealthiest Jews. From the socioeconomic standpoint it was also
very important that nowhere in Italy, and particularly not in the
Papal States, did feudalism become as rampant as it was north of
the Alps and Pyrenees. Although its final elimination came very
late, the landed aristocracy never commanded as dominant a position there as it did in other European countries.[35]

In the fourteenth century the limelight switched to Avignon,
the five Avignonese popes themselves being of French descent.
Several did not even deign to set foot in Rome. Of course, they did
not abandon their sovereignty over their ancient capital, and some
enactments issued by the Avignonese popes affected also their
Italian possessions, but Rome's municipal authorities succeeded
during that period in expanding their legislative and administrative functions also with respect to Jews. It is small wonder, then,
that on February 8, 1310 it was "the Roman people assembled in
the city's public parliament" which enacted the most comprehensive privilege for the Jewish community.

Among the important provisions of this privilege, extant in a
somewhat expanded version confirmed by Martin V in 1418, was
one freeing Jewish elders forever from displaying the badge. The
same concession was granted to Roman Jews traveling outside the
city, as well as to foreign visitors during the first ten days of their
stay. Anyone trying to force Jews to appear before any but the
Capitol court and any official or head of an artisan guild illegally
imposing upon them his will was to be subject to a severe fine of
25 pounds. More sweepingly, the privilege declared

that all Jews and Jewesses, living in the city or residing therein, collectively and severally, together with their families, shall be treated in
the city and regarded as Roman citizens in all matters; they shall thus
be viewed and considered in all respects and shall enjoy the privileges
of Roman citizens notwithstanding anything the statutes or laws may
say to the contrary. Similarly, . . . we ordain that Jews and Jewesses

living outside the city should be able freely to come to the city, reside in it, and leave it notwithstanding [any contrary provisions].

Jews were also to be freed from all local taxes except for 1,130(?) florins they were wont to pay to the municipal treasury, and 100 florins to the papal vicar. Nor were they to be forced to take part in the repairs of streets and houses except in their own quarter. A later formulation added a special permit for the Jewish physicians, Magister Angelo and his sons, freely to move about the city without a badge, exercise their profession, and collect their usual fees. As Roman burghers Jews were admitted to membership in the merchant guild. A papal intervention secured for some such Roman merchants freedom from customs duties even in the Neapolitan possessions.[36]

A similar egalitarian treatment was exacted in 1313 by ten Roman Jewish bankers from the city of Orvieto, when that city badly needed a loan of 15,000 florins. The fourteen articles of that interesting compact included the provision that these Jews, their heirs and persons designated by them, would all be "treated as genuine and original citizens and members [*popolari*] of the city, as well as guild members entitled to exercise crafts with all the benefits appertaining to those who exercise them" (Art. 1). Curiously, the Jews also stipulated that "no other Jew except the aforementioned persons" shall be allowed to stay in Orvieto without their consent, under the penalty of 10 lire "for every day" of unauthorized sojourn (Art. 9).[37]

In contrast, the Papacy's French municipalities often demanded sharp limitations of Jewish rights. The Avignon bishops also exerted great influence ever since 1178, when Frederick I Barbarossa subjected the Jews to their jurisdiction in order to weaken the baronial controls. In Carpentras, where the Jewish community had had a long and checkered career, interrupted by an expulsion in the early thirteenth century and readmission in 1263, Bishop Pierre III Rostaing formally agreed with the sixty-four resident Jewish families on the amount of their annual contributions. The various Avignon church councils likewise debated the Jewish question. True, the antiusury provisions of the Council of 1209, which were aimed at Jews as well as Christians, were not repeated in the sessions of 1279, 1282, 1326, and 1341. (They were formally repudiated by Robert of Anjou with respect to Jewish lenders.) Those of 1457 and 1459 threatened with ecclesiastical penalties only Christian usurers. Even the extensive compilation of synodal statutes, prepared in 1441 by the Avignon bishop, Alain de Coëtivy, included no provisions against Jewish moneylending, while the local notaries of the fourteenth and fifteenth centuries frequently recorded Jewish credit transactions. From 1274 on, moreover, the constitutional situation was in so far confused, as the popes long had to share their sovereignty with the counts of the Provence. Even after Joanna I definitely gave up her claims to that area in 1348, the pontiffs still had to respect the established authority of the lords, both lay and ecclesiastical, and of the municipalities. These varying checks and balances, based upon ancient custom, also accounted for the differences in the status of Jews in the major communities of the area, Avignon, Carpentras, Cavaillon, and L'Isle-sur-la-Sorgue, often called in Hebrew briefly the *Arba qehillot* (Four Communities).[38]

Only under John XXII (1316–34) did the decrees of 1317 and 1320 definitely place the Avignonese and Carpentras Jews under the direct control of the papal vicars. Yet as late as 1343 the Carpentras community had to reach an agreement with Bishop Hugh pledging itself not to increase its membership beyond the existing ninety families. This restriction was not fully observed, however, and in 1408 the municipal authorities protested against their Jewry's continued growth, which was not stemmed by the establishment, in 1461, of a separate Jewish quarter. Twenty-five years later the Carpentras council demanded both a reduction of the area assigned to that quarter and a complete stoppage of further Jewish immigration. Avignon, too, was growing at an even faster pace. It attracted a great many settlers from various lands, including Jews, although the two hundred and ten Jewish heads of families who in 1358 took an oath of loyalty to the pope constituted but a small minority of the population of more than 30,000 which raised Avignon to the rank of the second largest city in France. But the Jews' commercial influence far exceeded their numerical strength. Their moneylending, pursued with the obvious toleration of clerical authorities, often transcended the boundaries of the papal possessions. An Avignon Jewess in 1377 extended credit not only to clients throughout the Comtat but also to some residing in the principality of Orange, the Provence, Languedoc, and the county of Roussillon. Certain branches of commerce, too, and particularly the trade in textiles, had strong Jewish participation. An oath taken in 1374 by 94 cloth brokers included no fewer than 87 Jewish names. Another list of 62 lumber brokers embraced 41 Jews. The medical profession, too, included many Jewish physicians and surgeons, some of high standing. This relative prosperity was made possible by the popes' liberal economic legislation, which also opened to Jews vast opportunities for the acquisition of real estate. Jews could even control feudal fiefs and influentially serve as collectors of feudal dues and other taxes for the papal administration. The latter occupation is the more noteworthy, as the municipality of Avignon had, as early as 1215, specifically stipulated that Jews would "at no time be appointed as gatherers of feudal revenues." [39]

Popes were far from consistent, however. John XXII extended to Jews effective protection against the Pastoureaux and during the so-called lepers' conspiracy, but, according to some rather obscure reports by later Jewish chroniclers, he soon thereafter ordered their expulsion from all papal possessions (1321–22). His bull, allegedly inspired by his sister "Sancha," was reputedly revoked only after the intercession by King Robert of Anjou and Naples assisted by a douceur for Sancha which is variously quoted as of 20,000 or 100,000 ducats. The authenticity of these reports is highly questionable; if true, this would have meant a total break with the traditional papal acceptance of the permanent presence of Jews, which was to continue even during the tidal wave of intolerance in the era of Counter Reformation. These reports may have been based upon exaggerating rumors about the renewed outlawry of the Talmud by John XXII. True, the synagogues of Carpentras and Bédarrides were really confiscated. In February 1321, John XXII approved the appointment of three priests to serve at three altars of a church which had replaced the Bédarrides synagogue. That of Carpentras apparently was not reestablished until 1343, when Bishop Hugh allowed the Jews to erect one of exactly the same dimensions. For some reason Jews apparently left the city in 1350, but returned in 1367, when they renewed their agreement of 1343 with the bishop. But these manifestations of local intolerance need not be attributed to the papal regime as such. In general, John's successors, Clement VI (1342–52), Innocent VI (1352–62), and Urban V (1362–70), continued to treat the Jews with much fairness and general adherence to the traditional *modus vivendi*. As a result, the massacres which, starting in neighboring Savoy, engulfed many Jewish communities in 1348–49, were effectively checked by the papal administration. Clement VI, about whom the Jews and other Roman citizens chanted, *Clemens nomine, clemens re* (Clement by name, clement in fact), reissued the bull, *Sicut Judaeis,* and Urban V reconfirmed it in 1363. One of the latter's successors, "Antipope" Clement VII (1378–94), who had come from Florence on a ship owned by a Jew and had thus been saved from his enemies, made the Jewish shipowner, Joshua d'Arnaud, his influential adviser. Joshua had to undergo baptism, however. The famous French chronicler, Jean Froissart, who as a child had witnessed the ravages of the Black Death, observed: "The Jews were at that time burned and chased by the whole world and their property was seized by the lords under whom they lived, except in Avignon and the lands of the Church, under the keys [*clés*] of the pope." [40]

In the meantime the pope's Jewish subjects in Italy, left to the tutelage of the papal bureaucracy and the municipal authorities, shared the vicissitudes of their non-Jewish compatriots. The ceremonies connected with the appearance in Rome of Emperor Henry VII in 1312 were largely paid for by a special tax imposed upon the Jewish community. Similarly when Louis the Bavarian entered Rome in 1328 and demanded from the city a contribution of 30,000 guilders, the Jews were made to contribute one-third, the same amount as the clergy and the non-Jewish burghers. Rome's total contribution was somewhat smaller, however, than that exacted from Milan and Pisa. Jews also suffered from the serious local earthquake and subsequent famine in 1329–30.[41]

Nor were they spared the ill effects of the constant factional strife which dominated the domestic evolution. They generally steered clear of direct involvement. But when in 1344 Cola di Rienzo, the people's tribune and nationalist dreamer, seized power they joined the majority in hailing the new regime, which offered a glittering reform program including a substantial tax reduction. Some Jews, moreover, might have been personally acquainted with the young revolutionary leader, who according to contemporary reports had been born in 1313 in the vicinity of a synagogue. Like the rivaling Neapolitan rulers, Jews of other Italian provinces submitted a controversy to his decision. Reciprocally, Rienzo in trying to impress Emperor Charles IV boasted that even in Jerusalem the news about the Roman "reformation" brought by Christian pilgrims caused "both Christians and Jews to celebrate new festivities and indulge in unwonted rejoicing." Yet when it turned out that the new dictator, particularly during the second phase of his administration, had to resort to ever new taxes, Jews joined their Christian compatriots in opposing him. After his assassination they allegedly nurtured the flames in which his earthly remains were consumed.[42]

Of more permanent interest were the city ordinances prohibiting Jews as well as non-Jews from burying their dead in the streets, thus forcing the community to enlarge its cemetery (1360). Other Roman ordinances prescribed in more detail the Jewish taxes and clothing, but their enforcement was so lax that in order to encourage denunciations the city promised the informers fully 50 percent of the fines collected from transgressors. Yet these were relatively minor chicaneries, and the Roman community seems to have grown accustomed to living under an absentee sovereign. Apparently taken by surprise when Clement VII had decided to return to the city in 1378 (thus marking the end of the "Babylonian Exile"), it braced itself with fasting and prayers before it extended the traditional welcome to its ruler. But its fears were quickly dispelled by the antipope's liberal regime, which lasted to his death in 1394. During the following decades of the Western Schism, Jewish life continued to be affected by the struggle between the rivaling popes. They fared worse in Avignon under Antipope Benedict XIII (1394–1423), whose antagonistic Spanish bull of 1415 extended to his French residence. But compared with the Spanish Jews, whose Christian neighbors wholeheartedly supported their compatriot on the papal throne, Avignonese Jewry seems to have suffered little from his hostility, which left the Italian Jews practically unaffected. Boniface IX, who after the

repudiation of Clement VII assumed the tiara in 1389, soon thereafter extended special privileges to the Jews of Rome and Rieti
(1391–92). In 1401 he exempted the Jews of Velletri from certain
local taxes, because they had already contributed their share to the
capital's Jewish taxation. Two years later he even protected the
Jews against certain excesses of the Inquisition.[43]

A complete change came only under the regime of the generally
recognized pope, Martin V (1417–31). Although early in his
reign he penalized the Avignonese Jews, who, according to Odori-
cus Raynaldus, "had been evoking demons with magic chants
infecting simple Christians with the Jewish superstition and exercising the usurious craft with impunity," Martin soon imposed
great restraint on the southern French inquisitor, Ponce Feugey-
ron, from whom this accusation had emanated. More significantly,
after several years of complaints and countercomplaints, Martin decided in 1421, as a matter of general policy, that the inquisitorial
courts should not follow their customary practice of withholding
from accused Jews the names of their accusers. The usual objections of prosecutors that witnesses might be intimidated by powerful defendants evidently carried little weight in the case of Jews
who were hardly in a position seriously to threaten Christian
witnesses.[44]

Martin also insisted upon the undisturbed validity of Jewish law
in matters of marriage and divorce among Jews, although whenever it served Church interests he readily followed a more restrictive interpretation. Thus, in the case of a converted Jew who
wished to take along with him his grandchildren against the will
of their parents—a legal problem debated for a while with much
learning and ingenuity among the canonists—Martin decided in
favor of the grandfather, primarily because his son, the father of
the children, had not yet come of age. The latter qualification did
not, however, restrain later canon jurists from citing this decision
as a general precedent that the will of a single grandparent sufficed
to secure conversion. Nor did Martin hesitate to reverse decisions
favorable to Jews, wherever his own interests or remonstrations by
his councilors made it advisable. Not surprisingly, some interested
Jewish parties at times preferred to invoke the earlier favorable
rulings, causing the irate pope to declare that from the outset the

latter "had been extorted from Us through circumvention and importunity" and that, hence, "they had justly been declared inefficacious and invalid." Yet despite his obvious inconsistencies, Martin generally tried to act toward Jews as a benevolent sovereign toward faithful and useful subjects, rather than as the head of a church toward a group of recalcitrant infidels. He endeavored to live up to the program he had enunciated in one of his earliest bulls, *Romanae ecclesiae,* of December 2, 1417:

We shall gladly listen to petitions by [the Jewish] subjects of the Roman Church who are entrusted to Our government. In particular such as are likely to mitigate disagreements arising among them and through which their common welfare would best be safeguarded.

Internationally, too, he tried to calm the rising waves of intolerance whipped up by Benedict XIII and other leading churchmen. He speedily renewed the bull, *Sicut Judaeis,* of which, according to a contemporary notarial record, nine copies were immediately prepared, evidently at the request of Jews eager to distribute them among various communities in strategic areas. Martin also prohibited the delivery of anti-Jewish sermons, including those preached by Bernardino da Siena.[45]

Martin's moderate policies were at first pursued also by his successor, Eugenius IV (1431–47). True, the latter's bull, *Dudum ad nostram,* of 1442 largely extended to Italy Benedict XIII's sharply discriminatory edict of 1415. But a Jewish delegation persuaded the pope to revoke it in 1443. In several earlier decrees, moreover, Eugenius had not only granted favors to such physicians as Elia di Sabbato, but in 1435 he had also forbidden anti-Jewish sermons. This mild decree aimed at such preachments aroused sufficient protests among the general public to bring about its ultimate withdrawal by Eugenius himself in 1442. That withdrawal, rather than the original order, was confirmed by Nicholas V soon after his accession to the throne in 1447.[46]

Otherwise, however, Nicholas V (1447–55) was even less consistent than his immediate predecessor. From the outset he protected the Jews against both the Inquisition and Jew-baiting agitators. But he would, or could, not prevent John Capistrano from staging a public disputation in 1450 with an unknown Jew, Gamaliel. This was during one of the greatest jubilee years in the annals of the Papacy; it attracted masses of pilgrims from all over the Christian world to the papal capital. (According to one doubtless exaggerating contemporary report, they numbered fully 1,000,000.) As a result of that disputation, we are told, Gamaliel and forty other Roman Jews accepted baptism. Nor were the Jewish apprehensions, voiced at the beginning of Nicholas' reign by the elders of Recanati to those of Ancona, allayed by the impression that the vacillating pope usually agreed with him who happened to have his ear at the moment. Just as his restated withdrawal of Eugenius IV's protective bull of 1435 followed by only five weeks his own very liberal decree in behalf of Spanish Jewry dated November 2, 1447 (he justified that abrogation by recriminations of the Christian public), so he nullified to all intents and purposes his intervening pro-Jewish enactments by a sharply intolerant bull of February 25, 1450. This bull, allegedly issued because of widespread complaints from all parts of Italy against the behavior of both Jews and Saracens, renewed almost all segregationist and discriminatory provisions of the older canon law, and even forbade Jews to collect any interest from Christians. The pope appointed, moreover, a Palermitan Franciscan, Lorenzo, as his special envoy to visit the various Italian courts and to induce the princes, if need be by threats of ecclesiastical censure, to enforce the entire bull.[47]

Stringent measures of this kind did not prevent Nicholas, however, from specifically allowing the Jews of Ferrara, Parma, and Lucca to engage in moneylending on interest (1448–52). If in these localities he yielded to the entreaties of local rulers who clamored that the drying up of Jewish credit would ruin many of their subjects, the pope similarly reversed, on Emperor Frederick III's protest, the anti-Jewish decisions adopted by various German synods under the prompting of his own legate, Nicolaus of Cusa. Locally, too, he broke his own prohibition in 1451 by allowing the Jews Dattilo and his son Guglielmo to establish their medical practice in Corneto (Tarquinia), Monte Alto, and Civitavecchia; he merely stipulated that in cases of fatal illness they would not administer any medicine until after the patient had received the sacraments. In his economic policies, too, Nicholas largely favored his Jewish subjects in both his Italian and French possessions. Listening to Jewish complaints about their suffering from endless legal chicaneries, he ordered in 1451 that in all civil litigations against Jews the statute of limitations should begin to operate after the passage of but a single year. Similarly, he yielded to entreaties of the Avignonese community concerning its inability to meet payments on its accumulated debt, especially the arrears on its rentals for a flour mill. Without some relief, the Jewish elders contended, Jews might have to leave Avignon. The pope granted them a two-year moratorium; subsequently they were to pay off the debts in equal instalments over a period of twenty years. But with his usual inconsistency he soon modified these provisions in favor of two Christian creditors whom he considered special hardship cases.[48]

No less moderate were Nicholas' successors, including Calixtus III (1455–58) and the humanist, Pius II (1458–64). To be sure, perhaps because he had grown up in Spain under the impact of Benedict XIII's anti-Jewish policies, Calixtus eagerly renewed in 1456 Eugenius IV's *Dudum ad nostram*. But he may have been more interested in the resulting revenue than in the bull's purely ecclesiastical effects. Panicked by the Turkish conquest of Constantinople, the pope frantically tried to organize a Crusade, and in order to finance it he not only imposed upon the Jews a new tithe but provided that violators of the bull *Dudum* should suffer confiscation of property. His successor, Pius II, previously well known as the humanist writer, Ennea Silvio Piccolomini, too, endeavored to raise funds for such a campaign in 1460 by taxing Jews at the rate of one-twentieth of their property, while the clergy was to contribute fully one-tenth, and the Christian laymen only one-thirtieth. At the same time, yielding to reiterated complaints from Avignon and Carpentras, Pius did not hesitate to interfere with Comtat Jewry's earning capacity by forbidding it to sell any kind of foodstuffs to Christians and making some Jews forswear moneylending on interest. He even recalled in 1459 his effective Avignonese rector, Angelo Geraldini, only because the latter's allegedly pro-Jewish administration had aroused the ire of local leaders. In the same year, on the other hand, Pius retraced his steps when he first abolished, and then speedily restored, the practice of entrusting Jews with the collection of papal revenue, a practice instituted by Martin V in 1423 and frequently opposed later by both the local Christian taxpayers and the more rigid canonists.[49]

There was little change under Paul II (1464–71), except for his extraordinary love for sports, which in 1466 led to the participation of Jews in the carnival track races. At first, Jews seem to have willingly, perhaps even joyously, participated in the games. Ultimately, a day of the week-long sporting event was set aside for Jewish races, just as two other days were filled with races of children and aged persons. In time, however, this spectacle aroused many anti-Jewish passions and ultimately turned into a degrading performance.[50]

One need not see in these vagaries any impact of humanism, although these popes' interest in classical and Hebraic studies may indeed have undermined their naive acceptance of the traditional rationales for the treatment of Jews in canon law. Paul's successor, Sixtus IV (1471–84), responded mainly to the numerous strains and stresses to which he was subjected at home and abroad. Although he had to collaborate with the Catholic monarchs in establishing the Spanish Inquisition, he soon publicly censored its excesses (1482). He also favored converts, but he did not mind making use of Jewish physicians. Most significantly, he forbade anyone to spread the news of the Jewish Blood Accusation of Trent in 1475, which before long became a *cause célèbre* and ultimately led to the canonization of the alleged boy martyr, Simeon of Trent. In 1476 the pope also publicly permitted the Jews to charge interest.[51]

Under the following regimes of Innocent VIII (1484–92) and the much-discussed Alexander VI of the Spanish house of Borgia (1492–1503), Jewish life in the Papal States as elsewhere was complicated by the large influx of both Marranos and professing Jews from the Iberian Peninsula. Even the learned Sicilian convert, Guglielmo Raimondo Moncada, was not above suspicion. Although on his arrival in Rome in 1477 he served as chaplain to the future Pope Innocent VIII, taught theology to the clergy, and impressed the public with his two-hour-long sermons interlaced with original Hebrew and Arabic quotations, he lost in 1483 his sinecure in the school "for Jews" in Girgenti. In 1493 the Catholic monarchs of Spain instructed their ambassador to express to Alexander their "amazement" at the admission of Marranos to Rome. Further aroused by the self-assertion of the Portuguese Marranos, who sent a delegation to the Holy See to submit grievances against their home authorities, the pope ordered the incarceration of some 280 Neo-Christians. Unlike the Spanish Inquisition, however, the papal courts were satisfied with a mere act of abjuration and a promise of good behavior. Understandably, the Roman Jewish community feared serious complications from the presence in its midst of numerous crypto-Jews. Economically, too, it viewed this sudden influx of impoverished yet haughty refugees from the Iberian Peninsula with mixed feelings. At one point it actually requested the pope to suspend further Jewish immigration, a step which aroused Alexander's ire and induced him to impose a fine of 2,000 florins on his inhospitable subjects. The Roman Jews were also affected in 1495 by one of the recurrent floods of the Tiber and the French occupation of the city, which despite Charles VIII's attempted protection led to the plunder of many Jewish homes. Twice (in 1488 and 1500) Jews had to pay new heavy war taxes. In 1500 all Jews living in Christian lands were expected to contribute fully five percent of all their property because, the pope argued, they had long been enjoying the protection of Christian rulers and hence ought to help stave off the Turkish menace. The clergy was again expected to contribute 10 percent, but Christian laymen were not to be taxed. Tax evaders were to be severely punished.[52]

While the Jews' political and legal status had thus remained largely intact, the impact of the ever growing taxation (the three war taxes of 5 percent each in 1480, 1488, and 1500 alone could be quite ruinous) and the increasing popular hostility, particularly in the Papacy's French possessions, helped to undermine their economic well-being. The municipal elders of Avignon showered the papal administration with complaints against their Jewish fellow-citizens, and in 1480 disavowed their own envoys to Rome who had secured a pro-Jewish bull. Jean Rosa, papal deputy-legate, charged with investigation of that disavowal, decided that the decree had been elicited by Jewish manipulations, rather than by the Avignonese envoys, and urged its revocation. In substance, however, that bull contained few innovations. It mainly tried to renew Nicholas V's concession of a twenty-year term for the liquidation of the Jewish communal debts and generally to safeguard Jews against unlawful attacks. Such riots were not infrequent; there was a particularly serious assault on the Jewish quarter of Cavaillon in 1485. Avignon, too, had to double the size of its usual guard in 1484 to counteract anti-Jewish agitators who assured the populace that, with the demise of Sixtus IV, the Jews might be assailed with impunity. Certainly, the complaint of Avignonese Jewry that as a result of wars and taxes its members had "become so impoverished and so deprived of possessions, both movable and immovable, that their indigence makes it impossible for them to sustain their miserable life" was not devoid of justification.[53]

Under the early sixteenth-century popes Julius II (1503–13) and Leo X (1513–21), the Renaissance splendor of the papal court reached its height, and some rays of its glory fell also upon the Jewish community. The new humanism affected the very welcoming ceremony for new popes. While handing Julius the customary Torah scroll, the Spaniard, Samuel (bearing the somewhat misleading family name of Sarfati or Frenchman), physician-in-ordinary to the pope, delivered a lengthy Latin oration, very likely in the then widely emulated Ciceronian style. The pope replied with the traditional rebuke of the Jewish interpretation. In his hatred of Alexander VI, Julius often styled this member of the house of Borgia a Marrano or even a Jew, and toward the end of his life ordered the incarceration of a number of prominent Marranos. But the Venetian envoy reporting that Marrano prosecution to his home government on January 16, 1513 regarded it as a mere financial operation, "for most offices in Rome are in their [the Marranos'] hands and it is expected that, through this measure, he [the pope] will secure 50,000 ducats." Leo X, a scion of the famous house of Medici, likewise proved quite friendly, although he, too, started with the usual negative reply to the welcoming Jewish delegation, using the somewhat milder formula: *Confirmanus sed non consentimus* (We confirm but do not agree). The enlightened pope must have felt the awkwardness of the entire ceremony, which after him was completely abandoned. More importantly, in his bull of 1519 Leo not only renewed all traditional privileges of Roman Jewry, but also eliminated the special Jewish tax of one gold ducat per family and of 10 ducats for each banking establishment. We shall see that, in the controversy over the Talmud, he was on the side of the German humanist, Johannes Reuchlin, against the Dominican accusers. We do not know to what extent the pope was influenced by his Jewish court physician, Bonet de Lattes, to whom Reuchlin had appealed in a remarkable Hebrew letter which included such flattering phrases as, "I have heard that Your Honor is constantly at the papal curia and that the care of His Holiness' body is entrusted to your wisdom." At any rate, Leo's humanistically oriented attitude toward the Talmud marked a total reversal of the Papacy's long-standing policies, initiated by Gregory IX in 1239. He actually promoted the printing of the Talmud! Both Julius and Leo, moreover, held the gates of Rome open to Jewish immigration from southern Italy in 1510–11. The only qualification inserted in Leo's bull of 1519 concerned the number of Jewish houses of worship in Rome, which was not to exceed eleven. Certainly, Froissart's aforementioned remark, contrasting the toleration of the Jews in the Papal States to their exclusion from other Western lands, would have been doubly justified in the first two decades of the sixteenth century.[54]

In fact, all of western Europe from Scotland to southern Spain and even large parts of Italy and Germany had at that time been completely emptied of Jewish settlers, whereas the Jewish community of Rome seems to have increased at as rapid a pace as that of the rest of the inhabitants. The best estimates available show that in 1526–27 Rome's total population amounted to 55,000, or about 60 percent more than it was half a millennium earlier. The Jewish population, estimated at 285 families or about 1,500 souls, had maintained its old ratio after recovering from an intervening decline. It grew sufficiently to be able to support some nine to ten synagogues at the end of the fifteenth century, and eleven in 1519. So long as there existed no compulsory ghetto, Roman Jewry built its houses of worship in the vicinity of its residential quarters scattered throughout the city, a practice recorded in ancient times. The cosmopolitan character of the city's Jewish settlers was reflected in their varied rituals and the ensuing predilection of worshipers to hold services of their own rite. Nevertheless, the presence of eleven synagogues, vastly exceeding the number of Jewish houses of worship in most other western metropolises, presupposed the existence of a sizable and fairly affluent community.[55]

Outside the capital the Jewish communities in the Italian States of the Church were small, and for the most part rather young. Apart from the general fluidity of frontiers and the rise of new independent duchies and city states, the growing decentralization of Jewish life throughout the Peninsula would make the enumeration of all communities located in the Papal States an arduous and, from the purely historical point of view, unrewarding task. This would be a good project for a comprehensive historico-geographical dictionary, a sort of *Italia Judaica,* similar in nature to the dictionaries now available for early medieval Germany and, in part, for France. Our knowledge of the historic evolution, sometimes the very existence, of most lesser central Italian communities is largely derived from a few chance records relating to individual Jews, particularly moneylenders and physicians.

Even Ancona, which as the main papal harbor on the Adriatic Sea was to play a great role in the Levant trade and for this reason was soon to embrace the second largest Italian Jewish community under papal suzerainty, was for a while an independent republic. During that period the community, whose synagogue had suffered from an earthquake of 1267 (an individual Jew had been mentioned in a real estate transfer in Ancona's vicinity as early as 967), was reinforced by refugees from the Black Death massacres in 1348. The first formal privilege, however, was apparently enacted only after Pope Martin V took over the city in 1429. Similarly Fano, though acknowledging papal suzerainty, was long controlled by local patricians, particularly the family Malatesta. Apart from some stray records relating to Jews there from 1214 on, we learn about Jewish bankers lending Galeatto Malatesta 1,000 ducats in 1332. From the expulsion of heretics in 1367 Jews were specifically exempted, while their considerable privileges were confirmed in 1430. So interested were the Malatestas in Jewish taxes, which in the fourteenth century often approximated half their revenue from the city, that in 1447 they tried to resist papal "encroachments." It was this resistance, rather than the implied favoritism shown to Jews, which brought down upon the city four papal excommunications within forty years. Although the badge was introduced in 1464, the municipal administration effectively protected the Jews against incendiary sermons; in 1492 it forbade a preacher to discuss the Blood Accusation of Trent. But it did not prevent the establishment of a *monte di pietà* in 1471. Among the Jewish professionals, it may be noted, there was a Jewess by the name of Perna who in 1460 applied for a medical license—a phenomenon not altogether exceptional in Italian Jewry. The community also boasted of an array of scholars and scribes and even of a distinguished printing press, established by Gershom (Hieronymus) Soncino, which published books in Hebrew, Greek, Latin, and Italian. A leading Jewish physician, Mose da Rieti, of neighboring Fabriano during the fifteenth century, has been the subject of special monographs. Mose, who had been the personal physician of Pius II and a poet, sometimes styled the Hebrew Dante, was invited to Fabriano in 1458 after a vain search for a Christian doctor.[56]

For the most part, however, we hear about Jewish communities in the papal provinces primarily in connection with the establishment of either Jewish loan banks, or with that of their rivals, the *monti di pietà*. In order to counteract the exorbitant rates of interest charged by Florentine and other Christian usurers, city after city, with the encouragement of the papal administration, invited Jewish bankers to settle in its midst and extend loans to the "needy" population at moderate rates. Treaties to this effect, going under the name of *condottas* (conveyances), were first recorded in Matelica, Umbria, in 1287, and in neighboring Todi five years later. In 1297 the city of Orvieto followed suit, and despite certain domestic vagaries reiteratedly upheld the essential Jewish privileges. On one occasion (in 1334) the elders even made use of the diplomatic skill of a Jewish envoy. Early in the fourteenth century the city of Urbino attracted a scholar-banker, Magister Daniel of Viterbo, endowing him with almost monopolistic rights. For many years thereafter any new Jewish moncylender settling in the city had to indemnify Daniel or his heirs by a stipulated annual fee. Such privileged Jewish loan banks are recorded during that period in no less than twenty-seven places in the Marches alone.[57]

Before long, however, a reaction set in. Anti-Jewish preachers often traversed the entire region sowing seeds of hostility. One such eminent homilist, San Giacomo della Marca, not only attacked Jewish moneylending but also sought to interfere with the sale of Jewish meat and wine and generally sharply to segregate Jews from their neighbors. He also objected to the display of luxuries by Jews or the participation of Christian guests at Jewish weddings. Wherever he delivered such sermons, particularly in Fermo, Recanati, San Severino, and Terni, he inspired both sharp popular reactions and anti-Jewish legislation. These preachers registered their first success in the city of Perugia, which the Jews had been formally expelled from in 1279, but probably had never left. At any rate they were there in 1310 and embraced in 1381 a total of thirty-three families, who were formally granted rights of citizenship for themselves and their descendants. In 1402 the city itself had to borrow one hundred gold florins from Jews for defense. Yet thirty years later it felt free to limit interest rates and to introduce the Jewish badge. With the new turn of events, Perugia became the first city to establish a *monte di pietà* in 1462 under the prompting of Fra Michele Carcano of Milan (not, as has long been assumed, of Fra Barnaba Manassei of Terni). Curiously, a year later the city forced the Jews to lend 1,200 gold florins to their new competitor! Other communities of that region for which we have more or less detailed data are those of Amelia, Ascoli, Foligno, Macerata, Montegiorgio, Terracina, Tivoli, Velletri and Viterbo.[58]

PAPAL DEPENDENCIES AND TUSCANY

North of the Marches and Umbria was located the old Republic of San Marino, which until today has preserved its independence. Among its earliest Jewish records is one relating to a loan extended to its government by Emanuele of Rimini in 1367. Occasional Jewish names appear in criminal prosecutions in the 1450s (an alleged thief, a traitor, and a counterfeiter), while in

1462 one Musetto lent the authorities money to entertain visitors. These stray references attest the presence of Jews in the republic, but they do not necessarily indicate the existence of an organized community, the full development of which was to come only after 1500. In contrast, medieval Ravenna Jewry was much more important than the modern community. We recall that in 519 the city had been the scene of a mob assault on the synagogue, which was followed by Theodoric the Great's punitive action. Four centuries later (930) we get another glimpse through a religious disputation with one Solomon b. Tanḥum appearing as the Jewish representative. Again centuries passed, and Emperor Frederick II intervened in 1226 in behalf of a Jew Donfolino against an attempted extortion by the city council. In 1248 Ravenna was annexed by the Papacy, and except for some 68 years (1441–1509) when it was under Venetian rule, the Jewish community shared the destinies of its Roman coreligionists. Even during the Venetian interlude the new rulers were bound by treaty to respect the local Jewish privileges. Early provincial synods, to be sure, meeting in 1311 and 1317 in Ravenna and Bologna, respectively, renewed the canonical demands that Jews be allowed to settle only in places having synagogues and be made to wear badges, here described as wheels of red color. (Ravenna itself had such a synagogue, which for some unexplained reason was removed in 1489 to another locality.) But their very repetition proves that these restrictive demands by churchmen were not taken too seriously by the municipal authorities.[59]

During the fourteenth and fifteenth centuries, Jewish communities spread also to many smaller localities in the Romagna and Emilia, for instance, to Lugo and Faenza. Although apparently not large, the community of Rimini played a considerable role in the affairs of Italian Jewry; a member, we recall, Menaḥem b. Nathan, upon his death in 1392, left bequests for the repair of the harbor of Rimini, the place of his residence, and for that of the walls of Rome, the place of his birth. The neighboring community of Forlì secured in 1359 a significant privilege, in which the municipal elders spoke, without any malice aforethought, of "Jews and other usurers." In 1488 we hear of a Forlì Jewish quarter, which, however, was not necessarily the exclusive locale of the

Jewish inhabitants, just as their economic well-being may well have been much brighter than it was represented in 1469 in the community's grievances against excessive papal taxation. It may be noted, however, that a long list of the city's creditors in December 1407 includes no Jewish names. Forlì is also remembered as the meeting place of representatives of many Italian communities in 1418, who sought a coordinated program for negotiations with the newly elected Pope Martin V.[60]

A similar intercommunal consultation had taken place two years earlier in Bologna, a leading commercial and intellectual center of central Italy. Here, too, the Jewish settlement reached back to ancient times, and, according to a local tradition, two Christian martyrs had been buried in the Bologna Jewish cemetery in 302. Even a decree of expulsion, promulgated for unknown reasons in 1171, hardly interrupted the community's historic continuity. A Jewish quarter is mentioned in Bologna in 1366, but Jews could also live and own houses in various other parts of town. A beautiful synagogue was erected in 1394 by two Roman Jews, Moses and Elijah, scions of the venerable Jewish family De' Ne'arim. The community's intellectual vigor is also illustrated by the presence there in 1454 of a fine private library, assembled by a branch of the family Finzi, which, apparently originating in Germany, was to play a considerable role in the destinies of the Italian and Middle Eastern Jews. The Jewish settlement continued to grow, and despite a number of restrictive ordinances (including two relating to the badge in 1417 and 1458) it was able to maintain eleven synagogues in the mid-sixteenth century. It also embraced a Jewish guild of silk weavers, who not only carried on with this time-honored Jewish manufacture but also served as patrons of Jewish learning. Needless to say, its fate was also deeply affected by the frequent clashes between the pro- and the antipapal factions, and the great international conflicts between the French and the Habsburg dynasties.[61]

Somewhat less intimately tied to the papal administration were the Emilian cities which in the fifteenth and sixteenth centuries lived under the enlightened regime of the house of Este. Jews were settled, in particular, in Ferrara, Modena, and Reggio. In Ferrara they were mentioned in 1088 (according to a somewhat dubious communal record), but their first known privilege is dated in 1275. The community must, nevertheless, have been sufficiently important then for the anti-Maimonidean controversy to have been fought there between a leading opponent, Solomon Petit, and some defenders of the philosopher, possibly including Hillel of Verona. The Ferrara community also actively participated in regional conferences. Of course, there also were some anti-Jewish spokesmen among both preachers and laymen. In two sonnets written in 1376, the poet Francesco di Vannozzo sharply attacked the city for its failure to receive him graciously. Blaming his misfortunes on the "Jewish sect" as well as the climate, he exclaimed in an oft-copied poem, "There is No Virtue Where the Faith is Scarce." But both the municipal authorities and the dukes upheld the rights of Jews. Of particular importance were Duke Borso's enactments of 1455 and 1464, reserving the jurisdiction over mixed Judeo-Christian litigations and in criminal cases, such as cohabitation with Christian women, to the *giudice dei savi,* that is, the supreme court of the city. Those privileges were confirmed in 1489. Ercole I d'Este argued with the pope in 1471 that Jewish contributions to his country's economy were so great that they should be freed from all papal taxes, a concession already secured by his predecessor, Borso. Two years later Ercole actually refunded to the Jews some amounts they had previously paid to the papal Treasury. The duke and his successors continued to tax them heavily for local needs, however, especially for the erection of some of those magnificent buildings which have perpetuated the memory of the great D'Este patrons of the Italian Renaissance. Here, too, we may observe numerous inconsistencies. On the one hand, the Inquisition was allowed in 1458 to prosecute the Jews of Ferrara, Modena, and other cities for having illicitly erected synagogues. It was appeased only after sharing with the House of Este the large fine of 5,000 gold scudi paid by the Ferrara Jews. On the other hand, perhaps learning from this experience, Samuel Melli, a native of Rome, secured in 1481 an advance permit for the erection of a new Jewish house of worship in Ferrara, which overshadowed in its splendor that of the other nine synagogues in the city. The same Ercole I who forced Bernardino da Feltre in 1493 to discontinue his rousing anti-Jewish sermons decreed three years later

that Jews must attend missionary homilies and wear badges—
orders which were largely observed in their breach. Similarly his
wife, Eleonora of Naples, who, as we recall, had been persuaded by
Bernardino da Feltre to argue with her Neapolitan brother and father against the Jews, and on another occasion was requested to
intercede in behalf of a Reggio murderer of a young Jew, nevertheless helped persuade the authorities of Ferrara to admit twenty-
one Jewish refugees from the south who had been stranded in
Genoa. The deep humanistic interests of both court and society
ultimately made it possible for the Jew, Abraham Farissol, to engage in a rather free religious disputation with a Christian cleric,
and for another, Abraham Sarfati, to teach Hebrew at the University of Ferrara.[62]

Ducal favoritism was, of course, not wholly disinterested; it was
largely the result of the major role played by Jewish moneylending in the country. Even the later renowned community of
Modena owed its origin to Jewish bankers. Though the presence
of Jews is sporadically attested in previous centuries—one
Ardingus Judaeus (if he was a Jew) actually served as collector of
ecclesiastical tithes in 1025—their communal history did not begin
until 1373 when a combine of Jewish moneylenders from Perugia,
Fermo, and Rimini successfully negotiated the establishment of a
Jewish bank in Modena. We have the text of another relatively
early privilege of this type, enacted by the municipality of Reggio
on July 30, 1413. Written in the form of Jewish stipulations and
the municipality's acceptance, modification, or rejection thereof,
and composed in a curious mixture of Latin and the local Italian
dialect, these "Cappitulla" provided among other matters:

I. In the first place, the syndics of the said community of Reggio in
possession of the legitimate mandate have made the plain and firm
commitment to the said Muso that if anything should be taken from
him by force and violence of the burghers or of any other person,
public or private, the said municipality will be held and obliged to indemnify him for it. Particularly all citizens of Reggio who can be
forced throughout the territory of Reggio by contracting this instrument [will adhere to its provisions]. . . . The reply of the said municipality of Reggio to this stipulation is: Let it be thus. . . .

II. Also that they [the Jews] may observe all their festivals and adhere
to their laws without contravention by any person, public or private.

The reply of the said municipality of Reggio to this stipulation is: Let it be thus so long as they observe their festivals in a private, not in a public location.

Understandably, the contracting parties laid the main emphasis upon provisions concerning loans, pawns, the free possession of houses, and the like. Although limited as to time and personnel, this "treaty" laid the foundation for a significant expansion of the Jewish community. So certain were the Jews of their indispensability that on occasion they threatened to leave the city. The very popes recognized that need, Nicholas V issuing in 1451 a special authorization for the Jews in the neighboring district of Parma (which was for the most part an independent duchy, except for the years 1512–45 when it became subject to direct papal suzerainty) to lend money on interest. The pope cited similar Jewish practices in the diocese of Ferrara and in the Marches. The Reggio Jews were expressly freed from distinguishing marks, and after prolonged negotiations were also allowed to sell their surplus meats to non-Jews. Before long, to be sure, *monti di pietà* were established in Parma, Modena, and Reggio in the years 1488–94, but they did not put an end to Jewish banking. On the contrary, by stimulating Jewish moneylenders to disperse their activities more widely over the countryside, they gave rise to numerous new Jewish settlements in the smaller localities. In general, the municipal authorities and princes, and particularly the house of Este as long as it lasted, opened up many opportunities for Jewish economic as well as intellectual creativity.[63]

In Tuscany Jews appeared sporadically in the earlier Middle Ages, but continuous settlements developed only from the twelfth century on. Lucca alone had a Jewish community in the tenth century, at a time when southern Italy had attracted a large and affluent Jewish population. The story of Kalonymus, who at the battle of Cotrone in 982 allegedly saved Emperor Otto II and thereby set in motion the Kalonymide emigration to Mayence, may not be wholly historical, but it reflects the indisputably great cultural, religious, and communal influences emanating from Italy which decisively shaped the outlook and communal life of Ashkenazic Jewry. Yet even in the 1160s, when Benjamin traveled in Tuscany, he found only forty Jewish families in Lucca and twenty more in neighboring Pisa. These communities must have been the leading Jewish settlements north of the Papal States. Lucca was able to attract the world traveler, Abraham ibn Ezra, who seems to have made a living there by teaching Hebrew grammar while pursuing his literary and scientific studies.

In the subsequent decades Lucca in general, and with it its Jewish community, declined in importance, while first Pisa and later Florence took over the leadership of the entire Tuscan region. In Lucca a bank was established by one Gaio of Forlì in the early 1400s. Gaio left Lucca in 1433 because of a heavy tax of 1,050 gold florins imposed upon him by Emperor Sigismund (who was then marching on Rome), but his work was continued by other Jewish bankers, Angelo di Gaio and Isacco di Emanuele, who in 1432 secured a favorable *condotta* allowing them to charge 33⅓ percent per annum. Among later leaders there stood out David di Dattalo of Tivoli. Probably to answer some carping critics, the city, moved by "conscientious scruples," appealed in 1452 to Pope Nicholas V, who had legalized Jewish usury in Parma and other communities during the preceding year. The pope responded favorably. "Although Jewish infidelity," he wrote, "ought to be reproved, their [the Jews'] relationships with Christians are nevertheless useful, as is demonstrated through the test of experience in our time. Hence since they are created by the Creator of all, they ought not to be shunned by faithful Christians." The pope absolved the Luccan burghers from all sins connected with their permission for Jews to settle in their midst and to grant loans at moderate rates of interest. The compact with the Jews was renewed, with some modifications, in 1468, 1477, and 1487. Before long, however, the Jewish bankers suffered serious reverses as a result of the agitation for a *monte di pietà*, the supporters of which included a local monk who claimed to have had a vision of Jesus demanding its establishment. Bernardino da Feltre's successful propaganda not only resulted in an immediate fine of 1,300 florins imposed upon Jewish objectors in 1489, but also made Jewish life in Lucca untenable in the long run. In the sixteenth century Jews were eliminated entirely from their ancient habitat.[64]

Pisa's thirteenth-century municipal statutes indirectly attest the presence of a Jewish community, since they include provisions for a badge and against the admission of Jewish witnesses. Pisa was, in fact, one of the first Italian cities to implement, as early as 1221, the pertinent resolution of the Fourth Latheran Council. Nonetheless, in three documents of 1317 Jews appear as "Pisan burghers." The flowering of the Pisan community came only after 1354, however, when the city issued its first invitation to Jewish moneylenders and subsequently negotiated a *condotta* with them. In 1406 one Yeḥiel b. Mattathiah, of the distinguished Roman family *Min ha-knesset* (De Sinagoga), was allowed to establish a loan bank; he became the founder of the famous family Da Pisa, whose members played a great role in both high finance and culture during the following two centuries. Yeḥiel himself represented the Pisan community at the conferences of Bologna and Forlì. His grandson and namesake (Yeḥiel b. Isaac) combined banking with literary activity; he wrote a particularly significant treatise on Jewish banking. He also corresponded with Don Isaac Abravanel, while he and other members of the family took care of such new arrivals as the Iberian refugees or David Reubeni (1525). Even the agitation for a Pisan *monte* in 1471 was accompanied only by a brief assault on Jews. A quarter century later, Isaac da Pisa (the first Yeḥiel's son) was actually instrumental in helping establish the *monte* by supplying it with more than half of its needed capital. The Pisan community not only persisted on the mainland, but under its influence the Jewry of the long-embattled island of Corsica, so long as it was dominated by Pisa, likewise continued into the modern period.[65]

Equally dramatic were the vicissitudes of the community of Siena. Well established in 1229, it did not enjoy the monopoly in banking given to some other Jewries by their *condottas*, since Siena did not formally outlaw Christian usury. The municipal statute of 1309–10 spoke without much emphasis about restitution of usury, but insisted that a usurer not be disqualified as a witness unless he "otherwise be a person of ill fame or of suspect opinions and way of life." Nonetheless the local treaties, successively renewed, gave the Jews extensive rights. One provision stated succinctly: "In every cause, civil or criminal, they [the Jews] ought to be held, treated and respected like true and native citizens of the city of Siena and be able to enjoy all the privileges

. . . for the duration of the present stipulations." Perhaps because they always had had to compete with Christian moneylenders, the Sienese Jews overcame with greater ease the difficulties occasioned by the establishment of a *monte de pietà* in 1471. Jewish bankers, including one Jacob of Padua, who had reached new agreements with the city in 1456–57, continued undisturbedly until the establishment in Siena of a formal ghetto in 1571 and beyond. Culturally, too, the integration of Jews into Renaissance mores and artistic predilections seems to have gone further than in most other Italian communities. At least there is no evidence that the presence in the Jewish quarter of a statue of Moses ever elicited indignant protests from orthodox members. True, the sculptor was a Christian, Antonio Federighi, but the community must have acquiesced in its erection, if it did not altogether order it. These friendly Judeo-Christian relations are also evidenced by the request of the city elders in 1373 that their bishop, Guglielmo, intercede with the pope in behalf of the local Jewish council and secure the abolition of the Jewish badge. With rather unaccustomed rudeness the bishop replied, "You ought to know that it is necessary that Jews be distinguished from us by clothing just as much as by faith." [66]

As elsewhere, these relationships deteriorated in the fifteenth century. Certainly, San Bernardino da Siena, whose influence outside his native city may have been greater than at home, did not, in the Jewish case, "disseminate peace, harmony, and unity," to cite the enthusiastic praise of his sermons by his devoted disciple, San Giacomo della Marca. Apart from these two anti-Jewish preachers, we need but mention Antonio da Rimini and John Capistrano, all Franciscans. In asking the pope's intercession with Antonio that he come to preach in their city, the city council described him as being "beloved with the highest devotion by our people." However, the Papacy intervened here, too, for the Jews, and at the height of agitation for a *monte di pietà* Innocent VIII ordered the vicar general of the Siena archbishopric to absolve the municipal authorities from any ecclesiastical penalties for their contractual agreement with Jewish usurers. Not surprisingly, therefore, Sienese Jewry weathered the reaction which was soon to set in throughout Tuscany better than most other communities, although neither the city nor the Jewry ever recaptured its medieval glory. In contrast, the great harbor city of Leghorn was to attract Jews in significant numbers only in the early modern period, when it was ultimately to embrace one of Italy's largest and most influential Jewish communities.[67]

Overshadowing all Tuscan communities in importance was that of Florence; not because of its own intrinsic strength, be it in numbers, financial power, or cultural achievement, but rather because in the Late Middle Ages Florence had become the great world center of both banking and the Italian Renaissance, and the cynosure of all eyes among Western scholars and artists. Politically and militarily, too, Florence succeeded in gradually extending its rule over Lucca, Pisa, Leghorn, and Siena, and ultimately, as the capital of the Grand Duchy of Tuscany under the Medici, played a considerable role in international affairs as well.

The Jewish community, on the other hand, had a rather brief medieval career. Although the nearby municipality of San Gimignano, then in financial straights, sent an envoy to Siena in 1309 to secure a loan and "to induce the Jews residing there to come to San Gimignano as they had promised," only a few Jewish-sounding names sporadically appear in the fourteenth-century Florentine records. In 1437, however, the city council concluded a treaty with one Abramo di Dattilo and his associates for the establishment of a loan bank for ten years. Although Abramo's family had operated credit institutions in the neighboring locality of San Miniato since 1393, it had not been allowed to penetrate Florence until the credit "pinch" on the local population became extremely acute after the formerly leading world banks of the Peruzzi and Bardi had suffered serious reverses. Christian lenders were still allowed to charge interest, but their severe extortions under the existing shortage of liquid capital forced the authorities to consider the admission of Jews. After debates carried on during the 1420s, the city elders decided on June 12, 1430 to admit Jews so that

the poor of Florence should, particularly at this time of the pestilence, not be ruined by such grave usuries as are practiced by those who extend loans. Also that whenever the necessity should arise, they [the poor] should be able to provide for their affairs in the least burdensome way.

The agreement of 1437 was renewed in the following decades, although not without extended debates and occasional delays of several months or even a year. The Florentine Jews also had difficulty in safeguarding their accustomed communal and judicial autonomy. The *Otto di Guardia e Balia* reserved for themselves exclusive jurisdiction, demanding that Jews wishing to appear before any other court, even before an ecclesiastical tribunal in cases involving clerics, should first secure a permit from their office. The *Otto* also expected to deal with internal Jewish litigations in accordance with the provisions of common law, and recognized Jewish law only in matrimonial cases. But Jewish parties could insist on the application of Jewish law, particularly in courts of arbitration recognized by the state, or else repair to rabbinic courts outside the city. Similarly, the handling of ritually slaughtered meats, which by decree of 1477 was to be controlled by a single Christian butcher, was soon modified to meet Jewish objections. In 1481 the city divided this operation between two butchers, and restricted the prices charged to Jewish customers to those currently prevailing in the general market.[68]

At this juncture Bernardino da Feltre intervened. At first the authorities, and especially the real ruler of the city, Lorenzo the Magnificent, forbade Bernardino in 1488 to preach against Jews. Without this strong emotional incentive his agitation for a *monte* languished, just as an earlier effort led by a Fra Francesco in 1473 had quickly spent itself. But when, after the French invasion in 1494, the Medici were expelled and a new republic was proclaimed, Bernardino was allowed to resume his propaganda. It led to the establishment of a charitable loan bank in 1495, Bernardino's success being facilitated by the severe financial crisis of 1494. Not all partisans of a *monte*, to be sure, were anti-Jewish. A Jewish banker, Manuele da Camerino, actually left it a bequest of 200 lire. The popular leader, Fra Girolamo Savonarola, though a supporter of the *monte*, once informed the authorities of Lucca that, in his opinion, Jews already engaged in moneylending were fully entitled to pursue their trade. Nevertheless, the mere operation of such a loan bank made the presence of Jewish bankers seemingly superfluous. In 1496 the Signoria not only canceled its agreement with them, but also ordered them to leave the city. Most bankers, however, obtained an extension of three years, and, after lending the municipality 16,000 florins, another extension until the repayment of that debt. This proviso enabled the bankers to secure further extensions, which expired in 1508. Subsequently, too, many remained by giving up banking and joining the fairly large group of Jews who derived their livelihood from other occupations. If in 1527 the city Senate decreed an expulsion of Jews, it did not make clear whether it wished to remove all Jewish inhabitants or only the moneylenders. In any case, with the restoration of a Medicean regime three years later, this decree was never implemented. Combined with the establishment soon thereafter of the Grand Duchy of Tuscany, this transformation of the character of the Jewish community and particularly of its leadership opened a new chapter in its history.[69]

ITALY'S NORTHWEST

In northern Italy there was even less consistency in the admission or rejection of Jews. Many cities, long independent, were gradually incorporated into larger states, but they often changed allegiance from one principality or republic to another. Each such change created conditions affecting the Jewish settlement. The domestic situation likewise varied greatly from locality to locality. Moreover, the close proximity of France and the Holy Roman Empire invited emulation of their intolerant policies, but it also opened the gates to the influx of Jewish immigrants from these countries. Northern Italy, which had been the matrix of Ashkenazic communities north of the Alps, now received much reinforcement from Franco-German Jewish settlers, particularly after each wave of massacres and decrees of expulsion in their home countries.

Local economic transformations and the frequently felt need for Jewish bankers contributed to the rise of the North-Italian communities, whereas the growing anti-Jewish reaction, including the agitation for *monti di pietà,* served as a major deterrent. Any attempt at generalization, therefore, of the prevailing trends in the policies of these territories is extremely hazardous. One may confidently assert only that this region, which had very few Jews in the thirteenth century, witnessed the rise of many communities toward the end of the Middle Ages. By the sixteenth century some of them, especially those of Venice, Padua, and Mantua, achieved a status in international Jewish life far exceeding their numerical strength.

Tuscany's immediate neighbor, Genoa, pursued policies far more akin to those of its Florentine than of its Pisan rivals. From ancient times Jews had sporadically appeared in that Ligurian city. In fact, in two letters preserved by Cassiodorus, Theodoric the Great tried to protect the Genoese Jews and their synagogue, just as he did somewhat more drastically in Ravenna. In 1134 a special Jewish tax was, ironically, collected for the benefit of a local church. Yet when Benjamin of Tudela arrived in that city some thirty years later he found there only two Jewish brothers, seemingly fairly recent arrivals from North Africa. Nor did the Genoese, whose famous banking system developed along different lines from that of Florence, prove more tolerant in the later medieval centuries, although stray records indicate the presence of some Jews there in the middle of the thirteenth century. In 1492 a group of Spanish exiles made its appearance. Their ships having suffered severe damage at sea, crews and passengers asked asylum in the Genoese harbor; they were perforce tolerated for a short time. "And while they were making their preparations to journey further," observes Bartolomeo Senarega, the Republic's chancellor in his oft-quoted pathetic description of the plight of these new arrivals, "winter came on, and many died on the wharves." Finally, as we recall, Ferrara admitted twenty-one refugees, and only a few Jews seem to have remained in Genoa. They did not organize a community until 1550, when several individuals obtained formal permission to reside in the city for a few years. Nor did Genoa extend greater protection to Jews wishing to settle in the provincial communities under its sway. Even the island of Sardinia, we remember, was not really to admit Jewish settlers until after the replacement of the Genoese by Aragonese rule.[70]

Neighboring Piedmont underwent many changes in political

controls. Ultimately united with Savoy, it embarked upon its great historic career which culminated in the nineteenth-century unification of Italy. In the Middle Ages, however, the two sections often pursued diverse Jewish policies. Savoy largely followed the French example, whereas Piedmontese Jewry grew only after 1348 and the final expulsion from most of France in 1394, although, according to a somewhat uncertain report, Count Edward the Liberal (1323–39) had submitted to the Estates proposals "to stem the widespread usury of Jews." When, during the fifteenth century, Jewish settlements sprang up in various Piedmontese communities, including Turin, some newcomers were forced by foreign litigants under various pretexts and threats to appear before courts in their former places of residence. Such summonses caused much expense and aggravation to the defendants, and many preferred to settle out of court. Together with Jewish representatives at the Council of Florence, Amadeus VIII of Savoy (1391–1451) secured on February 13, 1429 from Pope Martin V a bull providing that:

Jews, both indigenous and foreign, of whatever kind who, before the start of the litigation, have chosen to reside within the Duchy of Savoy or your dominion, shall not, for whatever reason or cause, even the pretext of some privileges conferred upon Jews or anyone else by the Apostolic See, be summoned to justice outside the said duchy and dominion, be excommunicated, aggravated, or pressured with other sentences.

To insure obedience, the pope threatened all transgressors with "the wrath of the omnipotent God and of the Apostles Peter and Paul." Fifteen years later Amadeus himself, who by a curious historical twist served at that time as the supreme pontiff under the name of Felix V, renewed Martin's bull. Of more general significance for Piedmontese Jewry was his comprehensive *condotta* of 1430 (adumbrated by his provisions of 1403), however, which promised it and its religious observances full protection for a period of ten years. On the other hand, Jews were to wear badges, live in a ghetto, and promise not to erect any new synagogues, as if all synagogues of the region had not been relatively new. While the personally pious duke was evidently prompted by a mixture of humanitarian and fiscal motivations, his son, Louis, was more subject to temporary moods and greedy impulses. In 1436 he ordered the removal of Jews from certain Turin houses so as to make them available for students. Five years later he sharply reacted to complaints reaching him from both nobles and commoners that Jews not only charged excessive rates of interest but often concealed usurious transactions behind contracts relating to the sale of grain or other objects. The duke insisted, therefore, that Jews should not charge more than one penny per florin a week without compound interest. More radically, in 1452 and 1454 Louis twice decreed the expulsion of Jews, only to revoke his edicts within one and five months respectively after receiving substantial payments from the Jewish communities. On the whole, the status of Piedmontese, like that of Savoyard, Jewry remained unchanged during the regime of Louis' immediate successors.[71]

Apart from the regulations issued by the dukes (up to 1406, counts) of Savoy, a number of municipal ordinances and local developments deeply affected the Piedmontese communities. The municipal council of Turin debated on December 14, 1425 a proposal to confine "all Jews" in the city to one quarter in order "the better to supervise them lest they lend money on usury." Characteristically, the high-sounding phrase, "all Jews," referred to but four families recorded in the census of 1428-29. The subsequent two annual censuses of 1429-31 showed an increase to eleven families, enumerated by names of husbands and wives for the assessment of a poll tax of one ounce each, from which, however, several individuals were exempted. The physician Elia Almandi (probably derived from Alemani) was included among the taxpayers in the first census, but was exempt according to the subsequent enumerations. Local capitoli were also arranged by the Marquess of Mortara with a Jew, Moses, while other Jews entered the city of Novara over the protests of Novarese burghers. Jews established themselves also in Savigliano, where Bonafede de Chalon concluded agreements with them in 1430-47. More or less similar arrangements were made in Vercelli and Cuneo (1446-52), while the subsequently important community of Casale, in the duchy of Monferrato, seems not to have been formed until the beginning of the sixteenth century, although a Monferrato inhabitant was severely fined in 1432 for having "spoken words injurious to Jews." [72]

During the fifteenth and sixteenth centuries Piedmont became an important center of Jewish life and a meeting place for three streams of Jewish immigrants coming from France, the Holy Roman Empire, and central Italy. The French immigrants made an interesting contribution to Jewish liturgy. Settling in the small communities of Asti, Fossano, and Moncalvo, they modified their traditional prayers and created the so-called ritual of APAM (representing the Hebrew initials of the three cities). The history of Piedmontese Jewry as a whole was to become both more significant and better recorded under the reigns of Emanuel Philibert (1553–80) and Charles Emanuel I (1580–1630) when, as we shall see in a later context, periods of intolerance alternated with those of relative calm.[73]

Alessandria, one of the major Piedmontese cities, had long been under Milanese domination. In 1391 it requested from Gian Galeazzo Sforza (1378–1402) a permit for the Jewish banker, Abraham, to reside in the city with full burgher's rights. Although the Visconti and Sforza dynasties were quite favorable to Jews (we recall in particular the negotiations relating to Jews between Francesco Sforza and the pope), the animosity of Milanese burghers kept the Jews out of the capital more effectively than did similar efforts of the municipalities of Turin or Novara. This was the more remarkable as the Jewish question had been discussed in Milan in the days of ancient Rome, when it became the subject of the first major clash between the Church and the Christian Roman Empire in St. Ambrose's sharp attack on Emperor Theodosius I in 388. While we hear little more about Milanese Jews in the High Middle Ages, they seem to have constituted a regular community. In 1225 the city issued a decree of expulsion of infidels, which, though principally intended to suppress the strong local heretical movements, apparently put an end to all organized Jewish life as well. The *podestà*, to be sure, reserved the right to readmit Jews with the archbishop's permission, but neither such a request nor a permission is recorded, at least until the establishment of the powerful regime of the Viscontis. In 1396 King Wenceslaus transferred to Gian Galeazzo Visconti, in a typically Germanic fashion, various imperial lands in Lombardy together with the jurisdiction "over pastures, fisheries, customs duties, and Jews." Even before this royal conferral Gian Galeazzo

had been admitting Jews; he guaranteed them in 1387 the enjoy-
ment of civil rights on a par with other citizens, promised not to
tax them, and allowed them to lend money "at whatever price
they wish and are able to." The Sforzas went further in protecting
Jewish rights. Beginning with Francesco (1450–66), who had
himself been heavily indebted to one Solaam di Bonsignore (a
loan at 14 per cent is recorded in 1447), they made efforts to attract more Jews to their possessions. Perhaps learning from his
experiences in southern Italy, particularly Bari, he also maintained at his court a number of Jewish oculists, dentists, and
physicians.[74]

Before long, however, the Milanese Jews encountered serious
difficulties with both inquisitors and preachers. It was against such
feared interventions that Francesco Sforza provided in his privilege for Jacopo di Vital and Salomone da Bologna, who wished to
settle in Castell'Arquato, that:

No bishop, legate, inquisitor, vicar or other judge, rector or any other
kind of official, be he ecclesiastical or secular, should be able or dare
to proceed against, or in any form to summon, etc., the said Jews, etc.,
or proceed against their exercising the profession of physicians, etc.,
under the pretext of some article or provision of the Christian faith.
Nor shall any priest in regular fashion be able or presume to baptize,
etc., any Jewish person, male or female, other than one aged fourteen
years or more, without the consent, agreement, and will of the parents
of such a person under the penalty for each transgressor, if he be a
layman, of 100 gold ducats to be paid to the Treasury and, if he be an
ecclesiastic, under the penalty of disgrace. And, in so far as someone
should be baptized in the said way, the official of the said city shall
be obliged to offer aid and assistance to restore such a person to his
parents and to give him back his freedom.

But the clergy did not yield readily. Particularly under the reign
of Lodovico "il Moro" (1488–99), whose somewhat shaky regime
needed popular support, the ecclesiastical party assailed ever more
sharply this liberal attitude. Francesco Sforza's earlier decision in
favor of the Talmud was heatedly debated at a church council in
Piacenza in 1490. As reported by a participant, Bernardino de'
Busti, this *Concilium contra Judaeos* argued that had the duke
closely examined the books submitted to him he would not have
declared them free of blasphemies. With typical sophistry, the

ecclesiastics added that even if the duke had intended to free the Jews from responsibility for past transgressions, he had not really allowed them to go on blaspheming against Christianity. More sweepingly, they declared that such dismissal of charges against the Talmud by the duke could safely be disregarded, since privileges enacted by the very emperors and popes were null and void if they controverted the principles of the Christian faith and the Gospels.[75]

The clergy's agitation began to yield considerable legislative fruits in the last three decades of the fifteenth century. Originally, the Jews of Milan seemingly wore no distinguishing marks. But on August 27, 1473 Galeazzo Maria Sforza (1466–76) ordered the Jews to display badges under the severe penalty of four lashes and 1,000 gold ducats for each transgression. Similarly, the penalties for sex relations with Christian women, set in 1439 at 100 lire or four months in prison, were sharpened to capital punishment in 1470. Bernardino de' Busti also led the movement to establish a *monte di pietà.* He wrote a *Defensorium sacratissimi Montis Pietatis,* published in Milan in 1497 and aimed at the Dominican detractors of that institution because it was charging some interest to cover its expenses. He was answered by a leading Dominican, Tommaso de Vio, known as Cardinal Cajetan (Gaetano), who in his *Trattato di cambi,* published in Milan in 1499, argued against the permissibility of any service charges for loans. Here, too, the Franciscans prevailed and received the support of both the state and the Church. In 1496 Lodovico "the Moor" approved the *monte*'s statute, while beginning in 1497 the popes lent their sup port by promising papal indulgences for ten years to all contributors and testators in its favor, as well as thirty days for each florin deposited in it. More formal approval came in the papal bulls issued by Alexander VI on June 18, 1501, and by Leo X on May 4, 1515, the latter specifically authorizing the *monte* to charge small fees.[76]

Outside the capital, the important organized Jewish community of Cremona dated back to the 1278 agreement between the city and some Jewish moneylenders. It speedily developed into a major center of Jewish learning and became the seat of famous Hebrew printing presses. Although this propitious growth at times evoked the animosity of burghers—who in 1466–68, without asking for the expulsion of Jews living in the city, petitioned Bianca Maria Sforza, Francesco's widow, for complete stoppage of further Jewish immigration—Jewish economic and cultural life was not seriously disturbed. The Cremona Jewish moneylenders jealously guarded their rights against intruders, combating, for example, the attempt of one Aaron of Bassano to establish another loan bank in the city. The latter appealed to the governor, claiming that he would perform "a greater service for, and confer more benefits on, the poor than would the others." The outcome of this controversy is not known. In another interesting litigation the *podestà* decided in favor of one Moses, forbidding the community to molest or excommunicate him, or otherwise enforce against him the regulations of Jewish law. But such governmental interference with Jewish autonomy was quite exceptional. So generally recognized was Cremona as the focal community of all Lombardy, that elections to the Jewish communal boards of other cities often took place there. For a moment, to be sure, the community was threatened with extinction when the French occupation forces decreed its banishment in 1509. But this decree was never carried out, and even the subsequent Spanish administration protected the Jews.[77]

Another important community was established in Pavia, Lombardy's ancient capital, which had been the scene of a religious disputation heard by Alcuin. But according to a Ticinese chronicler there had been no Jews settled in the city since 836. Apart from a somewhat doubtful entry of 1374 in a Hebrew manuscript, the first positive notices relate to a remarkable treaty concluded in 1387 between Gian Galeazzo Visconti and a group of Jews from Germany and to residential permits granted them in 1388–89. They were assigned a "house in which three families could live comfortably." As a university town Pavia required both shopkeepers and bankers to provide wares and credit for teachers and students. Fuller documentation begins, however, only upon the arrival of a banker, Averlino di Vicenza, and his family soon after 1430. The burghers, spearheaded by the Christian banker Niccolino Colleoni, were as a rule quite unfriendly. In 1479 they were stimulated by the Trent rumors to produce a Blood Accusation of their own. If, owing to the ducal governor's protection, Jews did not suffer immediately, they were seriously threatened in the following years by the reiterated appearances of Bernardino da Feltre (1480, 1493, and 1494). The preacher left such a permanent imprint upon the Pavian people that in 1527 the burghers took an oath on his shade to expel the Jews, in order to appease the divine wrath during the French siege. This oath did not save the city from the French occupation, but it served in the following decades as both a reminder and an excuse for the city's reiterated petitions for the total elimination of Jews. This request was finally granted when all Jews of the duchy were banished in 1597.[78]

Many other Jewish communities in the Milanese provinces are likewise mentioned in connection either with the establishment of Jewish loan banks or with Blood Accusations, which spread like wildfire after Trent. Jewish banks are recorded in Lodi in 1420, Como in 1437, and Bellinzona in 1455, while Blood Accusations appeared in 1479 in such small localities as Valenza, Monte Castello, and Bormio, as well as Pavia. In Bergamo, then temporarily under Venetian domination, Doge Giovanni Mocenigo allowed one Lucas Hebraeus to open a loan bank, but six weeks later he revoked this concession because of the burghers' protests (July 3, 1479). On the other hand, the small municipality of Vigevano borrowed 150 ducats from a Jewish banker, Dattilo (1450). It sought the duke's approval of its agreement, including the remarkable clause that if for some reason the municipality should fail to repay this loan on the due date, the Jewish creditor would be free to seize the person and property of any citizen.[79]

VENETIAN REPUBLIC AND ITS NEIGHBORS

One of the more significant communities east of the duchy of Milan was founded in Brescia at the beginning of the fifteenth century. Most early records, to be sure, concern such incidents as the solemn conversion of a Jew, Paul, to Christianity in 1434, possibly a delayed result of San Bernardino da Siena's stirring sermons there in 1427. About the same time a number of Jewish bankers received concessions to settle in several localities in and outside the city. Although some of them became involved in protracted controversies—for instance, one Simon was prosecuted by the neighboring community of the Orzinuovi in 1445—they continued to ply their trade under the protection of both the local and the Venetian authorities. In 1463 the Serenissima formally ordered the Brescians to respect the rights of Jewish moneylenders, an order upheld, with reference to Sixtus IV's bull, during the Blood Accusation of Trent, which caused serious repercussions in Brescia too. Following Venetian instructions of November 5, 1475, the local authorities issued a proclamation citing that combined intervention by pope and doge and stating that:

No person, lay and secular of whatever station, must paint pictures on the walls or elsewhere, nor sell such pictures of the martyr or blessed [child]. Nor must anyone preach *per zeratani* or in any other form, nor write epistles, nor sell anything written about that small child called Simeon who, it is said, had died at the hand of Jews in the city of Trent. Nor must one keep such pictures in public or in private, because his Holiness, the supreme Pontiff, has decreed otherwise. Transgressors will be subject to a fine of twenty-five lire de *planeti* which will be collected and applied one-half for the ducal Chamber and the other half for the accuser, if he is not a Jew.

But neither these orders nor their renewal by the Venetian government two years later stopped the anti-Jewish agitation. Under the pressure of an aroused public opinion, the Serenissima herself conceded in 1481 the city's right not to tolerate Jews, but merely argued that so long as they were allowed to stay in Brescia the Jews' lives and property must be duly protected. The city could only insist on their strict segregation from Christians, their wearing badges, and otherwise observing the traditionally restrictive laws. Brescia proceeded immediately to threaten with severe penalties Jews having carnal intercourse with Christian women, even prostitutes, or giving instruction to Christian children in their schools for dancing and singing. With respect to the badge, however, the city was confronted by the often contradictory Venetian laws of 1480, 1489, and 1495. The following years were a sad period for Brescian Jewry, as a side effect of the war and French occupation rather than as a result of any anti-Jewish bias. Peace was not restored until Brescia's reoccupation by Venice in 1516, when the old protective laws were largely reinstated, to be more or less effectively enforced throughout the sixteenth century.[80]

Among the oldest communities of the region was Verona, where, as we recall, Jews had been assailed by the tenth-century Archbishop Ratherius. Their subsequent expulsion seems to have been effective, and we hear little about them until the city came under Venetian rule in 1408, when they were allowed to erect a synagogue in the center of the city and engage in moneylending. A Jewish house of worship must have existed much earlier, however, since the thirteenth-century Viennese rabbi, Issac b. Moses Or Zaru'a, mentions decisions by Jewish courts in both Verona and Mantua. Except for some difficulties with the badge, Jews led a rather peaceful life. Starting with a yellow wheel in 1422, the badge was changed into a star in 1443, but restored to a wheel in 1480. These changes indicate that the law was as a rule observed in its breach. In 1443 Jews were shut out of various professional activities. But the great menace to their survival came only with the Blood Accusation in Trent in 1475, when a contemporary chronicler even accused Pope Sixtus IV of having been bribed by Jews to suppress it. It is small wonder, then, that in 1481 a local blood libel also found willing ears, and the ensuing condemnation of a Jewish shoemaker by a local court was confirmed by the *avvogadori* of the municipality. By 1498–99 the Verona city council yielded to popular pressure and banished the Jews altogether, but recalled them after a short-lived experience with rapacious Christian usurers. In 1526, on the petition of burghers, the city again prohibited Jewish moneylending; it renewed that prohibition in 1548. Nonetheless, Jews continued to flourish in Verona, which in the sixteenth and seventeenth centuries attracted more and more settlers and became a major center of Jewish learning. Smaller Jewish settlements in the vicinity included Bassano, where a petty Jewish landowner was recorded as early as 1264; the little village of Lonato, where a medieval Jewish tombstone was discovered; and the more important center of Treviso, with the adjoining townships of Asolo and Vicenza.[81]

Neighboring Mantua long maintained its independence under the house of Gonzaga. Although the city had been the place of activity of Abraham ibn Ezra as early as 1145 (there he composed his well-known grammatical treatise Ṣaḥot), and other Jewish residents are mentioned by German rabbis of the twelfth and thirteenth centuries, no actual legislation concerning Jews is recorded before the end of the fourteenth century. Soon after reaching an agreement in 1386 with Benjamino di Musetto (Moses) of Perugia for the establishment of a loan bank in Revere, Giovan Francesco I Gonzaga (1382–1407) also drew up a similar compact with Abramo di Bonaventura (Meshullam) of Forlì and four of his associates residing in Rimini, Bologna and Ancona. They were to start the first Jewish bank in the city of Mantua itself (1389). Other such conventions speedily followed, so that by 1428 seven groups, including eleven families, operated in Mantua. Their interterritorial character was emphasized not only by the provenance of six of these families from various localities in Italy, four from Germany and one from France, but also by the fact that many partners retained their permanent residences in other Italian cities. True, the government still manifested deep-rooted suspicions of usurers, Christian and Jewish. In reissuing (some time between 1393 and 1407) the older *Statuti Bonacolsiani*, Giovan Francesco inserted a clause prohibiting the appearance of any usurer as attorney for either a Jew or a Christian and providing for the automatic expiration of all loan deeds after six years. But in 1401 he himself petitioned Pope Boniface IX for approval of his pacts with the Jews, since he had to employ "foreign usurers, as few or no native-born ones exist." Apart from bankers the city also attracted numerous Jewish merchants and scholars. That the community must have grown substantially in the first half of the fifteenth century is evident from the sizable tax of 2,000 ducats imposed upon it in 1459 (reduced, because of Jewish protests, to 600 ducats). More significantly, the community was able to attract such distinguished scholars as Joseph b. Solomon Colon (Colombo or Jonah of the Trabotto family) from France, and Yehudah ben Yeḥiel Messer Leon from Bologna and Venice. Colon soon achieved wide renown as a leading jurist, while Messer Leon composed in Mantua his well-known rhetoric *Nofet Ṣufim,* and translated Aristotle's *Physics* into Hebrew. But the community seems to have been too small as yet to accommodate two such diverse individuals, and the ensuing protracted controversy between them generated such tensions that Ludovico Gonzaga expelled them both in 1475. It appears that after settling in Naples, Messer Leon proceeded in 1490 to Moscow at Ivan III's invitation. But having failed to cure Ivan's son and namesake of a mortal illness, he was executed, in truly oriental fashion.[82]

Although in 1476 the Jews of Mantua were specifically permitted by the pope to charge interest, Bernardino da Feltre succeeded eight years later in establishing there a *monte di pietà* and in securing for it Innocent VIII's approval in 1486. His enthusiastic sermons doubly appealed to the Mantuan population, since it had long been prone to riot against Jews. After the events in Trent in 1475, the tensions had constantly mounted, although a local Blood Accusation of 1478 was quickly quashed when the purported child victim was found unharmed. The rulers, who ever since 1435 kept urging restraint upon their subjects, had to repeat their appeals in constant reiteration. (Four proclamations are recorded for the years 1435, 1437, 1455, and 1471, but no less than thirteen were issued in the two decades of 1479–99.) Some leading Jews had to be given permission to bear arms for self-defense.

Another incident added fuel to the existing animosity. In 1495 the rich banker Daniel Norsi was allowed to acquire a building in a fine residential section. Because of religious scruples he secured permission to remove a painting of the Virgin which he had found in the house. Rumors about this "desecration" quickly spread among the populace and gave rise to a riot which might have had untoward consequences for Daniel had he not been absent from the city. Although granted an "amnesty" by the authorities, he had to agree to pay for a new representation of the Virgin. No less an artist than Andrea Montegna was commissioned to execute this order, for the handsome sum of 120 ducats at Daniel's expense. For some reason this masterpiece, now exhibited at the Louvre, was not hung in Daniel's house, which had been interveningly converted into the church of Santa Maria della Vittoria to commemorate Giovan Francesco III Gonzaga's (1484–1519) "victory" over the French at Fornovo. Montegna's painting was replaced by a much inferior one prepared by an anonymous artist, again at Daniel's expense. Historically, however, this lesser painting had the advantage of including the portraits of four members of the Norsa family, rare specimens indeed of medieval Jewish portraiture. Understandably, another anti-Jewish preacher, Dominico da Ponzone, arriving in Mantua in 1496, was greeted with great acclaim and deeply impressed even Isabella d'Este, who reigned in the absence of her militant husband Giovan Francesco. However, a renewal of the badge, a prohibition against Jews' employing Christian servants except for necessary tasks on the Sabbath, and restrictions on the sale of Jewish meat to Christians were the only legislative results of the popular agitation. None of them was strictly applied in the following decades. Certainly, these hostile moves did not interrupt the growth of the Mantuan community, whose influence during the sixteenth century made itself felt on Jews far beyond the confines of Italy. Particularly some of its communal ordinances (there are probably more communal statutes extant from early modern Mantua than from any other community of that period) served as models for similar legislation in other cities.[83]

No less important was the community of Padua. Here, too, few earlier records are extant, such as that of the Jew, Jacob Bonacosa (Tobiah?), who in 1255 translated Averroës' *Colliget* into Latin! The real history of the community begins in the years 1369–83, when three Jewish loan banks were founded with capital resources of 6,500, 9,000, and 3,500 ducats respectively. For the most part the partners had lived in various parts of central Italy, but now they or their agents established their permanent residence in Padua. They were soon joined by immigrants from other lands, notarial documents of 1403 mentioning without much ado Jews hailing from Barcelona and Candia. This trend was accelerated after the city's incorporation into the Venetian Republic in 1405. The new arrivals, including some German immigrants, established banks of their own not only in Padua but also in several neighboring small communities such as Montagnana, Este, and particularly Piove di Sacco, where even before 1373 *capitoli* had been concluded by Francesco da Carrara, the ruler of Padua, with a Jewish banker Abramo. Piove was to play an eminent historic role also as one of the birthplaces of Hebrew printing.[84]

Generally treated as citizens, the Jews of Padua possessed a synagogue and cemetery, and freely acquired other real estate. Jewish banking was needed not only for the city's permanent inhabitants, but also for the numerous visiting professors and students of its famed university. When in 1415, the Venetian Senate tried to impose new terms unacceptable to the Jewish bankers, the latter merely had to close their establishments in order to force the hand of the authorities. However, despite generations of Jewish banking, the city elders, egged on by itinerant preachers, still had conscientious scruples about allowing this prohibited trade. Many citizens must also have been cognizant of Dante's memorable description of the sufferings in the Inferno of the earlier Christian usurers of their city. In 1453 Padua secured, therefore, from the Venetian authorities the outlawry of all Jewish moneylending in its territory. But this prohibition merely forced the credit transactions underground (many were executed under the names of Piove residents) and caused the rise of interest rates from the formerly permissible 15 per cent to 30 per cent or more. Reversing their previous stand, the authorities appealed to the newly elected pope, Calixtus III, for a special dispensation. They wrote:

Our municipality has in past times become involved on many occasions in bringing in Jews to lend on usury under diverse stipulations, and many burghers of our city have rented houses to usurers in which they could exercise their occupation. It has been stated that, because these proceedings are prohibited by law, they subject our souls to infernal penalties for which we have no absolution. And hence we, citizens and community, live under the gravest danger.

The presence of university students may also have accounted for the unusually long and detailed decree of 1420, outlawing carnal intercourse between Jews and Christians. According to this law, a Jew cohabiting with a prostitute living in a bordello was to be flogged three times around the palace and incarcerated for six months. If the woman was unmarried but not a prostitute, the penalty was raised to a year's imprisonment. If, however, he committed adultery with a married Christian woman he was to be burned. The penalty for the Christian partner was scaled from treble floggings for the prostitute to six months incarceration for the single girl and burning for the married woman. If, on the other hand, a Christian cohabited with a Jewess, both were to be condemned to treble flogging and a year's imprisonment, but they could escape corporal punishment by the payment of 1,000 lire. Here no distinction of marital status was indicated. These Judeo-Christian social contacts continued unabated during the following decades despite the fulminations of preachers. Da Feltre succeeded in establishing a *monte* in 1491, but the Jewish bankers continued to ply their trade, weathering many storms, including the severe sack of Padua by the enemies of Venice in 1509.[85]

Overshadowing all these communities in political and economic influence was the great Jewish center in the City of the Lagoons. We remember the doge's efforts in 932 to persuade the German emperor and diet to banish Jews from the whole Empire, followed by the Venetian decree of 945 prohibiting their transportation on Venetian ships. Yet Jews lived in Venice, particularly, it appears, in the section called Giudecca (this district is first mentioned in a document of 1252). They were numerous enough for a local census, prepared a century earlier, to record the presence of 1,300 Jews—a gross exaggeration. Although in 1290 the city imposed a special tax of 5 per cent on Jewish imports and exports, this branch of commerce became ever more important as Jews helped Venice colonize the eastern Mediterranean islands, beginning with the capture of Corfu in 1386. Nor were Jewish bankers unwelcome; the city merely preferred to keep them for a while in the adjacent community of Mestre. True, the interest rate of 4 per cent, provided in 1366, proved untenable and soon had to be raised to 10–12 per cent, but the city readily issued a full-fledged *condotta* in 1386 which spelled out many privileges for Jews including some arriving from the Levant. Jews were to pay 4,000 ducats annually, but were to be freed from all other imposts except customs duties. Three years later the Serenissima made a special arrangement with a banker named Levi and his wife, which the city renewed in 1390 for the other Jews as well. All such agreements being by their very nature revocable, Jews anticipated an expulsion in 1396 and retired to Mestre, but were soon allowed to return to the city for fifteen days at a time. This provision enabled some individuals to maintain a permanent residence in Venice by interrupting it every fortnight through a short stay outside its limits. But such evasions were soon checked by the city through a required interval of four months, later extended to one year, between each sojourn.[86]

Although forbidden in 1423 to acquire any real estate in Venice and in 1434 again told to wear a badge (which here changed in form gradually from a yellow wheel to a yellow cap and ultimately a red cap), the Jews steadily grew in number and affluence. When the agitation against Jewish moneylenders became more violent, the Senate inquired in 1463 from Cardinal Bessarione as to the legitimacy of interest. Since the cardinal gave it qualified approval, Venice fiercely resisted the establishment of a *monte di pietà*. It expelled Da Feltre and even in 1534 the Council of Ten declared that "one may not nor ought one to propose any more, or to speak of such matters as *monti di pietà* without the express license and deliberation of this Council." In their place the authorities arranged with the Jewish community for the establishment of the *banchi del ghetto* to serve, at its expense, as charitable loan banks for the Christian population. The first formal decree allowing Jews to practice medicine was enacted in 1443, but a special privilege for one Leone, generally held in high esteem, is recorded as early as 1331. As a rule, Jewish doctors were even exempt from wearing badges. In 1515, in consideration for a loan of 5,000 ducats, the Serenissima also allowed Jews to open nine (later ten) shops for trade in secondhand clothing. Above all, she encouraged them to cultivate international trade with the Levantine communities.[87]

Because of the Republic's ramified connections, the Jewish settlement in and around Venice assumed an increasingly cosmopolitan character and occasionally had international repercussions. When a Syracuse Jewish merchant was murdered in 1306 near Zara, then under Venetian control, the king of Sicily saw to it that the property was restored to the victim's heirs. On the other hand, King Wenceslaus of the Holy Roman Empire, after canceling in 1390 all debts owed to Jews, tried to prevent Jewish creditors from seizing merchandise held by their debtors while on a visit to Venice. A local Jew, Anselmo, who together with two correligionists from Verona and Vicenza had caused the arrest of his Christian partner for the latter's alleged debts, was in turn prosecuted by the Venetian authorities and condemned to a four months' term in prison. We also recall the interesting convention in 1395 between Desiderato Lucio, Venetian envoy to Henry III of Castile, and the Jew, Dumzagus (Don Çag or Issac) b. Abraham Levi of Burgos and his associates, whereby Venetian merchants arriving in Santander and other Castilian ports were to be charged but a third of the usual customs duties. We do not learn what compensation the Republic had offered in return for this substantial concession. On the other hand, because of the alleged Jewish part in the destruction of the Franciscan monastery on Mount Zion, the Serenissima not only imposed a tax on her own Jews but also forbade Venetian merchant ships to transport Jewish pilgrims to the Holy Land, affecting, among others, the famous scholar-traveler, Obadiah di Bertinoro.[88]

Outside the Venetian-controlled *terra firma*, some Jewish communities soon came under the sway of the Holy Roman Empire. Although it never became the seat of an important Jewish community, Trent achieved historical significance in the annals of Jewish history through its Blood Accusation of 1475. To the east, individual Jews appeared in Trieste in the earlier Middle Ages (in 1236, a Carinthian Jew lent money to its bishop; a Hebrew tombstone was allegedly inscribed there in 1325) but it embraced a Jewish community only after it came under Austrian domination in 1382. Other seats of Jewish banking, sometimes operating alongside the *monti di pietà*, are recorded in such smaller localities as Capodistria, Gemona, and Venzone near Udine, the castles of Porcia and Brugnera in the district of Friuli, Cherso near Fiume, and Pirano near Pola. Independently, Jews also spread across the Adriatic Sea to Dalmatia. Here they met a native Jewish population dating from ancient times, as well as many newcomers from the Balkans.[89]

MEDITERRANEAN LIGHTS AND SHADOWS

Unlike the countries north of the Alps and Pyrenees, the states of southern and central Italy embraced deeply rooted, populous, and affluent Jewish settlements which had long constituted an integral part of their ethnographic and religious structures. Often dating back to Roman times, these communities had behind them a rich and variegated history under the moderately friendly regimes of Muslim and Norman rulers and of most popes from Gregory I to Alexander III. The Jews' great adaptability to the ever changing conditions, combined with their frequent display of pioneering ingenuity, wide economic diversification, and cultural creativity, made them welcome accretions to these countries' basic human resources.

For these reasons even the fanatical spirit of the Crusades interfered but little with the intimate collaboration of Jews and Christians during the Late Middle Ages. Only the cities located north of the States of the Church remained sparsely, if at all, populated by Jews. But this was the effect of economic jealousies and self-sufficiency of the enterprising and expansive North-Italian merchant class, rather than of religious intolerance as such. Before long, however, the relative decline in the prosperity of that class, occasioned by the economic crisis of the fourteenth and fifteenth centuries, forced one northern city after another to admit ever new groups of Jews. At the same time Sicily and Naples, however unwillingly, followed the orders of their Aragonese masters in totally suppressing their age-old Jewish communities.

Jews, thus suddenly ousted from their ancient positions of strength in the south, often found a more or less grudging reception in areas where they had never lived before in significant numbers. From their main center in Rome, where they maintained a steady if equivocal mode of living under the general polarity of Church policies toward Jews and Judaism, they began spreading northward through central and northern Italy. First settling in the Papal provinces, including those which paid only formal allegiance to the Holy See, they soon penetrated also most of the independent republics and principalities. Here they encountered waves of Jewish refugees from the Holy Roman Empire and France.

It was especially the oft-resented system of petty usury and pawnbroking which was now more and more delegated to the Jewish newcomers, with whom one Italian city after another concluded specific treaties, the so-called *condottas*. From the outset limited in time, though renewable, these agreements established a rather novel status for Jewish settlers. On the one hand, for the duration of their pacts with the respective cities or dukes, Jews enjoyed rights similar to those of Christian burghers. On the other hand, because of the need for constant renegotiation of these agreements, the Jews, as well as their enemies, fully realized the precariousness of their sojourn. With the growing anti-Jewish agitation during the fifteenth century, climaxed by the rabble-rousing propaganda for the establishment of *monti di pietà,* whose charitable loans to the poor undermined the basic rationale of these *condottas,* Jewish residence in some localities lost its *raison d'être.* Yet in many cities, such as Venice, Mantua, Padua, Verona, and Ferrara, Jews successfully weathered this concerted onslaught. Their communities persisted through the era of the Catholic Restoration and became, from the sixteenth century on, important centers of Jewish culture and economic enterprise.

NOTES

ABBREVIATIONS

AFH	Archivum franciscanum historicum
AHDE	Anuario de historia del derecho español
AHR	American Historical Review
AKKR	Archiv für katolisches Kirchenrecht
AS	Archivio storico
ASI	Archivio Storico Italiano
ASPN	*AS* per le provincie napoletane
APH	Acta Poloniae historica
Baer Jub. Vol.	Sefer Yobel le-Yitzhak Baer (Yitzhak Baer Jubilee Volume), ed. by Salo W. Baron *et al.* Jerusalem, 1960
BAH	Boletín de la R. Academia de la Historia, Madrid
BEC	Bibliothèque de l'École des Chartes
BEP	Bulletin des études portugaises
BIHR	Bulletin of the Institute of Historical Research, London
BZIH	Biuletyn of the Żydowski Instytut Historyczny, Warsaw
CH	Church History
CHE	Cuadernos de historia de España
DAGM	Deutsches Archiv für Geschichte des Mittelalters
EEM	Estudios de la Edad media de la Corona de Aragón
EHR	English Historical Review
ES	Evreiskaia Starina
Freidus Mem. Vol.	Studies in Jewish Bibliography and Related Subjects in Memory of Abraham Solomon Freidus (1867–1923). New York, 1929
GS	Gesammelte Schriften
Gulak-Klein Mem. Vol.	Sefer Zikkaron (Studies in Memory of Asher Gulak and Samuel Klein). Jerusalem, 1942
HJ	Historia Judaica
HJB	Historisches Jahrbuch der Görres-Gesellschaft
Homenaje Millás	Homenaje a Millás-Vallicrosa. 2 vols. Barcelona, 1954–56
JJLG	Jahrbuch der Jüdisch-Literarischen Gesellschaft, Frankfurt a.M.
JJS	Journal of Jewish Studies

JSS	Jewish Social Studies
JQR	Jewish Quarterly Review
KH	Kwartalnik Historyczny
Marx Jub. Vol.	Alexander Marx Jubilee Volume. Two vols., New York, 1950. A volume each of English and Hebrew essays
MGH	Monumenta Germaniae Historica
MGWJ	Monatsschrift für Geschichte und Wissenschaft des Judentums
MHJ	Monumenta Hungariae Judaica (Magyar-Zsidó Oklevéltár)
MIOG	Mitteilungen of the Institut für österreichische Geschichtsforschung
MMAH	Monumenta medii aevi historica ad gesta Poloniae illustrantia
MPH	Monumenta Poloniae historica
MZ	Miesięcznik żydowski
MZS	Magyar-Zsidó Szemle (Hungarian Jewish Review)
Neuman Jub. Vol.	Studies and Essays in Honor of Abraham A. Neuman. Leiden, 1962
PL	Patrologiae cursus completus, series Latina
RABM	Revista de Archivos, Bibliotecas y Museos
RBPH	Revue belge de philologie et d'histoire
REJ	Revue des études juives
RH	Revue historique
RHE	Revue d'histoire ecclésiastique
RMI	Rassegna mensile di Israel
RSI	Rivista storica italiana
TJHSE	Transactions of the Jewish Historical Society of England
TRHS	Transactions of the Royal Historical Society
VSW	Vierteljahrsschrift für Sozial- und Wirtschaftsgeschichte
ZGJD	Zeitschrift für die Geschichte der Juden in Deutschland
ZHB	Zeitschrift für hebräische Bibliographie
ZRG	Zeitschrift der Savigny-Stiftung für Rechtsgeschichte

NOTES

CHAPTER XLII: GERMANY'S NEIGHBORS

1. The formation of the Swiss *Eidgenossenschaft* was so slow and gradual that even the medieval chroniclers were quite confused about it. It has also been the subject of endless debates among modern scholars, and even today there is hardly a complete consensus among specialists. However, to all intents and purposes the independence of the main Swiss cantons was firmly established at the end of the medieval period, and the Treaty of Westphalia merely gave formal sanction to what had long been an established historical fact. See T. Mayer, "Die Schweizer Eidgenossenschaft und das deutsche Reich im Mittelalter," *DAGM*, VII, 239–88 (with a sharp polemic against K. Meyer); B. Meyer, "Die Entstehung der Eidgenossenschaft. Der Stand der heutigen Anschauungen," *Schweizerische Zeitschrift für Geschichte*, II, 153–205; and other literature as well as critical comments in *Das Handbuch der deutschen Geschichte*, newly ed. by L. Just *et al.*, I, Part 5, pp. 155 f. See also, from another angle, K. Mommsen, *Eidgenossen, Kaiser und Reich. Studien zur Stellung der Eidgenossenschaft innerhalb des heiligen römischen Reiches*.

2. The antiquity of the linguistic divisions in present-day Switzerland, and their impact upon the subsequent historical developments of its various regions, were discussed at a *Kollegium* held in Zurich on May 11, 1963. See the presentation by M. Beck *et al.*, "Volks- und Sprachgrenzen in der Schweiz im Frühmittelalter. Mit besonderer Berücksichtigung der burgundisch-alemannischen Grenze," *Schweizerische Zeitschrift für Geschichte*, XII, 133–587.

3. J. Trouillat, ed., *Monuments de l'histoire de l'ancien évêché de Bâle*, I, 96 f. No. 50, cap. 8 (*ne Judaismo capiantur*), 463 No. 303, 491 f. No. 328 (see also the agreement between the Jewish community and the convent of St. Léonard of 1293, *ibid.*, II, 543 f. No. 421); S. Grayzel, *The Church and the Jews*, pp. 294 f. No. 133; J. Aronius, *Regesten zur Geschichte der Juden*, pp. 173 f. No. 392, 188 No. 424, 254 f. No. 596, 286 No. 692; M. Ginsburger, "Die Juden in Basel," *Basler Zeitschrift für Geschichte und Altertumskunde*, VIII, 315–436 (also reprint), esp. pp. 315 ff., 326 ff.; L. Löwenstein, *Geschichte der Juden am Bodensee und Umgebung*, I, 19 ff.; T. Schiess and B. Meyer, eds., *Quellenwerk zur Entstehung der Schweizerischen Eidgenossenschaft*, Abt. I: Urkunden, I, 765 ff. No. 1662. The formulation in the latter source concerning the Murbach loan is somewhat suspect. The emphasis on the sale of property to repay the loan owed to Jews and the rather casual reference to additional property the monastery wished to acquire with the proceeds of that sale, give the impression of a deliberate effort to place the blame on Jews, rather than on the possibly imprudent exchange of some pieces of real estate for others. A similar excuse was offered also, in 1295, by Countess Elizabeth of Homberg. *Ibid.*, II, 43 No. 695; *Urkundenbuch der Stadt und Landschaft Zürich*, ed. by J. Escher and P.

Schweizer, VI, 290 ff. No. 2325. The presence of Asher b. Yeḥiel in Basel has rightly been doubted. Although his whereabouts in 1293, the year of Meir b. Baruch's death, are uncertain, he probably spent most of the years of his master's imprisonment in Erfurt and vicinity. See A. Freimann, "Ascher b. Jechiel. Sein Leben und Wirken," *JJLG*, XII, 248 f. A. Nordmann actually claims that "Rasor" was a barber rather than a rabbi, although he may have been designated "Rabbi" in accordance with the then growing anti-Karaite custom. See Nordmann's "Glanes otomalogiques," *REJ*, LXXXII, 485 f.; and *supra*, Vol. V, pp. 283, 416 n. 85. On the Basel Jewish contribution of 40 marks in 1241 (against one of 200 marks by the city) and its relation to those of other German communities, see the data analyzed by I. Rösel in "Die Reichssteuern der deutschen Judengemeinden," *MGWJ*, LIII, 702 No. 28 (offprint, p. 32; shows that—apart from the 1241 list, republished by J. Schwalm in "Noticia de precariis civitatum et villarum," *MGH*, Constitutiones, III, 2 ff., esp. p. 3 Nos. 38 and 47—Basel is not mentioned in the pertinent records); and *infra*, Chap. LIV. See also T. Nordmann's more recent survey, *Zur Geschichte der Juden in Basel . . . . . . Jubiläumsschrift der Israelitischen Gemeinde Basel,* which is, however, mainly concerned with the "third" community of Basel since 1805.

Swiss Jewry was quite fortunate in finding a careful and, on the whole, quite sympathetic investigator in the eighteenth-century Zurich pastor, Johann Caspar Ulrich. After indefatigably assembling much documentary material, particularly from the Zurich archives, Ulrich compiled his comprehensive work, entitled *Sammlung jüdischer Geschichten, welche sich mit diesem Volk in dem XIII. und folgenden Jahrhunderten bis auf MDCCLX. in der Schweitz von Zeit zu Zeit zugetragen,* which appeared in Basel, 1768, the year of the author's death. A theologian, primarily animated by a remarkable blend of "enlightened" tolerance with missionary aspirations, Ulrich was at his best in accurately reproducing his source materials, rather than in his historical critique or interpretation. See the careful analysis by L. Rothschild in his "Johann Caspar Ulrich von Zürich und seine 'Sammlung jüdischer Geschichten in der Schweiz,' " *Schweizer Studien zur Geschichtswissenschaft,* XVII, 189–270 (also reprint). Ulrich's large volume has served as the fountainhead of all subsequent researches in this field. Much more concise and likewise based upon extensive archival and library research, is A. Steinberg's systematic analysis, *Studien zur Geschichte der Juden in der Schweiz während des Mittelalters,* which also lists most of the intervening monographic literature up to 1902. Since then quite a few additional monographs have appeared, but a comprehensive new history of the Jews in Switzerland, undertaken in the early 1930s by the Swiss Jewish *Gemeindebund,* has not progressed beyond the planning stage. See M. Ginsburger, "Zur Geschichte der Juden in der Schweiz unter Kaiser Sigismund (1411–1437)," *ZGJD*, IV, 77. The recent brief survey of *Die Juden in der Schweiz,* by F. Guggenheim-Grünberg, does not quite fill the lacuna of a well-documented synthetic treatment. Some of the more important monographs will be mentioned in the following notes.

4. Steinberg, *Studien*, pp. 11, 111 f.; J. Tonjola, ed., *Basilea sepulta, detecta, continuata, passim* (this important collection of tombstone inscriptions begun by Pastor Johannes Grossius in 1619 and published by Tonjola in 1661 includes such Hebrew epitaphs of Christian humanists as that of Johannes Frobenius dated 3. of Kislev 5275 [Nov. 21, 1514]; it also has four lines in Greek; p. 117); Ginsburger in *Basler Zeitschrift,* VIII, 429 ff. (reproducing nine Hebrew inscriptions in corrected versions

with 3 facsimiles, a German translation and notes), esp. No. 5; J. Kollman and Kahnt, "Schädel und Skelettreste aus einem Judenfriedhofe des 13. und 14. Jahrhunderts zu Basel," *Verhandlungen* of the Naturforschende Gesellschaft, VII, 648 f. See also P. Buxtorf's more recent study of *Die Lateinischen Grabinschriften in der Stadt Basel;* and the six Zurich tombstone inscriptions, reproduced with Latin and German trans., in Ulrich's *Sammlung*, pp. 39 ff., all of which date, however, from the period after the Black Death.

5. On the Berne Blood Accusation, see the chronicles excerpted in Ulrich's *Sammlung*, pp. 143 ff. In his *'Emeq ha-bakha*, ed. by Letteris, p. 56 (in Wiener's German trans., pp. 45, 179 f. n. 178), Joseph ha-Kohen places the early Berne events in 1287 and associates them with Rudolph I's futile siege of the city. This confusion of the Jewish historian was shared not only by his source, Sebastian Münster, but also by many other writers until 1888. See Steinberg, p. 125 n. 2. The historic events underlying these distortions are discussed in O. Redlich's *Rudolf von Habsburg*, pp. 624 ff. The earlier Interlaken reference and the Fribourg data are found in the *Fontes rerum bernensium (Bern's Geschichtsquellen)*, ed. by M. von Stürler *et al.*, II, 492 f. No. 473, 584 f. No. 550, 703 No. 641 (Aronius, *Regesten*, pp. 270 No. 643, 286 No. 689, 308 No. 730); G. Tobler's "Zur Geschichte der Juden im alten Bern bis 1427," *Archiv* of the Historischer Verein des Kantons Berns, XII, 336–67; and other sources listed by Steinberg in her *Studien*, pp. 10 f.; and by A. Favre in "Les Médécins juifs à Fribourg dans les siècles passés," *Archives* of the Société d'histoire du Canton de Fribourg, VII, 25–35. Equally accidental documentary entries reveal to us the presence of Jews in some rural communities, such as those in the Lies Valley near Basel. See H. Boos, *Urkundenbuch der Landschaft Basel*, p. 296 No. 339. From another document we learn that the entire community of the valley of Frutigen borrowed 168 marks from Jews in Berne in 1263 in order to pay 140 marks it owed to Bishop Henry I of Sitten (Sion). See T. Schiess *et al.*, eds., *Quellenwerk*, Abt. I, Vol. I, p. 425 No. 939.

6. M. Wiener, *Regesten*, pp. 34 f. Nos. 71 and 77, 47 No. 155; J. E. Scherer, *Rechtsverhältnisse*, p. 362 n. 1; Frederick the Handsome's decree of 1317, published from the Constance archives by L. Löwenstein in his *Geschichte der Juden am Bodensee*, pp. 114 f. n. 20; Leopold II's treaty with Charles of 1324, excerpted from the Paris original MS in R. Wackernagel and R. Thommen, eds., *Urkundenbuch der Stadt Basel*, IV, 51 No. 54. The Austrian dukes' treatment of the Swiss Jews was as utilitarian and inconsistent as that of other German princes. Duke Leopold III, to whom all Jewish taxation in Basel was assigned by Charles IV's order of 1374, ten years later mortgaged his Jewish revenue in Schaffhausen to its bailiff in payment of a debt of 600 florins. See Wiener, pp. 231 No. 104, 234 No. 131. During the stormy years of the German *Interregnum* the bishop and city of Basel joined an alliance of Mayence, Cologne, Worms, Spires, and Strasbourg, to guarantee a truce. In its proclamation of 1254, the alliance guaranteed peace for ten years to all inhabitants, great or small, clerics, laymen, or Jews. Almost a century later, shortly before the Black Death crisis, the city of Basel (but not the bishop) joined a similar alliance of cities and nobles in 1345 to guarantee public order for five years. Once again Jews were specifically included. See *Urkundenbuch der Stadt Basel*, ed. by R. Wackernagel and R. Thommen, I, 199 No. 274 (or rather the sources indicated there); IV, 152 ff. No. 163; Aronius, *Regesten*, pp. 256 f. Nos. 601–602; Wiener, *Regesten*, p. 50

No. 179; and *supra*, Chap. XL, n. 18. Other examples of German city alliances were mentioned *supra*, Chaps. XL, n. 29; XLI, n. 26.

7. Konrad Justinger, *Berner Chronik bis 1425*, ed. by G. Studer, pp. 29 f.; Johannes of Winterthur (Johannes Vitoduranus), *Chronicon*, ed. by G. von Wyss, pp. 97 f.; and other sources cited by Ulrich, *Sammlung*, pp. 375 ff.; L. Löwenstein, *Geschichte......Bodensee*, pp. 25 ff., 58 ff., 79 ff.; A. Steinberg, *Studien*, pp. 124 ff.; and Ginsburger in *Basler Zeitschrift*, VIII, 340 ff. On the events in Kyburg, see the chronicle for the years 1316–1361 by Henry (Henricus) Dapifer de Diessenhofen in J. F. Böhmer, ed., *Fontes rerum germanicarum*, IV, 16–126, esp. pp. 72 and 74; Scherer, *Rechtsverhältnisse*, pp. 369 ff.; and, more generally, S. Salfeld, *Das Martyrologium*, pp. 69 f., 81 ff. (Hebrew), 244 ff., 280 ff. (German); and *infra*, Chap. LIV. As pointed out by Löwenstein and by Rothschild, it was long believed that the Schaffhausen Jews were among the few Swiss communities which escaped the slaughter in 1349. However, an arbitration award by Queen Agnes of Hungary regarding the division of the Schaffhausen spoils was expressly called "the judgment when the Jews were burned." See the texts reproduced by Löwenstein, pp. 141 ff. nn. 57–58; and Rothschild's observations in *Schweizer Studien*, XVII, 234. Apart from these major tragedies, there were many other instances in which individual Jews became the subjects of false accusation and persecution. An unnamed Jew in Basel was sentenced in 1396 to the large fine of 500 florins because he had allegedly spoken ill of St. Catherine. See Wackernagel and Thommen, eds., *Urkundenbuch . . . Basel*, V, 226 No. 223. A Constance Jew and his daughter were burned in 1424, because they had allegedly testified falsely that a member of King Sigismund's family had entertained illicit relations with a Jewess. Löwenstein, p. 39.

8. Ulrich, *Sammlung*, pp. 382 Doc. H, 441 Doc. P; Löwenstein, *Geschichte . . . Bodensee*, pp. 30 f., 85 ff.; A. Steinberg, *Studien*, pp. 136 ff. On the readmission of Jews to Berne, see the interesting document reproduced by Tobler in the *Archiv* of the Historischer Verein des Kantons Berns, XII, 360 f., 362 ff. On the other hand, the reappearance of Jews in Lucerne in 1349 reinforces the impression that they had never been completely eliminated during the Black Death frenzy.

9. Wackernagel and Thommen, eds., *Urkundenbuch . . . Basel*, IV, 258 f. No. 287, 368 f. No. 379; V, 84 ff. No. 78 (with the corrections by Ginsburger in *Basler Zeitschrift*, VIII, 345 ff., 360 f.). In addition to the regular Jewish residents, most communities embraced also visitors and other temporary sojourners. As a rule such visits were rather strictly supervised by the cities. Only in Fribourg after 1381 were Jews, accepted as "resident burghers" (*ingessessne Burger*), allowed to accommodate foreign coreligionists without limitation in either the number of guests or the duration of their stay. During their residence these visitors were promised by the authorities full protection for their lives and property. At the other extreme, in its contract of 1398 with the Jewish city doctor, Gutleben, Basel expressly stipulated that he might entertain alien coreligionists during the day, but that he must not keep them overnight. Other local regulations varied, Fribourg itself abandoning its liberal legislation in 1412 and limiting its hospitality to but four days, unless extended by a special municipal permit. This limitation evidently did not apply to the family (broadly conceived) and associates of the physician Ackinus, whom the city invited in 1420 for ten years to practice medicine. See *Recueil diplomatique du*

canton de Fribourg, [ed. by Canon Fontaines *et al.*], IV, 156 No. cclxxi; VII, 19 f. No. ccccxxxviii, 109 ff. No. cccclxxiii; and the next note.

10. Wackernagel and Thommen, *Urkundenbuch* . . . *Basel*, V, 56 No. 46, 63 f. Nos. 55–57, 92 ff. No. 85, 153 ff. Nos. 143–44 and 146, 223 No. 220, 262 f. No. 243; M. Ginsburger in *Basler Zeitschrift*, VIII, 369, 386 ff.; Löwenstein, *Geschichte . . . Bodensee*, pp. 31 ff.; Favre in *Archives* of the Société d'histoire du Canton de Fribourg, VII, 30; and more generally, Steinberg, *Studien*, pp. 88 ff. Clearly, the employment of a Jewish physician by a city and the rather mild punishment for a Jew's sex relations with a Christian woman ran counter to the demands of canon law. But this conflict seems to have little disturbed the Swiss city fathers. In similar cases in 1323–24, the Zurich council banished two Christian mistresses of Jews "for ever." If later apprehended in the city, either was to be imprisoned for a year and banished again. See Schiess *et al.*, *Quellenwerk*, II, 600 No. 1191; and *infra*, Chap. XLVIII. On Wenceslaus' cancellation of debts, see *supra*, Chap. XL, nn. 29–30; and the literature mentioned there. His opposite order of 1397 is reproduced by J. J. Hisely and J. Gremaux in their ed. of *Monuments de l'histoire du comté de Gruyère et d'autres fiefs de la maison souveraine de ce nom*, I, 251 ff. No. 156. See also Hisely's *Histoire du comté de Gruyère*, I, 374 ff. It may be noted that Wenceslaus' successor, Rupert, continued to collect the one-half of the Jewish tax from Constance (the other half went to the city) arranged by Wenceslaus. An original receipt, signed in 1404 by Johannes Winheim and covering the payment of 25 florins each for the preceding two years, is found in the archives of Karlsruhe. See M. Stern, *König Ruprecht*, pp. 14 f. No. 16.

11. Wackernagel and Thommen, *Urkundenbuch* . . . *Basel*, V, 273 ff. No. 252, 309 No. 284, 335 f. No. 320, with the interpretation thereof and several additional documents by M. Ginsburger in *Basler Zeitschrift*, VIII, 394 ff., 472 f. Nos. xxviii–xxx; J. H. Schreiber, *Urkundenbuch der Stadt Freiburg*, II, 167 ff. (reporting the correspondence with Schaffhausen and Zurich about the blood libel of 1401); Löwenstein, *Geschichte . . . Bodensee*, pp. 64 f., 82 ff., 143 ff. nn. 59 ff. and 68 (also pointing out that the libel and the subsequent trial were recorded neither in the major local chronicle of Diessenhofen nor in any extant archival record there); Ulrich, *Sammlung*, p. 382 App. G. Additional information has been made available by A. Nordmann in a series of articles including his "Geschichte der Juden in Basel seit dem Ende der zweiten Gemeinde bis zur Einführung der Glaubens- und Gewissensfreiheit, 1397–1875," *Basler Zeitschrift für Geschichte*, XIII, 1–190, which continues the history of the Jews in Basel where Ginsburger leaves off; and idem, "Die Juden im Kanton Baselland," *Basler Jahrbuch*, 1914, pp. 180–249. Nordmann stresses, in particular, the economic motivations of Basel's intolerance after 1397; see his observations, pp. 10 ff., and the documents pp. 165 ff. Nos. i, ii, v–vii.

12. Ulrich, *Sammlung*, pp. 462 ff. App. Aa; Löwenstein, *Geschichte . . . Bodensee*, pp. 66 ff. Interesting new data on the first half of the fifteenth century have been made available by such documentary publications as R. Thommen's *Urkunden zur Schweizer Geschichte aus österreichischen Archiven*. The Jewish material contained in its Volume III, covering the years 1411–39, was analyzed by M. Ginsburger in his aforementioned article in *ZGJD*, IV, 77–82. Other volumes likewise contain significant data relating to Jews; for instance, the important privilege issued by Duke

Albert for the Jews of the Austrian dependencies on October 20, 1446, in Vol. V, pp. 73 ff. No. 62. Other interesting data were yielded by H. Chone's "Zur Geschichte der Juden in Konstanz," *ZGJD*, VI, 3–16. This essay is largely based upon the extensive business documents preserved in the so-called Ammann courts of Constance; covering the years 1423–34, they contain much material of Jewish interest. Chone had planned to publish some of this material in full (only three documentary excerpts are included in his essay, pp. 13 ff.), but for some reason this project was never realized except through H. Ammann's more recent article, "Die Judengeschäfte im Konstanzer Ammann-Gerichtsbuch 1423–1434," *Schriften* of the Verein für Geschichte des Bodensees, LXXI, 37–84. Of course, the main contribution of these studies and the significant monographic literature cited there is to Jewish economic history of the period, and they will frequently be referred to *infra*, Chaps. LII and LIV. Chone also published an informative article, "Zur Geschichte der Juden in Zürich im 15. Jahrhundert," *ZGJD*, VI, 198–209, which is of interest beyond the local Zurich developments (see esp. pp. 205 f. regarding Löw of Constance); and another on Constance mentioned in the next note. See also F. Wyler's juridical analysis of *Die Staatsrechtliche Stellung der israelitischen Religionsgenossenschaften in der Schweiz* (in *Glarner Beiträge zur Geschichte, Rechtswissenschaft und Wirtschaftskunde*, X), which sheds some light also on the medieval status.

13. Löwenstein, *Geschichte . . . Bodensee*, p. 47; and *supra*, n. 10. On the general impact of the ecumenical councils of Constance and Basel on the history of the Jews in Central Europe, including these two Swiss cities themselves, see M. Simonsohn's study of *Die Kirchliche Judengestzgebung im Zeitalter der Reformkonzilien von Konstanz und Basel*; A. Nordmann's observations in *Basler Zeitschrift*, XIII, 5 ff.; and H. Chone, "Die Juden in Konstanz nach dem Konstanzer Konzil," *Nathan Stein-Schrift*, pp. 22–34.

14. A. Nordmann, "Histoire des Juifs à Genève de 1281 à 1780," *REJ*, LXXX, 1–41; idem, "Les Juifs dans les pays de Vaud 1278–1875," *ibid.*, LXXXI, 146–68; idem, "Documents relatifs à l'histoire des Juifs à Genève, dans le pays de Vaud et en Savoie," *ibid.*, LXXXIII, 63–73; LXXXIV, 81–91. The evolution here reveals certain peculiarities accountable by the controls exercised over that region by both the counts of Savoy and French bishops, which will be treated in next chapter. See also, more generally, P. Duparc, *Le Comté de Genève IX–XV siècle*, esp. pp. 401 f. (reference to a Jewish physician Ysac), 493, 521 f. (few Jews in the countryside; no Jewish quarter except in Geneva and possibly Annecy); and the data assembled in Steinberg's *Studien*, pp. 144 ff. The specific as well as the general forces behind that gradual elimination of Jews from all Swiss cities in the decisive stages of their struggle for national independence during the fifteenth and early sixteenth centuries would certainly merit further detailed monographic treatment. See also, *infra*, Chap. L.

15. T. H. Reed, *Government and Politics of Belgium*, p. 4. Although nominally under the overlordship of the Holy Roman Empire, many Flemish and Brabant areas gravitated toward France. This was even more the case of Burgundy proper which likewise occupied a somewhat intermediary position, although it ultimately threw in its lot with the French realm. On the history of the Jews there, see *infra*, Chap. XLIII, nn. 25 f.

16. See *supra*, Vols. IV, pp. 57, 265 f. n. 74; VI, pp. 48, 344 n. 52; Chap. XXXVII, n. 52; Raphael Levy, *The Astrological Works of Abraham ibn Ezra*, pp. 24 ff.; Caesarius of Heisterbach, *Dialogus miraculorum*, ed. by J. Strange, I, 95 ff.; Thomas of Cantimpré (Cantimpratensis), *Bonum universale de Apibus*, ed. by G. Colvenerius, Douai, 1627 ed., pp. 295 f.; E. Ouverleaux, "Notes et documents sur les Juifs de Belgique sous l'ancien régime," *REJ*, VII, 117–38, 252–71; VIII, 206–34; IX, 264–89 (also reprint), esp. VII, 127 f.; J. Stengers, *Les Juifs dans les Pays-Bas au Moyen Age*, esp. p. 15. Stengers's suggestion (p. 97 n. 36) that Rebecca's tombstone inscription be read "jardin d'Edom," that is, "in a strange land," rather than the usual "jardin d'Eden," is not acceptable. Otherwise, however, his volume offers a most remarkable documentation for the history of medieval Jewry in the Low Countries. Subject to some minor reservations, such as formulated in my review of this work in *Speculum*, XXVI, 407–409, it is one of the fullest monographs on Jewish history in any medieval region. In his bibliography (pp. 67 ff.) and his extensive notes covering more than half the volume, Stengers also quotes almost all the pertinent earlier literature. See also the old but still valuable work by H. J. Koenen, *Geschiedenis der Joden in Nederland*, pp. 57 ff.; supplemented by his "The Vicissitudes of the Jews, particularly in the Netherlands" (Dutch), *Bijdragen voor vaderlandsche geschiedenis*, VI, 75–92; S. Ullmann, *Histoire des Juifs en Belgique jusqu'au 18e siècle (Notes et documents)* (much too harshly judged by Stengers, p. 76); and J. Zwarts, *Hoofdstukken uit de geschiedenis der Joden in Nederland* (Principal Data on the History of Jews in the Netherlands), which includes an essay, "The Decline of the Medieval Jewish Communities in the Netherlands," pp. 1–38, with a map of Jewish settlements at the beginning of the 14th century; and another on "Utrecht Jewry and a Medieval Jewish Quarter," pp. 39–62. See also Zwarts's bibliographical survey, "A Source Publication for the History of Jews in the Netherlands" (Dutch), *Tijdschrift voor Geschiedenis*, XL. On the other hand, the more recent comprehensive *Geschiedenis der Joden in Nederland*, ed. by H. Brugmans and A. Frank, Vol. I, deals almost exclusively with the modern period.

17. E. Gachet, "Un Cartulaire de Guillaume Ier, comte de Hainaut," *Bulletin* of the Commission royale d'histoire, 2d ser. IV, 72 f., 100 (safe-conducts of 1307 and 1308); L. Devillers, ed., *Monuments pour servir à l'histoire des provinces de Namur, de Hainaut et de Luxembourg*, III, 460 ff. Nos. 344–45, 594 ff. No. 429 (safe-conducts of 1310 and 1337, together with the list of Jewish taxpayers in the county of Hainaut in 1337); F. Meyer, "Essai sur l'histoire des Juifs du Hainaut au XIVe siècle," *Annales de l'Est*, [2d ser.] III, 321–43; H. Poppers, *De Joden in Overijssel* (Jews in O. from their Settlement to 1814), pp. 1 ff.; J. Zwarts, *Hoofdstukken*, pp. 31 f. Stengers, who carefully reviewed all this material, has also checked the texts published by Gachet against the originals preserved in the archives of Mons, and found them substantially correct. See his observations, p. 115 nn. 104–105.

18. See the data carefully reviewed by Stengers, *passim*. The "sacrilege of Cambron" had been the subject of many writings, both belletristic and scholarly. As far back as 1897, F. Hachez was able to utilize a large bibliography on this subject in his critical review of "La Littérature du sacrilège de Cambron," *Annales* of the Cercle archéologique de Mons, XXVII, 97–152. See also the more recent literature, cited *infra*, Chap. XLIX.

19. See P. Lefèvre, "À propos du trafic de l'argent exercé par les Juifs de Bruxelles au XIVᵉ siècle," *RBPH*, IX, 906, rightly arguing against the earlier exaggerations of the size of the Brussels community. The "holy sacrament of the miracle" of 1370 in Brussels has stimulated many artists and writers and has been subjected to scholarly scrutiny for many generations. See the extensive bibliography cited by Stengers, pp. 134 ff. n. 169. A Hebrew poet commemorated the Jewish martyrs in a dirge, reproduced in French trans. by E. Carmoly in his "Essai sur l'histoire des Juifs de Belgique," *Revue orientale*, I, 173. In contrast to the tragedy of the Black Death, on which see the extensive literature quoted by Stengers (pp. 119 ff.) and others, the later pestilences seem to have had no effect on the Jews. See W. Vangassen's recent Ghent dissertation, *De Pestepidemieën na 1350* (The Pest Epidemics after 1350, Especially Those of 1400 and 1438 in Flanders and Hainaut). Apart from the presence of but a few Jewish survivors from the previous catastrophe who may have aroused little enmity, returning sanity must have caused some remorse among thinking people. All these tragic events and their underlying popular suspicions will be treated more fully, *infra*, Chaps. XLIX and L.

20. E. Ouverleaux in *REJ*, VII, 126; VIII, 207; J. F. Böhmer, *Regesta imperii*, VIII, ed. by A. Huber, p. 87 No. 1079; S. Salfeld, *Das Martyrologium*, p. 286 No. 36; the chapter, "Die Juden im Luxemburger Lande" included in N. van Werveke's *Kurze Geschichte des Luxemburger Landes mit besonderer Berücksichtigung der Kulturgeschichte*, pp. 232 ff.; and, on the situation under the Burgundian regime, *infra*, Chap. XLIII, n. 25. See also U. von Dietze's typescript dissertation, *Luxemburg zwischen Deutschland und Burgund (1383–1443)*; and, for some comparative data, J. Vannerus, "Les Lombards dans l'ancien pays de Luxembourg," *Bulletin* of the Institut historique belge de Rome, XXVII, 415–50.

21. While Hungary's partial dependence on both Germany and the Papacy has long been explored, that on the Byzantine civilization has but recently been more fully clarified. Gyula Moravcsik, a leading expert in this field, came to the conclusion that "the Byzantine influence in the early period of the Arpads was stronger and more meaningful than was assumed by earlier scholars." See "Die Problematik der byzantinisch-ungarischen Beziehungen," *Byzantinoslavica*, 1958, p. 209. See also his more detailed illustrations in *Die Byzantinische Kultur und das mittelalterliche Ungarn;* his chapter on "Hungary and Byzantium in the Middle Ages," *Cambridge Medieval History*, 2d ed., IV; and, from the Byzantine angle, F. Dölger's "Ungarn in der byzantinischen Reichspolitik," *Archivum Europae Centro-Orientalis*, VIII, 315–42. On the much-debated internal ethnic divisions, see, for instance, E. Mályusz's "Hungary's Nationality Policies in the Middle Ages" (Hungarian), *Századok* (Centuries), LXXIII, 257–94, 385–448.

22. See the resolutions of the Council of Gran (Esztergom) of 1112, can. lx; and Coloman's *Decretum*, Art. lxxiv in S. F. L. Endlicher, ed., *Rerum hungaricarum Monumenta Arpadiana*, II, 349 ff., 358 ff., 371 f.; Scherer, *Rechtsverhältnisse*, pp. 58 ff.; *supra*, Vols. III, 211 ff., 332 f. nn. 50–51; IV, 106 f., 293 f. n. 22; and Chap. XL, n. 16. On Teka's Hungarian activities, see B. Mandel, "Materials for the History of Some Jews in Medieval Hungary" (Hungarian), *MZS*, XXXV, 58–65, also discussing the Viennese David Steuss's commercial relations with Hungary. As early as the tenth century Ḥisdai ibn Shapruṭ envisaged Jewish traders traveling through Hun-

gary as readily available bearers of his message to the king of Khazaria. Some knowledge of Hungarian conditions was available also to such eleventh-century Franco-German scholars as Yehudah ha-Kohen and Rashi. See Meir b. Baruch's *Resp.*, Prague ed., fol. 89bc Nos. 903–904, 94a No. 935 (referring to a Hungarian Jew sent on a mission by the queen and to another who had brought merchandise for sale in Mayence); and Rashi's *Commentary* on Talmud Yoma 11a *s.v. Eḥad sha'are*, together with S. Kohn's comments thereon in "Das Land 'Hagar' in der hebräisch-mittelalterlichen Literatur," *MGWJ*, XXX, 145–61, 193–201. The early epigraphic evidence reaching back to ancient times is now available in the comprehensive publication by A. Scheiber, entitled, *Magyarországi zsidó feliratok* (Corpus inscriptionum Hungariae judaicarum, a temporibus saeculi III., quae exstant, usque ad annum 1686). On the other hand, the fanciful explanation of a tombstone dating from 1130 which was found in the small Carinthian town of St. Stephan and which commemorated the passing of a Jewish leader, Shabbetai, supposedly slain in Hungary, has turned out to be based upon a simple misreading. See J. Babad, "Jüdische Grabsteine in Kärnten," *MGWJ*, LXXX, 52–57, esp. pp. 53 f.; and D. Herzog's comments in his "Jüdische Grabsteine und Urkunden," *ibid.*, pp. 64 f. n. 22.

23. Andrew II's Golden Bull, Art. xxiv, now readily available in its Latin original with a German trans., ed. by W. Näf in his *Herrschaftsverträge des Spätmittelalters: Die Goldene Bulle Andreas' II von Ungarn, 1222, etc.*, pp. 9 (Latin), 14 (German); his *Decretum II* of 1231, Art. 31 and his *Juramentum de reformando regno* of 1233 in Endlicher's ed. of *Rerum hungaricarum Monumenta Arpadiana*, p. 436; Scherer, *Rechtsverhältnisse*, pp. 59 f.; Innocent III's circular letter of August 17, 1198 (some seven months after his ascending the throne of St. Peter) in his *Epistolae*, i.336, in *PL*, CCXIV, 311 f.; Honorius III's letter of August 23, 1225, reproduced in *MHJ*, I, 6 ff. No. 10; and Gregory IX's letter of March 3, 1231, *ibid.*, pp. 10 ff. No. 12, all also in Grayzel, *The Church and the Jews*, pp. 67 n. 114, 86 f. No. 1, 170 ff. No. 53, 184 ff. No. 61. See I. Csetényi's succinct remarks on "Hungarian Jews in the Period of the Golden Bull" (Hungarian), *MZS*, XI., 113–15.

In "Der Weg zur Goldenen Bulle Andreas' II von 1222," *Schweizer Beiträge zur allgemeinen Geschichte*, X, 104–38, J. Deér has shown how much Andrew II followed here West-European models. However, Deér himself warned against the earlier assumption of an overwhelming German influence on Hungary ever since Otto III, and specifically denied that Hungary had ever become a vassal state of the Empire. See his "Die Entstehung des ungarischen Königtums," *Archivum Europae Centro-Orientalis*, VIII, 52–148. Apart from the influence of the more distant popes, the newly founded Dominican order likewise made its presence strongly felt. One of its leaders, Julian, was a close adviser of King Béla IV and was sent by him in 1235 or 1236 to Constantinople and southern Russia to secure whatever information he could about the extent and nature of the new Mongolian menace. See N. Pfeiffer, *Die Ungarische Dominikanerprovinz von ihrer Gründung 1221 bis zur Tartarenverwüstung (1241 bis 1242)*; and, more generally, E. Lederer, "The Role of the Church during the Arpadian Period" (Hungarian), *Századok*, LXXXIII, 79–105 (also reprint).

It may also be noted that, despite the availability of an extensive monographic literature, some of which will be mentioned in the following notes, no comprehensive history of Hungarian Jewry is available even in the Hungarian language. J. Bergl's almost century-old *Geschichte der ungarischen Juden*; or Y. J. (L.) Greenwald's more recent sketch, *Toiznt yor yidish leben in Ungarn* (A Thousand Years of Jewish Life in Hungary), are but poor substitutes. Nor has the legal status of medieval Hungarian Jewry been systematically analyzed and it is doubly to be regretted that J. Scherer was unable to keep his promise of 1901 to furnish such a detailed review in the second volume of his *Beiträge* (a sequel to his *Rechtsverhält-nisse*).

24. Gregory IX's letter to King Béla of December 10 or 11, 1239, in *Registres,* ed. by Auvray, III, 147 No. 5001 (see also *ibid.,* I, 454 ff. No. 733; and Grayzel, *The Church,* pp. 244 ff. No. 100); *Continuatio IV Gestorum Treverorum, 1190–1242,* vii, ed. by G. Waitz *et al.,* in *MGH,* Scriptores, XXIV, 390–404, esp. p. 404; Richer, *Gesta Senonensis Ecclesiae,* xx, *ibid.,* XXV, 249–345, esp. p. 310 (also stressing the nearly total depopulation of Hungary); both reproduced with comments by F. A. Gombos in his *Catalogus fontium historiae Hungaricae aevo ducum et regum ex stirpe Arpad,* I, 771 f.; III, 2052 No. 4427. See also the excerpts in *MHJ,* I, 21 No. 20; and V, Part 1, pp. 10 f. No. 6.

25. See the Hebrew text and German translation of the elegy by S. Salfeld in *Das Martyrologium,* pp. 334 ff.; and in S. Bettelheim's "Geschichte der Pressburger Jeschiba," in *Die Juden und die Judengemeinde Bratislava in Vergangenheit und Gegenwart,* ed. by H. Gold, p. 63; Isaac b. Moses, *Sefer Or Zaru'a* (a halakhic work), I, fols. 50d f. No. 366. This observation by the Viennese scholar is also in so far noteworthy as it reveals the legalistic concern in these two Hungarian communities about the use of naturally warm waters for ritualistic ablutions, of which R. Isaac approved. The connection between Jonah's martyrdom, which is vaguely dated between 1250 and 1300, and the Tartar invasion is far from clear. Although the Tartars invaded Hungary again in 1258, this time unsuccessfully, and their menace was felt long thereafter, their direct impact on the anti-Jewish feeling is uncertain. At the most, the sense of helplessness generated by the great catastrophe may have enhanced the influence of popular preachers and stimulated the spread of folkloris-tic accusations against Jews, including that of the desecration of hosts. See, in general, the contemporary account by Canon Roger in his *Miserabile Carmen* or *Historia super destructione regni Hungariae temporibus Belae IV. regis per Tartaros facta,* ed. by I. G. Schwandtner in his *Scriptores rerum hungaricarum veteres, ac genuini,* I, 292–321; or in the new ed. by L. Juhász in E. Szentpétery's *Scriptores rerum hungaricarum tempore ducum regumque stirpis Arpadianae gestarum,* II, 543–88; and such recent analyses as E. Lederer's "The Tartar Invasion in Hungary and Its International Connections" (Hungarian), *Századok,* LXXXVI, 327–63 (also repeated in Russian in the *Acta Historica* of the Hungarian Academy of Science, II, 1–45, with a French summary, pp. 44 f.). Here the authoress emphasizes the lack of support for the Hungarians by the western Christian powers. Not only did Frederick II of Austria use the opportunity to seize Hungarian territory, but the king of France and the very pope later concluded an alliance with the Tartars. It is quite possible, therefore, that the West-German chronicler's observation concerning the Jewish messianic expectations in 1241 reflected more German than contemporary Hungarian reactions.

26. Béla IV's decree of 1251 was published in 1782 in S. Katona's comprehensive *Historia critica regum Hungariae stirpis Arpadianae, ex fide domesticorum et ex-*

ternorum scriptorum, VI, 158 ff. No. xlvii (later also in *MHJ,* I, 23 ff. No. 22) and it has been frequently analyzed since. See the more incidental references in J. E. Scherer's *Rechtsverhältnisse,* pp. 173 ff., where it is treated in connection with the text and detailed review of the individual provisions of Frederick II's prototype charter of 1244. More recently Alexander Büchler reedited the text of that privilege from its confirmation by King Sigismund on August 22, 1422, and noted some minor deviations in its still later confirmation by Wladislaus II of January 10, 1494. Both texts have been well preserved in the Pressburg Archives. On the other hand, as Büchler observed, nothing was heard about that privilege between 1251 and the discovery in 1396 of its copy prepared in 1256 by the Chapter of the Cathedral at Stuhlweissenburg (Szekesfehervár). At that time it was publicized at the request of two Jews. Nevertheless Büchler expressed no doubts of its authenticity. See his brief remarks and text edition in "Das Judenprivilegium Bélas IV vom Jahre 1251," *Jubilee Volume in Honor of Bernhard Heller,* ed. by A. Scheiber, pp. 139–46. See also *supra,* Chap. XL, n. 16; and *infra,* n. 53.

27. *MHJ,* I, 52 ff. Nos. 29–30 and 32. Andrew III's Pressburg privilege of 1291 is preserved in the Pressburg Municipal Museum. It is partially reproduced in photostat by D. Gross in his "Äusserer Verlauf der Geschichte der Juden [in Bratislava]," in H. Gold's ed. of *Die Juden und die Judengemeinde Bratislava,* p. 5.

28. See Joannes de Turóczi's *Chronica Hungarorum,* III, xli, in *Scriptores rerum Hungaricarum,* ed. by J. G. Schwandtner, I, 194; *MHJ,* V, Part 1, pp. 15 f. Nos. 18–19. Turóczi's brief statements leave many questions unanswered. They certainly do not explain Louis' sudden conversionist impulses and his early reconsideration. It appears that he and his advisers hastily reacted to the people's sufferings during the pestilence. They may also have been temporarily impressed by the anti-Jewish rumors and outbreaks occasioned by that pestilence in the neighboring countries. On the other hand, Rudolph IV's hospitable reception of these refugees into the Austrian lands (following the example set by his father Albert II in the preceding years) may have taught Louis a lesson in statesmanship. See Joseph b. Joshua ha-Kohen's *'Emeq ha-bakha* (Valley of Tears, a chronicle), ed. by M. Letteris, p. 68; in M. Wiener's German trans., p. 54; and *supra,* Chap. XLI, n. 3. Nonetheless, as late as 1368 the mayor and judge of Haimburg still demanded from the Pressburg Jews the delivery of the writs of indebtedness held by them on Pressburg residents. See *MHJ,* I, 76 f. No. 46.

29. *MHJ,* I, 78 f. No. 48, 106 ff. No. 71–72; V, Part 1, pp. 14 No. 15, 52 ff. No. 121, 76 No. 179, 86 ff. No. 194. The value of such interest accumulations was enhanced by the relative stability of the currency since the monetary reform of Charles I in 1323. If F. Kováts is right, the coins produced by the Hungarian mints in the Angevin period actually increased in their metallic content. See his "The Circulation of Money in Hungary during the Angevin Period, II: Standards of Weight in Hungary" (Hungarian), *Numizmatikai Közlöny* (Numismatic Bulletin), L–LI, 20–26. These high interest rates merely reflected the great scarcity of capital in the rapidly expanding economy under Sigismund's predecessors which Erik Molnár equates with early capitalism. See his succinct survey of "Les Débuts du capitalisme en Hongrie (1200–1350)," *Revue d'histoire comparée,* XXV, Part 2, pp. 22–41.

30. *MHJ*, I, 100 ff. Nos. 68–69; D. Gross in H. Gold's ed. of *Die Juden* . . . *Bratislava*, p. 4. On the general economic evolution in medieval Hungary, see E. Molnár's twin studies, *A Magyar társadalom története as öskortól as Árpádkorig* (A History of Hungarian Society from Prehistoric Times to the Arpadian Period), 2d ed.; and *A Magyar társadalom története as Árpád-kortól Mohácsig* (A History of Hungarian Society from the Arpadian Period to the Catastrophe of Mohács). Although writing from a Marxist point of view, Molnár was criticized by some more extreme colleagues because he had given due credit to the progressive role played by the gentry and the upper peasant class. See the summaries in the *Bibliographie d'oeuvres choisies de la science historique hongroise 1945–1959*, published by the Historical Institute of the Hungarian Academy of Sciences, pp. 68 f. Nos. 405–406 and 408; and, more generally, D. Kosary's comprehensive *Bevezetés a magyar történelem farrásaiba és irodalmaba* (Introduction to the Sources and Literature of Hungarian History), Vol. I (to 1711).

31. *MHJ*, V, Part 1, p. 106 No. 236. The development of craft guilds in Hungary was retarded also by the extensive importation of industrial goods from western lands, despite the operation of various protective tariffs. See J. Szücs, *Városok és kézmü vesség a XV. századi Magyarországon* (Cities and Artisanship in Fifteenth-Century Hungary), based upon a careful analysis of ten cities. The Ödenburg tailors, largely recruited from recently immigrated Germans (this is also indicated by the German language in which their demand is recorded), tried to employ here the methods used by their confreres in the Empire. See the concise remarks by K. Mollay in "Ödenburg at the End of the Middle Ages" (Hungarian), *Soproni Szemle* (Sopron Review), X, 31–42. These tailors paid little attention to the antiquity of the local Jewish settlement, reaching back to Roman Scarbantia, and ts significant history long before any Germans appeared on the scene. See the literature cited *supra*, Vol. III, p. 332 n. 50.

32. *MHJ*, V, Part 1, pp. 66 No. 156, 70 f. No. 167, 130 f. No. 268; I. Goldberger, "History of the Jews in Tatatóváros" (Hungarian), *MZS*, LIII, 216–31. The Mendl family was also engaged in far-flung commercial transactions. For instance, Fekethe Mendl issued in 1511 a quitclaim to an agent of Marquess George of Brandenburg. *MHJ*, V, Part 1, pp. 119 f. No. 256. On Matthias' occupation of Lower Austria see K. Schober, *Die Eroberung Niederösterreichs durch Matthias Corvinus in den Jahren 1482–90*. See also T. Kardos, "The Hussite Movement and Matthias Hunyadi's Role in the Formation of a National Church in Hungary" (Hungarian), *Századok*, LXXXIV, 121–77; and, more generally, H. Schönebaum, *Das Zeitalter der Hunyadi in politischer und kulturgeschichtlicher Bedeutung*.

33. *MHJ*, I, 222 No. 175; V, Part 1, pp. 87 f. No. 195 (following Bonfini's account); J. Bergl, *Geschichte der ungarischen Juden*, pp. 54 ff.; the anonymous dirge, *Aqonen be-marah be-khol shanah* (I Shall Bitterly Lament Every Year), cited from a Cracow MS by S. Kohn in his *A Zsidák Története Magyarországom* (A History of the Jews in Hungary), I, 441 ff. To alleviate the sufferings of the debtors (*compatientes paupertati fidelium nostrorum*), Wladislaus again canceled all interest due to Jewish lenders (1508–1511). In one case he repeated such a cancellation in 1516, when the debt amounted to only one florin. *MHJ*, V, Part 1, pp. 112 f. Nos. 247–48, 129 f. No. 267. Otherwise, however, Wladislaus maintained close personal relations with some

Jews as when he called the Jewish physician Zacharias from Pressburg to Buda in 1511. Such use of Jewish medical assistance was no more exceptional here than it was in other Christian countries. Ercole d'Este, Queen Beatrice's nephew, who under her pressure had been appointed archbishop of Gran and primate of Hungary at the age of nine, made use of Jewish apothecaries and other suppliers, as well as bankers. See esp. *ibid.*, p. 101 No. 224. Isaac's appointment to the mint of Kaschau in defiance of the express royal pledges in the Golden Bull and in later enactments was doubly significant as Kaschau had become a major commercial center of northern Hungary. See E. Fügedi's "Kaschau, eine osteuropäische Handelsstadt am Ende des 15. Jahrhunderts," *Studia Slavica* of the Hungarian Academy of Science, II, 185–213, showing, among other matters, how greatly the city had suffered from lack of capital and how often the clergy (Jews are not mentioned) appear in the records as creditors for substantial sums.

34. *MHJ*, V, Part 1, p. 97 No. 212. See also A. Scheiber, "Recent Additions to the Medieval History of Hungarian Jewry," *HJ*, XIV, 154; and the more detailed analysis by E. Winkler, "The Jewish Oath in Hungary" (Hungarian), *MZS*, XLIV, 29–47. This simple oath was replaced by a far more elaborate one included in Stephen Werböczy's *Codex tripartitum* of 1514. See *supra*, Chap. XXXVII; and E. Molnár, "Werböczy and the Feudal Law" (Hungarian), *Társadalmi Szemle* (Social Review), II, 109–114.

35. See, for instance, the photographic reproduction of a fragment from Jacob b. Asher's *Ṭurim* published with brief comments by S. (A.) Büchler in "The Mediaeval Hebrew Codex-Fragment of *Turim* in Körmend" (Hungarian) in *Semitic Studies in Memory of Immanuel Löw*, ed. by A. Scheiber, p. 311; Scheiber's report in *HJ*, XIV, 157 f.; and L. (Y. J.) Grünwald's list in *Ha-Jehudim be-Hungaria* (Geschichte der Juden in Ungarn. Biographien von Rabbinern und Gelehrten Ungarns), I, esp. p. 17 No. 1. Among other medieval Hungarian scholars one might mention the namesakes Judah Liebermann of the thirteenth and fifteenth centuries, the former a grandson of the distinguished Tosafist, Eliezer b. Nathan. As in the case of Isaac of Tyrnau, however, their very existence has become known to us mainly because of their western connections. Even in the case of Rabbi Eliakum b. Kalonymus Feiwelmann, for whom we possess a local Pressburg record of 1484, we owe its preservation to the archives of Wiener Neustadt, where he served as head of the academy in the following years. See S. Bettelheim's remarks in *Die Juden . . . Bratislava,* ed. by. H. Gold, pp. 62 f.

36. W. Kadłubek, *Chronicon Polonorum*, ed. by A. Bielowski (Monumenta Poloniae historica, II); Eliezer b. Isaac's letter cited by Meir b. Baruch in his *Responsa*, Lwów, 1860 ed., fol. 6d No. 112; Isaac b. Moses, *Sefer Or Zaru'a*, I, fol. 20d No. 113; *supra*, Vol. III, p. 338 n. 57. Yehudah the Pious' inquiry may have been prompted by his general dislike of synagogue readers, as suggested by A. (V.) Aptowitzer in his *Mabo le-Sefer Rabiah*, pp. 311, 347 n. 17. However, R. Eliezer was perfectly right that, in the struggling communities of east-central Europe, the elders had no alternative. The singular privilege granted the Cistercians of Koprzywnica need not have been as anti-Jewish as it sounds. According to the text reproduced in *Kodeks dyplomatyczny Małopolski* (Documents of Little Poland), ed. by F. Piekosiński, I, No. 60, this privilege merely gave the abbot and members of the

Order the power to invite people, *praeterquam Judeos*, apparently reserving for the duke himself the right of settling the few available Jews in localities of his choice. If so, the reservation was part of a broader ducal policy looking beyond the expected taxes from Jews, as suggested by I. Schipper in his *Studya nad stosunkami gospadarczymi Żydów w Polsce podczas średniowiecza* (Studies in the Economic Conditions of the Jews in Poland during the Middle Ages), pp. 42 ff.; and in the revised Yiddish translation entitled *Virtshaftsgeshikhte fun di Yidn in Poiln be'esn mitelalter*, pp. 51 f.

37. See the summary of a thesis submitted in 1935 to the Jewish Theological Seminary in Breslau on "The Oldest Jewish Communities in Silesia," by F. Rosenthal, published in the Polish trans. by D. Dąbrowska in *BZIH*, 1960, No. 34, pp. 3–27 (with an English résumé, p. 171); the sources cited by M. Balaban in his *Dzieje Żydów w Krakowie i na Kazimierzu* (A History of the Jews in Cracow and Kazimierz, 1304–1868), I, 3 ff.; and L. Zunz, "Aelteste Nachrichten über Juden und jüdische Gelehrte in Polen, Slavonien, Russland," reprinted in his *GS*, III, 82–87. Since the publication of this essay in 1846, little new information has been forthcoming. See A. Eisenstein's more recent review of "The Earliest References to the Intellectual Stance of the Jews in Poland" (Polish), *MZ*, III, 478–81.

The story of the Cracow rabbi Jacob ha-Kohen is characteristic. So sure were modern scholars of the nonexistence of that learned Jew in thirteenth-century Cracow that they sought to identify the city of "Cracow," mentioned in a responsum by Meir b. Baruch, with similar-sounding localities in Bohemia or Mecklenburg. Only recently did E. (F.) Kupfer discover in a Vatican MS (No. 176) the express identification of that city with Cracow in Poland. However, a residuum of doubt still remains, since that identification might well have been inserted into the MS by the scribe Abraham b. Aaron who, writing in 1543, was familiar with the prominence of the Polish capital. As has been pointed out, no less than eleven localities in Hungary alone bore the names of Karakó, Karko, or Krakó before the sixteenth century, a Polish scholar suggesting that all these names may have been derived from some pagan cultic designation. See E. (F.) Kupfer, "From Near and Far" (Hebrew), *Sefer ha-Yobel le-Nathan Michael Gelber* (The N. M. G. Jubilee Volume), pp. 217–19; and the debate between J. Staszewski in his *Słownik geograficzny* (Geographic Dictionary: The Origin and Meaning of Geographic Names), 2d ed. rev., p. 153; and his reviewers' L. Papp and L. Kiss in *Studia slavica*, VII, 243–63, esp. p. 253. Staszewski accepted that stricture in his "Einige Bemerkungen des Verfassers zur Besprechung seines Buches," *ibid.*, VIII, 453–57. This debate has underscored the extreme difficulty of deriving definite historical conclusions from possible connections of certain geographic names with ethnic groups. Franz von Miklosich has rightly observed that, "with good will, one could without too much ingenuity explain even Mecca and Medina as being of Slavic origin." This circumstance places further question marks before I. Schipper's long-debated theory that the numerous localities in Little Poland and Red Russia bearing such names as Zidów or Kozarzów are necessarily indications of Jewish or Khazar settlements there. See his *Studya*, pp. 31 ff. We recall similar difficulties with German localities or persons named Judenburg or Jude which, in many cases, may have had nothing to do with Jews.

38. A. Gieysztor and K. Dąbrowski, eds., *Osiemnaście wieków Kalisza* (Eighteen Centuries of Kalisz: Studies and Materials for the History of the City and District

of Kalisz, with English and Russian summaries); Yehudah b. Meir ha-Kohen's *responsum*, reproduced and commented on by F. (E.) Kupfer and T. Lewicki in their *Źródła hebrajskie do dziejów Słowian* (Hebrew Sources for the History of the Slavs and Some Other Peoples of Central and Eastern Europe), I, 36 f., 41 f.; Vitovt's Brest privilege of 1388 reproduced by M. Bersohn in his *Dyplomataryusz dotyczący Żydów w dawnej Polsce* (Documents Relating to Jews in Old Poland: Derived from Archival Sources, 1388–1782), pp. 15 ff. No. 1; and T. Lalik's comments in his "Recherches sur les origines des villes en Pologne," *APH*, II, 118 f.; *infra*, n. 56. The identification of "Primut" with Przemyśl, first suggested by Julius Brutzkus, remains uncertain, despite Kupfer's and Lewicki's argument. It is doubly suspect as we do not hear of any other Przemyśl Jew until 1466. See M. Schorr, *Żydzi w Przemyślu* (Jews in Przemyśl to the End of the Eighteenth Century), pp. 2 f.

In addition there must have been quite a few converted Jews in the country. If Pope John XXI mentioned in his letter of Sept. 28, 1276 to Roland of Radomsk the death of one Peter "called Jew [*dicti Judei*]" who had served as canon of a church in Łęczyca, the latter probably received that name from his Jewish origin. See J. Ptaśnik, ed., *Analecta Vaticana 1202–1366*, pp. 58 f. No. 101; and *supra*, Chap. XL, n. 45; and *infra*, Chap. XLVI, n. 81. Numerous other details which had become known by the beginning of this century were analyzed by I. Schipper in "The Early Stages of Jewish Colonization in Poland" (Russian), *ES*, IV, 161–79, 348–71; his *Studya*, esp. pp. 62 ff.; and his *Virtshaftsgeshikhte*, pp. 72 ff. The few extant data on the early history of Lithuanian Jewry have recently been summarized by B. Mark in *Di Geshikhte fun Yidn in Poiln* (A History of the Jews in Poland to the End of the Fifteenth Century), pp. 357 ff. See also R. Mahler's *Toledot ha-Yehudim be-Polin* (History of the Jews in Poland: To the Nineteenth Century, Economy, Society, the Legal Status), trans. from the Yiddish MS by A. Hameiri and ed. by D. B. Malkhim, pp. 25 ff. On the general background and particularly the few relevant archaeological contributions see A. Gieysztor, "The Genesis of the Polish State in the Light of More Recent Researches" (Polish), *KH*, LXI, 103–36; and other sources listed *supra*, Vol. III, p. 388 n. 57.

39. G. Labuda, "The War with the Tartars in 1241" (Polish), *Przegląd historyczny*, L, 189–224; A. Szyszman, *Osadnictwo karaimskie na ziemiach Wielkiego Księstwa Litewskiego* (Karaite Settlements in the Territories of the Grand Duchy of Lithuania). See also *supra*, nn. 2 and 24.

40. J. Ptaśnik, ed., *Analecta Vaticana 1202–1766*, pp. 466 f. No. 515; the Kalisz resolutions, critically ed. by B. Ulanowski *et al.* in *Studia i materiały do historii ustawodawstwa synodalnego w Polsce* (Studies and Sources for the History of the Synodal Legislation in Poland); the older but still valuable analysis thereof by W. Abraham in "The Statutes of the Provincial Synod of Kalisz of 1420" (Polish), *Rozprawy* of the Akademia umiejętności of Cracow, Hist.-phil. section, 1888; and T. Silnicki's biography of *Arcybiskup Mikołaj Trąba* (Archbishop M. T.), esp. pp. 193 ff.

Not surprisingly, however, the churches were not always able to keep their own houses in order. In a lengthy litigation before the papal legate in 1310, Abbot Nicholas of St. Mary's monastery in Breslau was accused of many misdeeds. The procurator of the abbey named Henry claimed that, after Nicholas' deposition, he had been obliged to spend 126 marks on redeeming from Jewish lenders chalices, crosses, silver containers for hosts, books, and other church ornaments, and that many such objects still were under pledge. See the text in Ptaśnik, pp. 138 ff. No. 133, esp. pp. 146 f.

41. W. Kuhn, *Geschichte der deutschen Ostsiedlung in der Neuzeit,* esp. II, 141 ff. On the German immigrants' municipal autonomy see G. C. von Unruh, "Die Selbstverwaltung deutscher Gemeinden in Polen im Spiegel örtlicher Satzungen," *Zeitschrift für Ostforschung,* IV, 590–602. Some literature relating to the controversy concerning the extent of German colonization of Poland is quoted *infra,* n. 52.

42. Matteo Villani, *Chronicle of Oliva* in *MPH,* VI, 347; S. Salfeld, *Das Martyrologium des Nürnberger Memorbuches,* pp. 249, 282; Ṣiyyon arayavekh (poem) in *'Amude ha-'abodah,* ed. by L. Landshut, App. p. vi; *Annales Mechovienses,* ed. by R. Ropell in *MGH,* Scriptores, XIX, 670 (describes only "great mortality" in Hungary, though it mentions the Flagellants there and *de aliis partibus*). See A. Eisenstein, *Die Stellung der Juden in Polen im XIII und XIV Jahrhundert,* pp. 81 ff. It is noteworthy, however, that besides Cracow and Kalisz no Polish city, except those in half-Germanized Silesia, are mentioned in these sources. Not even the few more populous communities of Great Poland seem to have suffered severely.

This fact casts some doubts upon the seriousness of the events in Cracow as well. Majer Balaban's effort to reinforce that tradition by the disappearance of Jewish names from the business and other records in the Cracow archives during the years 1349–56 (see his *Dzieje Żydów w Krakowie,* I, 5) is inconclusive, since the silence of those sources during the preceding seven-year period of 1342–49 would still require explanation. It appears that the tremendous loss of life occasioned by the Black Death was largely limited to western and central Europe, but that the eastern territories suffered much less. It should also be noted that Matteo Villani merely speaks of the population blaming "the presence of Jews" for the spread of the disease. If the *Chronicle of Oliva* does refer to the poisoning libel, it doubtless had Germany rather than Poland in mind. See also *infra,* Chap. XLIX.

43. J. Perles, *Geschichte der Juden in Posen;* P. Mojecki, *Żydowskie okrucieństwa mordy i zabobony* (Jewish Cruelties, Murders and Superstitions), Cracow, 1598; Justus Ludwig Dietz (Iodocus Ludovicus Decius), *De Sigismundi regis temporibus liber,* ed. by W. Czermak; in the Polish trans., entitled *Księga o czasach Króla Zygmunta,* ed. by T. Bieńkowski, p. 31; Jan Długosz (Longinus), *Historiae polonicae libri XII,* Book x *ad* 1407, ed. with notes by G. Groddecki, Leipzig, 1711–12 ed., Part 2, cols. 186 ff.; A. Z. Helcel, *Starodawne prawa polskiego pomniki* (Monuments of the Ancient Polish Law), II, 281 No. 1937 *ad* 1423; Schipper, *Studya,* pp. 134 ff., 327 ff. Apps. i–ii. As elsewhere, some rioters pursued antigovernmental as well as anti-Jewish aims. While Poland did not quite reveal the same sharp class conflicts as characterized the late medieval Italian and German cities, there existed enough inflammable material in the dissensions between the craftsmen and the patrician merchants for the latter to seek to divert some of that popular discontent into anti-Jewish channels. It was quite natural for even purely economic conflicts to clothe themselves in religious ideologies. See the data assembled by S. Piekarczyk in his *Studia z dziejów miast polskich w XIII i XIV w.* (Studies in the History of Polish Cities in the Thirteenth and Fourteenth Centuries), which, however, exaggerates the

element of class struggle and entirely neglects the Jewish segment of the population; W. Swoboda's pertinent remarks in his review of E. Engelmann's ed. of *Städtische Volksbewegungen im 14. Jahrhundert* in *Roczniki historyczne*, XXIX, 287–94.

The story of the Polish blood and host accusations has never been told in full. Much information is available in the general sources, especially the works by H. Strack and others to be cited *infra*, Chap. XLIX. Some additional material may be found in M. Balaban's "Episodes from the History of the Ritual Murder Trials and the Anti-Jewish Literature in Poland (16th–18th Centuries)" (Russian), *ES*, VII, 163–81, 318–27; and such detailed monographs as R. Prümers, "Der Hostiendiebstahl zu Posen im Jahre 1399," *Zeitschrift* of the Historische Gesellschaft für die Provinz Posen, XX, 293–317, showing how the alleged involvement of Jews, first briefly told by Długosz, was completely ignored in the official pronouncements, beginning with that by Jagiello dated in 1406. It was blown up into a full-fledged miracle tale by one Thomas Treter in 1609.

44. I. Schipper, "The Jewish Dispersion in Poland and Lithuania," in the *Istoriia evreiskago naroda* (A History of the Jewish People), ed. by M. Balaban *et al.*, Vol. XI (the only volume published), pp. 21–29; idem, "The Development of the Jewish Population on the Territories of the Old Republic" (Polish) in his *et al.* ed. of *Żydzi w Polsce Odrodzonej* (Jews in Resurrected Poland), I, 21–36; and R. Mahler, *Toledot*, pp. 28 f., 93 ff., 145 ff. Clearly, all such estimates are highly conjectural, although Berl Mark's stricture that the Jews could not have increased from 30,000 to 150,000 in the course of the sixteenth century (*Geshikhte*, p. 253) is inconclusive. The mass immigration during that century could readily have accounted for even more than a fivefold increase. See also, more generally, such Polish debates as J. Mitkowski's "Remarks on Poland's Population at the Beginning of Casimir the Great's Reign," *Roczniki dziejów społecznych i gospodarczych* (Annals of Social and Economic History), X, 121–33. The significant evolution of the Jewish population in Poland will be more fully analyzed in connection with the far richer documentation of the early modern period in a later chapter.

45. L. Wadding, *Annales Minorum*, 2d ed. by J. M. Fonseca de Evoca, XII, 232 No. lxxvii; the decree of expulsion from Warsaw in 1527 and its renewals in 1570, 1580, and 1633, reproduced by T. Wierzbowski in his *Przywileje królewskiego miasta stołecznego Starej Warszawy* (Privileges of the Royal Capital of Warsaw 1370–1772), pp. 35 f. No. 33, 86 ff. No. 76, 101 f. No. 85, 120 ff. No. 100; other sources cited by E. Ringelblum in his *Żydzi w Warszawie* (Jews in Warsaw), Vol. I: From the Earliest Times to Their Expulsion in 1527, pp. 15 ff.; and the data summarized by I. Schiper (Schipper) in his *Dzieje handlu żydowskiego na ziemiach polskich* (A History of Jewish Commerce in Polish Lands, esp. p. 27 listing nineteen cities which had secured privileges *de non tolerandis Judaeis* in the years 1520–97 alone); and Mahler in his *Toledot*, pp. 92 ff. On the date of the Jews' settlement in Warsaw and their legal status in neighboring Płock, see now I. Trunk's *Shtudies in yidisher geshikhte in Poiln* (Studies of Jewish History in Poland), pp. 11 ff., 25 ff. These uncertainties are the less astonishing as even the main Mazovian statutes have neither been well preserved nor, in so far as they are extant, have they been well edited. See S. Russocki's pertinent observations "On the Investigation of the Statutes Promulgated by the Mazovian Dukes of the XIV and XV Centuries" (Polish),

Czasopismo prawno-historyczne, VIII, 27–52. On Capistrano and the impact of his visit in Poland, which proved to be much less tragic than in neighboring Silesia, see *infra*, n. 58.

46. Bersohn, *Dyplomataryusz*, pp. 77 ff. Nos. 106, 109; M. Balaban, *Die Judenstadt von Lublin*, pp. 7 ff.; idem, *Dzieje Żydów w Krakowie*, pp. 47 ff. The text of the Cracow covenant of 1485 was published in its Hebrew text and a contemporary German translation by F. H. Wettstein in his *Mi-Pinqese ha-qahal bi-Qraqa* (From Communal Minute Books in Cracow), pp. i f.; and in its Latin form by F. Pikosiński in his *Kodeks dyplomatyczny miasta Krakowa* (Documentary Collection for the City of Cracow). It continued to be invoked later on many occasions.

The immediate cause of the 1495 expulsion was one of the recurrent fires which destroyed much Jewish as well as Christian property, and which the burghers blamed on the Jews. It is described by contemporary chroniclers, including Matthew of Miechow (Maciej z Miechowa) in his *Chronica Polonorum*. Published in 1519–23, this chronicle is up to 1480 largely a restatement of Jan Długosz' narrative, but from then on it contains much firsthand information. Despite his fine humanistic education in Italy, Matthew shared many of his predecessor's prejudices. See the two recent biographical studies by H. Barycz, *Maciej z Miechowa* (Matthew of Miechow 1457–1523: Historian, Geographer, Physician and Organizer of Science); and L. Hajdukiewicz, *Biblioteka Macieja z Miechowa* (Matthew of Miechow's Library). On the early relations between Cracow and Kazimierz see J. Dąbrowski's query, "Were Kazimierz and Kleparz Founded as Cracow's Competitor Cities?" (Polish), *Prace z dziejów Polski feudalnej* (Studies in the History of Feudal Poland in Honor of Roman Grodecki), pp. 181–87, which is answered in the negative. Nevertheless, especially after the transplantation there of Jews, Kazimierz became an important commercial center.

The example set by the capital also inspired the Lwów burghers to try to curtail the commercial rights of their Jewish fellow townsmen. Although greatly outnumbered by the so-called minorities of Ruthenians, Jews, Muslims, and Armenians, these burghers invoked their city's privileges placing it substantially on a par with Cracow, and succeeded in securing in 1488 a general prohibition of Jewish retail trade in cloth. Similar prohibitions were also pushed through in Poznań, Sandomierz, and Danzig. See *Akta grodzkie i ziemskie* (Town and Country Documents), published by the Galician Provincial Committee, VII, 163 f. No. lxxxix; and L. Charawiczowa's comprehensive analysis of "The Economic Restrictions of the Schismatic Nations and the Jews of Lwów in the Fifteenth and Sixteenth Centuries" (Polish), *KH*, XXXIX, 193–227, esp. pp. 215 ff. These developments will become clearer in our treatment of medieval Jewish economic history and that of early modern Polish Jewry in later chapters.

47. S. A. Bershadskii, *Litovskie Evrei* (Lithuanian Jews: a Story of Their Legal and Social Conditions in Lithuania from Vitovt to the Union of Lublin, 1388–1569), pp. 247 ff.; T. Wierzbowski, *Matricularum regni Poloniae summaria*, II, 1498 No. 1241. On the important Judaizing movement in contemporary Muscovy see D. Oljancyn, "Aus dem Kultur- und Geistesleben der Ukraine, I: Was ist die Häresie der 'Judaisierenden'?" *Kyrios*, I, 176–89; the more general suggestive observations by M. Mieses in his "Judaizers in Eastern Europe" (Polish), *MZ*, III, 41–62, 169–85; IV, 147–59, 241–60, 342–58, esp. III, 173 ff.; and my *The Russian Jew under Tsars and*

Soviets, p. 8. On the tremendous impression made by the Spanish expulsion all over Europe, see *infra*, Chap. L. The fear of Jewish proselytization may well have been one of the phobias instilled in Alexander during the years of anti-Jewish training he had received in his youth from his tutor, Jan Długosz, on whose intolerant views see S. Goldshtein, "From the History of the Fifteenth-Century Jewish Community in Cracow: the Historian Jan Długosz and the Cracow Jews" (Russian), *ES*, III, 624–31. Remarkably, Alexander's brother, John Albert, although likewise under Długosz' influence, not only upheld, upon his accession to the Polish throne in 1492, the toleration of the Jews in the "Crown" but he also accepted without demurrer the influx of Lithuanian refugees. See his decree of June 29, 1498 (renewing one issued in the preceding year), in S. A. Bershadskii *et al.*, eds., *Russko-evreiskii Arkhiv* (Russian-Jewish Archive: Documents and Materials for the History of the Jews in Russia), III, 34 No. 13. This was in line with the Jews' general freedom of movement throughout the realm granted them by the royal charters. On the privilege in Ezekiel's favor see *ibid.*, p. 40 No. 20.

48. M. Bersohn, *Dyplomataryusz*, pp. 26 f. No. 11, 226 ff. Nos. 411–13, 424, 428 and 433; S. A. Bershadskii *et al.*, eds., *Russko-evreiskii Arkhiv*, III, 63 ff. No. 42, 80 f. No. 54, 88 f. No. 61, 92 f. No. 67. The two nobles who brought back from Jerusalem the report about Isaac (sometimes called in the documents by the diminutive Izaczko, once Jacob Isaac) were by no means rare exceptions, since Poles made frequent pilgrimages to Palestine. Of course, but few left behind such travelogues as are analyzed by K. Hartleb in his "Voyages de Polonais en Orient au XVIme siècle," *La Pologne au VIIe Congrès international des sciences historiques*, Warsaw, 1933, III, 217–26.

49. A. Lewicki, ed., *Codex epistolaris saeculi decimi quinti*, Vol. III, pp. 70 f. No. 57, 583 f. No. 75; Bersohn, *Dyplomataryusz*, pp. 238 ff. Nos. 451, 454–55 and 458; Bershadskii *et al.*, *Russko-evreiskii Arkhiv*, pp. 128 ff. Nos. 98, 104, 109 and 121–22. Of other foreign interventions one might mention especially that by Pope Boniface IX of April 24, 1392. On the complaint of a Cracow official, Klemens of Kurow, the pope ordered an investigation of the alleged usurious exactions by the then leading Jewish financier, Lewko son of Jordan. The pope insisted that, if true, Lewko "should return the extorted amounts to the plaintiff and subsequently desist from usurious exactions" under the usual warning that otherwise all faithful Christians would abstain from any communication with him. This interesting document is reproduced, from the original preserved in the Dominican monastery in Cracow, by S. Kutrzeba in "The Legal Status of the Jews in Poland in the Fifteenth Century" (Polish), *Przewodnik naukowy i literacki*, XXIX, 1007–18, 1147–65, esp. p. 1155 App. i. The papal intervention seems to have secured for Klemens no more than a temporary respite, however, since his entire debt was ultimately liquidated in 1410 by his son Nicholas, then serving as archbishop of Gniezno and primate of Poland.

50. The long-accepted term of royal "privileges" for Jews is justified if one accepts, with Jan Łaski, the definition of the *summa . . . Raimundi* that "a privilege is a benefit enacted contrary to common law, and nothing may be called a privilege, unless it grants a special exception." See his ed. of *Commune incliti Polonie regni privilegium*, Cracow, 1506 ed., fol. iiia. At the same time, since their observance was universally obligatory, one might also call them "statutes" or "char-

ters." See the discussion of a similar dualism applying to the so-called Nieszawa statutes or privileges in R. Hube's "The Nieszawa Statutes" (Polish), reproduced in his *Pisma* (Works), ed. with a Biographical-Critical Sketch by K. Dunin, II, 165.

51. F. Papée, ed., *Akta Aleksandra króla polskiego* . . . *(1501–1506)* (The Documents of Alexander, King of Poland, 1501–1506), pp. 111 ff. No. 91, 527 f. No. 314.

52. See, for instance, the data analyzed by H. Weczerka in his "Herkunft und Volkzugehörigkeit der Lemberger Neubürger im 15. Jahrhundert," *Zeitschrift für Ostforschung*, IV, 506–30. See also G. Schubert-Finketscher, *Die Verbreitung der deutschen Stadtrechte in Osteuropa;* and, more generally, P. Dąbkowski, *Tolerancja narodowościowa w dawnej Polsce* (National Tolerance in Old Poland); and E. von Puttkammer, *"Menschenrechte" und "Bürgerrechte" in der Verfassungsentwicklung Osteuropas bis zum 16. Jahrhundert.* There has been considerable interest in recent years in the origin and structure of the medieval Polish cities. Of the vast literature on the subject we need but mention here the thirteen papers submitted at a 1957 symposium, ed. by P. Francastel in *Les Origines des villes polonaises;* and other writings reviewed by T. Lalik in his "Recherches sur les origines des villes en Pologne," *APH*, II, 101–31. See also such monographic essays as S. Piekarczyk's aforementioned *Studia z dziejów miast polskich.*

Of similarly great interest have been the recent debates on the extent of the German colonization in Poland and its impact upon the Polish economy and culture, which had been a bone of contention between nationalistic Germans and Poles for generations. Only the recent cooperation between the Polish and East-German Peoples' Republics has enabled scholars to seek some more balanced interpretations. A number of such recent studies are cited in S. Trawkowski's review article, "Zur Erforschung der deutschen Kolonisation auf polnischem Boden in 13. Jhd.," *APH*, VII, 79–95; and his own interpretation, "On the Question of the German Colonization in the Transformation of the Material Culture in Polish Lands during the Thirteenth Century" (Polish), *Kwartalnik historii kultury materialnej*, VIII, 183–207. In time, however, the Polonization of these German settlers had progressed far enough that even in a border city like Danzig the bourgeoisie began to be recruited in an increasing degree from native-born inhabitants. There also were Flemish, English, and other elements in the population. See the careful archival study by H. Penners-Ellwart, *Die Danziger Bürgerschaft nach Herkunft und Beruf 1537–1709.* On the contrast with growing West-European nationalism and its intolerance toward Jews, see *infra*, Chap. LIV.

53. Boleslas' statute of 1264 is no longer extant; it can be reconstructed only from its greatly altered confirmation by Casimir the Great. Frequently reproduced, it was provided with detailed comments by L. Gumplowicz in his *Prawodawstwo polskie względem Żydów* (The Polish Legislation Relating to Jews), pp. 121 ff. (On the life and work of this pioneer in the study of the legal history of Polish Jewry, who later developed into an outstanding sociologist, see B. Zebrowski, *Ludwig Gumplowicz. Eine Bio-Bibliographie*). The statute of 1264 has been more fully reconstructed by P. Bloch in *Die General-Privilegien der polnischen Judenschaft;* it has also frequently been compared with its Austrian, Hungarian and Czech prototypes. See the texts of the decrees by Frederick II of Austria of 1244 in J. E. Scherer's *Rechtsverhältnisse*, pp. 135 ff.; Béla IV's Hungarian decree of 1251 in A. Friss *et al.*, eds., *Monumenta Hungariae Judaica*, I, 23 ff. No. 22; and those issued by Přemysl Ottakar II in

1254–55 in Bondy and Dworský, *Zur Geschichte der Juden,* I, 17 ff. No. 24, where additional sources and particularly the extant MSS of these texts are recorded. See also the further data cited *supra,* n. 27; and Chap. XL, n. 16. Analytical studies include Scherer, *loc. cit.;* P. Bloch, *Die General-Privilegien,* pp. 4 ff.; and Schipper, *Studya,* pp. 45 ff., the latter emphasizing particularly the economic aspects of Boleslas' decree. On its local background see now J. Sieradzki, "Boleslas the Pious and the 'Kalisz Statute' for the Jews of the Year 1264" (Polish), in A. Gieysztor and K. Dąbrowski's ed. of *Osiemnaście wieków Kalisza,* I, 131–42 (with an English summary, p. 370); and, on the impact of German law and commercial relations on the city's thirteenth-century evolution, Z. Kaczmarczyk, "Kalisz's Historic Role in the Middle Ages" (Polish), *Przegląd zachodni,* VII, Part 3, pp. 32–46. It may also be noted that, despite the influence exerted by Hungary's Golden Bull of 1222 on Poland's legal evolution and particularly the protection of the rights of the gentry (see A. Divéky's *Pochodzenie węgierskiej Złotej Buly* [The Origin of the Hungarian Golden Bull and Its Impact on Polish Law]), Jews were not immediately barred from such semipublic occupations as those of fiscal agents. Even the prohibition of lending on rural estates was not enacted before the statute of Warta of 1423. See *infra,* n. 56.

54. L. Gumplowicz, *Prawodawstwo polskie,* pp. 29 ff. (Art. xxvi); E. Jarra, "The Juristic Creativity of the Polish Clergy (966–1800)" (Polish), *Sacrum Poloniae Millennium,* I, 253–390, esp. pp. 262 f.; and, more generally, O. Balzer, ed., *Les Statuts de Casimir le Grand.* According to Berl Mark, the 1364 text, still extant in the Count Krasiński Library in Cracow in the 1930s, was lost during the Second World War. See his *Geshikhte,* p. 295. It is possible, however, that this particular passage in the 1347 statute was inserted by a later anti-Jewish interpolator. On the highly unsatisfactory state of preservation of the original text of that so-called *Statut Wiślicki,* promulgated in a Wiślica assembly *ca.* 1347, see the century-old debate summarized by J. Bardach *et al.* in *Historia państwa i prawa Polski* (A History of Poland's State and Law), I, 376 n. 5. The polarity of Casimir's attitude to the contemporary Polish Church is well analyzed by Z. Kaczmarczyk in his *Monarchia Kazimierza Wielkego* (The Monarchy of Casimir the Great: Organization of the Church, Arts and Sciences), esp. pp. 172 ff., 235 ff.

Some modern scholars who voiced doubts about the historicity of Długosz' account of Esterka argued in particular that this Polish historian had generally revealed both an anti-Jewish animus and an excessive interest in the amours of Casimir and the other princes. See *supra,* n. 47; and E. S. Swieżawski's *Zarysy badań krytycznuch nad dziejami historyjografiją i mitologiją* (Outlines of Critical Studies in History, Historiography and Mythology), Vol. III: Esterka and Other Women of Casimir the Great. However, the deeper sociopolitical reasons motivating Casimir's policies toward Jews have not yet been monographically analyzed. For the time being see A. Eisenstein, *Die Stellung der Juden;* and such more general recent treatments as J. Baszkiewicz, *Powstanie zjednoczonego państwa polskiego na przełomice XIII i XIV wieku* (The Rise of a United Polish State at the Turn from the Thirteenth to the Fourteenth Centuries); and O. Balzer's older but still very useful three-volume study of *Królestwo polskie 1295–1370* (The Kingdom of Poland, 1295–1370). See also *infra,* n. 55.

55. Stanisław Ciołko's *"Liber cancellariae:* Ein Formelbuch der polnischen Königskanzlei aus der Zeit der husitischen Bewegung," ed. by J. Caro in *Archiv für*

österreichische Geschichte, XLV, Part 2, pp. 319–545, esp. pp. 385 f. No. xxx; F. Piekosiński, ed., *Rachunki dworu króla Władysława Jagiełły i królowej Jadwigi* (Accounts of the Court of King Wladislaw Jagiello and Queen Jadwiga for the Years 1388–1420), p. 268 (dated July 5, 1394); *Akta grodzkie i ziemskie*, II, 77 f. Nos. xlvi and xlix. Such social relations of kings with big merchants were not exceptional. See, for instance, E. Maschke, *Krakauer Bürger als Geldgeber und Gastgeber von Königen*, 3d ed. rev. and enlarged by V. Kauder (on the fourteenth-century family Wersing). See also the analysis of Jagiello's attitude to Wołczko and the Lwów Jews in general, in M. Balaban's pertinent essay reprinted in his *Z historji Żydów w Polsce* (From the History of the Jews in Poland: Sketches and Studies), pp. 3–17; and I. Schipper's critique thereof in his "Disputable Points in the History of the Jews during the Reign of Wladislaw Jagiello" (Russian), *ES*, VI, 102–107.

56. Jadwiga's and Jagiello's decrees, reproduced by J. W. Bandtkie in his ed. of *Jus polonicum*, pp. 212 ff.; "Statuta . . . praeside Nicolao II. Trąba . . . in synodo provinciali Vieluno-Calissiensi," in A. Z. Helcel, ed., *Starodawne prawa polskiego pomniki*, IV, 171 ff., 238 ff.; *Akta grodzkie i ziemskie*, III, 75 f. No. xlii. "On the Date of the Origin of the Statute of Warta" which, after a long dispute, was definitely settled as that of 1423, see S. Roman's pertinent Polish article in *Czasopismo prawno-historyczne*, III, 155–92, with an additional note thereon by J. Sobalski, *ibid.*, VII, Part 2, pp. 307–308. Vitovt's decrees in favor of the Jews of Brest, Troki, and Grodno of 1388–89 are reproduced in M. Bersohn, *Dyplomataryusz*, pp. 15 ff. No. 1; and S. A. Bershadskii *et al.*, eds., *Russko-evreiskii Arkhiv*, I, 1 ff. No. 1; III, 7 ff. No. 2. Their indebtedness to the preceding Polish and other East-Central European decrees is quite obvious.

In "The Legal and Social Status of Jews in the Ukraine from the Fifteenth to the Seventeenth Centuries" (Hebrew), *Zion*, XX, 128–52, esp. p. 129 nn. 5–6, S. Ettinger argues against Bershadskii that the original Vitovt decrees of 1388 extended to the rest of Lithuania as well and that Volhynia's privilege of 1432 was but preparatory to its ultimate incorporation into the Polish Crown. This question remains open, however. See also, more broadly, J. Deveiké, "The Legal Aspect of the Last Religious Conversion in Europe," *Slavonic and East European Review*, XXXII, 117–31 (on the Lithuanian developments from the tenth to the fifteenth centuries); and on the simultaneous evolution of the legal status of the Lithuanian nobility, see O. P. Backus, "Die Rechtsstellung der litauischen Bojaren 1387–1506," *Jahrbücher für Geschichte Osteuropas*, n.s. VI, 132 (also stressing the equivocal nature of that term in fifteenth-century Lithuania).

57. The important "undated privilege" (see *supra*, n. 54) was originally issued by Casimir the Great, but through Casimir IV's confirmation in 1453 it became, despite its temporary revocation a year later, the basis for the entire legal status of Polish-Lithuanian Jewry. See the text, German translation, and comments by P. Bloch in *Die General-Privilegien*, pp. 41 ff., 102 ff. (the privilege is here designated as "the Boleslas-Casimir statute"); and A. Eisenstein's comments in his "Echtheit des undatierten Privilegs der grosspolnishen Judenschaft," *MGWJ*, LXXVII, 211–28. These arguments have not completely dispelled, however, all doubts in the authenticity of that charter. See, in addition to the extensive discussions by Hube and others, S. Kutrzeba's observation in *Przewodnik naukowy*, XXIX, 1010 n. 1. Whatever its origin, through its subsequent royal confirmations, this document attained uncontested legal validity.

58. Zbigniew Oleśnicki's missive to Casimir IV of 1454 in *Monumenta medii aevi, codex epistolaris saeculi XV*, Vol. II, Part 2, p. 146; John Capistrano's letters to the king of April 28, 1454, and to Pope Nicholas V of October 13, 1454, in Wadding's *Annales minorum*, XII, 196 f.; and other data analyzed by M. Dzieduszycki in his comprehensive biography of *Zbigniew Oleśnicki* (includes an interesting undated letter sent by Capistrano to Pope Nicholas V relating to the Prague Jewish convert Magister Paul, whom Capistrano had arrested with Oleśnicki's approval but ultimately had to release; pp. xci ff. [Latin], 413 ff. [Polish]); and J. Hofer, *Johannes von Capestrano*, pp. 530 ff. The sharpness of the conflict between the king and his chief ecclesiastical adviser had reached its climax when, at the Estates' assembly of Piotrków in 1453, Oleśnicki threatened to urge the king's deposition. Casimir avoided the complete break by repeating the oath he had taken in 1440, which, however, was substantially meaningless. All along Długosz, our main witness, sided with Oleśnicki and made his peace with the king only in 1463. See M. Bobrzyński and S. Smolka, *Jan Długosz, jego życie i stanowisko w piśmiennictwie* (J. D.: His Life and Position in Literature, esp. pp. 46 ff., 185 ff. Here as often elsewhere Długosz allowed his dislike of Jews and his amity for Oleśnicki to run away with his better historical judgment. See the perceptive analysis by I. Chrzanowski in his "Jan Długosz: an Attempt at Characterization of the Man" (Polish), *Studia historyczne* (Historical Studies) in Honor of Stanisław Kutrzeba, II, 99–115. In any case, Oleśnicki's threat of an interdict must have sounded quite hollow to the king who was on very friendly terms with Nicholas V. In 1447 he had recognized the pope's election over the objections of his councilors, lay and ecclesiastical, many of whom were espousing the highly controversial theory of Conciliar supremacy over the Papacy.

Casimir IV's resistance to the encroachments of the Church, as represented by his vigorous counterpart, was part of his effort to strengthen the monarchical power in the direction of what was called "protoabsolutism." This policy involved the promotion of the interests of the Crown's loyal Jewish subjects, although by fostering also the power of the burghers it enhanced the possibilities of conflict between the two groups. This involuntary ambiguity explains also the aforementioned restrictions on Jewish trade in Cracow, Lwów, and elsewhere during the last decade of Casimir's reign, which could not have occurred without royal sanction. See K. Górski, "The Domestic Regime of Casimir the Jagiellon in the Crown" (Polish), *KH*, LXVI, 726–59; and *supra*, n. 46.

59. On Callimach and the gentry's opposition to him see J. Szujski's *Dzieje Polski* (History of Poland), II, in his *Dzieła* (Collected Works), 2d ser. II, 152 f., 156; J. Zathey, "Quelques recherches sur l'humaniste Kallimach (Filippo Buonaccorsi, 1437–1496)" in *Umanesimo e esoterismo* (Atti of the Convegno internazionale di studi umanisti, Oberhofen, Sept. 1960), ed. by E. Castelli, pp. 123–39 (a well-informed, though undocumented, study of Callimach's distinguished family background and his general liberal outlook); B. Mark and F. Kupfer, "The Polish Jews in the Period of the Renaissance" (Polish), *BZIH*, 1953, Nos. 2–3 (6–7), pp. 3–55, esp. pp. 24 ff.

60. See Boleslas' privilege, esp. Arts. 9–11, 20–21, 25, in Jan Łaski, ed., *Commune incliti Poloniae regni privilegium*, 1506. fol. 163; J. W. Bandtkie, *Jus polonicum*, pp. 1 ff.; the analysis thereof in P. Bloch, *Die General-Privilegien*, pp. 4 ff.; I. Schipper, *Kultur-Geshikhte fun di Yidn in Poiln* (Cultural History of the Jews in Poland during the Middle Ages), pp. 99 ff.; and *supra*, n. 46. Of some interest also are F.

Papée's biography of *Jan Olbracht,* which minimizes Callimach's influence upon the king (pp. 127 ff., 225 f.); and that of the king's even more conservative brother, *Królewicz Kardynał Fryderyk Jagielloński* (Prince Royal Frederick the Jagiellon as Bishop of Cracow and Archbishop of Gniezno) by H. Rebus.

61. The texts of the respective confirmations are extant in various archives and have often been reprinted. An original confirmation issued by John Casimir in 1640 was reproduced from the Poznań State Archives by J. Perles in his *Geschichte der Juden in Posen,* pp. 129 ff. Another such confirmation, promulgated by John Sobieski in 1676, was published by L. Gumplowicz in his *Prawodawstwo polskie,* pp. 161 ff. The compilation submitted to the Prussian authorities in 1793 was used by P. Bloch in *Die General-Privilegien* (p. 1 n. 1), while that preserved in the Cracow communal archives and bearing the title, *Sumaryusz przywilejów generalnych nadanych Żydom w Polsce* (A Summary of the General Privileges Granted the Jews in Poland and particularly in Cracow since Most Ancient Times), was ed. with an Intro. by M. Schorr in "A Cracow Compilation of Jewish Statutes and Privileges" (Russian), *ES,* I, 247–64; II, 76–100, 223–45; and further analyzed by him in "Die Hauptprivilegien der polnischen Judenschaft," *Festschrift Adolf Schwarz,* pp. 519–38. See also I. Lewin, *The Protection of Jewish Religious Rights by Royal Edicts in Ancient Poland;* and, more generally, J. Bardach *et al., Historia państwa i prawa Polski, passim.*

62. See O. Halecki's pertinent remarks on "The Significance of the Christianization of Poland in European History," *The Polish Review,* VI, Parts 1–2, pp. 3–17. It is possible, though it is nowhere documented, that Jews, arriving from either the West, Byzantium, or the Caliphate, brought with them some knowledge of the more advanced techniques of agricultural production, which in time were emulated by the local populations. More directly, they exerted their influence through creating certain channels of export trade, at least in the articles mentioned by Ibn Khurdadhbah, and thus stimulated their production. Despite the growing interest in Poland's agricultural history, which has been greatly advanced by the Marxist-oriented Polish historians of recent years, no data have as yet been made available which would justify any reasonable hypotheses on this score. See M. M. Fryde's critical review of "Recent Studies in Polish Agrarian History," *The Polish Review,* VI, Parts 1–2, pp. 19–32; VII, Part 4, pp. 37–54. On many of the pre-Christian developments and, in particular, also on the exaggerations concerning the extent of the Jewish slave trade at the end of the first millennium, see *supra,* Vol. IV, esp. pp. 175 f., 180 f., 196, 325 f. n. 31, 328 f. n. 39, 336 ff. n. 59.

CHAPTER XLIII: FRANCE AND ENGLAND

1. Henry de Bracton, *De legibus et consuetudinibus Angliae*, v.6, 6, ed. by T. Twiss, VI, 50 f., ed. by C. E. Woodbine, II, 305; Philip the Fair's statement of 1302 in Pierre Dupuy, *Histoire du différend d'entre le pape Boniface VIII et Philippe le Bel Roy de France*, Preuves, pp. 68 f.; and *supra*, Vol. IV, pp. 62 f., 269 f. n. 81; and Chap. XXXVII, nn. 40 and 55. Frederick II's moderation in his foreign correspondence is well illustrated by his circular letters to Louis IX of France, Henry III of England, and other monarchs cited by R. W. Carlyle and A. J. Carlyle in *A History of Mediaeval Political Theory in the West*, V, 285 ff., 302 ff. The neutrality, on the other hand, maintained in these struggles between Frederick and the popes, even by so pious a Christian king as Louis IX, reflected the growing trend toward national self-determination which was deeply to affect also the destinies of medieval Jewry. See W. Holtzmann, *Das mittelalterliche Imperium und die werdenden Nationen;* my "Medieval Nationalism and Jewish Serfdom" in *Neuman Jub. Vol.*, pp. 17–48; and *infra*, Chaps. XLVII and L.

2. King Edward the Confessor, *Leges ecclesiasticae e secularibus suis depromptae*, xxi, in *PL*, CLI, 1193 f.; Bracton, *De legibus*, v.6, 6, *loc. cit.;* F. Pollock and F. W. Maitland, *The History of English Law Before the Time of Edward I*, 2d ed., I, 471 f.; J. M. Rigg, ed., *Select Pleas, Starrs and Other Records from the Rolls of the Exchequer of the Jews A. D. 1220–1284*, pp. lvi ff., 2 f. Bracton seems to have written his treatise about 1259. See the extensive literature cited by E. H. Kantorowicz in *The King's Two Bodies*, pp. 143 ff., esp. p. 145 n. 172; and, more generally, W. Fesefeldt, *Englische Staatstheorie des 13. Jahrhunderts. Henry de Bracton und sein Werk*. The jurist clearly reflected the Crown's official position, which had found expression in Henry III's mandate of 1253 to the justices assigned to the custody of the Jews. Here the king specifically stated "that no Jew remain in England unless he do the King's service [*servicium*], and that no sooner be a Jew, whether male or female, born than he serve [*serviat*] Us in some way." See T. Rymer and R. Sanderson, *Foedera*, ed. by A. Clarke, F. Holbrooke, and J. Caley, I, Part 1, p. 293; and Rigg in his *Select Pleas*, pp. xlviii f. The authenticity of Edward the Confessor's statement has rightly been disputed; it is generally agreed that it dates from the twelfth century rather than the tenth. See F. Liebermann, *Über die Leges Edwardi Confessoris*, pp. 66 f.; H. S. Q. Henriques, *The Jews and the English Law*, pp. 52 f.; *supra*, Vol. IV, pp. 78 ff., 278 f.; and *infra*, n. 46.

3. *Forum Turolii*, Art. 425, ed. by F. Aznar y Navarro (in *Colección de documentos para el estudio de la historia de Aragón*, II), pp. 223 ff.; in the old Romance trans. entitled *El Fuero de Teruel*, ed. by M. Gorosch, p. 320 No. 568; F. Baer, *Die Juden im christlichen Spanien*, I, Part 1, pp. 896 ff. No. 554, 1043; Part 2, pp. 36 No. 107, 214 No. 221; James I's letter to the authorities of Montpellier, published by S. Kahn in his "Documents inédits sur les Juifs de Montpellier," *REJ*, XIX, 261 n. 2; and other sources cited by Baer in his *Studien zur Geschichte der Juden im König-*

reich Aragonien, pp. 11 ff. See also *infra,* Chap. XLIV, n. 11. The meaning of such declarations will become clearer in our forthcoming analysis of the legal status of Spanish Jewry. Here we need but add that, to safeguard their own revenue, the kings of Castile and Aragon forbade the sale of Jews into slavery for debts either by themselves or by creditors. At times the monarchs rode roughshod even over the established rights of local authorities. For instance, in order to encourage Jewish resettlement in Lérida after the ravages of Martinez' "holy war" of 1391, King Martin ordered the local lords and the Jewish communities not to interfere with the later departures of such new settlers. He invoked to this effect "the plenitude of his royal power" and his general protection over Jews, "his chests and his treasure." See Baer, *Die Juden,* I, Part 1, p. 762 No. 472; Part 2, p. 169 No. 176, etc.

4. E. J. de Laurière, D. F. Secousse *et al.,* eds., *Ordonnances des roys de France de la troisième race,* I, 47, 53; III, 475 Art. 3; Council of Béziers, canon 27, in G. D. Mansi, *Sacrorum conciliorum nova et amplissima collectio,* XXIII, 883; and *supra,* Vol. IV, pp. 59, 62 f., 266 f. n. 76, 269 f. n. 81. On the growth of national sentiment in France, which had affected and become the tool of the French monarchy ever since the twelfth century, see L. Boehm, "Gedanken zum Frankreich-Bewusstsein im frühen 12. Jahrhundert," *HJB,* LXXIV, 681–87. It was particularly the leading role played by Frenchmen in the Crusades which made possible such lyrical assertions as that by Robert Monachus who spoke of the happy French nation, "whose God is the Lord; the people whom He hath chosen for His own inheritance." See his *Historia Hierosolymitana,* Prolegomena in *PL,* CLV, 670, with reference to Ps. 33:12. This new feeling naturally implied the French monarchy's independence of the Empire. Of the vast literature on this subject see, for instance, A. H. Benna, "Der Kaiser und der König von Frankreich im Recht des späten Mittelalters," *ZRG,* Germanistische Abteilung, LXVIII, 397–410; and, more generally, P. E. Schramm's comprehensive analysis of *Der König von Frankreich—Das Wesen der Monarchie vom 9. bis zum 16. Jahrhundert,* 2d ed. rev., esp. I, 180 ff., 192 ff., 222 ff.; II, 111 f., 139 ff.; and *infra,* Chaps. XLVII and L.

We shall see how the growth of French centralization during the fourteenth century, especially after the readmission of the Jews in 1315, enabled the kings to arrogate to themselves full control over the Jews residing in the possessions of their vassals even without such mutual agreements. See J. Parkes, *The Jew in the Medieval Community,* pp. 119 ff.; and *infra,* nn. 23 ff. While this centralization opened the gates to boundless fiscal exactions, it secured at least some protection against overzealous local officials, and particularly against fanatical inquisitors. Already Philip the Fair ordered his bailiffs to stem the zeal of inquisitors in prosecutions for alleged unlawful usuries or acts of sorcery. In 1377 the royal attorney of Saint Denis withdrew Mouce de Senlis, supposedly a relapsed Jewish convert, from the inquisitor's clutches, although his alleged crime clearly fell within the authority of the inquisitorial courts. Less equivocal was a case twelve years later of an accused murderer in Reims, where the royal jurisdiction was successfully upheld by the local officials. See C. V. Langlois, "Formulaires et lettres du XIIe, du XIIIe et du XIVe siècle," *Notices et extraits des manuscrits de la Bibliothèque Nationale,* XXXIV, Part 1, pp. 19 f. No. 14; R. Anchel, *Les Juifs de France,* pp. 98, 116 f. Here Anchel also quotes briefly some examples of the charters granted to individual Jewish communities by their local rulers (pp. 120 ff.).

5. See H. F. Delabordes and C. Petit-Dutaillis, eds., *Recueil des Actes de Philippe Auguste*, II, Nos. 582–83, 678, 776, 900; the excerpts in U. Robert, "Catalogue d'actes relatifs aux Juifs pendant le moyen âge," *REJ*, III, 212 ff., summarizing, in Nos. 7, 17–18 and 20, the mutual agreements with the counts of Champagne of 1210, 1224, and 1228; A. Teulet *et al.*, eds., *Layettes du Trésor des Chartes*, I, 197ab No. 479, 350 Nos. 922–23, 373 No. 977, 487 f. No. 1360; II, 14 f. No. 1610, 15 No. 1612, 16 No. 1615, 18 No. 1620, 30 No. 1648, 153 No. 1996, 174 No. 2049, 192 f. No. 2085; C. Petit-Dutaillis, *Étude sur la vie et le règne de Louis VIII (1187–1226)*, p. 459 No. 79; and, more generally, *ibid.*, pp. 414 ff., 426 f., 452 ff. Nos. 26–28, 54 and 73, 474 No. 183; with the comments thereon by Israel Lévi in his "Louis VIII et les Juifs," *REJ*, XXX, 284–88; the careful reexamination of all issues involved in the Jewish treaties between the kings and barons by G. I. Langmuir in his "'Judei nostri' and the Beginning of Capetian Legislation," *Traditio*, XVI, 203–39; *supra*, n. 4; and Vol. IV, pp. 62 f., 269 f. n. 81. Between 1223 and 1230, another decree enacted at the beginning of Louis IX's reign concerned itself particularly with Jewish usury; it tried to stop the enforced collection of debts owed to Jews antedating the ordinance of 1223, unless the lenders possessed specific authorizations from Louis VIII or Louis IX. This decree was dated by its editors, E. Martène and U. Durand (in their *Veterum scriptorum . . . amplissima collectio*, I, 1294) in 1245, but G. Caro has cogently argued for its dating in 1227. See his *Sozial- und Wirtschaftsgeschichte der Juden im Mittelalter*, I, 370, 507.

The treaty of Melun thus merely reaffirmed and expanded the agreements made by Louis IX's predecessors. As Petit-Dutaillis and Lévi have pointed out, these treaties directly obligated only the signatories. Yet there was an implied promise of assistance to the king in enforcing similar provisions in other vassal territories. Petit-Dutaillis has plausibly argued, moreover (pp. 426 f.), that even the cosigners of the treaty of 1223 had merely sworn to adhere to provisions stipulated by the king. See also Langmuir's remarks in *Traditio*, XVI, 216 ff., 235. On Louis IX's role in the prosecution of the Talmud and the Paris disputation of 1240, at which his mother Blanche of Castile still served as the presiding officer, see *supra*, Chap. XXXVIII; and M. Brion's biography of *Blanche de Castille, femme de Louis VIII, mère de Saint Louis, 1188–1252* (also appeared in the Spanish trans. by F. Durán).

6. Count A. A. Beugnot, ed., *Les Olim, ou registres des arrêts rendus par la cour du roi*, I, 122 f. No. xiii, 364 f., 791 No. iv, 795 No. vii, 811 No. xxxii, 821 f. No. xvi, 1015 n. 149, etc.; P. Varin, *Archives administratives et législatives de la ville de Reims*, I, 906 No. cccliii and the extensive note thereon (referring to a fascicle of 37 documents relating to Jews in medieval Reims which was then [1839] still extant in the Royal Library), II, 18 ff. On the other hand, in the medieval section of his *Les Juifs à Reims*, E. Cahen offers little more than a rehash of Varin's documents and notes. Louis IX's personal interest in Jewish affairs is also illustrated by the report in 1240 of Archbishop Galterus of Sens about an agreement signed by three royal Jews in the king's presence (*coram domino rege*) with a nobleman to whom they had ceded lands inherited from their father. See A. Teulet *et al.*, eds., *Layettes du Trésor des Chartes*, II, 430 ff. No. 2875. See also U. Robert, "Catalogue," *REJ*, III, 213 f. Nos. 15 and 22. Perhaps it is not too sanguine a hope that the vast judicial source material extant from medieval France, which goes far beyond the data assembled by Beugnot, Boutaric, and others, will, on closer investigation, shed some

new light also on neglected phases of medieval French Jewish history as well. See M. Antzine *et al.*, eds., *Guide des recherches dans les fonds judiciares de l'ancien régime*, esp. on the Paris Parlement, pp. 65 ff. (the Index has no entry on Jews).

7. F. A. Isambert *et al.*, eds., *Recueil général des anciennes lois françaises*, I, 272 f. No. 32; Laurière *et al.*, *Ordonnances des roys de France de la troisième race*, I, 75, 85; *Ordonnances du Louvre*, I, 44, 49, 85; L. Lazard, "Les Juifs de Touraine," *REJ*, XVII, 213; idem, "Les Revenus tirés des Juifs de France dans le domaine royal (XIIIᵉ siècle)," *ibid.*, XV, 235; *supra*, Chap. XXXVIII, nn. 13–14 and 29; R. Anchel, *Les Juifs de France*, pp. 111 f.; T. Manteuffel, "A Contribution to the History of Thirteenth-Century Paris" (Polish), *Prace z dziejów Polski Feudalnej* (Roman Grodecki Jubilee Volume), pp. 149–52. On Louis' way of life see J. Levron, *Saint Louis ou l'apogée du moyen âge*, p. 174; and L. K. Little, "St. Louis' Involvement with the Friars," *CH*, XXXIII, 125–48. True, as Anchel points out, some of the child converts may have been recruited from Muslim captives brought back by Louis from his North-African expedition. However, a substantial percentage undoubtedly were former Jews—a sizable number, indeed, within the relatively small Jewish population of northern France. See G. Nahon, "Contribution à l'histoire des Juifs en France sous Philippe le Bel," *REJ*, CXXI, 76 n. 2; and *infra*, Chap. L.

8. B. Guérard, ed., *Cartulaire de l'église Notre Dame de Paris* (Collection des documents inédits, II), pp. 447 ff.; M. Roblin, "Les Cimetières juifs de Paris au moyan âge," *Mémoires* of the Fédération des Sociétés historiques et archéologiques de Paris, IV, 7–19, esp. pp. 11 ff. Louis' negative attitude to Jewish usury was adumbrated by his order to the bailiffs in 1234 that "Christian bodies shall not be seized for a debt to Jews nor shall Christians be forced to sell their hereditary estates for that purpose." On this occasion the king also proclaimed a general forgiveness of one-third of all debts owed the Jews. See the text of the ordinance, enacted through Louis' son, in E. Martène and U. Durand, eds., *Thesaurus novus anecdotorum*, I, 984. See also the report by Guillaume de Chartres, "De vita et actibus Ludovici," in M. Bouquet, *Recueil des historiens des Gaules et de la France*, ed. by L. Delisle, XXIV, Part 2, pp. 34 ff. Louis IX's legislation was doubtless prompted, in part, by the numerous complaints of his subjects not only about the oppressive accumulation of their debts, but also about the frequent abuses committed by his officials in enforcing their collection. For the years 1247–48 alone, see the various regional *Quaerimonia*, reproduced in Bouquet's *Recueil*, XXIV, Part 2, pp. 215 f. Nos. 1458–65, 743 ff. Nos. 145–54, etc. But it appears to have been mere wishful thinking when some French chroniclers attributed to Saint Louis an expulsion of all French Jews in 1251 or 1252. See *ibid.*, XXIII, 214 f., 402, and the fuller discussion *infra*, Chap. L.

With all his piety, however, Louis was by no means a blind tool of churchmen. His independence, which came to the fore in the limitations he imposed on the use of ecclesiastical censures, also made him treat his Jewish subjects from the standpoint of their usefulness to the state. On the former see G. J. Campbell, "The Attitude of the Monarchy toward the Use of Ecclesiastical Censures in the Reign of Saint Louis," *Speculum*, XXXV, 535–55. See, also, more generally, M. Bloch's searching observations in his lectures on *La France sous les derniers Capétiens 1223–1328*. Nor were, for that matter, the French churchmen of the period wholly intolerant. While generally supporting the then unfolding segregationist program of the ambitious popes, they also clearly echoed the papal insistence upon the protection of Jewish lives and property against attacks of the frenzied crusading mobs. A strongly worded resolution to this effect was adopted, for instance, in 1236, by the synod of Tours. Its tenor resembled the letter on the same subject written by Gregory IX. See Mansi, *Collectio*, XXIII, 411; L. de Grandmaison, "Le Cimetière de Juifs de Tours," *REJ*, XVIII, 262 f., 270 ff.; *supra*, Chap. XXXVII, n. 8.

9. A. Teulet *et al.*, eds., *Layettes du Trésor des Chartes*, III, 72 f. Nos. 3782-83; H. Clouzot, *Cens et rentes dus au comte de Poitiers, à Niort, au XIIIe siècle*, p. 41; A. Molinier, ed., *Correspondance administrative d'Alphonse de Poitiers*, I, 402 ff. Nos. 646-50, 408 No. 652, 429 No. 681, 492 No. 760, etc. Upon his return from the Crusade, Alphonse allegedly forbade the Jews in 1252 to leave their houses on Fridays and to erect new synagogues. This decree, cited by J. Guérinière, is denied by [J. B.] Vincent in *Les Juifs en Poitou au bas moyen âge*, p. 14. Vincent also points out that, despite his Catholic piety which resembled that of his brother, Alphonse did not hesitate to invite in 1253 a Jewish ophthalmologist, Ibrahim of Lunel, to give him medical advice. According to Alphonse's informant in Lunel, the local Jews attested Ibrahim's high competence. The doctor, when told about the nature of the disease which had caused the count's partial paralysis, was prepared to "heal it in a short time at the risk of his life [*in capitis sui periculo*]." Teulet *et al.*, III, 183ab No. 4055. Alphonse's officials proved even more liberal, and in 1260 Bishop Hugh de Chateauroux complained to the count that the seneschal of Poitou favored Jews over Christians.

The documentation for Alphonse's Jewish policies is quite rich, his administrative correspondence alone containing some threescore references to them. See Molinier's edition, in the numbers incompletely listed in the Index, II, 686. See also M. Jusselin, "Documents financiers concernant les mesures prises par Alphonse de Poitiers contre les Juifs (1268-1269)," *BEC*, LXVIII, 130-49 (includes a long list of Jewish possessions, pp. 141 ff.); E. Boutaric, *Saint Louis et Alphonse de Poitiers*, which includes certain archival data relating to Jews; and G. Caro's careful summary in his *Sozial- und Wirtschaftsgeschichte der Juden*, I, 381 ff., 509.

10. G. Saige, *Les Juifs du Languedoc*, pp. 212 f. No. xliii, 2; N. Brussel, ed., *Nouvel examen de l'usage général des fiefs en France*, I, 599 ff.; Laurière *et al.*, *Ordonnances*, I, 312 f. (undated but placed about 1283); A. A. Beugnot, ed., *Les Olim*, II, 185 No. xxii, 195 No. xxiii, 212 No. xxx, 218 No. xlv, 869 f.; Mansi, *Collectio*, XXIV, 984 (briefly dismissed by C. J. Hefele in his *Histoire des conciles*, VI, 265); A. Neubauer, "Literary Gleanings, VIII," *JQR*, [o.s.] V, 713 f. The king was also bent upon safeguarding the jurisdiction of royal officials against encroachments of both the clergy and municipal elders, a policy even more firmly pursued by his successor. See Beugnot, pp. 278 No. xiii, 322 f. No. i; C. Devic and J. Vaissète, *Histoire générale de Languedoc*, X, Part 1, col. 157.

The French Parlements were busy adjudicating the authority over Jews to various claimants. In 1270, for example, two Jews were assigned to the lords of Marli because "neither they nor their fathers had descended from Jews of [royal] France." Two years later, on the other hand, a prioress was given the right to expel two Jews from her land unless they accepted baptism, because she enjoyed exclusive jurisdiction over them. In 1275 the Parlement agreed with the contention of the burghers of Chauny (in Aisne) that they need not tolerate more than the four Jewish families originally settled there by order of Louis IX. See Beugnot, I, 821 f. No. xvi, 893 f. No. xxxvi, 944 No. xlvi. See also, more generally, C. V. Langlois, *Le Règne de Philippe III le Hardi*, esp. pp. 295, 298 f., 341, 411 No. 151, 418 Nos. 179–80, 440 No. xxi; Vincent, *Les Juifs en Poitou*, pp. 22 ff.; and *infra*, Chap. XLVII.

11. H. Guéraud, ed., "Paris sous Philippe le-Bel . . . contenant le rôle de la taille . . . en 1292," in *Collection des documents inédits*, 1st ser., [VI], pp. 1 ff., 178 f., 465 ff., 549 ff.; L. Lazard, "Les Juifs de Touraine," *REJ*, XVII, 212. If the "Lombard" taxpayers of 1292 obviously included also a number of non-Lombards, this deficiency was made up by Lombards listed under the respective quarters. See Guéraud, pp. 176, 520 f.

12. See C. Baudon de Mony, "La Mort et les funérailles de Philippe le Bel," *BEC*, LVIII, 12; and J. R. Strayer's more general observations on "Philip the Fair—a 'Constitutional' King," *AHR*, LXII, 18–32.

13. C. V. Langlois, "Formulaires," *Notices et extraits des manuscrits de la Bibliothèque Nationale*, XXXIV, Part 1, pp. 18 f. No. 11; Isambert *et al.*, *Recueil*, II, 683 No. 291 (1290), 747 No. 358 (1302); Laurière *et al.*, *Ordonnances*, I, 333 (1299), 545 f. (1303); S. Luce, "Catalogue des documents du Trésor des Chartes relatifs aux Juifs sous le règne de Philippe le Bel," *REJ*, II, 15–72, esp. pp. 24 ff. Nos. v–vi; Brussel, *Nouvel examen*, I, 684; A. Darmsteter, "L'Autodafé de Troyes (24 Avril 1288)," *REJ*, II, 199–247 (supplemented by his ed. of "Deux élégies du Vatican" on that subject in *Romania*, III, 443–86, both reprinted in his *Reliques scientifiques*, I, 217–64, 265–307); U. Robert, "Catalogue," *REJ*, III, 219 No. 59, 221 Nos. 74 and 76, 223 No. 90, 224 No. 96; L. Lazard, "Les Revenus," *REJ*, XV, 236 ff.; T. Reinach, "Charles de Valois et les Juifs," *ibid.*, XLII, 103–10 (with reference to Joseph Petit's dissertation, *Charles de Valois*); J. Havet, "Comte du Trésor du Louvre (Toussaint 1296)," *BEC*, XLV, 245 f. Nos. 83 (*tallia Judeorum*), 93 ff. (*finatio Judeorum*), 247 No. 120 (*per receptorem focagii pro expulsione Judeorum de Pict[avia]* 3300 livres), see *Index*, p. 283 *s.v.* Judei; I. Loeb, "Notes et extraits divers," *REJ*, IX, 138; Vincent, *Les Juifs*, pp. 24 ff. The Jewish community of Troyes, it may be noted, sympathized with the martyrs of 1288, and as soon as the passions calmed down tried to regain their confiscated real estate, especially if located within the Jewish quarter. We have the record of such a repurchase, by two Jewish representatives, acting together with their spiritual leader Diex le beine (Berakhiah?), of five such houses *sitas in Judaria tercensi* in Nov. 1294. See P. Piétresson de Saint-Aubin, "Document inédit relatif aux Juifs de Troyes," *Moyen Âge*, XXXI, 84–87.

Philip the Fair's sharp methods of tax collection are also illustrated by his two successive orders to the seneschal of Carcassonne (in 1290 and 1292) to arrest all Jewish taxpayers who had arrears of 10 livres or more and to send them to Paris. See Robert in *REJ*, III, 220 ff. Nos. 71 and 84. The number and size of Jewish financial contributions to Philip IV's Treasury is well illustrated by the numerous entries in the royal accounts for the period of 1285–1306. The Index to the three-volume work, ed. by R. Fawtier in his *Comptes royaux 1285–1314*, lists no less than 181 entries relating to Jewish payments. Characteristically, the largest group consisted of payments in grain rather than money during the fiscal year of June 1302 to June 1303 (I, 180 ff. Nos. 14,032–14,130). Much larger sums were involved in the collection of Jewish fines (*de finatione Judeorum*), reflected in the accounts of the Trésor de

Louvre where individual bailiwicks contributed amounts up to 2,000 livres and more. See the list in R. Fawtier, ed., *Comptes du Trésor (1290, 1316, 1384, 1477)*, p. 14 No. 288 (here the Jew Kalot appears as an important collector of that revenue). See also *ibid.*, p. 14 No. 304; and C. V. Langlois *et al.*, eds., *Inventaires d'anciens comptes royaux*, pp. 146 No. 1146 (mentioning a Jewish tax of 4,462 livres in 1295), 170 No. 1362, 172 no. 1372, 245 No. 1975, 264 No. 2113. See also G. Nahon's "Contribution," *REJ*, CXXI, 59–80, which summarizes to very good advantage the data offered by Fawtier's ed. of the *Comptes royaux*.

Remarkably, these voluminous Treasury records contribute relatively little to our knowledge of the liquidation of Jewish property after the expulsion of 1306. The king's protection of the Jewish judiciary was likewise aimed more at withdrawing them from under the jurisdiction of local municipalities and barons than at securing for them a higher measure of justice. In fact, in 1291, he sent a circular letter to the seneschals of Toulouse, Carcassonne, Beaucaire, and others, ordering them to suppress the special Jewish judges and subject the Jews to their own jurisdiction, on a par with the Christians. *Ibid.*, p. 221 No. 77. But this order apparently had no bearing on the rabbinic jurisdiction in the internal litigations among Jews. See also, more generally, E. Boutaric, *La France sous Philippe le Bel*, esp. pp. 82 ff., 120 ff., 415 ff.

14. The text of the 1306 decree of banishment is not extant. We must rely, therefore, on contemporary chroniclers who are neither precise nor even in agreement as to the exact date. Some Christian writers speak vaguely of its occurrence "around the feast of Madeleine [July 22]," in August, or September, while the author of the Hebrew *Minḥat qena'ot* sets it more exactly on August 10. See G. Saige, *Les Juifs de Languedoc antérieurement au XIVᵉ siècle*, p. 92; P. Girard, "Histoire sociale: Les Juifs de Paris sous Philippe le Bel," *Science historique*, n.s., XXXVIII, No. 17, pp. 8–11; No. 18, pp. 43–46; and, particularly, I. Loeb, "Les Expulsions des Juifs de France au XIVᵉ siècle," *Jubelschrift . . . H. Graetz*, pp. 39–56; and G. Nahon's aforementioned essay in *REJ*, CXXI, 59 ff.

The confiscations connected with the stabilization of the currency seem to have preceded the large scale expropriations of both Jews and Templars. We do not possess Philip's letter to the pope, but its import has been reconstructed from Clement V's bull preserved in a seventeenth-century work. Although it is not dated, Armand Grunzweig has plausibly argued that it was written in 1305 and that hence it did not refer to the decree of expulsion promulgated a year later. See his "Les Incidences internationales des mutations monétaires de Philippe le Bel," *Moyen Age*, LIX, 141 f. For a comparison of the Jewish and the Templars' financial operations see L. Delisle's detailed "Mémoire sur les opérations financières des Templiers," *Mémoires* of the Institut National de France of the Academie des Inscriptions, XXXIII, Part 2, pp. 1–248. Examples of the use of returning Jews in 1311–12 to locate and punish the official embezzlers of Jewish property are given in Beugnot, *Les Olim*, III, 675 No. xl, 749 No. xxxii. The story of that and later expulsions, as well as their basic causes and more permanent effects, will be more fully discussed *infra*, Chap. L.

15. Laurière *et al.*, *Ordonnances*, I, 595 ff.; the anonymous chronicle in the *Extraits des chroniques de Saint-Denis* in Bouquet's *Recueil*, XXI, 139 (written in 1356 or soon thereafter). Understandably, despite the alleged restoration of the previous status and the assignment of many Jews to baronial overlordship, royal authority

now reigned supreme. In the name of the king, the Paris Parlement frequently intervened in behalf of Jews accused of various crimes by enemies or blackmailers. Characteristically, the tribunal continued its pursuits even after the new expulsion of Jews from royal France in 1322. (See the next note.) In 1323 it reconfirmed an earlier fine of 1,000 livres imposed upon the consuls of Saverdun for hanging a Jew caught in an adulterous act with a Christian woman. The Jew's guilt was not denied, but the court saw in this procedure an infringement of the exclusive royal jurisdiction. See E. Boutaric, ed., *Actes du Parlement,* II, 222 No. 5218, 238 f. No. 5376, 263 No. 5615, 459 No. 6849, 491 No. 7026.

16. Laurière *et al., Ordonnances,* I, 645 ff.; Isambert, *Recueil,* III, 156 ff.; Ph[i-lippe] G[uignard], "Mandement de Philippe le Long relatif aux Juifs de Troyes," *BEC,* X, 413–15; A. Assier, "Les Juifs et les Templiers de la Champagne et de la Brie," *Nouvelle Bibliothèque de l'amateur champenois,* VI, 49 f. No. 7. By February 1318 Philip the Tall dropped all pretenses and issued a decree regulating in some detail Jewish moneylending. See the text in Isambert's *Recueil,* III, 201 ff. No. 560. However, the other regulations of the decree of April 1317 remained in force; among them the provision that Jews must not be treated as slaves, that they should be able freely to inherit the estates of their relatives, and that, except in the case of evident murder, they must not be forced to defend themselves in a judicial duel. See Laurière *et al., loc. cit.* In 1319 Philip expressly ordered the bailiff of Meaux to withdraw Jews accused of crimes from the jurisdiction of ecclesiastical courts except when those crimes directly "related to the Christian faith." See Boutaric, *Actes du Parlement,* II, 291 No. 5848. Needless to say, Jews paid heavily for these concessions. A partial entry in the Treasury's account book of 1316 mentions the receipt of 2,700 livres by "the men of King Louis" from a compact they had made with Jews returning from their exile. See R. Fawtier, ed., *Comptes de Trésor,* p. 29 No. 504. Other receipts of that year are listed *ibid.,* p. 40 No. 672; and in F. Maillard, ed., *Comptes royaux (1314–1328),* I, 132 No. 1894.

17. Bouquet, *Recueil,* XX, 628 ff.; XXI, 56 f., 140, 673 f.; XXII, 25 f.; Brussel, *Nouvel examen,* I, 622 f.; Devic and Vaissète, *Histoire générale,* IX, 402 ff., 415 f.; X, Preuves, pp. 616 ff. No. lxx; F. Maillard, ed., *Comptes royaux (1314–1328),* I, 98 ff. Nos. 1488–1506, 285 ff. Nos. 4858–91; Laurière *et al., Ordonnances,* II, 143. See also J. M. Vidal, "L'Emeute des Pastoureaux en 1320," *Annales de Saint Louis des Français,* III, 121–74; *infra,* n. 43; and Chap. L. Notwithstanding the short period of but seven years during which Jews were allowed to live in France again, the liquidation of their property became quite arduous. At least in the case of the distinguished banker Héliot of Vesoul (about whom see *infra,* Chap. LIII), whose house was given away by the king in 1324, the rest of his property was still under liquidation fourteen years later. See L. Gauthier, "Les Juifs dans les Deux Bourgognes," *Mémoires* of the Société d'émulation du Jura, 9th ser. III, 96 f.; and *infra,* n. 26.

In his essay in *Jubelschrift . . . H. Graetz,* pp. 51 f., I. Loeb has convincingly denied the historicity of the readmission of Jews in 1328 and their renewed expulsion in 1346 (or 1348). His arguments, to be sure, are based largely upon the absence of references to Jews during that period in the *Actes normands de la Chambre des Comptes sous Philippe de Valois (1328–1350),* ed. by L. Delisle; and in the *Actes du Parlement de Paris,* ed. by Boutaric. Quite apart from the general precariousness of *argumenta a silentio,* that related to Boutaric's compilation is completely meaning-less, since the volumes published in Loeb's lifetime covered court decisions only till 1328, that is, to the year of the purported readmission. But Loeb guessed right, for the partial continuation of Boutaric's work, ed. by H. Furgeot in his *Actes du Parlements de Paris,* 2d ser., Vol. I: Jugés 1328–1342, indeed does not seem to contain any references to decisions affecting Jews. Moreover, the subsequent govern-ment account books mention only receipts from Jewish loans, which probably still were under liquidation in 1331, and, if Charles V. Langlois correctly filled in a lacuna, also from finances of "banished" Jews in five different provinces in 1334. See his *Inventaire,* pp. 373 ff. Nos. xviii, xxx. At the same time Loeb's interpretation of Laurière *et al.,* II, 143, as referring only to Jews residing abroad, remains somewhat questionable. On the other hand, the presence of Lombards in Paris under Philip VI is attested, for instance, by F. Lehoux, in her "À Paris sous Philippe VI: Les opérations d'un Lombard," *Annales, Économies, Sociétés, Civilisations,* IX, 55–62. See also *supra,* n. 6. This problem will be more fully reviewed *infra,* Chap. LIII.

18. Laurière *et al., Ordonnances,* III, 473 ff. (dated March, 1360), 487 f.; Isambert, *Recueil,* V, 61 No. 292 (1359), 114 ff. No. 315 (text of repeal also dated March, 1360), 124 No. 329 (1361); and R. Cazelles's interesting data on "Les Mouvements révolu-tionnaires du milieu du XIVᵉ siècle et le cycle de l'action politique," *RH,* CCXXVIII, 279–312. The law of 1361 which regulated the status of Jews, their moneylending and commerce, and, to some extent, even their self-government under both a royal *gardien général* and a chief rabbinate, will be discussed in many contexts. See also J. Parkes's analysis of this document and its comparison with the earlier decree enacted by the dauphin in his own province in 1356 (see *infra,* n. 29) in *The Jew in the Medieval Community,* pp. 174 ff., 193 f., 396 ff. (reprinting the royal charter of 1361); together with an earlier draft of the French charter, differing in many details from the final product published by M. Jusselin in his "Projet d'ordonnance concernant la situation des Juifs sous Jean II le Bon," *REJ,* LIV, 142–46 (reproducing the text of a MS in the Bibliothèque Nationale). Charles V even went so far as to restore to the Jewish community fifteen Hebrew manuscripts from the *Trésor des Chartes.* See S. Luce, "Les Juifs sous Charles V et le fonds hébraïque du Trésor des Chartes, en 1372," *RII,* VII, 362–70 (includes a catalogue of these books as well as of those Hebraica which had been retained by the king or given to his astronomer Thomas de Pisan [de Boulogne]. Notwithstanding this respect for Jewish judicial autonomy, the Paris Parlement felt free on February 3, 1374 to rule that the Jews "should not make use in our French realm of the said sentences or proclamations of a *niddui, samatha* and *herem* [the three states of excommunication] among themselves." Cited by C. du Cange in his *Glossarium mediae et infimae latinitatis,* III, 434. See also G. Tessier, "L'Activité de la Chancel-lerie royale française au temps de Charles V," *Moyen Age,* XLVIII, 14–52, 81–113 (includes formulas for royal orders in favor of both debtors and creditors, pp. 102 ff.). As we shall see (*infra,* Chap. L), this benevolent policy of the monarchy was not supported by public opinion. It actually evoked many a popular outbreak, and protests from several municipalities even in southern France.

19. Laurière *et al., Ordonnances,* III, 351 f., 601 f., 648; Vincent, *Les Juifs,* pp. 37 ff. The text of the appointment of the *gardien général* in 1359 is not extant. But it is cited here from a letter to D'Outreleau reprinted by Laurière *et al.,* because it

underlay the ordinance which they included in their collection. See also the chapter on the Jews under Charles V in S. Luce, *La France pendant la guerre de cent ans*, pp. 161–75, esp. pp. 164, 170 f. Luce, who otherwise waxes quite lyrical about the humane qualities of Charles V, often surnamed the Sage, nonetheless assumes that in 1367–68 that king had promulgated a decree of expulsion. True, we actually possess the text of a decree dated Feb. 6, 1367, ordering the expulsion of the Jews and the inventory of their property. See L. Delisle, ed., *Mandements et actes divers de Charles V (1364–1380)*, pp. 216 f. No. 430. Yet this order seems never to have gone beyond the range of a proposal. In fact, in 1369 Charles ordered the seneschals of Beaucaire, Carcassonne, and Toulouse to discontinue the enforced attendance of Jews at missionary sermons. See Laurière, *Ordonnances*, V, 167 f.; Isambert, *Recueil*, V, 320 ff. No. 442. Another order in Delisle's collection, dated Aug. 11, 1377, assigned to the king's cousin, Charles d'Artois, 500 francs from the royal revenue from Jews. At the same time, Charles was sufficiently pious a Christian to serve personally as a godfather at the baptism of a Castilian Jew, Mousse. He gave the convert his own name, Charles, and provided him with special letters against possible molestation because of his former faith. See Delisle, *Mandements*, pp. 726 No. 1426, 748 f. No. 1483 (Oct. 16, 1377). See also R. Delachenal's comprehensive *Histoire de Charles V* (vols. IV–V revised by Léon le Grand); and other data cited *infra*, Chap. L.

20. The controversy between Jacob de Sainte Maxence and the two communal leaders as tried at the Paris Parlement is briefly summarized by R. Anchel in "Deux documents inédits sur les Juifs de Paris au XIVme siècle," *Revue juive de Genève*, IV, 63–66. Regrettably, the author had no opportunity to present the texts of these documents. The controversy over the chief rabbinate in 1391 will be discussed more fully in a later chapter. For the time being see Israel Lévi, "La Lutte entre Isaïe fils d'Abba Mari, et Yohanan, fils de Matatia pour le rabbinat de France à la fin du XIVe siècle," *REJ*, XXXIX, 85–94; and other essays cited in my *The Jewish Community*, III, 68 f. n. 12a.

21. L. Bellaguet, ed., *Chronique du religieux de Saint Denys, contenant le règne de Charles VI, de 1380 à 1422*, I, 52 ff.; Charles VI's decrees of 1387 and 1389 in Laurière *et al.*, *Ordonnances*, VI, 171; VII, 170 f., 225 f.; and Devic and Vaissète, *Histoire générale*, X, 1783 f. No. 718 (under slightly different dates). "Les Folies du roi Charles VI" are discussed by E. Delamare in *Ecrits de Paris*, 209 (1962), 72–80. The intolerant winds blowing at Charles VI's court were also illustrated by such local decrees as that issued by the archbishop of Reims with the king's approval on June 12, 1389. Here Christian butchers were forbidden either to have animals slaughtered for Jews unless the latter bought the entire carcass, or to purchase any meat from them under the penalty of both losing their merchandise and paying a fine of five sous. See P. Varin, *Archives administratives*, pp. 711 ff. No. cmxxiv. In two successive decrees of 1392 and 1393 Charles VI specifically provided that converts should not be deprived of their possessions. In the latter year he also ordained that if Christian debtors contracted with their Jewish lenders for the use of physical compulsion in enforcing the contracts, such stipulations should not be executed by the courts. See Laurière *et al.*, VII, 557 f., 589 f., 792 f. But all these were minor pinpricks compared with the tragedy of the sudden banishment in 1394, the causes of which will be more fully analyzed *infra*, Chap. L. How seriously Charles took this

policy of exclusion may also be noted in his letter of April 23, 1397 in favor of foreign merchants visiting the generally hospitable southern fairs. He mentions specifically Provençal, Catalan, Piedmontese, and Savoy merchants, but passes over in silence Jewish traders from Avignon, as well as the Provence and Savoy, who might have wished to visit these fairs. See J. Combes, "Montpellier et les foires de Pézenas et de Montagnac au XIVe siècle et au commencement du XVe," *Congrès régional des Fédérations historiques de Languedoc, Carcassonne, 24–26 Mai, 1952,* p. 12 n. 44.

22. See esp. L. I. Rabinowitz, *The Social Life of the Jews of Northern France in the XII–XIV Centuries as Reflected in the Rabbinical Literature of the Period;* Mansi, *Collectio,* XXIV, 176 (also Hefele, *Histoire des Conciles,* VI, Part 1, p. 233); C. Douais, *L'Inquisitions. Ses origines, sa procédure,* pp. 357, 360; Anchel, *Les Juifs,* pp. 106 f.; and *supra,* Chap. XXXVIII, n. 3. On the more subtle rather than formal influence exerted by the burghers on the French legislation see F. Dumont's pertinent observations in his "Gouvernants et gouvernés en France au moyen âge et au XVIe siècle," *Schweizer Beiträge zur allgemeinen Geschichte,* XX, 188–99. The resolution of the Council of Bourges was widely disobeyed even in the district around Tours, however. See L. Lazard's data in *REJ,* XVII, 215, 217.

Because of this wide dispersal of French Jewry many monographs relating to individual regions and localities offer important supplementary information on its position in royal France. Some of these have been listed *supra,* Vol. IV, esp. pp. 267 f. n. 77; and in our previous notes in this chapter. Many other studies have appeared in the *REJ* and can readily be located with the aid of the excellent index covering the first fifty volumes, and the list of articles in Vols. LI–C. The more recent volumes, on the other hand, have added but little new information on the local history of northern French Jewry. This relative neglect is doubly noteworthy as the general French historiography of the last decades has evinced particular interest in local and regional developments. See K. F. Werner, "Hauptströmungen der neuen französischen Mittelalterforschungen," *Welt als Geschichte,* XIII, 187–97. See also the following monographs arranged in the alphabetical order of their authors: T. Cochard, *La Juiverie d'Orléans du VIe au XVe siècle;* G. Jeanton, *Les Juifs en Mâconnais* (with reference to L. Gauthier's "Les Juifs dans les Deux Bourgognes"); F. Meyer, "Essai sur l'histoire des Juifs du Hainaut au XIVe siècle," *Annales de l'Est et du Nord,* [2d ser.] III, 321–43; and various studies mentioned in the forthcoming notes. Many more are listed in B. Blumenkranz's *Bibliographie des Juifs en France,* a preliminary draft of which, prepared in 1961, was available to me. Needless to say, many general local histories also contain references to Jews. See also the brief survey by F. L. Ganshof, *Études sur le développement des villes entre Loire et Rhin au Moyen Age.*

It is not surprising that the great local variations and constant changes in legislation, with its sudden shifts from broad tolerance to extreme intolerance and back again, make a careful study of the Jewish status in France extremely difficult. Certainly the two analyses by X. Gasnos, *Étude historique sur la condition des Juifs dans l'ancien droit français;* and by H. Prado-Gaillard, *La Condition des Juifs dans l'ancienne France,* leave much to be desired. The latter, in particular, is much too superficial for a Paris juridical thesis. Of considerable interest are also the data on "La Tolérance au Moyen-Âge," included in R. Anchel, *Les Juifs de France,* pp. 93–124.

23. See R. Fawtier's suggestive "Communication: Comment, au début du XIVe siècle un roi de France pouvait-il se représenter son royaume?" *Comptes rendus* of the Académie des Inscriptions, 1960 (1959), pp. 117–22; F. Lehoux, "Le Duc de Berri, les Juifs et les Lombards," *RH,* CCXV, 38–57. H. Graetz's claim, without further proof, that 100,000 Jews were banished from France in 1306, is exaggerated, although it comes close to the population estimates submitted by G. Nahon on the basis of the revenues collected by Philip the Fair. These Jewish taxpayers resided in large numbers, however, in possessions of vassals, some of whom failed to carry out the decree of banishment to the full. See Graetz's *Geschichte,* 4th ed., VII, 246; and Nahon's data in *REJ,* CXXI, 70 ff. These problems of medieval Jewish demography will be discussed *infra,* Chap. LI.

24. The history of Lorraine Jewry, possibly reaching back to Roman times, is inextricably tied up with that of its major communities of Metz and Nancy, which have been fully investigated only with respect to the modern period. See *supra,* Vol. VI, pp. 48, 344 n. 52; R. Clément, *La Condition des Juifs de Metz sous l'ancien régime;* N. Netter, *Vingt siècles d'histoire d'une communauté juive (Metz et son grand passé);* N. S. Doniach, "Le Poème de Benjamin le Scribe sur R. Samson le Martyr," *REJ,* XCIII, 84–92; J. Weill, "Un Juif brûlé à Metz vers 1385 pour profanation d'hostie," *ibid.,* LIII, 270–72. Weill rightly doubts the veracity of the latter story, which he had found only in a Paris transcript of a Turin MS. Evidently Jewish moneylenders were quickly replaced here by Lombards who, as early as 1227–29, lent a substantial amount to the bishop of Metz. The dukes themselves, who had begun merely as guarantors of loans, ultimately turned debtors. See J. Schneider, "Les Activités des marchands et financiers italiens dans la région Lorraine aux XIIIe et XIVe siècles," *Comptes rendus* of the Académie des Inscriptions et Belles Lettres, 1951, pp. 327–30; and, more generally, idem, *La Ville de Metz au XIIIe et XIVe siècle.* True, Bishop Conrad Bayer de Boppard's privilege of 1422 specifically provided for the right of Jews to lend money on pledges or writs of indebtedness. See the text paraphrased by Clément, pp. 14 ff. But Clément minimizes the importance of that charter because the city had long before emancipated itself from the bishop's tutelage. In the following year, indeed, Emperor Sigismund allegedly recognized the local situation by decreeing that only Catholics should exercise the banking profession. This statement reported by Clément from an unpublished *Histoire ecclésiastique et civile de la ville et du diocèse de Metz,* by Benoist Picard, is very questionable, however. No such ordinance is recorded in W. Altmann's ed. of *Die Urkunden Kaiser Siegmunds,* which includes some two score references to Metz, both the city and the bishopric.

This example illustrates the numerous obscurities in the history of a community which was destined to play a major role in the evolution of French Jewry in the subsequent centuries. Not surprisingly, we know even less about the medieval developments in the other Jewish communities of the region including Nancy and Lunéville. On the latter see the series of articles by P. Lang, "Les Juifs de Lunéville et la petite histoire," *Revue juive de Lorraine,* XI–XIV. A comprehensive study of the Jews of medieval Lorraine would, therefore, fill an important lacuna.

25. B. Blumenkranz, "Cultuvateurs et vignerons juifs en Bourgogne du IXe au XIe siècle," *Bulletin philologique et historique* of the Comité des Travaux historiques et scientifiques, 1959 [1960], pp. 120–36; J. Simonnet, "Juifs et Lombards [en

Bourgogne]," *Mémoires* of the Académie des sciences de Dijon, 2d ser. XIII, 145–272; L. Gauthier, *Les Lombards dans les Deux Bourgognes*, esp. pp. 50 f., 55 ff., 180 No. 2; G. Jeanton, *Les Juifs en Mâconnais*, pp. 21 f.; and above all L. Gauthier's fully documented study of "Les Juifs dans les Deux Bourgognes: Étude sur le commerce d'argent aux XIIIᵉ et XIVᵉ siècles," *Mémoires* of the Société d'émulation du Jura, 9th ser. III, 57–232, esp. pp. 180 No. 2, 182 ff. No. 5. Gauthier reprints here, with some revisions and additional lists and documents, an article which had appeared a decade earlier in *REJ*, XLVIII, 208–29; XLIX, 1–17, 244–61. Of some interest is a reference of 1221 to a Jewish quarter (*vicus Judaeorum*) in Chalon-sur-Saône which, apparently because of conflicting jurisdictions, was divided between the bishop and the duchess of Burgundy. See A. Teulet, ed., *Layettes*, I, 522 f. No. 1463. See also R. Anchel, *Les Juifs*, pp. 120 ff.; M. H. Clément-Janin, *Notice sur la communauté israélite de Dijon*, esp. p. 50; J. Marilier, "Les Établissements juifs à Dijon au début du XIVᵉ siècle," *Mémoires* of the Commission des antiquités de la Côte-d'Or (Dijon), XXIV, 171–78; J. Richard, *Les Ducs de Bourgogne et la formation du duché du XIᵉ au XIVᵉ siècle*, esp. pp. 379 ff.; his more popular *Histoire de la Bourgogne*, supplemented by his observations on "Les États de Bourgogne," *Schweizer Beiträge zur allgemeinen Geschichte*, XX, 230–48. Richard also furnishes interesting material on the tug of war between the cities and the duke. While in 1187 Hugh III had still reserved for himself the authority over Jews, nine years later Odo III formally transferred the control over Dijon Jewry to the city. Yet, even after his confirmation of that act Hugh IV continued to insist upon his final authority over "nostre Juifs." See *Les Ducs*, pp. 340 ff., 360 ff.

26. J. Morey, "Les Juifs en Franche-Comté au XIVᵉ siècle," *REJ*, VII, 1–39; Gauthier in *Mémoires* of the Société d'émulation du Jura, 9th ser. III, 182 ff. No. 5. Héliot of Vesoul, his ramified business transactions and interesting records will be discussed *infra*, Chap. LIII. These bankers often associated, as well as competed, with the Christian Lombards to such an extent that in the eyes of the populace, and occasionally even in those of legislators, they appeared as a single category. See the text of Duke Hugh's decree republished by Gauthier in the *Mémories* of Jura, III, 219 No. 28. See also *ibid.*, pp. 224 f. No. 31, where interesting data are offered showing the presence of Jews and their continued moneylending in both sections of Burgundy during the years of 1333 to 1336; and, more generally, L. Febvre's *Histoire de Franche-Comté*, new ed.

27. J. Auscher, "Notice sur les Israélites de Bésançon et de la Comté," *Archives israélites*, XXXI, 440–42, 472–75, 592–94 (was to be continued), esp. pp. 472 ff. and 592 ff.; I. Loeb, "Expulsion des Juifs de Salins et Bracon en 1374," *REJ*, XV, 298–301. Auscher mentions here Philip the Tall's gift of Héliot's house in Vesoul to his wife Jeanne of Burgundy as a sign of his forgiveness of her adultery. Auscher's contention, however, that Bésançon had admitted Jews in 1394 only out of fear of some pro-Jewish lords in that region is not substantiated by any documents. Among the creditors of the powerful Duke Philip the Good of Burgundy (1419–67), who succeeded in extending his reign over the Lowlands, Luxembourg, and parts of Switzerland, we find one Richard Juif as lender of 1,350 gold philippi in 1440. But he may well have been one of the numerous Christians bearing that designation whom we have encountered in various parts of Europe. See also *infra*, n. 32. On these and other loans see G. Bigwood, *Le Régime juridique et économique du*

commerce de l'argent dans la Belgique du moyen âge, I, 41; R. Vaughan's biography of *Philip the Bold: the Formation of the Burgundian State;* and, on the imperial connections, see R. Hoke, "Die Freigrafschaft Burgund, Savoyen und die Reichsstadt Besançon im Verbande des mittelalterlichen deutschen Reiches," *ZRG,* Germanistische Abt., LXXIX, 106–194.

28. The fullest information on the Dauphiny was made available by A. Prudhomme in "Les Juifs en Dauphiné au XIVᵉ et XVᵉ siècles," *Bulletin* of the Académie Delphinale, 3d ser. XVII, 129–237 (with a "Réponse" by Pres. Charaux, *ibid.,* pp. 238–47), esp. pp. 137, 141 f., 150; and in his "Notes et documents sur les Juifs du Dauphiné," *REJ,* IX, 231–63. See also Grayzel, *The Church,* pp. 262 ff. Nos. 113–14, 292 f. No. 131 with the literature listed there; and *supra,* Chap. XXXVII, n. 7. Occasional intercommunal cooperation is illustrated by the assembly of representatives of ten Dauphiny communities, held in Moras in 1337. See Prudhomme in *Bulletin,* pp. 144 f.

29. A. Prudhomme in *Bulletin* of the Académie Delphinale, 3d ser. XVII, 164 ff., also summarizing the charter of 1355; idem in *REJ,* IX, 238 f. See also the succinct observation by B. Blumenkranz in "Le 'Siècle d'or' en Dauphiné et en Provence," *Evidences,* XII, No. 88, pp. 29–33.

30. C. de Beauregard, "Notes et documents sur la condition des Juifs de Savoie," *Mémoires* of the Académie royale de Savoie, 2d ser. II (1854); M. Gerson, "Notes sur les Juifs des états de la Savoie et particulièrement de la Bresse, de Bugey et Gex pendant les XIIIᵉ, XIVᵉ et XVᵉ siècles," *REJ,* VIII, 235–42; I. Loeb, "Un Episode de l'histoire des Juifs de Savoie," *ibid.,* X, 32–59; idem, "Notes et extraits divers," *ibid.,* X, 289 (summarizing an interesting report by C. Poma in the Turin *Gazetta letteraria* of Dec. 6, 1884); M. Stern, *Urkundliche Beiträge,* I, 7 ff. No. 2; M. Esposito, "Un Procès contre les Juifs de la Savoie en 1329," *RHE,* XXXIV, 785–801. These papal bulls were discussed *supra,* Chap. XXXVII, nn. 7 and 44. The episode relating to Sansinus is documented by M. Bruchet in *Le Château de Ripaille,* pp. 174 f., 382 f. No. xxxiii.

31. See ex-queen Marie José's much too admiring biography of the "duke who became pope" in *La Maison de Savoie,* Vol. II. *Amédée VIII;* and *infra,* Chap. XLVII; also the sources cited in the last note. Despite the continued independence of the respective sections of the country, much of what will be said about the Piedmontese development in Chap. XLVI will also have a bearing on the situation of Savoy Jewry. Even before their unification with Piedmont under the house of Savoy, however, these southeastern French areas often felt the impact of Spanish as well as Italian developments. According to Joseph ha-Kohen, Vicente Ferrer's sermons led to anti-Jewish riots in Savoy in 1394. Solomon ibn Verga reports a general persecution of Jews in Savoy and Piedmont in 1490. See Joseph ha-Kohen, *'Emeq ha-bakha* (Valley of Tears; a chronicle), ed. by M. Letteris, pp. 71 f.; in the German trans. by M. Wiener, p. 57; Ibn Verga, *Shebeṭ Yehudah,* xi, ed. by M. Wiener, p. 33; in Wiener's German trans. pp. 65 f.; ed. by Shohet, pp. 56, 181 f. However, Ibn Verga himself admits that he had found no documentation for his story, which is, indeed, unconfirmed by any contemporary Christian chroniclers, who on the other hand furnish ample evidence for the massacres of 1348. See *infra,* Chap. L. It may be of interest

to note here that the evolution of the Jewish community in the principality of Orange revealed certain similarities to both the neighboring Dauphiny and Savoy. See H. Chabaut, "Notes sur les Juifs de la principauté d'Orange et sur leur charte de libertés du 14 février 1353," *REJ*, Cbis, 62–70, summarizing that decree and citing earlier publications.

32. G. Saige, "De la condition des Juifs dans le comté de Toulouse avant le XIV⁴ siècle," *BEC*, XXXIX, 255–322, 432–80; XL, 424–56; idem, *Les Juifs du Languedoc antérieurement au XIVᵉ siècle* (with excellent archival documentation); Devic and Vaissète, *Histoire générale*, III, 330; S. Kahn, "Les Juifs de la Sénéchaussée de Beaucaire," *REJ*, LXV, 181–95; LXVI, 75–97; A. de Boüard, *Actes et lettres de Charles Iᵉʳ Roi de Sicile concernant la France (1257–1284)*, esp. pp. 293 No. 946, 305 No. 985; Willy Cohn, "Die Judenpolitik König Karls I. von Sizilien in Anjou und in der Provence," *MGWJ*, LXXIV, 429–37, esp. pp. 434 f. See also J. H. Mundy, *Liberty and Political Power in Toulouse 1050–1230*, esp. pp. 8 f. with the notes thereto; and the earlier literature listed in R. Limouzin-Lamothe's *Bibliographie critique de l'histoire municipale de Toulouse des origines à 1789*. However, Jean le Juif or Johannes Judeus mentioned in documents as a tax collector in Carcassonne in 1360 and in Toulouse in 1375–77 need not have been Jewish despite that onomatological emphasis in both French and Latin. See Devic and Vaissète, X, 1222 ff., 1246 ff., 1523, 1541 f. On the Albigensian Crusade, Alphonse de Poitiers' persecution, the southern French Inquisition, and Charles I's rather moderate insistence upon the Jewish badge—despite his indebtedness to the Papacy for his Sicilian conquests—see *supra*, n. 9; Chap. XXXVII, nn. 9, 43 and 49; and Vol. IV, pp. 132, 236 n. 54. Because of their proximity the Jews of Avignon and the Comtat Venaissin maintained intimate relations with their southern French coreligionists. One can, therefore, learn much about the latter from the aforementioned monographic studies on these papal areas by Bardinet, De Maulde, and Mossé.

33. R. André-Michel, "Une Accusation de meurtre rituel contre les Juifs d'Uzès en 1297," *BEC*, LXXV, 59–66; *Anciennes coutumes d'Alais* reproduced in the App. to A. A. Beugnot, *Olim*, pp. 1458 ff.; *Libertates et consuetudines Carcassonensis civitatis*, Art. xx, and *Addilamenta* to the Montpellier *Consuetudines* of 1205, both cited in A. Teulet *et al.*, *Layettes*, I, 272 ff. No. 745, 290b No. 760 Art. 16. Even in Toulouse there was a conflict between the city consuls and the royal officials regarding their respective jurisdictional rights over Jews. The consuls claimed that exemption from municipal jurisdiction would make the Jews "more privileged than the Christians, which is against human and divine law and against the welfare of the land." After a discussion thereon at the Paris Parlement in 1279, Philip III ordered the *viguier* (provost) to protect the rights of the royal courts. See Devic and Vaissète, *Histoire générale*, X, Part 1, p. 157 col. 2; Part 2 (Preuves), pp. 159 ff. No. 27. On the general defense of royal prerogatives, see Y. Dossat, "La Lutte contre les usurpations domaniales dans la sénéchaussée de Toulouse sous les derniers Capétiens," *Annales de Midi*, LXXIII, 129–64.

34. G. Saige, *Les Juifs de Languedoc*, pp. 30 ff., 200 ff. No. xli, 213 ff., and *passim*; G. Caumes's dissertation, *Les Jurisdictions royales et seigneuriales de la ville de Béziers de 1229 à 1789*; B. Gaillard, "Une Charte inédite du XIIIᵉ siècle en faveur

des Juifs de Narbonne," *Mémoires* of the Société d'archéologie de Montpellier, 2d ser. VIII, 102–11 (a document of 1269); E. Boutaric, ed., *Actes du Parlement*, II, 351 No. 6330; D. Kaufmann, "Le Pourim de Narbonne," *REJ*, XXXII, 129–30; J. Régné, *Étude sur la condition des Juifs à Narbonne du Ve au XIVe siècle* (enlarged reprint of *REJ*, LV–LXIII). See also "Dr." Cuyla, "Nouveaux aspects de Narbonne au cours du premier tiers du XIVe siècle," *Bulletin* of the Commission archéologique de Narbonne, XXV, 26–46; and, more generally, P. Carbonnel, *Histoire de Narbonne*. In view of the intimate connections between Narbonne and Aragon the numerous studies and documentary publications by Régné and others relating to the latter kingdom have a considerable bearing on the history of the Jews in the French city as well. See also *infra*, Chaps. XLIV and LV.

35. L. Ménard, *Histoire civile, ecclésiastique et littéraire de la ville de Nismes*, I, 412 ff. (text), 125 f. No. xciii (*preuves*). On Ibrahim, the Lunel ophthalmologist called to the ailing Alphonse de Poitiers, see *supra*, n. 9.

36. E. Azémard, *Étude sur les Israélites de Montpellier au Moyen Âge;* supplemented by S. Kahn's "Documents inédits sur les Juifs de Montpellier au moyen âge," *REJ*, XIX, 259–81; XXII, 264–79; XXIII, 265–78, esp. XIX, 261 n. 2, 267 ff. App. i, 274 ff. Apps. vi–vii. See also F. de Bofarull y Sans, "Jaime el Conquistador y la communidad judía de Montpeller," *Boletín* of the R. Academia de Buenas Letras de Barcelona, V, 484–92; and A. E. Sayous and J. Combes, "Les Commerçants et les capitalistes de Montpellier aux XIIIe et XIVe siècles," *RH*, CLXXXVIII–IX, 341–77, showing the relatively broad occupational range among the local Jews. The decline of Montpellier's population and university after 1348 is discussed by J. C. Russell in "L'Évolution démographique de Montpellier au Moyen Âge," *Annales de Midi*, LXXIV, 345–60. See also *infra*, n. 37. Other southern communities have been treated in the following additional monographs: J. Simon, *Histoire des Juifs de Nîmes au Moyen Âge;* S. Kahn, *Notice sur les Israélites de Nîmes (672–1808)*; idem, "Les Juifs de Posquières et de Saint Gilles au moyen âge," *Mémoires* of the Académie de Nîmes, 7th ser. XXXV, Part 3, pp. 1–21. See also *supra*, Vol. IV, pp. 267 f. n. 77; and the next notes.

37. Devic and Vaissète, *Histoire générale*, IX, 293 f. (with an informative note by A. Molinier); X, 616 ff. No. lxxx; Laurière *et al., Ordonnances*, III, 351 f.; Luce in *RH*, VII, 367. The local officials cooperated but halfheartedly or else sought their private gain from that expropriation of Jews. As late as 1342, royal agents sold several houses from the estate of one dishonest clerk. On the *gardien général* and southern French taxation, see *infra*, Chaps. XLVII and LIV.

38. R. Limouzin-Lamothe, *La Commune de Toulouse et les sources de son histoire (1120–1249)*, pp. 231, 296 f. No. xix; A. Blanc, "Le Livre de comptes de Jacme Olivier," *Bulletin* of the Commission archéologique de Narbonne, III–VII, 562, cited by R. W. Emery, *Heresy and Inquisition in Narbonne*, pp. 22 f.; John II's *lettres patentes* of 1360 in S. Kahn's "Les Juifs de la Sénéchaussée de Beaucaire," *REJ*, LXVI, 90 f. App. iii; P. Wolff, "Midi aquitain et midi méditerranéen: Toulouse et les foires de Pézenas à la fin du XIVe et au début du XVe siècle," *Congrès régional* of the Fédérations historiques de Languedoc, Carcassonne, 24–26 Mai 1952, pp. 79–83; idem, "Trois études de démographie médiévale en France méridionale,"

Studi in onore di Armando Sapori, I, 493–503; and particularly his comprehensive study of *Commerces et marchands de Toulouse vers 1350—vers 1450,* esp. pp. 19 f., 70, 97 ff. The estimate of but fifteen Jewish families in Toulouse here given is probably an understatement. Wolff himself admits that Jews had resisted the tax on which this estimate is based. These economic and demographic aspects will be more fully analyzed in later chapters.

It may also be noted that Beaucaire and its district figure prominently in the numerous decisions by the Paris Parlement recorded in *Les Olim,* ed. by Beugnot, in the passages listed in the *Index rerum* to each of the 3 vols., *s.v.* Judei; and in E. Boutaric's ed. of *Actes du Parlement de Paris,* 1st ser., esp. Vol. II, pp. 291 No. 5848 (1319), 353 No. 6355 (1321). These proceedings are partially summarized by Caro in his *Sozial- und Wirtschaftsgeschichte,* I, 387 ff.; and by Anchel in *Les Juifs,* pp. 104 f. See also the various passages in Devic and Vaissète's *Histoire générale,* discussed by A. Molinier in his note thereon, IX, 270 n. 1.

39. A. Crémieux, "Les Juifs de Marseille au moyen âge," *REJ,* XLVI, 1–47, 246–68; XLVII, 62–86, 243–61, esp. XLVI, 3 ff. (citing among other documents the city statute of 1257 reading: *Civis Massilie, Christianus vel Judaeus*); the archival documents listed in E. Isnard's *Ville de Marseille, Inventaire sommaire chronologique de chartes, lettres-patentes, lettres missives et titres divers antérieurs à 1500;* the *Histoire du Commerce de Marseille,* ed. by G. Rambert *et al.* (esp. Vols. I–II covering the period to 1480; see, in particular, Vols. I, pp. 292 f.; II, pp. 89 ff., 684 ff., 788 ff.; III, pp. 24 ff.); E. Camau, *Les Juifs en Provence* (reprinted from his *La Provence à travers les siècles,* IV, 249–367), p. 312, citing, with respect to Jewish physicians, L. Barthélemy's observations in *Les Médecins à Marseille avant et pendant le moyen âge,* p. 353; M. Zarb, *Histoire d'une autonomie communale. Les privilèges de la ville de Marseille du X*e *siècle à la Révolution,* p. 329. On the restriction of Jewish sea travel, see R. Pernoud, ed., *Les Statuts municipaux de Marseille,* IV, 22.

Originally the Jewish communities in Marseilles and Arles were mainly under the bishops' jurisdiction, an authority confirmed by an 1164 ordinance addressed to Bishop Peter II by Emperor Frederick I Barbarossa (Judeis omnes de Massilia, tam de episcopali villa quam de vicecomitali). See J. H. Albanès, ed., *Gallia Christiana novissima: Histoire des archevêchés, évêchés et abbayes de France,* completed and revised by U. Chevalier, *Marseille,* cols. 81 ff. No. 164; Zarb, p. 90. The authenticity of some of these imperial ordinances, to be sure, has been impugned by H. Hirsch in his *Urkundenfälschungen aus dem Regnum Arelatense.* But his overcritical remarks have since been greatly modified, if not repudiated, by a member of his own Austrian Historical Institute, U. Brummer in her "Zur Frage der Echtheit der ersten Stauferdiplome für südburgundische Empfänger," *MIOG,* LVII, 279–338; and by J. de Font-Réaulx in essays including his "Diplomes de Conrad III et Frédéric Barberousse pour le Royaume d'Arles," *BEC,* CVIII, 124–26. The important function performed by commercial agents during the Middle Ages is emphasized by J. van Houtte in "Les Courtiers au moyen âge," *Revue historique de droit français et étranger,* 4th ser. XV, 105–141. On the occupational activities of Marseilles Jewry and the interlocking of the city's commercial interests with its general hospitality toward her Jews, see *infra,* Chaps. LI–LIII.

40. See Boüard, *Actes et lettres;* and Willy Cohn's essay mentioned *supra,* n. 32; C. Arnaud, *Essai sur la condition des Juifs en Provence, au moyen âge,* esp. pp. 28 f.,

38 ff. (this essay has often been sharply criticized by later scholars); Camau, *Les Juifs*, p. 337 and *passim* (like Arnaud and others, extensively citing from the Archives des Bouches-du-Rhône); H. Gross, "Zur Geschichte der Juden in Arles," *MGWJ*, XXVII–XXIX; and his "Nachträge," *ibid.*, XXXI, 465–71, 496–523; P. Hildenfinger, "Documents relatifs aux Juifs d'Arles," *REJ*, XLI, 62–97; XLVII. 221–42; XLVIII, 48–81, 265–72. See also E. Engelmann, *Zur städtischen Volksbewegung in Süd-frankreich. Kommunefreiheit und Gesellschaft Arles (1200–1250)*, pp. 84 ff., with the comments thereon by L. Stouff in "La Commune d'Arles au XIIIᵉ siècle à propos d'un livre récent," *Provence historique*, XI, 293–316; *supra*, Vols. II, pp. 179, 398 n. 10; IV, pp. 55 f., 59, 60 f., 265 ff. nn. 73, 76 and 78; and the literature listed in the last note. In contrast to royal France, the conditions in Arles, as in the rest of the Provence, were more favorable to Jews in the fourteenth and early fifteenth centuries than in the thirteenth.

41. See R. Busquet's searching examination of "Les Privilèges généraux et la conservation des privilèges des Juifs de Provence," *Mémoires* of the Institut historique de Provence, IV, 68–86; idem, *Études sur l'ancienne Provence. Institutions et points d'histoire*, esp. p. 114 (on the role of the conservators). The important functions of the royal officials in the internal affairs of the Jewish communities will be discussed in later chapters.

42. G. Arnaud d'Agnel, "La Politique de René envers les Juifs de Provence," *Bulletin historique et philologique* of the Comité des travaux historiques, 1908, pp. 247–76; R. Busquet in *Mémoires* of the Institut historique, IV, 81. The situation of Provençal Jewry has long been extensively studied. See the literature listed in n. 40. Much can also be learned from the detailed accounts presented by G. Arnaud d'Agnel in *Les Comptes du roi René*. The Index contains no less than 60 entries under "Juifs" and 14 under "Juives" in addition to two entries relating to the "Juiverie." A single group of entries of 1472 records Jewish payments to the Treasurer of 2,662; 3,000; and 18,000 florins. *Ibid.*, II, 45 f. Nos. 3004–3007. See also E. Baratier, *La Démographie provençale du XIIIᵉ au XVᵉ siècle, avec chiffres de comparaison pour l'XVIIIᵉ siècle*. A great deal of information is also included in the host of monographs pertaining to local history or to that of various phases of economics, politics, or religion in the area, including the numerous pertinent dissertations written at southern French universities. See, for one example, R. Aubenas, "L'Histoire de Provence à travers les dernières thèses soutenues devant la Faculté du Droit et des Sciences économiques d'Aix," *Provence historique*, XII, 276–93.

Local monographs relating to Jews include: H. de Gérin-Ricard, "Traitement d'égalité . . . accordé aux Juifs par les seigneurs de Tretz (B.-d.-R.) aux XIVᵉ et XVᵉ siècles," *Répertoire des travaux* of the Société de statistique de Marseille; S. Kahn, "Les Juifs de Tarascon au moyen âge," *REJ*, XXXIX, 95–112, 261–98; and V. Emanuel, *Les Juifs à Nice, 1400–1800*. See also those listed in R. Anchel's *Les Juifs de France*, pp. 279 ff.; and B. Blumenkranz's *Bibliographie*. On the Comtat Roussillon and especially Perpignan, see P. Vidal, "Les Juifs des anciens comtés de Roussillon et de Cerdagne," *REJ*, XV, 19–55; XVI, 1–23, 170–203; and I. Loeb, "Histoire d'une taille levée sur les Juifs de Perpignan en 1413–1414," *ibid.*, XIV, 55–79 (based on a Hebrew MS in Perpignan's Municipal Library). Some interesting misreadings of documents by Vidal have been corrected by R. W. Emery in *The Jews of Perpignan in the Thirteenth Century.* In this carefully documented study Emery stresses mainly the economic developments, but incidentally sheds light also on the Jews' political and legal status.

43. Devic and Vaissète, *Histoire générale,* V, 1369 No. ccxxi; and A. Crémieux, "Les Juifs de Toulon au moyen âge et le massacre du 13 avril 1348," *REJ,* LXXXIX, 33–72; XC, 43–64; J. P. Moret de Valbonnais, *Histoire du Dauphiné,* II, 625. See also G. Arnaud d'Agnel, *Politique des rois de France en Provence. Louis XI et Charles VIII,* I, 165 and *passim;* R. Busquet, *Études sur l'ancienne Provence,* pp. 179 ff.; G. Rambert *et al., Histoire du Commerce de Marseille,* II, 684 ff. Of some interest also is the epigraphic material turning up from time to time in the locales of former southern French Jewish communities. See for example, R. Boyer and A. Dupont-Sommer, "Une Épitaphe hébraïque trouvée à la Martelle (Var)," *Semitica,* III, 61–66, which the authors deciphered as that of Jonah Duran, "the head of his people," who passed away in 1625 (?). If the date is correct, a ritual burial of a Jew in that late period in the district of Var would be quite surprising. A similar conclusion was reached by R. Boyer, this time working in cooperation with Jacob Leveen and Cyril Moss, in their article, "Epitaph of Jonah Duran Found Near Toulon," *JJS,* I, 194–96 (which seemingly appeared slightly earlier than the essay in *Semitica,* though it is not mentioned there). This article gave rise to a debate with C. Roth, *ibid.,* II, 57, 158 and 176. The only question was whether the date of 1625 should be emended to 1630. Various reasons, often quite farfetched, were advanced as to how this tombstone found its way into the Provence more than a century after the expulsion of the Jews from that area. All these speculations may appear superfluous if, as is far more likely, the epitaph refers only to the last letter *heh,* or to the last two letters *nun* and *heh* of the crucial word *ha-Shekhinah* in line 12. (Only one or both of these letters appear stressed according to the facsimile published in both articles. Such stress on individual letters within longer words or sentences for purposes of dating was quite customary also on title pages.) In that case Jonah died in 1245, or 1295, in the midst of a flourishing Provençal Jewish community. This scion of a distinguished family, which, according to one of its later descendants, emigrated from the Provence in 1306—one Moses Duran having been recorded there in 1280—may indeed have been the "judge of his community" as he is styled in the inscription.

44. The policies of Louis XI (1461–83) and of Charles VIII (1483–98) after the reunification of the Provence in 1481, are fully documented in C. Arnaud d'Agnel's *Politique des rois de France en Provence.* Their effects on the Jews are well summarized by Camau in *Les Juifs,* pp. 340 ff., showing that, even after the decree of expulsion of 1493, the Jews did not leave their ancient habitat in Arles until 1500, when the decree was confirmed by Louis XII (1498–1515). This despite the fact that the Jewish quarter had already been destroyed in 1498. Less certain is the date of the Jews' departure from Marseilles. See R. Busquet, "La Fin de la communauté juive de Marseille au XV⁰ siècle," *REJ,* LXXXIII, 163–83, arguing for November 1500 as marking the end of the Jewish settlement there, which had begun under the Romans. The sporadic appearance of Jews in the following century is mentioned by Vincent in *Les Juifs en Poitou,* p. 39 n. 148; and, more generally, by S. Ben Sidoun in "Les Juifs en France au XVI⁰ siècle," *Trait d'Union,* III, 36–41; and F. Secret, in

"Glanes pour servir à l'histoire des Juifs en France, à la Renaissance," *REJ*, CXV, 87–107. The fascinating story of the Spanish-Portuguese Marranos in early modern France will be treated in later chapters.

45. *Rotuli litterarum patentium*, ed. by T. D. Hardy, I, 62, 480; Vincent, *Les Juifs en Poitou*, pp. 5 f. The incipient signs of English Jewry's intellectual independence during the thirteenth century will be treated in connection with the intellectual history of that period in a later volume. Not surprisingly, most English exiles after 1290 turned toward France, and, despite barriers against their immigration erected by Philip the Fair, a few were able to settle even in Paris. See *supra*, n. 13; *infra*, n. 73.

46. J. Jacobs, *The Jews of Angevin England*, pp. 134 ff., 212 ff. A slightly different translation of John's charter, together with the Latin text, is offered by J. M. Rigg in his *Select Pleas, Starrs, and Other Records from the Rolls of the Exchequer of the Jews A.D. 1220–1284*, pp. 1 ff. The text of Pseudo-Edward the Confessor's *Leges ecclesiasticae*, xxi, is cited here from *PL*, CLI, 1193; and F. Liebermann's ed. of *Die Gesetze der Angelsachsen*, I, 627 ff. See also *supra*, n. 2. Although generally recognized as a later forgery, "Edward's" laws enjoyed sufficient authority for the historian Roger Howden (Hovedene) to associate them with the name of the distinguished jurist, Ranulf de Glanville (d. 1190). See Howden's *Chronica*, ed. by W. Stubbs, II, 215 ff., 231. See also F. Liebermann, *Über die Leges Edwardi Confessoris*, pp. 66 f.; and *supra*, Vol. IV, pp. 79, 278 n. 103. In his important recent work on *The English Jewry under Angevin Kings*, pp. 12 f., H. G. Richardson has tentatively suggested that the presence, early in Henry II's reign, of Jews at Bungay and Thetford, towns belonging to Hugh Bigord, earl of Norfolk, suggest that, because of the generally disturbed conditions in the country, Stephen had encouraged Jewish settlement under the protection of local magnates. However, he could point to no source referring to such a royal concession, and it appears likely that these tiny settlements resulted from some private arrangements between the Jews and the lords. The temporary nature of these compacts may account for the apparently unpunished murder of a Jew in Thetford some time before 1192 and the speedy disappearance of both settlements after the riots of 1190. Even Henry III's mortgage of English Jewry with his brother Richard, or his son Edward (see *infra*, n. 65) merely involved the Crown's temporary renunciation of its revenue from Jews, with neither the latter nor the princely lenders being at all certain that a royal whim would not suddenly impose some new payments upon the Jewish taxpayers.

47. T. D. Hardy, ed., *Rotuli litterarum clausarum* (Close Rolls), I, 1b, 33b, 34a, 73a, 89a, 107a, 220a, 261b, 272b; idem, *Rotuli Normanniae*, I, 47, 52, 60, 61, 68, 72, 116, 118, etc.; idem, *Rotuli de Liberate et de misis et praestatis regnante Johanne* (Liberate Rolls), pp. 24, 34, 44, 48, 73, etc.; *Patent Rolls of the Reign of Henry III*, A.D. *1216–1225*, pp. 179 f.; S. Painter, *The Reign of King John*, pp. 140 ff.; Rigg, *Select Pleas*, pp. xx f.; and, for a reconstruction of the rather confusing sequence of the various justices mentioned in the records after John's death, see C. A. F. Meekings, "Justices of the Jews, 1218–68: a Provisional List," *BIHR*, XXVIII, 173–88. Litigations among Jewish parties were, with few exceptions, settled in Jewish courts, and the revenue accruing to the judges helped to relieve the budgetary needs of the Jewish communities.

48. Johannes of Oxenedes, *Chronica*, ed. by H. Ellis, p. 126. Some contemporary chroniclers speak of the imprisonment of all Jews in 1210. The continuation of the *Chronicon* by Florence of Worcester (ed. by B. Thorpe, II, 169) states succinctly that "throughout the whole of England, the Jews, both men and women, were incarcerated." More moderately, the author of the *Annals of Dunstaple* (in H. R. Luard's ed. of *Annales monastici*, III, 32) speaks only of the despoliation of all English Jewry and adds: "all the rich men were imprisoned and many of them died." See also *ibid.*, I, 29 (Margam); II, 81 (Winchester), 264 (Waverley), 451 (Bermondsey); IV, 54 (Oseney), often almost literally repetitious; and on the protracted efforts to collect that tallage, C. Roth, *The Jews of Medieval Oxford*, pp. 16 f. In "The Economic and Financial Position of the Jews in Mediaeval England," *TJHSE*, VIII, 179 ff., Sir Lionel Abrahams impugned the veracity not only of the story relating to the dental extractions of the unnamed Bristol Jew, whom Myer Davis had identified with one Abraham, son of Vives, but also of the amount of the levy of 1210. The latter is substantially confirmed, however, by the plea of one Ursell of Winchester in 1218 "that, being sent to Southhampton with mandate to make distraint upon the debtors of the Jews at the time when all the Jews of England were arrested by command of the King to render him 60,000 marks. . . ." See J. M. Rigg, *Calendar of the Plea Rolls of the Exchequer of the Jews Preserved in the Public Record Office*, I, 4. On the other hand, the story of the Bristol Jew is told only by the unreliable chronicler, Roger of Wendower in his *Flores historiarum* (The Flowers of History: world chronicle), ed. by H. G. Hewlett, II, 54 f.; and repeated from him by Matthew Paris in his *Chronica Majora* (English History), ed. by H. R. Luard, II, 528. See also M. Adler, *Jews of Medieval England*, pp. 64 n. 7., 201 ff.; and C. Roth, *A History of the Jews in England*, p. 35.

49. T. D. Hardy, ed., *Rotuli litterarum clausarum*, I, 186b; S. Krauss, "L'Émigration de 300 rabbins en Palestine en l'an 1211," *REJ*, LXXXII, 332–52; and E. N. Adler's note thereon, *ibid.*, LXXXV, 70–71. On the two articles in the Magna Carta relating to Jews, their background and effects, see *infra*, n. 60.

50. Henry III's treaty and ordinances in T. Rymer and R. Sanderson, *Foedera*, ed. by Clarke, Holbrooke and Caley, I, 148; *Patent Rolls of the Reign of Henry III, A.D. 1216–1225*, pp. 180 f.; Hardy, *Rotuli litterarum clausarum*, I, 186b, 354b, 357a, 359b, 378b; D'B. Tovey, *Anglia Judaica*, pp. 77, 79, 81 ff. On the legislation concerning the synagogue and the Jewish badge in England, see *infra*, Chaps. XLVII–VIII. In view of these protective measures, Hubert and the king doubtless felt doubly justified to impose upon the Jews in November 1225 a substantial tallage, which according to a contemporary chronicler yielded 5,000 marks. See *Patent Rolls, 1216–1225*, p. 496; *Annales Monasterii de Waverleia* (Waverley), ad 1225, ed. by H. R. Luard in his *Annales Monastici*, II, 301. See also S. Painter, *William Marshal, Knight-Errant, Baron, and Regent of England*, pp. 228 ff.; C. Ellis, *Hubert de Burgh: a Study in Constancy*. On Stephen Langton and the thirteenth-century synods see *infra*, n. 57.

51. Tovey, *Anglia Judaica*, pp. 106 ff.; H. G. Richardson, "Glanville Continued," *Law Quarterly Review*, LIV, 393 f. (publishing the text of the ordinance of April 4, 1233 and plausibly arguing for its authenticity); Henry III's speech reported by Matthew Paris in his *Chronica majora*, ed. by Luard, V, 487 f., in the partial

English translation by J. A. Giles, entitled *English History from the Year 1235 to 1273*, III, 114. Fuller lists of Jewish taxes during Henry's regime were given as early as 1830 by J. E. Blunt in *A History of the Establishment and Residence of the Jews in England*, pp. 38 f., and again by P. Elman in "The Economic Causes of the Expulsion of the Jews in 1290," *Economic History Review*, VII, 153 f.; and C. Roth in *A History of the Jews in England*, pp. 270 f. According to F. M. Powicke, however, the latter table "requires drastic reduction." See his *King Henry III and the Lord Edward*, I, 311. All such estimates are essentially based on recorded revenues of the Treasury, the unreliability of which, however, is illustrated, for instance, in F. A. Cazel, Jr., "The Fifteenth of 1225," *BIHR*, XXXIV, 67–81. See also, more generally, S. K. Mitchell, *Studies in Taxation under John and Henry III*; idem, *Taxation in Medieval England*, ed. by S. Painter. Neither volume discusses the Jewish imposts more than tangentially, but they contribute much to the understanding of contemporary procedures and terms. These expropriatory taxes will be more fully analyzed *infra*, Chap. LIV.

52. *Patent Rolls, 1232–1247*, p. 187; *Close Rolls, 1234–1237*, p. 81; *supra*, Chap. XXXVIII, n. 16. The *auxilium* of 1221 was analyzed by H. M. Chew in "A Jewish Aid to Marry, A.D. 1221," *TJHSE*, XI, 92–111. On other fiscal contributions to queens and royal princes see H. P. Stokes, "The Relationship between the Jews and the Royal Family of England in the Thirteenth Century," *ibid.*, VIII, 153–70. Here all pretense of the voluntary nature of such Jewish "aids" was abandoned; the Jewish taxpayers probably did not even discuss with the royal councilors whether their payments were to be considered an *auxilium* or a *tallagium*, as did the city of London in 1255. See Mitchell, *Taxation*, pp. 324 ff. Hence the rabbinic equation of a royal *mattanah* (*donum*) with an extralegal exaction (see *infra*, n. 54) was perfectly realistic. Clearly, even more than their Christian neighbors, the English Jews thus suffered severely from the hazy distinction between private and public funds characteristic of most royal finances of that period.

53. Matthew Paris, *Chronica majora*, ed. by Luard, IV, 260, 263; in Giles's English trans., I, 459, 461. On Eleanor's expulsion of Jews from Gloucester and other towns, see *infra*, n. 67.

54. M. Adler, *Jews of Medieval England*, p. 206; H. P. Stokes, *Studies in Anglo-Jewish History*, pp. 250 f. The institution of Jewish "presbyters" or "archpresbyters," their relation to Jewish "bishops" and their status within the Jewish community, though often analyzed, still is full of obscurities. See H. G. Richardson, *The English Jewry under Angevin Kings*, pp. 121 ff.; and *supra*, Vol. V, p. 319 n. 77. The fullest discussion of the six successive "archpresbyters" of English Jewry and of the Worcester Parliament of 1241 is found in Stokes, *Studies*, esp. pp. 23 ff., 44 f., 83 ff., 243 ff. Only one of these men, however, namely Aaron of York, has been the subject of a more comprehensive biographical study by Michael Adler in his "Aaron of York and King Henry III," reprinted in his *Jews*, pp. 125–73. Additional documents pertaining to Aaron and his community have more recently been made available by E. Birnbaum in "Starrs of Aaron of York in the Dean and Chapter Muniments of Durham," *TJHSE*, XIX, 199–205; and by E. Brunskill in "The Jews in Medieval York," *ibid.*, XX, 239–45. See also A. Raine's *Medieval York: a Topographical Survey*.

The method of holding an individual Jew responsible for any arbitrary impost on the whole community was also frequently applied on the Continent, but there it aroused much rabbinic opposition. According to R. Ḥayyim Or Zaru'a, in such cases the communities did not feel obliged to indemnify the arrested leaders. In connection, perhaps, with this procedure a London rabbi, cited by Mordecai b. Hillel ha-Kohen, drew the distinction between regular taxes which were to be recognized as a legitimate exercise of royal authority in consonance with the old rabbinic principle that the "law of the kingdom is law," and certain extraordinary fines or *dona* which were considered illegitimate and could be repudiated by the community. See Ḥayyim b. Isaac Or Zaru'a, *Resp.*, ed. by J. Rosenberg, fols. 88d f. No. 253; Mordecai b. Hillel ha-Kohen, *Sefer Mordecai* (Halakhic commentary on Alfasi), on Baba Qama, Nos. 151 f.; I. Epstein, "Pre-Expulsion England in the Responsa," *TJHSE*, XIV, 194.

55. On the Jewish Exchequer, which became so important in the life of medieval English Jewry, see the older, but still valuable study by C. Gross, "The Exchequer of the Jews of England in the Middle Ages," *Papers Read at the Anglo-Jewish Historical Exhibition*, pp. 170–230; H. Jenkinson, "The Records of Exchequer Receipts from the English Jewry," *TJHSE*, VIII, 19–54; and the more recent succinct analysis by A. C. Cramer, "The Jewish Exchequer: an Inquiry into Its Fiscal Functions," *AHR*, XLV, 327–37 (concluding that it performed both judicial and administrative functions). See also *supra*, Vol. IV, pp. 82 ff., 280 f. nn. 109 and 111, 341 n. 69; and H. G. Richardson's demonstration of the frequent inefficacy of this system in *The English Jewry*, pp. 146 ff.

56. J. R. Green, *History of the English People*, I, 271; *Patent Rolls, 1247–1258*, pp. 43a ff.; T. Madox, *History and Antiquities of the Exchequer of the King of England, 1066–1327*, 2d ed., I, 225; *Close Rolls, 1237–1242*, p. 31, *1242–1247*, p. 275; H. G. Richardson, *The English Jewry*, p. 115; Matthew Paris, *Chronica majora*, ed. by Luard, V, 441, 487, in Giles's English trans., III, 76, 114; M. Adler, *Jews of Medieval England*, pp. 148 f., 155, 161. According to Matthew, Henry extorted from Aaron, on a single occasion, 14,000 marks silver, in addition to 10,000 marks in gold, "for the use of the queen" (ed. by Luard, V, 136, in Giles's English trans., II, 357). As a single payment this amount, especially the gold marks (the term *auri* is missing in some texts and written over an erasure in another), is doubtless exaggerated, even if the chronicler added a number of items covering a period of several years. An interesting light on the manifold exactions from Jews by the "Poitevins" is shed by "The Testimony of the London Jewry against the Ministers of Henry III," published from the *Curia Regis Roll* for 1234 by M. Adler in *TJHSE*, XIV, 141–85. Here (pp. 156 ff.) Adler summarizes also the trial and discharge of two corrupt justices of the Jews in 1286, after they had held that office for fourteen years. The generally widespread corruption even among judges was stigmatized, for instance, in the interesting Latin song, published by T. Wright in *The Political Songs of England from the Reign of John to that of Edward II*, pp. 224 ff., 382.

57. Peter de Blois, *Epistolae*, No. clvi; and his pamphlet *Contra perfidiam Judaeorum* in his *Opera omnia*, in *PL*, CCVII, 450, 825–70; D. Wilkins, ed., *Conciliae Magnae Brittaniae et Hiberniae*, I, 570 f., 585 ff., 626, 671, 675, 746 ff.; Mansi, *Collectio*, XXII, 1147 ff.; XXIII, 543 (canons 56–58), 714, 912, 973 ff., 1067 f.; C. J.

Hefele, *Histoire*, V, Part 2, pp. 1429 ff.; VI, Part 1, pp. 88 f., 97 ff. (summaries, mostly omitting the anti-Jewish canons); Tovey, *Anglia Judaica*, pp. 81 ff. See also E. S. Cohn, "The Manuscript Evidence for the Letters of Peter of Blois," *EHR*, XLI, 43–60. The prohibition against refusing victuals to Jews was repeated in 1235 by the king himself. See *Close Rolls, 1234–1237*, p. 329. Langton's animosity toward Jews may have been reinforced by the memory of the events of 1187, when Canterbury Jews and burghers had aided the monks of St. Augustine against the troops of Archbishop Baldwin. See *supra*, Vol. IV, pp. 84, 280 f. n. 110. A critical edition of the canons of 1222, rightly observes F. M. Powicke, "is badly needed, if only to bring them into relation with the constitutions issued during the period by the English bishops." See his biography of *Stephen Langton*, p. 152; and on the archbishop's relations with Hubert de Burgh during those years, C. Ellis's aforementioned biographical essay, *Hubert de Burgh*, pp. 67 ff. See also F. A. Cazel, Jr., "The Last Years of Stephen Langton," *EHR*, LXXIX, 673–97.

58. *Close Rolls, 1237–1242*, p. 238; C. Roth, *A History of the Jews in England*, pp. 40, 130; Honorius IV's bull, *Turbato corde*, and its several successors, discussed *supra*, Chap. XXXVII, n. 24. Robert of Reading's conversion to Judaism, described in the continuation of Florence of Worcester's *Chronicon* (ed. by B. Thorpe, II, 214) under the date of 1275, is so obscure that the friar was readily confused with the Oxford deacon of 1222. In medieval Jewish historiography Robert and other Christian proselytes were blamed for the sharp rise of English Jew-baiting which resulted in the expulsion of 1290. See Samuel Usque, *Consolaçam às tribulaçoens de Israel*, Ferrara, 1553 ed., iii.12; in M. A. Cohen's English trans., *Consolation for the Tribulations of Israel*, pp. 180 ff. On this attribution, combined by Usque with an erroneous date of the expulsion, see Roth, *A History*, pp. 41, 83, 273 f.; I. Abrahams, "The Deacon and the Jewess," *TJHSE*, VI, 254–59, with reference to F. W. Maitland's paper under the same title, reprinted *ibid.*, pp. 260–76; and in Maitland's *Collected Papers*, I, 385–406; and *infra*, Chap. L.

59. *Patent Rolls, Henry III, 1247–1258*, pp. 543 f.; M. Adler, *Jews of Medieval England*, pp. 150 ff., 154 ff.; I. Abrahams and H. P. Stokes, eds., *Starrs and Jewish Charters Preserved in the British Museum*, I, 4 ff. No. ii, 20 ff. No. v, etc.; R. Lennard, "Peasant Tithe-Collectors in Norman England," *EHR*, LXIX, 590. Other telling examples of the progressive concentration of landholdings via Jewish money-lending are adduced by P. Elman in "The Economic Causes," *Economic History Review*, VII, 149 f. On the price trends in thirteenth-century England see E. Kosminsky, "The Evolution of Feudal Rent in England from the XIth to the XVth Centuries," *Past and Present*, VII, 12–36, emending the computation of wheat prices from 1160 to 1319 made by M. M. Postan in *Cambridge Economic History*, II, 121 ff. This situation, creating much discontent among the nobles, greatly contributed to the development of the English parliamentary system and, ultimately, also to the growth of democratic liberties for Jews as well. But its immediate effect was extreme intolerance and efforts to oust them from England altogether.

60. Magna Carta, Arts. x and xi; Statute of Merton, in A. Luders *et al.*, eds., *Statutes of the Realm (1235–1713)*, I, 1 ff., with the observations thereon by F. M. Powicke in his *King Henry III and the Lord Edward*, I, 148 ff.; II, 769 ff. (Appendix D). On the much debated evolution of the Magna Carta, see, for instance, W. S.

McKechnie, *Magna Carta: a Commentary on the Great Charter of King John*, esp. pp. 164 ff., 265 ff.; and F. Thompson, *The First Century of Magna Carta*.

61. See the barons' petition of 1258, Art. xxv, in W. Stubbs, *Select Charters and Other Illustrations of the English Constitutional History from the Earliest Times to the Reign of Edward I*, pp. 385 f.; the reports of the various ecclesiastical chroniclers in H. R. Luard's ed. of *Annales monastici*, I, 442 (Burton); II, 101 (Winchester), 363, 371 (Waverley); III, 230 (Dunstaple); IV, 141 f. (Wykes), 145 (Oseney), 450 (Worcester); Rigg, *Select Pleas*, pp. xxxvii f.; idem, *Calendar of the Plea Rolls of the Exchequer of the Jews*, I, 133, 139, 146; and, more generally, R. F. Treharne, "The Knights in the Period of Reform and Rebellion, 1258–67: a Critical Phase in the Rise of a New Class," *BIHR*, XXI, 1–12; and E. F. Jacob, *Studies in the Period of Baronial Reform and Rebellion, 1258–1267*, esp. pp. 236, 337 ff. App. i, 395 ff. App. x. See also the next note.

62. Jacobs, *The Jews of Angevin England*, pp. 217 f.; *Close Rolls, 1231–1234*, pp. 466, 515; *1234–1237*, pp. 20, 275, 425; *1237–1242*, p. 393; *1242–1247*, p. 149; Rigg, *Select Pleas*, pp. xlviii f. Not that these intolerant local decrees were necessarily carried out right away. In the case of Leicester we know that the actual expulsion was delayed until 1253, when Simon de Montfort promised in his charter for the burghers "that at no time during my life or the lives of my heirs, and to the end of the world" would any Jew be allowed to live within the city's boundaries. An *archa* is also recorded in Warwick in 1261. See J. Nichols, *The History and Antiquities of the County of Leicester*, I, Part 2, Appendix, p. 38; C. Roth, *A History of the Jews in England*, p. 58; and, on the attitude of Bishop Robert Grosseteste, L. M. Friedman, *Robert Grosseteste and the Jews*, pp. 12 ff., 23 f.; and *supra*, Chaps. XXXVII, n. 15; XXXIX, n. 4.

63. J. Z. Titow, "Some Evidence of the Thirteenth Century Population Increase," *Economic History Review*, XIV, 218–23; G. H. Martin, "The English Borough in the Thirteenth Century," *TRHS*, 5th ser. XIII, 123–44; C. Roth, *A History . . . in England*, pp. 55 f., 272 (c); Matthew Paris, *Chronica majora*, ed. by Luard, V, 114 f.; in Giles's English trans., II, 340 f. On the Blood Accusation of Lincoln see esp. Matthew Paris, *ibid.*, V, 516 ff.; in Giles's trans., III, 138 ff.; F. Michel, *Hugues de Lincolne: recueil de ballades anglo-normandes et écossaises;* J. Jacobs, "Little St. Hugh of Lincoln," *TJHSE*, I, 89–135, reprinted in his *Jewish Ideals and Other Essays*, pp. 192–224; and *infra*, Chap. XLIX.

64. Rigg, *Select Pleas*, pp. 35 f.; Adler, *Jews of Medieval England*, pp. 83, 111 f. No. ix with the adjoining plate; H. G. Richardson, *The English Jewry*, pp. 16 f. Much information on the Jewish relations with the burghers is available in monographs pertaining to individual cities. Unfortunately, the most important of these, London, has not yet received the detailed treatment it deserves. E. N. Adler's *London* offers some interesting sidelights and bibliographical curiosities, rather than a detailed history of the community, especially during the medieval period. More informative are the essays by Michael Adler on "The Jews of Medieval Canterbury," and "The Jews of Medieval Bristol," reprinted in his *Jews of Medieval England*, pp. 47–124, 175–231. Other important monographs include: idem, "The Jews of Medieval Exeter," *Transactions of the Devonshire Association*, LXIII, 221–40; R. Davies,

"The Mediaeval Jews of York," *Yorkshire Archaeological Journal*, III, 147–97; H. P. Stokes, "The Jews in Cambridge till 1275," in his *Studies in Anglo-Jewish History*, pp. 103–204; M. D. Davis, "The Mediaeval Jews of Lincoln," *Archaeological Journal*, XXXVIII, 178–200; C. Roth, *Medieval Lincoln Jewry and Its Synagogue;* idem, *The Jews of Medieval Oxford;* and other monographs recorded in his *Magna Bibliotheca Anglo-Judaica*, pp. 84 ff.; and by R. P. Lehmann in her *Nova Bibliotheca Anglo-Judaica*, pp. 28 ff. Of considerable interest also are the general city histories such as J. W. F. Hill, *Medieval Lincoln*, esp. pp. 217 ff.; or the studies relating to thirteenth-century London, cited *infra*, n. 67.

65. *Patent Rolls, 1255*, pp. 400 f., 439 f.; *1262*, p. 233; *1263*, p. 263; Matthew Paris, *Chronica majora*, ed. by Luard, V, 487 f.; in Giles's English trans., III, 114 f.; *supra*, Chap. XL, n. 18. On Prince Edward's personality and general attitudes see E. Jenks's biography, *Edward Plantagenet (Edward I.) the English Justinian; or, the Making of the Common Law*. Matthew's account is the more significant as Richard himself had been one of his chief informants. See R. Vaughan, *Matthew Paris*, pp. 13, 135 f., 148. Long before assuming temporary control over all of English Jewry, the king's brother had many dealings with individual Jews. Among his protégés was Abraham of Berkhamsted, then one of the wealthiest English Jews, whose clients included residents of half the counties in England, but who, like his master, was quite unscrupulous. It was for the benefit of Richard and his tenants that an *archa* was established in Berkhamsted in 1235, to be removed seven years later, together with the Jewish community and all its privileges, to Wallingford. See *Close Rolls, 1234–1237*, p. 46; *1237–1241*, p. 393; Richardson, *The English Jewry*, pp. 16 f. See also J. P. Trabut-Cussac, "Le Financement de la croisade anglaise de 1270," *BEC*, CXIX, 113–21. Though not discussing the fund raising in England proper, the author shows Prince Edward's financial straits after he had incurred a large debt from Louis IX in 1269 to defray the costs of the Crusade.

66. *Close Rolls, 1250–1253*, pp. 312 f.; H. G. Richardson, *The English Jewry*, pp. 293 f. App. xii; J. M. Rigg, ed., *Select Pleas*, pp. xlviii ff. Nos. iii–iv; idem and H. Jenkinson, eds., *Calendar of the Plea Rolls of the Exchequer of the Jews*, I, 243; C. Roth, "Rabbi Berechiah of Nicole (Benedict of Lincoln)," *JJS*, I, 69. On the Jewish right to own land, see C. M. Picciotto's observations in "The Legal Position of the Jews in Pre-Expulsion England, as Shown by the Plea Rolls of the Jewish Exchequer," *TJHSE*, IX, 77, citing documentation from the years 1244, 1253, and 1267. The attempt to prevent Jews from accumulating land was doubly significant, as landowners, large and small, belonged to the main debtors of Jewry. What Sarah Cohen wrote about the Jews of Oxford applied also to the rest of the country. She found that a large group of the moneylenders' clients was "made up of great landowners, tenants-in-chief (or sub-tenants) of the king in Oxfordshire and of knights holding direct from the manors or honors, which lay within the county boundary." On the basis of records relating to Abraham of Berkhamsted, Peter Elman generalized that, among the debtors of Jews, some 70 percent were recruited from agricultural classes. See S. Cohen, "The Oxford Jewry in the Thirteenth Century," *TJHSE*, XIII, 306 f.; P. Elman, "The Economic Causes of the Expulsion of the Jews in 1290," *Economic History Review*, VII, 148.

In contrast to this pure self-interest of the knightly class, the clergy's motivations were partly ideological. Through its support of these restrictive measures, the

Church obviously helped to undermine a major factor in the constant growth of its landholdings, but, by weakening the fiscal strength of Jewry, it forced the king to look for financial support from other groups, including the clergy. It was no mere coincidence that, beginning in 1272, its fiscal contributions constantly increased, often with the blessings of the Papacy. The Canterbury Fifteenth and York Tenth of 1279-81 were speedily followed by the York Thirtieth allotted in 1286 for three years, and many other imposts. See H. S. Deighton, "Clerical Taxation by Consent, 1279-1301," *EHR*, LXVIII, 161-92; and *infra*, Chaps. XLVIII and LIV.

67. J. M. Rigg and H. Jenkinson, eds., *Calendar of the Plea Rolls*, II, 64 f.; III, 290 ff.; M. Adler, *Jews of Medieval England*, p. 225; R. R. Sharpe, ed., *Calendar of Letter-Books......of the City of London at the Guildhall*, I, 215. On the coin-clipping affair of 1278-79, see Richardson's justified reservations in *The English Jewry*, pp. 218 ff. It will be more fully analyzed *infra*, Chap. LIII. Although the words *et judaeos* are crossed out in Letter-Book A, they undoubtedly were an integral part of the ordinance. Otherwise the preceding *inter Christianos* becomes meaningless. See also M. Weinbaum, *London unter Eduard I. und II. Verfassungs- und wirtschaftsgeschichtliche Studien*, pp. 63, 80 n. 65, 84 f.

68. Edward I's *Statutum de judeismo* in A. Luders *et al.*, *Statutes of the Realm*, I, 221 f.; J. E. Blunt, *A History of the Establishment . . . of the Jews in England*, p. 55 note; John Selden, *De jure naturali et gentium juxta disciplinam Ebraeorum*, Leipzig, 1695 ed., pp. 188 ff.; M. Schwab, *Inscriptions hébraïques de la France*, p. 162; and the observations thereon by C. Roth in *A History of the Jews in England*, p. 273 note (c). See also, more generally, T. F. T. Plucknett's Ford Lectures on the *Legislation of Edward I*; with such correctives (only tangentially related to the Jewish issue) as are suggested by N. D. Hurnard in her "Did Edward I Revise Henry II's Policy upon Seisin?" *EHR*, LXIX, 129-53.

Royal encouragement of general Jewish commerce was quite tenuous, however. Jews were not given any opportunity to compete on equal terms with Christian merchants. In the so called Statute of Merchants of Easter 1285 (often confused with the Statute of Acton Burnell of October 1283) the discrimination was quite blatant. This statute was enacted in response to the grievances of English merchants about their inability to collect on the due date the debt owed them for the goods sold. "Because of this many merchants refrained to come into this realm with their merchandise, to the damage both of the merchants and of the whole realm." Thenceforth a simplified procedure was to enable the seller to recover the sale price. But the statute added that this procedure was open "to all except Jews." See B. Wilkinson, *Constitutional History of Medieval England 1216-1399*, III, 317 f. No. xxix; Plucknett, *Legislation*, pp. 138 ff. Similarly, the limitation of Jewish leaseholds of tillable land to but fifteen years may indicate that, from the outset, Edward envisaged the possibility of failure of this short-term experiment which then might be followed by a total banishment of Jews. If this be true, the decree of 1290 was well planned by the king in advance, at least as a possible alternative, which would not be surprising with an admirer of the French monarchy, and especially of his idol, Louis IX.

69. W. Stubbs, *The Constitutional History of England in Its Origin and Development*, 4th ed., II, 276 n. 2; B. Wilkinson, *Constitutional History*, III, 144 No. xvi; K.

Knoll, *London im Mittelalter. Seine wirtschaftliche, politische und kulturelle Bedeutung für das britische Volk*, pp. 130 f.; G. A. Williams, "London and Edward I," *TRHS*, 5th ser. XI, 81–99; W. E. Rhodes, "The Italian Bankers in England and Their Loans to Edward I and Edward II," in *Historical Essays* by Members of the Owen College, Manchester, ed. by T. F. Tout and J. Tait, pp. 137–68. Archbishop John Peckham (or Pecham), an able administrator rather than theologian and pietist, acted also in the Jewish question out of political considerations and in response to the prevailing hostility toward Jews. While the authenticity of some of his enactments has rightly been questioned, there is no doubt about his complaint to Edward regarding the frequent relapses of Jewish converts and the alleged spread of "Judaic superstitions." See C. R. Cheney, "The So-Called Statutes of John Pecham and Robert Winchelsey for the Province of Canterbury," *Journal of Ecclesiastical History*, XII, 14–34; and D. L. Douie's biography, *Archbishop Pecham.*

Among Edward's creditors were more Italians than Cahorsins. The latter, called by Matthew Paris "an abominable pest," had largely disappeared from the scene after 1275, except for those who decided to live in England; for instance Guillaume Servat, who continued to play a weighty role in the English capital. See F. Arens, "Wilhelm Servat von Cahors als Kaufmann zu London (1273–1320)," *VSW*, XI, 477–514; and Y. Renouard, "Les Cahorsins, hommes d'affaires français du XIIIe siècle," *TRHS*, 5th ser. XI, 43–67. On the perennial Judeo-Lombard competition in England, as well as on the Continent, see A. Sapori, "Le Compagnie italiane in Inghilterra (secoli XII–XV)," *Studi di storia economica (secoli XIII–XIV–XV)*, 3d ed., II, 1039 ff.; and *infra*, Chap. LIII.

70. T. Rymer and R. Sanderson, *Foedera*, I, Part 2, pp. 598 f.; F. Michel, *Rôles Gasconnes. Transcrits et publiés*, II, 329 No. 1067, 335 f. Nos. 1117 and 1128, 486 f. No. 1571. Although the expulsion of the Jews from Gascony in 1288–89 was doubtless owing in part to local conditions which greatly differed from those in England, it adumbrated the English developments as well. It is doubly to be regretted, therefore, that so little work has hitherto been done on elucidating the underlying causes of this intolerant outburst. Even its connection with Edward I's ordinances of May and June, 1289, aimed at revamping the administrative system in the French provinces, has not yet been subjected to careful scrutiny. See F. M. Powicke, *The Thirteenth Century 1216–1307*, 2d ed., pp. 274 n. 1, 277 f. n. 2, 298 ff. (referring to the text reproduced in the unpublished dissertation on Edward in Gascony by J. C. Trabut-Cussac); and, more generally, C. Bémont, ed., *Recueil des actes relatifs à l'administration des rois d'Angleterre en Guyenne au XIIe siècle;* and E. C. Lodge, *Gascony under English Rule*, esp. pp. 45 ff.

71. J. M. Rigg, ed., *Select Pleas*, pp. xi f. Although much has been written on the subject, some legal aspects and immediate antecedents of the decree of 1290 still are unclarified. For example, the much discussed British Museum manuscript pertaining to "articles touching the Jewry" and printed in both the French original and an English translation in Rigg's *Select Pleas*, pp. liv ff., is of highly uncertain provenance. This decree may never have been enacted; perhaps it was not even considered until about 1287. In any case, its impact upon the destinies of English Jewry was questionable. The forces driving toward the expulsion and the ultimate catastrophe itself will be more fully discussed *infra*, Chap. L. For the time being, see the older but still valuable studies by G. H. Leonard, "Expulsion of the Jews from England by

Edward I: an Essay in Explanation of the Exodus, A. D. 1290," *TRHS*, V, 103–46; and by B. L. Abrahams, "The Expulsion of the Jews from England in 1290," *JQR*, [o.s.] VII, 75–100, 236–58, 428–58 (also reprint); P. Elman, "The Economic Causes of the Expulsion of the Jews in 1290," *Economic History Review*, VII, 145–54; and, particularly, H. G. Richardson's new data in *The English Jewry*, pp. 213 ff. With his unmatched familiarity with the medieval English archives relating to Jews, the latter author was able to supply many new facts and correct numerous prevailing misconceptions, including the predilection of many modern English historians to exonerate Edward I personally from mercenary motives. However, as elsewhere in his important work, Richardson often fails to see the forest for the trees and does not penetrate to the essence of the factors underlying the outburst of total intolerance. To that extent G. J. Langmuir's otherwise rather diffuse and unperceptive critique is not unjustified. See his "The Jews and the Archives of Angevin England: Reflections on Medieval Anti-Semitism," *Traditio*, XIX, 183–244.

Incidentally, the evaluation of Edward I by modern historians has long ranged from that of an ambitious tyrant, or competent but conventional ruler, to that of a mighty king of destiny. See G. Templeman, "Edward I and the Historians," *Cambridge History Journal*, X, 16–35. Similarly divided are the opinions of scholars concerning the ultimate effects of the expulsion on both the English economy and the European Jewish community. Some historians have attributed to it Edward I's great financial difficulties from 1294 on. See W. Stubbs, *The Constitutional History of England*, 4th ed., II, 560; W. Cunningham, *The Growth of English Industry and Commerce during the Early and Middle Ages*, 3d ed., I, 150 f. The effects on the Jewish people will become more apparent in the forthcoming chapters.

72. F. Michel, *Rôles Gasconnes*, III, 55 No. 2054, 461 No. 4786; C. T. Martin, "Gascon Rolls," *TJHSE*, II, 170–79, esp. pp. 176 ff. Nos. 12–17; J. W. F. Hill, *Medieval Lincoln*, p. 238. Inmates of the *Domus Conversorum* after 1290 are discussed by M. Adler in "The History of the Domus Conversorum," reprinted in his *Jews of Medieval England*, pp. 307 ff. Other data were gathered some three-quarters of a century ago by L. Wolf in "The Middle Age of Anglo-Jewish History (1290–1656)," *Papers Read at the Anglo-Jewish Historical Exhibition*, pp. 53–79; and, more recently, by C. Roth in *A History of the Jews in England*, pp. 132 ff. This problem will be discussed more fully in a later volume.

73. After a long period of hesitancy by modern scholars we now possess some documentation for more or less significant literary contributions by medieval English rabbis. See A. Marmorstein, "New Material for the Literary History of the English Jews before the Expulsion," *TJHSE*, XII, 103–15; and C. Roth's brief survey of *The Intellectual Activities of Medieval English Jewry*. See, however, the important caveats suggested by J. L. Teicher in his review of the latter essay in *JJS*, II, 58–60. At the same time some Christian scholars cultivated Hebrew studies with great vigor. See B. Smalley's *Hebrew Scholarship Among Christians in XIII Century England*. This entire evolution will be treated more fully in later chapters. In any case, contributions to Jewish Bible studies, Hebrew grammar, or even liturgy and law shed but little light on the daily life of the people. As far as decisions in legal cases are concerned, even the sources quoted by I. Epstein in his "Pre-Expulsion England in the Responsa," *TJHSE*, XIV, 187–205, are largely of non-English origin.

CHAPTER XLIV: RISE OF IBERIAN JEWRY

1. As is well known, the numbering of the early Castilian kings has caused medieval chroniclers many difficulties, particularly since they appeared under different numbers as kings of Leon. See J. Gimeno Casalduero's pertinent remarks in "Sobre las numeraciones de los Reyes de Castilla," *Nueva Revista de Filologia Hispanica*, XIV, 272–94. In our treatment we intend to adhere to the more widely accepted Castilian system.

2. See the documents excerpted by F. Baer in *Die Juden im christlichen Spanien*, I, Part 2, esp. pp. 50 ff. No. 67, 58 ff. No. 76; P. León Tello, "Nuevos documentos sobre la judería de Haro," *Sefarad*, XV, 161 ff.; and *infra*, n. 13. The document of 1266, which includes some 90 entries relating to the assignment of houses to the Jews of Jerez, is particularly interesting. Long known from F. Fita's "Jerez de la Frontera. Su judería en 1266," *BAH*, X, 465–84, this distribution has been frequently scrutinized. The names of recipients were corrected by Yitzhak (Fritz) Baer and, whenever possible, identified from other sources. See also H. Sancho de Sopranis, "Contribución a la historia de la judería de Jerez de la Frontera," *Sefarad*, XI, 349–70, mainly supplying data of a later period.

The earlier allotment of houses and land in Seville (1253), on the other hand, can now be studied in the critical edition by J. González of the *Repartimiento de Sevilla, Estudio y edición preparada*, esp. I, 361 ff., although the author's assumption that Jews had totally disappeared from that Almohade capital before the Reconquest doubtless goes too far. The resurrected Jewish quarter in the city and the life therein is described with extensive documentation by A. Ballesteros in his *Sevilla en el siglo XIII*, pp. 219 ff. See also M. Méndez Bejarano, *Histoire de la juiverie de Seville;* J. Espín Rael, "De la conquista y repartimientos de tierras a los conquistadores y pobladores de Lorca," *Anales* of the Centro de Cultura Valenciana, 2d ser. XXV, 93–102 (the redistribution of land began only after the definitive occupation in 1265); H. Sancho de Sopranis, "La Repoblación y el ripartimiento de Cadiz por Alfonso X," *Hispania* (Madrid), XV, 483–539 (in contrast to neighboring Jerez, Jews seem to have taken little part in the resettlement and land distribution here; only one Jew is recorded in the incomplete lists of 1264–75; p. 514); and, more generally, the papers read at the Conference held at Jaca in August 1947 and devoted to the various aspects of *La Reconquista española y la repoblación del país*.

Despite the friendly attitude of the conquerors, not all communities formerly under the rule of Islam recovered their strength, which had been sapped by both Almohade intolerance and the warlike devastation. For one example, the once magnificent center of Jewish learning in Lucena never regained its preeminence, demographically or intellectually. See F. Cantera y Burgos, "La Judería de Lucena," *Sefarad*, XIII, 343–52, mainly quoting excerpts from early modern historians relating to local antiquities, with little bearing on the Jewish community. Parallel developments during the earlier period of resettlement were discussed *supra*, Vol. IV, pp. 27 ff., 245 ff. See also the extensive literature cited there.

3. Baer, *Die Juden*, II, 21 f. No. 40; J. González, *El Reino de Castilla en la época de Alfonso VIII*, I, 131; II, 472 f., 807 f. (Alphonso's decree of 1187 is reproduced here with minor variations); F. Cantera, "La Judería de Calahorra," *Sefarad*, XV, 353–72; XVI, 73–112, esp. XV, 354; XVI, 74 No. iii; Innocent III's letter of May 5, 1205, in his *Espistolae*, viii.50 in *PL*, CCXV, 616 f.; and that by Gregory IX to the bishop of Cordova dated August 29, 1239, in Grayzel, *The Church*, pp. 112 f. No. 17, 244 f. No. 99. Gregory's letter (not reproduced in his *Registres*, ed. by L. Auvray) was first published from a Cordova original by F. Fita in "La Sinagoga de Córdoba," *BAH*, V, 363 f. No. 1, where, however, the date is given as of September 10, 1239. This dating is also followed by Baer, pp. 27 f. No. 53.

The problem of ecclesiastical tithes had engaged the attention of many kings, popes, and ecclesiastical councils during the eleventh and twelfth centuries. See *supra*, Vol. IV, pp. 13, 43, 58, 153 f., 239 n. 11, 256 n. 54, 313 n. 5. After 1215, it seems to have been adjusted more or less to the satisfaction of the Church, notwithstanding the ensuing diminution of the Jews' taxable property available to the king. But the Jews, understandably, continued to resist a tax which they considered a direct contribution to the support of an alien faith. On Burgos itself see the documents cited by D. Mansilla in "La Diócesis de Burgos a través de la documentación del archivo capitular en los siglos XIII y XIV," *Anthologica annua*, IX, 417–73. This is the less surprising as "Resistance to the Tithes in the Middle Ages" was well-nigh universal even among the Christians. See G. Constable's pertinent data in *JEH*, XIII, 172–85, despite the author's efforts to minimize and explain that resistance. The clergy's segregationist agitation, including the introduction of a distinguishing badge, encountered even stiffer Jewish opposition supported, in part, by both the state and society. We shall see that only after a prolonged struggle over several generations did the Spanish people achieve sufficient homogeneity to convert the Jewish community into a more distinctly "alien" segment of the population which could more formally be separated from the majority.

4. Baer, *Die Juden*, I, Part 1, pp. 49 ff. Nos. 61–63, 94 ff. No. 92, 177 ff. No. 153, etc.; Part 2, pp. 66 f. No. 84, 77 f. No. 93, 88 f. No. 98, etc. The vicissitudes of the leading Jewish tax farmers and fiscal agents are reviewed by Baer in his *Toledot ha-Yehudim bi-Sefarad ha-noṣrit* (A History of the Jews in Christian Spain), 2d ed. rev., pp. 45 ff.; and in the English trans. by L. Schoffmann entitled *A History of the Jews in Christian Spain*, I, 78 ff. Baer has also succeeded in interpreting many allusions in the recalcitrant mass of contemporary Hebrew poetry and integrating these often uncertain data into the total picture of the historical evolution. See, for instance, his "The Life and Times of Todros ben Yehudah ha-Levi" (Hebrew), *Zion*, II, 19–55. See also *supra*, Vol. IV, p. 246 n. 30; and *infra*, n. 17. A Jewish soldier who took part in the "liberation" of Orihuela is described by J. Garcia Sorano in "La Reconquista de Orihuela," *BAH*, CIV, 216. This participation of Jewish combatants in the earlier Spanish wars was mentioned *supra*, Vol. IV, pp. 36, 251 n. 43, with reference to the rabbinic sources here quoted. Its subsequent decline will be more fully analyzed in a later chapter.

5. Baer, *Die Juden*, I, Part 2, pp. 24 f. No. 47, 55 ff. Nos. 70–71, 66 ff. No. 84, 78 f. No. 94. The last mentioned document refers to the Order of Santiago farming, in 1287, its revenue to two Jews in return for the debts owed them. On that order's commercial relations with Jews, see the interesting documents reproduced *ibid.*, pp.

62 ff. No. 82. See also E. Benito Ruano's "Deudas y pagos del Maestre de Santiago don Pelay Pérez Correa," *Hispania* (Madrid), LXXXV, 23–37. The execution of Çag de la Maleha in 1279 is mentioned in the *Chronicle* of Alphonso X (*La Crónica del rey don Alfonso Décimo*), lxix–lxxii, ed. by C. Rosell y López, in his *Cronicas de los reyes de Castilla*, I, 53 ff. See J. Amador de los Rios, *Historia social, política y religiosa de los Judios de España y Portugal*, I, 492 ff. That the ruthless crown prince, whose subsequent regime as Sancho IV *el Bravo* (the Bully; 1284–95) was characterized by many cruelties, would not mind jeopardizing the life of his father's faithful servant is less astonishing than the impulsive action of Alphonso X, styled *el Sabio* (the Wise). See the recent biographies by P. Bernardou, *Alphonse le Savant;* E. S. Procter, *Alfonso X of Castile, Patron of Literature and Learning*, esp. pp. 123 ff.; and *infra*, n. 6. See also R. Menéndez Pidal *et al.*, eds., *Primera crónica general de España que mandó componer Alfonso el Sabio y se continuaba bajo Sancho IV en 1289*, Vol. I: Texto; and N. Guglielmi's Buenos Aires dissertation on *La Administración regia de León y Castilla de Fernando I a Alfonso X*, summarized in the *Revista de la Universidad de Buenos Aires*, 5th ser. II, 141–43.

6. J. Rodriguez, "Judería de Sahagún," *Archivos Leoneses*, VII, 58 f. App. 2; idem, "Judería de Céa," *ibid.*, IX, 46 No. 8; the Palencia decrees of 1177, 1185, and 1256 extant in its Cathedral archive and included in the fascicle, *Pergaminos, 1175–1564*, Nos. 13, 18 and 60, microfilms of which are available in the Archivo Histórico Nacional in Madrid. An even more permanent difficulty, however, for the communal administration arose, as we shall see, from the frequent tax exemptions granted by the king to individual members. Such withdrawal of wealthy taxpayers usually placed a very heavy tax burden squarely on the shoulders of the less affluent members.

7. Alphonso X, *Las Siete Partidas*, i.iv, 119 (on behavior during Christian processions); iii.xi, 20 (Jewish oath); iv.ii, 15 (intermarriage), x, 3 (dissolution of matrimony with an unconverted spouse); vii.xxiv, *passim;* new ed. by G. Lopez, I, 147; II, 545 f.; III, 30 f., 82; IV, 643 ff.; U. R. Burke, *A History of Spain from the Earliest Times to the Death of Ferdinand the Catholic*, 2d ed., with additional notes and an introduction by M. A. S. Hume, I, 282. On the text and origin of the *Siete Partidas*, see also A. Garcia Gallo, "El 'Libro de las Leyes' de Alfonso el Sabio. Del Espéculo a las Partidas," *AHDE*, XXI–XXII, 345–528. Though during the years of its compilation (1256–65) Castile was spared the religious frenzy generated in Aragon by the disputation of Barcelona, the easily swayed king yielded to his ecclesiastical advisers and inserted some anti-Jewish clauses into his famous code. On the specific provisions relating to Jews, see O. Belmonte's "Glosas a la legislación sobre los Judíos en las Partidas," *Boletin* of the R. Academia de Ciencias de Córdoba, XXVI, 41–66; and, more generally, J. Iturrioz, "Fundamentos sociológicos en las Partidas de Alfonso X el Sabio," *Estudios de historia social de España*, III, 5–100.

8. Alphonso X, *Las Siete Partidas*, vii.xxiv, ed. by G. Lopez, IV, 643 ff.; José Giménez y Martínez de Carvajal, "San Raimundo de Peñafort y las Partidas de Alfonso X el Sabio," *Anthologica annua*, III, 201–338, esp. pp. 324 f.; J. Amador de los Rios, *Historia social*, I, 494 ff. Giménez correctly points out a minor conflict between Peñaforte's statement in his *Diplomatario*, ed. by J. Ruis Serra, p. 281, and his *Raymundiana*, I, 32. See A. Collel (Costa), "Raymundiana. Apéndice a un diplomatario," *Analecta sacra Tarraconensia*, XXX, 63–95. According to the *Diplo-*

matario, the college was established for the purpose of teaching Arabic, whereas in the *Raymundiana* instruction in Hebrew is stressed as its equally valid objective. Here the argument is advanced that the alumni of the college could not only "convince Jews of their malice and errors" but also were enabled to emend some corruptions in the Hebrew Bible intended "to conceal the mysteries of the Passion and other sacraments of the faith." Evidently both languages were to be taught with equal intensity since the conversion of both Muslims and Jews was high on the agenda of the churchmen and, to a lesser extent, of many leading statesmen in the two Spanish realms. See also Giménez's "El Decreto y las decretales fuentes de la primera Partida de Alfonso el Sabio," *Anthologica annua,* II, 239–348; and *supra,* Chap. XXXVIII, n. 22. Nor was Spanish folklore devoid of deeply religious biases. If, therefore, Alphonso's famous *Cantigas de Santa Maria* betrayed the deep impact on him of Spain's popular beliefs and superstitions, he clearly could not divorce himself completely from the prevailing misconceptions concerning Jews and Judaism in his legislative work, too. See J. E. Keller, "Folklore in the *Cantigas* of Alfonso el Sabio," *Southern Folklore Quarterly,* XXIII, 175–83; and, on the general influence of anti-Jewish folklore, see *infra,* Chap. XLIX.

Religious concerns were evident also in Alphonso's other enactments. Even when the assembled Cortes at Seville of 1252 addressed themselves to the more secular aspects of the civil procedure in litigations among Christians and Jews, the king nevertheless added prohibitions relating to the employment of Christian nurses by Jews or Moors and even to the conversion of the latter to Judaism or *vice versa.* Moorish and Jewish converts to each other's religion were threatened by perpetual enslavement to the Treasury. See A. Ballesteros, "Las Cortes de 1252," *Anales of the Junta por ampliación de estudios y investigaciones científicas,* III, 109–43, esp. pp. 121, 139 ff.; and *infra,* n. 10.

9. Honorius III's letter of March 20, 1219, in his *Regesta,* ed. by P. Presutti, I, 321 No. 1943; Grayzel, *The Church,* pp. 150 f. No. 38. The pope may also have given some weight to the financial losses which many Spanish churches might sustain from such a forced departure of wealthy Jews. His consent to the exemption of Castilian Jewry from the badge must be read in the context of the two earlier communications he had addressed to the same Archbishop Roderic on Jan. 26, 1218 and March 18, 1219 (the latter only two days before this concession) in which he had insisted upon the full payment by Jews of the ecclesiastical tithes even if the Jewish owners had built houses on property acquired by them from Christians. It may also be noted that three months later Roderic himself reached an agreement with the Jews in which he accepted a poll tax in lieu of the tithe. See Baer, *Die Juden,* I, Part 2, pp. 24 f. Nos. 46–47; and Grayzel, *The Church,* p. 147. See also D. Mansilla Reoyo, "Inocencio III y los reinos hispanos," *Anthologica annua,* II, 9–49; *supra,* n. 6; and Vol. IV, pp. 255 f. Innocent's successors, too, insistently demanded the payment of the tithe by Jews. See the letters issued by Innocent IV in 1252 and Urban VI in 1264 and reproduced by F. Cantera in "La Judería de Calahorra," *Sefarad,* XV, 355; XVI, 75 f. Nos. vi–vii; and *supra,* Chap. XXXVII, nn. 55–56. See also Cantera's "Documentos de compraventa hebraicos de la catedral de Calahorra," *Sefarad,* VI, 37–61.

10. See the sources cited *supra,* Vol. IV, pp. 253 f. n. 49. Survivals of the Visigothic age, both overt and underground, were to haunt Jewish life on the Iberian Peninsula forever after. The decisions of the seventh-century Toledan Councils, in partic-

ular, were to play a complicating role in the progress of canon law, even if some of their most antagonistic postulates had been quietly dropped by such codifiers as Gratian or the popes. They appealed to many Spaniards particularly in periods of great tension, which is the less surprising as even today some scholars strain their ingenuity to offer excuses for these early excesses. See, for instance, A. Echánove's recent "Precisiones acerca de la legislación conciliar toledana sobre los judíos," *Hispania sacra*, XIV, 260–80. However, during the *Reconquista*, when the need for Jewish cooperation was widely felt, this Visigothic heritage was generally toned down.

11. *El Fuero real de España*, I, v.5, ix.4; III, v.8, vi.16, viii.3, ix.2; IV, i.1, ii.1–7, xx.2, in *Los Códigos españoles concordados y anotados*, 2d ed., I, 353, 357, 382, 385–87, 402 f., 417; *Libro de los Fueros de Castilla*, ed. by G. Sanchez, Arts. 30, 33–34, 47, 57, 62, 73, 92, 96, 107, 140, 216–17, 219–21, 234, 306, with the comments thereon by Baer in *Die Juden*, I, Part 2, pp. 34 ff. Nos. 60–61. Apart from these more general compilations applicable in many localities, there existed numerous local *fueros* whose validity was geographically circumscribed. This is particularly true of the older districts around Leon where Judeo-Christian coexistence had been shaped during several centuries of living together under the shadow of a powerful Muslim Caliphate. See the texts of such local *fueros* included in A. Castro and F. de Onís, eds., *Fueros Leoneses de Zamora, Salamanca, Ledesma y Alba de Tormes*, I, esp. pp. 170, 201 f. (Salamanca, Arts. 259, 341), 271, 284 f. (Ledesma, Arts. 315, 389), 297, 308 f. (Alba de Tormes, Arts. 12, 39–40), and the excerpts therefrom in Baer, *Die Juden*, I, Part 2, pp. 30 ff. Nos. 57–59. On the royal mastery over Jews, cited in the text from the *Libro de los Fueros de Castilla*, Art. 107, see *supra*, Chap. XLIII, n. 3. The translation here of the adjective *ricos* as "great lords" rather than "rich men" follows U. R. Burke, *A History of Spain*, I, 254 n. 2, which correctly traces the etymology of that term to the German word, *reich*, or literally "men of empire." Alphonso X may have been confirmed in his views on Jewish serfdom by his futile excursion into German politics and his aspirations to serve as Roman emperor of the German nation. See W. Freiherr von Schoen's biography of *Alfons X von Kastilien, ein ungekrönter deutscher König*. However, the Spanish doctrine had much more in common with the royal than with the imperial theory of Jewish serfdom.

12. See A. Ballestros Baretta, "Burgos y la rebelión del infante Don Sancho," *BAH*, CXIX, 93–194; Baer, *Die Juden*, I, Part 2, pp. 76 No. 90, 94 ff. No. 100. Curiously, so concerned were the thirteenth-century Spanish kings about losing their Jewish subjects that they even experimented with the procedure initiated by Philip II Augustus. In 1291 Sancho IV made an agreement with James II of Aragon for the extradition of each other's Jews together with their possessions. Baer, p. 88 No. 97. However, we hear little of the implementation of that treaty or of its renewal in later years. See also Baer, *Toledot*, 2d ed., pp. 78 ff.; idem, *A History of the Jews in Christian Spain*, I, 130 ff.; and, more generally, M. Gaibrois de Ballestero's comprehensive work on the *Historia del reinado de Sancho IV de Castilla* (which includes, for instance, the Treasury's receipts from the *juderías* listed in Vol. I, p. cxv).

13. A Pons, "Los Judíos del reino de Mallorca durante los siglos XIII y XIV," *Hispania*, XVI (Madrid), 163–255, 335–426, 503–94, esp. pp. 525 f.; Baer, *Die Juden*, I, Part 1, pp. 94 ff. No. 97, 119 f. No. 107; *infra*, n. 16; and Chap. XLVII. Much

additional information is given in F. de Bofarull y Sans, *Los Judíos en el territorio de Barcelona (siglos X al XIII): Reinado de Jaime I, 1213-1276;* F. Fita and G. Llabrés, "Privilegios de los Hebreos mallorquines en el Codice Puayo," *BAH,* XXXVI, 19; and in J. Régné's "Catalogue" for the years 1213-1327, esp. in *REJ,* LX, 168 No. 36, 180 No. 101. Sometimes the land distribution took place in stages. For example, the district of Lorca was reconquered first by the Aragonese, then came partially into the hands of the Castilians, and was finally reoccupied by James I in 1265. It was the latter reassignment which established permanent property rights. See J. Espín Rael's aforementioned essay in *Anales* of the Centro de Cultura Valenciana, 2d ser. XXV, 93-102, esp. pp. 93 f., 102. Nor were feudal restrictions too arduous. Many Jews owned and freely disposed of vineyards and other landed property to other Jews as well as non-Jews. See the extensive illustrations of such transactions included in J. Miret y Sans and M. Schwab, eds., "Documents sur les Juifs catalans aux XIe, XIIe et XIII siècles," *REJ,* LXVIII, 49-83, 174-97.

Of some value still, despite Régné and Baer, are the brief notations taken during a short scientific journey through Spain in 1888 by Joseph Jacobs and summarized by him in *An Inquiry into the Sources of the History of the Jews in Spain.* Apart from stopping with the year 1327 (to cover the whole period to 1492 would have required the review of 4,000 additional registers), Régné was, regrettably, unable to supply the promised introduction and index. He himself recognized these shortcomings in his subsequent review of his "Catalogue" in *RH,* CXLVIII, 117-18. See also, more generally, D. Romano, "Analisis de los repertorios documentales de Jacobs y Régné," *Sefarad,* XIV, 247-64.

14. Régné, "Catalogue," *REJ,* LX, 180, No. 101; Baer, *Die Juden,* I, Part 1, pp. 112 f. No. 103, 120 No. 108. The respective sizes of the Jewish communities are, of course, but partially reflected in their fiscal contributions which depended on a variety of local and temporary factors. Certainly, the reduction of Perpignan's share from 15,000 to 5,000 solidi in the two assessments did not represent any decline in the Jewish population. On the contrary, the community, then in its early stages of evolution, was probably growing numerically in those years. See R. W. Emery, *The Jews of Perpignan,* pp. 11 ff. Moreover, the wealth of a whole community was frequently determined by that of a few leading families. See *infra,* Chap. LIV. Nevertheless, the documents recording tax assessments are quite instructive from many angles. In addition to the lists mentioned in the text, see also D. Romano, "El Reparto del subsidio en 1282 entre las aljamas cataláns," *Sefarad,* XIII, 73-86.

The sharp displacement of the Muslim population may be seen from recent estimates that, before the reconquest, Valencia alone had had some 15,000 Moors who were not fully replaced by the new Christian and Jewish settlers. See C. de la Véronne, "Recherches sur le chiffre de la population musulmane de Valence en 1238," *Bulletin hispanique,* LI, 423-26. See also M. Gual Camarena, "Precedentes e la Reconquista valenciana," *Estudios medievales,* I, Part 5, pp. 167-246; and F. A. Roca Traver, "Un Siglo de vida mudéjar en la Valencia medieval (1238-1338)," *EEM,* V, 115-208.

15. J. Miret y Sans, *Itinerari de Jaume I "El Conqueridor,"* pp. 34 f., 200, 330 f. On many other fiscal and commercial privileges for churches and monasteries which were to complicate Aragon's fiscal administration and economic endeavors in the following generations, see the data assembled by J. Vincke in his *Staat und Kirche in*

Katalonien und Aragon während des Mittelalters, I, 27 ff., 32 ff. See also, more generally, C. de Tourtoulon's aforementioned older biography of *Jacme Ier le conquerant roi d'Aragon.*

16. Baer, *Die Juden,* I, Part 1, pp. 87 ff. No. 88. The contrast between the newly conquered provinces and the older Catalan settlements comes to the fore also in such regional collections of documents and monographs as J. E. Martínez Ferrando, *Catálogo de la documentación relativa al antiguo Reino de Valencia* (see, for instance, the numerous documents relating to Jucef Abinçaprut and Jucef Ravaya and listed in the Indices, Vols. I, p. 461; II, p. 499); J. Busquets Mulet, "El Codice latinoarábigo del Repartimiento de Mallorca," *Boletín* of the Sociedad arqueológica Luliana, XXX, 708–58 (Latin text), and *Homenaje Millás,* I, 243–300 (Arabic text); A. Pons, "Los Judíos," *Hispania,* XVI; idem, "Erección del Call en Inca de Mallorca. Su lenta y fatigosa gestación (siglo XIV)," *Sefarad,* XV, 69–87 (negotiations, begun in 1346, continued till 1372); J. Sanchez Real, "La Judería de Tarragona," *Sefarad,* XI, 339–48 (to 1391); L. Torres Balbás, "La Judería de Zaragoza y su baño," *Al-Andalus,* XXI, 172–90.

17. D. Kaufmann, "Jewish Informers in the Middle Ages," *JQR,* [o.s.] VIII, 217–38; Baer, *Die Juden,* I, Part 1, pp. 92 ff. No. 91. At times royal generosity went very far indeed. James not only generally confirmed all existing Jewish privileges in Perpignan, Roussillon, and Cerdagne and ordered all officials "not to molest them [Jews], nor to allow anybody else to molest them in any fashion or for any reason," but on one occasion he proclaimed a blanket forgiveness to all Jewish inhabitants of these districts with respect to any civil or criminal proceedings instituted against them. See the texts cited by F. de Bofarull y Sans in *Los Judíos en el territorio de Barcelona,* pp. 121 f. Nos. cliv and clvi. This exceptional treatment is understandable in the light of the uncertainties connected with the Aragonese domination over, and the peculiar conditions prevailing in, these outlying southern French districts. See the studies by R. W. Emery and S. Kahn, cited *supra,* Chap. XLIII, n. 35; and F. de Bofarull y Sans, "Jaime el Conquistador y la communidad judía de Montpeller," *Boletín* of the Academia de Buenas Letras de Barcelona, V, 484–92 (includes interesting excerpts from documents of 1262–74). The intricate problems of Jewish capital jurisdiction in Spain, unparalleled in other countries, are briefly discussed *supra,* Vol. V, pp. 45 f., 312 n. 55. They will be more fully analyzed in later chapters.

18. See F. de Bofarull y Sans, *Los Judíos en el territorio de Barcelona,* pp. 45 Nos. xiii–xiv, 47 f. No. xviii, 57 Nos. xxxii–xxxiii. Sometimes such exemptions became almost ludicrous. In 1257 James conceded to a widow, Bonafilia, that if for some reason she should be obliged to take an oath she would be allowed to swear in her own home and no one might compel her to do it outside her dwelling. If the king wished thereby to underscore the sanctity of the Jewish home he did it even more effectively when, in 1260, he granted the entire Barcelona community a general exemption from billeting the royal household, including the king's own family, in the Jewish quarter. *Ibid.,* pp. 42 No. viii, 49 No. xx. Such exemption from billeting was welcomed on both sides for social as well as ritualistic reasons and it was frequently enacted elsewhere. See *infra,* Chaps. XLVIII and LIV.

19. Régné, "Catalogue," *REJ*, LX, 162 No. 4, 164 Nos. 9–10, 166 f. No. 28, 176 No. 77, 187 No. 139; *Cortes de los antiguos reinos de Aragón y Valencia y Principado de Cataluña*, published by the R. Academia de Historia (Vols. I–XXVI cover only the medieval Cortes of Catalonia), I, 120 f., 126, 131, 133 ff.; Baer, *Toledot*, 2d ed., pp. 58 ff.; idem, *A History of the Jews in Christian Spain*, I, 148 ff. See also Y. Renouard, "Les Principaux aspects économiques et sociaux de l'histoire des pays de la Couronne d'Aragon aux XIIᵉ, XIIIᵉ et XIVᵉ siècles," *VII Congreso de Historia de la Corona de Aragón-Ponencias*, Barcelona, 1962, pp. 231–64; and *infra*, Chap. LIII.

20. Régné, "Catalogue," *REJ*, LX, 164 No. 9, 171 No. 46; LXI, 1 f. No. 215; LXII, 52 No. 562; J. Sanchez Real, "Los Judíos de Tarragona," *Boletín arqueológico* [*de Tarragona*], XLIV, 18 f.; G. Tilander's ed. of *Los Fueros de Aragón, según el manoscrito 458 de la Biblioteca Nacional de Madrid;* Baer, *Toledot*, 2d ed., pp. 90 f.; idem, *A History*, I, 150 ff.; *supra*, n. 11; Chap. XXXVIII, nn. 21 ff. and 34 ff. Even more than in Castile the royal legislation was supplemented by numerous local Aragonese *fueros*, such as have been, or will be, mentioned here in various connections. See J. E. Rivas, "Notas para el estudio de la influencia de la Iglesia en la compilación aragonese de 1247," *AHDE*, XX, 758–74; *supra*, Vol. IV, pp. 39 ff., 253 ff.; and *infra*, n. 26; Chaps. XLVII–XLVIII. See also J. L. Lecruz Berdejo, "Fueros de Aragón hasta 1265," *Anuario de derecho aragonès*, II; J. Bergua Camón, "Fueros de Aragón de 1265 a 1381," *ibid.*, V; E. Wohlhaupter, "Die Lokalen Fueros Aragons in ihrer Verbreitung," *Festschrift Ernest Heymann*, I, 110 ff.; J. Vincke's analysis of *Staat und Kirche in Katalonien und Aragon*, Vol. I.

21. J. Miret y Sans, *Itinerari de Jaume I*, pp. 406, 407 n. 1 (with a small correction in the excerpt published in Régné's "Catalogue"), 491 f. Vives was probably identical with Vives Abenvives to be mentioned presently, while Astrug was a member of the influential Ravaya family. In return for these loans, both men doubtless received many favors from Pedro, as crown prince and later as king. See *infra*, n. 24.

22. A. Michavilla y Villa, "Apuntes para el estudio de la vida social del reino de Valencia en la época de los reyes de la casa de Aragón," *III Congrès d'Historia de la Corona d'Aragó*, II, 118; Pedro II's decree of March 31, 1211, in the Archivo Histórico Nacional, Madrid, Sección de códices, Cod. 650B, pp. 563 ff. No. 554 (the king had issued a related decree on Sept. 5, 1210, available in the same archive, Sección Ordenes Militares, Leg. 160 No. 8); the extensive *Cartulario* pertaining to the Templars in the same archival collection Cod. 597B mem. 171. There are similar data in some of the published sources. See, more generally, J. L. Shneidman's essays, "Jews as Royal Bailiffs in Thirteenth Century Aragon," *HJ*, XIX, 55–66; and "Political Theory and Reality in Thirteenth Century Aragon," *Hispania* (Madrid), XXII, 171–85, both based, in part, on the Registers of the Crowns of Aragon in the State Archive of Saragossa. See also R. B. Merriman's brief study of "The Cortes of the Spanish Kingdoms in the later Middle Ages," *AHR*, XVI, 476–95; P. E. Schramm, "Der König von Aragonien. Seine Stellung im Staatsrecht (1276–1410)," *HJB*, LXXIV, 99–123; and, more generally, M. R. Madden, *Political Theory and Law in Medieval Spain;* and J. A. Maravall, "Sobre el concepto de monarquía en la edad media española," *Estudios dedicados a Menéndez Pidal*, V, 401–17; and his "El Pensiamento político en España del año 400 al 1300," *Journal*

of World History, IV, 818–32. On the religious controversies of the period see *supra*, Chap. XXXVIII.

23. Honorius III's letters of Nov. 4, 1220, in his *Regesta*, ed. by P. Presutti, I, 457 f. No. 2578; Grayzel, *The Church*, pp. 158 f. No. 45; Régné, "Catalogue," *REJ*, LXXIII, 198 f. Nos. 2386–87; and other data assembled by A. A. Neuman in *The Jews in Spain*, II, 221 ff. An interesting description of the activities of a Jewish diplomat at the beginning of the fourteenth century is offered, with ample documentation by J. Vernet in "Un Embajador judío de Jaime II: Selomó b. Menassé," *Sefarad*, XII, 125–54. See also *infra*, n. 24.

24. Régné, "Catalogue," *REJ*, LXI, 17 f. Nos. 309–11, 20 No. 326, 21 ff. Nos. 338, 340–41 and 346, 27 Nos. 372–73; LXIII, 245 ff. Nos. 659, 663, 677, 680, 682, 704, etc.; Baer, *Die Juden*, I, Part 1, pp. 100 ff. No. 96, 110 ff. No. 102, 113 ff. Nos. 104–105, 121 ff. Nos. 109–11 and 113, 131 ff. Nos. 119–20, etc.; Part 2, pp. 50 ff. No. 67, 66 ff. No. 84, 85 and 87, 77 f. No. 93, etc.; J. Miret y Sans, *Itinerari de Jaume I*, p. 506. See also J. E. Martínez Ferrando's *Catálogo* (cited *supra*, n. 16); and, more generally, Baer's excursus on the Jewish share in the financial administration of Aragon during the thirteenth century in his *Studien zur Geschichte der Juden im Königreich Aragonien*, pp. 174 ff.; his aforementioned Hebrew essay in *Zion*, II, 19–55; and the additional data summarized in his *Toledot*, 2d ed., pp. 71 ff., 78 ff., 86 f., 97 f., 490 ff.; his *A History*, I, 120 ff., 129 ff., 144 ff., 162 ff.; and by A. A. Neuman in *The Jews in Spain*, II, 221 ff. Some interesting additional data from the Registers of the Crowns of Aragon were supplied by J. L. Shneidman's aforementioned essay on "Jews as Royal Bailiffs in Thirteenth Century Aragon," *HJ*, XIX, 55–66; and his "Jews in the Royal Administration of Thirteenth Century Aragon," *ibid.*, XXI, 37–52. These leading Jewish families would deserve extensive monographic treatment, but thus far only a few detailed studies have been written. See esp. D. Romano Ventura's Madrid dissertation, *Estudio histórico de la familia Ravaya, bailes de los reyes de Aragón en el siglo XIII* (typescript); and its summary in the *Revista de la Universidad de Madrid*, I.

25. See H. Wieruszowski's stimulating essay, "Peter der Grosse von Katalonien-Aragon und die Juden, eine Politik des gerechten Ausgleichs," *Homenatge a Antoni Rubio y Lluch*, III, 239–62; D. Romano, "Los Hermanos Abenmenasse al servicio de Pedro el Grande de Aragón," *Homenaje Millás*, II, 243–92; and *infra*, n. 36.

Needless to say, despite all the furor against the royal councilors, some lesser lords, both lay and ecclesiastical, made good use of the services of Jewish financiers and doctors. For example, in his remarkable will of October 12, 1252 Don Vidal de Cañellas, bishop of Huesca, left a legacy of 20 maravedis to his physician, Abraym Aberalle, doubtless in recognition of the latter's services. He also provided that a converted Jewess, Urraca, receive 300 solidi, "beyond what we owe her." See R. del Arco, "La Judería de Huesca," *BAH*, LXVI, 328 f.

26. Baer, *Die Juden*, I, Part 2, pp. 102 f. Nos. 113 and 115, 106 f. Nos. 118–20, 114 No. 123, 117 f. No. 132, 131 ff. Nos. 138–39, etc.; Régné, "Catalogue," *REJ*, LX, 176 No. 77 (Barcelona, Villafranca, Tarragona, 1257), 187 No. 139 (Barbastro, 1260–61); LXI, 14 No. 286 (Perpignan, 1264), etc. On the varying attitudes of the individual monarchs see such biographical studies as those relating to Pedro III of Aragon and

his successors, Alphonso III, James II, and Alphonso IV, by F. Soldevila, *Pere el Gran*, Part I: L'Infant; and J. E. Martínez Ferrando *et al., Els Descendents de Pere el Gran, Alfons el Franc, Jaume II, Alfons el Benigne*, esp. p. 14. The middle section (pp. 55–145), dealing with James II, is but a summary of Martínez Ferrando's comprehensive biography of *Jaime II de Aragón. Su vida familiar.* See II, 272 No. 306, 307 No. 425. On the Castilian rulers, see esp. L. Suárez Fernández, *Juan I, rey de Castilla* (*1379–1390*).

The burghers' attitude toward Jews came to the fore particularly in the local custumals (*fueros*). The important *fuero* of Sepúlveda, which secured a royal confirmation in 1309, is now available in an excellent critical edition accompanied by historical-juridical, as well as linguistic, analyses by various specialists. See E. Saez *et al.*, eds., *Los Fueros de Sepúlveda*. It is supplemented by Saez's *Colección diplomática de Sepúlveda*. With a Foreword by P. Marín Perez. Other critical editions include H. Keniston, *Fuero de Guadalajara (1219)* (with no direct mention of Jews); L. M. de Uriarte Lebario, *El Fuero de Ayala*; G. Sanchez, *Fueros castellanos de Soria y Alcalá de Henares*; F. Cantera Burgos, *Fuero de Miranda de Ebro*; M. Gorosch, *El Fuero de Teruel*; G. Tilander, *Los Fueros de la Novenara*; V. Martínez Morellá, *Fueros de Benidorm*; and those mentioned *supra*, nn. 11 and 20. Some other local ordinances also have incidental references to specific Jewish rights or disabilities. See, for instance, F. Valls Taberner, ed., *Los Consuetudos i franqueses de Barcelona de 1284 o "Recognoverunt proceres,"* whose Arts. 94–95 (pp. 88 f.) regulate slaveholdings by Saracens and Jews. See also such critical analyses as M. A. Ortí Belmonte, "El Fuero de Córboda y las clases sociales en la ciudad. Mudéjares y judíos en la Edad Media," *Boletin* of the Real Academia de Córdoba, XXV, 5–94.

Much new information is also available in the various monographs on Jewish communities which appeared in such older journals as the *BAH* or *REJ*, or in the more recent *Sefarad* and *Archivos Leoneses*. See esp. R. del Arco, "La Judería de Huesca," *DAII*, LXVI, 321–54; idem, "La Aljama judaica de Huesca," *Sefarad*, VII, 271–301; idem and F. Balaguer, "Nuevas noticias de la aljama de Huesca," *ibid.*, IX, 351–92; F. Carreras Candi, *L'Aljama dels juheus de Tortosa;* F. Cantera Burgos, "La Judería de Miranda del Ebro (1093–1492)," *Sefarad*, I, 89–140; II, 325–75; idem, "La Judería de Burgos," *ibid.*, XII, 59–104, supplemented by L. Huidobro and his "Juderías burgalesas (Belña, Belorado)," *ibid.*, XIII, 35–59; J. Sanchez Real, "Los Judíos en Tarragona," *Boletín arqueológico de Tarragona*, XLIX, 15–39; idem, "La Judería de Tarragona," *Sefarad*, XI, 339–48; L. Piles Ros, "La Judería de Burriana (Apuntes para su estudio)," *ibid.*, XII, 105–24; D. Romano, "Restos judíos en Lérida," *ibid.*, XX, 50–65; L. Piles, "La Judería de Alcira (Notas para su estudio)," *ibid.*, pp. 363–76; R. del Arco, "Las Juderías de Jaca y Zaragoza," *ibid.*, XIV, 79–98 (chiefly relating to the fifteenth century); J. Rodriguez Fernandez, "Juderías de León," *Archivos Leoneses*, I, 33–72; II, 3–113; IV, 11–52; idem, "Judería de Sahagún," *ibid.*, VII, 5–77; idem, "Judería de Céa," *ibid.*, IX, 5–46; idem, "Judería de Valderas," *ibid.*, XVI, 59–83 (in the fourteenth century this Leonese city played a certain role as the capital of the so-called *siete villas de Campos*). On the ancient *fuero* of Leon, the critical edition of which was being prepared by L. Varquez de Parga, see his preliminary study, "El Fuero de León," *AHDE*, XV, 464–98. See also J. Salarrullana de Dios's "Estudios históricos acerca de la ciudad de Fraga. La Aljama de Judíos de Fraga," *RABM*, XL, 69–90, 183–206, 431–46 (reproducing, among other matters, the lengthy and important charter granted the community in 1328; pp. 71 ff.); L. Batlle y Prats's succinct analysis of the later "Ordenaciónes relativas a los Judíos gerundeses," *Homenaje Millás*, I, 83–92 (also publishing four municipal ordinances of 1445–49), supplemented by his and J. M. Millás Vallicrosa's "Noticias sobre la aljama de Gerona a fines del siglo XIV," *Sefarad*, V, 131–45. Of considerable importance is a well-documented comprehensive monograph by P. León Tello, *Judíos de Ávila*. No less important are the comprehensive studies of individual Spanish cities. For one example, E. Bayerri y Bertomeu's voluminous *Historia de Tortosa y su Comarca*, includes some material of Jewish interest (for instance, his reference to an agreement reached between the city and the Jewish community in 1296; VIII, 94). See also the studies related to the topography of the Jewish and Moorish quarters and the more general analysis of the treatment of these minorities in medieval Spain listed *supra*, Vol. IV, pp. 248 ff.; and in the forthcoming notes.

27. Baer, *Die Juden*, I, Part 1, pp. 152 f. Nos. 137–38; Part 2, pp. 181 No. 188. See L. Torres Balbás, "Mozarabías y Juderías de las ciudades hispanomusulmanas," *Al-Andalus*, XIX, 172–97, esp. pp. 189 ff.; idem, *Algunos aspectos del mudejarismo urbano medieval;* T. López Mata, "Morería y judería," *BAH*, CXXIX, 335–84 (with special reference to Burgos; includes archival documents). How close the relations between the two minorities frequently were may be seen from the numerous commercial and other deeds written in Arabic or Hebrew as late as the fourteenth century which have come down to us from the city of Toledo. See A. González Palencia's comprehensive publication, *Los Mozárabes de Toledo en siglos XII y XIII*. On the presence of foreign merchants in Spanish cities see, for instance, J. Lladonosa Pujol, "Marchands toulousains à Lérida aux XIIe et XIIIe siècles," *Annales du Midi*, LXX, 223–30 (they included a number of Christian and Jewish moneylenders, one Astruc taking over some mills in the vicinity of Lérida in 1249 and lending the Templars money without interest in 1251; p. 229). Another aspect of the close Franco-Spanish interrelations was the similarity of the two countries' municipal constitutions, particularly in Catalonia which had deep-rooted ties to southern France. See J. M. Font Rius, "Un Problème de rapports: gouvernements urbains en France et en Catalogne (XIIe et XIIIe siècles)," *Annales du Midi*, LXIX, 293–306. See also, more generally, L. Torres Balbás *et al., Resumén histórico del urbanismo en España;* and *infra*, nn. 43 and 47.

Despite the availability of a large body of literature, the Spanish cities' governmental and socioeconomic structure have thus far not been so intensively studied as those of the other West-European countries. Possibly the lesser role the municipalities played in Spain's political life than in that of Italy or Germany, and their even greater regional diversities, have discouraged modern investigators. See, however, such studies as those analyzed a decade ago by J. M. Font Rius in his "Neuere Arbeiten zur spanischen Städtegeschichte," *VSW*, XLII, 137–51.

28. M. Kayserling, "Notes sur l'histoire des Juifs en Espagne," *REJ*, XXVII, 148–49; E. Müller, *Das Konzil von Vienne, 1311–1312*, esp. pp. 155 ff., 696 f.; J. E. Martínez Ferrando, *Jaime II de Aragón. Su vida familiar*, II, 272 No. 366, 307 No. 425; Baer, *Die Juden*, I, Part 1, pp. 184 f. No. 157 (1305), 204 f. No. 166 (1312), 209 ff. No. 171 (1318). On the compulsory attendance at conversionist sermons and Lull's general missionary efforts see *supra*, Chaps. XXXVIII, n. 22; XXXIX, n. 4 item 2. Of primary concern to churchmen as a missionary vehicle, the Hebrew language also interested many Spaniards, both ecclesiastical and lay, because of its major role in

the transmission of Eastern learning to the West. Some clerics actually collaborated with Jewish scholars in translations from the Arabic into Latin. These manifold relations between the clergy and the Jews, already discussed *supra*, Vols. IV, pp. 32 f., 248 n. 35; VIII, pp. 310 n. 19, 364 n. 41; and Chaps. XXXVII–XXXVIII, will be further treated in various connections in our forthcoming chapters.

29. Baer, *Die Juden,* I, Part 2, pp. 100 f. No. 110, 188 No. 196, 218 No. 222, 220 ff. No. 227, 227 No. 235; *supra*, Vol. IV, pp. 175, 263 f. n. 68, 324 f. n. 30. Such inconsistencies are not at all astonishing, since the Spanish episcopate, like that of other medieval countries, particularly Germany, also had many sociopolitical concerns in the areas under its direct administration. Ensuing demands for its reform reached from time to time the papal Curia. See, for one example, J. Goñi Gaztambide, "Una Bula de Juan XXII sobre la reforma del episcopado castellano," *Hispania sacra*, VIII, 409–413. We must also bear in mind that even in the tense year of 1384 a provincial synod could meet in Ávila without discussing relations with Jews within the wide range of transgressions, the absolution for which was reserved to the bishop himself. See the text of the "Constituciones sinodales abulenses de 1384," ed. by T. Sobrino Chomón, *ibid.*, XV, 465 f.

30. Baer, *Die Juden,* I, Part 1, pp. 157 No. 141, 327 f. No. 232; Part 2, pp. 100 f. No. 110, 133 f. No. 140, 163 f. No. 167; K. Eubel, "Zu dem Verhalten der Päpste gegen die Juden," *Römische Quartalschrift*, XIII, 31 No. 3; and other documents referred to in M. Mercedes Costa's "Documentos pontíficos para la Corona de Aragón según los registros del Archivo Vaticano, Benedicto XII (1334–1342)," *Analecta Sacra Tarraconensia*, XXXIV, 73–102. In 1311, Bishop Francisco Poholac of Tortosa forbade the diocesan clergy to place their bread or meats in Jewish baking kilns (*hornos*), evidently a measure which combined segregationist with prestige aims. See E. Bayerri y Bertomeu, *Historia de Tortosa*, VIII, 295. Synodal regulations against Jews became particularly numerous in the fourteenth century. While the texts of their resolutions have long been available, they are, for the most part, still awaiting such careful analyses as those offered by J. M. Ochoa Martinez de Soria in the essays listed *infra*, n. 31.

31. J. Amador de los Rios, *Historia*, II, 155 ff., 561 ff. (reproducing the full text of the decisions at Zamora, 1313: a copy is still available among the MSS of the Biblioteca Nacional, Madrid, No. 13,116); Baer, *Die Juden,* I, Part 2, pp. 110 ff. No. 121, 118 f. No. 133, 159 No. 160. The provincial Council of Salamanca in 1335, however, although adopting a special canon (xii) against the Jews and the Moors, merely outlawed usury under *ipso facto* excommunication (canon xiv) without mentioning Jews. See Mansi, *Collectio*, XXV, 1055 f. See also the recent studies by J. M. Ochoa Martinez de Soria, "Los Dos sínodos de Zaragoza bajo el pontificado de D. Pedro López de Luna, 1317–1345," *Scriptorium Victoriense*, II, 118–59; idem, "Los Sínodos de Zaragoza promulgados por el arzobispo don Lope Fernández de Luna, 1351–1382," *ibid.*, pp. 311–70; and particularly F. Cantera Burgos, "La Usura judía en Castilla," *La Ciencia Tomista*, XXIII, 5–26. The struggle against Jewish money-lending in Spain and the changeable governmental policies on this score will be more fully discussed *infra*, Chap. LIII.

32. Alphonso IV's ordinance of 1333 was first published by F. de Bofarull y Sans in "Los Dos textos catalan y aragonès de las ordinaciones de 1333 para los Judíos de la

Corona de Aragón," *Boletín* of the R. Academia de Buenas Letras, Barcelona, VII, 153–63. It was subsequently summarized and commented upon by Baer in *Die Juden,* I, Part 1, pp. 273 ff. No. 201, the latter also referring to Pedro IV's futile attempt of 1346. The restrictions and governmental interventions against Jewish moneylending increased in number and intensity as the fourteenth century wore on. If, as a result of the Papal Schism, the influence of the Church greatly diminished in the century's last decades, so did also the monarchical power, that theretofore staunchest defender of Jewish rights. On the other hand, a case was actually made, though in a somewhat exaggerating fashion, for the contention that it was the decline of the Church's generally moderating influence which accounted for the growing insecurity of Jewish life after the Civil War in Castile. See F. V. Beltrán de Heredia, "Castilla, cisma y la crisis conciliar," *La Ciencia tomista,* 277, pp. 167–71; and A. Jimenez Soler, "Los Judíos españoles a fines del siglo XIV y principios del XV," *Universidad* (Saragossa), XXVII, 362 f. On the economic views and practices of the period, see D. Iparragine, "Los Fuentes del pensamiento económico en España en los siglos XI al XVI," *Estudios de Dustro,* II, 79–113; Y. Renouard's aforementioned paper at the *VII Congreso de Historia de la Corona de Aragón-Ponencias,* pp. 231–64; and *infra,* Vol. XII.

33. Baer, *Die Juden,* I, Part 1, pp. 222 ff. Nos. 176–77, 324 ff. Nos. 230–32; Part 2, pp. 200 No. 209 (excerpt from Samuel Zarza's *Meqor ḥayyim,* or Fountain of Life); J. Miret y Sans, "Le Massacre des Juifs de Montclus en 1320. Épisode de l'entrée des Pastoureaux dans l'Aragon," *REJ,* LIII, 255–66; and M. de los Angeles Masiá, "Aportaciónes al estudio de los 'Pastorellos' en la Corona de Aragón," *Homenaje Millás,* II, 9–30 (includes a good documentary appendix). These disturbances were repeated in the following years in several communities of Navarre (1328) and in Gerona (1331). See *infra,* n. 35; and J. M. Millás Vallicrosa and L. Batlle y Prats, "Un Alboroto contra el call de Gerona en el año 1331," *Sefarad,* XII, 297–335. On the events in 1348–49 see A. Pons, "Erección del call en Inca de Mallorca," *Sefarad,* XV, 69–87 (also in his essay in *Hispania,* XVI, 191 ff.); and, more generally, the important data assembled from the Archives of the Corona de Aragón by A. López de Meneses in her "Documentos acerca de la peste negra de la Corona de Aragón," *EEM,* VI, 291–347; and "Una Consequencia de la peste negra en Cataluña; el pogrom de 1348," *Sefarad,* XIX, 93–131, 321–64; with the comments thereon by J. Gautier-Dalché in "La Peste noire dans les États de la Couronne d'Aragon," *Bulletin Hispanique,* LXIV*bis,* 65–80. On the expansion of cemeteries see F. Cantera Burgos's brief remarks in his "Cementerios hebreos de España," *Sefarad,* XIII, 362–67. A fuller study is clearly indicated; thus far only the tombstone inscriptions have been carefully investigated, particularly in F. Cantera Burgos and J. M. Millás's monumental study of *Las Inscripciones hebraicas de España.* This volume also includes, of course, inscriptions found in synagogues and elsewhere. See, for instance, the Toledo epigraphy to be mentioned *infra,* n. 35. On the long-range effects of the Black Death, see also C. Verlinden, "La Grande Peste de 1348 en Espagne. Contributions à l'étude de ses conséquences économiques et sociales," *RBPH,* XVII, 103–146; and J. Iglesies Fort, "El Fogaje de 1365–70. Contribución al conocimiento de la población de Cataluña en la segunda mitad del siglo XIV," *Memorias* of the Academia de Ciencias y Artes de Barcelona, 3d ser. XXXIV, 247–356, showing a 20 percent drop in the Catalan population between 1366–70 and 1378–85, which also helps to explain the shift in the center of gravity of Spanish Jewry from Aragon to Castile.

34. Among the contemporary testimonies of Jewish sufferings during the Castilian Civil War, one may also mention the poet Santob de Carrion's *Viddui* (Confession). See Baer's observations in the Yellin Jubilee Volume, *Minḥah le-David*, pp. 201 f. As a reflection of the growing tensions we also learn of the spread of folkloristic accusations, for instance in Huesca in 1377. See J. Miret y Sans, "El Procès de les hosties contra els Juheus d'Osca in 1377," *Anuari* of the Institut d'Estudis Catalans, IV, 59–80. Jews rarely benefited even from tax reductions owing to their severe financial losses. In 1370, the small Jewry of Aguilar de Campóo claimed that, as a result of its depopulation and impoverishment following the bloodshed and plunder by the English invaders, it had secured from its count, Don Tello, a reduction of its annual tax from 3,000 to 1,200 maravedis and that, consequently, it owed the local monastery only a tithe of the reduced amount. Unable, however, to prove its contention by documentary evidence, it was sentenced to the payment of the full tithe of 300 maravedis in addition to the costs of the trial. See A. Benavides, ed., *Memorias de Don Fernando IV de Castilla*, II, 787 f. No. dxxxix; Baer, *Die Juden*, I, Part 2, pp. 117 No. 130, 205 No. 215; L. Huidobro and F. Cantera, "Los Judíos en Aguilar de Campóo," *Sefarad*, XIV, 339 f. The foreign interventions during the Civil War between Pedro the Cruel and Henry II of Castile have been comprehensively treated by A. Gutiérez de Velasco in "Los Ingleses en España (siglo XIV)," *EEM*, IV, 215–319; and by P. E. Russell in *The English Intervention in Spain and Portugal in the Time of Edward III and Richard II*. See esp. *ibid.*, pp. 21 n. 2, 113 n. 1, 165 n. 1. Tax reductions such as were allegedly granted the Jews in Aguilar de Campóo were quite exceptional. On the contrary, since the royal treasuries were usually most depleted after widespread disturbances, the taxes as a rule became even more burdensome.

35. Ibn Verga, *Shebeṭ Yehudah*, x, ed. by Wiener, pp. 30 f. (Hebrew), 60 ff. (German); ed. by Shohet, pp. 53 ff., with F. Baer's comments thereon in his *Untersuchungen über Quellen und Komposition des Schebet Jehuda*, pp. 47 ff., citing three additional Hebrew sources. See also A. Ballestero's biographical sketch of "Don Juçaf de Ecija," who had served for many years as royal tax gatherer (*almojarife*) under Alphonso XI, in *Sefarad*, VI, 253–57. The events leading up to the asassination of Samuel ha-Levi in 1361 or 1362 and the other atrocities committed by King Pedro, which earned him the designation, "The Cruel," are graphically described by the historian Pedro López de Ayala in his *Crónica del rey don Pedro*, conveniently available in C. Rosell y López's ed. in *Biblioteca de Autores españoles*, LXVI, 393–614. The latter's veracity has, however, been both strongly impugned and heatedly defended. See the recent essays by C. Sanchez-Albornoz, "El Canciller Ayala, historiador," *Humanitas*, I, 13–46; R. B. Tate, "Lopez de Ayala, Humanist, Historian," *Hispanic Review*, XXV, 157–74; and B. Sánchez Alonso, *Historia de la historiografía española*, 2d ed. rev. See also Baer, *Toledot*, 2d ed., pp. 216 f., 517 n. 51; idem, *A History*, I, 362 ff.; and on Samuel ha-Levi's Toledan synagogue, F. Cantera Burgos's comprehensive study of the *Sinagogas españoles con especial estudio dela de Córdoba y la toledana de El Tránsito*, pp. 65 ff., with special attention to its architecture and inscriptions (also listing the large earlier bibliography). Its communal and artistic aspects will be treated in later chapters.

36. See A. A. Neuman's pertinent observations in *The Jews in Spain*, II, 221 ff.; Baer, *Toledot*, 2d ed., pp. 190 f., 210 ff., 216 f., 232 f., and *passim*. Interesting new

data are furnished by J. Vernet in his aforementioned sketch of Solomon b. Menasseh in *Sefarad*, XII, 125–54, referring in particular to negotiations in the years 1309–17; and by D. Romano in "Los Hermanos Abenmenasse al servicio de Pedro el Grande de Aragón," *Homenaje Millás*, II, 243–92. See also *supra*, n. 23. These developments can be understood only against the background of the international affairs of the period and particularly of the diplomatic relations between the courts of Castile and Aragon and those of their Muslim neighbors. See, for instance, P. Prieto y Llovera, *Política aragonesa en Africa hasta la muerte de Fernando el Católico*. Among the Jewish physicians were quite a few women. In her "Cincas catalanas licenciadas en medicina por el Pedro el Ceremonioso (1374–82)," *Correo erudito*, V, 316–17, A. López de Meneses has shown that four of these five female doctors were Jewish. See also A. Cardoner Planas, "Seis mujeres hebreas practicando la medicina en el reino de Aragón," *Sefarad*, IX, 441–45; his several biographical studies of Jewish physicians, in part belonging to the fifteenth century, *ibid.*, Vols. I–VII (the last in collaboration with F. Vendrell Gallostra); J. Miret y Sans, "Les Médecins juifs de Pierre, roi d'Aragon," in *REJ*, LVII, 268–78: and other data relating to the Jewish share in that important profession, which will be discussed in later chapters.

37. M. Kayserling, *Die Juden in Navarra, den Baskenlaendern und auf den Balearen*, pp. 28 ff.; Gregory IX's letter of Nov. 29, 1238, and those of Innocent IV of June 12 and July 6, 1247, in Gregory's *Registres*, ed. by L. Auvray, II, 1169 f. No. 4601; A. Potthast, *Regesta pontificum*, I, 904 No. 10673; II, 1060 No. 12563; and Grayzel, *The Church*, pp. 236 f. No. 92, 268 f. No. 115, 272 f. No. 117. Innocent's successor, Alexander IV, was far less friendly, however. In his letter of 1256 or 1257 to Thibaut II he urged the king not only to outlaw Jewish usury, but also to confiscate the possessions they had thus acquired and either return them to the original debtors or else use them for pious causes. In his *Historia social*, II, 22 f., J. Amador de los Rios cites that bull from the Navarrese archives and dates it in 1256, while L. Cadier, in his *Bulles originales de XIIIme siècle* (p. 54), attributes it more specifically to October 13, 1257. See Grayzel, p. 236 n. 2.

38. N. Brussel, *Nouvel examen de l'usage général des fiefs en France*, I, 595; II, 596; F. de Mendoza, "Con los Judíos de Estella," *Principe de Viana*, XII, 237 f.; J. Goñi Gaztambide, "La Orden de Grandmont en España," *Hispania sacra*, XIII, 401–411; and, more generally, idem, *Historia de la Bula de la Cruzada en España*; and such monographs as P. Sagüés Azcona, "El Reino de Navarra en la contienda entre Felipe el Hermoso y Bonifacio VIII (1303–1304)," *Archivo Ibero-americano*, 2d ser. XXIII. On the destruction of the Navarrería in Pamplona in 1276–77, see *infra*, n. 42. Taking a leaf out of the royal book, some officials allowed themselves liberties with the Jews under their control. In 1308, the seneschal of Estella ordered the incarceration of all Jews in his district. However, the Jews were able to appeal to King Louis, who immediately transferred the jurisdiction over the imprisoned Jews to the seneschal of Pamplona and informed the latter that the captives were under his special protection until the final disposition of their case. See M. Kayserling, *Die Juden in Navarra*, p. 35, citing the older standard history of the kingdom by J. Yanguas y Miranda, *Historia de Navarra*, II, 113.

39. Baer, *Die Juden*, I, Part 1, pp. 935 ff. Nos. 579–80; Solomon ibn Adret, *Resp.*, IV, 84 f. No. 268; I. Epstein, *The "Responsa" of R. Solomon ben Adreth of Barce-*

lona (1235–1310) as a Source of the History of Spain, p. 92; supra, Vol. IV, pp. 35 f., 251 n. 42. This fair treatment of the Jews did not extend, however, to religious transgressions, which were strenuously prosecuted. In 1351 one Salomon Embolat was condemned to the huge fine of 80 pounds for having forced his entry into a church seeking to prevent the baptism of his nephew. A convert was publicly flogged for an alleged blasphemy against the Virgin and another was burned for relapse to Judaism. See F. de Mendoza in Principe de Viana, XII, 255; Baer, Die Juden, I, Part 1, p. 948 No. 585.

40. The massacre of 1328 is described by one of its Estella survivors, Menahem b. Aaron ibn Zeraḥ, in his Ṣedah la-derekh (Provision for the Way; a code of laws), Intro., Sabionetta, 1567 ed., fol. 16a. Later Jewish chroniclers had little independent information. The non-Jewish sources, though frequently analyzed, still leave many questions open. They largely concentrate on the few major localities, whereas the swift royal retribution shows that many other places were also affected. See the next note. The views of earlier historians on the Estella events are well summarized by F. de Mendoza in Principe de Viana, XII, 260. More recently, A. Goñi Gaztambide has subjected these reports to renewed scrutiny. See his "La Matanza de Judíos en Navarra en 1328," Hispania sacra, XII, 5–33. This tragic episode will be more fully treated infra, Chap. L. The prosecution of Shem Ṭob ibn Shapruṭ in Tarazona has been retold, with much new documentation, by J. M. Sanz Artibucilla in "Los Judíos en Aragón y Navarra: Nuevos datos biográficos relativos a Sem Ṭob ben Isḥaq Šapruṭ," Sefarad, V, 337–66. See also supra, Chaps. XXXVIII, n. 28; and XXXIX, n. 7 item 10. Other interesting cases of Navarre Jews condemned by courts for various violent actions (including a woman condemned for wounding another Jewess), are cited by De Mendoza, pp. 247 f.

41. Kayserling, Die Juden in Navarra, pp. 200 f. App. G, reproducing Art. 13 of Philip III's decree of 1330, which added insult to injury by stating that the law was enacted "in order to restrain the malice of the Jews and Moors." The large number of localities condemned to fines, ranging from 20 livres payable over four years for Baigorri to Estella's 10,000 livres due in instalments over eleven years, reveals not only the contagious nature of the disturbances but also the presence of Jews in many smaller places throughout the country, about which little is known from other sources. See F. de Mendoza in Principe de Viana, XII, 265 ff., the author also pointing out that the Estella Jewish community had sufficiently recovered in two years to be able, together with that of Funes, to lend the king 1,600 livres. The absence of any large-scale conversions of Jews, that usual by-product of massacres, is also noteworthy. This at least is the conclusion drawn by De Mendoza from his perusal of the records of the Chamber of Accounts. See ibid., pp. 253 f. On Jewish jugglers (one Gento is mentioned in 1328), see ibid., p. 245; and F. Idoate Iraqui's excerpt ibid., XVIII, 586 No. 76 (see the next note).

42. Baer, Die Juden, I, Part 1, pp. 964 f. No. 590. The order that Jews return to the Navarrería was part of the government's attempt to rebuild that entire section of the capital, which had been thoroughly devastated by the French invaders, as graphically described by Guillem (Guillaume) Anelier of Toulouse. It is said to have been inhabited by only one family in 1301. Its reconstruction began in earnest in 1323 and by 1350 the quarter embraced 263 hearths. See Guillem Anelier of

Toulouse's *Histoire de la guerre de Navarre en 1276 et 1277,* ed. with a translation, introduction, and notes by F. Michel, esp. pp. 306 v. 4774, 308 v. 4780, with the editor's notes thereon *ibid.* and pp. 639 f. (also mentioning the request of Jews that they be assigned ground to build houses in lieu of those destroyed during the "rebellion" in which, they claimed, they had taken no part); and, more generally, J. J. Uranga, "La Población de la Navarrería de Pamplona en 1350," *Principe de Viana,* XIII, 67–106, esp. pp. 72 f., 77, 79, 83 f. The district figures prominently again in 1366, in connection with the French and English troop movements in support of the contending parties during the Castilian Civil War. At that time the Navarre government ordered all inhabitants including the Jews, to help fortify the Navarrería. Jews were also involved in similar works of fortification in Tudela, Estella, and other cities, through both financial contributions and personal labor. On one occasion the Moors of Tudela were told to cease working on strengthening the walls of the *juderia,* for their own *moreria* was in equal need of repairs. On the other hand, the government was quite liberal in admitting Castilian refugees, the Jews being expressly mentioned among those who were to be hospitably received. See the highly informative collection of excerpts from the registers of the Chancery for the years 1365–66, preserved in the Archivo General de Navarra and published by F. Idoate Iraqui in "Un Registro de Cancelleria del siglo XIV," *Principe de Viana,* XVIII, 573–94; XIX, 179–228, 337–57; XX, 109–126, esp. XVIII, 582 No. 42; XIX, 187 No. 194, 197 No. 260, 200 No. 287, 205 No. 322, 225 No. 475, 337 No. 505, 339 No. 520; XX, 114 No. 692, 123 No. 755.

It doubtless was in connection with these generally disturbed conditions that the king felt the need to issue, on December 5, 1365, a general safe-conduct for the Jews of the entire kingdom condemning all assailants of their persons or property as "bruisers" (*machechores*). Two months later the bailiff of Pamplona was told that, "in view of the hatred, ill will and evil deeds with which the high lords [*grandes gentes*] passing on their way to Spain treat Jews especially," he should allow the local Jews to leave their quarter and seek shelter in the rest of the city, where they were to be "received with love [*amorablement*]." At the same time the government appealed to the Jewries of the country urgently to advance it the funds needed to pay the Navarrese troops. From time to time Jews were also called upon not only to man the walls of their own quarter, but also to participate in the defense of certain forts. On February 20, 1366 the commander of the castle of Ruesta was ordered to evacuate the Jewish women and children to Sangüesa, because the Jews as well as the Christians had sworn to defend the castle. See *ibid.,* XIX, 191 No. 217, 218 No. 418, 220 No. 434, 339 No. 517, 341 No. 532.

43. F. Idoate Iraqui in *Principe de Viana,* XVIII–XX, *passim,* esp. XIX, 228 No. 499; Baer, *Die Juden,* I, Part 1, pp. 965 f. No. 591, 969 ff. No. 595 with the informative notes thereon; and, more generally, S. H. Duvergé's brief *Notes sur la politique économique de Charles le Mauvais en Navarre;* and J. M. Lacarra's *El Desarollo urbano de las ciudades de Navarra y Aragón en la edad media.* The comeback staged by the younger Ezmel de Ablitas is the more remarkable since he had been involved in the difficult liquidation of his grandfather's estate in 1342 and was even forced on this occasion to take a rather unusual oath, cited by Kayserling in *Die Juden in Navarra,* p. 55.

Our knowledge of the history of Navarre Jewry still leaves much to be desired. Although a century old, Kayserling's work has not yet been superseded. Much documentary evidence, however, has been added, especially by J. Jacobs in *An Inquiry*, pp. xxxv ff., 82 ff. (from the Pamplona archives); and by Baer in *Die Juden*, I, Part 1, pp. 919–1005, 1034–37. There also have been some monographs on certain phases of that history, such as J. M. Millás Vallicrosa, ed., "Contratos de Judíos y Moriscos del reino de Navarra," *AHDE*, X, 273–86; F. Idoate Iraqui, "Historia menuda. Moros y Judíos en Tudela en 1343," *El Pensamiento navarro* (Oct. 12, 1954); and, more generally, J. R. Castro's ed. of the "Memorias históricas de Tudela de Fray José Vicente Diaz Bravo," *Principe de Viana*, XI, 251–65; XII, 289–303; XIII, 149–66, 378–404; XIV, 99–124, 276–345; XV, 157–94.

44. J. Jacobs, *An Inquiry*, p. 92 No. 3459. As elsewhere, the statistical data for the medieval Jewish population in Navarre are both scarce and unreliable. Even more than in other parts of the Peninsula, Jews seem to have lived scattered through many small localities, including some villages, from which no records have come down to us. See *supra*, n. 41. Some data for Pamplona, Tudela, Sangüesa, and Tafalla in 1366 have been supplied by Joseph Jacobs, who always evinced great interest in Jewish demography. See pp. 150 f. More comprehensive are the figures suggested by Baer in *Die Juden*, I, Part 1, pp. 941 ff. No. 385, 971 ff. No. 596 and his note thereon, pp. 976 f.; and by F. de Mendoza in *Principe de Viana*, XII, 263 f. These problems will be more fully discussed *infra*, Chap. LI.

45. C. Erdmann, *Papsturkunden in Portugal*, p. 23. This relative neglect is doubly remarkable, as there had been some interest in Portuguese-Jewish history even in non-Jewish scholarly circles in Italy in the mid-nineteenth century. See *supra*, Vol. IV, p. 250 n. 40. For this reason, like his book on Navarre, M. Kayserling's *Geschichte der Juden in Portugal* still is of considerable value today. Amador de los Rios's *Historia social*, which was supposed to cover Portugal as well as Spain, is much weaker in its Portuguese sections. Nor has J. Mendes dos Remedios in his *Os Judeus em Portugal* greatly advanced our knowledge of medieval history, although he has helped to elucidate many phases of Marrano life during the period following the so-called expulsion of the Jews in 1496–97. Even the monographic literature is rather scarce, which fact will also explain the relative paucity of bibliographical references in the forthcoming notes. Some data may be derived, however, particularly in the realm of folklore, from such general surveys as J. A. Lima de Pires's *Mouros, judeos i negros na historia de Portugal*; and the comparative materials offered by F. Pérez Embid in *El Mudejarismo portugués*, 2d ed. See also, more generally, J. Verissimo Serrão's suggestive recent observations, "Da possibilidade de uma nova 'história de Portugal': método e fontes," *Anais* of the Academia portuguesa de história, 2d ser. XIII, 109–37.

46. Gregory IX's *Registres*, ed. by L. Auvray, I, 454 ff. No. 733; III, 146 f. Nos. 5000–5001; A. Potthast, *Regesta pontificum*, I, 824 No. 9673, 911 No. 10768; Grayzel, *The Church*, pp. 190 ff., 242 f.; and *supra*, Chaps. XXXVII, n. 40; XLII, n. 28. Portugal's general submission to the papal will and the considerable influence of the episcopate on all political affairs are attested by many contemporary documents. See especially the data assembled by C. Erdmann in *Das Papstum und Portugal in ersten Jahrhundert der portugiesischen Geschichte* (mainly dealing with the twelfth century); and by A. E. Reuter in her *Königtum und Episkopat in Portugal im 13. Jahrhundert*. The royal resistance, therefore, to this combined papal-episcopal on-

slaught is doubly noteworthy. See also, more generally, M. de Oliveira's *História ecclesiástica de Portugal*.

47. *Portugaliae Monumenta Historica, a saeculo octavo post Christum usque ad quintumdecimum*, published by the Academy of Science of Lisbon, *Leges et consuetudines*, pp. 739–939: Costumes e foros, esp. pp. 760, 777 f., 789, 823, 864 f., 880, 882, 910 f., 924 f.; *Collecção de livros inéditos de história portugueza*, likewise published by that Academy (José Correa da Serra, Secretary), IV, 527 ff., 555, 557 f., 566, 568; V, 456 ff., 475, 479, 483, 503, 505 f., 508, 513 f., 520 ff., in part excerpted by Kayserling in his *Geschichte der Juden in Portugal*, pp. 339 ff.; *Fuero de Usagre*, ed. by R. de Ureña y Smenjaud and A. Bonilla y San Martin, pp. 28, 85, 108 f., 138, 141; Baer, *Die Juden*, I, Part 2, pp. 28 f. No. 56. The mutual borrowings of Portuguese and Castilian *fueros* is the less surprising as Portugal had emerged into full independence only in the twelfth century, and local customs often disregarded such recent political divisions. See esp. E. Mayer, "Studien zur spanischen Rechtsgeschichte, I: Das Fuero de Sobrarbe," *ZRG*, Germanistische Abteilung, XL, 237. See also T. B. de Souza Soares, "Notas para a estudo das instituções municipais de Reconquista," *Revista portuguesa de história*, I, 71–92; II, 265–91; and the literature cited *supra*, nn. 27 and 43; and Vol. IV, pp. 253 ff. nn. 49–54.

48. The petitions of the Portuguese bishops are cited from archival sources by A. Herculano in his classical *Historia de Portugal*, III, 107, 128; and from there by Kayserling in his *Geschichte*, pp. 4 f. On Theotonio see *supra*, Vol. III, pp. 160, 308 n. 45. The agreement between Dinis and the Jews of Braganza is recorded by F. Brandão in his *Monarchia Lusitana*, V, 265a; VI, 26; Kayserling, pp. 18 f., 342 f. App. iii. This agreement reflects Dinis' great concern for the reconstruction of his old and newly won territories, a concern which dominated his thinking for nearly half a century. Like his Castilian and, to a lesser extent, his Aragonese contemporaries, he did not allow ecclesiastical demands and popular prejudices, inherited from the Visigothic age, to deter him from his major endeavors. See also *Crónica de D. Dinis*, ed. from an unpublished MS by C. da Silva Tarouca; ed. from a Porto MS by Ruy de Pina, *passim*. The freedom with which Jews otherwise dealt in real estate is illustrated by the contract of sale negotiated by one Moysen and his wife Auicibia with a Don Johan and his wife Marina for the sale of a house (*casal*) in Cintra (1272). See P. A. d'Azevedo, "Livro de João de Portel," *Archivo histórico portuguez*, V, 464 f. No. cxx.

49. *Documento de Bragança*, cited from I. de S. Roca de Viterbo's *Elucidario de palavras que em Portugal antiguamente se usarão*, I, 131, by Kayserling in his *Geschichte*, p. 9 n. 1. This important office of *arrabi moor*, similar in nature to the Castilian "rabbinate of the Court" and the English "archpresbyterate," will be discussed more fully in connection with other Jewish communal organizations in a later chapter.

50. The complaint of the Portuguese clergy of 1309 is quoted by F. Brandão in his *Monarchia Lusitana*, VII, 85; it is also later alluded to in the *Ordenaçoens do Senhor Rey Don Affonso V*, II, xv.26 f., 36 and 38. On the Cortes of Évora see Brandão, VIII, 243. See also the inventory prepared for an exhibition in 1940, ed. by A. A. Oliveira Neves [Toste] in his *Córtes do Reino de Portugal*. Despite his

personal unfriendliness, Alphonso IV effectively protected his Jewish subjects against any popular outbreaks during the Black Death. See Brandão, VII, 524; and on the serious effects of the plague on Portugal's population and economy, A. H. de Oliveira Marques and his associates' researches, *Para a estudo da Peste Negra em Portugal*, a preliminary report on which was submitted by Oliveira Marques in November 1959, to the Congresso histórico de Portugal medievo in Braga. See the summary in the *Revista portuguesa de história*, IX, 336. Interesting sidelights on the career of a foreigner living in that period in Lisbon are shed by Y. Renouard's biographical sketch of "Un Français du Sud-Ouest, évêque de Lisbonne au XIVème siècle: Thibaud de Castillon (1348–1356), sa fortune, ses placements et ses relations avec les hommes d'affaires de son temps," *BEP*, XIII, 29–51, which shows that it took the bishop four years from his appointment to reach his episcopal see in 1352. With considerable modifications Thibaud's experiences might have been duplicated by a prominent Jewish immigrant during the Black Death era.

51. Fernão Lopes, *Chronica de Senhor Rei Pedro I*, v–vi, in the aforementioned *Collecção dos livros inéditos de história portuguesa*, IV, 18 ff.; idem, *Chronica d'el rey D. Fernando*, *ibid.*, IV, 121–525, esp. pp. 502 ff. See A. Brásio's observations on "Da Autoria da Crónica de D. Pedro I e da história geral do reino," *Anais* of the Academia portuguesa de história, 2d ser. VIII, 339–68 (attributes it mainly to Gomes Eannes de Zurara); Baer, *Die Juden*, I, Part 2, pp. 179 No. 187 n., 224 f. No. 230. The complexities of succession to Ferdinand and the subsequent war between the two pretenders are described at considerable length by S. Dias Arnaut in *A Crise nacional dos fins do século XIV*, Vol. I: A Successão de D. Fernando.

52. Fernão Lopes, *Chronica de [del rei] D. João I*, reedited from a manuscript in the National Archives of Tôrre de Tombo with a Foreword by A. Sérgio, Vol. I, pp. 34 ff., 128, 147, 155 ff., 248. The passage here quoted is given in a somewhat different form in E. Prestage's English trans. in *The Chronicles of Fernão Lopes and Gomes Eannes de Zurara*, pp. 41 f. On David Negro's role during the Portuguese-Castilian hostilities of 1383–84, see the observations and the document published by P. A. d'Azevedo in his "Culpas de David Negro," *Archivo histórico portuguez*, I, 53–57 (showing that David's services in Castile led in 1389 to his indictment on seventeen counts in Lisbon and the confiscation of all his remaining Portuguese possessions); and, with a bit of its customary confusion, Gedaliah ibn Yahya's chronicle *Shalshelet ha-qabbalah* (Chain of Tradition), Venice, 1587 ed., fol. 57b. See also Baer, *Die Juden*, I, Part 2, pp. 224 f. No. 230.

In view of Lopes' crucial significance for our knowledge also of the relations between the Jewish grandees and the Portuguese Crown, a critical reexamination of his veracity is quite important. Fortunately, many Portuguese and foreign historians have discussed and rediscussed the works of this writer, whom the Englishman Robert Southey called with abandon, "the greatest chronicler of any age or nation." Among recent studies one might mention especially A. E. Beau's "Os Elementos panegiricos nas Crónicas de Fernão Lopes" (1951) and "Caracteristicas da manifestação de sentimento nacional em Fernão Lopes" (1940), both reprinted in his *Estudos*, I, 41–61, 63–72. See also, more generally, the critical problems discussed by S. da Silva Neto in his *Textos medievais portuguêses e seus problemas;* and by A. Pimenta in the introduction and notes to his collection of *Fontes medievais da história de Portugal*, Vol. I.

53. Samuel Usque, *Consolaçam às tribulaçoens de Israel,* ed. with a Preface by J. Mendes dos Remedios, iii.21, in Part III, pp. xxii ff.; in M. A. Cohen's English trans., *Consolation for the Tribulations of Israel,* p. 194; and briefly repeated by Joseph b. Joshua ha-Kohen in his '*Emeq ha-bakha,* ed. by M. Letteris, p. 71 (Hebrew), and in M. Wiener's (slightly inexact) German trans., p. 66; Kayserling, *Geschichte der Juden in Portugal,* pp. 38 ff.; Boniface IX's bull of July 2, 1389, reproduced in Portuguese trans. in Alphonso (Affonso) V's *Ordenaçoens,* ii.94, 120, Vol. II, pp. 514 ff. See also J. P. Oliveira Martins, *Os Filhos de D. João I,* pp. 175 ff., 179 n. 1 (reprinting the trans. of the papal bull); and M. Caetano, "As Cortes de 1385," *Revista portuguesa de história,* V, 5–86, which confirmed John's election but had little to say about Jews. The story of Ferrer's nonadmission was doubtless overdramatized by rumors circulating among the Jews and thus reached Usque a century later in a distorted form. However, the fact that the preacher failed to extend his farflung missionary journeys to Portugal is best explained by such royal refusal. Even his purported earlier attendance at the Council of Santarém of 1381 is rightly denied by S. Brettle in his *San Vicente Ferrer und sein literarischer Nachlass,* p. 39 n. 3. See also the literature cited *supra,* Chap. XXXVIII, nn. 45–46.

54. See the text of the lengthy inscription, reproduced in Hebrew with a Spanish trans. and comments by F. Cantera, in his and J. M. Millás's ed. of *Las Inscripciones hebraicas de España,* pp. 338 ff.

CHAPTER XLV: DECLINE OF IBERIAN JEWRY

1. See the succinct summary offered by A. Ubieto *et al.*, in their recent *Introducción a la Historia de España*, pp. 152 ff.

2. D. S. Sassoon, "Thesaurus of Mediaeval Hebrew Poetry," *JQR*, XXI, 89–150 (a review of I. Davidson's *Oṣar ha-Shirah ve-ha-Piyyuṭ*), esp. p. 105, citing from his own MS Sassoon No. 670 item 84 (also in his *Ohel Dawid, Descriptive Catalogue of the Hebrew and Samaritan Manuscripts in the Sassoon Library*, II, 909 f.); Baer, *Die Juden*, I, Part 2, pp. 232 ff. No. 248, 236 No. 251. On the destruction of these two communities see also F. Fita, "La Judería de Madrid en 1391," *BAH*, VIII, 439–66, esp. pp. 454 f.; R. Ramirez de Arellano, "Matanzas judías en Córdoba, 1391," *ibid.*, XXXVIII, 294–311; and, more generally, L. Suárez Fernández, "Problemas políticos en la minoridad de Enrique III," *Hispania* (Madrid), XII, 163–231, esp. pp. 222 ff. App. ii. The estimate of 140,000 apostates is given by Reuben b. Nissim Gerondi in his flyleaf entry on the scroll of law handwritten by his father and now extant in Tiberias. See the text published, with an English trans., by A. M. Hershman in his *Rabbi Isaac ben Sheshet Perfet and His Times*, pp. 194 ff. Reuben's figure probably was but part of the larger total of 200,000 converts, cited by Abraham Zacuto in his *Sefer Yuḥasin*, ed. by H. Filipowski, p. 225a. See *infra*, n. 4; and, more fully, Chaps. LI and LVI.

3. Baer, *Die Juden*, I, Part 2, pp. 232 f. No. 248, 236 ff. Nos. 252–54. We shall see that some of the new converts, prompted either by the zeal of neophytes or by envy of the staunch orthodoxy of their former coreligionists, now became the source of much annoyance to the surviving communities. They not only kept on denouncing Jews to the authorities, but they also persistently preached conversion to their recalcitrant brethren.

4. On the role played by Solomon ha-Levi (Paul of Burgos) in the Regency Council of Castile during John II's minority, see L. Serrano, *Los Conversos D. Pablo de Santa Maria y D. Alfonso de Cartagena*, pp. 49 ff. Serrano passes over lightly the influence on Jewish status exerted by the former rabbi who had turned into an anti-Jewish controversialist. See *supra*, Chap. XXXIX n. 6 item 2.

5. See the data cited by A. Jiménez Soler in "Los Judíos españoles a fines del siglo XIV y principios del XV," *Universidad*, XXVII, 403 ff. Here, too, the death and exodus of many Jews led to the conversion of local synagogues into churches, often depriving the Jewish remnant of all houses of worship. Such a situation apparently arose in Fraga, which survived as a community but whose synagogue had been turned into a chapel. In a 1418 petition to the government, this building and its property rights were claimed by a priest who exaggeratingly asserted that the entire *aljama* had been converted to Christianity in 1391. See the text reproduced from a MS in the Vatican Archives by J. Goñi Gaztambide in "Conversión de la aljama de Fraga," *Hispania sacra*, XIII, 205–206. Other Aragonese communities are treated by J.

M. Sanz Artibucilla in "Los Judíos de Tarazona en 1391," *Sefarad*, VII, 63–92; J. Sánchez Real in "Los Judíos en Tarragona," *Boletín arqueológico* [*de Tarragona*], XLIV, 14–45; and in F. Delsors Coy's dissertation, *Los Judíos en Cataluña a fines del siglo XIV*, summarized in the *Revista de la Universidad de Madrid*, I. Other pertinent publications have been, or will be, mentioned in other notes.

6. Amador de los Rios, *Historia social*, II, 424 ff., 426 n. 1; F. Palacký, *Documenta Mag. Joannis Hus*, p. 540 No. 68; *supra*, Chap. XXXVIII, n. 8; Abraham b. Samuel Zacuto, *Sefer Yuḥasin* (Liber Juchassin sive lexicon biographicum et historicum), ed. by H. Filipowski, p. 225. See also the other sources cited by Graetz in his *Geschichte*, 4th ed., VIII, 113 n. 1. The divergent estimates of Ferrer's conversions mentioned by various chroniclers and modern historians, which range from 20,000 to 50,000, are noted by B. Llorca in his "San Vicente Ferrer y su labor en la conversión de los Judíos. En el centenario de su canonización," *Razón y Fé*, CLII, 277–96 (with further bibliographical data), esp. p. 296. They will be more fully discussed *infra*, Chap. LI.

Few of the protagonists, including the kings of both Castile and Aragon, in this great drama extending from 1391 to 1415, have been treated in comprehensive monographs. Next to Vicente Ferrer, for whom we possess a large—perhaps too large and repetitious—series of studies, only Pedro de Luna has thus far been the subject of a full-length biography. In addition to the literature cited *supra*, Chaps. XXXVIII, nn. 45–46; XXXIX, n. 2, see J. M. de Garganta and V. Forcada's *Biografía y escritos de San Vicente Ferrer*, offering a convenient collection of some of Ferrer's writings and sermons; and the following studies: J. E. Martínez Ferrando and F. Solsona Climent, "San Vicente Ferrer y la Casa Real de Aragón. Documentación conservada en el Archivo Real de Barcelona," *Analecta Sacra Tarraconensia*, XXVI, 1–143 (includes documentary appendix of 96 numbers); L. Batlle y Prats, "San Vicente Ferrer en Gerona," *ibid.*, pp. 145–50; A. C. Floriano, "San Vicente Ferrer y las aljamas turolenses," *BAH*, LXXXIV, 551–80 (includes a valuable documentary appendix, esp. p. 579 No. xxvii); F. Vendrell, "La Actividad proselitista de San Vicente Ferrer durante el reinado de Fernando I de Aragón," *Sefarad*, XIII, 87–104; V. Beltrán de Heredia, "San Vicente Ferrer, predicador de las sinagogas," *Salmanticensis*, II, 669–76. Some materials on the missionary activities of the renowned preacher were assembled in connection with his canonization in 1854. See M. Gual Camarena, *Trabajos para la canonización de San Vicente Ferrer*, Supplemento de Valencia, 1954, No. 6. On his part, Pedro de Luna found a recent apologist in A. Gascón de Gotor, who in his *Pedro de Luna. "El Pontífice que no cedió"* goes so far as to argue for the validity of Pedro's election to the papal throne. This view is, of course, not shared by the official Roman Church, in which Benedict XIII has always ranked among the rejected antipopes. See also F. Vendrell Gallostra, "La Política proselitista del rey D. Fernando I de Aragón," *Sefarad*, X, 349–66 (includes a documentary appendix, showing the special favors bestowed by the king on recent converts).

7. Baer, *Die Juden*, I, Part 1, pp. 654 ff. Nos. 409–10, 685 ff. Nos. 433–34; Part 2, pp. 259 f. No. 271; idem, *Toledot*, 2d ed., pp. 284 ff. On the subsequent growth of the Jewish community of Murviedro (Sagunto), see L. Piles Ros, "La Judería de Sagunto. Sus restos actuales," *Sefarad*, XVII, 352–73.

8. A. Morel-Fatio, "Notes et documents pour servir à l'histoire des Juifs des Baléares sous la domination aragonaise du XIIIᵉ au XVᵉ siècle," *REJ*, IV, 38 ff. Nos. 28–30, 36; A. L. Isaacs, *The Jews of Majorca*, pp. 76 ff.; and A. Pons's observations in "Los Judíos del reino de Mallorca," *Hispania* (Madrid), XVI.

9. The documents pertaining to the resettlement of the Jews in Barcelona and its ultimate failure have long been known from the *Colección de documentos inéditos del Archivo General de la Corona de Aragón*, VI, 438 ff.; and from F. Carreras y Candi, *La Ciutat de Barcelona*, pp. 496 f. See also M. Kayserling, "Zur Geschichte der Juden in Barcelona," *MGWJ*, XV, 81–95 (includes three documents dated 1392–97). On neighboring Valencia see L. Piles's brief observations in "Notas sobre Judíos del Reino de Valencia," *Sefarad*, XIII, 115 ff.; and his other studies listed *infra*, n. 13. We need not assume, however, that Jews totally disappeared from these important harbors. In 1436 Queen Maria, acting in behalf of Alphonso V, was sufficiently aroused by the purported close contacts between the Barcelona *conversos* and some professing Jews still living in that city that she renewed, and considerably amplified, the decree against such contacts, originally issued by King John I on April 13, 1393. See the text published by J. M. Madurell Marimón in "La Confradía de la Santa Trinidad de los conversos de Barcelona," *Sefarad*, XVIII, 72 ff. Evidently, many *conversos* had joined, perhaps even organized, this special brotherhood in order to camouflage more effectively their continuing relations with Jews. But the latter were no longer able to maintain an organized community of their own.

10. Luis Batlle y Prats, "Ordinaciones relativas a los Judios gerundenses," *Homenaje Millás*, I, 83–92 (includes a documentary appendix with the text of the four ordinances issued in 1445–48); M. de los Angeles Masiá, "Aportaciones al estudio del call gerundense," *Sefarad*, XIII, 287–308; Baer, *Die Juden*, I, Part 1, pp. 701 No. 447, 716 ff. No. 456, 732 ff. No. 464, with the notes thereon. See also L. Batlle y Prats and J. M. Millás Vallicrosa, "Noticias sobre la aljama de Gerona," *Sefarad*, V, 131–45. Notwithstanding its great difficulties and its small size the Gerona community still included a number of prominent Jewish families. See esp. S. Sobrequés Vidal, "Familias hebreas gerundenses. Los Zabarra y los Caravita," *Anales* of the Instituto de Estudios Gerundenses, II, 68–98. That throughout the fifteenth century the Jews remained but a small minority in the city's population is evident from the same author's study of the "Censo y profesión de los habitantes de Gerona en 1462," *ibid.*, VI, 193–246.

11. Baer, *Die Juden*, I, Part 1, pp. 758 ff. No. 472, 781 ff. No. 480, with the notes thereon. All these royal interventions failed to settle, however, the controversy between the Jewish community and the municipality of Lérida. As late as 1436, Queen Maria felt impelled to issue a new ordinance regulating the "modus vivendi et conversandi judaeorum . . . inter christianos." See the text published by Madurell Marimón in *Sefarad*, XVIII, 77 ff. No. 6. See also P. Sanahuja's rather colored description in *Lérida en sus luchas por la fé (Judíos, Moros, Conversos, Inquisición y Moriscos)*, which, however, mainly deals with the developments in the latter part of the fifteenth century. On Crescas see the brief sketch by J. M. Simón de Gilleuma, "Crescas Abnarrabi. Médico oculista de la Aljama Leridana," *Sefarad*, XVIII, 83–97.

12. Ḥisdai Crescas' Epistle to the communities of Avignon of 1391, reproduced in the Appendix to M. Wiener's ed. of Solomon ibn Verga's *Shebeṭ Yehuda*, pp. 128 f.; Baer, *Die Juden*, I, Part 1, pp. 724 ff. No. 461; M. Kayserling, *Die Juden in Navarra, den Baskenlaendern und auf den Balearen*, pp. 163 ff.; the order of the governor of Majorca of Nov. 22, 1393, published by A. Pons in *Hispania* (Madrid), XVI, 594 App. 69. See also A. L. Isaacs, *The Jews of Majorca*, pp. 80 ff.; *supra*, n. 8. For other monographic studies relating to Aragonese communities, see esp. J. Cabezudo Astrain, "Noticias y documentos sobre los Judíos zaragozanos en el siglo XV," *Sefarad*, XIV, 372–84 (includes interesting notarial documents), supplemented by his "La Expulsión de los Judíos zaragozanos," *ibid.*, XV, 103–36; and his "Médicos y curanderos zaragozanos en el siglo XV," *Archivo iberoamericano de historia de la medicina*, VII, 119–26 (identifying more than 40 Christian and about 25 Jewish physicians in the course of that century); and those listed in our earlier and forthcoming notes, esp. *supra*, Chap. XLIV, n. 26.

13. Baer, *Die Juden*, I, Part 1, pp. 712 ff. No. 453, 726 f. No. 462; the aforementioned studies by J. Sanchez Real in the *Boletín arqueológico*, XLIV, 14–45; and in *Sefarad*, XI, 339–48 (mainly for the period before 1391; includes notable reproductions); and L. Piles Ros's searching studies: "Los Judíos en la Valencia del siglo XV. El pago de deudas," *Sefarad*, VII, 151–56; "Judíos extranjeros en la Valencia del siglo XV," *ibid.*, pp. 354–60; "Los Judíos valencianos y la autoridad real," *ibid.*, VIII, 78–96; "Notas sobre Judíos del reino de Valencia," *ibid.*, XIII, 115–18; and, more broadly, "Situación económica de las aljamas aragonesas a comienzos del siglo XV," *ibid.*, X, 73–114, 367–84. On Fraga, see *supra*, n. 5.

14. J. Jacobs, *An Inquiry*, p. 76 Nos. 1317–18; K. Eubel, "Zu dem Verhalten der Päpste gegen die Juden," *Römische Quartalschrift*, XIII, 34 No. 5; Baer, *Die Juden*, I, Part 2, pp. 241 Nos. 256–57, 252 ff. Nos. 266–67, with the comments thereon. See also such local monographs as those by M. Méndez Bejarano, *Histoire de la juiverie de Seville*, for the starting point of Martinez' "unholy war"; F. Cantera Burgos, "La Judería de Burgos," *Sefarad*, XII, 59–104, esp. pp. 71 ff.; idem, *Alvar García de Santa María y su familia de conversos. Historia de la judería de Burgos y de sus conversos más egregios*, esp. pp. 9 ff.; and the other passages listed in the *Index* thereto, p. 606. With respect to the attitude of the Spanish cities to the Jews, one ought to consider also their general struggle for independence from both the Crown and the feudal lords. See, for instance, the stimulating summary by J. M. Lacarra, "El Desarollo urbano de las ciudades de Navarra y Aragón durante la Edad Media," *Pirineos*, VI, 5–34 (includes several fine maps and summaries in French, English, and German); other studies reviewed in the aforementioned bibliographical survey by J. M. Font Rius, in *VSW*, XLII, 137–51; and *supra*, Chap. XLIV, n. 27.

15. M. Lattes, "Una Convenzione daziaria fermata nel 1395 fra l'inviato veneto in Castiglia ed un Ebreo di Burgos," *Archivio Veneto*, V, 97–98; *infra*, Chap. XLVI, n. 88; and *supra*, Chap. XXXVIII, n. 46. See also Baer, *Die Juden*, I, Part 1, pp. 694 ff. Nos. 440–41, reproducing Hebrew letters by Astruc Rimoch of 1391, on the one hand containing Astruc's appeal for financial aid for the community which had to sell the costly implements of its synagogue, and on the other hand comforting his friend in Monzón whose father and brother had accepted baptism.

16. Baer, *Die Juden*, I, Part 1, pp. 740 ff. No. 467, 781 ff. No. 480 Art. 9, 984 No. 601. On the Jewish artisans and their role in both the Jewish economic and communal life, see, for instance, the interesting documents published by J. M. Madurell Marimón in "La Contratación laboral judaica y conversa en Barcelona (1349–1416). Documentos para su estudio," *Sefarad*, XVI, 33–71, 369–98; XVII, 73–102; and more fully *infra*, Chap. LI. Crescas and his associates were not necessarily permeated with antidemocratic feelings. Although it was quite natural for them to hold the wealthier and more educated members of their own entourage in higher esteem than the lower classes, they could justify their action by the existing emergency which taxed the best judgment and experience of communal leaders. At the same time the fiscal stringency of the communal budgets enforced rigid economies. Crescas' reform envisaged the subnormal daily stipend of 12 solidi for messengers engaged in communal missions and forbade any additional gifts to them, a limitation incidentally left untouched by the queen. This amount was insufficient to cover both the officials' travel expenses and the maintenance of their families at home. Moreover, Crescas himself experienced how difficult it was for him, even with royal aid, to collect from the impoverished communities the expenses he had incurred in their behalf. Hence only persons of independent means could afford to accept such assignments. On the progressive decline of the community of Tudela even before 1391 and the attempts at its reconstruction under the reign of Charles III, see Kayserling, *Die Juden in Navarra*, pp. 96 ff.

17. The fifteenth-century documents, to a large extent published and carefully scrutinized only in recent years, give but an inkling of the large number of converts during that crucial period between the riots of 1391 and the completion of the disputation of Tortosa in 1414. The figure of 200,000 mentioned by Abraham Zacuto may indeed not be too far from the truth. We possess, however, more detailed information only about a few leading individuals. See esp. the studies by F. Cantera Burgos, *La Conversión del célebre tamudista Salomon Levi (Pablo de Burgos)*; idem, *Alvar Garcia de Santa Maria*; L. Serrano y Pineda, *Los Conversos D. Pablo de Santa Maria y D. Alfonso de Cartagena*; F. Vendrell Gallostra, "Aportaciones documentales para el estudio de la familia Caballeria," *Sefarad*, III, 115–54; idem, "Concesión de nobleza a un converso," *ibid.*, VIII, 397–401 (includes the texts of two decrees of 1416 in favor of Egidio [Gil] Ruiz Najari, formerly Samuel Najari). The latter author has contributed much also to the understanding of the governmental policies of the time; see her aforementioned essays in *Sefarad*, X, 349–66; and XIII, 87–104. See also the additional notes assembled by Baer in his *Toledot*, esp. pp. 529 f. n. 38; *supra*, Chaps. XXXVII–XXXIX; and *infra*, nn. 39 ff. This entire subject will be more fully discussed *infra*, Chaps. LV–LVI.

18. J. Amador de los Rios, *Historia social*, II, 605 ff. App. xvi; Baer, *Die Juden*, I, Part 1, pp. 703 ff. No. 449, 755 Nos. 470–71, 796 f. No. 492, 807 f. No. 500, 816 ff. No. 505; Part 2, pp. 242 f. No. 258; J. Segura y Valls, *Aplech de documents curioses è inedits fahents per la historia de las costums de Catalunya, Jochs florals de Barcelona*, pp. 270 ff.; M. Serrano y Sanz, *Origenes de la dominación española en América*, I, p. xxxi. Serrano suggests that Gonzalo de la Cavalleria had gone to Rome rather than to Avignon. But the Roman antipope, John XXIII, generally evinced no interest in the Jewish question in Spain. Hence Baer (I, Part 1, p. 797) suggested that this "embassy" consisted merely in Gonzalo's original representation of Sara-

gossan Jewry at the disputation of Tortosa. However, it is quite likely that Gonzalo had made a trip to Avignon, perhaps in order to persuade Benedict to terminate the disputation. On its part, the government had to intervene from time to time against the people's excessive missionary propensities. On January 26, 1392 John I ordered the governor of Aragon to investigate the attempted forced conversion and robbery committed on two Jews of Daroca by the peasants of the vicinity and also the slaying of a Jew and his companion who were trying to collect debts in another village. *Ibid.*, Part 1, pp. 696 f. No. 443.

19. See the text published from the Vatican Archives by F. Perez-Aguado in "Un Congreso cristiano-rabbinico celebrado en Tortosa," *La Ciudad de Dios*, XXXIX, 111 ff.; and, more generally, A. Pacios Lopez, *La Disputa de Tortosa*, I, 44 f.; and *supra*, Chap. XXXVIII, nn. 39 ff. The impact of the disputation in many localities is well illustrated by a 1414 entry in the "Libro de los Jueces" of Teruel. Here a judge simply records a debate as to whether the messiah had already come and declares that "they found that he had come and many of the leading Jews turned Christian."

20. See *Cortes de los antiguos reinos de León y de Castilla*, II, 545 ff., cited in an abridged English trans. by E. H. Lindo in *The History of the Jews of Spain and Portugal*, pp. 182 ff.; Baer, *Die Juden*, I, Part 2, pp. 257 No. 268, 260 f. No. 273. See also M. Colmeiro's *Cortes de los antiguos reinos de León y de Castilla, Introducción*, I, 402 f. These vicissitudes in the legislation of the two realms will become clearer in our analysis in Chap. XLVIII.

21. J. Amador de los Rios, *Historia social*, II, 618 ff. App. xix; and, from another MS, Baer, *Die Juden*, I, Part 2, pp. 263 ff. No. 275; in A. H. Lindo's English trans. in *The History*, pp. 196 ff. It appears that, despite his considerable influence on the regents, Paul of Burgos had no direct share in the enactments of 1408 and 1412, as suggested by Amador de los Rios (II, 493 ff.). In the autumn of 1408 he was away on a mission in Perpignan, while in 1412 his influence as royal councilor was far behind that of Vicente Ferrer. See L. Serrano y Pineda, *Los Conversos*, pp. 54, 57 f.; and J. Torres Fontes, "Moros, Judíos y conversos en la regencia de Don Fernando de Antequera," *CHE*, XXXI–XXXII, 60–97, esp. p. 77 n. 19.

22. The Catalan version of Ferdinand I's decree was published by J. Villanueva in his *Viage literario a las iglesias de España*, ed. "con algunas observaciones" by J. L. Villanueva, XXII, 258 f. French and English summaries are offered by A. Morel-Fatio in *REJ*, IV, 40 ff. No. 38; and A. L. Isaacs in *The Jews of Majorca*, pp. 105 ff. See also Baer's comments in *Die Juden*, Part 1, pp. 790 f. No. 485. Benedict's bull, *Et si doctoris*, and its aftermath were discussed *supra*, Chap. XXXVIII, n. 46. See also F. Vendrell, "En torno a la confirmación real en Aragón de la Pragmática de Benedicto XIII," *Sefarad*, XX, 319–51; and, more generally, M. J. Tits-Dieuaide's ed. of *Documents relatifs au Grand Schisme. Lettres de Benoît XIII (1394–1422)*, II. The role of the two churchmen in the "Compromise of Caspe" is described by M. Luna in "Intervención de Benedicto XIII (D. Pedro de Luna) en el Compromiso de Caspe," *RABM*, 3d ser. XXVIII, (243–90) 343–90; and V. Genovés, *San Vicente Ferrer en la política de su tiempo*, pp. 29 ff. The participation of another ecclesiastical leader in these negotiations is discussed in S. d'Algaida's "Fra Joan Exemeno i la succesió a la Corona d'Aragón," *Estudios franciscanos*, XXXVII, 265–70; XXXVIII, 39–54. It

may be noted that to the Majorcan decree was added a postscript referring to specific dangers to the *conversos* of the Balearic Islands arising from the proximity of Jews.

At the same time Ferdinand did not hesitate to enact in 1413–14 two relatively tolerant decrees for the Jews of Fraga. See J. Salarrullana de Dios's data in *RABM*, XL, 204 f. His intervention in behalf of Nageri, mentioned in the text, is recorded in a document published by Baer in *Die Juden*, I, Part 1, pp. 794 f. No. 490. On the developments in Gerona and Teruel see *ibid.*, pp. 788 ff. Nos. 483–85 and 489, 829 ff. No. 515; E. C. Girbal, *Los Judíos en Gerona*, pp. 37 n. 2, 84 f. (citing the text of Ferdinand's order of February 25, 1413); J. de Chia, "El Ducado y el principado de Gerona: Apuntes históricos," *Revista de ciencias históricas*, III, 29 ff. (quoting excerpts from the resolution of Gerona's city council of January 9, 1414). Notwithstanding this sympathetic attitude of the city elders, the synagogue of Gerona was sealed as a result of Benedict's bull, an action which led to a lengthy litigation before the courts. It apparently ended with the return of the synagogue to the Jews. See M. de los Angeles Masiá's and other essays cited *supra*, n. 10; and C. Batlle Gallart, "Solución al problema de las dos sinagogas de Gerona," *Sefarad*, XIX, 301–20, based on a reconstruction from postexpulsion documents.

23. Solomon ibn Leḥamias Alami (Al'ammi), *Iggeret musar* (Epistle on Ethics), reed. by A. M. Habermann, p. 40; in L. Zunz's abridged German trans. under the title, "Eine alte Stimme" (1844), reprinted in his *GS*, II, 177–82. On this writer's unusual name, obviously of Arabic origin, see M. Steinschneider's comment in "An Introduction to the Arabic Literature of the Jews," *JQR*, [o.s.] XI, 486.

24. L. Serrano y Sanz, *Orígenes*, pp. 457 f.; Baer, *Die Juden*, I, Part 1, pp. 847 ff. No. 527 with the notes thereon; *supra*, Chap. XXXVIII, n. 16. Alphonso V's revocation of the anti-Jewish decrees of Ferdinand and Benedict is characterized even by a recent Spanish scholar as a "judaizing policy." See M. R. Jiménez Jiménez, "La Política judaizante de Alfonso V a la luz de las concesiones otorgadas en 1419 a la aljama de Murviedro," *Actas y comunicaciones* of the IV Congreso de historia de la Corona de Aragón, I, 325–36, publishing the decree addressed to Murviedro from the text preserved in the Municipal Archive of Saragossa. These Aragonese and Castilian monarchs and their reigns have been recorded in many contemporary sources and frequently discussed in modern literature. Among the chroniclers of the reign of the Castilian John II was the convert Alvar García de Santa María. See his "Crónica de Don Juan II de Castilla (1420–1434)," reedited by Marquis de la Fuensanta del Valle *et al.* in the *Colección de documentos inéditos*, XCIX, 79–495; C, 3–409; and M. Martínez's ed. of "Una Crónica inédita de Don Juan II de Castilla," *Ciudad de Dios*, LXXXVI, 90–105. Of some interest also are J. De Mata Carriazo's "Notas para una edición de la crónica de Alvar García," *Estudios . . . Menéndez Pidal*, III, 489–505; and his ed. of a "Sumario de la crónica de Juan II. Glosado por un converso en 1544," *Anales* of the Universidad hispalense (Seville), XII, 11–71. A good review of the extant MSS and the editions of Alvar's chronicle is offered by F. Cantera Burgos in his biography, *Alvar García de Santa María*, pp. 212 ff. Cantera neglects, however, that author's contributions to Spanish science on which see esp. the texts and comments in J. M. Millás Vallicrosa's more recent *Nuevos estudios sobre historia de la ciencia española*. On Henry IV's reign see esp. *Memorias de Don Enrique IV de Castilla;* and the somewhat colored biographical

sketch by J. Lucas Dubreton, *L'Espagne au quinzième siècle: Le Roi Sauvage*. See also F. Meregalli's succinct comments on *Cronisti e viaggiatori castigliani del quattrocento (1400–1474)*, pp. 7 ff., 83 ff.

Of importance also are studies of such leading statesmen as Álvaro de Luna, who for many years concentrated in his hands most of the governmental powers in Castile. J. Amador de los Rios's "Estudio histórico. El condestable D. Álvaro de Luna y sus doctrinas políticas y morales," *Revista de España*, XIX, 245–55, 469–86; and C. Silió's *Don Álvaro de Luna y su tiempo*, are therefore of considerable interest also for the position of Castilian Jewry. On the contemporary Aragonese kings, see esp. the series of papers presented at the Centro de cultura Valenciana entitled *Homenaje a Alfonso el Magnánimo*, and published with an introduction by S. Carreres Zacarés; and J. Vicens Vives's comprehensive biography of *Juan II de Aragón (1398–1479). Monarquía y revolución en la España del siglo XV*, esp. pp. 28, 54. Pope Martin V and his successors are discussed *infra*, Chap. XLVI, nn. 44 ff.

25. L. Luszczki, "La Predicazione del B. Matteo d'Agrigento a Barcellona e Valenza," *AFH*, XLIX, 225–351, esp. pp. 270, 294 ff. Nos. 28–29; A. Jiménez Soler in *Universidad*, XXVIII, 412 f.; the "Alba Bible" published under the title *Biblia (Antiguo Testamento). Traducida del hebreo al castellano por Rabi Mose Arragel de Guadalfajara (1422–1433?) y publicada por el Duque de Berwick y Alba*. On the illustrations in the remarkable manuscript of the Alba Bible see R. Vishnitzer (Wischnitzer), "Illuminated Haggadahs," *JQR*, XIII, 193 f. Arragel's was not the only translation into Spanish prepared by Jews, either for their own use or, after collaboration with Christian scholars, for the use of the Christian public. Often the purpose was not stated and it is mere guesswork whether one finds in these texts traces of apologetics or merely achievements of philologically trained translators interested in the accuracy of their versions. See M. Morreale's recent discussion of "El Códice de los 'Profetas' en latín y castellano que se conserven en la Biblioteca de la R. Academia de la Historia (87)," *BAH*, CL, 133–49; and her "Apuntes bibliográficos para la iniciación al estudio de las traducciones bíblicas medievales en castellano," *Sefarad*, XX, 66–109. See also J. Llama's detailed reviews of "La Antigua Biblia castellana de los Judíos españoles," *ibid.*, IV, 219–44; "Nueva Biblia medieval judía e inédita en romance castellano," *ibid.*, IX, 53–74; and "Antigua Biblia judía medieval romanceada," *ibid.*, XI, 289–304; T. Ayuso Marazuela's "La Biblia de Huesca: Otro importante códice aragonés," *Universidad* (Saragossa), XIII, 161–210 (trans. *ex hebraico;* also lists several of the author's earlier monographs relating to the Bibles of Calatayud, Calahorra, Lérida, and Oña); and the host of other writings which will be analyzed in a later chapter in connection with Spanish Jewry's contributions to biblical learning.

Growing hostility of large segments of public opinion toward both Jews and *conversos* is clearly reflected in contemporary art and belles lettres. Numerous illustrations can readily be found in J. Caro Baroja's comprehensive *Los Judíos en la España moderna y contemporanea*, esp. I, 83 ff., 100 ff. This suggestive work, written by an ethnologist rather than an historian, has been subjected to severe criticisms by both Spanish and Hebrew scholars. See the reviews by J. L. Lacave in *Sefarad*, XXIII, 377–88; and by H. Beinart in *KS*, XXXIX, 346–57 (Hebrew). However, the materials assembled and the insights presented by the author are quite valuable, especially for the period after the expulsion. See also A. Portnoy, *Los Judíos en la literatura española medieval;* S. Resnick's dissertation, *The Jew as Portrayed in*

Spanish Medieval Literature, briefly summarized in his article, "The Jew as Portrayed in Early Spanish Literature," *Hispania* (America), XXXIV, 54–58; E. Glaser, "Referencias antisemitas en la literatura peninsular de la Edad de Oro," *Nueva Revista de Filología hispánica,* VIII, 39–62 (mainly relating to *conversos*); and such more detailed analyses as F. Vendrell Gallostra, "Las Posición del poeta Juan de Dueñas respecto a los Judíos españoles de su época," *Sefarad,* XVIII, 108–13. Among the literary assailants of Jews and Judaism stand out in particular the authors of the vast polemical literature of the period, such as Alphonso de Spina, as well as the frequently anonymous poets who aimed the shafts of their bitter satires at both the Jews and the *conversos.* See *supra,* Chap. XXXVIII, n. 4 item 9; *infra,* n. 39. Those aspects of anti-Judaism primarily nurtured from folkloristic sources will be more fully dealt with *infra,* Chap. XLIX.

26. M. Serrano y Sanz, *Orígenes de la dominación española,* I, pp. clxxxv ff.; E. C. Girbal, "Un Testamento hebreo de la edad media," *Revista de Gerona,* VI, 104 ff.; J. Cabezudo Astrain, "Testamentos de Judíos aragoneses," *Sefarad,* XVI, 136–47 (dated in 1484–91). The polarity in feelings and actions often characterizing the relations between the Jews and the *conversos* will be more fully discussed *infra,* Chap. LVI.

27. L. Comenge, "Los Archiatros de la Corona de Aragón," *Boletín* of the R. Academia de Buenas Letras de Barcelona; J. Cabezudo Astrain, "Medicos y curanderos zaragozanos en el siglo XV," *Archivo iberoamericano de historia de medicina,* VII, 119–26; Kayserling, *Die Juden in Navarra,* pp. 88 f.; Baer, *Die Juden,* I, Part 1, pp. 992 ff. No. 603, 1001 f. No. 605. A Jewish astrologer, Mosen Bazo in Navarre is mentioned in a document of 1423, cited by F. de Mendoza in *Príncipe de Viana,* XII, 247. On the Spanish Jewish physicians see also the literature listed *supra,* Chap. XLIV, n. 36; and the general treatment of the Jewish role in medieval medicine in later chapters.

28. A. Millares Carlo, "Indice y extractos del *Libro horadado* del Concejo madrileño (siglos XV–XVI)," *Revista de la Biblioteca, Archivo y Museo,* I, 46–101, esp. pp. 49 f. Nos. 6 and 9, 69 No. 96, summarized by J. Weill in his "Notes sur l'histoire des Juifs en Espagne et Portugal au XVᵉ siècle," *REJ,* LXXVIII, 92; Baer, *Die Juden,* I, Part 1, pp. 877 No. 548; Part 2, pp. 313 f. No. 299, 325 ff. No. 313. On the incident in Haro see also P. León Tello, "Nuevos documentos sobre la judería de Haro," *Sefarad,* XV, 157–69 (includes a royal decree with renewals to 1342 and a judgment in a tax litigation between the city and the community rendered in 1476). These generally favorable actions of the Castilian Crown did not prevent Henry IV, however, from renewing in 1456, at the request of certain localities in the district of Rioja, the highly discriminatory decree of 1405. See the text published by F. Cantera in *La Usura judía en Castilla* (reprinted from *La Ciencia tomista*), 2d ed., pp. 24 ff.; and *supra,* n. 20.

29. The tragic end of Don Meir Alguades is known to us mainly from the biased account of Alphonso de Spina, who claims to have heard the story indirectly from an eyewitness. See his *Fortalitium fidei,* end; and other sources briefly analyzed by Graetz in his *Geschichte,* 4th ed., VIII, 95 f. n. 1. Graetz cogently argues that, despite the hearsay nature of De Spina's report unsupported by any Jewish source, we need not doubt Meir's unnatural death. A remarkable summary of the Valladolid

resolutions of 1432 was edited, almost a century ago, from a Paris MS, by F. Fernández González in his "Ordenamiento formado por los procuradores de las aljamas hebreas, pertenecientes al territorio de los estados de Castilla, en la asamblea celebrada en Valladolid el año 1432," *BAH*, VII, 145–89, 275–305, 395–413; VIII, 10–27. It was translated into German by M. Kayserling in "Das Castilianische Gemeinde-Statut (*Taqqanah*). Zugleich ein Beitrag zu den Rechts-, Rabbinats- und Gemeinde-Verhältnissen der Juden in Spanien," *Jahrbuch für die Geschichte der Juden*, IV, 263–334; and reproduced in an abridged English rendition in L. Finkelstein's *Jewish Self-Government in the Middle Ages*, pp. 348 ff. See also I. Loeb's comparative study of the "Règlement des Juifs de Castille en 1432 comparé avec les règlements des Juifs en Sicile et d'autres pays," *REJ*, XIII, 187–216. Many details had to be modified, however, in the light of the much-improved version of the same Paris MS published by Baer in *Die Juden*, I, Part 2, pp. 280 ff. No. 287. See also my *The Jewish Community*, esp. the passages listed in its Index, Vol. III, p. 385.

The provisions of this important synod as well as the functions of the various court rabbis of Castile during the fifteenth century will be more fully analyzed in a later chapter. But this document furnishes also new insights into the government's interest in Jewish autonomy and the latter's frequent utilization of the chief rabbis' authority for better fiscal exploitation. Needless to say, respect for Jewish self-government did not prevent the kings from interfering in the communities' inner affairs whenever it pleased them. On one occasion, John II of Aragon simply ordered the community of Huesca to appoint one Isach Arrundi as its communal rabbi, notwithstanding its earlier election of a "foreign Jew" to that office (1460). See Baer, Part 1, p. 877 No. 547.

30. V. Beltrán de Heredia, "San Vicente Ferrer," *Salmanticensis*, II, 673; Baer, *Die Juden*, I, Part 1, pp. 856 ff. No. 533, 864 ff. No. 543; Part 2, pp. 275 ff. No. 281; E. C. Girbal, *Los Judíos en Gerona*; S. Sobrequés Vidal, "Contribución a la historia de los Judíos de Gerona. Familias hebreas gerundenses: Los Zabarra y los Caravita," *Anales* of the Instituto de Estudios Gerundenses, II, 68–98; his "Familias hebreas gerundenses: Los Falcó," *ibid.*, III, 113–26; Serrano, *Origenes de la dominación española*, p. cccclxvi (App. No. xxvii). See also F. Vendrell de Millás, "Al margen de la organización de la aljama judaica de Zaragoza," *Sefarad*, XXIV, 81–106, publishing a new constitution of 1415. One wonders how the community of Saragossa managed to enforce the collection of any dues from apostates. That provision is, indeed, omitted from the text of the statutes governing the wine as well as the meat taxes in Saragossa, published by Serrano in *Origenes*, pp. cccclxviii ff. (App. Nos. xxviii and xxix).

The destruction of the community of Ocaña in 1391 is recorded by Solomon ibn Verga following his main source, Shem Ṭob ibn Shem Ṭob. This author was identical with either the well-known kabbalist of that name or his grandson, writing in the early or late fifteenth century, respectively. Neither had been an eyewitness to these events, and his report had evidently undergone many changes before it reached Ibn Verga. See the latter's *Shebeṭ Yehudah*, xlviii, ed. by Wiener, p. 88; in Wiener's German trans., pp. 179 f.; ed. by Shohet, p. 119; and the comments thereon by F. Baer in his *Untersuchungen über Quellen und Komposition des Schebet Jehuda*, pp. 34 ff. However, the fact itself of the massacre and of the decline of Ocaña Jewry need not be doubted. On the communities of that entire district see also F. Giménez de Gregorio, "La Población en la Jara toledana," *Estudios geográficos*, XLIV, 527–81.

31. Baer, *Die Juden*, I, Part 1, pp. 875 f. Nos. 544–45, 883 ff. No. 550 (with the notes thereon); Part 2, pp. 313 No. 298, 331 ff. Nos. 319–20. John's intervention in behalf of the two Tudelan Jews, in his capacity as king of Navarre through his marriage to Charles III's daughter, Blanche, may have been but part of a broader diplomatic action, although the purported treaty between Aragon and England, allegedly concluded in Valencia in 1459, has recently been rejected by A. Fernández Torregrosa in his "Aspectos de la política exterior de Juan II de Aragón," *Estudios de historia moderna*, II, 99–132. In Aragon, too, where he resided more or less permanently, John was forced to issue, in 1459, special orders for the protection of the Jews of Lérida against assaults by students, as well as of those of Teruel who had left their city because of a raging pestilence. See Baer, Part 1, p. 876.

32. The Segovia sermon of June 17, 1452 is briefly excerpted in H. Hirschfeld's *Descriptive Catalogue of the Hebrew MSS. of the Montefiore Library*, p. 13 No. 61, 2. The attacks in, and subsequent expulsion of the Jews from, Cordova are reflected in an interesting testament by a *converso*, analyzed by S. Mitrani-Samarian in "Le Sac de Cordoue et le testament d'Anton de Montoro," *REJ*, LIV, 236–40. See also, more generally, M. S. Ortí Belmonte, "El Fuero de Córdoba y las clases sociales en la ciudad. Mudéjares y Judíos en la edad media," *Boletín* of the R. Academia de Córdoba, XXV, 5–94. The legends concerning Antichrist may the more readily have come to the attention of *conversos*, as that subject had been heatedly debated in Spanish theological circles. See esp. J. Carreras Artau, "La Polémica gerundense sobre el Anticristo entre Arnau de Vilanova y los dominicanos," *Anales* of the Instituto de Estudios Gerundenses, V, 5–72.

The Jewish part, both active and passive, in the various dramatic events of the period has never been fully analyzed; it can be gleaned mainly from the numerous local histories, such as those mentioned *supra*, Chap. XLIV, nn. 6 and 26. See also A. Rodríguez Herrero, *Valmaseda en el siglo XV y la aljama de los Judíos*, esp. pp. 141 ff., 177 ff., 255, which is of interest mainly for the last years before the expulsion. Much can also be learned from general monographs shedding tangential light on the Jewish situation as well; for instance, S. Sobrequés Vidal, "Los Orígenes de la revolución catalana del siglo XV—Las Cortes de Barcelona de 1454–1458," *Estudios de historia moderna*, II, 1–96; and various essays published in the *Estudios de historia social de España*, particularly M. J. Aragoneses, "Los Movimientos y luchas sociales en la baja edad media," I, 275–423; and L. Piles, "La Situación social de los Moros de realengo en la Valencia del siglo XV," *ibid.*, pp. 225–74.

33. U. R. Burke, *A History of Spain*, I, 384 ff.; Cortes of Burgos of 1430 in *Cortes . . . de León y de Castilla*, III, 88; Lindo, *The History*, pp. 217 f.; Baer, *Die Juden*, I, Part 2, pp. 279 ff. Nos. 286–87, 320 No. 305 and n. 1; Neuman, *The Jews in Spain*, II, 365 ff. On the date and proceedings of the Cortes of Burgos, see M. Colmeiro's *Cortes de los antiguos reinos de León y de Castilla. Introducción*, I, 444 ff. ("They give a very sad notion of John II's reign"). That despite his need of friends the king could so readily brush aside the wishes of the Estates was constitutionally quite permissible. See V. K. (W.) Piskorskii's analysis of *Kastilskie kortezy v perekhodnuiu epoku (1180–1520)* (The Cortes of Castile in the Transition Period from the Middle Ages to Modern Times, 1180–1520), or in the Spanish trans. by C. Sanchez Albornoz entitled *Las Cortes de Castilla*, pp. 128 ff.

Much too little has thus far been written about the life and work of Joseph ibn Shem Ṭob as both statesman and writer. In fact, no significant biographical or literary data have been published since the days of S. Munk and H. Graetz during the last century. See the former's *Mélanges de philosophie juive et arabe*, pp. 507 f.; and Graetz, *Geschichte der Juden*, 4th ed., VIII, esp. Excursus iv.2, pp. 421 f. Many of Joseph's controversial tracts and other works are still dormant in manuscripts; see the few references to his polemical works *supra*, Chaps. XXXVIII, n. 28; XXXIX, n. 7 item 10. Surely a comprehensive biographical study of this physician, scholar, apologist, and statesman would shed some interesting new light also on the equivocal status of Castilian Jewry in the crucial years before the reign of Isabella.

34. M. Stern, *Urkundliche Beiträge über die Stellung der Päpste zu den Juden*, I, 37 No. 26, 45 f. Nos. 38–40; *Bullarium romanum, ad* 1442 No. xxix, Turin, 1860 ed., V, 67 ff.; *supra*, Chap. XXXVII, nn. 36 and 47; and *infra*, Chap. XLVI, nn. 46–47. Nicholas V's confirmatory decree on March 1, 1451 is reproduced in O. Raynaldus, *Annales ecclesiastici ad* 1451 No. v, Vol. IX, pp. 570 f. The respective popes' attitudes toward *conversos* will be treated in other contexts. As a matter of fact the Spanish clergy had difficulties in enforcing the anti-Jewish canonical provisions among its own adherents. On his inspection tour through the archdiocese of Toledo in 1436, one Matheos Sanchez found much neglect of both the general requirements of canon law and the specific resolutions of the synods of Alcalá held under the archbishop's chairmanship. He pointed out, therefore, to the inhabitants of Brihuega that they must not allow Jews to keep Christian employees in their homes or eat with them; that they should forbid Jews and Moors to work in public on Sundays and holidays; and that no Jewish or Moorish physician or carpenter should be permitted to visit a convent except in the company of a Christian. According to Sanchez, the contrary practices could be observed daily. In 1449, Pope Nicholas V was told that to stave off a pestilence the Jews of Seville had staged a public procession in exact emulation of the Christian rites and at a time when Christian processions were traversing the streets of the city, thus causing much annoyance to their Christian neighbors. Most remarkably, a canon who had violently objected to that practice was excommunicated by archepiscopal officials and, after ultimately being cleared in Rome, he was put in prison by them. This incredible complaint of a disgruntled cleric sufficiently impressed the pope to demand a careful inquiry and, if such abuse of ecclesiastical authority should really have occurred, the payment of an indemnity to the canon and the punishment of all guilty persons. See Stern, I, 48 No. 43; Baer, *Die Juden*, I, Part 2, pp. 302 No. 289, 315 No. 301.

35. J. Amador de los Rios, *Historia social*, III, 583 ff. (App. ii), here given in a variant of the English trans. by Lindo in *The History*, pp. 221 ff.

36. F. Fita, "La Judería de Jerez de la Frontera," *BAH*, XII, 72 ff., 75; Baer, *Die Juden*, I, Part 2, pp. 327 f. No. 314, 329 ff. Nos. 316 and 318. On Oropesa and his general attitude toward Jews and Judaism see J. de Sigüenza, *Historia de la orden de San Jeronimo*, ed. by J. Catalina García, pp. 361 ff.

37. Baer, *Die Juden*, I, Part 1, pp. 858 ff. Nos. 535–37, 876 ff. Nos. 545–47, 883 ff. Nos. 550–52; A. L. Isaacs, *The Jews of Majorca*, pp. 110 ff.; J. M. Millás Vallicrosa, "Notas históricas sobre la judería de Vich," *Sefarad*, XXII, 312–20 (mainly using

thirteenth-century materials). Another interesting royal intervention in behalf of a Jewish tailor is recorded in 1434, with reference to one Abraham Abayn in Paterna, in the province of Valencia. See L. Piles Ros, "Notas sobre Judíos del reino de Valencia," *Sefarad*, XIII, 115 ff. In general, however, after the breakdown of 1391 and 1413–14 Aragonese Jewry never regained its former strength and decidedly ranked far behind the more populous, affluent, and culturally leading communities of Castile. This relative decline was true also in the general relations between the two Spanish kingdoms.

38. M. Kayserling, *Die Juden in Navarra*, pp. 101 ff., 211 f. App. K; F. de Mendoza in *Principe Viana*, XII, 247 f. On the Jewish quarter in the Navarrería of Pamplona see J. J. Uranga, "La Población de la Navarrería de Pamplona," *ibid.*, XIII, 80 ff.; and other sources listed *supra*, Chap. XLIV, nn. 37 ff.

39. H. Pflaum, "Une Ancienne satire espagnole contre les Marranes," *REJ*, LXXXVI, 131–50; and, more generally, M. Menéndez Pelayo, "La Sátira política en tiempo de Enrique IV," *Estudios de Deusto* (Bilbao), LXXX, 19–37. Of course, satires were two-edged swords, the *conversos* reciprocating by sharply criticizing the existing social order. See their numerous satirical works cited by Américo Castro in his *La Réalidad histórica de España*, p. 531 n. 17. Examples of the entry of numerous *conversos* into the ranks of nobility, learned professions, and city councils are given in F. Vendrell's aforementioned data on the conferral of nobility on Samuel Najari in *Sefarad*, VIII, 397–401; as well as in the following essays: J. M. Madurell Marimón, *Documentos para la historia de la imprenta y librería en Barcelona (1474–1553)*, ed. with notes by J. Rubió y Balaguer (showing that almost all librarians were *conversos*); F. Márquez Villanueva, "Conversos y cargos concejiles en el siglo XV," *RABM*, 5th ser. LXIII, 503–40. (The first forty years of the fifteenth century mark the period of "their penetration, slow, efficacious, and propitious, into the various councils," especially in Andalusia.) See also A. Santamaría Arández, "En torno a la situación de los Judíos conversos de Mallorca en el siglo XV," *Boletín* of the Sociedad Arqueológica Luliana, XXXI, 185–97. The obvious racial overtones in the anti-Marrano movement, which led to the circulation of the *Libro verde de Aragón* and similar tracts in Castile and elsewhere, have long been recognized. They will be discussed in some detail *infra*, Chap. LVI.

Needless to say, such prominent *conversos* as Alvar García de Santa María, Paul of Burgos, and the latter's son, Alonso of Cartagena, who succeeded his father in the bishopric of Burgos, managed to live beyond any cloud of suspicion. In fact, Alonso courageously took up the cudgel for his suspected confreres in a tractate apparently written under the impact of the events of 1449. See the new edition of his *Defensorium unitatis christianae* (tratado en favor de los Judíos conversos), ed. with an Introduction and Notes by M. Alonso. See also M. Martínez Burgos, "Don Alonso de Cartagena, obispo de Burgos. Su Testamento," *RABM*, LXIII, 81–110 (Latin with a Spanish trans.); and the literature listed *supra*, n. 25; and Chap. XXXVIII, n. 8. This effective defense was shortly thereafter supported by the influential voice of Cardinal Juan de Torquemada in his *Tractatus contra Madianitas et Ismaelitas* (Defensa de los judíos conversos), ed. with an Introduction and Notes by N. López Martínez and V. Proaño Gil. Yet the venom of *anticonverso* sentiment spread ever more widely, ultimately contributing greatly to the tragic dénouement of 1492.

40. Raynaldus, *Annales ecclesiastici ad* 1449 No. xii, *ad* 1451 No. vi (Vol. IX, pp. 540 f., 571 f.); Stern, *Urkundliche Beiträge*, I, 50 No. 45, 57 No. 51; Baer, *Die Juden*, I, Part 2, pp. 315 f. Nos. 302, 304 and 308; and B. Llorca's *Bulario pontificio de la Inquisición española en su periodo constitucional (1478–1525)*. The uprising in Toledo is recorded, not without many ambiguities, in the *Memorias de Don Enrique IV*. On the likely toning down of its anti-Marrano references by a later *converso* copyist, see Baer's remark, p. 318; and, more generally, Alonso de Palencia, *Crónica de Enrique IV*, trans. by A. Paz y Mélia, I, 15 f. Some information may also be gathered from the biased account in Alphonso de Spina's *Fortalitium fidei* (Fortress of Faith), discussed *supra*, Chap. XXXIX, n. 4 item 9; and other sources analyzed by E. Benito Ruano in his "Don Pero Sarmiento, Repostero Mayor de Juan II de Castilla," *Hispania* (Madrid), XVII, 483–504; and "La 'Sentencia-Estatuto' de Pero Sarmiento contra los conversos toledanos," *Revista de la Universidad de Madrid*, VI, 277–306. See also, more generally, his *Toledo en el siglo XV* (with another volume promised relating to the city's socioeconomic and administrative evolution during that century). Of interest also is F. Jiménez de Gregorio's *Toledo y sus constantes*, showing a certain continuity in the city's attitudes also to its religious minorities.

This is not the place to discuss at length the Spanish Inquisition and its impact upon the Marranos, which will be done *infra*, Chaps. LV–LVI. For the time being it will suffice to refer to H. C. Lea's standard works, *A History of the Inquisition of the Middle Ages;* and *A History of the Inquisition in Spain;* C. Roth, *A History of the Marranos;* B. Llorca, "La Inquisición española y los conversos judíos o 'marranos,'" *Sefarad*, II, 113–51 (includes the records of a Teruel trial in 1484–85); and A. Domínguez Ortiz, "Los 'Cristianos Nuevos.' Notas para el estudio de una clase social," *Boletín* of the University of Granada, XXI, 249–97. See also J. Caro Baroja's suggestive observations in *Los Judíos en la España moderna*, I, 115 ff.; and B. Netanyahu's analysis of "The Marranos According to the Hebrew Sources of the 15th and Early 16th Centuries," *Proceedings* of the American Academy for Jewish Research, XXXI, 81–164. Of course, in view of the secrecy surrounding all Marrano life we must lean heavily upon the data uncovered in various inquisitorial trials. In spite of the obvious bias of the prosecutors and the frequent unfairness of the proceedings, the testimonies gathered in these trials cannot be so lightly dismissed as is done by E. Rivkin in "The Utilization of Non-Jewish Sources for the Reconstruction of Jewish History," *JQR*, XLVIII, 183–203. These "confessions" and other attestations are accepted at their face value by no one, not even by most apologists for the Inquisition. But to discard them entirely because of some preconceived "structural configuration" would be an even more blatantly uncritical approach. See *infra*, n. 47; and Chap. LVI.

41. The literature on the "Catholic kings" is enormous. Since the story of both the expulsion of the Jews from Spain and the impact of the Inquisition on their lives before and after will be more fully considered in other connections (esp. Chaps. L and LV–LVI), we need but concern ourselves here with certain other sociopolitical developments as well as the more personal aspects of the royal pair and their relations with Jews. Some Jews, and particularly *conversos*, took a hand in the dangerous intrigues and negotiations (including the transportation of the famous pearl necklace estimated at 40,000 gold florins in value) which ended in the marriage of the Castilian princess to her cousin, the Infante of Aragon. On the numerous

legends spun around this marriage, including the alleged Jewish role in it, see esp. the report included by Elijah Capsali in his *De-be Eliyahu* (Chronicle), ed. by M. Lattes under the title *Liqquṭim shonim mi-Sefer De-be Eliyahu* (Various Fragments from the Chronicle *De-be Eliyahu*), pp. 47, 60 f. Although Capsali had heard these stories "from the mouths of sages and elders" among the Spanish exiles, including one Jacob who had reconstructed for him Ferdinand's alleged Jewish ancestry going back to a love affair between the Castilian admiral Don Frederico Henriques and a Jewess, Paloma, we may almost wholly disregard that hearsay account. But there is no question about the part played by Seneor and especially by the distinguished *conversos*, Pedro and Alphonso de Cavalleria, in these crucial events, as described in Alonso de Palencia's *Crónica de Enrique IV*, trans. by A. Paz y Mélia, Vols. II, pp. 233, 242; III, pp. 183 f., 278, 316, 320, 332 ff., 337. See also the additional documents cited by Paz y Mélia in his biographical study of *El Cronista Alonso de Palencia. Su vida y sus obras; sus "Décadas" y las Crónicas contemporáneas*, esp. pp. 88 ff. No. 23 (1469), 368 f., 429; Serrano, *Orígenes*, pp. cxcii ff.; and Baer, *Toledot*, pp. 396 f., 538 n. 42. On Lorenzo Badoç and his ministrations to the queen see A. de la Torre, "Un Médico de los Reyes Católicos," *Hispania* (Madrid), No. xiv (1944), p. 69.

The subsequent reign of the Catholic kings and their attitude to the Jews, as well as their general missionary policies, have likewise often been analyzed. Apart from the general descriptions by Graetz, Lindo, Amador de los Rios, and Baer, see the large new collection of *Documentos acerca de la expulsión de los Judíos*, ed. and annotated by L. Suárez Fernández; and such general summaries as the popular essay by M. Mahn-Lot, "Isabelle la Catholique et les Juifs," *Mercure de France*, CCCIX, 491–500; J. Weill's more detailed data on "Les Juifs de Soria et Isabelle la Catholique," *REJ*, LXXIV, 98–103 (mainly analyzing a document relating to a forced loan of over 300,000 maravedis imposed upon the wealthiest Jews of the community in 1483); C. Bayle Gutiérez, "La Política religiosa de los Reyes Católicos en España hasta la conquista de Granada," *Miscelanea Comillas*, published by the Pontifical University of Comillas (Santander), XVIII, 227–69; idem, "Ideales misioneres de los reyes Católicos," *Missionalia hispanica*, IX, 209–31 (mainly concerned with the activities in the New World). It was, indeed, not only for political reasons that Pope Alexander VI conferred the title "Catholic" upon the royal couple in 1496. See E. Rey, "La Bula de Alejandro VI otorgando el título de 'Católicos' a Fernando e Isabel," *Razón y Fé*, CXLVI, 59–75, 324–47, esp. pp. 338 ff. (the pope emphasizing among other reasons the fact of the expulsion of Jews at great sacrifice to the Crown). See also R. Menéndez Pidal's analysis of "Significación del reinado de Isabel la Católica según sus coetaneos," in his *España y su historia*, ed. by G. Menéndez Pidal, II, 9–45; W. T. Walsh's colored *Isabella of Spain: The Last Crusader;* the essays on "Pensiamento político, política internacional y religiosa de Fernando el Católico," *V Congreso de Historia de la Corona de Aragón (1451–1504)*; and some of the older writings listed by F. López Estrada in his "Breve orientación bibliográfica sobre el reinado de los Reyes Católicos," *Archivo hispalense*, XIV, 339–47.

42. M. de Foronda y Aguilera, "Honras por Enrique IV y proclamación de Isabel la Católica en la ciudad de Ávila," *BAH*, LXIII, 432. Understandably, some Jews "bet on the wrong horse." A Jewish physician, Rabbi Jacob of Madrid, joined the lord of that city, the Marquess de Villena, one of the most powerful of Castile's grandees, in supporting the rival candidacy of Alphonso (Affonso) V of Portugal to

the Castilian throne. In retribution Isabella confiscated all of Jacob's Madrid property and rewarded one of her own partisans with its possession for life. See Baer, *Die Juden*, I, Part 2, pp. 337 f. No. 328.

43. L. Suárez Fernández, ed., *Documentos acerca de la expulsión de los Judíos*, pp. 13 ff., 82 f. No. 2, 88 f. No. 6, 106 ff. No. 14, 110 ff. Nos. 16–20; Baer, *Die Juden*, I, Part 2, pp. 336 No. 324, 346 No. 334. It was almost self-understood that the Jews need not contribute to the expenses of church festivals. Nevertheless attempts to force them to do so were not lacking, and in 1488 the Catholic monarchs were obliged to stop the city of Soria from collecting Jewish contributions to the so-called "Festival of the Nuptials of St. Mary." See Suárez Fernández, pp. 296 f. No. 108.

Not surprisingly, there were many inconsistencies in the new legislation as well. If on Dec. 23, 1490 the monarchs ordered the authorities of Medina del Campo to see to it that the Jews "should not be able to keep and hold stores and shops where they might work or do anything except in the said quarter or *judería*," less than four weeks later, at the intervention of Abraham Serrano in behalf of the Jewish community, they permitted the occupancy of such shops outside the Jewish quarter "so long as they would not eat or sleep there as is reported it being done in many parts of Our kingdoms." *Ibid.*, pp. 348 ff. Nos. 145–46. In addition there were the usual exemptions for individual Jews. In 1475, the queen freed the royal cobbler Yucef Çulama of Ávila of all military duties toward the city in consonance with the privileges he had received from John II and Henry IV. Baer, Part 2, p. 337 No. 326. Ávila frequently appears in the documents of the late fifteenth century because it was one of the most populous and affluent communities of the realm. See P. León Tello, "La Judería de Ávila durante el reinado de los Reyes Católicos," *Sefarad*, XXIII, 36–53, esp. pp. 38 f., 41 f., 46 ff.; and *infra*, Chap. LI.

44. *Cortes de los antiguos reinos de León y de Castilla*, IV, 103 f.; Amador de los Rios, *Historia social*, III, 282; L. Suárez Fernández, *Documentos*, pp. 94 ff. Nos. 10–11, 149 ff. No. 35; Baer, *Die Juden*, I, Part 1, pp. 896 ff. No. 554; Part 2, pp. 363 ff. Nos. 348–49, 382 f. No. 356; MS in the Ávila Municipal Archive, Legajo No. 1 (microfilm in National Archives in Madrid). See also P. León Tello, *Judíos de Ávila;* her article in *Sefarad*, XXIII, 38 ff.; and L. Huidobro y Serna, "La Judería de Castrojeriz," *ibid.*, VII, 137–45 (referring to earlier developments).

With their absolutist proclivities the Catholic kings were even more inclined than their predecessors to intervene in internal Jewish affairs. Quite early in Isabella's reign (March 25, 1475) she had to decide concerning a complaint of many Ávila Jews against their own tax collectors, who for more than ten or eleven years had failed to submit accounts of the communal incomes and expenditures. Isabella ordered the corregidor of Ávila to convoke a general communal assembly in order to elect four persons to audit these accounts. In the case of the Jews' inability to agree on the personnel of such a committee, the corregidor himself should make the selection. Two years later Ferdinand, somewhat shamefacedly, revoked his appointment of Don Vidal Astori as chief judge, rabbi, and tax distributor of the "other side" of Burgos, because this appointment ran counter to the powers conferred by the queen on Abraham Seneor. See Baer, Part 2, pp. 336 f. No. 325; Suárez Fernández, pp. 108 f. No. 15. These examples could readily be multiplied, especially from the later years of these monarchs' reign when they felt more secure on their thrones and began more effectively to control the various groups of the population.

45. *Cortes de los antiguos reinos de León y de Castilla*, II, 310 f.; IV, 68 f., 94 f., 101 ff., 149 f.; Amador de los Rios, *Historia social*, II, 282 ff.; L. Suárez Fernández, *Documentos*, pp. 23 ff., 104 ff. No. 13, 133 ff. Nos. 25–30, 145 f. No. 32, 151 ff. No. 36, 193 ff. Nos. 57–58, etc.; Baer, *Die Juden*, I, Part 1, pp. 912 f. No. 563; Part 2, pp. 220 ff. No. 227, 340 f. No. 330, 346 f. No. 335, 348 ff. No. 337.

It would be futile to look in these activities, too, for genuine consistency. Only five years before she proclaimed the banishment of the Jews from Seville, Isabella herself had issued a special decree of protection for that community and ordered its public proclamation in the main thoroughfares of the city and its vicinity. In the same year (1483), moreover, when he consented to the expulsion of Jews from Andalusia, Ferdinand reorganized the Jewish community of Tauste so that there should be sufficient persons "who would take care of the preservation and increase of the said Jews." Similar ordinances were issued in favor of the communities of Saragossa and Teruel. This did not prevent the king from reversing himself in regard to Saragossa three years later. But at the same time Ferdinand rejected an attempt to exclude Jews from the city of Valmaseda. See Suárez Fernández, pp. 146 ff. No. 33; Baer, Part 1, pp. 908 f. No. 558, 912 f. No. 563; Part 2, pp. 348 f. No. 337, 383 No. 357; and A. Rodríguez Herrero, *Valmaseda en siglo XV*, pp. 255 ff. (publishing an agreement concluded on the basis of the royal order between the city of Valmaseda and its Jewry). See also H. Sancho de Sopranis, "La Judería del Puerto de Santa María de 1483 a 1492," *Sefarad*, XIII, 309–24, showing the persistence of that southern community; and, from another angle, his *Historia social de Jerez de la Frontera al fin de la Edad Media*, esp. Vol. III. Of considerable interest also is Ferdinand's liberality in 1479 in conceding to the Jewish community of Gerona various privileges in recognition of its services at the city's siege, which had apparently been rendered some seventeen years before. Baer, Part 1, pp. 893 f. No. 553; and L. Batlle y Prats, "El Rey Católico y la Ciudad de Gerona," *Anales* of the Instituto de estudios gerundenses, VII, 156–266.

46. Nikolaus von Popplau (Nicholas of Popielowo), *Schlesien ehedem und jetzt*, in the Spanish translation in Javier (Ksawery) Liske's *Viages de estrangeros por España y Portugal en los siglos XV, XVI y XVIII* [1878], trans. into Spanish and annotated by F. R., p. 47 (the translator claims that the passage relating to the queen's Jewish descent is untranslatable); Baer, *Die Juden*, I, Part 1, pp. 909 f. No. 559; Part 2, pp. 347 f. No. 336, 384 No. 959, 987 f. No. 362, 398 f. No. 372; L. Suárez Fernández, *Documentos*, pp. 162 f. No. 39, 243 ff. No. 78, 246 f. No. 80, 297 ff. No. 109, 420 ff. No. 192, 472 f. No. 224. The number of Jews in Granada during the conquest of 1492 may be compared with the general estimates offered by L. Torres Balbás in his "Esquema demográfico de la ciudad de Granada," *Al-Andalus*, XXI, 131–46; and by C. de la Véronne in his "Recherches sur la population musulmane de la región de Málaga à la fin du XVe siècle d'après les 'Repartimientos,'" *Bulletin hispanique*, LXIV, 216–19 (showing that, for instance, Vélez-Málaga in 1487 embraced some 50 Jews among 2,500 to 3,000 Muslims and a few Christians). On the conditions under the declining Muslim regime in Granada, see also G. Levi della Vida, "Il Regno di Granada nel 1465–66 nei ricordi di un viaggiatore egiziano," *Al-Andalus*, I, 307–34 (from a Vatican MS of Al-Malati); J. Torres Fontes, "Las Relaciones castellano-granadinas desde 1475 a 1478," *Hispania* (Madrid), XXII, 186–229; idem, "Las Treguas con Granada de 1462 y 1463," *ibid.*, XXIII, 163–99.

A contemporary Jewish letter writer, to be sure, voiced a mild complaint against the war tax of a castellano per family, but even he extolled the king as "a man of righteousness and justice" and gloried in the presence at court of Abraham Seneor, whom he likened to the Babylonian exilarch. See his Hebrew letter addressed in 1487 to Rome and Lombardy, a copy of which was found by A. Marx on the back of the Constantinople, 1520 (?) ed. of Maimonides' *Teshubot she'elot ve-iggarot* (Responsa and Letters) extant at the Jewish Theological Seminary of America. It is briefly referred to in A. Marx's "The Expulsion of the Jews from Spain," *JQR,* [o.s.] XX, 247 (reprinted in his *Studies in Jewish History and Booklore,* p. 82); and more fully reproduced by Baer, Part 2, pp. 384 f. No. 360.

The remarkable careers of Don Isaac Abravanel and his family in three countries have often been treated; they will be mentioned here, too, in various connections. For the present we need but refer to B. Netanyahu's comprehensive biography, *Don Isaac Abravanel Statesman and Philosopher.* Of course, the effectiveness of the Jewish fiscal agents increased with the general rise in production and economic prosperity in the country. See R. Carande's brief survey of "La Economía y la expansión de España bajo el gobierno de los Reyes Católicos," *BAH,* CXXX, 213–55, esp. pp. 230 ff.; and, from another angle, L. Drèz del Carral, "L'Expérience historique nationale et supranationale de l'Espagne," *Journal of World History,* VI, 919–47.

47. Sixtus IV's bull, of November 1, 1478, included in Ferdinand and Isabella's decree of Sept. 27, 1480 and published by F. Fita in his "Nuevas fuentes [or 'Nuevos datos'] para escribir la historia de los Hebreos españoles," *BAH,* XV, 449 ff. (Baer, *Die Juden,* I, Part 2, pp. 344 ff. No. 333). See also the text and comments in B. Llorca's *Bulario pontificio,* pp. 48 ff. No. 3. This bull laid the foundations for the momentous evolution of the Spanish Inquisition, which will be analyzed *infra,* Chaps. LV–LVI, where large selections from the vast and controversial literature on this subject will also be listed. See also *supra,* nn. 39–40. For the time being we need but mention the divergent approaches on the part of both accusers and defenders of the Inquisition as illustrated by the following two recent dissertations: the Hebrew University dissertation by H. Beinart, *Ha-Mishpaṭim mi-ṭa'am ha-inqviziṣiah be-Toledo neged ha-mityahadim* (Trials of Judaizers by the Toledan Inquisition: From its Establishment till the Beginning of the Sixteenth Century); N. López Martínez's dissertation at the Pontifical University of Salamanca, *Los Judaizantes castellanos y la Inquisición en tiempo de Isabel la Católica,* which constantly harps on the theme of the *converso* "danger" to Spanish unity. See also his more succinct essay, "El Peligro de los conversos," *Hispania Sacra,* III, 3–61. Similar disparities also permeate much of the other abundantly rich literature on the entire reign of the Catholic kings, a sample of which was given *supra,* n. 41.

48. The much-debated decree of expulsion of Spanish Jewry, dated Granada, March 31, 1492, has often been reprinted. Among the better texts are those edited by F. Fita in his "Edicto de los Reyes Católicos (31 March, 1492) desterrando de sus estados a todos los Judíos," *BAH,* XI, 512–28; and repeated in Baer, *Die Juden,* I, Part 2, pp. 404 ff. No. 378; and in L. Suárez Fernández's *Documentos,* pp. 391 ff. No. 177. Although Fita's text was published from original copies circulated by the Spanish authorities, Baer is right in urging a new critical edition of that text based

upon all extant contemporary manuscripts. Its tenor clearly stemmed from the king's clerical advisers, but, as we shall see, the decisive factors behind the expulsion were not exclusively religious. Its immediate antecedents, including the Blood Accusation of La Guardia, will be more fully scrutinized *infra*, Chaps. XLIX–L. Here we need but mention F. Fita's still basic studies, esp. his "La Verdad sobre el martirio del Santo Niño de La Guardia ó sea el proceso y quema (16 Nov. 1491) del Judío Jucé Franco en Ávila," *BAH*, XI, 7–134; his "Memoria del Santo Niño de La Guardia, escrita en 1544," *ibid.*, pp. 135–60; and Baer's *Toledot*, pp. 450 ff., 546 f. More generally, see H. Sancho, "Un Documento interesante sobre la expulsión de los Judíos," *Archivo hispalense*, 2d ser. V, 225–28 (showing the opposition of some southern lords to the expulsion); the weak apologia for the expulsion offered by the Duke de Maura in his "Nueva luz sobre la expulsión de los Judíos en 1492," *BAH*, CXXXVII, 187–200; and J. Cabezudo Astrain's "La Expulsión de los Judíos zaragozanos," *Sefarad*, XV, 103–136 (also citing the instruction to the inquisitors of April 1492 against the acquisition of the exiles' property; p. 104). See also Baer's analysis in "The Expulsion of the Jews from Spain" (Hebrew), *Aḥdut ha-'Abodah*, III, 298–307; his *Toledot*, pp. 401 ff.; and, on a more popular level, V. Marcu, *The Expulsion of the Jews from Spain*, English trans. from the German by Moray Firth (pseud.).

49. See the literature cited *supra*, n. 39; and *infra*, Chap. XLIX. The antisemitic reinterpretation of the Jewish role in medieval Spain served as a keynote for C. F. Rühs's arguments against Jewish emancipation; see esp. his *Ueber die Ansprüche der Juden an das deutsche Bürgerrecht*, published in 1815–16. The anthropological data from Valladolid have been analyzed by M. Bañuelos in his "Antropología actual," *Valladolid, Revista financiera del Banco de Viscaya* (Bilboa), No. 79, pp. 182–86. More far-reaching are Américo Castro's views, first formulated in his *España en su historia: cristianos, moros y judíos* (translated into English by E. L. King under the title, *The Structure of Spanish History*), and slightly revised in its 2d ed. entitled, *La Realidad histórica de España*. See also his *Aspectos del vivir hispánico· espiritualismo, mesianismo, actitud personal en los siglos XIV al XVI*; and his debate with M. Bataillon in the latter's open letter to Castro entitled, "L'Espagne religieuse dans son histoire"; and Castro's reply, "Quelques précisions au sujet de España en su historia," *Bulletin hispanique*, LII, 5–26; LIII, 5–12. The critical discussions evoked by the first publication of his work include: Y. Malkiel, "The Jewish Heritage of Spain: on the Occasion of Américo Castro's *España en su historia*," *Hispanic Review*, XVIII, 328–40; C. Sanchez-Albornoz, "Ante 'España en su historia,'" *CHE*, XIX, 129–45; and other studies analyzed by E. Rey in "La Polémica suscitada por Américo Castro en torno a la interpretación de España," *Razón y Fé*, CLVII, 343–62. See also E. Nuñez Martinez, *La Influencia judía en la España medieval;* and *infra*, Chap. LV.

50. A. C. Sousa, *Provas de historia genealogica da casa real portuguesa*, I, 507, 650; III, 624; Kayserling, *Geschichte der Juden in Portugal*, pp. 25, 46, 56, 73; Baer, *Die Juden*, I, Part 2, pp. 179 No. 187, 320 No. 305, 338 ff. No. 329 with notes thereon; *supra*, n. 44. See also F. de S. Bonaventura, *Summário da vida, acçõens e gloriosa morte de senhor D. Fernando, chamado o Infante Sacro* (reprinting a Portuguese translation of a Vatican Latin MS which was first published in Modena in 1836); and J. Goulven, *L'Infant Ferdinand, prince et martyr (1402–1443)*. The matrimonial negotiations between Castile and Portugal in 1453–55 are briefly summarized in L. Suárez Fernández, "Aragón y Portugal en la política de don Álvaro de Luna,"

RABM, LIX, 132 n. 68. On Isaac Abravanel's considerable services to the Crown and his subsequent condemnation on May 30, 1485 after his flight to Castile in 1481, see A. Brancamp Freire, "As Conspirações no reinado de D. João II. Documentos, Part VI: Sentença de Isaque Bravanel," *Archivo histórico portuguez*, II, 31–33 (this text is reprinted in the Appendix v to Ruy de Pina, *Crónica d'el Rei D. João II*, new ed. by A. Martins de Carvalho, pp. 235 ff.); and B. Netanyahu's aforementioned biography, *Don Isaac Abravanel*, pp. 18 ff. Of some interest also is the letter written by Don Isaac in 1470 or 1471 to Count Alphonso de Farão. See the text republished with a lengthy introduction by J. de Carvalho in his "Uma epístola de Isaac Abarbanel," *Revista de estudos hebraicos*, I, 231–38 and reprinted in his *Estudos sobre a cultura portuguesa de século XV*, I, 253–68. See also the earlier ed. of that letter with a German trans. by J. Schwerin (geb. Abarbanel) in "Ein Brief Don Isaac Abarbanels in portugiesischer Sprache," *Magazin für die Wissenschaft des Judentums*, XVIII, 133–45.

51. Cortes of 1481–82 meeting in Évora, in the English rendition by J. C. Branner in his trans. of A. Herculano's *History of the Origin and Establishment of the Inquisition in Portugal*, pp. 241 ff. Complaints about excessive Jewish luxuries were often heard in Jewish quarters as well. Solomon Alami's aforementioned ethical treatise of 1415 referred to the shortcomings of all Iberian Jewry. See *supra*, n. 23. As we shall see, the Portuguese Jewish leaders felt induced to issue from time to time sumptuary ordinances to prevent such excesses. However, the propensity of the wealthy classes to display their riches could not be stemmed by either the state or the community. They became a source of continuous friction with the non-Jewish populace, although among the latter, too, expensive attire was generally regarded as a high status symbol.

52. F. Lopes, *Chronica do Senhor Rei Pedro I*, v, in *Colecção de livros inéditos*, IV, 16 f.; Gomes Eannes de Zurara, *Chronica de Conde Dom Pedro de Menezes*, xv, *ibid.*, II, 259; Sousa Viterbo, "Occorrencias da vida judaica," *Archivo histórico portuguez*, II, 180 ff.; *Ordenaçoens de Senhor Rey D. Affonso V*, ii.67, 76, 80, 86 and 91, Vol. II, pp. 423 ff., 455 ff., 471 ff., 499 ff., 509 f. On Zurara and his even more eminent predecessor, Fernão Lopes, whose chronicles serve to elucidate also many phases of fifteenth-century Portuguese Jewish life, see E. Prestage, *The Chronicles of Fernão Lopes and Gomes Eannes de Zurara*. The laws, dating from various periods, were included in the comprehensive *Ordenaçoens* which, though largely completed in 1446, were not officially promulgated by Alphonso V until 1472. They will be more fully considered in connection with the development of the medieval ghetto and badge.

53. C. E. Nowell, *A History of Portugal*, pp. 32 f.; A. L. Lebeson, "Jewish Cartographers: a Forgotten Chapter of Jewish History," *HJ*, X, 155–74. The extensive Jewish collaboration in Portugal's economic and cultural life, particularly during the fifteenth century, will be discussed at length in other connections. Here the following literature ought to suffice: J. de Carvalho's aforementioned *Estudos*, I, 120–39 ("Escritores israelitas e árabes"); I. González Llubera, "Two Old Portuguese Astrological Texts in Hebrew Characters," *Romance Philology*, VI, 267–71; J. Bensaude, *L'Astronomie nautique au Portugal à l'époque des grandes découvertes*; idem, *Histoire de science nautique portugaise, collection de documents* (both refer-

ring to the extensive Jewish contributions to medieval Portuguese science in that field); M. Kayserling, "Theilnahme von Juden an den portugiesischen Entdeckungen," *Jahrbuch für die Geschichte der Juden*, III, 303–17; A. Freimann, "Die Hebräischen Inkunabeln der Druckereien in Spanien und Portugal," *Gutenberg Festschrift zur Feier des 25-jährigen Bestehens des Gutenbergmuseums in Mainz*, ed. by A. Ruppel, pp. 203–206; M. B. Amzalak, *A Tipografia hebraica em Portugal no século XV*, esp. pp. 19 ff. It may also be noted that the distinguished Spanish Jewish astronomer and historian, Abraham Zacuto, was in Lisbon in 1493 (after the expulsion from his native land) where he signed in Hebrew with the title of "royal astronomer." See F. Cantera Burgos's biographical sketch, *El Judío salmantino Abraham Zacut. Notas para la historia de la España medieval* (reprinted from *Revista de la Academia de Ciencias*, Madrid, 2d ser. XXVIII), p. 24.

Active Jewish participation was somewhat hampered by the great influence of the Papacy, although the Renaissance popes themselves were on the whole more tolerant than their thirteenth-century predecessors. See, for instance, C. M. de Witte, "Les Bulles pontificales et l'expansion portugaise au XVᵉ siècle," *RHE*, XLVIII, 683–718; XLIX, 438–61; LI, 413–53, 809–36; and, more generally, J. P. Oliveira Martins, *The Golden Age of Prince Henry the Navigator*, English translation by J. J. Abraham and W. E. Reynolds; M. Bataillon, *Études sur le Portugal au temps de l'humanisme*. So impressed were the Iberian Jews by the explorers' reports, particularly their tales about the alleged discovery of a distant Jewish island and the implied confirmation of the old legends concerning the mythical river, Sambation, that the Castilian leaders felt impelled very cautiously to relate these stories to their Italian coreligionists ("all this is told you from hearsay, not from direct observation"). See Baer, *Die Juden*, I, Part 2, pp. 384 f. No. 360.

54. The letter of the unnamed friar of São Marcos to Alphonso V is cited here in J. C. Branner's English trans. of Herculano's *History of the Origin*, p. 241; Ruy de Pina, *Chronica do Senhor Rey D. Affonso V*, xxx, in the *Colecção de livros inéditos de história portugueza*, I, 439 f.; Sousa Viterbo's observations in *Archivo histórico portuguez*, II, 185 f., reproducing two excerpts from petitions submitted in 1451; in both cases the accused pleaded complete innocence. The secular argumentation of the monk of São Marcos reflects in part the high degree of secularization of fifteenth-century Portuguese life under the impact of both commercialization and incipient humanism. Nevertheless the Church still exerted considerable influence on the country's public affairs. See F. de Almeida, *História da igreja de Portugal*.

55. The Cortes of Santarém, 1451; of Lisbon, 1455 and 1460; of Cintra, 1461; of Coimbra, 1473 and 1475, summarized in *Ordenaçoens Affonso V*, ii, *passim*. It doubtless was a concession to the Christian burghers that the Jewish notaries were forbidden to use the Hebrew language in their documents. But as usual the king made exceptions, as in his favorable reply of 1452 to a Jewish notary of Setúbal who, when fined for the use of Hebrew, had pleaded ignorance of the law. See Sousa Viterbo in *Archivo histórico portuguez*, II, 182 ff., also referring to documents which mention the appointment of Jewish notaries in Lisbon in 1445, Setúbal in 1482, and Porto in 1486. Behind the opposition of the Cortes also loomed the rise of Portuguese nationalism which unfavorably affected also the status of the Muslim population. However, the latter never played in Portugal quite the same role as it did in Spain. See A. E. Beau, *Die Entwicklung des portugiesischen Nationalbewusstseins;* F.

Pérez Embid, *El Mudéjarismo portugués,* 2d ed. Many of these parliamentary debates are briefly referred to in Alphonso's compilation, because they led to legal enactments. However, a careful monograph on these debates referring to the Jewish question, with due consideration of the spokesmen for the anti-Jewish majority, their class origins and personal motivations, would help clarify many a moot point in Portuguese history. Certainly, the general literature on the Cortes does not yield sufficient data on our problem, even if it consists of such a careful examination of the record, as is offered, with respect to a single session, by M. Caetano in "As Cortes de 1385," *Revista portuguesa de história,* V, 5–86. See, in general, A. A. Oliveira Neves [Toste], *Córtes do Reino de Portugal. Inventario de documentação existente.* We know even less about the relations between individual municipalities and the Jews. That ever since the *Reconquista* the Portuguese municipal autonomy was playing an increasing role in the country's affairs has rightly been emphasized by T. de Souza Soares in his "Notas para a estudo das instituções municipais da Reconquista," *Revista portuguesa de história,* I, 71–92; II, 265–91.

56. Foro de Beja in F. Brandão, *Monarchia Lusitana,* V, xviii, p. 18; *Ordinaçoens Affonso V,* ii.89, Vol. II, pp. 507 f. See the aforementioned general works by Herculano and Kayserling, as well as J. L. d'Azevedo, *História dos Christãos Novos portugueses.* The subject of the Portuguese *conversos* and the related operations of the Portuguese Inquisition will be discussed more fully *infra,* Chaps. LV–LVI. But before 1496 neither the number of the Portuguese *conversos* nor their influence on society stirred up much controversy, the Jewish question being generally debated in terms of professing Jews as such.

57. *Ordenaçoens Affonso V,* ii.72 and 79, Vol. II, pp. 434 f., 465 ff.

58. Nowell, *History of Portugal,* p. 48; Cortes of 1490 cited in Herculano's *History of the Origin,* pp. 243 f. One must distinguish here between Jewish tax farming, which was a semicommercial enterprise—the enterpreneur usually contracting to pay the Treasury a certain lump sum and keeping the surplus or absorbing the loss—and tax collecting, which was a governmental function. Although official tax gatherers probably were more moderate in their exactions, they could easily be replaced, for there always were many willing Christian candidates. The loss of revenue sustained because of the employment of inefficient collectors also was less immediately apparent than that arising from competitive bidding. See Ruy de Pina, "Chrónica d'el Rei D. João II," in the *Colecção de livros inéditos, II,* 5–204; or in the new ed. by J. Martins de Carvalho.

59. See Ruy de Pina, *Crónica d'el Rei D. João II,* lxv, reed. by J. Martins de Carvalho, esp. pp. 179 ff. See also A. de la Torre and L. Suárez Fernández, eds., *Documentos referentes a las relaciones con Portugal durante el reinado de los Reyes Católicos,* Vol. I.

60. Damião de Góis (Goes), *Crónica do felicissimo rei D. Manuel,* i.10, 18 and 20, new edition with notes and intro. by J. Martins Teixeira de Carvalho and D. Lopes, I, 21 f., 35 f., 38 ff. The story of this tragic dénouement in Portugal, as well as that of a year later in Navarre, will be more fully told *infra,* Chap. L. It may be noted here, however, that the Portuguese government, like its Spanish counterpart, did not issue

the same intolerant regulations for the Muslim minority. Apart from the latter's relatively small number, the presence of powerful Muslim states in North Africa, which could retaliate by sharply discriminating against their Christian subjects, served as a deterrent. Nevertheless, the two religious minorities show many parallels in their Portuguese evolution. See especially, J. A. Pires de Lima, *Mouros, judeus e negros na história de Portugal,* esp. pp. 30 ff. (while unduly critical of Mendes dos Remedios it offers some literary and folkloristic data, particularly of the 16th century); H. da Gama Barros, "Judeus e Mouros em Portugal em tempos passados (apontamentos histórico-etnográficos)," *Revista lusitana,* XXXIV, 165–205; XXXV. Much of the aforementioned debate (*supra,* n. 49) concerning the Jewish and Muslim roles in the evolution of medieval Spain applies also, with minor modifications, to their share in the development of the medieval Portuguese state and culture.

61. See Santob de Carrión, *Proverbios morales,* ed. with an intro. by I. González Llubera; and E. Alarcos Llorach's observations on "La Lengua de los 'Proverbios morales' de don Sem Tob," *Revista de Filologia española,* XXXV, 249–309.

CHAPTER XLVI: ITALIAN POTPOURRI

1. G. Prezzolini, *Fascism*, English trans. from the Italian by K. Macmillan, p. vii. See also my *Modern Nationalism and Religion, passim.*

2. Scholarly interest in southern Italian Jewry has been as long and sustained as that in the Spanish Jews. Among the early careful studies was Giovanni di Giovanni's *L'Ebraismo della Sicilia, ricercato ed esposto,* published in Palermo, 1748. It laid the foundation for all subsequent researches, including the important essay by L. Zunz, "Geschichte der Juden in Sicilien" in his *Zur Geschichte und Literatur,* Vol. I, pp. 484–534. This essay was translated into Italian by P. Perreau, and published under the title "Storia degli Ebrei in Sicilia" in *AS Siciliano,* n.s. IV, 69–113. Much new material has become available, however, through the extensive documentary publication of *Codice diplomatico dei Giudei di Sicilia,* compiled by B. Lagumina and G. Lagumina, Part 1, Vols. I–III. Of interest is also the juridical analysis by Q. Senigaglia, "La Condizione giuridica degli Ebrei in Sicilia," *Rivista italiana per le scienze giuridiche,* XLI, 75–102.

Less intensive have been the researches relating to the Neapolitan provinces. The main works in this field have been N. Tamassia, "Stranieri ed Ebrei nell'Italia meridionale dall'età romana alla sueva," *Atti* of the R. Istituto Veneto di scienze, lettere ed arti, LXIII, 757–839, esp. pp. 796 ff.; and N. Ferorelli, *Gli Ebrei nell'Italia meridionale dall'età romana al secolo XVIII.* See also E. Munkácsi, *Der Jude von Neapel: die historischen und kunstgeschichtlichen Denkmäler des süditalienischen Judentums;* O. Dito, *La Storia calabrese e la dimora degli Ebrei in Calabria dal secolo V alla seconda metà del secolo XVI;* and G. Summo, *Gli Ebrei in Puglia dall'XI al XVI secolo;* and *infra,* nn. 10 and 22–23. Understandably, little work has been done on the far less significant Jewries of the other islands. C. Roth and A. Milano wrote comprehensive syntheses of *The History of the Jews of Italy* and the *Storia degli Ebrei in Italia,* respectively, the latter with brief notes and a selected bibliography.

Of course, there is a host of special monographs on certain localities, persons, or specific Jewish activities, many of which will be mentioned in the following notes. These are well listed in the bibliographical handbooks by G. Gabrieli, *Italia judaica; saggio d'una bibliografia storica e archeologica degli Ebrei d'Italia,* and A. Milano, *Bibliotheca historica italo-judaica,* together with a *Supplemento 1954–1963* thereto. Needless to say, a great deal can also be learned from the numerous general histories of the area; for instance, the "Cinque storie della Sicilia," published in 1948–55 and aptly reviewed in conjunction with other recent publications by R. Zapperi in *Società,* XII, 514–28. Of considerable assistance also are such general bibliographical surveys as B. C. de Frede's "Bollettino bibliografico per la storia del Mezzogiorno d'Italia, 1939–1950," *ASPN,* LXXI, 217–350, supplemented by G. Pizzuti's "Correzioni e aggiunte" thereto in *Calabria nobilissima,* VII, 43–53, 95–110; and various regional bibliographies such as M. Zuccarini's *Contributi alla bibliografia abruzzese,* Vol. I, covering the publications of 1890–1955 available in the Provincial Library of Chieti.

3. To the sources cited *supra*, Vol. IV, pp. 242 ff. nn. 20 ff., add S. M. Stern, "Un Circolo di poeti siciliani ebrei nel secolo XII," *Bollettino* of the Centro di studi filologici e linguistici siciliani, IV, 39–59. On the emperor's relations with the Byzantine and Muslim worlds, see S. Borsari, "Federico II et l'Oriente bizantino," *RSI*, LXIII, 279–91; F. Gabrieli, "Federico II e la cultura musulmana," *ibid.*, LXIV, 5–18; and, more generally, P. Charanis, "On the Question of the Hellenization of Sicily and Southern Italy during the Middle Ages," *AHR*, LII, 74–87 (discussing the earlier period); R. Weiss, "The Greek Culture of South Italy in the Middle Ages," *Proceedings* of the British Academy, XXXVII, 23–50; and the literature listed by F. Gabrieli in his review article "Un Secolo di studi arabo-siculi," *Studia islamica*, II, 89–102. See also *infra*, n. 12; and N. Tamassia's general survey cited *supra*, n. 2.

4. See *supra*, Chap. XL, nn. 9 ff.; B. Lagumina and G. Lagumina, *Codice diplomatico*, I, 12 ff. Nos. xvi–xix; A. Marongiu, "Gli Ebrei di Salerno nei documenti dei secoli X–XIII," *ASPN*, LXII, 238–66, esp. pp. 256 ff.; N. Ferorelli, *Gli Ebrei nell'Italia meridionale*, pp. 44 f.; and some additional data supplied by L. Erler in "Die Judenverfolgungen des Mittelalters," *AKKR*, XLVIII, 14 ff.; and R. Straus, *Die Juden im Königreich Sizilien unter Normannen und Staufern*, pp. 20 ff. An alleged decree by Frederick II of 1224 provided that the jurisdiction over "excesses of Jews and other infidels in all matters relating not only to our most sacred religion but also to their illicit relations with any Christian person" should belong to the inquisitors of the Holy Office. Jews were also supposed to help support transient inquisitors, although their contributions were limited to a maximum annual payment of a Roman *paolo*. This decree is cited, from its confirmation by Alphonso V in 1452, by Ludovicus Paramus, a sixteenth-century historian of the Inquisition. See his *De origine et progressu officii Sanctae Inquisitionis*, ii.11, 7–8, pp. 199 ff. But its attribution to the Hohenstaufen emperor has rightly been denied by J. Ficker in his ed. of *Die Regesten des Kaiserreichs unter Philipp, Otto IV, Friedrich II, Heinrich (VII), Conrad IV, Heinrich Raspe, Wilhelm und Richard, 1198–1272* in J. F. Böhmer, *Regesta imperii*, V, 311 f. No. 1511. Ficker suggested that that law was probably issued by Frederick III of the Aragonese dynasty some time after 1295. Erler's arguments for the authenticity and original dating (*AKKR*, XLVIII, 24 n. 3) of that ordinance are not convincing; they are vitiated by his evident unfamiliarity with the text quoted by Paramus, which he knew only at second hand. It is also possible that the decree was altogether spurious. Remembering Frederick's general friendliness to the inquisitorial courts and his sharp prosecution of heresies, evidently for imperialistic reasons rather than out of personal conviction, some self-seeking later inquisitors may have submitted a forged decree of the Hohenstaufen emperor to Alphonso V who blindly confirmed it.

5. Frederick II's *Constitutiones regni Siciliae* in J. L. A. Huillard-Bréholles, *Historia diplomatica Friderici Secundi*, IV, 1–178, esp. pp. 28 f.; Lagumina and Lagumina, *Codice diplomatico*, I, 17 ff. Nos. xx–xxii; C. Carucci, "Gli Ebrei in Salerno nei secoli XI e XII," *AS della provincia di Salerno*, I, 78 f. The decree of 1239 relating to the settlement of the Jews from Djerba clearly illustrates Frederick's deep interest in Jewish immigration from Muslim lands and his employment of the new arrivals in meeting the country's industrial and agricultural needs rather than in moneylending. As pointed out by several scholars, including Straus (p. 64), no Jewish name has been identified among the numerous creditors of the much-

harassed emperor. Perhaps Frederick was not considered a good credit risk by Jews who feared that the Treasury, taking seriously the term "serfs," might view all their property as part of the royal domain and prove less inclined to repay their loans. Certainly, wealthy Jewish merchants could, through various legal subterfuges, secure from private borrowers interest ranging from 36 to 66 percent annually as did their Christian competitors. See the data cited by Erler in *AKKR*, XLVIII, 26 f. In any case, credit transactions were to play but a relatively minor role among the southern Italian Jews even in later generations.

6. Lagumina and Lagumina, *Codice diplomatico*, I, 21 No. xxiii; K. Rodenberg, ed., *Epistolae saeculi XIII*, III, 335 No. 370; Usque, *Concolaçam*, iii.11, ed. by Mendes dos Remedios, Part 3, fols. x f.; in M. A. Cohen's English trans. entitled *Consolation for the Tribulation of Israel*, pp. 180 ff.; Joseph ha-Kohen, *'Emeq ha-bakha*, ed. by Letteris, pp. 50 ff.; in M. Wiener's German trans., pp. 40 f., 176 n. 170; Solomon ibn Verga, *Shebeṭ Yehuda*, xix, ed. by Wiener, p. 43; in his German trans., pp. 85 f.; ed. by Shohet, pp. 66 f. These legends doubtless were but rationalizations of what later happened in Trani and other Neapolitan communities. See, *infra*, n. 8.

7. G. del Giudice, *Codice diplomatico del regno di Carlo I⁰ e II⁰ d'Angiò*, I, 314 ff. No. cxvi, with the note thereon; II, 212 ff. No. lxix; III, 127 ff. No. lxxv, 200 ff. No. cxxii; Ferorelli, *Gli Ebrei*, pp. 53 f.; R. Filangieri *et al.*, eds., *I Registri della cancelleria angioina*, XI, 101 No. 8; Erler, *AKKR*, XLVIII, 32 f.; and, more generally, U. Cassuto, "Sulla storia degli Ebrei nell'Italia meridionale nell'età angionia," *Il Vessillo israelitico*, LIX, 282–85, 338–41, 422–24 (also reprint); and E. Artom, "Gli Ebrei in Italia sotto il dominio degli Angioini e dei Durazzeschi," *RMI*, XV, 80–84. There is no evidence of any Jewish participation in the Sicilian Vespers, although Aragonese Jewry had evinced much sympathy for Pedro II's African campaign. Perhaps having become inured to Frederick II's extreme fiscal exactions and having suffered from the chaotic conditions after his death, the Sicilian Jews were more prone to appreciate the stability achieved under Charles I. Individual Jews, moreover, were well received at Charles' court, and, as we have seen, that king's policy in his Angevin and Provençal possessions favorably contrasted with the Jews' insecurity in other parts of France. See Willy Cohn, "Jüdische Uebersetzer am Hofe Karls I. von Anjou, Königs von Sizilien (1266–1285)," *MGWJ*, LXXIX, 246–60; idem, "Die Judenpolitik König Karls I von Sizilien in Anjou und in der Provence," *ibid.*, LXXIV, 429–37; *supra*, Chap. XLIII, nn. 32, 40; and, more generally, S. Runciman, *The Sicilian Vespers: a History of the Mediterranean World in the Later Thirteenth Century* (has only a brief and rather incorrect statement concerning Jews, p. 129).

8. See Ferorelli, *Gli Ebrei*, pp. 53 ff. The sequence of the events which led to the mass conversions of the 1290s and the fate of the professing Jews then and soon thereafter is far from clarified. Much new light was shed by several studies and inscriptions published by U. Cassuto. See esp. "Un Ignoto capitolo di storia ebraica," *Judaica, Festschrift Hermann Cohen*, pp. 389–404; idem, "The Destruction of Jewish Academies in Southern Italy in the Thirteenth Century" (Hebrew), *Gulak-Klein Mem. Vol.*, pp. 139–52; and J. Starr, "The Mass Conversion of Jews in Southern Italy (1290–1293)," *Speculum*, XXI, 203–11. See also Cassuto, "Iscrizioni ebraiche a Trani," *Rivista degli studi orientali*, XIII, 172–80; idem, "Iscrizioni ebraiche a Bari,"

ibid., XV, 316–22; idem, "One More Hebrew Inscription from the City of Trani," *Marx Jub. Vol.*, Hebrew section, pp. 387–89; V. Vitale, "Un Particolare ignorato di storia pugliese: neofiti e mercanti," *Studi di storia napoletana in onore di Michelangelo Schipa*, pp. 233–46. On the *relapsi*, see, for instance, the document reproduced in R. Filangieri *et al.*, eds., *Registri della cancelleria angioina*, IV, 158 f. The complex problems of these *neofiti*, which came to plague the officials, both secular and ecclesiastical, as well as the Jewish elders, will be more fully discussed *infra*, Chap. LVI.

Needless to say, the Church, which had brought the Angevin dynasty to power, continued to enhance its own authority over the local Jews. Yet, when in 1292 the archbishop of Salerno tried to appropriate the heirless estate of a Jewish widow Letula, "a special vassal of the Salernitan church," the Treasury protested vigorously and, it appears, successfully. We are not told, however, whether the Jewish community had in any way become a beneficiary of the heirless property of that former member, as was customary in many European countries. See the texts published by A. Marongiu in "Gli Ebrei di Salerno," *ASPN*, LXII, 242 f., 264. This case was exceptional, however, inasmuch as Letula had, before her demise, been convicted by the Inquisition "because of a certain crime against the faith"—probably consisting of no more than aiding some *relapsi* in the observance of Jewish rituals after the mass conversion. In fact, the Dominican Fra Bartolomeo da Aquila, who condemned her, also sentenced the Jewish elders of Salerno for having "known and consented" to the circumcision in the synagogue of a Christian named Moses and the ablution there of one Azzaria who thus wished to wash off the effects of his baptism. See Marongiu in *ASPN*, LXII, 242 f., 261 f., 264 f. No. ii.

9. Council of Benevento of 1374, cited by P. Lonardo in *Gli Ebrei a Benevento*, p. 12; Ferorelli, *Gli Ebrei*, pp. 56 ff., 60 ff. On the intellectual contacts between Robert and the Jews see M. Steinschneider's "Robert von Anjou und sein Verhältnis zu einigen gelehrten Juden," *MGWJ*, XLVIII, 713–17. Interesting additional documentation is available in the comprehensive biographical work by R. Caggese, *Roberto d'Angiò e i suoi tempi*, esp. I, 295–310, which also offers significant data on both the high rates of interest charged, and the exorbitant taxes paid, by Jews. Shortly before his demise (Dec. 1, 1342), it may be noted, Robert suspended an ordinance calling for separate Jewish quarters. *Ibid.*, II, 300. See also E. G. Léonard's comprehensive *Histoire de Jeanne Ière, Reine de Naples*, which offers interesting demographic data for 1337 (I, 12 ff.).

10. Ferorelli, *Gli Ebrei*, pp. 64 ff. See the text cited by C. Minieri-Riccio in his *Notizie storiche tratte da 62 registri angioini dell'Archivio di Stato di Napoli*, pp. 92 f. Much information for this entire period may also be derived from the numerous local histories and monographs on individual Jewish communities. See, for example, G. B. Beltrani's note "Degli Ebrei chi dimoravano nella città di Trani e de importanza di uno studio speciale sulle colonie che gli stessi ebbero nei regni di Puglia," in his *Sugli antichi ordinamenti marittimi della città di Trani*, I, 55–88 (supplemented by his article cited in the next note); F. Cerone, "Sei documenti inediti sugli Ebrei di Salerno dal 1125 al 1269," *Studi di storia napoletana in onore di Michelangelo Schipa*, pp. 59–73 (includes deeds recording transfers of land); C. Carucci, "Gli Ebrei in Salerno nei secoli XI e XII," *AS della provincia di Salerno*, I, 74–79; D. Spanò Bolani, "I Giudei in Reggio di Calabria dal secolo XIII sino al

primo decennio del secolo XVI," *ASPN*, VI, 336–46; R. Cotroneo, "Gli Ebrei della giudecca de Reggio Calabria," *Rivista storica calabrese*, 3rd ser. XI, 390–418; G. Carano-Donvito, "Gli Ebrei nella storia economica di Puglia," *Rivista di politica economica*, XXIII, 836–43; G. Guerrieri, "Gli Ebrei a Brindisi ed a Lecce (1409–1497). Contributo allo studio dell'usura nell'Italia meridionale," *Studi senesi*, XVII, 225–52; N. Vacca, "Per la storia degli Ebrei in Taranto: 1) Un tumulto antisemita nell 1411; 2) l'usure nel 1474," *Rinascenza salentina*, n.s. IV, 221–29; and the literature listed *supra*, n. 30; and Chap. XLII, n. 28. See also A. Cutolo's comprehensive biography of *Re Ladislao d'Angiò-Durazzo*. It may be noted that, although generally a rather effective ruler, Ladislaus, like most of his predecessors and successors, was seriously hampered by his kingdom's large, heavy-handed and disunited bureaucracy. See *ibid.*, I, 149 ff.; II, 50 ff.

11. The interesting Catanzaro document was published by C. Minieri-Riccio in his *Di alcune pergameni, ecc.*, p. 411. On Joanna II's reign in general, see esp. G. B. Beltrani, "Il Conte Alberigo da Barbiano, la regina Giovanna Seconda e gli Ebrei di Trani," *Il Buonarotti*, 2d ser. XI, 175–86; and J. Starr, "Johanna II and the Jews," *JQR*, XXXI, 67–78. The figure of 638 contributors including women and children is quoted from a MS in the Lanciano Public Library by C. Marciani in his "Ebrei a Lanciano dal XII al XVIII secolo," *ASPN*, LXXXI, 175. John Capistrano's activities during that period are briefly described by J. Hofer in *Johannes von Capestrano. Ein Leben im Kampf um die Reform der Kirche*, pp. 151 ff. In his anti-Jewish agitation Capistrano had quite a few local assistants, some of whom he even took along with him to Germany. See A. Chiappini, "I Compagni abruzzesi di S. Giovanni da Capistrano nell'impéro tedesco," *Bollettino* of the Deputazione abruzzese di storia patria, 4th ser. XLVI, 61–70; the source study by F. Banfi, "Le Fonti per la storia di S. Giovanni da Capistrano," *Studi francescani*, LVIII, 299–344; Ferorelli, *Gli Ebrei*, p. 66; and *infra*, n. 47. It should be noted, on the other hand, that the visit of the even more influential preacher, Saint Bernardino da Siena, in the Neapolitan provinces had no deleterious effects on the Jews or on their relations with their neighbors. Although he left a lasting impression in the region (in Campagna, for instance, for generations thereafter the community held special services twice a year praying for the saint's intercession with the Deity), and although one of his laudations included the phrase that he had been *zelator paupertatis*, "zealous exponent of poverty," a phrase which could also reflect attacks on Jewish moneylending and luxuries, there is no record that Jews in any way suffered from his rousing sermons. See F. Cioffi, "Ricordi di San Bernardino da Siena nella provincia francescana di Principato," *AS della provincia di Salerno*, n.s. III, 117–23. See also M. F. Faraglia, *Storia della regina Giovanna II*; and, more generally, E. G. Léonard, *Les Angevins de Naples;* and the older literature reviewed in G. M. Monti's *Nuovi studi angioini,* which includes the bibliographical survey, "Gli Angioini di Napoli negli studi dell' ultimo cinquantennio," covering the years of 1886 to 1936 (pp. 1–102).

12. S. (P.) Cassel, "Juden," *Allgemeine Encyclopädie*, ed. by J. S. Ersch and J. G. Gruber, 2d ser. XXVII, pp. 1–238, esp. p. 144; G. di Giovanni, *L'Ebraismo della Sicilia,* pp. 182 ff.; Lagumina and Lagumina, *Codice diplomatico*, I, 116 ff. Nos. lxxi ff., 131 ff. Nos. lxxxvii and lxxxviii. See also, more generally, the works analyzed by F. Giunta in his "Alcuni recenti studi sulla Sicilia aragonese," *AS Siciliano*, 3d ser. VII, 413–16; F. Gabrieli, "Arabi di Sicilia e Arabi di Spagna," *Al-Andalus*, XV, 27–45;

and *infra*, n. 16. On Sicily's persistent Saracen and Greek traditions see *supra*, n. 3; Vol. IV, pp. 20 ff., 242 ff.; and A. Guillou's recent "Inchiesta sulla popolazione greca della Sicilia e della Calabria nel medioevo," *RSI*, LXXV, 53–68.

13. Lagumina and Lagumina, *Codice diplomatico*, I, 28 ff. Nos. xxxi–xxxii, 31 ff. Nos. xxxiv–xxxv (including p. 31 n. 2), 39 f. No. xxxix. Other archival studies shedding indirect light on the conditions of Jews in the Aragonese possessions in Italy are reviewed by J. Mazzoleni in his "Fonti per la storia dell'epoca aragonese esistenti nell'Archivio di Stato di Napoli," *ASPN*, LXXII, 125–54; LXXIV, 351–73. See esp. G. La Mantia, *Codice diplomatico dei re aragonesi de Sicilia . . . dalla rivoluzione siciliana del 1282 sino al 1355*, I, 172 f. No. lxxxvi; the second volume was posthumously edited by A. de Stefano and F. Giunta. Of some interest are also the complementary biographical studies by R. O. Bertrand, *Un rei de llegenda. Frederic III de Sicilia;* and A. de Stefano, *Federico III d'Aragona re di Sicilia (1296–1337)*, 2d ed. On King Frederick III's possible authorship of the decree of 1224 attributed to Emperor Frederick II, see *supra*, n. 4.

14. Lagumina and Lagumina, *Codice diplomatico*, I, 42 ff. No. xli, 50 ff. Nos. xliii–xliv with reference to the earlier decrees, *ibid.*, pp. 12 ff. Nos. xvi–xviii, 47 ff. No. xlii. Not that such supremacy of the bishops was necessarily prejudicial to Jews. In 1278, under Charles I's regime, Archbishop Jacob of Messina had proclaimed the general principle of the equality of rights of Jews and Christians in that city. See S. V. Bozzo, *Note storiche siciliane del secolo XIV*, pp. 307 f. On the meaning of "equality" see *infra*, Chap. XLVII. The bishop of Mazzara confirmed a Jew bearing the characteristic name Suleiman, in the office of "priest" (*sacerdos*), to which he had been elected and ordained by the community of Trapani. See the text cited by C. Minieri-Riccio in *Il Regno di Carlo di Angiò negli anni 1271–1272*, p. 113. All of this naturally did not prevent the Church from keeping up a running battle with the Crown over both the Jewish revenue and the application to Jews of the more rigid provisions of canon law.

15. *Consuetudines Palermitanae*, xv, xxvii, xxxvi, lxvii; *Consuetudines et statuta* of Messina, xlvii; *Consuetudines* of Syracuse, xxiv, all ed. by W. von Brünneck in *Sicilien's mittelalterliche Stadtrechte*, I–II. The authors of the Palermo custumal were particularly concerned about Jewish economic competition. At the same time they tried to preserve the revenue from Jews as the city's exclusive domain (Art. lvi), a right strenuously denied it by the royal officials. Brünneck, I, 47 ff., 50.

16. Lagumina and Lagumina, *Codice diplomatico*, I, 85 ff. Nos. lviii–lxii; and *supra*, n. 13. In a somewhat exceptional move Frederick IV approved in 1374 Marsala's agreement with the Jewish elders concerning the enlargement of the local synagogue. See *ibid.*, pp. 90 ff. No. lxiii; Erler in *AKKR*, XLVIII, 37. On the "custodian of the red wheel" and the antecedents of that office, see *infra*, Chap. XLVIII. To understand the nature of these local custumals and their bearing on Jews, one must realize the vast range of municipal autonomy which the Sicilian cities succeeded in preserving under their changing regimes. See esp. M. Gaudioso, *Natura giuridica delle autonomie cittadine nel "regnum Siciliae."* Its interrelations with the equally extensive Jewish self-government will be discussed in a later chapter.

17. Lagumina and Lagumina, *Codice diplomatico*, I, 131 ff. Nos. lxxxvii–xcii, 191 ff. Nos. cxlviii–cxlix, 215 ff. No. clxii, 231 ff. No. clxxvi, 321 No. ccliii. To what length some cities were prepared to go in circumventing royal decrees may be seen in a subterfuge used by the municipal elders of Marsala; after making the Jews surrender to them the original royal privilege of 1399, they subsequently refused to return it. The Jewish representatives had considerable difficulty, and doubtless also much expense, in securing from the king a renewal of that enactment (1405). The Inquisitor, Fra Matteo, insisted moreover upon the continued desirability of submitting Jews to conversionist sermons, although the ceremonial connected with these oratorical performances was somewhat mitigated. See the documentation in F. Lionti, "Gli Ebrei e la festa di S. Stefano Protomartire," *AS Siciliano*, n.s. VIII, 463–82.

Many of these protective regulations were obtained on the intervention of the community of Palermo, which now had begun to act "as the head and the principal community of all those of Our entire Sicilian kingdom." Lagumina and Lagumina, pp. 131 f. No. lxxxvii. On the growth of the communal organization in Sicily during the fourteenth and fifteenth centuries, see especially the older studies by F. Lionti, "Le Magistrature presso gli Ebrei di Sicilia," *AS Siciliano*, n.s. IX, 328–71; idem, "I Ministri della religione presso gli Ebrei di Sicilia," *ibid.*, n.s. X, 130–36; I. Sonne, "The General Council in Italy—Model for the Council of Four Lands in Poland" (Hebrew), *Hatekufah*, XXXII–XXXIII, 617–89 (deals mainly with north-central Italy); and, more generally, my *The Jewish Community*, esp. I, 315 ff.; III, 78 ff. This aspect will be more fully clarified in a later chapter. Incidentally, the expulsion from Vizzini was facilitated by Martin's earlier donation of the town to Huguest di Sancta Pace (1393). Cited from R. Gregorio's edition of *Scriptores rerum aragonarum*, II, 506, 511 by Erler in *AKKR*, XLVIII, 38. See also, more generally, the biographical data reviewed by D. Girona y Llagostera, "Itinerari del rey en Marti (1396–1402 y 1403–1410)," *Anuari* of the Institut d'estudis catalans, Barcelona, IV, 81–184; V, 515–655.

18. Lagumina and Lagumina, *Codice diplomatico*, I, 525 ff. No. cdi, 573 ff. Nos. cdxxxii–xxxiii; L. La Rocca, "Gli Ebrei di Catania nell'osservanza delle feste di rito romano," *AS per la Sicilia orientale*, V, 235–41, esp. pp. 240 f. No. iii. That such occasional fiscal favoritism aroused considerable resistance on the part of the cities is not at all surprising. The municipality of Catania actually sought from the viceroy permission to separate the Jewish community from its tax rolls and to make it contribute its payments independently. Lagumina and Lagumina, pp. 494 ff. No. ccclxxxv, 536 ff. Nos. cdiii–iv. Alphonso and his viceroy Simone de Bononia, Archbishop of Palermo, had to issue many further regulations to reduce the fiscal controversies between the Jews and the burghers. The usually disproportionate size of Jewish fiscal contributions is discussed by A. Milano in his "Vicende economiche degli Ebrei nell'Italia meridionale ed insulare durante il medioevo," *RMI*, XX, 378 f.; and his *Storia degli Ebrei*, pp. 172 f. See also, more generally, *infra*, Chap. LIV.

19. F. Lionti's data in *AS Siciliano*, n.s. VIII, 477 ff.; Lagumina and Lagumina, *Codice diplomatico*, I, 494 ff. No. ccclxxxv, 530 ff. No. cdii; A. Amore, "Nuovi documenti sull'attività del B. Matteo d'Agrigento nella Spagna ed in Sicilia," *AFH*, LII, 32 f. No. 18, 38 ff. On Alphonso's great piety, which, among other manifesta-

tions, made him vigorously promote the canonization of such outspokenly anti-Jewish preachers as Vicente Ferrer and Bernardino da Siena, see esp. J. Ametller y Viñas, *Alfonso V de Aragón en Italia y la crisis religiosa del siglo XV*, ed. by J. Collell *et al.*; and S. Sobrequés Vidal, "Sobre el ideal de cruzada de Alfonso V de Aragona," *Hispania* (Madrid), XII, 232–52. See also other biographical data, with special reference to his reign in the Italian provinces, in A. Jiménez (Gimenez) Soler, *Itinerario del rey Don Alonso* [or *Alfonso V*] *de Aragón el que ganó Nápoles;* F. de Bofarull y Sans, "Alfonso V de Aragón en Nápoles," *Homenaje a Menéndez y Pelayo*, I, 615–35, which includes a brief description of the royal library and the newly founded Alphonsine Academy; and the literature cited *supra*, Chap. XLV, n. 24.

20. Ferorelli, *Gli Ebrei*, pp. 173 ff.; P. M. Lonardo, "Un'Abiura di Ebrei a Lucera nel 1454," *Studi storici*, ed. by A. Crivellucci, XVI, 581–91; R. Gregorio, "Considerazioni sopra la storia di Sicilia" in his *Opere scelte*, pp. 446, 448 f. Since Alphonso's attempt to establish full royal supremacy over Jews ran counter to many privileges of individual barons and bishops, the ensuing clashes contributed to the spreading disaffection with his royal "absolutism." They led to severe disturbances after Alphonso's death in 1458 and the division of the Italian possessions of the Aragonese dynasty. See Ferorelli, pp. 175 ff.; and G. F. Ryder, "La Politica italiana di Alfonso d'Aragona (1442–1458)," *ASPN*, LXXVII, 43–106.

21. A. Caldarella, "L'Impresa di Martino I, re di Sicilia in Sardegna (a. 1408–1409)," *Atti* of the Accademia di scienze in Palermo, 4th ser. XIV, Part 2, pp. 55 f.; Ferorelli, *Gli Ebrei*, p. 17; Lagumina and Lagumina, *Codice diplomatico*, I, 304 No. ccxxxii; and *infra*, n. 23. On the background of the Sicilian government's manifold negotiations with Tunisia see A. Flandina, "La Spedizione di Alfonso nell'isola delle Gerbe e la presidenza del regno di Sicilia in quell'epoca," *AS Siciliano*, n.s. I, 422–53; F. Cerone, "A proposito di alcuni documenti sulla seconda spedizione di Alfonso V contra l'isola Gerba," *Anuari* of the Institut d'estudis catalans, Barcelona, III, 51–90; idem, "Alfonso il Magnanimo ed Abu 'Omer Othmân. Trattative e negoziati tra il Regno di Sicilia di qua e di là dal Faro ed il Regno di Tunisi (1432–1457)," *AS per la Sicilia orientale*, IX, 45–70.

22. Tacitus, *Annales*, ii.85, in his *Histories*, ed. with an English trans. by H. Moore and J. Jackson (the Loeb Classical Library), II, 516 f.; J. B. Frey, *Corpus inscriptionum iudaicarum*, I, 472 f. Nos. 656–60; P. Amat di S. Filippo, "Indagini e studi sulla storia economica della Sardegna. Memoria postuma," *Miscellanea di storia italiana*, XXXIX, 351 ff.; *supra*, Vol. I, pp. 246, 405 n. 43. Less reliable are the anthropological measurements of five skulls found in the ruins of Tharros which, according to some archaeologists, reveal decidedly Semitic features. See the report dated 1865 and cited by Amat, p. 353 n. 1. If certain suggestions connecting the biblical ships going to "Tarshish" with Sardinia are correct (see *supra*, Vol. I, p. 321 n. 3), the relations between ancient Jewry and that island may indeed reach back to the Israelitic monarchy.

23. E. Putzulu, "Carte reali aragonesi e spagnole dell'Archivio comunale di Cagliari (1358–1719)," *AS Sardo*, XXVI, 27 f. No. 61, 51 No. 118; Amat di S. Filippo in *Miscellanea di storia italiana*, XXXIX, 406 ff.; the slightly colored presentations

by L. Falchi, *Gli Ebrei nella storia e nella poesia populare dei Sardi;* and *La Dominazione ebraica in Sardegna,* with the independently valuable comments thereon by Eliezer ben David (Guido Bedarrida) in his "Ebrei di Sardegna," *RMI,* XI, 328–58, 424–43 (includes a noteworthy onomastic study); and A. Boscolo, "Gli Ebrei in Sardegna durante la dominazione aragonese," *Annali* of the Faculty of Letters of the University of Cagliari, XIX, Part 2, pp. 162–71 (includes data on Jewish merchants and fiscal agents).

24. To the literature cited in the last note add A. Caldarella's data in *Atti* of the Accademia di scienze, Palermo, 4th ser. XIV, pp. 55 f. (relating to Elia, brother of Samuele Sala, Martin's envoy to the king of Tunisia; Elia had been sent to Cagliari also to report orally on the progress of these negotiations; see *supra,* n. 21); L. Arezio, "La Sardegna e Alfonso il Magnanimo dalla battaglia di Ponza alla pace con Genova (1435–1444)," *AS Sardo,* III, 157–210; and, more generally, E. Besta's institutional history, *La Sardegna medioevale.* While apparently playing no active role in local political struggles, Jews were nonetheless their involuntary participants both as taxpayers and as prospective victims or beneficiaries. On the Jewish role in Sardinian mining, see also *infra,* Chap. LI.

25. See the analysis by A. Era of *Il Parlamento sardo del 1481–1485;* idem, "Contributi alla storia dei parlamenti sardi," *Studi sassaresi,* 2d ser. XXVI, 1–32; and, more generally, A. Solmi, *Studi storici sulle istituzioni della Sardegna nel medio evo.* See also the literature listed *supra,* nn. 22–23; and other studies relating to all phases of Sardinian history in R. Ciasca's comprehensive *Bibliografia sarda.*

26. Ferorelli, *Gli Ebrei,* esp. pp. 72 f., 191; G. Guerrieri's data in *Studi senesi,* XVII, 225–52; G. Pansa, "Gli Ebrei in Aquila nel secolo XV, l'opera dei frati minori e il Monte de pietà istituito da San Giacomo della Marca," *Bollettino* of the Società di Storia patria A. L. Antinori negli Abruzzi, 2d ser. XVI, 206 n. 3; C. Marciani in *ASPN,* LXXXI, 175 f. In 1463 the burghers of Bari tried in vain to force Jews to live in separate quarters. Following Alphonso's example, Ferrante insisted upon the exclusive royal control over Jews against any infringement by the bishop of Cantanzaro or the archbishop of Reggio (1468, 1491). Only the archbishop of Bari succeeded in inducing the king in 1465 to recognize the archepiscopal privileges dating back to the Norman period. Nor did the king and the royal family hesitate to support Neapolitan Jewish merchants abroad. On Ferrante's request, the authorities of Lucca extended in 1489 favored treatment to a Neapolitan Jewish businessman who had formerly resided in their city, and to the latter's father who had remained in Lucca. In 1466 Duchess Ippolita Maria of Calabria asked her mother, the duchess of Milan, to take a Neapolitan Jew, "whom We hold dear among Our faithful" under her protection. Six years later she asked the duke of Milan to free "her most faithful servant," Benedetto of Cremona, a resident of Naples, from his share in the severe tax imposed upon the Jewish community of Cremona. See Ferorelli, pp. 74 ff., 100, 175 f.; and R. Cotroneo's observations in *Rivista storica calabrese,* 3rd ser. XI, 390–418. See also G. Carano-Donvito in *Rivista di politica economica,* XXIII, 836–43; P. Sposato, "Saggio di ricerche archivistiche per la storia degli Ebrei in Calabria nella seconda metà del secolo XV," *Calabria nobilissima,* VIII, 41–48, 109–23 (includes 8 unpublished documents); G. Coniglio, "Mercanti forestieri a Napoli attraverso gli

atti del notaio Petruccio Pisano (1465–66)," *Samnium,* XXVIII, 78–85; E. Pontieri's comprehensive study, *Per la storia del regno di Ferrante I d'Aragona re di Napoli;* and other studies listed *supra,* n. 10; and *infra,* n. 29.

27. "De B. Bernardino Feltriensi" (a biography), in *Acta Sanctorum,* September, VII, 814–914, esp. pp. 851 f., 855; G. Pansa, "Gli Ebrei in Aquila nel secolo XV," *Bollettino* of the Società di Storia patria . . . negli Abruzzi, 2d ser. XVI; L. Rivera, "S. Bernardino da Siena e la città dell'Aquila," *Bollettino* of the Deputazione abruzzese di storia patria, 5th ser. VI, 47–119; L. Chiappini, *Eleonora d'Aragona prima duchessa di Ferrara.* On Bernardino da Siena, whose works have recently appeared in a new comprehensive edition by the College of St. Bonaventura, and his general contribution to the economic theories of the fifteenth-century Church, see *infra,* nn. 62, 67. The movement to establish *monti di pietà* spread from northern through southern Italy. One of the earliest to be established by Giacomo della Marca was that in his own birthplace of Ascoli Piceno in 1458. See G. Fabiani, *Gli Ebrei e il Monte di pietà in Ascoli;* and other works listed by G. Mira in his "Cenni bibliografici sugli studi relativi alla costituzione e alla prima fase di sviluppo dei Monti di pietà," *Archivi storici delle Aziende di Credito,* I, 343–80. See also *supra,* Chap. XXXVII, nn. 60–61; and *infra,* Chap. LIII.

28. Lagumina and Lagumina, *Codice diplomatico,* I, 403 ff. No. cccxxxii; II, 59 f. No. d, 127 ff. Nos. dxlvii–lii, 145 ff. No. dlix, 150 ff. Nos. dlxii–iv, 157 ff. No. dlxvi, 160 ff. No. dlxviii, 164 No. dlxxii, 480 ff. No. dcclxvii; R. Starrabba, "Di un documento riguardante la Giudecca di Palermo," *AS Siciliano,* I, 89–102 (a letter from Pietro di Bologna, Secretary of Palermo, to Viceroy Ferrando d'Acugna, dated Aug. 27, 1492; see Lagumina and Lagumina, III, 154 ff. No. dccclxx); idem, "Transazione tra il Comune e la Giudecca di Palermo del 2. novembre 1491," *ibid.,* n.s. I, 454–68; and, on the social unrest, C. Trasselli, *La "Questione sociale" in Sicilia e la rivolta di Messina del 1464.* The "Prammatica" of King John II of 1468, appointing Ferdinand coregent of Sicily, was published by J. Vicens Vives in his *El Principe Don Fernando (El Católico), Rey de Sicilia,* pp. 33 f. In this connection Vicens cites also a Sicilian chronicler's description of the Palermitan festivities on the occasion of Ferdinand's marriage to Isabella: "The Jews marched alongside the burghers with torches in their hands" (pp. 31 f.). See also, more generally, the same author's *Fernando el Católico, príncipe de Aragón, rey de Sicilia, 1458–1478.*

29. Lagumina and Lagumina, *Codice diplomatico,* I, 403 ff. No. cccxxxii; II, 59 f. No. d, 403 No. dccxxxiii; III, 2 ff. Nos. dccclxxi–lxxii, 9 f. No. dccclxxv; R. Starrabba, "Guglielmo Raimondo Moncada. Ebreo convertito siciliano del secolo XV," *AS Siciliano,* n.s. III, 15–91. Not that all, or even most, of the clergy necessarily participated in the anti-Jewish agitation. Some churchmen were financially interested in the preservation of Jews. For instance, the abbott of Santa Maria di Nova Luce concluded in 1474 a new agreement with the Jews of Catania concerning an old excise tax on their silk manufacture paid to the monastery. See Lagumina and Lagumina, II, 183 f. No. dlxxxiii; and, more generally, A. Petino, "L'Arte ed il consolato della seta a Catania nei secoli XIV–XIX," *Bollettino storico catanese* (continuation of the *AS per la Sicilia orientale*), VII–VIII, 15–78, esp. pp. 18 f. See also C. Fontana, *Gli Ebrei in Catania nel secolo XV.*

30. Lagumina and Lagumina, *Codice diplomatico*, III, 7 ff. Nos. dccclxxiv–lxxvi, 17 ff. Nos. dccclxxxi–xcii. See also A. Milano, "The Number of the Jews in Sicily at the Time of their Expulsion in 1492," *JSS*, XV, 25–32 (appeared also in Italian in *RMI*, XX, 16–24); the lower estimates given by C. Trasselli in his "Sull'espulsione degli Ebrei dalla Sicilia," *Annali* of the University of Palermo, Faculty of Economics and Commerce, VIII, 129–51; and, on the subsequent destinies of the refugees, B. (C.) Roth's Hebrew essay, "A Contribution to the History of the Exiles from Sicily," *Eretz-Israel*, III, 230–34. This entire subject will be more fully elucidated *infra*, Chaps. L and LVI.

31. S. H. Margulies, "La Famiglia Abravanel in Italia," *Rivista israelitica*, III, 97–107, 147–53; B. Netanyahu, *Don Isaac Abravanel*, pp. 61 ff. On southern Italy's printing presses, see the data assembled by J. Bloch in his "Hebrew Printing in Naples," *Bulletin* of the New York Public Library, XLVI, 489–514; and R. Frattarolo, *Tipografi e librai, ebrei e non, nel Napoletano, all fine del XV secolo*.

Unfortunately, the history of the declining years of the Neapolitan regime before it was taken over by Spain, including the Jewish aspects thereof, can now be investigated only with some difficulty. The vast collections of the Neapolitan State Archives were removed at the beginning of the Second World War from Naples to a small locality in its vicinity. No one could foresee that, before their retreat in November 1943, the Germans would purposely set fire to this irreplaceable collection. This catastrophe cannot fully be remedied even by the extremely ambitious and relatively successful effort at reconstructing these archives from various other sources, undertaken in recent years by R. Filangieri and his associates. See their compilation of *I Registri della cancelleria angioina ricostruiti*, of which Vols. I–XVII have appeared until 1963, covering the early years of 1265 ff. See also J. Mazzoleni, ed., *Regesto della cancelleria aragonesa di Napoli*.

32. L. I. Serrano y Pineda, "Correspondencia de los Reyes Católicos con el Gran Capitán durante las campañas de Italia," *RABM*, 3d ser. XXI, 353 No. xxi; XXIII, 500 No. xliii; P. Villari, ed., *Dispacci di Antonio Giustinian, ambasciatore veneto in Roma del 1502 al 1505*, III, 51 f.; P. Gasparrini, "Un Ignorato parlamento generale napoletano del 1504 e un altro poco noto del 1507," *ASPN*, LXXV, 203–10; D. Spanò Bolani's observations on "I Giudei in Reggio di Calabria," *ibid.*, VI, 339; and C. Marciani's data, *ibid.*, LXXXI, 177 f. Hernandez Gonzalo de Cordova's recommendation of an Inquisition is contained in his letter to the Catholic kings dated July 6, 1504. See the excerpt from that letter cited in an English trans. by A. Marx in his report on "The Library," *Register* of the Jewish Theological Seminary of America, 1940–41, pp. 65 f. Incidentally, Marx mentions here that the Seminary Library owns a "unique copy of the Proclamation ordering the expulsion of all Jews and Marranos from the Kingdom of Naples." It is dated June 22, 1510. On that significant stage in Neapolitan history, in general, see esp. the studies reviewed by P. Villani in his "Nuove ricerche sul dominio spagnolo in Italia," *Società*, XII, 707–14. See also F. Ruiz Martín, "La Expulsión de los Judíos del Reino de Nápoles," *Hispania* (Madrid), IX, 28–76, 179–240; and *infra*, Chap. L.

The regime of the Catholic monarchs in southern Italy has aroused almost as much interest as their rule over their Spanish homeland. Italian historians, in particular, have spent much time and effort in elucidating the various phases of that reign, including its international and domestic aspects. See, for instance, E. Pontieri's analysis of "Ferdinando il Cattolico e i regni di Napoli e di Sicilia nella storiografia italiana dell'ultimo cinquantennio," *RSI*, LXIV, 399–422. The specific problems of the establishment of the Inquisition in Naples along Spanish lines in 1509 and its subsequent effects on the history of that region are discussed by F. Ruiz Martín in "Fernando il Católico y la Inquisición en el reino de Nápoles: génesis de un mito," *Pensamiento político, política internacional y religiosa de Fernando el Católico,* pp. 314–36. Ruiz Martín's attempt, however, to minimize the impact of the dead hand of the Inquisition and its coresponsibility for the retardation of that region's economy and cultural evolution is too apologetically colored to be taken seriously. See also *infra,* Chap. LV. On the permanent Jewish heritage see also C. Trasselli's succinct philological and folkloristic data in his "Sulla diffusione degli Ebrei e sull'importanza della cultura e della lingua ebraica in Sicilia, particolarmente in Trapani e in Palermo, nel secolo XV," *Bollettino* of the Centro di studi filologici e linguistici siciliani, II, 376–82.

33. See *supra,* Chap. XXXVII and the literature listed there. This constant interplay of international and local factors in the policies of the Papal States has made it difficult for historians to present a clear-cut picture of what happened to Rome's own Jewish subjects. See the two standard works, titled *Geschichte der Juden in Rome,* by A. Berliner and by H. Vogelstein and P. Rieger. (The latter is summarized with but minor changes by Vogelstein in his *Rome* in the Jewish Communities Series.) More remarkably, despite the passage of nearly seventy years, little scholarly progress has since been made in the investigation of the local history of Roman Jewry. Both G. Blustein in his *Storia degli Ebrei in Roma dal II° secolo avanti Cristo;* and A. Milano in his recent summaries, "The Church and Roman Jewry in the Thirteenth and Fourteenth Centuries" (Hebrew), *Eretz-Israel,* III, 223–29; and *Storia degli Ebrei in Italia,* pp. 78 ff., 146 ff., still lean heavily on Vogelstein and Rieger, Milano adding significant data mainly with respect to the occupational life of the Roman Jews. Of some independent value still are E. Rodocanachi, *Le Saint-Siège et les Juifs: Le ghetto à Rome;* and the graphic description of some surviving monuments of ancient and medieval Jewry by E. Loevinson in his *Roma Israelitica.* On the basic *Constitutio pro Judaeis,* see also S. Grayzel's recent analysis of "The Papal Bull *Sicut Judeis,*" *Neuman Jub. Vol.,* pp. 243–80.

Nor is the differentiation between the local history of Rome or the papal provinces and the international history of the Papacy clearly drawn in the existing general literature. Hence here, too, old standard works, by Gregorovius and Pastor, still serve as the most comprehensive guides to the history of the States of the Church as well. See F. Gregorovius, *Geschichte der Stadt Rom im Mittelalter,* available also in a thin-paper edition with an intro. and notes by F. Schillmann and in the English translation by A. Hamilton entitled *History of the City of Rome in the Middle Ages* (supplemented in regard to our subject by Gregorovius's essay on *The Ghetto and the Jews of Rome,* trans. from the German by M. Hadas); and L. Pastor, *The History of the Popes from the Close of the Middle Ages* (despite the title, the first six volumes deal essentially with the medieval popes reigning in the years 1305–1513).

Needless to say, the twentieth century has accumulated a vast additional literature for which even the bibliographical aids are rather inadequate, except for the data included in recent years in the annual *Bibliografia storica nazionale,* published by the Giunta Centrale per gli studi storici (since 1939); and the *Bibliografia romana* ed. by Ceccharino for the Istituto di studi romani, Vols. I–IX (for the years 1945–53). See also, for instance, the fairly recent analyses by R. Folz, "La Papauté médiévale vue par quelques-uns de ses historiens récents," *RH*, CCXVIII, 32–63; R. Manselli, "Storia di Roma e del papato nel medioevo," *Studi romani*, V, 316–22; and the literature cited in the forthcoming notes.

34. Bismarck's observations, reproduced by H. Bastgen in *Die Römische Frage, Dokumente und Stimmen*, III, Part 1, pp. 3 ff., esp. p. 14; Benjamin b. Abraham 'Anav's poems, esp. *El mi anusah le-'ezrah* (To Whom Shall I Flee for Help), ed. from a Ferrara MS of the Roman *Maḥzor* (Prayer Book for Holidays) by Isaac Baruch ha-Levi, in a collection entitled *Taḥnune bene Yisrael* (Prayers of the Children of Israel) with Notes and Additions by S. Z. H. Halberstam in *Qobeṣ 'al yad* (Sammelband), IV, Part 2, pp. 6 ff.; Vogelstein and Rieger, *Geschichte der Juden in Rom*, I, 234 ff., 246 ff.; Clement IV's *Turbato corde* of 1267 in *Bullarium romanum*, Turin, 1857 ff. ed., III, 785 ff. No. xxiv; *supra*, Chap. XXXVII, *passim*. On Charles I's election as Roman senator see F. Bock, "Le Trattative per la senatoria di Roma e Carlo d'Angió," *Archivio* of the Società romana di storia patria, LXXVIII, 69–105. See also E. Nasalli Rocca di Corneliano's interesting analysis of *Problemi religiosi e politici del Duecento nell'opera di due grandi Italiani: il Cardinale Giacomo da Pecovara e il Pontefice B. Gregorio X*. Giacomo, it may be noted, served as papal legate in France during the crucial years of 1239–41, and the actual burning of the Talmud may have been owing to his personal perseverance as much as to Louis IX's religious zeal and neutralism in the struggle between the Papacy and the Empire. See *supra*, Chap. XXXVIII, nn. 12 ff.

35. L. Wadding, *Annales Minorum*, ed. by J. M. Fonseca, V, 232; Potthast, *Regesta pontificum*, II, 1865 f. No. 23170; Erler in *AKKR*, L, 3 n. 2 (proving that the bull *Vineam sorec* in *Bullarium romanum*, IV, 95 ff. No. iii, was addressed to the entire Dominican and Franciscan orders, and not only to their provincials in Lombardy and in Austria); M. da Alatri, *L'Inquisizione francescana nell'Italia centrale nel secolo XIII;* F. Pericolo, "L'Abolizione della feodalità negli Stati della Chiesa," *Rivista araldica*, LIV, 100–116; and *infra*, Chap. LIX. Martin IV's order to the bishops and inquisitors in France of October 21, 1281 not to extend the right of asylum in churches to heretics and relapsed Jews likewise applied in practice only to France and had no direct bearing on the life of the pope's Italian subjects. See O. Raynaldus, *Annales ecclesiastici*, III, 525 (*ad* 1281, xviii); Potthast, II, 1763 No. 21806; Erler, p. 4 n. 4. The general impact of feudalism on the status of European Jewry will become clearer in our forthcoming Vols. XI–XII.

36. The statute of 1310, as renewed in 1402 and confirmed in 1418, was published from a Vatican MS by Vogelstein and Rieger in their *Geschichte der Juden in Rom*, I, 490 ff. Appendix 5. Unfortunately, the text is not completely legible. The lacuna preceding the words *mille centum triginta florinorum*, which the Jews were supposed to pay to the municipal treasury, is particularly regrettable. The reference to Angelo and his sons was evidently inserted first into the renewal of 1402. We also possess the text of another privilege, previously extended to Angelo and his father Manuel by members of the Roman Senate and the heads of the society of ship dressers and flag makers (*pavesatororum et banderensium*). In this privilege, dated

April 29, 1376, shortly before Gregory XI's return to Rome, Manuel and Angelo are described as "Jewish surgeons most expert in their art who have daily performed many services for the Roman burghers and are most useful to the city, particularly since they are the physicians of our society and have the duty to cure its members." For this reason the two doctors were to be free from all taxation and not be "aggrieved" therein by the Jewish community or any other agency or person. See M. Stern, *Urkundliche Beiträge über die Stellung der Päpste zu den Juden*, I, 14 ff. No. 3. This privilege, renewed by the Senate in 1385, was confirmed by Boniface in 1392 and 1399. See the summaries by Stern, p. 17 Nos. 5–6; and *supra*, Chap. XXXVII, n. 49. On other privileged Jewish physicians see Chap. LII.

37. The curious treaty of Orvieto is reproduced by L. Fumi in his *Codice diplomatico della città d'Orvieto*, pp. 418 f. As stressed by Vogelstein and Rieger, I, 305 n. 1, the famous Hebrew poet, Immanuel b. Solomon of Rome, though not one of the lenders, took an active interest in this transaction and referred to it, obliquely but intelligibly, at the end of his classic *Maḥbarot* (Maqamae). See the *Sefer Gezerot Ashkenaz ve-Ṣarefat*, ed. by A. M. Habermann, pp. 851 f.; and the interpretation of that passage by B. (C.) Roth in "The Historic Background of Immanuel's *Maḥbarot*" (Hebrew), *Sefer Assaf* (Simḥah Assaf Jubilee Volume), pp. 444–58, esp. pp. 448 f. (also available in an Italian translation entitled "Lo Sfondo storico della poesia di Immanuel Romano," *RMI*, XVII, 424–46, esp. pp. 430 f.). As in the rest of Italy, it may be noted, the Black Death which devastated Orvieto did not lead to any serious anti-Jewish reactions, although the bankers were hampered for many years in recovering even a portion of their loans antedating 1348. On the extent of the plague see E. Carpentier, *Une Ville devant la peste: Orvieto et la Peste Noire de 1348*, esp. pp. 60 f., 206 f.

38. The main data on the Jews of Avignon and the Comtat Venaissin esp. during the popes' "Babylonian Exile" were assembled by L. Bardinet in his "Condition civile des Juifs du Comtat Venaissin pendant le séjour des Papes à Avignon (1309–1376)," *RH*, XII, 1–47; idem, "Condition civile des Juifs du Comtat Venaissin pendant le XVe siècle (1409–1513)," *REJ*, VI, 1–40; idem, "Les Juifs du Comtat Venaissin au moyen âge. Leur rôle économique et intellectuel," *RH*, XIV, 1–60; idem, "Antiquité et organisation des juiveries du Comtat Venaissin," *REJ*, I, 262–92; and R. de Maulde, *Les Juifs dans les états français du Saint-Siège au moyen âge*, which consists of a lengthy introduction and an extensive collection of documents. Although writing some six years after Bardinet, De Maulde fails to indicate his frequent indebtedness to this predecessor. See esp. pp. 9 ff. See also the monographic studies by I. Loeb, "Les Juifs de Carpentras sous le gouvernement pontifical," *REJ*, XII, 34–64, 161–235 (among other matters, plausibly arguing against the alleged expulsions of Jews in 1269 and 1350, pp. 39 f., 51 f.); J. Bauer, "Les Juifs de Bédarrides," *ibid.*, XXIX, 254–65 (mainly of interest for the Counter Reformation); and the more general surveys by A. Mossé, *Histoire des Juifs d'Avignon et du Comtat Venaissin;* and S. Grayzel, "The Avignon Popes and the Jews," *HJ*, II, 1–12. Of interest are also the general histories of the Avignon papacy including G. Mollat, *Les Papes d'Avignon (1305–1378)*, 9th ed.; or in the English trans. from that ed. by J. Love entitled *The Popes of Avignon (1305–1378)*; and Y. Rénouard, *La Papauté à Avignon;* as well as B. Guillemain, *La Cour pontificale d'Avignon (1309–1376): Étude d'une société*.

39. Bardinet in *RH*, XII, 10 f., 38 ff.; XIV, 8, 13 ff., 18, 36, 41, 44 ff.; De Maulde, *Les Juifs, passim*. See also *supra*, Chap. XLIII, n. 38. Interesting examples of Jewish tax gatherers in the Comtat during the fourteenth century are cited by C. Faure in his *Étude sur l'administration et l'histoire du Comtat-Venaissin du XIIIᵉ au XVᵉ siècle (1229-1417)*, pp. 106 f. The astounding growth of the population of Avignon during the popes' "Babylonian Exile" often led to exaggerations. Among others. Bardinet assumed a population of 100,000. More moderately, B. Guillemain pointed out that after the ambitious reconstruction of the city in 1355 its area covered somewhat less than 152 hectares (*ca.* 380 acres) which, assuming a considerable population density, accommodated little more than 30,000 inhabitants. See his "Punti di vista sul papato avignonese," *ASI*, CXI, 181–206, esp. p. 187; and *infra*, Chap. LI.

Not surprisingly, the steady increase in the Jewish population created problems also for the Jewish community. According to a later manuscript record, the local Jewish cemetery speedily filled up. Apparently unable to enlarge its area or to acquire another cemetery, since permits of that kind were obtained only with great difficulty, "it occurred to them to place earth upon the graves and to put [subsequent] graves one on top of the other." See the text published by A. Neubauer in his "Documents inédits XV: Documents sur Avignon," *REJ*, X, 94 No. v. This practice is also known from other communities.

Needless to say, the papal friendliness was greatly affected by the Treasury's incessant needs, since John XXII, Innocent VI, and Gregory XI had to expend a large percentage of their budgets for war purposes. See Y. Rénouard's avowedly incomplete estimates in *Les Relations des papes d'Avignon et des compagnies commerciales et bancaires de 1316 à 1378*, pp. 32 ff. Compared, however, with the vast contributions flowing from many Christian lands, the Jewish share in both the payment and the handling of papal imposts appears to have been rather moderate. (Rénouard claims to have found the records of only two Jews, Bonaccorso di Saul of Lucca and Vergudonus Capelle of Sardinia, who were actually used in the transfer of papal funds, p. 106 n. 1.) Suffice it to mention that on his death in 1334 John left behind a huge Treasury accumulation. See *infra*, n. 40 end; and, more generally, W. E. Lunt, *Papal Revenues in the Middle Ages*; F. Baethgen, "Quellen und Untersuchungen zur Geschichte der päpstlichen Hof- und Finanzverwaltung unter Bonifaz VIII," reprinted in his *Mediaevalia: Aufsätze, Nachrufe, Besprechungen*, pp. 228–95; H. Hoberg, ed., *Die Inventare des päpstlichen Schatzes in Avignon, 1314-1376*, esp. pp. 38 ff., 50 ff. (showing the Treasury accumulations in 1342); and *supra*, Chap. XXXVII, n. 50.

40. John XXII, *Lettres communes analysées d'après les registres d'Avignon et du Vatican*, ed. by G. Mollat, III, 362 f. Nos. 14244–45, relating to the former synagogue in Bédarrides; Samuel Usque, *Consolaçam*, iii.17, ed. by Mendes dos Remedios, III, fol. xviiib; in M. A. Cohen's English trans., p. 190; Ibn Verga, *Shebeṭ Yehudah*, xiv, ed. by M. Wiener, pp. 37 f.; in the latter's German trans., pp. 74 ff.; ed. by Shohet, pp. 60 f.; Joseph ha-Kohen, *'Emeq ha-bakha*, ed. by Letteris, pp. 61 f.; in Wiener's German trans., p. 49; Bardinet in *RH*, XII, 16 ff.; Jean Froissart, *Chroniques*, 1.2, in his *Oeuvres*, ed. by J. M. B. C. Kervyn de Lettenhove, V, 275 (see also the somewhat different versions, *ibid.*, p. 277; XVII, 274).

The story of the intended expulsion and burning of the Talmud in 1321–22 still is full of obscurities. Apart from the confused records of the aforementioned Hebrew chroniclers, all of whom may have derived their information from Profiat Duran's lost account of anti-Jewish persecutions, who in turn used some surviving contemporary sources (see F. Baer, *Untersuchungen über Quellen . . . des Schebet Jehuda*, pp. 23 ff.), we only have the positive data concerning the synagogues in Bédarrides and Carpentras. However, the papal decrees relating to that Bédarrides synagogue are dated February 20 and 27, 1321, which would place them chronologically before the alleged decree of expulsion and its revocation. Even the burning of the Talmud is mainly recorded in connection with a Jewish delegation petitioning John XXII against the execution of that decree and the proclamation, by some Italian Jewish communities, of a fast day during which a number of new prayers were recited. These liturgical pieces were included in the manuscript *Maḥzor* of the Italian rite written *ca.* 1420 and now at the Jewish Theological Seminary of America. See A. Marx's report in the *Register* of the Jewish Theological Seminary, 1938–39, p. 69; Letteris's note in his ed. of *'Emeq*, pp. 62 f.; and *supra*, Chap. XXXVIII, n. 19. These obscurities will not be resolved until some possible new discoveries in the papal registry during the reign of John XXII might yield some fresh information. On the unsatisfactory state of preservation of that registry, see, however, F. Bock, "Neue Forschungen zum Registerwesen Johannes XXII," *Forschungen und Fortschritte*, XIV, 23 ff. See also *infra*, Chap. L.

Robert of Anjou's role in these negotiations, though not confirmed by other sources, is not implausible. We know that he entertained very close relations with the new pope. See esp. G. Tabacco, *La Casa di Francia nell'azione politica di papa Giovanni XXII*, which includes the text of a very friendly letter written by the pope to Robert on June 15, 1318 (see esp. pp. 170 ff., 189 ff., 251 ff.). It may also be noted that John extended the inquisitorial jurisdiction to all cases of sorcery even if unconnected with heresy, but he did not include Jews. This restriction contrasted, for instance, with the specific inclusion of Jews temporarily secured a century later by the southern French inquisitors. See *infra*, nn. 43 and 44; and A. Maier, "Eine Verfügung Johanns XXII über die Zuständigkeit der Inquisition für Zaubereiprozesse," *Archivum fratrum praedicatorum*, XXII, 226–46. All these measures were doubtless in some way affected by the pope's fiscal interest which might have made him readily accessible to such gifts as a share in the 20,000–100,000 ducats allegedly paid by the Jewish communities. It was not without certain questionable practices that John succeeded in leaving behind a papal Treasury allegedly filled with cash valued at 15,000,000–25,000,000 florins. See V. Verlaque, *Jean XXII, sa vie et ses oeuvres, d'après des documents inédits*, pp. 205 f.

41. Giovanni Villani, *Historie fiorentine*, x.67, ed. by G. B. Recanati, in *Rerum italicarum scriptores*, ed. by L. A. Muratori, XIII, 640; Vogelstein and Rieger, *Geschichte*, I, 303 ff. Upon entering Rome, emperors received a ceremonial welcome similar to that of popes. They also seem to have followed the popes' example in accepting the Jewish scroll of law, but repudiating its Jewish interpretations. We possess a graphic description of such a welcoming ceremony by Balduin of Treves, a witness of Emperor Henry VII's expedition to Rome. Although the accompanying picture presenting Jews wearing the characteristic Jewish hats was drawn from Balduin's memory, it doubtless represented an approximation of the event. True, on the one occasion when both emperor and pope were welcomed by Jews, namely after the election of Martin V by the Council of Constance on November 21, 1417, eyewitnesses recorded somewhat different reactions. According to one reporter,

Martin refused to accept the scroll from the Constance Jews. Emperor Sigismund allegedly took it saying, "Your laws are just and good, none of Us rejects them; only you do not observe any of them as you should." Only after he returned the scroll to the Jews did the pope speak up, "May the Omnipotent Lord remove the veil from your eyes and make you perceive the light of life eternal." The Vienna MS record of the Council of Constance, however, refers to the pope as returning the scroll to the Jews with the observation, "You have the law but you do not understand it; the old things have receded, everything is new." See H. von der Hardt, ed., *Magnum oecumenicum Constantiense concilium de universali ecclesiae reformatione, unione ac fide*, IV, 1491.

42. E. Amadei, "Gli Ebrei in Roma," *Capitolium*, VIII, 253–60, esp. p. 255; Cola di Rienzo, *Briefwechsel*, ed. by K. Burdach and P. Piur, III, 198 ff., 208 No. 50; E. Rodocanachi, *Cola di Rienzo*, pp. 404 f., 438; Vogelstein and Rieger, *Geschichte*, I, 310 ff. Supposedly, it was a Jew who sounded the church bell calling the population to arms in 1347 to save the revolution. Such actions by individual Jews, however, whether betraying a friendly or unfriendly attitude toward Rienzo, did not necessarily represent the will of the community or its elders. It is quite possible that even at that critical moment in Rome's history the communal leadership held aloof from the partisan struggles. In any case, the reestablished papal regime enacted no reprisals against the community.

43. C. Rè, ed., *Statuti della città di Roma*, p. 191; K. Eubel, "Weitere Urkunden zu dem Verhalten der Päpste gegen die Juden," *Römische Quartalschrift*, XVII, 184 ff.; Vogelstein and Rieger, *Geschichte*, I, 315 ff.; *supra*, Chaps. XXXVII, n. 49; XXXVIII, n. 46. Taxation loomed large in all relations between Roman-Avignonese Jewry and the papal administration. The contributions of the provincial communities to the papal Treasury were relatively minor during the thirteeth century, probably because few Jews resided outside the capital. But with the growth of Jewish settlements in the vicinity of Rome, as well as in Umbria and Romagna, the Roman elders often regarded it a matter of both necessity and equity to have those outside communities share in their increasing burdens. See *infra*, nn. 55 ff.; and Chap. LIV.

44. O. Raynaldus, *Annales ecclesiastici*, VIII, 503 *ad* 1419 ii. The annalist places this Avignonese repression in the year preceding Martin V's arrival in Mantua in February 1419, but it may have occurred soon after his election in 1417. On the very complex inquisitorial procedures see *infra*, Chap. LV.

45. F. Vernet, "Le Pape Martin V et les Juifs," *Revue des questions historiques*, LI, 373–423, esp. the documentary excerpts, pp. 409 ff.; *supra*, Chap. XXXVII, nn. 14–16; and, more generally, P. Partner, *The Papal State under Martin V: The Administration and Government of the Temporal Power in the Early Fifteenth Century*. Needless to say, the registration of pro-Jewish bulls was also turned into a source of revenue. The Treasury recorded, for instance, the receipt of the substantial amount of 40 florins from the Jews of Padua, Bologna, and Ferrara "for the registration or tax of one bull in the register of bulls" (Feb. 7, 1419). See Lunt, *Papal Revenues*, II, 509. In 1421 Martin, evidently prompted by the Roman Jewish elders, broadened the earlier provisions and ordered not only the communities of the Campagna, Romagna, and Ancona, but also those of Tuscany, to share in the taxes

paid by the Jews in Rome. He also granted substantial privileges to Roman Jewish physicians, including Elia di Sabbato, who since 1405 had been a naturalized Roman "burgher." It was characteristic of the rising humanistic interests in antiquity for the pope to listen to a lecture on the biblical cherubim, delivered at court by a foreign Jew, Aaron b. Gershom Abulrabi. Not surprisingly, therefore, even the anti-Jewish furor, caused in Italy by the alleged responsibility of Jerusalem Jews for the destruction of the Franciscan chapel on Mount Zion in 1428, entailed no untoward consequences for their coreligionists in the Papal States, except that the communities of the Marches were singled out for sharing with the Jewries of the Venetian Republic the payment of an indemnity to the Jerusalem monks. See M. Stern, *Urkundliche Beiträge*, I, 25 ff. Nos. 11, 12, 20, 22 and 30; Vogelstein and Rieger, I, 323 ff.

46. M. Stern, *Urkundliche Beiträge*, I, 45 f. Nos. 38 and 40; and *supra*, Chaps. XXXVII, nn. 32 and 36; XL, n. 38. Curiously, we hear practically of no public protests against the pope's favorite treatment of Jewish physicians. Although their very employment ran counter to long-established canon law, the Roman public must have become sufficiently inured to the services of Jewish doctors to accept without demurrer even the extraordinary privileges granted to them by various popes. See V. Rocchi, "Gli Ebrei e l'esercizio della medicina di fronte alle leggi della Chiesa e del governo di Roma papale," *Rivista di storia, letteratura e scienza*, I, 32–39; and such local monographs as R. Mosti's "Medici ebrei del XIV–XV secolo a Tivoli (Per un disegno storico della medicina tiburtina)," *Atti e memorie* of the Società tiburtina di storia e d'arte, XXVII, 109–56.

47. M. Stern, *Urkundliche Beiträge*, I, 46 ff. Nos. 39–41, 43 and 46; the older archival study by F. Kayser, "Papst Nicolaus V (1447–55) und die Juden," *AKKR*, LIII, 209–20 (particularly interesting because of his data on the pope's attitude toward the Spanish *conversos*); D. Kaufmann, "Correspondance échangée entre les communautés juives de Recanati et d'Ancone en 1448," *REJ*, XXIII, 249–55; Vogelstein and Rieger, *Geschichte*, II, 9 ff., 427 f. No. 19. On the papal attitude to John Capistrano, see the essays published in 1956 on the occasion of the 500th Anniversary of his death in *Bullettino* of the Deputazione di storia patria per gli Abruzzi, XLVI; *supra*, n. 11; and Chap. XXXVII, n. 32. The story that Capistrano "once offered a large ship to his Holiness Eugenius IV in order to transport the Jews across the sea," frequently cited, is founded on no better evidence than some anonymous notes preserved in a Vatican MS and quoted by Vogelstein and Rieger, II, 427 f. Written in the seventeenth century, this story is probably apocryphal. Some such stories may have circulated, however, among contemporaries, who were doubtless perplexed by the constant vagaries of the pope's Jewish policies.

48. M. Stern, *Urkundliche Beiträge*, I, 47 ff. Nos. 42, 47–50, 52–55 and 57; E. Vansteenberghe, *Le Cardinal Nicolas de Cues (1401–1464); l'action, la pensée*, pp. 134 f.; R. Aubenas and R. Ricard, *L'Église et la Renaissance (1449–1517)*, in *Histoire de l'Église*, ed. by A. Fliche and V. Martin, XV, pp. 20 ff., 383 ff.; and *supra*, Chaps. XXXVII, n. 32; XL, n. 38. The impression created upon a German observer is illustrated by a letter to Duke Henry of Bavaria of June 29, 1449 from the Dominican Hainrich Kalteisen, who looked at the papal court from the close range of the small town of Spoleto, in which the pope and his entourage sought

refuge from a pestilence then raging in Rome. Though clearly biased, Kalteisen doubtless reflected the general anti-Jewish sentiments then permeating the papal court. See the text reproduced from a Munich MS by M. Stern, pp. 48 ff. No. 44.

49. R. de Maulde, *Les Juifs dans les états français du Saint-Siège,* esp. pp. 8 n. 3, 11, 13 n. 7, 18, 29 n. 1; the documents analyzed by Bardinet in *REJ,* VII, 145 f.; and G. B. Picotti in his "D'una questione tra Pio II e Francesco Sforza per la ventesima sui beni degli Ebrei," *AS Lombardo,* 4th ser. XX, 184–213; Rodocanachi, *Le Saint-Siège et les Juifs,* pp. 152 ff. Picotti shows how divided the Italian states were in their interpretation of the Jewish tax. Pius himself clearly had a property tax of five percent in mind. In his *Commentarii rerum memorabilium,* xii, he recorded without hesitation that he had wanted the Jews to pay "omnium bonorum vigesimae." See the Frankfort 1614 ed., p. 333; and F. A. Gragg's English trans. in *Smith College Studies in History,* XLIII, 812 (or in the abridged ed. entitled *Memoirs of a Renaissance Pope,* p. 143); and, more generally, R. J. Mitchell, *The Laurels and the Tiara: Pope Pius II 1458–1464,* esp. pp. 143, 176 f. Accordingly, Pius demanded such payments from both Bologna and Florence. The Republic of Venice, however, interested in safeguarding the fiscal resources of its Jewish subjects, gave it the meaning of a mere income tax of 5 percent. In fact, the Venetians had previously objected to the large property tax imposed by Calixtus III in 1456. Now they were joined by Milan, Francisco Sforza arguing with the pope that a 5 percent property tax would constitute "a wholly unbearable burden." See the texts published by L. Pastor in his *Ungedruckte Akten zur Geschichte der Päpste,* I, 52 ff. Nos. 38–39, 116 f. No. 86, 202 ff. No. 152, 240 ff. No. 170, 261 No. 176; by Picotti, pp. 204 ff. Nos. i–ii; and *infra,* Chap. LIV. All of these remonstrations did not deter later popes, as we shall presently see, from endeavoring to collect similar taxes.

50. The later forms of the Roman Carnival, which the game-loving Roman populace turned into one of the city's most widely renowned celebrations while investing the Jewish role therein with an aura of contumely, are extensively discussed by A. Ademollo, *Alessandro VI, Giulio II e Leone X nel Carnevale di Roma. Documenti inediti (1499–1520);* idem, *Il Carnevale di Roma nei secoli XVII e XVIII;* F. Clementi, *Il Carnivale romano nelle cronache contemporanee dalle origini al secolo XVII,* I, 55 ff., 556 ff.; II, 75 ff.; and E. Toaff, "Il Carnevale di Roma e gli Ebrei," *Scritti in Memoria di Sally Mayer,* pp. 325–43, the latter furnishing data on the eighteenth century. On its papal initiator see also the recent biography by R. Weiss, *Un Umanista veneziano: Papa Paolo II,* emphasizing that the pope's humanist interests were far less literary than "esthetic-antiquarian," an attitude which could readily breed indifference toward the contemporary anti-Jewish discrimination. It may also be noted that, by giving in 1464 and 1467 their stamp of approval to the first *monte di pietà* established in Perugia in 1462, both Pius and Paul greatly strengthened the hand of the Franciscan protagonists of that institution in their fierce battle against its Dominican detractors.

51. E. Martène and U. Durand, *Veterum scriptorum et monumentorum amplissima collectio,* II, 1516, 1519; and other sources cited in Rodocanachi, *Le Saint-Siège,* pp. 155 ff.; Vogelstein and Rieger, *Geschichte,* II, 18 ff. The attitude of the popes to the Spanish Inquisition and the Marranos will be discussed more fully *infra,* Chaps. LV–LVI.

52. R. Starrabba, "Guglielmo Raimondo Moncada," *AS Siciliano*, n.s. III, 15–91, esp. pp. 40 ff.; Z. Hermann, "The Relations between Pope Alexander VI and the Jews," *Scritti in Memoria di Sally Mayer*, Hebrew section, pp. 115–19 (mainly with respect to the Inquisition and the Marranos); and, more generally, G. Soranzo's brief critical review, "A proposito degli ultimi studi su papa Alessandro VI e sul Savonarola," *Aevum*, XXVII, 553–56. The flood of December 1495 led to the demolition of many houses and caused the death of numerous domestic animals, particularly in the district of Trastevere, where most Jews had lived since ancient times. Its effects are briefly noted in a notarial entry cited from a MS in the Archivio del Collegio dei Notai Capitolini by C. Traselli in his "Note sugli atti del Tribunale civile del Senatore di Roma del secolo XV," *Archivi*, III, 103.

53. R. de Maulde, *Les Juifs*, pp. 18 n. 5, 20, 23 f., 29 n. 1, 176 ff. (reproducing Rosa's noteworthy decision). Curiously, the municipality of Avignon, which frequently complained to the popes about Jewish business methods, nevertheless protested in 1488 against the 5 percent war tax which it considered a clear infringement of its municipal franchise. *Ibid.*, p. 29 n. 1. On the Jewish share in papal taxation in general, see *infra*, Chap. LIV. The Papacy's self-interest in the preservation of the financial strength of the Jewish communities did not prevent, even the friendly pontiffs from encouraging the growth of the *monti di pietà*. See the bulls issued in favor of the Bologna *monte* alone by Innocent VIII in May 1488, Julius II in March 1506 and Leo X in May 1515, and published, together with twelve similar enactments, in the anonymous collection *Bolle e provisioni per il sacro Monte di pietà di Bologna*, in Bologna, [*ca.* 1623]. Leo's decree stresses that it was promulgated "with the approval of the sacred Council."

54. Marino Sanuto, *Diarii*, January, 1513, ed. by F. Stefani *et al.*, XV, 504; L. Geiger, *Johann Reuchlin. Sein Leben und seine Werke*, pp. 105 ff., 290 ff., 297; F. Gregorovius, *The Ghetto and the Jews of Rome*, English trans., pp. 57 ff.; Vogelstein and Rieger, *Geschichte*, II, 29 ff.; and *infra*, Chap. LVII. The text of Leo X's important bull of 1519 was published from a Modena MS (evidently a copy had been obtained by the Jewish community of that city) by D. Kaufmann in his "Léon X et les Juifs de Rome," *REJ*, XXI, 285–89. Individual privileges went even further. One, issued in 1504 by Julius II in favor of Samuel Sarfati and his son Joseph, was subsequently renewed by both Leo X and Clement VII; it is reproduced in Stern's *Urkundliche Beiträge*, I, 68 ff. Nos. 65, 69. Remarkably, even Sarfati, who was allowed to hold private services at home, was told not to erect a new synagogue. But this prohibition did not prevent the Jews from adding to their houses of worship to meet the exigencies of their large and variegated immigration. Some Jewish merchants and artisans likewise secured favorable privileges or specific intercessions by papal authorities. When the Jewish dyers complained to Leo that the fiscal officials, failing to identify pieces of cloth on which the tax had previously been paid, tried to collect another tax, the pope, as in some other cases, specifically prohibited double taxation. See Rodocanachi, "La Communauté juive à Rome au temps de Jules II et de Léon X," *REJ*, LXI, 71–81.

55. F. Castiglioni, *Della popolazione di Roma dalle origini ai nostri tempi*, p. 166; R. Rocca, "Gli Israeliti di Roma nell'evo antico e medio," *Annali di statistica*, 3d ser. IX, 163–67; A. Milano, "Le Sinagoghe del vecchio ghetto di Roma," *Studi*

romani, VI, 138–59, esp. pp. 143 f.; *supra*, Vol. II, pp. 239 f. n. 12; *infra*, Chap. LI. This proliferation of synagogues for worshipers of different countries of origin is the less surprising as even Christian arrivals preferred to pray in churches of their own national provenance. See, for instance, J. Fernández Alonso, "Las Iglesias nacionales de España en Roma. Sus origenes," *Anthologica annua*, IV, 9–96.

56. C. Ciavarini, *Memorie storiche degli Israeliti in Ancona;* G. Luzzatto, *I Banchieri ebrei in Urbino nell'età ducale*, esp. pp. 13 f., 18 f., 27, 30; E. Menghetti, "I Primitivi capitoli del Monte di pietà di Fano," *Archivi*, 2d ser. XXIII, 323–42; R. Sassi, "Un Famoso medico ebreo a Fabriano [Ancona] nel secolo XV," *Studia Picena*, VI, 113–23. See also G. Castellani, "Il Primo libro stampato a Fano," *Bibliofilia*, XXVIII, 267–80, showing that Hieronymus or Girolamo Soncino settled in Fano in 1501 and soon thereafter entered the publishing field. Castellani also reproduces the dedicatory letter by Laurentius Abstemius to Fra Franciscus Georgius of Venice, dated March 1502, in which Soncino is described as that friar's "most beloved." See also M. Marx, "Gershom (Hieronymus) Soncino's Wander-Years in Italy, 1498–1527, Exemplar judaicae vitae," *HUCA*, XI, 427–501, esp. pp. 457 ff. The fascinating story of Italian Jewish printing will be dealt with in a later chapter. Interdependence of these communities was so great that their fate was determined by general more than by local regulations, giving rise to such common actions as are reflected in the aforementioned correspondence between the communities of Recanati and Ancona, published by D. Kaufmann. See *supra*, n. 47. A remarkable joint intervention occurred in 1498, when delegates of the Jewish communities of the papal Marches appeared in Rome to protest against the unwonted services as well as unrepaid forced loans imposed upon them by the municipalities of Fermo, Ascoli, Ancona, and Recanati. In his decree of June 20, 1498 Alexander VI ordered the four municipalities to discontinue their unjust persecution of Jews and abrogated the pertinent statutes. See V. E. Aleandri, *Gli Ebrei, le loro banche d'usura ed il Monte di Pietà in Sanseverino Marche: Memorie dal secolo XIV° al XVII°*, pp. 22 f. See also A. Menchetti, "Un Banco di Ebrei in Montalboddo nel 1423," *Atti e memorie* of the R. Deputazione di storia patria per le Marche, 3d ser. I, 198–208.

57. G. Luzzatto, "I Prestiti comunali e gli Ebrei a Matelica nel secolo XIII," *Le Marche*, n.s. VII, 249–72; idem, *I Banchieri ebrei in Urbino nell'età ducale*; L. Leonij, "Documenti tratti dall'Archivio segreto di Todi," *ASI*, 3d ser. XXII, 175–98 (including Part III: Capitoli del Comune di Todi cogli Ebrei. Vi si uniscono i capitoli del Comune di Arezzo [1420], pp. 182–88; the earlier Arezzo capitoli are dated 1399, pp. 188–90); and "Decreti del Comune di Todi contro gli Ebrei e giustizia loro resa da Francesco Sforza," *ibid.*, 4th ser. VII, 25–28 (relating to a controversy of 1438). In the fifteenth century, it may be noted, the community of Orvieto was sufficiently important to become the battleground for the aforementioned religious disputation between Elijah Ḥayyim da Genazzano and Fra Francesco di Aquapendente. See J. Bergmann, "Deux Polémistes juifs italiens," *REJ*, XL, 188–205; J. Rosenthal, ed., "A Judeo-Christian Debate at the End of the Fifteenth Century" (Hebrew), *Sura*, I, 156–77; and *supra*, Chap. XXXIX, n. 7 item 19. See also the literature listed in the next note.

58. A. Fabretti, ed., *Sulla condizione degli Ebrei in Perugia dal XII al XVIII secolo*, esp. pp. 8 f., 23 f. No. viii, 28 ff. No. xi, 62 ff. Nos. xxii–xxvi; O. Scalvanti, *Il Mons Pietatis di Perugia con qualche notizia sul Monte di Gubbio e di Perugia;* P. Valugani, *Il Beato Michele Carcano da Milano*, pp. 85 ff.; A. Ghinato, "Un Propagatore dei Monti di pietà del'400: P. Fortunato Coppoli da Perugia, O. F. M. († 1477)," *Rivista di storia della chiesa in Italia*, X, 193–211 (includes an analysis of Coppoli's defense of the *monte* against Dominican assailants, posthumously published in Venice, 1498, under the title, *Consilium Montis pietatis* and fully discussed by M. Ciardini in 1905); G. Caselli, *Studi su S. Giacomo della Marca*, esp. I, 194 f., 347, 365 ff.; D. Pacetti, "Le Prediche autografe di S. Giacomo della Marca (1393–1476) con un saggio delle medesime," *AFH*, XXXV, 296–327; XXXVI, 75–97; A. Ghinato, "L'Apostolato religioso e sociale di S. Giacomo della Marca in Terni," *ibid.*, XLIX, 106–42, 352–90.

There exists a host of monographic studies on individual communities and personalities. Among those relating to Jewish settlements in the papal provinces of Lazio (Latium), Umbria, and the Marches, the following (arranged here in the alphabetical order of the communities) are of special interest: A. Ghinato, *Monte di pietà e monti frumentari di Amelia. Origine e antichi statuti* (enlarged ed. of his "Fondazione e statuti del Monte di pietà di Amelia," *AFH*, XLVIII, 324–80); G. Fabriani, *Gli Ebrei e il Monte di Pietà in Ascoli;* A. Messini, *Le Origini e i primordi del Monte di Pietà di Foligno (1463–1488)*; A. Ravenna, "Appunti storici sulle Comunità del Lazio. Da un antico manoscritto," *RMI*, XVII, 305–11, 377–82 (lists of circumcisions from three books of circumcisers for the years 1554–1622); L. Zdekauer, "La Fondazione del Monte Pio di Macerata e i primordi sua gestione," *Rivista italiana per le scienze giuridiche*, XXVII, 127–49; XXIX, 389–410; C. Pace, "Su la colonia ebrea di Montegiorgio (Marche): alcuni documenti," *Rivista abruzzese di scienze, lettere ed arti*, XVII, 98–108; XVIII, 1427–47; idem, "La Colonia ebrea di Montegiorgio: altri documenti," *Le Marche*, XI, 118–21; B. Ghetti, "Gli Ebrei e il Monte di pietà in Recanati nei secoli XV e XVI," *Atti e Memorie* of the R. Deputazione di storia patria per le Marche (Ancona), n.s. IV, 11–39; V. E. Aleandri, *Gli Ebrei, le loro banche d'usura ed il Monte di Pietà di Sanseverino Marche*, esp. pp. 18 ff.; A. Ghinato, "Primi tentativi per la fondazione di un Monte di pietà a Terni (1464–1472)," *AFH*, L, 379 440; idem, "I Francescani e il Monte di pietà Terni dal 1490 al 1515," *ibid.*, LII, 204–89; idem, "I Francescani e il Monte di pietà di Terni da Fra Agostino da Perugia al B. Bernardino da Feltre (1471–1489)," *ibid.*, LI, 95–160; E. Loevinson, "Zur Geschichte der Juden in Terracina," *MGWJ*, LXVI, 149–55; A. Gabrielli, *Alcuni capitoli del 1547 per un banco di prestito a pegno tenuto dagli Ebrei in Velletri;* C. Roth's brief notes on "Il Primo soggiorno degli Ebrei a Viterbo (Un capitolo della storia dei banchi di prestito ebrei)," *RMI*, XX, 367–71; and other data referred to by A. Milano in "I Primordi del prestito ebraico in Italia," *RMI*, XIX, 221–30, 272–80, 306–19, 360–71, 398–406, 450–60 (also reprint).

59. A. A. Bernardy, "Les Juifs dans la République de San-Marino du XIVe au XVIIe siècles," *REJ*, XLVIII, 241–64; XLIX, 89–97; idem, "Nouveaux documents pour servir à l'histoire des Juifs dans la République de San-Marin (XVe siècle)," *REJ*, L, 129–35; P. M. Lonardo, "Gli Ebrei nella repubblica di San Marino," *Atti e Memorie* of the R. Deputazione di storia patria per le Marche, 2d ser. II, 93–115; Mansi, *Sacrorum conciliorum collectio*, XXV, 450 ff., 461 (Ravenna, 1311 can. xxiii),

599 ff., 612 f. (synod of the Ravenna province meeting in Bologna, 1317, can. xiv); *supra*, Vol. III, p. 241 n. 31.

60. *Statuto di Forlì dell'anno MCCCLIX con la modificazione del MCCCLXXIII*, ii.22 and 26, ed. by E. Rinaldi, pp. 166 f.; and other data assembled by her in "Gli Ebrei in Forlì nei secoli XIV e XV," *Atti e Memorie* of the R. Deputazione di storia patria per le provincie di Romagna, 4th ser. X, 295–323, esp. pp. 300, 305 f., 313 ff. No. iv; A.. Garzanti, "Un Banco ebreo in Forlì," *La Romagna*, V, 266–79; G. Ballardini, "I Banchieri ebrei e le origini del Monte di Pietà di Faenza," *Studi romagnoli*, V, 445–51; G. Volli, "Gli Ebrei a Lugo," *ibid.*, IV, 143–83; G. Orlandelli, "Le Finanze della comunità di Forlì sotto il vicariato di Baldassare Cossa," *Studi romagnoli*, VII, 184 n. 5. The interesting will left by Menaḥem b. Nathan of Rimini dated August 14, 1392, was published by A. Berliner in his "Old Records" (Hebrew), *Ha-Medabber le-Yisrael*, ed. by Z. H. Itzkowski, I, 15, 31, 39, 47, 55, 63, 77, 81–82, esp. p. 47. See also E. S. Artom, "Notizie sugli Ebrei a Rimini e nelle Marche in un quesito rituale," *Miscellanea di studi ebraici . . . H. P. Chajes*, pp. 1–9 (from a responsum by Simon b. Ṣemaḥ Duran); and P. Norsa's brief remarks in his fine study of *Una Famiglia di banchieri; la famiglia Norsa (1350–1950)*, I, 3. (Norsa claims that he had found no data on Menaḥem's activities in the Rimini archives; p. 49 n. 8.) See also the next note.

61. E. Loevinson, "Notizie e dati statistici sugli Ebrei entrati a Bologna nel secolo XV," *Annuario di studi ebraici* of the Collegio rabbinico, II (= Angelo Sacerdoti Mem. Vol.), 125–73; and I. Sonne, "On the History of the Jewish Community of Bologna at the Beginning of the Sixteenth Century," *HUCA*, XVI, Hebrew section, pp. 35–98. See also G. Zucchini, "Artigiani a Bologna nei secoli XIV, XV e XVI," *Atti e Memorie* of the Deputazione di storia patria per la Emilia, XXI, 37–84; XXII, 113–59 (based upon a score of even more specialized monographs by the author). Interest in Hebrew manuscripts was by no means limited to the Bologna Jews. It doubtless was there that the Christian family Sabatini, forced to leave the city in 1488, had acquired the remarkable Hebrew manuscript collection which included a fourteenth-century Bible and a miscellany of halakhic writings, as well as a fifteenth-century copy of Rashi's Commentary on Deuteronomy. See G. Sabatini, "Pergamene conservate dalla famiglia Sabatini in Pescocostanzo e relative notizie storiche," *Bollettino* of the R. Deputazione Abruzzese di storia patria, XXX–XXXI, 57–116, esp. pp. 70 f. No. 31, 79 No. 69. See also, more generally, L. dal Pane's brief review of "Gli Studi sulla storia economica bolognese del medioevo al secolo XX°," *Giornale degli economisti e Annali de economia*, XVI, 135–47; G. Rossi, *Bologna nella storia*, 2d ed.; and other pertinent studies to be mentioned *infra*, Vol. XII. On the important assemblies of Bologna and Forlì, which passed a number of significant resolutions of permanent import to Italian Jewry, see the texts of "The Ancient Ordinances Adopted in Bologna and Forlì in the Years 1416 and 1418 in Behalf of All of Italy" (Hebrew), ed. with notes by S. Z. H. Halberstam, and a letter by M. Güdemann in *Jubelschrift . . . Graetz*, Hebrew section, pp. 53–64. They are reproduced with an English trans. in L. Finkelstein's *Jewish Self-Government in the Middle Ages*, pp. 281 ff. These and similar later resolutions, as well as the circumstances which led to the convocation of these assemblies, are discussed in my *The Jewish Community*, I, 319 ff.; III, 79 ff. n. 35; and in I. Sonne's aforementioned Hebrew essay in *Hatekufah*, XXXII–XXXIII, esp. p. 636. They will be more fully analyzed in a later chapter.

62. A. Pesaro, *Memorie storiche sulla Comunità israelitica ferrarese,* with the subsequent *Appendici* thereto; E. Levi, *Francesco di Vannozzo e la lirica nelle corti lombarde,* pp. 127 ff., 308; L. Chiappini, *Eleonora d'Aragona prima duchessa di Ferrara;* A. Balletti, *Gli Ebrei e gli Estensi; supra,* n. 27. The latter work, a revised and expanded edition of a study first published seventeen years before, gives extensive documentary data especially for Reggio. On Farissol's disputation, see *supra,* Chap. XXXIX, n. 7 item 20. As pointed out by A. Medin, Vannozzo's sonnet, "Non è virtù dov'è la fede rara," achieved greater popularity than any of his other poems. See his ed. of *Le Rime di Francesco di Vannozzo,* pp. 116 f. No. lxxx. Some attacks by prominent preachers were more oblique. If St. Bernardino da Siena addressed himself in his sermon in Ferrara to the general subject of luxury or spoke up against gambling in Bologna (in 1424), listeners readily connected such speeches with the preacher's frequent perorations against Jewish usury. See P. Thureau-Dangin, *Saint Bernardine of Siena,* English trans. from the French by Baroness G. von Hugel, pp. 68 ff. See also his violent diatribe against usury and usurers published by G. de Angelis in her ed. of "Quatro prediche inedite di S. Bernardino tenute a Siena in Piazza del Campo nel 1425," *Bullettino di studi Bernardiniani,* VI, 189 ff.; *infra,* n. 67; and, from another angle, M. Roberti, "Privilegi forensi degli Ebrei in Ferrara," *Atti e Memorie* of the Accademia di scienze . . . Padova, n.s. XXXIII, 155–66, esp. pp. 158, 163 ff. Nos. i–ii.

63. G. Cammeo, "Gli Ebrei di Modena sotto i duchi estensi," *Vessillo israelitico,* LX, 662–63; LXI, 71–73, 242–43, 357–58, 469–71, 525–28; LXII, 30–32, 126–28, 206–208, 386–88, 470–72, 502–505, 582–83, 646; Balletti, *Gli Ebrei e gli Estensi,* pp. 20 ff., 26 f.; Stern, *Urkundliche Beiträge,* I, 54 No. 48. In Parma the traditions of good will toward Jews had been sufficiently deep-rooted for the city's general assembly to include in the terms of its surrender to Duke Francesco Sforza of Milan in 1449 a clause safeguarding the existing privileges for the present and future Jewish settlers. Personally, Francesco probably was not averse to accepting that condition. See *infra,* n. 74.

64. *Inventario del R. Archivio de Stato di Lucca,* I, 208, 210–11, 302; II, 387–88; Stern, *Urkundliche Beiträge,* I, 60 ff. No. 54; *Memorie e documenti per servire alla storia di Lucca,* Vols. I–XIII, esp. Vol. III, Part 3 (containing the text of the *Statuto del Comune di Lucca* of 1308, which is expressively silent on the subject of Jews and moneylending, except for providing a penalty for anyone appealing to a court other than the Luccan municipal tribunal under the excuse that the loan had been usurious; lv.12, p. 257); E. Lazzareschi, "Il Beato Bernardino da Feltre, gli Ebrei e il Monte di pietà in Lucca," *Bollettino storico lucchese,* XIII, 12–43, esp. pp. 13 f., 16 f., 25 f. See also *supra,* Vols. IV, pp. 26, 273 n. 87; VII, pp. 50 ff.; VIII, pp. 171 f., 362 f. n. 38.

65. F. Bonaini, ed., *Statuti inediti della città di Pisa dal XII al XIV secolo,* II, 377 f., 689 n. 1, 776, 788, 867; P. M. Lonardo's well-documented study, "Gli Ebrei a Pisa sino alla fine del secolo XV," *Studi storici,* ed. by A. Crivellucci, VII, 171–213; VIII, 59–101. Obviously, Jews did not hold a monopoly on banking in the Tuscan cities, which in the Late Middle Ages were the leading banking centers in the world. On fourteenth-century Pisa see, e.g., F. Melis, *Note di storia della banca pisana nel trecento* (discusses 48 Christian merchant bankers after 1350, the Pisan contribution

to the origin of the check, and other early banking practices); and E. Cristiani, "Note sulla legislazione antiusuraria pisana (secoli XII–XV)," *Bollettino storico pisano*, 3d ser. XXII–XXIII, 3–53. Not surprisingly, with its general penchant for biographical and cultural data, Jewish historiography paid more attention to the Da Pisa family than to the community as a whole. See D. Kaufmann's "Ein Jahrhundert aus der Geschichte der Familie Jechiel von Pisas" (1893) and "Zur Geschichte der Familie Pisa" (1894), both reprinted in his *GS*, II, 257–76, 277–84; and U. Cassuto's *Sulla famiglia da Pisa* (reprinted from *Rivista israelitica*, V–VII, X). The significant changes brought about in the entire structure of the Jewish community of Pisa by the influx of the Marranos in the sixteenth and seventeenth centuries will be discussed *infra*, Chap. LVI. See also more generally, D. Herlihy, *Pisa in the Early Renaissance. A Study of Urban Growth*, showing how Pisa, which had been the largest Tuscan city in the twelfth century, gradually receded in both power and population and was finally conquered by Florence.

Information on the Jewish settlement on the island of Corsica is extremely scant. Much can be indirectly learned, however, from essays published in the *Archivio storico di Corsica*. Under the long Genoese domination, however, Jews were neither welcomed by the authorities, nor were the economic conditions good enough to make them defy such discouragement. The island, which even in antiquity had had a rather large and vigorous population, declined under the Genoese administration until in the seventeenth century it embraced no more than 80,000 inhabitants. See F. Borlandi's introductory remarks to his study, "Per la storia della popolazione della Corsica," *ibid.*, XV, 358–61.

66. N. Pavoncello, "Origine e sviluppo della comunità ebraica a Siena," *Nova Historia*, VII, Parts 5–6, pp. 31–51; L. Zdekauer, "I Capitoli Hebraeorum di Siena (1477–1526) con documenti inediti," *Archivio giuridico "Filippo Serafini,"* LXIV, 259–70 (analyzing six versions of these *Capitoli* adopted during that half century and reproducing the city's petition to the pope of 1477 in which the Priori argued that, despite the alleviation brought to the poor by the establishment of a *monte* in 1471, Jewish moneylenders still were badly needed by the community); N. Mengozzi and N. Piccolomini, *Il Monte dei Paschi di Siena e le aziende in esso riunite*, esp. I, 148; A. Lisini, ed., *Il Costituto del Comune di Siena volgarizzato nel MCCCIX–MCCCX*, i.1, 7; ii.2, 223, pp. 48, 484; his and F. Jacometti's as yet incomplete and unindexed ed. of *Cronache senesi* in L. A. Muratori's *Rerum italicarum scriptores*, new ed. XV, Part 6; Stern, *Urkundliche Beiträge*, I, 66 ff. No. 63. The request of the Sienese elders of 1373 and the bishop's reply thereto are published and analyzed by G. Mollat in his "Deux frères mineurs, Marc de Viterbe et Guillaume de' Guasconi, au service de la papauté (1363–1375)," *AFH*, XLVIII, 52–72, esp. pp. 61, 69 f. App. vii.

67. On the various anti-Jewish preachers in Siena, see in particular, A. Liberati, "La Repubblica di Siena e San Giovanni da Capistrano," *Bullettino senese di storia patria*, XLIV, 375–402 (with 46 excerpts from documents of 1444–50); E. Bulletti, "Predicazioni senesi di frate Antonio da Rimini (Documenti inediti)," *ibid.*, LXII–LXIII, 206–12, esp. p. 200 No. 4 (also in *Studi francescani*, LIV, 97–102); and most especially the works by and on San Bernardino da Siena. The praise of Bernardino's sermons cited in the text is included in a homily delivered by San Giacomo della Marca and reproduced by Pacetti in *AFH*, XXXVI, 82. In Bernardino's numerous

fulminations against usury (Sermons xxxix–xlv of his *Quadragesimale de Evanglio aeterno* are entirely devoted to these attacks) he even tried to deny the Jewish contention that biblical law had prohibited Jews to lend on usury only to other Jews. See esp. his Sermon xxxviii Part ii.2, in his *Opera omnia*, in the new critical ed. by the College of St. Bonaventura, IV, 255 f. See also his *Le Prediche volgari*, ed. by C. Comarozzi (Vols. VI–VII of series begun in 1934); and the analytical studies by P. Bargellini, *San Bernardino da Siena*, 4th ed.; and A. E. Tugenberger, *San Bernardino da Siena. Considerazioni sullo sviluppo dell'etica economica cristiana nel primo Rinascimento,* esp. pp. 93 ff. See also *supra,* n. 62; and, on the rise of Leghorn, *infra,* Chap. LIX.

68. R. Davidsohn, *Forschungen zur Geschichte von Florenz,* II, 271 f. No. 2096, 327 ff. Nos. 2459–68 (about Jews in San Gimignano in the years 1254–1392). Because of Florence's cultural eminence, its history has been treated in much greater detail than that of any other Italian city, except Rome and possibly Venice. The standard work by R. Davidsohn (also available in a revised Italian trans. by G. B. Klein, with revisions by R. Palmarocchi, entitled *Storia di Firenze*), has been supplemented by a host of specialized monographs. Among these, two excellent studies were devoted to the Jewish community, namely, M. Ciardini, *I Banchieri ebrei in Firenze nel secolo XV e il Monte di Pietà fondato da Girolamo Savonarola;* and U. Cassuto, *Gli Ebrei a Firenze nell'età del Rinascimento.* The deliberations of the Council in 1430 and the communal vicissitudes are cited here from Cassuto, pp. 18, 196 ff., 218, 364 f. No. iv. See also Cassuto's earlier study of "Un Rabbino fiorentino del secolo XV," *Rivista israelitica,* III, 116–28, 224–28; IV, 33–37, 151–61, 225–29; and S. H. Margulies, "Il Talmud Torà di Firenze," *ibid.,* V, 14–24, 48–54. (This institution was founded only after the establishment of the ghetto.)

Since the history of the Florentine community during the fifteenth century revolved so greatly around the group of licensed bankers, the careful study by Ciardini was effectively supplemented by Cassuto's publication of "Un Registro ebraico di pegni del secolo XV," *ZHB,* XV, 182–85; XVI, 127–42. For a better understanding of the propelling forces behind both the admission and ultimate rejection of the Jewish bankers, see the host of monographic studies relating to Florentine banking in the Middle Ages, including A. Sapori, *La Crisi delle compagnie mercantili dei Bardi e dei Peruzzi;* his *Studi di storia economica* (sec. XIII–XIV–XV), 3d ed.; and the recent essays by M. B. Becker, "Gualtieri di Brienne e la regolamentazione dell'usura a Firenze," *ASI,* CXIV, 734–40; "Nota dei processi riguardanti prestatori di danaro nei tribunali fiorentini dal 1343 al 1379," *ibid.,* pp. 741–48; and "Three Cases concerning the Restitution of Usury in Florence," *Journal of Economic History,* XVII, 445–50. The latter cases, all of 1377, curiously were a reflection of the antipapal feeling then rampant in the city.

69. Cassuto, *Gli Ebrei, passim;* A. Ghinato, "Un Propagatore," *Rivista di storia della chiesa in Italia,* X, 196 ff. On Savonarola's attitude toward the Jews see also F. R. Salter, "The Jews in Fifteenth-Century Florence and Savonarola's Establishment of a *Mons Pietatis,*" *The Cambridge Historical Journal,* V, 193–211, giving an excellent economic interpretation. Salter's data may now be supplemented by L. F. Marks's study of "La Crisi finanziaria a Firenze dal 1494 al 1502," *ASI,* CXII, 40–72. See also R. Ridolfi's comprehensive *Vita di Girolamo Savonarola* (the English trans. of that work by C. Grayson omits the extensive documentation); and G. Soranzo's

aforementioned critical review in *Aevum*, XXVII, 553–56. The attitude of the Medicean family, which when in power almost invariably was friendly to Jews, is analyzed by U. Cassuto in "La Famille des Médicis et les Juifs," *REJ*, LXXVI, 132–45. See also the biography of its leading protagonist by F. G. Fiori, *Lorenzo il Magnifico*, with the additional data to be gleaned from "Le Lettere di Lorenzo il Magnifico nell'Archivio di Stato di Firenze," ed. by M. del Piazzo in the *Rassegna degli Archivi di Stato*, XVI, 10–46 (listing 826 letters with their destination and dates, but rarely indicating their content); and, from another angle, G. R. B. Richards, ed., *Florentine Merchants in the Age of the Medici*.

Before and after the opening of Jewish loan banks in Florence, there existed similar establishments in many neighboring cities. Apart from the Jewish money-lenders of San Miniato, described by Cassuto in *Gli Ebrei*, pp. 32 f., see, for instance, L. Zdekauer, "Per la storia del prestito ebraico in Colle Valdelsa," *Miscellanea storica della Valdelsa*, XVII, 202–204. The far more significant intellectual relationships between the Jews and the great Florentines from the fourteenth to the sixteenth centuries, and particularly the Jewish impact on such Christian Hebraists as Giovanni Pico della Mirandola, will be discussed *infra*, Chap. LVII.

70. Bartolomeo Senarega, *De rebus Genuensibus Commentaria ab anno MCDLXXXVIII usque ad annum MDXIV*, ed. by E. Pandani, in L. A. Muratori's ed. of *Rerum italicarum scriptores*, new ed. by G. Carducci *et al.*, XXIV, Part 8, pp. 24 f.; Joseph ha-Kohen, *'Emeq ha-bakha*, ed. by Letteris, pp. 84 f.; in M. Wiener's German trans., pp. 66 f., 199 f. nn. 233a–234; M. Staglieno, "Degli Ebrei in Genoa," *Giornale ligustico di archeologia, storia e belle arti*, III, 173–86, 394–415; *supra*, n. 17; and Vols. III, pp. 26, 241 n. 31; IV, p. 26. That there was no organized Jewish community in medieval Genoa is generally conceded. But E. H. Byrne, who had pioneered in the study of Genoa's notarial archives, thought that he had identified two Jews, namely Soliman of Salerno, an important figure frequently recorded in 1156–61, and Solomon Blancardo, banker and cloth-dealer. See his "Easterners in Genoa," *Journal* of the American Oriental Society, XXXVIII, 176–87, esp. pp. 179 ff.; and, more generally, his "Genoese Trade with Syria in the Twelfth Century," *AHR*, XXV, 191–219. However, the Jewish identity of these two merchants has rightly been questioned. Soliman, whose Arabic-sounding name may have stemmed from his journeys to the Near East (he is recorded to have spent two years in Alexandria) was hardly a Jew if his daughter married into the "mighty" Mallone family. Blancardo's estate was handled in 1178 by the archbishop, who took into consideration his penitent deathbed renunciation of all usurious gains. See Byrne, *loc. cit.*, and particularly, B. N. Nelson, "Blancardo (the Jew?) of Genoa and the Restitution of Usury in Medieval Italy," *Studi in onore di Gino Luzzatto*, I, 96–116. (Many "Addenda et corrigenda" to this essay are available in mimeographed sheets attached to its reprints.)

More recently, however, C. Roth succeeded in identifying in the notarial documents of the mid-thirteenth century a few Jewish names. True, the Paganos Judaeus, recorded in a number of transactions of 1250, and Giovanni Judaeus, the cheese maker who was taught to manufacture soap in 1264, need not have been Jewish. See *infra*, n. 81. On the other hand, the fact that in 1231 twenty-eight Hebrew books were acquired from a Jew in Genoa, and the mention there of a Magister Elia in 1267, seem to indicate the occasional appearance of professing Jews. Genoa's intensive trade with both Spain and the eastern Mediterranean would likewise presuppose at least some temporary visits of foreign Jews, such as that of three Tortosa merchants mentioned in 1274. See C. Roth, "Genoese Jews in the Thirteenth Century," *Speculum*, XXV, 190–97. Possibly the appearance of Jews at that time was connected with the first great crisis of the Bank of Genoa, on which see R. S. Lopez, *La Prima crisi della banca di Genova (1250–1259)*; and, more generally, his *Studi sull'economia genovese nel medio evo*. On the later connections between Genoese merchants and some Sevillian Jewish financiers see F. Baer, *Die Juden im christlichen Spanien*, I, Part 2, pp. 116 No. 128, 407 No. 378 n. The intriguing question of the Spanish Jewish antecedents of Christopher Columbus, the great Genoese explorer, and the subsequent activities there of the historian Joseph ha-Kohen, will be discussed in later chapters.

71. Amadeus VIII's ordinance of 1430 is included in *Decreta Ducalia Sabaudie*, i.4–19, while his bull of August 31, 1444, was published by S. Foa in. "Una Bolla di Felice V per la giustizia da amministrarsi agli ebrei," *Bollettino storico-bibliografico subalpino*, LV, 482–87. See also *Historia patriae monumenta*, ed. at the order of King Charles Albert, *Leges municipales*, cols. 466 ff., 474a, 507b ff. Together with other documents the law of 1430 is analyzed by F. Gabotto in "La Politica di Casa Savoia verso gli Israeliti nella prima metà dal Quattrocento," one of a series of articles entitled, "Per una storia degli Israeliti in Piemonte nel medio evo, IV," *Vessillo israelitico*, LXVI, 288–92. See also the more general reviews by G. Volino, *Condizione giuridica degli Ebrei in Piemonte prima dell'emancipazione;* and by M. D. Anfossi, *Gli Ebrei in Piemonte loro condizioni giuridico-sociali dal 1430 all'emancipazione;* the somewhat colored analysis by G. Marrò, "Gli Ebrei negli statuti di Amedeo VIII," *Razza e Civiltà*, I, 319–32; and, more generally, G. C. Buraggi, "Gli Statuti di Amedeo VIII di Savoia del 31 luglio 1403," *Memorie* of the Accademia di scienze of Turin, Classe di scienze morali, 2d ser. LXX, 1–38 (the authors consider these statutes, here first published, the "embryo" of the legislative reform of 1430, esp. p. 10 Art. 2, *de iudois*); and the comprehensive biographies of the dukes of Savoy bearing that name by ex-queen Maria José of Italy in *La Maison de Savoie*, Vol. II. Needless to say, the Jews' legal status in Piedmont was deeply intertwined with that in the French possessions of the House of Savoy, on which see *supra*, Chap. XLIII, nn. 30–31.

72. F. Gabotto, "Per una storia," *Vessillo israelitico*, LXV, 433–37 (on Turin, 1425–30), 548–55 (on Savigliano in the early fifteenth century); LXVI, 123–26 (on Savigliano and Bonafede de Chalon in 1430–47); G. Morandi, "I Capitoli di Opicino Caccia marchese di Mortara a Moyses ebreo," *Bollettino storico per la provincia di Novara*, I, 19–33 (reproducing the text dated May 31, 1570); A. Viglio, "I Novaresi contro l'introduzione degli Ebrei," *ibid.*, XVI, 218 ff. The most significant communities were those in Casale and Alessandria. On the former, see the detailed monograph by S. Foa, *Gli Ebrei nel Monferrato nei secoli XVI e XVII*, supplemented by his "Appunti d'archivio di storia ebraica monferrina," *RMI*, XV, 113–21; and his "L'Istituzione del ghetto a Moncalvo (1722)," *ibid.*, XVI, 188–201. All offer mainly data on the later period. On Alessandria, see the literature cited *infra*, n. 74.

73. "Il Rito di Asti-Fossano-Moncalvo (APAM)" is briefly discussed by D. Disegni in *Scritti in Memoria di Sally Mayer*, pp. 78–81. Though mainly reproducing MSS of the eighteenth century, his data shed light also on the earlier period of gradual

growth. See also D. Goldschmidt, "The Maḥzor (APAM)" (Hebrew), *Kirjath Sepher*, XXX, 118–36, 264–78. The crucial mid-sixteenth century developments will be discussed more fully *infra*, Chap. LIX.

74. L. Osio, *Documenti diplomatici tratti dagli archivi milanesi*, I, 259 f. No. cxci; C. Canetta, "Gli Ebrei del ducato milanese," *AS Lombardo*, VIII, 632–35 (reproducing the duke's order to his *oratori* in Rome of Jan. 23, 1456, and the latter's petition to the pope including a draft of the proposed *capitoli* with the Jews); G. Barbieri, *Economia e politica nel ducato di Milano, 1386–1535*, esp. pp. 59 f., 124 ff.; E. A. Motta, "Oculisti, dentisti e medici ebrei nella seconda metà del secolo XV alla corte milanese," *Annali universali di medicina*, CCLXXXIII, 326–28; L. Fumi, "L'Inquisizione romana e lo stato di Milano. Saggio di ricerche nell'Archivio di Stato," *AS Lombardo*, XXXVII, 5–124, 285–414; XXXVIII, 145–220, particularly XXXVII, 285 ff., which offers the relatively fullest data on the Jews in the duchy of Milan. See also *supra*, Vol. II, pp. 189, 401 n. 24; S. Schaerf, "Appunti storici sugli Ebrei della Lombardia," *RMI*, II, [33]–49 (listing also the tiny Jewish settlements in Valenza, Monte Castello, Bormio, Borgi di Abbiategrasso, and Tortona; p. [43]); and, more generally, C. Santoro, "Contributi alla storia dell'amministrazione Sforzesca," *AS Lombardo*, n.s. IV, 27–114; T. Zerbi, *Studi e problemi di storia economica*, Vol. I: Credito ed interesse in Lombardia nei secoli XIV e XV. The Jews of Alessandria are treated by E. Biagi, "Notizie e ricerche sugli Ebrei di Alessandria—secolo XV (Ducato di Milano ed altri comuni della Lombardia)," *Rivista di storia, arte, archeologia . . . Provincia di Alessandria* (1955–56), 160 ff.; and, more fully, by S. Foa, "Gli Ebrei in Alessandria," *RMI*, XXIII, 547–56; XXIV, 121–29, 181–87, 215–20, 320–24, 463–71.

Otherwise, too, the Sforzas' connections with southern Italy and Germany accrued to the benefit of the Lombard Jews. King Alphonso himself interceded, through the influential minister Cicco Simonetta in behalf of a Jew, Leone of Lodi, with the Jewish community council in Pavia. Similarly, Duchess Ippolita Maria of Calabria asked her Milanese mother to intervene for a Jew Vitale and also to secure tax exemption for one Benedetto of Cremona. See A. C.'s review of Ferorelli's *Gli Ebrei nell'Italia meridionale* in *AS Lombardo*, XLIII, 234–36; and *supra*, n. 26. On the other hand, Francesco Sforza tried to promote Jewish trade by persuading his Swiss allies to facilitate the transit of Jews from Lombardy to Germany without the usual special permits for each journey. See Fumi, *ibid.*, XXXVII, 296.

75. L. Fumi in *AS Lombardo*, XXXVII, 295 f. (undated document of the fifteenth century); Bernardino de' Busti, *Rosarium sermonum predicabilium* (1498), summarized by H. Élie in his "Contribution à l'étude du statut des Juifs en Italie aux XVᵉ et XVIᵉ siècles. L'Opinion de Bernardin de Busti," *RHR*, CXLII, 67–97, esp. pp. 70 f. De' Busti's compilation of sample sermons included some ten discourses aimed at Jews. The most important section deals with the *Concilium contra Judaeos*, the proceedings of which are reproduced at considerable length. See Hagenau, 1508 ed., fols. lxxxviib–xcv.

76. C. Morbio, *Codice Visconteo-Sforzesco*, pp. 418 f.; C. Invernizzi, "Gli Ebrei a Pavia. Contributo alla storia dell'Ebraismo nel ducato di Milano," *Bollettino* of the Società Pavese di storia patria, V, 194 f.; the documents summarized in G. Barbieri's *Aspetti dell'economia lombarda durante la dominazione visconteo-sforzesca*, pp. 38 ff.

In his agitation for a *monte* and in his general anti-Jewish attitude, De' Busti followed in the footsteps of his teacher Michele da Carcano, who in turn had taken over his hostility toward Jews from his master, John Capistrano. Michele's agitation became so obnoxious to the authorities that he was expelled from the entire Duchy of Milan. See *infra*, n. 79; and *supra*, Chap. XXXVII, nn. 60–61.

77. C. Bonetti, *Gli Ebrei a Cremona, 1278–1630. Note ed appunti;* L. Fumi in *AS Lombardo,* XXXVII, 293 (from an undated archival document of the sixteenth century). Hebrew typography in Cremona has long attracted considerable attention. See the early study by I. Bianchi, *Sulle tipografie ebraiche di Cremona nel secolo XVI,* published in Cremona, 1807. See also the more recent literature cited *infra,* n. 89. It is noteworthy that the well-developed mercantile guilds of the city never seriously interfered with the pursuit of Jewish business. Only the *Statuta Mercatorum* of 1388 contained a few restrictive provisions on pawnbroking (Art. 67). See U. Gualazzini, *I Mercanti di Cremona, 1183–1260–1927. Cenni storici sulla loro organizzazione,* pp. 109 f., 113 nn. 39 and 41, also mentioning that the author had at his disposal C. Bonetti's personal copy of *Gli Ebrei a Cremona,* which contained additions and corrections from MSS consulted by Bonetti after the publication of his study.

78. See *supra,* Vol. IV, pp. 26, 245 n. 28; the well-documented narrative by C. Invernizzi, "Gli Ebrei a Pavia" in the *Bollettino* of the Società Pavese di storia patria, V, 191–240, 281–319; and V. Colorni's notes on "Prestito ebraico e comunità ebraiche nell'Italia centrale et settentrionale. Con particolare riguardo alla comunità di Mantova," *Rivista di storia del diritto italiano,* VIII, 444, 447 n. The University of Pavia (temporarily removed to Piacenza) played a much lesser role, both nationally and locally, than for instance that of Padua. It exerted, therefore, also less influence on the preservation of the Jewish community. On the other hand, because it lay on important crossroads and had long been the capital of a duchy, Pavia was generally quite hospitable to merchants from Germany, Flanders, France, and England. See G. Aleati, "Il Problema dell'ospitalità nella città di Pavia nel medioevo," *AS Lombardo,* LXXXIII, 182 ff.

79. E. A. Motta, "Ebrei in Como ed in altre città del ducato milanese. Documenti milanesi del secolo decimoquinto," *Periodico* of the Società storica per la provincia . . . di Como, V, 7–44; G. Antonucci, "Per la storia degli Ebrei in Bergamo," *Bergomum,* XXXV, 52–54; F. Fossati, "Gli Ebrei a Vigevano nel secolo XV," *AS Lombardo,* XXX, 199–215; idem, "Rapporti tra una 'terra' e i suoi signori (Vigevano e i duchi di Milano nel secolo XV)," *ibid.,* XLI, 109–86, esp. p. 116. A few cities even promised the Jews temporary tax exemptions in return for the services of their loan banks. Otherwise Jewish taxation differed widely. While Novara Jewry, then under Milanese domination, paid a tax of only 20 lire in 1447, the Como community was assessed 100 lire twenty-four years later and was told not to pay them from usurious income. The total tax revenue from Jews in the duchy supposedly amounted to 7,000 lire in 1463, but in Motta's estimate it really rose together with other imposts to some 20,000 lire (p. 10 n. 1). Jews also had difficulties with both inquisitors and preachers, particularly in connection with the growing agitation for the *monti di pietà.* Michele da Carcano played a particularly significant role in Como. See E. Motta, "Il Beato Michele da Carcano (Documenti milanesi inediti)," *Periodico* of the

Società storica per la provincia . . . di Como, V, 305–34; idem, "Inquisitori in Como nella seconda metà del secolo XV," *ibid.*, VI, 125–27.

80. F. Glissenti, *Gli Ebrei nel Bresciano al tempo della dominazione veneta. Saggio storico*, supplemented by his *Nuove ricerche e studi*; A. Gamba, *Gli Ebrei a Brescia nei secoli XV–XVI. Appunti per uno studio storico*. Glissenti mentions in passing also one Lazzaro and other Jews who received promises of protection in such small neighboring localities as Iseo, Gavardo, Palazzolo, and Gottolengo (p. 7). See also A. Milano, "I Primordi del prestito ebraico in Italia," *RMI*, XIX, 365 f.

81. See *supra*, Vol. IV, pp. 26, 244 n. 27; Isaac b. Moses, *Sefer Or Zaru'a*, I, No. 745; D. Fortis, "Gli Ebrei di Verona. Cenni storici," *Educatore israelita*, XI, 199–203, 301–305, 392–94; XII, 68–70, 110–12, 209–11; N. Pavoncello, *Gli Ebrei in Verona (dalle origini al secolo XX)*. A few early documents pertaining to the community of Verona are reproduced by G. Biscardo, "Attraverso le carte di S. Giorgio in Braida di Verona. Note storiche VII: Ebrei a Verona nei secoli XII e XIII," *Atti* of the Istituto Veneto di scienze, XLIV, 672–76. To be sure, the Ubertus Judeus whose testament of 1169 was to lead to an extensive litigation after his death five years later was definitely a Christian, though possibly a convert, perhaps the son of a convert named Adec. But the Helia Judeus and Samuelis Judeus who in 1204–1205 sold a house and other objects to Christians almost certainly were professing Jews. So were the three Jews mentioned by Biscardo from documents dated in 1194 to 1225. The frequency with which the name *Judaeus* was retained or adopted by Christian families, particularly in Italy, has often been noted. See the examples adduced by U. Cassuto in *Gli Ebrei a Firenze*, p. 3 n. 1, 431; V. Colorni, "Prestito ebraico," *Rivista di storia del diritto italiano*, VIII, 444 f. n.; and *supra*, n. 51. More extensive documentation on the Jews of Verona in the later medieval and early modern centuries was published from the then extant archival collections of the Jewish community by I. Sonne in his Hebrew studies, "Materials to the History of the Jews in Verona," *Zion*, III, 123–69, and *Kobez* [*Qobeṣ*] *'al yad*, XIII, Part 2, 143–83.

The anonymous Verona chronicler found the story of Simeon of Trent to be so "new and memorable a matter that contrary to my plan I shall narrate it at greater length." He also reported without any element of doubt a similar accusation in Verona itself in 1481. See G. Soranzo, ed., *Cronaca di anonimo veronese 1446–1488*, pp. 308 ff., 362 f. On the economic activities of Veronese Jewry, see also the incidental remarks in M. Lecce's *Vicende dell'industria della lana e della seta a Verona*. Some of the neighboring communities are treated in M. Lattes, "Documents et notices sur l'histoire politique et littéraire des Juifs en Italie," *REJ*, V, 219–37 (includes text and analysis of the *capitoli* arranged in Asolo in 1520, pp. 219 ff., 228 ff.); M. Osimo, *Narrazione della strage compiuta nel 1547 contro gli Ebrei di Asolo e cenni biografici della famiglia Koen-Cantarini* (among the victims of this riot were two of the original three recipients of the *capitoli* of 1520); G. Chiuppani, *Gli Ebrei a Bassano*; E. Morpurgo, "Monografie storiche sugli Ebrei del Veneto: I: Gli Ebrei a Treviso (905–1509, 1547–1590 dell' E.V.)," *Corriere israelitico*, XLVIII, 141–44, 170–72; "II: Gli Ebrei a Conegliano (1398–1896 dell' E.V.)," *ibid.*, pp. 188–91, 205–209; D. Carpi, "The Jews of Vicenza in the Period of Venetian Domination" (Hebrew), *Sefer ha-Yobel Nathan Michael Gelber* (the N. M. G. Jubilee Volume), pp. 199–203.

82. L. Carnevali, *Gli Israeliti a Mantova. Cenni storici* (esp. p. 7, citing the new version of the *Statuti Bonacolsiani*, ii.21a), supplemented by his *Il Ghetto di Mantova. Con appendice sui medici ebrei;* G. Amadei and F. Salvadori, *Gli Ebrei ed il loro soggiorno in Mantova. Scienza, storia, statistica;* V. Colorni, "Note per la biografia di alcuni dotti ebrei vissuti a Mantova nel secolo XV," *Annuario di studi ebraici*, I, 169–82; idem, "Prestito," in *Rivista di storia del diritto italiano*, VIII, 417 ff., 444 ff. These works are in part superseded now by S. Simonsohn's comprehensive *Toledot ha-Yehudim be-dukhsut Mantovah* (History of the Jews in the Duchy of Mantua), Vols. I–II. See H. Rabinowitz, "Rabbi Colon and Messer Leon," *JJS*, VI, 166–68; idem, "Rabbi Joseph Colon and the Jewish Ban," *HJ*, XXII, 61–70. Among other scientists who lived in fifteenth-century Mantua was Mordecai Finzi (flourished *ca.* 1443–76), a translator of various astronomical and mathematical treatises from Latin into Hebrew. Finzi betrayed his Spanish origins by the frequent use of Spanish technical terms. As early as 1454, his son Solomon had accumulated a remarkable collection of 206 Hebrew manuscripts. See C. Bernheimer, "Una Collezione privata di duecento manoscritti ebraici nel XV secolo," *Bibliografia*, XXVI, 300–325; Simonsohn, pp. 4 n. 6, 148 n. 15.

Not surprisingly, the art of copying Hebrew manuscripts was well developed in Mantua and the neighboring communities, such as small Sermide which, at one time, furnished this kind of employment also to the distinguished Jewish scientist and apologist, Abraham Farissol. See V. Colorni in "Gli Ebrei a Sermide, cinque secoli di storia," *Scritti in memoria di Sally Mayer*, pp. 35–72. A few data on Jews are also included in such comprehensive general works as F. Amedei, *Cronaca universale della città di Mantova*, ed. by G. Amadei *et al.* (includes a circumstantial narrative of the foundation of the *monte* in 1484 and some allegedly miraculous happenings connected with it; II, 270 ff.); and G. Coniglio, *Mantova, La Storia*. Planned for nine volumes to cover only the medieval period, this work has been appearing in instalments since 1958. On the confluence in northern Italy of the various streams of Jewish immigration from the neighboring lands, see also the brief sketch by J. L. Bato, "L'Immigrazione degli Ebrei tedeschi in Italia dal Trecento al cinquecento," *Scritti . . . Sally Mayer*, pp. 19–34; and other data cited by A. Milano in "I Primordi," *RMI*, XIX, 366 ff.

It is often asserted that Eugenius IV's bull, *Dudum ad nostram*, of 1442 gave new impetus to Jewish immigration from central Italy. Shlomo Simonsohn (I, 5 n. 21) has shown, however, that this contention was based upon the misreading of a note found by Vogelstein and Rieger in the papers of Élie Carmoly. As a matter of fact, most fifteenth-century Jewish arrivals in Mantua came from the Holy Roman Empire, where the outbreaks of intolerance were, of course, both more frequent and more violent. Mainly from the same sources were nurtured also the smaller Jewish settlements in the district of Mantua, of which no less than fourteen have been identified as recorded before 1500. They increased to twenty-one in the following forty years. See A. Milano, *Storia degli Ebrei*, pp. 204 f.

83. A. Parsons, "Bernardine of Feltre," *Franciscan Studies*, XXII, 24; V. Colorni, "Le Magistrature maggiori della comunità ebraica di Mantova," *Rivista di storia del diritto italiano*, IX, 57–128; idem, "Prestito," *ibid.*, VIII, 444 ff.; idem, in *Annuario di studi ebraici*, I, 175 n. 1; and particularly S. Simonsohn's *Toledot*, I, 8 ff. (also offering a reproduction of the anonymous painting at the Santa Maria della Vittoria

which includes the portraits of Daniel Norsa and three other members of his family; it bears the characteristic heading: *Debellata Judaeorum Temeritate*, or "Jewish Temerity Combated"). See also B. Blumenkranz's recent comments in *Juden und Judentum in der mittelalterlichen Kunst*, pp. 26, 83 n. 27; and *infra*, Chap. XLIX.

Mantua is particularly rich in its extant documentation. Apart from the papers accumulated in the local archives, both general and Jewish, many European and American libraries possess collections of statutes enacted by the Jewish community and its affiliated organizations. See, for instance, those assembled at the beginning of this century at the Jewish Theological Seminary of America and described by A. Marx in his "Italienische Statuten," *ZHB*, XI, 112–21; XV, 139–45. Of interest are also W. Braghirolli's note on "Isabella d'Este e gli Israeliti a Mantova," *Rivista storica mantovana*, I, 183–86; C. d'Arco and his *Documenti inediti intorno maestro Abramo medico mantovano del secolo XV*.

84. See M. Steinschneider, *Die Hebräischen Uebersetzungen des Mittelalters und die Juden als Dolmetscher*, pp. 671 ff.; the monographs by A. Ciscato, *Gli Ebrei in Padova (1300–1800)*, esp. pp. 18 ff., 229 ff. Nos. i–iii (reproducing the *capitoli* of Piove di Sacco and Montagnana of 1398, as well as the permission granted to the Jews of Padua to acquire a cemetery in 1384); and *Gli Ebrei a Este;* L. della Riva and A. Vergesi, *Capitoli concessi da Francesco Carrara signore di Padova all'ebreo Abramo, prestatore in Piove di Sacco*. The scarcity of reports concerning Jews in Padua before the late fourteenth century is well illustrated by P. Sambin's recent essays containing no direct reference to Jews. See his "Tre notizie per la storia culturale ed ecclesiastica di Padova (secoli XII e XIII)," *Archivio Veneto*, LXXXV, 1–11; and "Aspetti della organizzazione e della politica comunale nel territorio e nella città di Padova tra il XII e il XIII secolo," *ibid.*, LXXXVI, 1–16. See also V. Colorni, "Prestito," *Rivista di storia del diritto italiano*, VIII, 440 ff. On Hebrew printing in Piove see D. W. Amram, *The Makers of Hebrew Books in Italy*, pp. 22 ff.

85. Dante Alighieri, *La Divina Commedia, Inferno*, xvii.64–70, ed. by G. Campi, I, 429; in Henry Wadsworth Longfellow's English trans., Riverside ed., I, 96 f.; A. Ciscato, *Gli Ebrei in Padova*, esp. pp. 33 ff., 52 ff., 95 ff., 99, 243 ff. No. vi, 282 f. No. xxiv. It may be noted that the formula of the oath *more judaico* used in Padua was relatively mild, and steered clear of the extremes often found in other cities. *Ibid.*, p. 284 No. xxv. See also R. Cessi, "La Condizione degli Ebrei banchieri in Padova nei secoli XIV e XV," *Bollettino* of the Museo Civico of Padua, X, 201–14; XI, 8–22, denying that these conditions took a turn for the worse under Venetian domination after 1405; and, more generally, F. Pino-Branca, "Il Comune di Padova sotto la Dominante nel secolo XV (La politica economica di Venezia nel Comune padovano)," *Atti* of the Istituto Veneto di scienze morali, XCVI, Part 2, 739–74; XCVII, Part 2, 71–100.

86. See *supra*, Vol. IV, pp. 25, 183, 244 n. 26; B. Cecchetti, "Un Banco-Levi a Venezia nel 1389," *Archivio Veneto*, XXXII, 386–87; and other data assembled by R. Rocca *et al.* in "Cenni storici e statistici sulle comunità israelitiche di alcune provincie d'Italia," *Annali di statistica*, 3d ser. IX, 163–208; L. A. Schiavi, "Gli Ebrei a Venezia e nelle sue colonie. Appunti storici su documenti editi e inediti," *Nuova Antologia*, CXXXI, 309–333, 485–519; and C. Roth in his *Venice* in the "Jewish Community Series." Many other writings pertaining to the history of the Jews in Venice were listed half a century ago by E. Morpurgo in his "Bibliografia della storia degli

Ebrei nel Veneto," *Rivista israelitica*, VII, 180–90, 227–32; VIII, 14–29, 68–81, 106–26, 215–29; IX, 49–79, 127–52, 214–33. More recent studies are included in the afore-mentioned bibliographies by Gabrieli and Milano; see *supra*, n. 2.

87. See A. A. Viola, comp., *Compilazione delle leggi . . . in materia d'Officii, e banchi del ghetto*, IV, 381 ff.; and the literature listed in the last note. Regrettably, the rapid, if gradual, increase of the Venetian Jewish population cannot be ascertained statistically before the middle of the sixteenth century, although the City of the Lagoons could boast of better population data than almost any other contemporary locality. See *infra*, Chaps. LI and LIX. Some economic data on Jews are found in G. Luzzatto's *Studi di storia economica veneziana;* and the further bibliography listed in R. S. Lopez's comments thereon in his "Venezia e le grande linee dell'espansione commerciale nel secolo XIII," *La Civiltà veneziana del secolo di Marco Polo*, pp. 63 f.; and in F. C. Lane's "Recent Studies on the Economic History of Venice," *Journal of Economic History*, XXIII, 312–34.

88. A. Teja, *Aspetti della vita economica di Zara del 1289 al 1409*, Part 1; M. Lattes, "Gli Ebrei di Norimberga e la Repubblica di Venezia," *Archivio veneto*, IV, 149–54; idem, "Una Convenzione daziaria fermata nel 1395 fra l'inviato veneto in Castiglia ed un Ebreo di Burgos," *ibid.*, V, 97–98 (see *supra*, Chap. XLV, n. 15); idem, "Di un divieto fatto dalla Repubblica Veneta ai pellegrini ebrei di Palestina," *ibid.*, pp. 98–100; U. Inchiostri, "Accenni agli Ebrei nei documenti e statuti dalmati del medio evo," *AS per la Dalmazia*, VIII, 473; G. Matteucci, "I Francescani di Terra Santa, Venezia ed una lampada votiva nel S. Sepolcro," *Orientalia christiana periodica*, XXI, 232–55 ((includes a letter from the monastery's guardian, Bernardino di Collestati [?], to the Doge of September 21, 1569, which sheds light also on the earlier developments). This great Venetian sensitivity is fully understandable in the light of the impact of the Ottoman expansion, which caused many changes in the Republic's foreign policies. See F. Babinger, "Le Vicende veneziane nella lotta contro i Turchi durante il secolo XV," *La Civiltà veneziana del quattrocento*, pp. 49–73. On the repercussions of this affair in Rome and elsewhere see *supra*, nn. 11, 45.

89. G. Menestrina, "Gli Ebrei a Trento," *Tridentum*, VI, 304–16, 348–74, 385–411; *infra*, Chap. L; S. Sabbadini, "Di una lapide ebraica attributa al 1325," *Archeografo Triestino*, 4th ser. XII–XIII; R. Curiel, "Le Origini del ghetto di Trieste," *RMI*, VI, 440–72 (mainly after 1684); and Colorni, "Prestito," in *Rivista di storia del diritto italiano*, VIII, 436. It would lead us too far afield to try to discuss the details in the evolution of the lesser communities in that district. Suffice it to mention I. Zoller, "Il Codice diplomatico istriano quale fonte per la storia degli Israeliti nell'Istria," *Corriere Israelitico*, LI, 197–99; and to list the following monographs in the alphabetical order of the communities: (1) F. Luzzatto, "Ebrei in Aquileia (da un quaderno di appunti sulla storia degli Ebrei nel Friuli)," *Scritti in onore di Riccardo Bachi (RMI, XVI)*, pp. 140–46; (2) F. Majer, "Gli Ebrei feneratori a Capodistria," *Pagine istriane*, IX, 235–46, 272–76; X, 25–32, 182–85, 225–30, 275–79; XI, 31–42, 76–84, 129–30, 167–82 (also reprint); (3) A. Cella, "Il Monte di Pietà ed il banco feneratizio ebreo a Cherso," *Pagine istriane*, XII, 82–86, 109–114; (4) L. Billani, *Dei Toscani ed ebrei prestatori di danaro in Gemona. Note e documenti (1350–1575)*; (5) A. Ive, "Banques juives et Monts-de-Piété en Istrie. Les Capitoli des Juifs de Pirano," *REJ*, II, 175–98 (available also in an Italian

translation); (6) A. de Pellegrini, *Banchi di pegno degli Ebrei nei castelli di Porcia e Bruguera* [*Friuli*] (*1451–1604*); (7) E. Patriarca, *Il Monte di Pietà di S. Daniele del Friuli nel quadrante della storia patria;* (8) V. Joppi, *Di un banco di prestito a Venzone* [*Udine*]*: contratto (anno MCCCCXLIV).* On these and other localities which came under Austrian domination see also the data assembled by J. E. Scherer in *Die Rechtsverhältnisse der Juden,* pp. 616 ff. The Trent Blood Accusation and the historic Church Council which met there in the mid-sixteenth century will be discussed *infra,* Chaps. XLIX and LIX.